XML
In Plain English

Second Edition

XML
In Plain English

Second Edition

Sandra E. Eddy with B.K. DeLong

M&T Books

An imprint of IDG Books Worldwide, Inc.

Foster City, CA • Chicago, IL • Indianapolis, IN • New York, NY

XML In Plain English, Second Edition

Published by
M&T Books
An imprint of IDG Books Worldwide, Inc.
919 E. Hillsdale Blvd., Suite 400
Foster City, CA 94404
www.idgbooks.com (IDG Books Worldwide
Web site)

ISBN: 0-7645-4744-5

Printed in the United States of America

10 9 8 7 6 5 4 3 2 1

1O/RS/RS/QQ/FC

Distributed in the United States by IDG Books
Worldwide, Inc.

Distributed by CDG Books Canada Inc. for Canada;
by Transworld Publishers Limited in the United
Kingdom; by IDG Norge Books for Norway; by IDG
Sweden Books for Sweden; by IDG Books Australia
Publishing Corporation Pty. Ltd. for Australia and
New Zealand; by TransQuest Publishers Pte Ltd. for
Singapore, Malaysia, Thailand, Indonesia, and Hong
Kong; by Gotop Information Inc. for Taiwan; by ICG
Muse, Inc. for Japan; by Intersoft for South Africa;
by Eyrolles for France; by International Thomson
Publishing for Germany, Austria, and Switzerland;
by Distribuidora Cuspide for Argentina; by LR
International for Brazil; by Galileo Libros for Chile;
by Ediciones ZETA S.C.R. Ltda. for Peru; by WS
Computer Publishing Corporation, Inc., for the
Philippines; by Contemporanea de Ediciones for
Venezuela; by Express Computer Distributors for
the Caribbean and West Indies; by Micronesia
Media Distributor, Inc. for Micronesia; by Chips
Computadoras S.A. de C.V. for Mexico; by Editorial
Norma de Panama S.A. for Panama; by American
Bookshops for Finland.

For general information on IDG Books Worldwide's
books in the U.S., please call our Consumer
Customer Service department at 800-762-2974.
For reseller information, including discounts and
premium sales, please call our Reseller Customer
Service department at 800-434-3422.

For information on where to purchase IDG Books
Worldwide's books outside the U.S., please contact
our International Sales department at 317-596-5530
or fax 317-572-4002.

For consumer information on foreign language
translations, please contact our Customer Service
department at 800-434-3422, fax 317-572-4002,
or e-mail rights@idgbooks.com.

For information on licensing foreign or domestic
rights, please phone + 1-650-653-7098.

For sales inquiries and special prices for bulk quan-
tities, please contact our Order Services department
at 800-434-3422 or write to the address above.

For information on using IDG Books Worldwide's
books in the classroom or for ordering examination
copies, please contact our Educational Sales department at 800-434-2086 or fax 317-572-4005.

For press review copies, author interviews, or other
publicity information, please contact our Public
Relations department at 650-653-7000 or fax
650-653-7500.

For authorization to photocopy items for corporate,
personal, or educational use, please contact
Copyright Clearance Center, 222 Rosewood Drive,
Danvers, MA 01923, or fax 978-750-4470.

**Library of Congress Cataloging-in-Publication
Data**

Eddy, Sandra E.
    XML in plain English / Sandra E. Eddy.
        p. cm.
    ISBN 0-7645-4744-5 (alk. paper)
    1. XML (Document markup language)
I. Title.
QA76.76.H94 E33   2000
005.7'2--dc21   00-061346

is a registered trademark or trademark
under exclusive license to IDG Books Worldwide, Inc.
from International Data Group, Inc. in the
United States and/or other countries.

is a trademark of
IDG Books Worldwide, Inc.

ABOUT IDG BOOKS WORLDWIDE

Welcome to the world of IDG Books Worldwide.

IDG Books Worldwide, Inc., is a subsidiary of International Data Group, the world's largest publisher of computer-related information and the leading global provider of information services on information technology. IDG was founded more than 30 years ago by Patrick J. McGovern and now employs more than 9,000 people worldwide. IDG publishes more than 290 computer publications in over 75 countries. More than 90 million people read one or more IDG publications each month.

Launched in 1990, IDG Books Worldwide is today the #1 publisher of best-selling computer books in the United States. We are proud to have received eight awards from the Computer Press Association in recognition of editorial excellence and three from Computer Currents' First Annual Readers' Choice Awards. Our best-selling ...For Dummies® series has more than 50 million copies in print with translations in 31 languages. IDG Books Worldwide, through a joint venture with IDG's Hi-Tech Beijing, became the first U.S. publisher to publish a computer book in the People's Republic of China. In record time, IDG Books Worldwide has become the first choice for millions of readers around the world who want to learn how to better manage their businesses.

Our mission is simple: Every one of our books is designed to bring extra value and skill-building instructions to the reader. Our books are written by experts who understand and care about our readers. The knowledge base of our editorial staff comes from years of experience in publishing, education, and journalism — experience we use to produce books to carry us into the new millennium. In short, we care about books, so we attract the best people. We devote special attention to details such as audience, interior design, use of icons, and illustrations. And because we use an efficient process of authoring, editing, and desktop publishing our books electronically, we can spend more time ensuring superior content and less time on the technicalities of making books.

You can count on our commitment to deliver high-quality books at competitive prices on topics you want to read about. At IDG Books Worldwide, we continue in the IDG tradition of delivering quality for more than 30 years. You'll find no better book on a subject than one from IDG Books Worldwide.

John Kilcullen
Chairman and CEO
IDG Books Worldwide, Inc.

WINNER

*Eighth Annual
Computer Press
Awards ≥1992*

WINNER

*Ninth Annual
Computer Press
Awards ≥1993*

WINNER

*Tenth Annual
Computer Press
Awards ≥1994*

WINNER

*Eleventh Annual
Computer Press
Awards ≥1995*

Credits

Acquisitions Editor
Debra Williams Cauley

Project Editors
Andy Marinkovich
Michael Koch

Technical Editor
B.K. DeLong

Copy Editor
S.B. Kleinman

Proof Editors
Chris Jones
Cordelia Heaney

Project Coordinator
Joe Shines

Quality Control Technician
Dina F Quan

Graphics and Production Specialists
Bob Bihlmayer
Jude Levinson
Michael Lewis
Victor Pérez-Varela
Ramses Ramirez

Book Designers
London Road Design
Kurt Krames

Illustrator
Gabriele McCann

Proofreading and Indexing
York Production Services

Cover Image
© Noma/Images.com

About the Authors

Sandra Eddy has been writing about computers, the Internet, and Windows applications for almost two decades. Her publications for IDG Books include *HTML In Plain English, Second Edition; XML In Plain English;* and *XHTML In Plain English.*

   B.K. DeLong is Research Lead for the Web standards consultancy ZOT Group, staff member of computer security site Attrition.org, and general Web standards trouble maker (read: member) of the Web Standards Project steering committee. He lives on the North Shore of Massachusetts with his wife and two cats. He recently co-wrote *XHTML: Moving Toward XML* with Simon St.Laurent for IDG Books.

*In loving memory of Bart, a golden friend who
left us too soon*

Preface

Welcome to *XML In Plain English*. This reference hand-book and tutorial is designed to provide you with quick yet comprehensive information about the Extensible Markup Language (XML), which allows you to create custom markup languages; and the XLink Language and the XPointer Language, with which you can create sophisticated XML documents. In addition, one part and one chapter are devoted to the Extensible Stylesheet Language (XSL) styling language, and an appendix covers Universal Character Set (UCS), or Unicode 2.0, and the supported character sets. Also included are many examples, which you can use as templates for coding documents and as learning tools.

This handbook cuts to the heart of XML. When you want to create a new element, you don't need to learn about the back-ground of XML; all you need is the name of the *production* (that is, XML instructions or components that constitute instruc-tions) and purpose, its syntax, attributes, and practical examples. Although *XML In Plain English* does not cover Web programming and scripting, it leads you right up to those levels. So, this book is for all levels of XML developers — from first-time users to the most advanced.

XML In Plain English is the one essential XML handbook that should have a special place next to your personal computer.

How This Book Is Organized

XML In Plain English is designed to be easy to use, regardless of your level of experience.

XML In Plain English is organized into three parts — Part I: XML Reference, Part II: Style Sheet Reference, Part III: XML Tutorial — and Appendixes.

If you want to use a comprehensive reference and cross-references to the tutorial, browse through Part I: XML Reference, which includes the following sections:

- **XML in Plain English.** If you know what you want to do but can't remember the name of the XML, XLink, XPointer, or XPath production, element, attribute, or function, view this thumbnail list of plain-English tasks and related components. Then use the cross-reference to find the appropriate page in the reference or tutorial part.

- **XML A to Z.** If you know the name of the production or attribute you want to use, scan this alphabetically arranged list with brief descriptions. Once you have located a particular component, flip to a reference or tutorial page cited in the cross-reference.

- **XML Syntax.** If you know the production or attribute name but want to learn more about it or how to use one of its components, browse through these pages. In this part, you'll find each production or attribute, its *production number* (the superscript number that often appears on the right side of a production name is a cross-reference to the XML specification), along with its purpose, its complete syntax and components, usage notes, and related productions and attributes.

- **XLink Language.** XLinks, or extended links, which in conjunction with XPointers establish simple or extended hyperlinks in XML documents. This section is a comprehensive reference to all the components that make up XLinks.

- **XPointer Language.** XPointers, extended pointers, focus in on the location of XLink hyperlinks. This section is a thorough reference to XPointer productions and functions and their components.

- **XPath Language.** The XPath language supports both XPointers and XSL Transformations (XSLT). This section comprehensively covers XPath productions and functions as well as their components.

Throughout most of personal computing history, individuals creating word processor documents have set standard paragraph formats using style sheets. Then, they have applied individual properties, or styles, from the style sheets to paragraphs in both new and old documents. If you want to use a complete reference, which includes plenty of cross-references to the tutorial, visit Part II: Style Sheet Reference. This part includes the following sections:

- **Style Sheets in Plain English.** If you know how you want to style an element but have not memorized the CSS, XSL, or XSLT property name, view this thumbnail list of plain-English styles.

- **Style Sheets A to Z.** If you think that you know the name of the style sheet property you want to use, verify it by looking through this alphabetically arranged list with brief descriptions. Once you have located a particular property, go to a cross-referenced page.

- **Style Sheets by Category.** If you know the category (properties, pseudo-elements, pseudo-classes, at-rules, productions, functions, or formatting objects) of the style sheet component you want to use, look it up by using this list arranged by category. Once you have located a component, go to a cross-referenced page.

- **XSLT Component.** In conjunction with XSL style sheets (see the following section), you can use XSLT (Transformations) language (XSLT) to transform and style your XML documents. The XSLT (Transformations) language handles the job of transforming documents, and XSL uses declarations to create output. This section is a comprehensive reference to XSLT.

- **XSL Style Sheet Syntax.** You can use XSL style sheets to employ formats for XML documents. In this section, you'll find each XSL property along with its purpose, its complete syntax, usage notes, and related properties.

If you want to learn XML or some of the technologies that are re-lated to XML, browse through Part III: XML Tutorial, which contains cross-references to Part I and which includes the following chapters:

- **Chapter 1: Introducing XML.** This chapter introduces you to XML and other markup languages, narrates the history of hypertext, and presents XML in the context of its very close relatives SGML, HTML, and now XHTML. Finally, the chapter focuses on XML document structure and output.

- **Chapter 2: Introducing DTDs.** Document type definitions (DTDs) enable you to define elements and their attributes, entities, and notation. A DTD enables you to gently or forcefully guide those who develop XML documents. This chapter presents DTDs — both internal and external.

- **Chapter 3: Producing a DTD.** This chapter shows you how to construct a DTD — either in the current document or as a separate document. In this chapter, you'll learn how to declare the root element and all its descendant elements as well as how to define attributes, attribute types and values, and various types of entities.

- **Chapter 4: Constructing a Basic XML Document.** Once you have learned a little about XML and DTDs, you can build your first XML document. In this chapter, you'll find out how to add structure and content to a document.

- **Chapter 5: Using Custom XML Elements.** A simple XML document is composed of text, links, and occasional graphics (if your XML processor supports images). To make documents more interesting, you'll want to learn how to add lists and tables. And to better communicate with visitors to your pages, adding interactive forms is a very good idea. This chapter covers the basics of lists, tables, and forms.

- **Chapter 6: Adding Links and Pointers to an XML Document.** The main difference between HTML and XML documents is links. HTML documents support one type of link — simple. XML provides a variety of links, from simple to extended. This chapter presents an overview of links and extended pointers, which enable you to pinpoint link destinations.

- **Chapter 7: Styling Documents with XSL.** The Extensible Style sheet Language (XSL) allows writers and editors to write documents with which to transform, format, and enhance XML document output, using nested DSSSL Online (DSSSL-O) rules. This chapter provides an overview and examples of XSL style sheets based on the current XSL working draft.

The appendixes provide subsidiary information that helps you build your XML knowledge and get a better background of related, supported technologies:

- **Appendix A: Unicode Characters and Character Sets.** XML emphasizes internationalization, the use of many languages in documents. When you create documents using multiple languages, you use different alphabets and symbols, all of which should be supported. This appendix provides illustrated tables of characters and character sets, especially those commonly used by English-speaking people, and specifies non-English characters and character sets.

- **Appendix B: Country Codes.** When you create documents or parts of documents for an international audience, sometimes you must specify a country code, which names a particular country's version of a language. This appendix contains a tables of country codes.

- **Appendix C: Language Codes.** When you create documents or parts of documents for an international audience, you must explicitly name a language for an XHTML document using a two-letter language code. This appendix contains a table of language codes.

- **Appendix D: EBNF Reference.** The XML 1.0 recommendation uses Extended Backus-Naur Form (EBNF) notation to define XML documents and DTD syntax. To develop a custom language or to understand the XHTML document type definition (DTD) in which elements and attributes are declared, you should understand EBNF. This appendix contains tables of syntax and symbols.

The Syntax Used in This Book

The two types of syntax provided with each production is Extended Backus-Naur Form (EBNF) notation and standard programming syntax.

Extended Backus-Naur Form (EBNF) Notation

The XML 1.0 recommendation uses Extended Backus-Naur Form (EBNF) notation to define XML documents and DTD syntax. Developers can then write a DTD to specify the elements, attributes, entities, and special characters for one document or a document set. A DTD also sets the rules, limitations, and values for each of the components. EBNF uses certain conventions:

- Symbol|symbol ::= expression: Each statement, which is known as a *rule*, defines one production, or *symbol*, in the XML syntax, or *grammar*. XML is case-sensitive; symbols having initial uppercase characters indicate a *regular expression* (that is, a way of grouping characters or options), and all other symbols are all lowercase characters.

●—NOTE

When inserting an XML rule in a document, do not enter the symbol or ::=; enter the expression only.

- #xN: Enter #x and N, a hexadecimal integer matching any UCS-4 code value in ISO/IEC 10646. For more information about Unicode characters, see Chapter 1, "Overview," Appendix A, "Unicode Characters and Character Sets," and the "Webliography."
- [a-zA-Z], [#xN-#xN]: Enter one of the characters within the range a to z, A to Z, or #xN to #xN. In this book, brackets ([ ]) appear in a larger point size to standardize the appearance of other characters that enclose parts of expressions.
- [^a-z], [^#xN-#xN]: Do **not** enter any of the characters within the range adjacent to the **NOT** character.
- [^abc], [^#xN#xN#xN]: Do **not** enter any of the characters adjacent to the **NOT** character.
- "string": Enter the literal string enclosed within the quotation marks. Do **not** mix quotation marks (" ") and single quotation marks (' ') in an expression.

- 'string': Enter the literal string enclosed within the single quotation marks. Do **not** mix quotation marks (" ") and single quotation marks (' ') in an expression.

- (expression): Enter an expression composed of a combination of the previously listed parts of XML syntax and using the following syntax, where A represents an expression:

  - A?: An expression followed by a question mark indicates that the expression is optional.

  - A B: One expression followed by another must be matched exactly.

  - A|B: Expressions separated by pipe symbols indicate ORs. Choose one expression OR the other. In other words, just choose one. In this book, pipes appear in a larger point size to differentiate them from pipe characters within productions.

  - A - B: The first expression must be present, and the expression following the minus sign must be absent.

NOTE

A range (for example, A–B) contains no spaces, but the minus sign indicating an absent expression (A - B) is both preceded and succeeded by a space.

  - A+: The expression **must** appear one or more times.

  - A*: The expression **may** appear one or more times.

NOTE

In this book, the parentheses enclosing a range are in a larger point size to standardize the appearance of other characters that enclose parts of expressions.

Standard Programming Syntax

Standard programming syntax uses certain conventions:

- {}: You must choose one of the attributes, values, characters, or punctuation symbols within the braces. In this book, braces appear in a larger point size to standardize the appearance of other characters that enclose parts of expressions. In general, required attributes are listed before optional attributes.

- [ ]: You may choose one or more of the attributes, values, characters, or punctuation symbols within the brackets. In this book, brackets appear in a larger point size to differentiate them from bracket characters within productions and to standardize the appearance of other characters that enclose parts of expressions.

- |: A pipe symbol indicates an OR. Choose one attribute or value OR another. In other words, just choose one. In this book, pipes appear in a larger point size to differentiate them from pipe characters within productions.

- ^: Do **not** choose any of the characters or range of characters adjacent to the **NOT** character.

- . . . .: An ellipsis indicates an unlimited continuation of the preceding attribute and that the next attribute is the end of the series.

- *Italics*: Italicized text represents a variable (such as a folder/directory, file name, path, character, number, URI, and so on) that you enter. Most times, enclose a variable within quotation marks (" ") or single quotation marks (' '), making sure to use the standard syntax as a guide; never mix quotation marks and single quotation marks in a production.

- default: If an attribute or value is underlined, it is the default. In other words, if you do not use the attribute, your browser will automatically use the default attribute or value.

Conventions Used in This Book

Throughout this book, each production's description uses the same general format. The heading includes the name of the production, its superscript production number within brackets (for XML, XLink, and XPointer only), and a very brief description. Following that are a longer description, two types of syntax, information about components and other attributes that make up the syntax, notes about using the production, one or more examples, and a list of related productions.

● NOTE

A production number (for example, [84]) is useful when referring to the XML specification or working draft at the World Wide Web Consortium (W3C). In the W3C document, productions are arranged in production-number order and with related productions or components used to form XML documents.

A few attributes and functions warrant their own entries, primarily in "XML Syntax" and "XLink Language" in Part I of the book. Attributes and functions, which do not have production numbers, follow the same format as that for productions.

The conventions used in *XML In Plain English* are as follows:

- XML, XLink, and XPointer are case-sensitive, so type the exact combination of uppercase and lowercase characters.

- Productions, attributes, and entities that are to be typed into an XML document are displayed in a monospaced typeface.

- *Italicized* text represents both new terms and variables (such as a file name, number, or URL) that you name and enter. When you see italicized text, substitute the file name, number, or URL for the italicized text.

- In the XML, XLink, and XPointer chapters, examples are composed of both normal and **boldface** text. Boldface text highlights the part of the example affected by the current production or attribute.

- Default values, which are automatically supplied when you do not use a particular attribute, are underlined.

As you go through this book, you'll also notice the following two icons in nearly every section and chapter:

●─NOTE────────────────────────────

The Note icon is used to bring your attention to things you might otherwise be tempted to highlight with a marker, pen, or pencil.

●─CROSS-REFERENCE────────────────────

This icon points you to another section or chapter of the book where additional information on the current topic can be found.

How to Reach the Author

I would like to hear from you — especially if you can furnish tips, shortcuts, and tricks you have used to create innovative and praiseworthy XML documents. If I have missed an aspect of XML or an important example, be sure to let me know. My email address is eddygrp@sover.net.

Acknowledgments

There's no getting around it: The author whose name is on the cover of a computer or Internet book is only one of many people responsible for the birth of a book and its development into a finished product. Without the support of editors and experts, the author would be up the creek without a paddle, completely at sea, and well over her head — to re-coin a few nautical clichés. And there's nothing like the encouragement of family and friends to build the spirits — especially when deadlines loom, and reading and attempting to comprehend technical standards are the last things the author wants to do. In this section I'd like to thank all those whose support has been so important.

As always, a special thank you to Acquisitions Editor Debra Williams Cauley.

Thanks also to development editor Andy Marinkovich and a sincere and enthusiastic thank you to editor Michael Koch.

Thanks to the other people at IDG Books for making this a rewarding experience. Thanks to S.B. Kleinman for her wordsmithing.

For his XML expertise and attention to detail, thank you to the technical editor, B.K. DeLong.

Thank you and best regards to my agent, Matt Wagner of Waterside Productions.

For their continued encouragement, thanks to my family and friends.

For their special and continuing contributions — Eli and Grace. And always in loving memory of Indy and Toni.

Finally, thanks to the readers of *XML In Plain English*. I hope you'll let me know what you think of the book and how I can make the next edition even better.

Contents at a Glance

Preface ix
Acknowledgments xix

Part I: XML Reference 2

XML in Plain English 5
XML A to Z 19
XML Syntax 27
XLink Language 145
XPointer Language 165
XPath Language 181

Part II: Style Sheet Reference 230

Style Sheets in Plain English 233
Style Sheets A to Z 277
Style Sheets by Category 297
XSLT Component 319
XSL Style Sheet Syntax 369

Part III: XML Tutorial 650

Chapter 1: Introducing XML 653
Chapter 2: Introducing DTDs 669
Chapter 3: Producing a DTD 681
Chapter 4: Constructing a Basic XML Document 699
Chapter 5: Using Custom XML Elements 713
Chapter 6: Adding Links and Pointers to an XML Document . . 733
Chapter 7: Styling Documents with XSL 745

Appendix A: Unicode Characters and Character Sets 757
Appendix B: Country Codes 799
Appendix C: Language Codes 805
Appendix D: EBNF Reference 809

Index 814

Contents

Preface. ix

Acknowledgments xix

Part I: XML Reference 2

XML in Plain English 5

XML A to Z 19

XML Syntax 27

XLink Language 145

XPointer Language 165

XPath Language 181

Part II: Style Sheet Reference 230

Style Sheets in Plain English 233

Style Sheets A to Z 277

Style Sheets by Category 297

XSLT Component 319

XSL Style Sheet Syntax 369

Part III: XML Tutorial 650

Chapter 1: Introducing XML 653

The History of Hypertext 655
The History of Markup Languages 656
  SGML 656
  HTML and XHTML 657
  XML 657
  XHTML 659
XHTML and XML 659
  The similarities 659
  The differences 660

XML Document Structure 660
    The document prolog 660
    The document instance 662
XML Output 666

Chapter 2: Introducing DTDs **669**
What Is a DTD? 670
Learning About XML Document Types 670
    Well-formed documents 671
    Valid documents 672
Understanding Internal and External Subsets 673
    Internal DTD subsets 673
    External subsets 674
Introducing Extended Backus-Naur Form 676
Reading a DTD 677

Chapter 3: Producing a DTD **681**
Declaring an XML Document 682
Referring to a DTD 683
    The internal DTD 683
    The external DTD 684
Defining the Root Element and Its Child Elements 684
Specifying Element Occurrences 686
Declaring Child Elements and Listing Their Children 687
Declaring an Empty Element 687
Creating Attribute Lists and Values 687
    Setting an attribute type 688
    Making an attribute required or optional 690
    Specifying Attribute Values 691
Declaring Entities 692
    Parsed general entities 693
    Character and hexadecimal entities 694
    Parameter entities 694
    External entities 695
    Data entities 696

Chapter 4: Constructing a Basic XML Document **699**
Starting a Document 700
    Declaring XML characteristics 700
    Setting the document type and associating a DTD 701
Building Document Structure 702
    Inserting elements, start tags, and end tags 702
    Using empty elements 703

Adding attributes and attribute values 704
Inserting entities 705
Converting an HTML Document to XML 708
Considering DTDs 708
Allowing for style sheets 708
Declaring an XML document 709
Naming the root element 709
Following XML rules 710
Converting attributes and attribute values 710
Using entities 711

Chapter 5: Using Custom XML Elements 713

Using Lists 714
Declaring ordered and unordered list elements 714
Declaring definition-list elements 715
Nesting lists 716
Using Tables 716
Declaring table elements 717
Building a simple table 718
Sectioning a table 719
Organizing columns and rows 720
Building an XML Database 720
Declaring database elements 722
Converting a database to an XML document 724
Creating a Form 725
Learning about controls 726
Planning and designing a form 727
Declaring form elements 728
Defining a form 728
Processing a form 729

Chapter 6: Adding Links and Pointers to an XML Document . . 733

Calling the XLink Namespace 734
About URIs 734
Simple Links and Extended Links 735
Simple links 735
Extended links 737
Extended pointers 739

Chapter 7: Styling Documents with XSL 745

Learning About DSSSL and DSSSL-O 746
Introducing XSL 747
Evaluating Examples 750

Appendix A: Unicode Characters and Character Sets 757

Appendix B: Country Codes 799

Appendix C: Language Codes 805

Appendix D: EBNF Reference 809

Index 814

XML
In Plain English

Second Edition

XML Reference

Part I presents a comprehensive reference to XML and the associated technologies, Extended Links (XLink), Extended Pointers (XPointer), and the XML Path Language (XPath). The four major sections — XML Syntax, XLink Language, XPointer Language, XPath Language — are accompanied by two special tables of contents. If you know the task that you want to perform, but don't remember the name of the production, element, attribute, or function, review the tasks in "XML in Plain English" and find the appropriate page in either Part 1 or Part 3: "XML Tutorial." On the other hand, if you know the element or property name but want to find it in either the reference or tutorial, browse through the alphabetical list in "XML A to Z."

IN THIS PART

- XML in Plain English
- XML A to Z
- XML Syntax
- XLink Language
- XPointer Language
- XPath Language

XML in Plain English

This reference section is for those of you who know what you want to do in an XML document but may not remember the name of a particular production. This quick "cheat sheet" is composed of a three-column table. The left column contains the name of the production with which you'll accomplish your goal. The middle column lists tasks to be performed, organized alphabetically by *italicized* keywords. The right column lists the item's corresponding page number. For a complete description of the component, its syntax, its attributes, and more, you can go to "XML Syntax," "XLink Language," "XPointer Language," or "XPath Language," later in Part I.

Use this production, element, or attribute	If you want to...	Technology (page)
LocationPath	specify *absolute and relative steps* to a location	XPath (p. 203)
AbbreviatedAbsolute LocationPath	*abbreviate an absolute location path*	XPath (p. 182)
AbbreviatedAxis Specifier	*abbreviate an axis specifier*	XPath (p. 182)
AbbreviatedRelative LocationPath	*abbreviate a relative location path*	XPath (p. 183)
AbbreviatedStep	*abbreviate a step*	XPath (p. 184)
AbsoluteLocationPath	specify an *absolute step* and an optional series of relative steps to a location	XPath (p. 184)
actuate	*actuate link traversal* with or without a request	XLink (p. 146)
AdditiveExpr	act on one or more expressions through *addition* or subtraction	XPath (p. 185)
Letter	specify an *alphabetic character*	XML (p. 98)
from	specify an *arc link's starting point*	XLink (p. 149)
arcrole	specify an *arc's role* of content	XLink (p. 148)
Argument	represent an *argument*	XPath (p. 187)
MultiplyOperator	insert an *asterisk* (*) *multiply operator*	XPath (p. 205)
AttDef	define an *attribute*	XML (p. 28)
Attribute	name an *attribute*	XML (p. 31)
AttlistDecl	declare an element's *attribute list*	XML (p. 29)
AttType	specify an *attribute type*	XML (p. 32)
AttValue	give an *attribute value*	XML (p. 33)
DefaultDecl	declare an *attribute's default value*	XML (p. 58)
AxisName	give a predefined *axis name* to the current context node	XPath (p. 187)

Use this production, element, or attribute	If you want to...	Technology (page)
AxisSpecifier	give an *axis specifier*—an axis name and a predefined specifier	XPath (p. 188)
BaseChar	specify a *base character*	XML (p. 34)
arc	indicate the *beginning and end* of a link	XLink (p. 147)
boolean()	return an argument converted to a *boolean*	XPath (p. 189)
starts-with()	return a *boolean* depending on whether an argument string starts with another	XPath (p. 221)
FunctionCall	evaluate and process an expression and *call a function*	XPath (p. 198)
Char	specify one legal *character*	XML (p. 41)
NameChar	specify one *character* in a name	XML (p. 104)
CharRef	specify a legal *character code* from the ISO/IEC character set	XML (p. 43)
CData	represent *character data* within a character data section	XML (p. 37)
Mixed	mix *character data* and optional child elements	XML (p. 101)
CDSect	mark a *character data section*	XML (p. 39)
CDEnd	mark a *character data section end*	XML (p. 38)
CDStart	start a *character data section*	XML (p. 40)
Reference	name an entity reference or *character reference*	XML (p. 123)
children	list one or more *child elements*	XML (p. 44)
choice	list *child elements* from which a writer can choose	XML (p. 46)

Continued

Use this production, element, or attribute	If you want to...	Technology (page)
seq	list *child elements* in a set sequence	XML (p. 127)
ChildSeq	locate a target element by navigating *child elements* integer values	XPointer (p. 166)
choice	specify a *choice list* of child elements from which a writer can choose	XML (p. 46)
CombiningChar	specify a *combining character*	XML (p. 47)
Comment	indicate a non-displaying *comment*	XML (p. 49)
concat()	*concatenate* strings in an argument	XPath (p. 190)
conditionalSect	indicate a *conditional section*	XML (p. 50)
contains()	return a boolean depending on whether an argument string *contains* another	XPath (p. 191)
content	represent the *content* between the start and end tags	XML (p. 52)
cp	specify the *content particle* grammar in a child-elements list	XML (p. 55)
contentspec	write a *content specification*	XML (p. 53)
ignoreSectContents	define the *contents* of an ignored section	XML (p. 95)
position()	return a number equal to the *context position*	XPath (p. 226)
last()	return a *context size number*	XPath (p. 201)
count()	*count* the number of nodes in an argument's node-set	XPath (p. 191)
DeclSep	insert a parameter-entity reference or space between *declarations*	XML (p. 57)
doctypedecl	*declare* a document type declaration (doctype)	XML (p. 61)
elementdecl	*declare* an element	XML (p. 66)

Use this production, element, or attribute	If you want to...	Technology (page)
AttlistDecl	*declare* an element's attribute list	XML (p. 29)
DefaultDecl	declare an *attribute's default value*	XML (p. 58)
markupdecl	*declare* an element, attribute, entity, or notation in parameter entities	XML (p. 98)
EncodingDecl	*declare* an encoding	XML (p. 71)
extSubsetDecl	*declare* an external subset	XML (p. 88)
NotationDecl	*declare* a notation	XML (p. 110)
SDDecl	*declare* a standalone document	XML (p. 126)
XMLDecl	*declare* an XML document as such	XML (p. 137)
Digit	specify a *digit*	XML (p. 60)
Digits	specify one or more *digits*	XPath (p. 192)
MultiplicativeExpr	act on one or more expressions through *division,* multiplication, or finding a modulus	XPath (p. 204)
document	encompass an entire XML *document*	XML (p. 63)
doctypedecl	declare a *document type declaration* (doctype)	XML (p. 61)
elementdecl	declare an *element*	XML (p. 66)
element	specify an XML *element*	XML (p. 64)
EmptyElemTag	write an *empty element tag*	XML (p. 68)
EncodingDecl	declare an *encoding*	XML (p. 71)
EncName	specify an *encoding name*	XML (p. 70)
to	specify the *end point* for an arc link	XLink (p. 158)
end-point()	return the locations of the *end point type*	XPointer (p. 167)
ETag	define an *end tag* for all non-empty elements and some empty elements	XML (p. 83)

Continued

Use this production, element, or attribute	If you want to...	Technology (page)
EntityRef	specify an *entity reference*, a named general entity's content	XML (p. 77)
Enumeration	*enumerate* a list of name tokens for an attribute	XML (p. 81)
EnumeratedType	specify an *enumerated attribute*	XML (p. 80)
Eq	indicate an *equal sign* to an expression	XML (p. 82)
EqualityExpr	compare two operands for *equality or nonequality*	XPath (p. 192)
NodeTest	test the node type and the *expanded name* of the location-step nodes set	XPath (p. 208)
Expr	indicate an *expression*	XPath (p. 194)
RelationalExpr	test one *expression's relationship* to another	XPath (p. 218)
extended	indicate *extended links* that are local, remote, or both	XLink (p. 148)
Extender	insert an *extender symbol*	XML (p. 84)
ExtParsedEnt	specify a well-formed *external general parsed entity*	XML (p. 86)
ExternalID	identify an *external parsed entity*	XML (p. 84)
TextDecl	provide version and encoding information about an *external parsed entity*	XML (p. 132)
extSubsetDecl	declare an *external subset*	XML (p. 88)
extSubset	specify an *external subset*	XML (p. 87)
false()	return a boolean value of *false*	XPath (p. 197)
FilterExpr	*filter* one or more expressions	XPath (p. 197)
MultiplicativeExpr	act on one or more expressions through division, multiplication, or *finding a modulus*	XPath (p. 204)
FullXPtr	identify the a *full XPointer*	XPointer (p. 167)
FunctionName	provide a *function name*	XPath (p. 199)

Use this production, element, or attribute	If you want to...	Technology (page)
ENTITIES	list valid XML *general-entities list*	XML (p. 73)
GEDecl	declare a *general entity*	XML (p. 89)
EntityDef	define a *general entity*	XML (p. 76)
ENTITY	specify a valid XML *general entity*	XML (p. 73)
EntityDecl	declare a *general or parameter entity*	XML (p. 74)
Ideographic	specify a *glyph*	XML (p. 91)
floor()	return the *highest integer*	XPath (p. 198)
id()	return selected elements by *ID value*	XPath (p. 200)
ID	indicate that a valid XML *identifier* follows	XML (p. 91)
IDREF	indicate that a valid XML *identifier cross-reference* follows	XML (p. 92)
IDREFS	indicate that a valid XML *identifier cross-reference list* follows	XML (p. 93)
Ignore	mark an included section nested within an *ignored section*	XML (p. 94)
ignoreSect	name a conditionally *ignored section*	XML (p. 94)
includeSect	indicate an *included section*	XML (p. 97)
EntityValue	specify an *internal entity value*	XML (p. 79)
label	*label* a locator or resource-type	XLink (p. 151)
lang()	return a boolean after comparing context-node *language* and xml:lang of the context node	XPath (p. 201)
xml:lang	instruct XML to process selected text in the following XML *language code*	XML (p. 138)
role	specify the *link-content role*	XLink (p. 153)

Continued

Use this production, element, or attribute	If you want to...	Technology (page)
type	specify a *link type*: simple, extended, locator, arc, resource, or title	XLink (p. 160)
resource	indicate a *link's local resource*	XLink (p. 153)
locator	indicate a *link's remote resource*	XLink (p. 152)
NotationType	*list notation-names*	XML (p. 111)
Literal	represent a *literal*	XPath (p. 202)
local-name()	return the *local part* of the first node in an argument's node-set	XPath (p. 203)
RelativeLocationPath	specify a series of relative steps to a *location* in a target document	XPath (p. 219)
PathExpr	create a *location path*	XPath (p. 215)
Step	specify the contents of a *location step*	XPath (p. 221)
NodeType	identify the *location type* of a node	XPointer (p. 168)
AndExpr	evaluate two operands for a *logical and* result: both operands are true or both are false	XPath (p. 186)
Operator	provide a list of *mathematical and logical operators*	XPath (p. 212)
Misc	insert *miscellaneous information*	XML (p. 100)
MultiplicativeExpr	act on one or more expressions through division, *multiplication*, or finding a modulus	XPath (p. 204)
Name	specify a valid XML *name*, starting with a letter or underscore	XML (p. 102)
Nmtoken	specify a valid XML *name token*, starting with any character	XML (p. 107)

Use this production, element, or attribute	If you want to...	Technology (page)
NMTOKEN	indicate that a valid XML *name token* follows	XML (p. 107)
Nmtokens	specify a valid XML *name tokens list*	XML (p. 108)
NMTOKENS	indicate that a valid XML *name tokens list* follows	XML (p. 109)
Names	specify one or more valid XML *names lists*	XML (p. 105)
NameTest	check on a *namespace name collection* or a specific node name	XPath (p. 207)
namespace-uri()	return the *namespace URI* of the first node in the argument node-set	XPath (p. 206)
CharData	indicate any *non-markup character data*	XML (p. 42)
SchemeSpecificExpr	instruct an XML processor on interpreting a named *non-xpointer scheme*	XPointer (p. 173)
not()	apply a *not* to the value of an argument	XPath (p. 210)
NotationDecl	declare a *notation*	XML (p. 110)
Scheme	identify the *notation scheme* used to express the XPointer	XPointer (p. 172)
Number	represent a *number* made up of one or more digits	XPath (p. 210)
number()	return an argument that has been converted to a *number*	XPath (p. 211)
NodeType	identify the *number of the node* or its type	XPath (p. 208)
here()	return a *one-location* location-set	XPointer (p. 168)
OperatorName	insert a logical or mathematical *operator name*	XPath (p. 213)
OrExpr	evaluate two operands to find a logical *or* result: to find if each is true or false	XPath (p. 214)

Continued

Use this production, element, or attribute	If you want to...	Technology (page)
origin()	return an *out-of-line, one-location location-set*	XPointer (p. 170)
PEDecl	write a *parameter entity declaration*	XML (p. 112)
PEDef	define a *parameter entity*	XML (p. 114)
PEReference	name a *parameter entity reference*	XML (p. 115)
Predicate	insert a *predicate* expression	XPath (p. 216)
PredicateExpr	represent a *predicate expression*, which filters one or more nodes in a location path	XPath (p. 217)
PrimaryExpr	symbolize a *primary expression*	XPath (p. 217)
PI	issue an XML *processing instruction*	XML (p. 117)
PITarget	name a *processing-instruction's target* application	XML (p. 118)
PubidChar	specify a *public identifier character* within a public identifier literal	XML (p. 120)
PubidLiteral	name a *public identifier literal*	XML (p. 121)
name()	return a *QName* for the first node in the argument node-set	XPath (p. 206)
range-to()	return a *range* from the start of a context location to the end of it	XPointer (p. 172)
range()	return *ranges* for each location in a location-set	XPointer (p. 171)
range-inside()	return *ranges inside* a location-set	XPointer (p. 171)
href	name a *remote resource locator*	XLink (p. 150)
round()	*round an integer* so that it's closest in value to the argument	XPath (p. 220)

Use this production, element, or attribute	If you want to...	Technology (page)
show	*show* whether a link resource is displayed onscreen	XLink (p. 155)
simple	indicate a *simple link* with one starting point and one ending point	XLink (p. 156)
ceiling()	return the *smallest integer*	XPath (p. 190)
SDDecl	declare a *standalone document*	XML (p. 126)
start-point()	return the locations of the *start point type*	XPointer (p. 173)
STag	define a *start tag* for an element	XML (p. 129)
string()	return a *string* converted from an object	XPath (p. 222)
string-length()	return the argument's *string length*	XPath (p. 223)
StringType	specify a character data *string attribute type*	XML (p. 130)
string-range()	return each *string-match range location*	XPointer (p. 174)
StringWithBalanced Parens	match a *string's parentheses set*	XPointer (p. 175)
substring()	return a *substring* of the first argument string	XPath (p. 224)
substring-after()	return a *substring after* a specific character in the first argument string	XPath (p. 225)
substring-before()	return a *substring before* a specific character in the first argument string	XPath (p. 225)
AdditiveExpr	act on one or more expressions through *subtraction* or addition	XPath (p. 185)
sum()	return the *sum* of all nodes in a node-set	XPath (p. 226)
PublicID	resolve an external identifier into a *system identifier*	XML (p. 122)

Continued

Use this production, element, or attribute	If you want to...	Technology (page)
title (link type)	give *title information* to a link	XLink (p. 157)
title (attribute)	specify the *title of a link*	XLink (p. 157)
ExprToken	*tokenize* an expression character by character or name by name	XPath (p. 194)
TokenizedType	state that an attribute type is a *tokenized set*	XML (p. 134)
translate()	return the argument with third-string characters *translated* into certain second-string characters	XPath (p. 226)
true()	return *a true boolean* value	XPath (p. 227)
unique()	return a *true boolean* value of true if a location-set contains a unique location	XPointer (p. 175)
UnaryExpr	write a negative *unary* expression	XPath (p. 228)
UnionExpr	*unite* one or two expressions	XPath (p. 228)
SystemLiteral	specify the *URI of a system identifier*	XML (p. 131)
NDataDecl	write an *unparsed external entity declaration*	XML (p. 106)
VariableReference	specify the qualified name of a *variable reference*	XPath (p. 229)
VersionInfo	provide XML *version information*	XML (p. 135)
VersionNum	represent the XML *version number*	XML (p. 136)
S	insert *whitespace* in an XML document	XML (p. 124)
xml:space	control the *whitespace* in an XML document	XML (p. 140)
ExprWhitespace	insert *whitespace* in an expression	XPath (p. 196)
normalize-space()	return an argument with excess *whitespace* stripped out	XPath (p. 209)

Use this production, element, or attribute	If you want to...	Technology (page)
xlink	signal that an *XLink attribute and attribute value* follow	XLink (p. 161)
XMLDecl	declare an *XML document* as such	XML (p. 137)
prolog	describe an *XML document*	XML (p. 119)
XPointer	identify an *XPointer*	XPointer (p. 176)
XPtrExpr	instruct an XML processor in interpreting the *xpointer scheme*	XPointer (p. 177)
XPtrPart	locate an *XPointer's target element* by name, child elements, or part of a fragment identifier	XPointer (p. 177)

XML A to Z

This reference is a table of the productions and attributes covered comprehensively in "XML Syntax" (see p. 27), "XLink Language" (see p. 145), "XPointer Language" (see p. 165), and "XPath Language" (see p. 181) in this part of the book. The following table is an alphabetically arranged master list of XML, XLink, XPointer, and XPath productions and the sections and chapters in which they are located.

Element	Technology	Page Numbers
AbbreviatedAbsoluteLocationPath	XPath	182
AbbreviatedAxisSpecifier	XPath	182
AbbreviatedRelativeLocationPath	XPath	183
AbbreviatedStep	XPath	184
AbsoluteLocationPath	XPath	184
actuate	XLink	146, 735
AdditiveExpr	XPath	185
AndExpr	XPath	186
arc	XLink	147, 737
arcrole	XLink	148
Argument	XPath	187
AttDef	XML	28
AttlistDecl	XML	29, 679
Attribute	XML	31, 664
AttType	XML	32, 688
AttValue	XML	33, 691
AxisName	XPath	187, 740
AxisSpecifier	XPath	188
BaseChar	XML	34
boolean()	XPath	189
CData	XML	37
CDEnd	XML	38
CDSect	XML	39
CDStart	XML	40
ceiling()	XPath	190
Char	XML	41
CharData	XML	42
CharRef	XML	43
children	XML	44, 683
ChildSeq	XPointer	166
choice	XML	46, 686
CombiningChar	XML	47
Comment	XML	49, 685
concat()	XPath	190

XML A to Z

Element	Technology	Page Numbers
conditionalSect	XML	50
contains()	XPath	191
content	XML	52
contentspec	XML	53
count()	XPath	191
cp	XML	55
DeclSep	XML	57
DefaultDecl	XML	58
Digit	XML	60
Digits	XPath	192
doctypedecl	XML	61, 661
document	XML	63
element	XML	64, 663
elementdecl	XML	70, 661
EmptyElemTag	XML	167
EncName	XML	73, 689
EncodingDecl	XML	73, 689
end-point()	XPointer	167
ENTITIES	XML	73, 689
ENTITY	XML	73, 689
EntityDecl	XML	74, 675
EntityDef	XML	76
EntityRef	XML	77, 706
EntityValue	XML	79
EnumeratedType	XML	80, 690
Enumeration	XML	81
Eq	XML	82
EqualityExpr	XPath	192
ETag	XML	83, 663
Expr	XPath	194
ExprToken	XPath	194
ExprWhitespace	XPath	196
extended	XLink	148, 737

Continued

XML A to Z

Element	Technology	Page Numbers
Extender	XML	84
ExternalID	XML	84
extParsedEnt	XML	86, 666
extSubset	XML	87, 674
extSubsetDecl	XML	88, 674
false()	XPath	197
FilterExpr	XPath	197
floor()	XPath	198
from	XLink	149, 738
FullXPtr	XPointer	167
FunctionCall	XPath	198
FunctionName	XPath	199
GEDecl	XML	89, 666
here()	XPointer	168
href	XLink	150, 735
ID	XML	91, 688
id()	XPath	200
Ideographic	XML	91
IDREF	XML	92, 689
IDREFS	XML	93, 689
Ignore	XML	94
ignoreSect	XML	94
ignoreSectContents	XML	95
includeSect	XML	97
label	XLink	151, 738
lang()	XPath	201
last()	XPath	201
Letter	XML	98
Literal	XPath	202
local-name()	XPath	203
LocationPath	XPath	203, 741
locator	XLink	152, 737
markupdecl	XML	98
Misc	XML	100

Element	Technology	Page Numbers
Mixed	XML	101
MultiplicativeExpr	XPath	204
MultiplyOperator	XPath	205
Name	XML	102
name()	XPath	206
NameChar	XML	104
Names	XML	105
namespace-uri()	XPath	206
NameTest	XPath	207
NDataDecl	XML	106, 690
Nmtoken	XML	107, 689
NMTOKEN	XML	107, 689
Nmtokens	XML	108, 689
NMTOKENS	XML	109, 689
NodeTest	XPath	208, 742
NodeType	XPath	208
NodeType	XPointer	168
normalize-space()	XPath	209
not()	XPath	210
NotationDecl	XML	110
NotationType	XML	111
Number	XPath	210
number()	XPath	211
Operator	XPath	212
OperatorName	XPath	213
OrExpr	XPath	214
origin()	XPointer	170
PathExpr	XPath	215
PEDecl	XML	112, 666
PEDef	XML	114
PEReference	XML	115
PI	XML	117, 661
PITarget	XML	118

XML A to Z

Continued

Element	Technology	Page Numbers
position()	XPath	216
Predicate	XPath	216, 742
PredicateExpr	XPath	217
PrimaryExpr	XPath	217
prolog	XML	119, 660
PubidChar	XML	120
PubidLiteral	XML	121, 684
PublicID	XML	122
range()	XPointer	171
range-inside()	XPointer	171
range-to ()	XPointer	172
Reference	XML	123, 706
RelationalExpr	XPath	218
RelativeLocationPath	XPath	219
resource	XLink	153, 737
role	XLink	153, 736
round()	XPath	220
S	XML	124
Scheme	XPointer	172
SchemeSpecificExpr	XPointer	173
SDDecl	XML	126, 661
seq	XML	155, 736
show	XLink	155, 736
simple	XLink	156, 735
STag	XML	129, 663
start-point()	XPointer	173
starts-with()	XPath	221
Step	XPath	221
string()	XPath	222
string-length()	XPath	223
string-range()	XPointer	174
StringType	XML	130
StringWithBalancedParens	XPointer	175
substring()	XPath	224

Element	Technology	Page Numbers
substring-after()	XPath	225
substring-before()	XPath	225
sum()	XPath	226
SystemLiteral	XML	131
TextDecl	XML	132
title	XLink	157, 736
title	XLink	157, 736
to	XLink	158, 738
TokenizedType	XML	134, 689
translate()	XPath	226
true()	XPath	227
type	XLink	160, 735
UnaryExpr	XPath	228
UnionExpr	XPath	228
unique()	XPointer	175
VariableReference	XPath	229
VersionInfo	XML	135, 673
VersionNum	XML	136, 673
xlink	XLink	161, 658
xml:lang	XML	138
xml:space	XML	140
xml-stylesheet	XML	141
XMLDecl	XML	137, 660
XPointer	XPointer	176
XPtrExpr	XPointer	177
XPtrPart	XPointer	177

XML Syntax

This section is the cornerstone of this book: here, you will find detailed information about XML syntax, which is used to define custom markup languages.

AttDef [53]   Attribute Definition

Purpose

Defines a particular attribute, including its name, attribute type, and default value.

EBNF Syntax

```
AttDef ::= S Name S AttType S DefaultDecl
```

Standard Syntax

```
[ ... ]Name [ ... ]AttType[ ... ]DefaultDecl
```

Where

- S (p. 124) represents one or more whitespace characters: spaces, carriage returns, line feeds, or tabs. Syntax: { [#x20 | #x9 | #xD | #xA] [#x20 | #x9 | #xD | #xA] ... [#x20 | #x9 | #xD | #xA] }
- Name (p. 102) specifies a valid XML attribute name. Syntax: #xnnnn [#xnnnn] [_] [:] [#xnnnn] | [0 | 1 | 2 | 3 | 4 | 5 | 6 | 7 | 8 | 9] [.] | [-] [#xnnnn] [#xnnnn] ... [#xnnnn]
- AttType (p. 32) specifies an attribute type. Syntax: StringType | TokenizedType | EnumeratedType
- DefaultDecl (p. 58) declares whether a default value is required or optional. Syntax: #REQUIRED | #IMPLIED | [[#FIXED[...]]AttValue]

Notes

AttDef is a component of the AttlistDecl production.

Attributes are included within start tags and empty-element tags, not end tags.

Each attribute contains two components: a name and a value. Each name-value pair is known as an *attribute specification*.

An attribute adds extra information to the content that the associated element is marking up.

For an XML document to be well formed, each attribute assigned to an element — regardless of whether it has content — must be unique. The value of an attribute, however, does not have to be unique, and the order of attributes within a tag is not important.

For an XML document to be valid, each attribute must be declared in a DTD associated with the document. For an XML document to be well formed, it does not need a DTD. However, if a DTD exists, the attribute values of the document must not refer to external entities.

Use the AttlistDecl production to declare the list of attributes, attribute types, and attribute values for an element.

If you declare more than one attribute list for a particular element type, an XML processor merges them and may issue a warning message.

XML Syntax

●—NOTE

A *warning* message indicates that processing continues; an *error* message usually results in the end of processing.

If you declare more than one definition for a particular attribute, an XML processor recognizes the first definition, disregards the rest, and may issue a warning message.

Example

The following example shows the three attributes defined for the `frog` element:

```
<!ATTLIST frog
        id      ID       #REQUIRED
        name    CDATA    #IMPLIED
        type   (true|european|edible | leopard
        | wood | green|african|hairy)
>
```

Related Productions

AttlistDecl (p. 29), AttType (p. 32), DefaultDecl (p. 58), markupdecl (p. 98), Name (p. 102), S (p. 124)

AttlistDecl [52]   Attribute List Declaration

Purpose

Declares an element type's attribute list, including attribute names, data types, and default values.

EBNF Syntax

```
AttlistDecl ::= '<!ATTLIST' S Name AttDef* S? '>'
```

Standard Syntax

```
<!ATTLIST [ ... ]Name [AttDef[AttDef
   [...AttDef]]][ ... ]>
```

Where

- `<!ATTLIST` is an uppercase-only reserved keyword that indicates the start of an attribute list.
- `S` (p. 124) represents one or more whitespace characters: spaces, carriage returns, line feeds, or tabs. Syntax: `{[#x20|#x9|#xD|#xA][#x20| #x9|#xD|#xA]...[#x20|#x9|#xD|#xA]}`
- `Name` (p. 102) specifies a valid XML element-type name. Syntax: `#xnnnn [#xnnnn][_][:][#xnnnn]|[0|1|2|3|4|5|6|7|8|9][.]|[-][#xnnnn] [#xnnnn]...[#xnnnn]`

- *AttDef* (p. 28) writes an attribute definition. Syntax: *[...]Name [...]AttType[...]DefaultDecl*
- *>* indicates the end of an attribute list.

Notes

AttlistDecl is a component of the markupdecl production.

AttlistDecl is a representation of an attribute within a document type definition (DTD).

Attributes are included within start tags and empty-element tags, not end tags.

Each attribute contains two components: a name and a value. Each name-value pair is known as an *attribute specification*.

An attribute adds extra information to the content the associated element is marking up.

For an XML document to be valid, each attribute must be declared in a DTD associated with the document.

Use AttlistDecl to declare the list of attributes, attribute types, and attribute values for an element.

If you declare more than one attribute list for a particular element type, an XML processor merges them and may issue a warning message.

If you declare more than one definition for a particular attribute, an XML processor recognizes the first definition, disregards the rest, and may issue a warning message.

● NOTE

A *warning* message indicates that processing continues; an *error* message usually results in the end of processing.

Because the less-than symbol (<) is used to indicate the end of the attribute list, you should specify a less-than symbol within character data by using the entity <.

Example

The following example shows the three attributes defined for the frog element:

```
<!ATTLIST frog
          id       ID          #REQUIRED
          name     CDATA       #IMPLIED
          type     (true|european|edible | leopard | wood
          | green|african|hairy)
     >
```

Related Productions

AttDef (p. 28), AttType (p. 32), DefaultDecl (p. 58), markupdecl (p. 98), Name (p. 102), S (p. 124)

Attribute [41]   Attribute

Purpose

Names and gives a value to an attribute.

EBNF Syntax

```
Attribute ::= Name Eq AttValue
```

Standard Syntax

```
Name[ ... ]=[ ... ]AttValue
```

Where

- *Name* (p. 102) specifies a valid XML attribute name. Syntax: #xnnnn
  [#xnnnn][_][:][#xnnnn]|[0|1|2|3|4|5|6|7|8|9][.]|[-][#xnnnn]
  [#xnnnn]...[#xnnnn]
- *Eq* (p. 82) indicates an equal sign *(=)* preceded and followed by one or
  more spaces in an expression. Syntax: =
- *AttValue* (p. 33) states the value of an attribute. Syntax:
  {"[^<&"]]|'[^<&'}]}|[Reference[Reference[...Reference]]]{"|'}

Notes

Attribute is a component of the EmptyElemTag and STag productions.

Attributes are included within start tags and empty-element tags, never within end tags.

Each attribute contains two components: a name and a value. Each name-value pair is known as an *attribute specification.*

An attribute adds extra information to the content the associated element is marking up.

For an XML document to be well formed, each attribute under an element — regardless of whether it has content — must be unique. However, the value of an attribute does not have to be unique, and the order of attributes within a tag is not important.

For an XML document to be valid, each of its element types must have been declared in a DTD. An *element type*, or generic identifier (GI), is the declared element name in the start tag and end tag. For example, in the tags <speech> and </speech>, speech is the element type.

For an XML document to be valid, each attribute must be declared in a DTD associated with the document.

XML Syntax

For an XML document to be well formed, it does not need a DTD. However, if a DTD exists, the attribute values of the document must be within the internal subset (the part of the DTD that is located within the source document) and not refer to external entities.

Use the `AttlistDecl` production to declare the list of attributes, attribute types, and attribute values for an element.

The ampersand (&) and less-than symbol (<) are reserved; they indicate the start or end of markup, among other things. To specify an ampersand or less-than symbol within character data, use the entities & or <, respectively.

Example

The following example is a start tag with two attributes:

```
<hithere align="left" id="abc">
</hithere>
```

Related Productions

AttlistDecl (p. 29), content (p. 52), element (p. 64), EmptyElemTag (p. 68), Eq (p. 82), ETag (p. 83), STag (p. 129)

AttType [54]   Attribute Type

Purpose

Specifies a type for a declared attribute.

EBNF Syntax

```
AttType ::= StringType | TokenizedType | EnumeratedType
```

Standard Syntax

```
StringType|TokenizedType|EnumeratedType
```

Where

- *StringType* (p. 130) indicates that an attribute type is a character data string. Syntax: *CDATA*
- *TokenizedType* (p. 134) indicates that an attribute type is a tokenized set. Syntax: *ID|IDREF|IDREFS|ENTITY|ENTITIES|NMTOKEN|NMTOKENS*
- *EnumeratedType* (p. 80) indicates that an attribute type is composed of one or more enumerated notation names or name tokens. Syntax: *NotationType|Enumeration*

Notes

AttType is a component of the AttDef production.

Use the AttType production only within document type definitions (DTDs).

XML Syntax

An attribute type allows you to ensure that proper and valid data are entered in an XML document.

Attributes are included within start tags and empty-element tags, not end tags.

For an XML document to be valid, each attribute must be declared in a DTD associated with the document.

Example

The following example shows three attribute types — a tokenized type and two string types, respectively:

```
id       ID      #REQUIRED
name     CDATA   #IMPLIED
company  CDATA   #FIXED "Acme"
```

Related Productions

AttDef (p. 28), EnumeratedType (p. 80), StringType (p. 130), TokenizedType (p. 134)

AttValue [10]   Attribute Value

Purpose

States the value of an attribute.

EBNF Syntax

```
AttValue ::= '"' (^<&"] | Reference)* '"'
           | "'" (^<&'] | Reference)* "'"
```

Standard Syntax

```
{"[^<&"]]|'[^<&']]}|[Reference[Reference
   [ ...Reference]]]{"|'}
```

Where

- <, &, ", ', and] are characters *not* to be included in the production.
- *Reference* (p. 123) names an entity reference or character reference. Syntax: *EntityRef|CharRef*

Notes

AttValue is a component of the Attribute and DefaultDecl productions.

The *attribute value* is the value of an element's attribute.

A literal, such as AttValue, replaces the current value of an entity or attribute.

AttValue supports entity references, which must be preceded by a #. Each entity reference replaces one character.

The attribute value must follow the rules and constraints of the attribute type. For example, if the type is a decimal number, the value must also be a decimal number. And if the type is a string, the string must be enclosed within single quote marks or quotation marks.

The ampersand (&) and less-than symbol (<) are reserved: they indicate the start or end of markup, among other things. To specify an ampersand or less-than symbol within character data, use the entities & or <, respectively.

If you enclose a production, string, element, or other object within single quote marks, do not use single quote marks within the quoted object; if you enclose a production, string, element, or other object within quotation marks, do not use quotation marks within the quoted object. Within character data, you can use the apostrophe (') or quotation mark (") characters to indicate quote marks.

If a quotation mark is included in a string, enclose the string within single quote marks; if a single quote mark is included in a string, enclose the string within quotation marks.

Do not mix single quote marks and quotation marks; the quote marks at the beginning and end of a quoted object must match.

Examples

The following example shows a start tag, its two attributes, and their values:

```
<hithere align="left" id="abc">
</hithere>
```

The following example shows an attribute list with its element (pre_type), choices (default or preserve), and default value (preserve):

```
<!ATTLIST pre_type    xml:space    (default|preserve)
   'preserve'>
```

Related Productions

Attribute (p. 31), DefaultDecl (p. 58), EntityDef (p. 76), EntityValue (p. 79), PEDef (p. 114), PEReference (p. 115), PubidChar (p. 120), PubidLiteral (p. 121), Reference (p. 123), SystemLiteral (p. 131)

BaseChar [85]   Base Character

Purpose

Specifies a base character.

EBNF Syntax

```
BaseChar ::= [#x0041-#x005A] | [#x0061-#x007A]
           | [#x00C0-#x00D6] | [#x00D8-#x00F6]
           | [#x00F8-#x00FF] | [#x0100-#x0131]
           | [#x0134-#x013E] | [#x0141-#x0148]
```

```
| [#x014A-#x017E] | [#x0180-#x01C3]
| [#x01CD-#x01F0] | [#x01F4-#x01F5]
| [#x01FA-#x0217] | [#x0250-#x02A8]
| [#x02BB-#x02C1] | #x0386
| [#x0388-#x038A] | #x038C
| [#x038E-#x03A1] | [#x03A3-#x03CE]
| [#x03D0-#x03D6] | #x03DA | #x03DC
| #x03DE | #x03E0 | [#x03E2-#x03F3]
| [#x0401-#x040C] | [#x040E-#x044F]
| [#x0451-#x045C] | [#x045E-#x0481]
| [#x0490-#x04C4] | [#x04C7-#x04C8]
| [#x04CB-#x04CC] | [#x04D0-#x04EB]
| [#x04EE-#x04F5] | [#x04F8-#x04F9]
| [#x0531-#x0556] | #x0559
| [#x0561-#x0586] | [#x05D0-#x05EA]
| [#x05F0-#x05F2] | [#x0621-#x063A]
| [#x0641-#x064A] | [#x0671-#x06B7]
| [#x06BA-#x06BE] | [#x06C0-#x06CE]
| [#x06D0-#x06D3] | #x06D5
| [#x06E5-#x06E6] | [#x0905-#x0939]
| #x093D | [#x0958-#x0961]
| [#x0985-#x098C] | [#x098F-#x0990]
| [#x0993-#x09A8] | [#x09AA-#x09B0]
| #x09B2 | [#x09B6-#x09B9]
| [#x09DC-#x09DD] | [#x09DF-#x09E1]
| [#x09F0-#x09F1] | [#x0A05-#x0A0A]
| [#x0A0F-#x0A10] | [#x0A13-#x0A28]
| [#x0A2A-#x0A30] | [#x0A32-#x0A33]
| [#x0A35-#x0A36] | [#x0A38-#x0A39]
| [#x0A59-#x0A5C] | #x0A5E
| [#x0A72-#x0A74] | [#x0A85-#x0A8B]
| #x0A8D | [#x0A8F-#x0A91]
| [#x0A93-#x0AA8] | [#x0AAA-#x0AB0]
| [#x0AB2-#x0AB3] | [#x0AB5-#x0AB9]
| #x0ABD | #x0AE0 | [#x0B05-#x0B0C]
| [#x0B0F-#x0B10] | [#x0B13-#x0B28]
| [#x0B2A-#x0B30] | [#x0B32-#x0B33]
| [#x0B36-#x0B39] | #x0B3D
| [#x0B5C-#x0B5D] | [#x0B5F-#x0B61]
| [#x0B85-#x0B8A] | [#x0B8E-#x0B90]
| [#x0B92-#x0B95] | [#x0B99-#x0B9A]
| #x0B9C | [#x0B9E-#x0B9F]
| [#x0BA3-#x0BA4] | [#x0BA8-#x0BAA]
```

```
| [#x0BAE-#x0BB5] | [#x0BB7-#x0BB9]
| [#x0C05-#x0C0C] | [#x0C0E-#x0C10]
| [#x0C12-#x0C28] | [#x0C2A-#x0C33]
| [#x0C35-#x0C39] | [#x0C60-#x0C61]
| [#x0C85-#x0C8C] | [#x0C8E-#x0C90]
| [#x0C92-#x0CA8] | [#x0CAA-#x0CB3]
| [#x0CB5-#x0CB9] | #x0CDE
| [#x0CE0-#x0CE1] | [#x0D05-#x0D0C]
| [#x0D0E-#x0D10] | [#x0D12-#x0D28]
| [#x0D2A-#x0D39] | [#x0D60-#x0D61]
| [#x0E01-#x0E2E] | #x0E30
| [#x0E32-#x0E33] | [#x0E40-#x0E45]
| [#x0E81-#x0E82] | #x0E84
| [#x0E87-#x0E88] | #x0E8A | #x0E8D
| [#x0E94-#x0E97] | [#x0E99-#x0E9F]
| [#x0EA1-#x0EA3] | #x0EA5 | #x0EA7
| [#x0EAA-#x0EAB] | [#x0EAD-#x0EAE]
| #x0EB0 | [#x0EB2-#x0EB3] | #x0EBD
| [#x0EC0-#x0EC4] | [#x0F40-#x0F47]
| [#x0F49-#x0F69] | [#x10A0-#x10C5]
| [#x10D0-#x10F6] | #x1100
| [#x1102-#x1103] | [#x1105-#x1107]
| #x1109 | [#x110B-#x110C]
| [#x110E-#x1112] | #x113C | #x113E
| #x1140 | #x114C | #x114E | #x1150
| [#x1154-#x1155] | #x1159
| [#x115F-#x1161] | #x1163 | #x1165
| #x1167 | #x1169 | [#x116D-#x116E]
| [#x1172-#x1173] | #x1175 | #x119E
| #x11A8 | #x11AB | [#x11AE-#x11AF]
| [#x11B7-#x11B8] | #x11BA
| [#x11BC-#x11C2] | #x11EB | #x11F0
| #x11F9 | [#x1E00-#x1E9B]
| [#x1EA0-#x1EF9] | [#x1F00-#x1F15]
| [#x1F18-#x1F1D] | [#x1F20-#x1F45]
| [#x1F48-#x1F4D] | [#x1F50-#x1F57]
| #x1F59 | #x1F5B | #x1F5D
| [#x1F5F-#x1F7D] | [#x1F80-#x1FB4]
| [#x1FB6-#x1FBC] | #x1FBE
| [#x1FC2-#x1FC4] | [#x1FC6-#x1FCC]
| [#x1FD0-#x1FD3] | [#x1FD6-#x1FDB]
| [#x1FE0-#x1FEC] | [#x1FF2-#x1FF4]
| [#x1FF6-#x1FFC] | #x2126
```

```
|  [#x212A-#x212B]  |  #x212E
|  [#x2180-#x2182]  |  [#x3041-#x3094]
|  [#x30A1-#x30FA]  |  [#x3105-#x312C]
|  [#xAC00-#xD7A3]
```

Standard Syntax

```
#xnnnn
```

●─NOTE

The preceding EBNF syntax lists all the base characters supported by XML.

Where

- #xnnnn represents an alphabetic character supported by the Unicode Consortium. For a complete list of supported base characters, see Appendix A, "Unicode Characters and Character Sets" (p. 757). For more information about Unicode characters, see Chapter 2, "Introducing DTDs" (p. 669).

●─NOTE

BaseChar is a component of the Letter production.

Related Productions

Char (p. 41), CharRef (p.43), CombiningChar (p. 47), Digit (p. 60), EntityRef (p. 77), Extender (p. 84), Ideographic (p. 91), Letter (p. 98), Name (p. 102), PEReference (p. 115), Reference (p. 123)

CData [20]   Character Data

Purpose

Represents character data within a character data section.

EBNF Syntax

```
CData ::= (Char* - (Char* ']]>' Char*))
```

Standard Syntax

```
[[Char[Char[...Char]]]
```

Where

- Char (p. 41) specifies one legal character. Syntax: #xnnnn[n[n]]

Notes

CData is a component of the CDSect production.

A CDATA section cannot contain elements to be parsed. Although you can include markup such as tags in a CDATA section, an XML processor treats it strictly as character data.

Do not confuse the CData production with a CDATA section. (Notice the difference in case.) The CData production indicates the contents of a CDATA section.

Character data sections identify text blocks that are not XML markup but that may be confused with markup. You can use CDATA sections to organize a DTD.

Mark the start of a CDATA section with the string <![CDATA[and the end with the string]]>.

Within a CDATA section, you can use the ampersand (&) and less-than symbol (<) literally instead of their entity form (< and &), because these symbols are not reserved for any use within the section and are not seen as markup.

You cannot nest one CDATA section within another.

The CDATA type for attributes is related to the CDATA section; many of the same rules apply to both.

Example

You could consider this CDATA section example a cynical reaction to the typical programmer's greeting, "Hello, world!":

```
<![CDATA[<text>Goodbye, cruel world!</text>]]>
```

Related Productions

CDEnd (p. 38), CDSect (p. 39), CDStart (p. 40), Char (p. 41)

CDEnd [21]   Character Data Section End

Purpose

Marks the end of a section of character data.

EBNF Syntax

```
CDEnd ::= ']]>'
```

Standard Syntax

```
]]>
```

Where

- *]]>* marks the end of the character data section.

Notes

CDEnd is a component of the CDSect production.

Mark the start of a CDATA section with the string `<![CDATA[` and the end with the string `]]>`.

Within a CDATA section, you can use the ampersand (&) and less-than symbol (<) literally instead of their entity form (< and &), because these symbols are not reserved for any use within the section and are not seen as markup.

You cannot nest one CDATA section within another.

Example

You could consider this CDATA section example a cynical reaction to the typical programmer's greeting, "Hello, world!":

```
<![CDATA[<text>Goodbye, cruel world!</text>]]>
```

Related Productions

CData (p. 37), CDSect (p. 39), CDStart (p. 40)

CDSect [18]   Character Data Section

Purpose

Marks a character data section: the beginning, contents, and end.

EBNF Syntax

```
CDSect ::= CDStart CData CDEnd
```

Standard Syntax

```
CDStart CData CDEnd
```

Where

- *CDStart* (p. 40) marks the beginning of a character data section. Syntax: *<![CDATA[*
- *CData* (p. 37) represents character data within a character data section. Syntax: *[[Char[Char[...Char]]]*
- *CDEnd* (p. 38) marks the end of a section of character data. Syntax: *]]>*

Notes

CDSect is a component of the content production.

You can place a CDATA section wherever you would insert other character data.

A CDATA section cannot contain elements to be parsed. Although you can include markup such as tags in a CDATA section, an XML processor treats it strictly as character data.

Do not confuse the CData production with a CDATA section. (Notice the difference in case.) The CData production indicates the contents of a CDATA section.

Character data sections identify text blocks that are not XML markup but that may be confused with markup. You can use CDATA sections to organize a DTD.

Mark the start of a CDATA section with the string <![CDATA[and the end with the string]]>.

Within a CDATA section, you can use the ampersand (&) and less-than symbol (<) literally instead of their entity form (< and &), because these symbols are not reserved for any use within the section and are not seen as markup.

You cannot nest one CDATA section within another.

Example
You could consider this CDATA section example a cynical reaction to the typical programmer's greeting, "Hello, world!":

```
<![CDATA[<text>Goodbye, cruel world!</text>]]>
```

Related Productions
CData (p. 37), CDEnd (p. 38), CDStart (p. 40), content (p. 52)

CDStart [19]   Character Data Start

Purpose
Marks the beginning of a character data section.

EBNF Syntax
```
CDStart ::= '<![CDATA['
```

Standard Syntax
```
<![CDATA[
```

Where
- *<![CDATA[* is a reserved keyword-character combination that marks the start of a character data section.

Notes
CDStart is a component of the CDSect production.

Indicate the start of a CDATA section with the string <![CDATA[and the end with the string]]>. Do not use the <, [, and] characters within the section.

For additional notes, see the CDSect production.

Example
You could consider this CDATA section example a cynical reaction to the typical programmer's greeting, "Hello, world!":

```
<![CDATA[<text>Goodbye, cruel world!</text>]]>
```

Related Productions
CData (p. 37), CDEnd (p. 38), CDSect (p. 39)

Char [2]	Character

Purpose
Specifies one legal character.

EBNF Syntax
```
Char ::= #x9 | #xA | #xD | [#x20-#xD7FF]
       | [#xE000-#xFFFD] | [#x10000-#x10FFFF]
```

Standard Syntax
```
#x0009|#x000A|#x000D
|[#x0020-#xD7FF]|[#xE000-#xFFFD]
|[#x10000-#x10FFFF]
```

Where
- *#x9* (Unicode code *#x0009*) inserts a tab (HT). This control character moves the cursor to the next tab stop.
- *#xA* (Unicode code *#x000A*) inserts a line feed (LF). This control character moves the cursor to the next line below its present position.
- *#xD* (Unicode code *#x000D*) inserts a carriage return (CR). This control character moves the cursor to the beginning of the next line.
- *#x20-#xD7FF*, *#xE000-#xFFFD*, and *#x10000-#x10FFFF* are other characters defined by the Unicode Consortium. For more information about Unicode characters, see Chapter 2, "Introducing DTDs" (p. 669) and Appendix A, "Unicode Characters and Character Sets" (p. 757).

Notes
Char is a component of the CData, Comment, Ignore, and PI productions.

A character is the smallest component of markup and character data.

XML requires that processors support the UTF-8 (the default) and UTF-16 character codes. Processors can also support additional character codes such as ISO-10646-UCS-2, ISO-10646-UCS-4, ISO-8859-1, ISO-8859-2, and so on.

Character encodings supported by XML processors should be registered with the Internet Assigned Numbers Authority (IANA).

UTF-8 includes ASCII as a subset.

For more information about character encoding, see the following productions: EncodingDecl and EncName.

XML Syntax

For a list of character-class productions (that is, BaseChar, CombiningChar, Digit, Extender, Ideographic, and Letter), see Appendix A, "Unicode Characters and Character Sets" (p. 757). For more information about Unicode characters, see Chapter 2, "Introducing DTDs" (p. 669).

Related Productions

CData (p. 37), Comment (p. 49), EncName (p. 70), EncodingDecl (p. 71), Ignore (p. 94), PI (p. 117)

CharData [14]   Character Data

Purpose

Indicates any nonmarkup character data.

EBNF Syntax

```
CharData ::= [^<&]* - ([^<&]* ']]>' [^<&]*)
```

Standard Syntax

```
[[^<&][^<&]...[^<&]]
```

Where

- < and & are characters *not* to be included in the production.

Notes

CharData is a component of the content production.

Character data are one component of text; the other is markup. Character data are all the text that is not markup.

Do not use the]]> combination of characters as character data in a CDATA section; this combination is reserved and marks the end of the character-data section. (For more information about character-data sections, see the following productions: CData (p. 37), CDEnd (p. 38), CDSect (p. 39), and CDStart (p. 40)

The ampersand (&) and less-than symbol (<) are reserved; they indicate the start or end of markup, among other things. To specify an ampersand or less-than symbol within character data, use the entities & or <, respectively.

Example

The following example is an entire valid, self-contained XML document with one line of character data:

```
<?xml version="1.0"?>
<!DOCTYPE endstate[
<!ELEMENT endstate (#PCDATA)>
]>
<endstate>Goodbye, cruel world!</endstate>
```

Related Production
content (p. 52)

CharRef [66]	**Character Reference**

Purpose
Specifies a legal hexadecimal or decimal character code from the ISO/IEC 10646 character set.

EBNF Syntax
```
CharRef ::= '&#' [0-9]+ ';'
          | '&#x' [0-9a-fA-F]+ ';'
```

Standard Syntax
```
&#{0-9[0-9[...0-9]}; |&#x{0-9|a-f|A-F[0-9|a-f|A-F
[...0-9|a-f|A-F]]};
```

Where
- &# marks the start of a *hexadecimal* code. Valid values range from 0 to 9 and from case-insensitive A to F.
- &#x marks the start of a *decimal* code. Valid values range from 0 to 9.
- *0-9* are decimal or hexadecimal numbers from 0 to 9.
- *a-f* and *A-F* represent lowercase or uppercase hexadecimal numbers a, b, c, d, e, and f.
- ; terminates the character.

Notes
CharRef is a component of the Reference production.

A character reference is also known as a *nonprinting* or *nonkeyboard* character, although you can find some of these characters on some computer keyboards.

An entity always has content, and most entities have a name.

Character references and entities begin with a variety of characters, but all end with a semicolon (;):

- Decimal character references start with the &# characters and include the CharRef component.
- Hexadecimal character references start with the &#x characters and include the CharRef component.
- Parsed general entities start with an ampersand (&) and include the EntityRef component.
- Parameter-entity references start with a percent sign (%) and include the PEReference component.

The ASCII character set is supported by the UTF-8 version of Unicode. For a complete list of supported Unicode characters, see Chapter 2, "Introducing DTDs" (p. 669) and Appendix A, "Unicode Characters and Character Sets" (p. 757).

For an XML document to be well formed, its legal characters must conform to the rules set for the Char production. Also, all elements must be nested properly: all tags, elements, comments, processing instructions, character references, and entity references must be completely enclosed within one entity.

The ampersand (&) and less-than symbol (<) are reserved; they indicate the start or end of markup, among other things. To specify an ampersand or less-than symbol within character data, use the entities & or <, respectively.

Example
The following are examples of character references:

```
&#251;
&#x628;&#x631;&#x627;&#x64a;
```

Related Productions
BaseChar (p. 34), Char (p. 41), CombiningChar (p. 47), Digit (p. 60), EntityRef (p. 77), Extender (p. 84), Ideographic (p. 91), Letter (p. 98), Name (p. 102), PEReference (p. 115), Reference (p. 123)

children [47]   Child Element List

Purpose
Lists one or more child elements within a parent element declaration.

EBNF Syntax
```
children ::= (choice | seq) ('?' | '*' | '+' )?
```

Standard Syntax
```
{choice|seq}[?|*|+]
```

Where
- *choice* (p. 46) enables a user to choose the order in which child elements are used in a document. Syntax: *([...]cp[[...]|[...]cp [[...]|[...]cp[[...]|[...]cp]]][...])*
- *seq* (p. 127) forces a user to use child elements in a specific order in a document. Syntax: *([...]cp[[...],[...]cp][[...],[...] cp]...[[...],[...]cp][...])*
- *?* is a character indicating that a production or content particle can occur up to one time.
- *** is a character indicating that a production or content particle can occur an unlimited number of times.

XML Syntax

- + is a character indicating that a production or content particle *must* occur one or more times.

Notes

children is a component of the contentspec production.

Use the children production only within document type definitions (DTDs).

Use the following EBNF symbols to control the number of times a child element can appear in a document:

- ? indicates that an element can occur up to one time but does not have to occur at all.
- * indicates that an element can occur an unlimited number of times.
- + indicates that an element *must* occur one or more times.

If the ?, *, or + character is not present, the element occurs once.

For more information, see the Notes sections of the elementdecl and contentspec productions.

Examples

The following example declares the longdoc element, which includes three child elements, which must be selected in the order in which they are listed:

```
<!ELEMENT longdoc (intro, body, index)>
```

The following example declares the randdoc element, which includes three child elements, which may be selected in any order but just once each:

```
<!ELEMENT randdoc (normal|warning|note)>
```

The following example declares the randdoc element, which includes three child elements, which may be selected in any order; normal may selected any number of times or not at all, and warning and note are optional:

```
<!ELEMENT randdoc (normal*|warning?|note?)>
```

The following example declares the randdoc element, which includes three child elements, which may be selected in any order; normal must be selected at least once, and warning and note may be selected any number of times or not at all:

```
<!ELEMENT randdoc (normal+|warning*|note*)>
```

The following example declares the mixedtext element, which can contain both data and a child element (ital):

```
<!ELEMENT mixedtext (#PCDATA|ital)>
```

Related Productions

choice (p. 46), contentspec (p. 53), cp (p. 55), elementdecl (p. 66), Name (p. 102), S (p. 124), seq (p. 127)

XML Syntax

choice [49]	Choice List

Purpose

Enables a user to choose the order in which child elements are used in a document.

EBNF Syntax

```
choice ::= '(' S? cp ( S? '|' S? cp )+ S?
```

Standard Syntax

```
([ ... ]cp[[ ... ]|[ ... ]cp[[ ... ]|[ ... ]cp[[ ... ]
|[ ... ]cp]]][ ... ]
```

Where

- S (p. 124) represents one or more whitespace characters: spaces, carriage returns, line feeds, or tabs. Syntax: {[#x20|#x9|#xD|#xA][#x20|#x9|#xD|#xA]...[#x20|#x9|#xD|#xA]}
- cp (p. 55) specifies the content-particle grammar in a list of child elements. Syntax: {Name|choice|seq}[?|*|+]
- | is a character that separates one element from the next and indicates a choice of element use.

Notes

choice is a component of the children and cp productions.

Content models consist of *content particles* (CPs), which are names of child element types, as well as choice lists and sequence lists, which are, in turn, other content particles. This allows you to write very complex element-type declarations, which must be matched exactly during processing. Of course, the more complex a declaration, the more chances for errors exist in processing an XML document.

Use the following EBNF symbols to control the number of times a child element can appear in a document:

- ? indicates that an element can occur up to one time but does not have to occur at all.
- * indicates that an element can occur an unlimited number of times.
- + indicates that an element *must* occur one or more times.

If the ?, *, or + character is not present, the element occurs once.

For an XML document to be valid, any PEReference replacement text must be nested completely within its content particle in the following productions: choice, Mixed, and seq.

For an XML document to be valid, any PEReference replacement text cannot be empty and its first or last nonblank characters should not be a pipe (|) or ,) character combination.

XML Syntax

For more information, see the Notes sections of the `elementdecl` and `contentspec` productions.

Examples

The following example declares the `randdoc` element, which includes three child elements, which may be selected in any order — but just once:

```
<!ELEMENT randdoc (normal|warning|note)>
```

The following example declares the `randdoc` element, which includes three child elements, which may be selected in any order; `normal` must be selected at least once, and `warning` and `note` may be selected any number of times or not at all:

```
<!ELEMENT randdoc (normal+|warning*|note*)>
```

The following example declares the `randdoc` element, which includes three child elements, which may be selected in any order; `normal` may be selected any number of times or not at all, and `warning` and `note` are optional:

```
<!ELEMENT randdoc (normal*|warning?|note?)>
```

The following example declares the `mixedtext` element, which can contain both data and a child element, `ital`:

```
<!ELEMENT mixedtext (#PCDATA|ital)>
```

Related Productions

children (p. 44), contentspec (p. 53), cp (p. 55), elementdecl (p. 66), Mixed (p. 101), Name (p. 102), PEReference (p. 115), S (p. 124), seq (p. 127)

CombiningChar [87]   Combining Character

Purpose

Specifies a character that combines with letters of the alphabet and other characters to denote special pronunciation or meaning.

EBNF Syntax

```
CombiningChar ::= [#x0300-#x0345] | [#x0360-#x0361]
   | [#x0483-#x0486] | [#x0591-#x05A1]
   | [#x05A3-#x05B9] | [#x05BB-#x05BD]
   | #x05BF | [#x05C1-#x05C2] | #x05C4
   | [#x064B-#x0652] | #x0670 | #x06D6-#x06DC]
   | [#x06DD-#x06DF] | [#x06E0-#x06E4]
   | [#x06E7-#x06E8] | [#x06EA-#x06ED]
   | [#x0901-#x0903] | #x093C | [#x093E-#x094C]
   | #x094D | [#x0951-#x0954] | #x0962-#x0963]
   | [#x0981-#x0983] | #x09BC | #x09BE | #x09BF
```

```
| [#x09C0-#x09C4] | [#x09C7-#x09C8]
| [#x09CB-#x09CD] | #x09D7 | [#x09E2-#x09E3]
| #x0A02 | #x0A3C | #x0A3E | #x0A3F
| [#x0A40-#x0A42] | [#x0A47-#x0A48]
| [#x0A4B-#x0A4D] | [#x0A70-#x0A71]
| [#x0A81-#x0A83] | #x0ABC | [#x0ABE-#x0AC5]
| [#x0AC7-#x0AC9] | [#x0ACB-#x0ACD]
| [#x0B01-#x0B03] | #x0B3C | [#x0B3E-#x0B43]
| [#x0B47-#x0B48] | [#x0B4B-#x0B4D]
| [#x0B56-#x0B57] | [#x0B82-#x0B83]
| [#x0BBE-#x0BC2] | [#x0BC6-#x0BC8]
| [#x0BCA-#x0BCD] | #x0BD7 | [#x0C01-#x0C03]
| [#x0C3E-#x0C44] | [#x0C46-#x0C48]
| [#x0C4A-#x0C4D] | [#x0C55-#x0C56]
| [#x0C82-#x0C83] | [#x0CBE-#x0CC4]
| [#x0CC6-#x0CC8] | [#x0CCA-#x0CCD]
| [#x0CD5-#x0CD6] | [#x0D02-#x0D03]
| [#x0D3E-#x0D43] | [#x0D46-#x0D48]
| [#x0D4A-#x0D4D] | #x0D57 | #x0E31
| [#x0E34-#x0E3A] | [#x0E47-#x0E4E]
| #x0EB1 | [#x0EB4-#x0EB9] | [#x0EBB-#x0EBC]
| [#x0EC8-#x0ECD] | [#x0F18-#x0F19] | #x0F35
| #x0F37 | #x0F39 | #x0F3E | #x0F3F
| [#x0F71-#x0F84] | [#x0F86-#x0F8B]
| [#x0F90-#x0F95] | #x0F97 | [#x0F99-#x0FAD]
| [#x0FB1-#x0FB7] | #x0FB9 | [#x20D0-#x20DC]
| #x20E1 | [#x302A-#x302F] | #x3099 | #x309A
```

Standard Syntax

```
#xnnnn
```

●—NOTE

The preceding EBNF syntax lists all the combining characters supported by XML.

Where

- #xnnnn represents a combining character supported by the Unicode Consortium. For a complete list of supported combining characters, see Appendix A, "Unicode Characters and Character Sets" (p. 757). For more information about Unicode characters, see Chapter 2, "Introducing DTDs" (p. 669).

Note

CombiningChar is a component of the NameChar production.

Related Productions

BaseChar (p. 34), Char (p. 41), CharRef (p. 43), Digit (p. 60), EntityRef (p. 77), Extender (p. 84), Ideographic (p. 91), Letter (p. 98), Name (p. 102), NameChar (p. 104), PEReference (p. 115), Reference (p. 123)

Comment [15]   Comment

Purpose

Indicates a nonprinting, nonparsed comment.

EBNF Syntax

```
Comment ::= '<!--' ((Char - '-')
  | ('-' (Char - '-')))* '-->'
```

Standard Syntax

```
<!--[[Char]|[-Char][[Char]|[-Char]]...[[Char]
 |[-Char]]]-->
```

Where

- `<!--` marks the beginning of the comment.
- Char (p. 41) specifies one legal character. Syntax: #xnnnn[n[n]]
- `-->` marks the end of the comment.

Notes

Comment is a component of the content, markupdecl, and Misc productions.

Do not include one hyphen (-) or two hyphens in a comment; the hyphen is reserved for the start and end of the comment.

Do not include parameter entity references within comments.Comments describe markup, do not affect processing, and do not appear in printed output.

Do not include comments within a CDATA section or within markup.

An XML comment is much more restricted than an SGML comment. SGML comments can appear within declarations; XML comments cannot. However, declarations can appear within XML comments in the form of comments.

For an XML document to be well formed, all components must be nested properly: all tags, elements, comments, processing instructions, character references, and entity references must be completely enclosed within one entity.

XML applications do not have to be able to read comments, although some do. Use processing instructions (PIs) to instruct an application. For more information, see the PI production.

The Comment production is the counterpart to ! in HTML.

Example

The following example is a comment at the start of an element declaration:

```
<!--declaring paragraph element and attributes-->
```

Related Production

content (p. 52), markupdecl (p. 98), Misc (p. 100), PI (p. 117)

Conditional Section

Purpose

Indicates a conditional section.

EBNF Syntax

```
conditionalSect ::= includeSect | ignoreSect
```

Standard Syntax

```
includeSect|ignoreSect
```

Where

- *includeSect* (p. 97) names an included section. Syntax:
  <![[...]INCLUDE[...][[extSubsetDecl;][extSubsetDecl;]
  ...[extSubsetDecl;]]]>
- *ignoreSect* (p. 94) names a conditionally ignored section.
  Syntax: *<![[...]IGNORE[...][[ignoreSectContents]*
  [ignoreSectContents]...[ignoreSectContents]]]>

Notes

conditionalSect is a component of the extSubsetDecl production.

Use the conditionalSect production only within external document type definitions (DTDs).

A conditional section is either included or ignored during processing.

Use the conditionalSect production only within document type definitions (DTDs).

A conditional section can include declarations, comments, processing instructions, whitespace, and other conditional sections.

SGML and XML developers use conditional sections when they program validating parsers and when they develop sets of complex DTDs. The writer of a standard DTD does not need to use conditional sections.

If you are an accomplished XML developer, you can use PEReferences to identify and process particular conditional sections, instead of using the conditionalSect production and its components.

Only INCLUDEd conditional sections are an "official" part of a DTD; IGNOREd sections, including INCLUDEd sections nested within them, are not considered part of a DTD.

Properly programmed XML processors should process both INCLUDEd and IGNOREd sections.

If a conditional section's keyword is a PEReference, an XML processor should replace its content before including or ignoring particular conditional sections.

You can use conditional sections within external subsets (the part of a DTD that is stored in a separate document, completely outside the source document) but not within internal subsets (the part of the DTD that is located within the source document).

For an XML document to be valid, any <![, [, and]]> delimiters in parameter-entity reference replacement text must be enclosed in the same replacement text. Otherwise, a processor may confuse the delimiters with delimiters that set the boundaries of conditional sections.

Examples

The following example shows the reference to an external subset, quotes.dtd, in the source document, and some additional lines:

```
<?xml version="1.0"?>
<!DOCTYPE test SYSTEM "quotes.dtd">
<saying>
<para>
A stitch in time saves nine.
</para>
<para>
A fool and his money are soon parted.
</para></saying>
```

...and two elements defined within the quotes.dtd document:

```
<!ELEMENT saying (para*)>
<!ELEMENT para (#PCDATA)>
```

Note that para may be selected any number of times or not at all.

The following is a segment of an external subset with conditional sections:

```
<!ENTITY  %  hello    'INCLUDE' >
<!ENTITY  %  goodbye 'IGNORE'  >

<![%hello; [
<!ELEMENT histate (#PCDATA)>
]]>
```

XML Syntax

```
<![%goodbye; [
<!ELEMENT byestate (#PCDATA)>
]]>
```

Related Productions
extSubsetDecl (p. 88), Ignore (p. 94), ignoreSect (p. 94),
ignoreSectContents (p. 95), includeSect (p. 97), PEReference (p. 115),
S (p. 124)

content [43]	Element Content

Purpose
Represents element content within the start and end tags.

EBNF Syntax
```
content ::= CharData? ((element | Reference | CDSect | PI
    | Comment) CharData?)*
```

Standard Syntax
```
[[CharData] ((element | Reference | CDSect | PI | Comment)
[CharData])][[CharData] ((element | Reference | CDSect
| PI | Comment) [CharData])]...[[CharData]((element
| Reference | CDSect | PI | Comment) [CharData])]
```

Where
- *element* (p. 64) defines an XML element, with or without content.
  Syntax: *EmptyElemTag|STag content ETag*
- *CharData* (p. 42) indicates the character data that do not include markup
  characters. Syntax: *[[^<&][^<&]...[^<&]]*
- *Reference* (p. 123) names an entity reference or character reference.
  Syntax: *EntityRef|CharRef*
- *CDSect* (p. 39) marks a character data section: the beginning, contents,
  and end. Syntax: *CDStart CData CDEnd*
- *PI* (p. 117) specifies a process to be performed within a target applica-
  tion. Syntax: *<?PITarget [[...][Char[Char]...[Char]]?>*
- *Comment* (p. 49) indicates a nonprinting, nonparsed comment. Syntax:
  <!--[[Char]|[-Char][[Char]|[-Char]]...[[Char]|[-Char]]]-->

Notes
content is a component of the element and extParsedEnt productions.

All the text and child elements between the start tag and end tag of a non-
empty element are its content. An empty element has no content.

An internal general parsed entity is well formed if it is identical to its associated content production.

An external general parsed entity is well formed if it is identical to its associated `extParsedEnt` production.

The ampersand (`&`) and less-than symbol (`<`) are reserved; they indicate the start or end of markup, among other things. To specify an ampersand or less-than symbol within character data, use the entities `&amp;` or `&lt;`, respectively.

Use the `contentspec` production to specify an element's content type.

Examples

The following example is an entire valid, self-contained XML document with character data content within the start tag and end tag:

```
<?xml version="1.0"?>
<!DOCTYPE endstate[>
<!ELEMENT endstate (#PCDATA)>
]>
<endstate>Goodbye, cruel world!</endstate>
```

Related Productions

Attribute (p. 31), content (p. 52), contentspec (p. 53), element (p. 64), EmptyElemTag (p. 68), Eq (p. 82), ETag (p. 83), extParsedEnt (p. 86), STag (p. 129)

contentspec [46]   Content Type Specification

Purpose

Specifies an element's content type.

EBNF Syntax

```
contentspec ::= 'EMPTY' | 'ANY' | Mixed | children
```

Standard Syntax

EMPTY|ANY|Mixed|children

Where

- *EMPTY* is an uppercase-only reserved keyword that specifies an empty element that will be a placeholder for future content.
- *ANY* is an uppercase-only reserved keyword indicating that the current element can contain any of the other defined elements, including itself.
- *Mixed* (p. 101) indicates mixed-element content consisting of character data and, optionally, child elements. Syntax: *([...]#PCDATA[[[...] | [...]Name] [[...] | [...]Name]...[[...] | [...]Name]] [...])* | ([...]#PCDATA[...])*
- *children* (p. 44) lists one or more child elements within a parent element declaration. Syntax: *{choice|seq} [?|*|+]*

Notes

contentspec is a component of the elementdecl production.

Use the contentspec production only within document type definitions (DTDs).

If an element contains only child elements, you can control the order in which the child elements appear by separating the child elements with commas.

When you declare element content, you are implicitly following a *content model*, which sets valid child element types and the order in which they appear in the element content. The productions in the XML content-model category are children, choice, cp, and seq.

Mixed content defines the content of an element as both element content and character data.

ANY allows any content, as long as it abides by XML rules and constraints. ANY is a good way to bring old SGML and HTML documents into conformance with XML rules. To create a DTD quickly for one of these documents (that is, to enable a well-formed document to become a valid document), define all the element types in the document and declare each of their content as ANY. Then, at your convenience, you can edit each element type and content further.

For an XML document to be valid, a DTD containing element declarations must exist. Then, for each element type:

- If the element declaration contains the EMPTY reserved keyword, the element must be empty.
- If the element declaration contains the ANY reserved keyword, declare at least one child element, and possibly the current element, in the DTD.
- If the element declaration contains the Mixed component, the element can contain both character data and child elements.
- If the element declaration contains the children component, declare at least one child element in the DTD.

For an XML document to be valid, any PEReference replacement text must be nested completely within its content particle in one of the following productions: choice, Mixed, or seq.

For an XML document to be valid, any PEReference replacement text cannot be empty and its first or last nonblank characters should not be a pipe (|) or ,) character combination.

You cannot declare the same element type more than once in an XML document. However, you can declare attributes and entities more than once. Within a particular element declaration, attribute names must be unique.

Examples

The following example is an entire valid, self-contained XML document with one declared element:

```
<?xml version="1.0"?>
<!DOCTYPE endstate[>
<!ELEMENT endstate (#PCDATA)>
]>
<endstate>Goodbye, cruel world!</endstate>
```

The following example declares the longdoc element, which includes three child elements, each of which may be selected one time:

```
<!ELEMENT longdoc (intro, body, index)>
```

The following example declares the randdoc element, which includes three child elements, which may be selected in any order; normal must be selected at least once, and warning and note may be selected any number of times or not at all:

```
<!ELEMENT randdoc (normal+|warning*|note*)>
```

The following example declares the randdoc element, which includes three child elements, which may be selected in any order; normal may selected any number of times (hence the "*") or not at all, and warning and note are optional (hence the "?"):

```
<!ELEMENT randdoc (normal*|warning?|note?)>
```

The following example declares the empty image element:

```
<!ELEMENT image EMPTY>
```

The following ksink element can contain any contents:

```
<!ELEMENT ksink ANY>
```

The following example declares the mixedtext element, which can contain both data and another element:

```
<!ELEMENT mixedtext (#PCDATA|ital)>
```

Related Productions

children (p. 44), choice (p. 46), contentspec (p. 53), cp (p. 55), elementdecl (p. 66), Mixed (p. 101), Name (p. 102), PEReference (p. 115), S (p. 124), seq (p. 127)

cp [48]   Content Particle Grammar

Purpose

Specifies the content-particle grammar in a list of child elements.

XML Syntax

EBNF Syntax

```
cp ::= (Name | choice | seq) ('?' | '*' | '+')?
```

Standard Syntax

```
{Name|choice|seq}[?|*|+]
```

Where

- *Name* (p. 102) specifies a valid XML element-type name. Syntax: *#xnnnn [#xnnnn][_][:][#xnnnn]|[0|1|2|3|4|5|6|7|8|9][.]|[-][#xnnnn] [#xnnnn]...[#xnnnn]*
- *choice* (p. 46) enables a user to choose the order in which child elements are used in a document. Syntax: *([...]cp[[...]|[...] cp[[...]|[...]cp[[...]|[...]cp]]][...]*
- *seq* (p. 127) forces a user to use child elements in a specific order in a document. Syntax: *([...]cp[[...],[...]cp][[...], [...]cp]...[[...],[...]cp][...])*
- *?* is a character indicating that a production or content particle can occur up to one time.
- *** is a character indicating that a production or content particle can occur an unlimited number of times.
- *+* is a character indicating that a production or content particle *must* occur one or more times.

Notes

cp is a component of the choice and seq productions.

If the ?, *, or + character is not present, the element occurs once.

Content models consist of content particles (CPs), which are names of child element types, as well as choice lists and sequence lists, which are, in turn, other content particles. This enables you to write very complex element-type declarations, which must match exactly during processing. Of course, the more complex a declaration, the more chances exist for errors in processing an XML document.

For more information, see the Notes sections of the elementdecl and contentspec productions.

Examples

The following example declares the longdoc element, which includes three elements, each of which may be selected just once:

```
<!ELEMENT longdoc (intro, body, index)>
```

The following example declares the randdoc element, which includes three child elements, which may be selected in any order; normal must be selected at least once, and warning and note may be selected any number of times or not at all:

```
<!ELEMENT randdoc (normal+|warning*|note*)>
```

The following example declares the `randdoc` element, which includes three child elements, which may be selected in any order; `normal` may selected any number of times or not at all, and `warning` and `note` are optional:

```
<!ELEMENT randdoc (normal*|warning?|note?)>
```

The following example declares the `mixedtext` element, which can contain both data and a child element:

```
<!ELEMENT mixedtext (#PCDATA|ital)>
```

Related Productions

`children` (p. 44), `choice` (p. 46), `contentspec` (p. 53), `elementdecl` (p. 66), `Name` (p. 102), `S` (p. 124), `seq` (p. 127)

DeclSep [28a]   Declaration Separator

Purpose

Inserts a parameter-entity reference or space between declarations.

EBNF Syntax

```
DeclSep ::= PEReference | S
```

Standard Syntax

```
PEReference|[ ... ]
```

Where

- *PEReference* (p. 115) names a parameter-entity reference. Syntax: *%Name;*
- *S* (p. 124) represents one or more whitespace characters: spaces, carriage returns, line feeds, or tabs. Syntax: *{[#x20|#x9|#xD|#xA] [#x20| #x9|#xD|#xA]...[#x20|#x9|#xD|#xA]}*

Notes

`DeclSep` is a component of the `doctypedecl` production.

The document type declaration must precede any start tags in an XML document.

The document type declaration contains a document type definition (DTD).

For an XML document to be well-formed, a parameter-entity reference replacement text in `DeclSep` must be identical to that in the `extSubsetDecl` production.

According to the XML 1.0 (Second Edition) Review Version (http://www. w3.org/TR/REC-xml), "Like the internal subset, the external subset and any external parameter entities reference in a `DeclSep` must consist of a series of complete markup declarations of the types allowed by the non-terminal symbol `markupdecl`, interspersed with whitespace or parameter-entity references. However, portions of the contents of the external subset or of these external

XML Syntax

parameter entities may conditionally be ignored by using the conditional section construct; this is not allowed in the internal subset."

Parameter entities are processed first, resulting in replacement text being placed in the markup declarations.

Related Productions

doctypedecl (p.61), document (p. 63), ExternalID (p. 84), markupdecl (p. 98), Name (p. 102), PEReference (p. 115), prolog (p. 119), S (p. 124)

DefaultDecl [60]	Default Value Declaration

Purpose

Declares whether a particular attribute is required, optional, or fixed at a certain value.

EBNF Syntax

```
DefaultDecl ::= '#REQUIRED' | '#IMPLIED'
   | (('#FIXED' S)? AttValue)
```

Standard Syntax

```
#REQUIRED|#IMPLIED|[[#FIXED[ ... ]]AttValue]
```

Where

- *#REQUIRED* is an uppercase-only reserved keyword indicating that you *must* supply the defined attribute.
- *#IMPLIED* is an uppercase-only reserved keyword indicating that you *may* supply the defined attribute.
- *#FIXED* is an uppercase-only reserved keyword indicating that the defined attribute *must* always have the default attribute value.
- *S* (p. 124) represents one or more whitespace characters: spaces, carriage returns, line feeds, or tabs. Syntax: *{[#x20|#x9|#xD|#xA][#x20| #x9|#xD|#xA]...[#x20|#x9|#xD|#xA]}*
- *AttValue* (p. 33) states the value of an attribute. Syntax: *{"[^<&"]]|' [^<&']]}|[Reference[Reference[...Reference]]]{"|'}*

Notes

DefaultDecl is a component of the AttDef production.

Because they start with a #, you cannot confuse the #REQUIRED, #IMPLIED, and #FIXED reserved keywords with valid XML names.

Attributes are included within start tags and empty-element tags, not end tags.

Each attribute contains two components: a name and a value. Each name-value pair is known as an *attribute specification*.

An attribute adds extra information to the content that the associated element is marking up.

XML Syntax

A #FIXED attribute value declared for a particular element type means that you do not have to restate the value every time you specify the element type in an XML document.

For an XML document to be well formed, each attribute under an element, regardless of whether it has content, must be unique. However, the value of an attribute does not have to be unique, and the order of attributes within a tag is not important.

For an XML document to be valid, each of its element types must have been declared in a DTD. An *element type*, or generic identifier (GI), is the declared element name in the start tag and end tag. For example, in the tags <speech> and </speech>, speech is the element type.

For an XML document to be valid, each of its element's attributes must have been declared in a DTD and must match the declared type.

For an XML document to be valid, whenever an element type with a #REQUIRED attribute appears, the attribute and an attribute value must be present.

For an XML document to be valid, whenever an element type with an #IMPLIED attribute appears and does not have a value, the XML processor must report the missing value and continue processing.

For an XML document to be valid, whenever an element type is not #REQUIRED or #IMPLIED, the attribute value is the assigned default value.

For an XML document to be valid, whenever an element type with a #FIXED attribute appears with a value that is not the assigned default value, the XML processor should issue a fatal-error message.

For an XML document to be valid, whenever an element type with a #FIXED attribute appears without a value, the XML processor should supply the assigned default value.

An XML processor normalizes the attribute value in the following ways before sending it to the target application:

- It replaces or appends the #20 space character to line-end characters, normalized whitespace (S) characters, external parsed entities, and internal parsed entities.
- It replaces each entity reference with its replacement text.
- It appends other characters to normalized attribute values.
- It removes leading and trailing #x20 characters and removes instances of two or more succeeding #x20 characters.

For detailed information about attribute processing, refer to Section "3.3.3" in the XML 1.0 (Second Edition) recommendation (http://www.w3.org/TR/REC-xml).

Nonvalidating XML processors treat nondeclared attributes as if they had a CDATA value.

XML Syntax

The ampersand (&) and less-than symbol (<) are reserved; they indicate the start or end of markup, among other things. To specify an ampersand or less-than symbol within character data, use the entities & or <, respectively.

Example

The following example shows three attribute defaults:

```
<!ATTLIST frog
          id      ID      #REQUIRED
          name    CDATA   #IMPLIED
          company CDATA   #FIXED "Acme"
>
```

Related Productions

AttDef (p. 28), AttValue (p. 33), S (p. 124)

Digit [88]   Digit

Purpose

Specifies a digit.

EBNF Syntax

```
Digit ::= [#x0030-#x0039] | [#x0660-#x0669]
        | [#x06F0-#x06F9] | [#x0966-#x096F]
        | [#x09E6-#x09EF] | [#x0A66-#x0A6F]
        | [#x0AE6-#x0AEF] | [#x0B66-#x0B6F]
        | [#x0BE7-#x0BEF] | [#x0C66-#x0C6F]
        | [#x0CE6-#x0CEF] | [#x0D66-#x0D6F]
        | [#x0E50-#x0E59] | [#x0ED0-#x0ED9]
        | [#x0F20-#x0F29]
```

Standard Syntax

```
#xnnnn
```

●—NOTE

The preceding EBNF syntax lists all the digits supported by XML.

Where

- #xnnnn represents a digit supported by the Unicode Organization. For a complete list of supported digits, see Appendix A, "Unicode Characters and Character Sets" (p. 757). For more information about Unicode characters, see Chapter 2, "Introducing DTDs" (p. 669).

XML Syntax

Note

Digit is a component of the following productions: Instance, Length, NameChar, and Position.

Related Productions

BaseChar (p. 34), Char (p. 41), CharRef (p. 43), CombiningChar (p. 47), EntityRef (p. 77), Extender (p. 84), Ideographic (p. 91), Letter (p. 98), Name (p. 102), NameChar (p. 104), PEReference (p. 115), Reference (p. 123)

doctypedecl [28]	Document Type Declaration

Purpose

Declares an XML document type (or *doctype*).

EBNF Syntax

```
doctypedecl ::= '<!DOCTYPE' S Name (S ExternalID)? S?
('[' (markupdecl | DeclSep)* ']' S?)? '>'
```

Standard Syntax

```
<!DOCTYPE[ ... ]Name[[ ... ]ExternalID][ ...]
[[markupdecl|DeclSep[[markupdecl
|DeclSep...[[markupdecl|DeclSep
[ ... ]>
```

Where

- *<!DOCTYPE* is an uppercase-only reserved keyword that indicates the start of a document type declaration.
- *S* (p. 124) represents one or more whitespace characters: spaces, carriage returns, line feeds, or tabs. Syntax: *{[#x20|#x9|#xD|#xA][#x20| #x9|#xD|#xA]...[#x20|#x9|#xD|#xA]}*
- *Name* (p. 102) specifies a valid XML name of the document. Syntax: *#xnnnn [#xnnnn][_][:][#xnnnn]|[0|1|2|3|4|5|6|7|8|9][.]|[-] [#xnnnn][#xnnnn]...[#xnnnn]*
- *ExternalID* (p. 84) names a parsed external entity. Syntax: *SYSTEM[...] SystemLiteral|PUBLIC[...]PubidLiteral[...]SystemLiteral*
- *[* indicates the beginning of a markup declaration or parameter-entity reference.
- *markupdecl* (p. 98) declares markup of elements, attributes, entities, or notation. Syntax: *elementdecl|AttlistDecl|EntityDecl|NotationDecl| PI|Comment*
- *DeclSep* (p. 57) inserts a parameter-entity reference or space between declarations. Syntax: *PEReference|[...]*
- *]* indicates the end of a markup declaration or parameter-entity reference.
- *>* indicates the end of a document type declaration.

Notes

doctypedecl is a component of the prolog production.

A <!DOCTYPE declaration is required for an XML document to be valid; otherwise, the best the document can do is be well formed.

The document type declaration must precede any start tags in an XML document.

The document type declaration contains a document type definition (DTD).

A well-formed document can contain a document type declaration that does not contain an internal subset or refer to an external subset.

A document type declaration can point to both an *external subset* (an external parsed entity, the part of a DTD that is stored in a separate document, completely outside the source document) and an *internal subset* (the part of the DTD that is located within the source document), either or both of which may contain markup declarations that define an XML grammar, its attributes, and its constraints, for one or more documents, including the current one. This grammar is known as the document type definition (DTD). Note that document type *declarations* are *never* referred to as DTDs.

For an XML document to be valid, every element type in the document must have been declared in the DTD. An *element type*, or generic identifier (GI), is the declared element name in the start tag and end tag. For example, in the tags <speech> and </speech>, speech is the element type.

A DTD can be located in the internal subset (the part of the DTD that is located within the source document). In this case, the DTD is local. However, storing the DTD separately in an external subset (the part of a DTD that is stored in a separate document, completely outside the source document) is preferable, so that it can serve several documents.

Parameter entities are processed first, resulting in replacement text being placed in the markup declarations.

If an XML document is associated with a DTD, it does not necessarily have to be valid. For example, you can use a *nonvalidating* XML processor on the document; it doesn't validate the document and isn't required to read and validate the document against the external subset (the part of a DTD that is stored in a separate document, completely outside the source document).

For an XML document to be valid, the name in the doctype declaration must be identical to the name of the root element being defined.

Example

The following example specifies an internal subset:

```
<?xml version="1.0"?>
<!DOCTYPE endstate[>
<!ELEMENT endstate (#PCDATA)>
```

```
]>
<endstate>Goodbye, cruel world!</endstate>
```

The following example specifies an external subset, goodbye.dtd:

```
<?xml version="1.0"?>
<!DOCTYPE endstate SYSTEM "goodbye.dtd">
<endstate>Goodbye, cruel world!</endstate>
```

Related Productions

document (p. 63), ExternalID (p. 84), markupdecl (p. 98), Name (p. 102), PEReference (p. 115), prolog (p. 119), S (p. 124)

---

document [1]   Document Name

Purpose

Encompasses an entire XML document.

EBNF Syntax

```
document ::= prolog element Misc*
```

Standard Syntax

```
prolog element [Misc[Misc[...Misc]]]
```

Where

- *prolog* (p. 119) generally describes an XML document. Syntax:
  `[XMLDecl]`
  `[[Misc][Misc]...[Misc]][doctypedecl[[Misc][Misc]...[Misc]]]`
- *element* (p. 64) defines an XML element, with or without content.
  Syntax: `EmptyElemTag|STag content ETag`
- *Misc* (p. 100) indicates miscellaneous information. Syntax: `Comment|PI|`
  `[ ... ]`

Notes

This component identifies the current document, including the version of XML that was used to create it.

Although Misc enables you to add miscellaneous content — comments, processing instructions, and whitespace — to a document, use good syntax. Being careful helps links to work properly and XML processors to interpret XML statements correctly.

An XML document must contain at least one element, the root or document element, which encloses all other elements in the document. The root element is known as the parent of all other elements, which are known as child elements.

The *document entity* is the entire XML document as it will be read by a non-validating XML processor. This is in contrast to a *document module*, which is a part of the document distributed over a network.

For an XML document to be well formed, the document entity must be identical to the document production.

Examples

The following example is an entire valid, self-contained XML document, including a four-line prolog:

```
<?xml version="1.0"?>
<!DOCTYPE endstate[>
<!ELEMENT endstate (#PCDATA)>
]>
<endstate>Goodbye, cruel world!</endstate>
```

The following example is an XML document with a two-line prolog, including an external DTD:

```
<?xml version="1.0"?>
<!DOCTYPE endstate SYSTEM "goodbye.dtd">
<endstate>Goodbye, cruel world!</endstate>
```

Related Productions

Misc (p. 100), prolog (p. 119), VersionInfo (p. 135), XMLDecl (p. 137)

element [39]   Element

Purpose

Specifies an XML element, with or without content.

EBNF Syntax

```
element ::= EmptyElemTag | STag content ETag
```

Standard Syntax

```
EmptyElemTag|STag content ETag
```

Where

- *EmptyElemTag* (p. 68) writes an empty-element tag. Syntax: {*<Name*
  [[...]Attribute][[...]Attribute]...[[...]Attribute]]}
  [...]{/>}
- *STag* (p. 129) defines a start tag for all nonempty elements and optionally for some empty elements. Syntax: *<Name[[[...]Attribute][[*
  ...]Attribute]...[[...]Attribute]]][...]>
- *content* (p. 52) represents element content within the start and end tags. Syntax: *[element|CharData|Reference|CDSect|PI|Comment]*
  [element|CharData|Reference|CDSect|PI|Comment]...[element|
  CharData|Reference|CDSect|PI|Comment]
- *ETag* (p. 83) defines an end tag for an element. Syntax: *</Name[...]>*

Notes

element is a component of the content and document productions.

An XML document must contain at least one element, the root or document element, which encloses all other elements in the document. The root element is known as the parent of all other elements, which are known as child elements.

An element includes a start tag, an end tag, and the content within the tags.

An *element type*, or generic identifier (GI), is the declared element name in the start tag and end tag. For example, in the tags <speech> and </speech>, speech is the element type. The following HTML list includes five elements (every occurrence of <UL>/</UL> and <LI>/</LI>) and two element types (<UL>/</UL> and <LI>/</LI>).

```
<UL>
<LI>Beatles</LI>
<LI>Rolling Stones</LI>
<LI>Elvis</LI>
</UL>
```

Element types with content have start tags (see the STag production) and end tags (see the ETag production); empty element types have start tags and end tags or empty-element tags (see the EmptyElemTag production).

For an XML document to be well formed, the name of a particular element type must be the same for both the start tag and end tag.

For an XML document to be well-formed, all elements must be nested properly: all tags, elements, comments, processing instructions, character references, and entity references must be completely enclosed within one entity.

For an XML document to be valid, every element type in the document must have been declared in the DTD. For an XML document to be valid, there must be an element declaration and:

- If the element declaration contains the EMPTY reserved keyword, then the element is empty. (See the contentspec production.)
- If the element declaration contains the ANY reserved keyword, then at least one child element, and possibly the current element, have been declared. (See the contentspec production.)
- If the element declaration contains the Mixed component, then the element can contain both character data and child elements. (See the contentspec and Mixed productions.)
- If the element declaration contains the children component, then at least one child element has been declared. (See the contentspec and children productions.)

Use the elementdecl production to declare an element, its attributes, and its child elements.

Examples

The following example is an entire valid, self-contained XML document with one declared element:

```
<?xml version="1.0"?>
<!DOCTYPE endstate[>
<!ELEMENT endstate (#PCDATA)>
]>
<endstate>Goodbye, cruel world!</endstate>
```

The following examples show some empty elements:

```
<image align="left" id="bighome" src="bighouse.GIF"></image>
<br></br>
<br/>
```

Related Productions

children (p. 44), content (p. 52), contentspec (p. 53), document (p. 63), elementdecl (p. 66), EmptyElemTag (p. 68), Eq (p. 82), ETag (p. 83), Mixed (p. 101), STag (p. 129)

---

elementdecl [45]   Element Type Declaration

Purpose

Declares an element and its content.

EBNF Syntax

```
elementdecl ::= '<!ELEMENT' S Name S contentspec S? '>'
```

Standard Syntax

```
{<!ELEMENT[ ... ]Name[ ... ]contentspec}[ ... ]{>}
```

Where

- <!ELEMENT is an uppercase-only reserved keyword that marks the start of the element-type declaration.
- S (p. 124) represents one or more whitespace characters: spaces, carriage returns, line feeds, or tabs. Syntax: {[#x20|#x9|#xD|#xA][#x20|#x9|#xD|#xA]...[#x20|#x9|#xD|#xA]}
- Name (p. 102) specifies a valid XML element-type name. Syntax: #xnnnn [#xnnnn][_][:][#xnnnn]|[0|1|2|3|4|5|6|7|8|9][.]|[-][#xnnnn][#xnnnn]...[#xnnnn]
- contentspec (p. 53) specifies an element's content type. Syntax: EMPTY| ANY|Mixed|children
- > marks the end of the element-type declaration.

Notes

elementdecl is a component of the markupdecl production.

Use the elementdecl production only within document type definitions (DTDs).

Using an element declaration, you can fine-tune the definition and behavior of an element, its attributes, and its child elements.

The *element content* is one or more child elements in the content of a particular element type. Element content does not include any character data. If an element contains only child elements, you can control the order in which the child elements appear by separating them with commas. When you declare element content, you are implicitly following a *content model*, which sets valid child element types and the order in which they appear in the element content. The productions in the XML content-model category are children, cp, choice, and seq.

Mixed content defines the content of an element as both element content and character data.

You cannot declare the same element type more than once in an XML document. However, you can declare attributes and entities more than once.

Examples

The following example is an entire valid, self-contained XML document with one declared element:

```
<?xml version="1.0"?>
<!DOCTYPE endstate[>
<!ELEMENT endstate (#PCDATA)>
]>
<endstate>Goodbye, cruel world!</endstate>
```

The following example declares the longdoc element, which includes a sequence of three elements:

```
<!ELEMENT longdoc (intro, body, index)>
```

The following example declares the randdoc element, which includes three child elements, which may be selected in any order but just once each:

```
<!ELEMENT randdoc (normal|warning|note)>
```

The following example declares the randdoc element, which includes three child elements, which may be selected in any order; normal may selected any number of times or not at all, and warning and note are optional:

```
<!ELEMENT randdoc (normal*|warning?|note?)>
```

The following example declares the randdoc element, which includes three child elements, which may be selected in any order; normal must be selected at least once, and warning and note may be selected any number of times or not at all:

```
<!ELEMENT randdoc (normal+|warning*|note*)>
```

The following example declares the empty image element:

```
<!ELEMENT image EMPTY>
```

The following ksink element can contain any contents:

```
<!ELEMENT ksink ANY>
```

The following example declares the mixedtext element, which can contain both data and another element:

```
<!ELEMENT mixedtext (#PCDATA|ital)>
```

The following example declares the mixedtext element, which can contain both data and two parameter-entity references:

```
<!ELEMENT mixedtext (#PCDATA|%typeface;|%pointsize;)>
```

The following example from the Math Markup Language declares the EQ empty element:

```
<!ELEMENT EQ          EMPTY      >
```

Related Productions

children (p. 44), choice (p. 46), contentspec (p. 53), cp (p. 55), markupdecl (p. 98), Mixed (p. 101), Name (p. 102), S (p. 124), seq (p. 127)

EmptyElemTag [44]   Empty-Element Tag

Purpose

Writes an empty-element tag.

EBNF Syntax

```
EmptyElemTag ::= '<' Name (S Attribute)* S? '/>'
```

Standard Syntax

```
{<Name [[ ... ]Attribute][[ ... ]Attribute]
...[[ ... ]Attribute]]}[ ... ]{/>}
```

Where

- < marks the start of the empty-element tag.
- Name (p. 102) specifies a valid XML empty-element name. Syntax:
  #xnnnn [#xnnnn][_][:][#xnnnn]|[0|1|2|3|4|5|6|7|8|9][.]|
  [-][#xnnnn][#xnnnn]...[#xnnnn]

- *S* (p. 124) represents one or more whitespace characters: spaces, carriage returns, line feeds, or tabs. Syntax: { *[#x20 | #x9 | #xD | #xA] [#x20 | #x9 | #xD | #xA] ... [#x20 | #x9 | #xD | #xA]* }
- *Attribute* (p. 31) names and gives a value to an attribute. Syntax: *Name[...]=[...]AttValue*
- /> marks the end of the empty-element tag.

Notes

EmptyElemTag is a component of the element production.

An empty-element tag marks the future location of an object, such as a graphic or line break, in document output. In contrast, a nonempty element contains content that will be part of the document output.

You can insert an empty-element tag in an XML document in the following ways:

- Insert a start tag immediately followed by an end tag.
- Insert an empty-element tag by using the EmptyElemTag production.

Declare any empty element by using the contentspec production within the elementdecl production.

Use the EmptyElemTag production **only** for all elements that you declare to be EMPTY.

Although the EMPTY keyword is optional for empty elements, use it if you want your XML documents to process properly under a variety of computer platforms.

For an XML document to be well formed, each attribute under an element, regardless of whether it has content, must be unique. However, the value of an attribute does not have to be unique, and the order of attributes within a tag is not important.

For an XML document to be well formed, all elements must be nested properly: all tags, elements, comments, processing instructions, character references, and entity references must be completely enclosed within one entity.

For an XML document to be valid, each of its element types must have been declared in a DTD. An *element type*, or generic identifier (GI), is the declared element name in the start tag and end tag. For example, in the tags <speech> and </speech>, speech is the element type.

For an XML document to be valid, each attribute must be declared in a DTD associated with the document.

For an XML document to be well formed, it does not need a DTD. However, if a DTD exists, the attribute values of the document must be within the internal subset (the part of the DTD that is located within the source document) and not refer to external entities.

XML Syntax

A less-than symbol (<) is reserved; it indicates the start of markup, among other things. To specify a less-than symbol within character data, use the entity <.

Examples

These examples show two empty elements and two ways of expressing them:

```
<IMG align="left" id="bighome" src="bighouse.GIF"/>

<IMG align="left" id="bighome" src="bighouse.GIF"></IMG>

<br></br>

<br/>
```

Related Productions

Attribute (p. 31), content (p. 52), contentspec (p. 53), element (p. 64), EmptyElemTag (p. 68), ETag (p. 83), Eq (p. 82), STag (p. 129)

EncName [81]   Encoding Name

Purpose

Specifies an encoding name.

EBNF Syntax

```
EncName ::= [A-Za-z] ([A-Za-z0-9._] | '-')*
```

Standard Syntax

```
{[A-Z|a-z]}[[A-Z|a-z|0-9|.|_]|-][[A-Z|a-z|0-9|.|_]|-]
...[[A-Z|a-z|0-9|.|_]|-]
```

Where

- a-z and A-Z represent lowercase and uppercase letters of the current alphabet.
- 0-9 are numbers from 0 to 9.
- ., _, and - are supported characters.

Notes

EncName is a component of the EncodingDecl production.

Valid EncNames include:

- UTF-8, UTF-16, ISO-10646-UCS-2, and ISO-106046-UCS-4 for Unicode and ISO/IEC 10646.
- ISO-8859-1, ISO-8859-2, ISO-8859-3, ISO-8859-4, ISO-8859-5, ISO-8859-6, ISO-8859-7, ISO-8859-8, and ISO-8859-8 for ISO8859.
- ISO-2022-P, Shift_JIS, and EUC-P for JIS X-0208-1997.

- Encodings that are registered with the Internet Assigned Numbers Authority (IANA) at http://www.iana.org/.

IANA-registered names are case-insensitive.

For more information about encoding declarations, see the Notes section for the EncodingDecl production.

Example

The example shows an XML declaration including the ISO-8859-1 (Latin-1) encoding:

```
<?xml version="1.0" encoding="ISO-8859-1"?>
```

Related Productions

EncodingDecl (p. 71), Eq (p. 82), S (p. 124), TextDecl (p. 132), XMLDecl (p. 137)

EncodingDecl [80]   Encoding Declaration

Purpose
Declares the document's encoding name.

EBNF Syntax

```
EncodingDecl ::= S 'encoding' Eq ('"' EncName '"'
  | "'" EncName "'" )
```

Standard Syntax

```
[ ... ]encoding = {"|'}EncName{"|'}
```

Where

- S (p. 124) represents one or more whitespace characters: spaces, carriage returns, line feeds, or tabs. Syntax: {[#x20|#x9|#xD|#xA] [#x20| #x9|#xD|#xA]...[#x20|#x9|#xD|#xA]}
- encoding is a reserved keyword indicating that an encoding name follows.
- Eq (p. 82) indicates an equal sign (=) preceded and followed by one or more spaces in an expression. Syntax: =
- EncName (p. 70) specifies an encoding name. Syntax: {[A-Z|a-z]}[[A-Z|a-z|0-9|.|_]|-][[A-Z|a-z|0-9|.|_]|-]...[[A-Z|a-z|0-9|.|_]|-]

Notes

EncodingDecl is a component of the TextDecl and XMLDecl productions.

XML requires that processors support the UTF-8 (the default) and UTF-16 character codes. Processors can also support additional character codes.

UTF-8 includes ASCII as a subset.

Entities encoded with UTF-16 must start with the Byte Order Mark #xFEFF, which is the ZERO WIDTH NO-BREAK SPACE character, to distinguish them from entities encoded with UTF-8.

Each external parsed entity can use its own unique encoding.

If an external parsed entity uses an encoding that is *not* UTF-8 or UTF-16, it must contain an opening TextDecl that includes an EncodingDecl.

Valid EncNames include:

- UTF-8, UTF-16, ISO-10646-UCS-2, and ISO-106046-UCS-4 for Unicode and ISO/IEC 10646.
- ISO-8859-1, ISO-8859-2, ISO-8859-3, ISO-8859-4, ISO-8859-5, ISO-8859-6, ISO-8859-7, ISO-8859-8, and ISO-8859-8 for ISO8859.
- ISO-2022-P, Shift_JIS, and EUC-P for JIS X-0208-1997.
- Encodings that are registered with the Internet Assigned Numbers Authority (IANA) at http://www.iana.org/.

IANA-registered names are case-insensitive.

Each external parsed entity in an XML document that includes an EncodingDecl must use that declared encoding. If the encoding is different from the declared encoding, processing ends with a fatal error.

If an external parsed entity does not include an EncodingDecl or the Byte Order Mark, it must use UTF-8. Otherwise, a fatal error occurs.

If an EncodingDecl is not located in the proper location, at the beginning of its external parsed entity, a fatal error occurs.

If an XML processor does not recognize an encoding, declared or not, a fatal error occurs.

If you enclose a production, string, element, or other object within single quote marks, do not use single quote marks within the quoted object; if you enclose a production, string, element, or other object within quotation marks, do not use quotation marks within the quoted object.

Do not mix single quote marks and quotation marks; the quote marks at the beginning and end of a quoted object must match.

Example

The example shows an XML declaration including the ISO-8859-1 (Latin-1) encoding:

```
<?xml version="1.0" encoding="ISO-8859-1"?>
```

Related Productions

EncName (p. 70), Eq (p. 82), S (p. 124), TextDecl (p. 132), XMLDecl (p. 137)

XML Syntax

ENTITIES   General-Entity-List Attribute

Purpose
Specifies a list of valid XML general entities.

EBNF Syntax
See the TokenizedType production.

Standard Syntax
See the TokenizedType production.

Notes
ENTITIES is an uppercase-only reserved keyword indicating that a list of
ENTITYs follows.

For an XML document to be valid, the ENTITIES attribute must conform to
the Names production.

For more information, see the Notes section of the TokenizedType production, which is a component of the AttType production.

Related Productions
AttType (p. 32), Name (p. 102), Names (p. 105), Nmtoken (p. 107), Nmtokens
(p. 108), TokenizedType (p. 134)

Related Attributes
ENTITY (p. 73), ID (p. 91), IDREF (p. 92), IDREFS (p. 93), NMTOKEN (p. 107),
NMTOKENS (p. 109)

ENTITY   General-Entity Attribute

Purpose
Specifies a valid XML general entity.

EBNF Syntax
See the TokenizedType production.

Standard Syntax
See the TokenizedType production.

Notes
ENTITY is an uppercase-only reserved keyword indicating that the defined
attribute is an entity.

For an XML document to be valid, the ENTITY attribute must conform to the
Name production.

XML Syntax

For an XML document to be valid, each ENTITY must be an unparsed entity declared in the DTD.

For more information, see the Notes section of the TokenizedType production, which is a component of the AttType production.

Related Productions

AttType (p. 32), Name (p. 102), Names (p. 105), Nmtoken (p. 107), Nmtokens (p. 108), TokenizedType (p. 134)

Related Attributes

ENTITIES (p. 73), ID (p. 91), IDREF (p. 92), IDREFS (p. 93), NMTOKEN (p. 107), NMTOKENS (p. 109)

EntityDecl [70]   **Entity Declaration**

Purpose

Declares a general or parameter entity.

EBNF Syntax

```
EntityDecl ::= GEDecl | PEDecl
```

Standard Syntax

```
GEDecl|PEDecl
```

Where

- GEDecl (p. 89) declares a general entity. Syntax: <!ENTITY[...] Name[...]EntityDef[...]>
- PEDecl (p. 112) declares a parameter entity. Syntax: <!ENTITY[...] %[...]Name[...]PEDef[...]>

Notes

EntityDecl is a component of the markupdecl production.

Use the EntityDecl production only within DTDs.

All entities must have content and be named.

An *unparsed entity* contains unparsed data, which may or may not be valid, may not even be XML, and has not been processed through an XML parser. An unparsed entity has a named notation, which the XML processor sends to the target application.

A *parsed entity* contains parsed data, which is replacement text and which has been processed through an XML parser. A parsed entity has a name and is called by an entity reference.

An *internal entity* has its content stored completely within the DTD. An internal entity is a parsed EntityValue. Its content is declared within the current XML document. Any other entity is an external entity.

An *external entity* has its content stored in a separate file that is completely outside the XML document. An unparsed external entity has an NDataDecl declaration. All other external entities are parsed.

According to the XML specification, processors that check whether a document is well formed do not have to collect and expand external entities.

A *general entity* is a variable named within the text of the document instance. In contrast, a *parameter entity* is a variable named within markup. A general entity is preceded by an ampersand symbol (&) and followed by a semicolon (;). Valid general-entity categories are internal-parsed general, external-parsed general, and external-unparsed general.

An internal–parsed general entity is well formed if it is identical to its associated content production.

An external-parsed general entity is well-formed if it is identical to its associated extParsedEnt production.

A *parameter entity* (PE) is a variable that is named within markup in the prolog of a document, document type definition (DTD), or the document instance. A parameter entity is parsed, is preceded by a percent symbol (%), and is ended with a semicolon (;). Valid parameter-entity categories are internal parsed parameter and external parsed parameter. In other words, no unparsed parameter entities exist.

For an XML document to be well formed, all elements must be nested properly: all tags, elements, comments, processing instructions, character references, and entity references must be completely enclosed within one entity. In addition, internal parsed parameter entities must be syntactically correct.

Examples

The following example shows a general entity declaration:

```
<!ENTITY copyright "This document is copyrighted by
    the Eddy Group, Inc.">
```

The following example shows the parameter-entity declaration within the HTML INPUT element:

```
<!ENTITY % InputType
"(TEXT | PASSWORD | CHECKBOX |
    RADIO | SUBMIT | RESET |
    FILE | HIDDEN | IMAGE | BUTTON)"
>
```

The following example shows an external parameter entity for the Full Latin 1 character entity set and the related general entity:

```
<!ENTITY % HTMLlat1 PUBLIC
"-//W3C//ENTITIES Full Latin 1//EN//HTML">
%HTMLlat1;
```

XML Syntax

Related Productions

content (p. 52), EntityDef (p. 76), EntityValue (p. 79), ExternalID (p. 84), extParsedEnt (p. 86), GEDecl (p. 89), markupdecl (p. 98), Name (p. 102), NDataDecl (p. 106), PEDecl (p. 112), PEDef (p. 114), S (p. 124)

EntityDef [73]   Entity Definition

Purpose

Defines a general entity.

EBNF Syntax

```
EntityDef ::= EntityValue | (ExternalID NDataDecl?)
```

Standard Syntax

EntityValue|[ExternalID[NDataDecl]]

Where

- *EntityValue* (p. 79) specifies the value of an internal entity. Syntax: *{"[^%&"]|'[^%&']}[|PEReference|Reference][[|PEReference| Reference]...[|PEReference|Reference]{"|'}*
- *ExternalID* (p. 84) names a parsed external entity. Syntax: *SYSTEM[...] SystemLiteral|PUBLIC[...]PubidLiteral[...]SystemLiteral*
- *NDataDecl* (p. 106) declares an unparsed external entity. Syntax: *[...] NDATA[...]Name*

Notes

EntityDef is a component of the GEDecl production.

An *unparsed entity* contains unparsed data, which may or may not be valid, may not even be XML, and have not been processed through an XML parser. An unparsed entity has a named notation, which the XML processor sends to the target application.

A *parsed entity* contains parsed data, which are replacement text and which have been processed through an XML parser. A parsed entity has a name and is called by an entity reference.

An *internal entity* has its content stored completely within the DTD. An internal entity is a parsed EntityValue. Its content is declared within the current XML document. Any other entity is an external entity.

An *external entity* has its content stored in a separate file that is completely outside the XML document. An unparsed external entity has an NDataDecl declaration. All other external entities are parsed. Well-formedness checkers do not need to collect external entities.

A *general entity* is a variable named within the text of the document instance. In contrast, a parameter entity is a variable named within markup. A general entity is preceded by an ampersand symbol (&) and followed by a semicolon (;). Valid general entity categories are internal parsed general, external parsed general, and external unparsed general.

For a document to be well formed, its internal general parsed entities must be identical to their associated content production and its external general parsed entities must be identical to their associated extParsedEnt production.

The ampersand (&) and less-than symbol (<) are reserved; they indicate the start or end of markup, among other things. To specify an ampersand or less-than symbol within character data, use the entities & or <, respectively.

Example

The following example shows a general entity declaration, including an entity definition:

```
<!ENTITY copyright "This document is copyrighted by
    the Eddy Group, Inc.">
```

Related Productions

content (p. 52), EntityDecl (p. 74), EntityValue (p. 79), ExternalID (p. 84), extParsedEnt (p. 86), GEDecl (p. 89), markupdecl (p. 98), Name (p. 102), NDataDecl (p. 106), PEDecl (p. 112), PEDef (p. 114), S (p. 124)

XML Syntax

EntityRef [68]   Entity Reference

Purpose

Specifies an entity reference, a named general entity's content.

EBNF Syntax

```
EntityRef ::= '&' Name ';'
```

Standard Syntax

```
&Name;
```

Where

- & marks the beginning of the entity reference.
- *Name* (p. 102) specifies a valid XML entity reference name. Syntax:
  #xnnnn [#xnnnn][_][:][#xnnnn]|[0|1|2|3|4|5|6|7|8|9][.]
  |[-][#xnnnn][#xnnnn]...[#xnnnn]
- ; marks the end of the entity reference.

Notes

EntityRef is a component of the Reference production.

An entity always has content, and most entities have a name.

Character references and entities begin with a variety of characters, but all end with a semicolon (;):

- Decimal character references start with the &# characters and are defined using the CharRef production.
- Hexadecimal character references start with the &#x characters and are defined using the CharRef production.
- Parsed general entities start with an ampersand (&) and are defined using the EntityRef production.
- Parameter-entity references start with a percent sign (%) and are defined using the PEReference production.

For an XML document without a DTD to be well formed, the entity reference name must match the same name in an entity declaration, but a well-formed document doesn't need to declare amp, lt, gt, apos, or quot. Additionally, the entity must be declared before it is referred to.

For an XML document to be well formed, it does not need a DTD. However, if it has an internal DTD subset without any occurrence of the PEReference production, the entity reference name must match the same name in an entity declaration.

A well-formed document does not need to declare amp, lt, gt, apos, or quot.

You must declare the entity in a DTD before you refer to it.

For a stand-alone XML document to be well formed, it does not need a DTD. However, if it has a DTD, the entity reference name must match the same name in an entity declaration.

For an XML document to be well formed, its parsed entities must not have any recursive reference in their contents, all elements must be nested properly (all tags, elements, comments, processing instructions, character references, and entity references must be completely enclosed within one entity), and an entity reference must not have an unparsed entity name in its contents, but instead refer to unparsed entities using the following attribute values: ENTITY or ENTITIES.

For a nonstand-alone XML document with an external subset (the part of a DTD that is stored in a separate document, completely outside the source document) or external parameter entities to be valid, the entity reference name must match the same name in an entity declaration.

For a nonstand-alone XML document with an external subset (the part of a DTD that is stored in a separate document, completely outside the source document) or external parameter entities to be compatible with SGML, it should declare amp with the && character reference, lt with &<, gt with >, apos with ', or quot with ".

Examples

The following are examples of entity references:

```
&copyright;
&editdate;
```

Related Productions

AttValue (p. 33), BaseChar (p. 34), Char (p. 41), CharRef (p. 43), CombiningChar
(p. 47), content (p. 52), Digit (p. 60), EntityValue (p. 79), Extender (p. 84),
Ideographic (p. 91), Letter (p. 98), Name (p. 102), PEReference (p. 115),
Reference (p. 123)

Related Attributes

ENTITIES (p. 73) , ENTITY (p. 73)

EntityValue [9]   Internal Entity Value

Purpose

Specifies the value of an internal entity.

EBNF Syntax

```
EntityValue ::= '"' ([^%&"] | PEReference
   | Reference)* '"' | "'" ([^%&'] | PEReference
   | Reference)* "'"
```

Standard Syntax

```
{"[^%&"]|'[^%&']}[|PEReference|Reference]
  [|PEReference|Reference]
..[|PEReference|Reference]{"|'}
```

Where

- %, &, ", and ' are characters *not* to be included in the production.
- PEReference (p. 115) names a parameter-entity reference. Syntax: %Name;
- Reference (p. 123) names an entity reference or character reference.
  Syntax: EntityRef|CharRef

Notes

EntityValue is a component of the EntityDef and PEDef productions.

A literal such as EntityValue replaces the current value of an entity or
attribute.

EntityValue supports entity references, which must be preceded by a # symbol. Each entity reference replaces one character.

For an XML document to be well formed, each internal general parsed entity
must be identical to its associated content production.

If you enclose a production, string, element, or other object within single
quote marks, do not use single quote marks within the quoted object; if you
enclose a production, string, element, or other object within quotation
marks, do not use quotation marks within the quoted object.

XML Syntax

Within character data, you can use the apostrophe (') or quotation mark (") entities to indicate quote marks.

Do not mix single quote marks and quotation marks; the quote marks at the beginning and end of a quoted object must match.

The ampersand (&) is reserved; to specify an ampersand within character data, use the entity &.

Example

The following example shows a declared parameter entity from the Math Markup Language:

```
<!ENTITY % att-base        'base CDATA    "10"' >
```

Related Productions

AttValue (p. 33), content (p. 52), EntityDef (p. 76), PEDef (p. 114), PEReference (p. 115), PubidChar (p. 120), PubidLiteral (p. 121), Reference (p. 123), SystemLiteral (p. 131)

| **EnumeratedType** [57] | **Enumerated Name/Name Token** |

Purpose

Indicates that an attribute type is composed of one or more enumerated notation names or name tokens.

EBNF Syntax

```
EnumeratedType ::= NotationType | Enumeration
```

Standard Syntax

```
NotationType|Enumeration
```

Where

- *NotationType* (p. 111) lists all the possible names of a notation type.
  Syntax: *NOTATION[...]([...]Name[[[...]|[...]Name]*
  [[...]|[...]Name]...[[...]|[...]Name]][...])
- *Enumeration* (p. 81) lists all the possible name tokens for an attribute.
  Syntax: *([...]Nmtoken [[...]|[...]Nmtoken][[...]|*
  [...]Nmtoken]...[[...]|[...]Nmtoken][...])

Notes

EnumeratedType is a component of the AttType production.

Notation defines the elements of a body of knowledge by using a formalized set of symbols or an alphabet. Braille, musical notes, and even computer file formats are types of notation. In XML, a notation names the format of an unparsed entity or an element that contains a notation attribute, or names the target application of a processing instruction.

(XML Syntax)

An *enumeration* is a list of possible values.

For an XML document to be valid, each notation attribute type must match a declared notation name.

For an XML document to be valid, each enumeration type must match a declared Nmtoken token.

For an XML document to be valid and compatible with SGML, each Nmtoken token in a particular element type should be unique.

Examples

The following example presents a list of notation names:

```
NOTATION    (CGM  |  TIF  |  JPG  |  GIF)
```

The following example is an enumerated list of name tokens:

```
(1st  |  2nd  |  3rd  |  4th)
```

Related Productions

AttType (p. 32), Enumeration (p. 81), Nmtoken (p. 107), NotationType (p. 111),

Enumeration [59]   Enumeration

Purpose

Lists all the possible name tokens for an attribute.

EBNF Syntax

```
Enumeration ::= '(' S? Nmtoken (S? '|'
   S? Nmtoken)* S? ')'
```

Standard Syntax

```
([ ... ]Nmtoken [[ ... ]|[ ... ]Nmtoken][[ ... ]
|[ ... ]Nmtoken]...[[ ... ]|[ ... ]Nmtoken][ ... ])
```

Where

- *(* marks the start of the names on the list.
- *S* (p. 124) represents one or more whitespace characters: spaces, carriage returns, line feeds, or tabs. Syntax: *{ [#x20 | #x9 | #xD | #xA] [#x20 | #x9 | #xD | #xA]...[#x20 | #x9 | #xD | #xA] }*
- *Nmtoken* (p. 107) specifies a valid XML name token. Syntax: *NameChar [[NameChar]...[NameChar]]*
- *|* is a character that separates one name from the next.
- *)* marks the end of the names on the list.

Notes

Enumeration is a component of the EnumeratedType production.

An *enumeration* is a list of possible values for an attribute type.

For an XML document to be valid, each enumeration type must match a declared Nmtoken name token.

For an XML document to be valid and compatible with SGML, each Nmtoken token in a particular element type should be unique.

Example

The following example is an enumerated list of name tokens:

```
(1st | 2nd | 3rd | 4th)
```

Related Productions

EnumeratedType (p. 80), Nmtoken (p. 107), S (p. 124)

Eq [25]   Equal Sign

Purpose

Indicates an equal sign in an expression.

EBNF Syntax

```
Eq ::= S? '=' S?
```

Standard Syntax

```
[ ... ]=[ ... ]
```

Where

- *S* (p. 124) represents one or more whitespace characters: spaces, carriage returns, line feeds, or tabs. Syntax: {[#x20|#x9|#xD|#xA][#x20| #x9|#xD|#xA]...[#x20|#x9|#xD|#xA]}
- = is an equal sign.

Notes

Eq is a component of the Attribute, EncodingDecl, SDDecl, and VersionInfo productions.

Eq is a part of the XML specification. However, do not use the name Eq in DTDs and XML documents. Instead, use the equal sign (=).

Example

The following example declares a stand-alone document:

```
<?xml version="1.0" standalone="yes"?>
```

Related Productions

Attribute (p. 31), Comment (p. 49), doctypedecl (p. 61), document (p. 63), EncodingDecl (p. 71), Misc (p. 100), PI (p. 117), prolog (p. 119), S (p. 124), SDDecl (p. 126), VersionInfo (p. 135), VersionNum (p. 136), XMLDecl (p. 137)

ETag [42]   End Tag

Purpose
Defines an end tag for an element.

EBNF Syntax
```
ETag ::= '</' Name S? '>'
```

Standard Syntax
```
</Name[ ... ]>
```

Where
- </ marks the start of the end tag.
- *Name* (p. 102) specifies a valid XML element-type name. Syntax: *#xnnnn [#xnnnn][_][:][#xnnnn] | [0|1|2|3|4|5|6|7|8|9][.] | [-] [#xnnnn] [#xnnnn]...[#xnnnn]*
- *S* (p. 124) represents one or more whitespace characters: spaces, carriage returns, line feeds, or tabs. Syntax: *{ [#x20|#x9|#xD|#xA] [#x20| #x9|#xD|#xA]...[#x20|#x9|#xD|#xA] }*
- > marks the end of the end tag.

Notes
ETag is a component of the element production.

An end tag indicates the end of element content.

The element-type name for the start tag must match that for the end tag.

Every non-empty element with a start tag must also have an end tag. Empty elements either follow the syntax of the EmptyElemTag production or have a start tag (with or without attributes) immediately followed by an end tag. Requiring an end tag for every start tag is a difference from HTML 4.0 (and older versions), in which some end tags are optional and some are omitted altogether. Because XHTML is a subset of XML, it follows XML rules.

For an XML document to be well formed, all elements must be nested properly: All tags, elements, comments, processing instructions, character references, and entity references must be completely enclosed within one entity.

Example
The following example is an entire valid, self-contained XML document with one end tag:

```
<?xml version="1.0"?>
<!DOCTYPE endstate[>
<!ELEMENT endstate (#PCDATA)>
]>
<endstate>Goodbye, cruel world!</endstate>
```

XML Syntax

Related Productions
Attribute (p. 31), content (p. 52), element (p. 64), EmptyElemTag (p. 68), Eq (p. 82), STag (p. 129)

Extender [89]   Extender Symbol

Purpose
Inserts an extender symbol.

EBNF Syntax
```
Extender ::= #x00B7 | #x02D0 | #x02D1 | #x0387
  | #x0640 | #x0E46 | #x0EC6 | #x3005
  | [#x3031-#x3035] | [#x309D-#x309E]
  | [#x30FC-#x30FE]
```

Standard Syntax
```
#xnnnn
```

● NOTE
The preceding EBNF syntax lists all the extender symbols supported by XML.

Where
- #xnnnn represents an extender character supported by the Unicode Organization. For a complete list of supported extender characters, see Appendix A, "Unicode Characters and Character Sets" (p. 757). For more information about Unicode characters, see Chapter 2, "Introducing DTDs" (p. 669).

Note
Extender is a component of the NameChar production

Related Productions
BaseChar (p. 34), Char (p. 41), CharRef (p. 43), CombiningChar (p. 47), Digit (p. 60), EntityRef (p. 77), Extender (p. 84), Ideographic (p. 91), Letter (p. 98), Name (p. 102), NameChar (p. 104), PEReference (p. 115), Reference (p. 123)

ExternalID [75]   Parsed External Entity

Purpose
Identifies a parsed external entity.

XML Syntax

EBNF Syntax

```
ExternalID ::= 'SYSTEM' S SystemLiteral
             | 'PUBLIC' S PubidLiteral S
             SystemLiteral
```

Standard Syntax

```
SYSTEM[ ... ]SystemLiteral
|PUBLIC[ ... ]PubidLiteral[ ... ]SystemLiteral
```

Where

- *SYSTEM* is an uppercase-only reserved keyword indicating that a parsed external entity follows.
- *S* (p. 124) represents one or more whitespace characters: spaces, carriage returns, line feeds, or tabs. Syntax: {*[#x20|#x9|#xD|#xA][#x20|#x9|#xD|#xA]...[#x20|#x9|#xD|#xA]*}
- *SystemLiteral* (p. 131) specifies the URI of an external identifier. Syntax: {*"|'*}*URI*{*"|'*}
- *PUBLIC* is an uppercase-only reserved keyword indicating that a public identifier follows.
- *PubidLiteral* (p. 121) names a public identifier. Syntax: {*"|'*}*[[PubidChar][PubidChar]...[PubidChar]]*{*"|'*}

Notes

ExternalID is a component of the doctypedecl, EntityDef, NotationDecl, and PEDef productions.

All system identifiers are addresses (URI references).

A *parsed entity* contains parsed data, which is replacement text and which has been processed through an XML parser. A parsed entity has a name and is called by an entity reference.

An *external entity* has its content stored in a separate file that is completely outside the XML document. An unparsed external entity has an NDataDecl declaration. All other external entities are parsed.

A *parameter entity* (PE) is a variable that is named within markup in the prolog of a document, document type definition (DTD), or the document instance. A parameter entity is parsed, is preceded by a percent symbol (%), and is ended with a semicolon (;). Valid parameter-entity categories are internal parsed parameter and external parsed parameter. In other words, no unparsed parameter entities exist.

For an XML document to be well formed, internal parsed parameter entities must be syntactically correct.

For an XML document to be valid, a # and associated fragment identifier cannot be part of the system identifier URI.

For an XML document to be valid, a relative system identifier URI must relate back to the document resource in which the entity declaration resides — that is, the document entity, the external DTD subset entity, or an external parameter entity.

For an XML document to be valid, the XML processor converts non-ASCII characters (such as non-keyboard characters) in a system identifier URI to UTF-8 and then to hexadecimal.

Examples

The following example shows two external IDs:

```
<!ENTITY copyright SYSTEM "copyright.txt">
```

```
<!ENTITY copyright SYSTEM
    "http://www.myfiles.com/copyright.txt">
```

Related Productions

doctypedecl (p. 61), EntityDef (p. 76), NDataDecl (p. 106), NotationDecl (p. 110), PEDef (p. 114), S (p. 124), SystemLiteral (p. 131)

---

extParsedEnt [78]　　　　　External Parsed Entity

Purpose

Specifies a well-formed external general parsed entity.

EBNF Syntax

```
extParsedEnt ::= TextDecl? content
```

Standard Syntax

```
[TextDecl] content
```

Where

- *TextDecl* (p. 132) provides version and encoding information about an external subset or external parameter entity. Syntax: `<?xml [VersionInfo] EncodingDecl[ ... ]?>`
- *content* (p. 52) represents element content within the start and end tags. Syntax: `[element|CharData|Reference|CDSect|PI|Comment] [element|CharData|Reference|CDSect|PI|Comment]...[element| CharData|Reference|CDSect|PI|Comment]`

Notes

For an XML document to be well formed, all elements must be nested properly: All tags, elements, comments, processing instructions, character references, and entity references must be completely enclosed within one entity.

A *parsed entity* contains parsed data, which is replacement text and which has been processed through an XML parser. A parsed entity has a name and is called by an entity reference.

An *external entity* has its content stored in a separate file that is completely outside the XML document. An unparsed external entity has an NDataDecl declaration. All other external entities are parsed.

A *general entity* is a variable named within the text of the document instance. In contrast, a *parameter entity* is a variable named within markup. A general entity is preceded by an ampersand symbol (&) and followed by a semicolon (;). Valid general entity categories are internal parsed general, external parsed general, and external unparsed general.

An external general parsed entity is well formed if it is identical to its associated extParsedEnt production.

Example

The following example could be a very small external parsed entity named endstate.dtd:

```
<?xml version="1.0" encoding="UTF-8"?>
<!DOCTYPE endstate[>
<!ELEMENT endstate (#PCDATA)>
]>
<endstate>Goodbye, cruel world!</endstate>
```

If the preceding example is an external parsed entity, the current XML document must include an internal subset that refers to an external parsed entity:

```
<?xml version="1.0"?>
<!DOCTYPE endstate SYSTEM "endstate.dtd">
```

Related Productions

content (p. 52), extParsedEnt (p. 86), extSubsetDecl (p. 88), NDataDecl (p. 106), TextDecl (p. 132)

---

extSubset [30]   External Subset

Purpose

Specifies an external subset.

EBNF Syntax

```
extSubset ::= TextDecl? extSubsetDecl
```

Standard Syntax

```
[TextDecl] extSubsetDecl
```

Where

- *TextDecl* (p. 132) provides version and encoding information about an external subset or external parameter entity. Syntax: *<?xml[VersionInfo] EncodingDecl[...]?>*

- *extSubsetDecl* (p. 88) declares external subset markup, conditions, and/or parameter-entity references. Syntax: *[markupdecl|conditionalSect|PEReference|[...]][markupdecl|conditionalSect|PEReference|[...]]...[markupdecl|conditionalSect|PEReference|[...]]*

Notes

The external subset is an external parsed entity and the part of a DTD that is stored in a separate document, completely outside the source document.

Use the extSubset production only within external document type definitions (DTDs).

An external subset associated with a document or set of documents must be identical to the extSubset production.

An external subset can include a text declaration, which helps when the subset uses a particular Unicode encoding.

PEReferences are allowed within markup declarations in external subsets and external parameter entities.

Internal subsets (the part of the DTD that is located within the source document) are higher in precedence than external subsets.

You can use conditional sections within external subsets but not within internal subsets.

Example

The following example shows the reference to an external subset, quotes.dtd, in a source document:

```
<?xml version="1.0"?>
<!DOCTYPE test SYSTEM "quotes.dtd">
```

Related Productions

conditionalSect (p. 50), extSubsetDecl (p. 88), markupdecl (p. 98), PEReference (p. 115), TextDecl (p. 132), S (p. 124)

extSubsetDecl [31]   External Subset Declaration

Purpose

Declares external subset markup, conditions, and/or parameter-entity references.

EBNF Syntax

```
extSubsetDecl ::= ( markupdecl | conditionalSect
  | DeclSep )*
```

Standard Syntax

[*markupdecl* | *conditionalSect* | *DeclSep*]
[*markupdecl* | *conditionalSect* | *DeclSep*]
...[*markupdecl* | *conditionalSect* | *DeclSep*]

Where

- *markupdecl* (p. 98) declares markup of elements, attributes, entities, or notation. Syntax: *elementdecl* | *AttlistDecl* | *EntityDecl* | *NotationDecl* | *PI* | *Comment*
- *conditionalSect* (p. 50) indicates a conditional section. Syntax: *includeSect* | *ignoreSect*
- *DeclSep* (p. 57) inserts a parameter-entity reference or space between declarations. Syntax: *PEReference* | [...]

Notes

extSubsetDecl is a component of the extSubset and includeSect productions.

Use the extSubsetDecl production only within external document type definitions (DTDs).

For more information, see the Notes section of the extSubset production.

Example

The following example includes an external subset declaration:

```
<?xml version="1.0" encoding="UTF-8"?>
<!DOCTYPE test SYSTEM "endstate.dtd">
<endstate>Goodbye, cruel world!</endstate>
<!ELEMENT endstate (#PCDATA)>
```

Related Productions

conditionalSect (p. 50), extSubset (p. 87), includeSect (p. 97), markupdecl (p. 98), PEReference (p. 115), S (p. 124), TextDecl (p. 132)

GEDecl [71]   General Entity Declaration

Purpose

Declares a general entity.

EBNF Syntax

GEDecl ::= '<!ENTITY' S Name S EntityDef S? '>'

Standard Syntax

<!ENTITY[...]Name[...]EntityDef[...]>

Where

- *<!ENTITY* marks the start of the general entity declaration.

- *S* (p. 124) represents one or more whitespace characters: spaces, carriage returns, line feeds, or tabs. Syntax: { *[#x20|#x9|#xD|#xA] [#x20| #x9|#xD|#xA] ... [#x20|#x9|#xD|#xA]* }
- *Name* (p. 102) specifies a valid XML general-entity name. Syntax: *#xnnnn [#xnnnn][_][:][#xnnnn]|[0|1|2|3|4|5|6|7|8|9][.]|[-][#xnnnn] [#xnnnn]...[#xnnnn]*
- *EntityDef* (p. 76) prepares a general entity definition. Syntax: *EntityValue| [ExternalID[NDataDecl]]*
- > marks the end of the general entity declaration.

Notes

GEDecl is a component of the EntityDecl production.

An *unparsed entity* contains unparsed data, which may or may not be valid, may not even be XML, and has not been processed through an XML parser. An unparsed entity has a named notation, which the XML processor sends to the target application.

A *parsed entity* contains parsed data, which is replacement text and which has been processed through an XML parser. A parsed entity has a name and is called by an entity reference.

An *internal entity* has its content stored completely within the DTD. An internal entity is a parsed EntityValue. Its content is declared within the current XML document. Any other entity is an external entity.

An *external entity* has its content stored in a separate file that is completely outside the XML document. An unparsed external entity has an NDataDecl declaration. All other external entities are parsed.

A *general entity* is a variable named within the text of the document instance. In contrast, a *parameter entity* is a variable named within markup. A general entity is preceded by an ampersand symbol (&) and followed by a semicolon (;). Valid general entity categories are internal parsed general, external parsed general, and external unparsed general.

A document is well formed if its internal general parsed entities are identical to their associated content production and its external general parsed entities are identical to their associated extParsedEnt production.

Example

The following example shows a general entity declaration:

```
<!ENTITY copyright "This document is copyrighted by
    the Eddy Group, Inc.">
```

Related Productions

content (p. 52), EntityDecl (p. 74), EntityDef (p. 76), EntityValue (p. 79), ExternalID (p. 84), extParsedEnt (p. 86), markupdecl (p. 98), Name (p. 102), NDataDecl (p. 106), PEDecl (p. 112), PEDef (p. 114), S (p. 124)

ID   Identifier Attribute

Purpose
Indicates that a valid XML identifier follows.

EBNF Syntax
See the TokenizedType production (p. 134).

Standard Syntax
See the TokenizedType production.

Notes
ID is an uppercase-only reserved keyword indicating that the defined attribute is an identifier.

The ID attribute type enables complex linking and optional extended pointers. For more information, refer to "XLink Language" (p. 145) and "XPointer Language" (p. 165) in Part I, and Chapter 6, "Adding Links and Pointers to an XML Document" (p. 733).

Some nonvalidating XML processors assume that the default attribute type is ID. This allows a well-formed document to use identifiers for complex linking.

For an XML document to be valid and compatible with SGML, each element type can have only one ID attribute type.

For an XML document to be valid, the ID attribute must conform to the Name production.

For an XML document to be valid, each ID name must be unique.

For an XML document to be valid, each ID must have a default value of #IMPLIED or #REQUIRED.

For more information, see the Notes section of the TokenizedType production, which is a component of the AttType production.

Related Productions
AttType (p. 32), Name (p. 102), Names (p. 105), Nmtoken (p. 107), Nmtokens (p. 108), TokenizedType (p. 134)

Related Attributes
ENTITIES (p. 73), ENTITY (p. 73), IDREF (p. 92), IDREFS (p. 93), NMTOKEN (p. 107), NMTOKENS (p. 109)

Ideographic [86]   Ideographic Symbol

Purpose
Specifies an *ideogram*, a symbol or glyph that represents another character, a word, or other object.

XML Syntax

EBNF Syntax

```
Ideographic ::= [#x4E00-#x9FA5] | #x3007
    | #x3021-#x3029]
```

Standard Syntax

```
#xnnnn
```

●─NOTE───────────────────

The preceding EBNF syntax lists all the ideographic symbols supported by XML.

Where

- #xnnnn represents an ideographic character supported by the Unicode Organization. For a complete list of supported ideographic characters, see Appendix A, "Unicode Characters and Character Sets" (p. 757). For more information about Unicode characters, see Chapter 2, "Introducing DTDs" (p. 669).

Note

Ideographic is a component of the Letter production.

Related Productions

BaseChar (p. 34), Char (p. 41), CharRef (p. 43), CombiningChar (p. 47), Digit (p. 60), EntityRef (p. 77), Extender (p. 84), Letter (p. 98), Name (p. 102), PEReference (p. 115), Reference (p. 123)

IDREF   Identifier Cross-Reference Attribute

Purpose

Indicates that a valid XML identifier cross-reference follows.

EBNF Syntax

See the TokenizedType production (p. 134).

Standard Syntax

See the TokenizedType production.

Notes

IDREF is an uppercase-only reserved keyword indicating that the defined attribute is an identifier cross-reference.

The IDREF attribute type enables complex linking and optional extended pointers. For more information, refer to "XLink Language" (p. 145) and "XPointer Language" (p. 165) in Part I , and Chapter 6, "Adding Links and Pointers to an XML Document" (p. 723).

XML Syntax

For an XML document to be valid, the IDREF attribute must conform to the Name production.

For an XML document to be valid, each IDREF name must match the value of an ID.

For more information, see the Notes section of the TokenizedType production, which is a component of the AttType production.

Related Productions

AttType (p. 32), Name (p. 102), Names (p. 105), Nmtoken (p. 107), Nmtokens (p. 108), TokenizedType (p. 134)

Related Attributes

ENTITIES (p. 73), ENTITY (p. 73), ID (p. 91), IDREFS (p. 93), NMTOKEN (p. 107), NMTOKENS (p. 109)

IDREFS   Identifier Cross-Reference List Attribute

Purpose

Indicates that a list of valid XML cross-references follows.

EBNF Syntax

See the TokenizedType production. (p. 134)

Standard Syntax

See the TokenizedType production.

Notes

IDREFS is an uppercase-only reserved keyword indicating that a list of ID cross-references follows.

For an XML document to be valid, the IDREFS attribute must conform to the Names production.

For more information, see the Notes section of the TokenizedType production, which is a component of the AttType production.

Related Productions

AttType (p. 32), Name (p. 102), Names (p. 105), Nmtoken (p. 107), Nmtokens (p. 108), TokenizedType (p. 134)

Related Attributes

ENTITIES (p. 73), ENTITY (p. 73), ID (p. 91), IDREF (p. 92), NMTOKEN (p. 107), NMTOKENS (p. 109)

Ignore [65]   Ignore

Purpose
Indicates the beginning and end of an included section nested in an ignored section.

EBNF Syntax
```
Ignore ::= Char* - (Char* ('<![' | ']]>') Char*)
```

Standard Syntax
```
[Char[Char]...[Char]]
```

Where
- *Char* (p. 41) specifies one legal character. Syntax: #*xnnnn[n[n]]*

Notes
Ignore is a component of the ignoreSectContents production.

Use the Ignore production only within external document type definitions (DTDs).

Do not use the <, [, and] characters; combinations of those characters indicate the start and end of a character data section.

For more information, see the Notes section of the conditionalSect production.

Example
The following example from the XML specification shows two sections — one included and one ignored:

```
<!ENTITY % draft 'INCLUDE' >
<!ENTITY % final 'IGNORE' >
<![%draft;[
<!ELEMENT book (comments*, title, body, supplements?)>
]]><![%final;[
<!ELEMENT book (title, body, supplements?)>
]]>
```

Related Productions
Char (p. 41), conditionalSect (p. 50), extSubsetDecl (p. 88), ignoreSect (p. 94), ignoreSectContents (p. 95), includeSect (p. 97), S (p. 124)

ignoreSect [63]   Ignored Section

Purpose
Names a conditionally ignored section.

EBNF Syntax

```
ignoreSect ::= '<![' S? 'IGNORE' S?
  '[' ignoreSectContents* ']]>'
```

Standard Syntax

```
<![[ ... ]IGNORE[ ... ][[ignoreSectContents]
[ignoreSectContents]...[ignoreSectContents]]]>
```

Where

- `<![` marks the start of the ignored character data section.
- *S* (p. 124) represents one or more whitespace characters: spaces, carriage returns, line feeds, or tabs. Syntax: { *[#x20|#x9|#xD|#xA] [#x20| #x9|#xD|#xA]...[#x20|#x9|#xD|#xA]* }
- *IGNORE* is an uppercase-only reserved keyword indicating that the character data section should be ignored in XML processing.
- *[* marks the start of the contents of the ignored section.
- *ignoreSectContents* (p. 95) defines an ignored section's contents. Syntax: *Ignore [<![ignoreSectContents]]> Ignore][<![ignore SectContents]]> Ignore]...[<![ignoreSectContents]]> Ignore]*
- *]]>* marks the end of the ignored section.

Notes

ignoreSect is a component of the conditionalSect production.

Use the ignoreSect production only within external document type definitions (DTDs).

For more information, see the Notes section of the conditionalSect production.

Example

The following is a small ignored section:

```
<![ IGNORE [
<!ELEMENT byestate (#PCDATA)>
]]>
```

Related Productions

conditionalSect (p. 50), extSubsetDecl (p. 88), Ignore (p. 94), ignoreSectContents (p. 95), includeSect (p. 97), S (p. 124)

---

ignoreSectContents [64]   Ignored Section Contents

Purpose

Defines an ignored section's contents.

EBNF Syntax

```
ignoreSectContents ::= Ignore
('<![' ignoreSectContents ']]>' Ignore)*
```

Standard Syntax

```
Ignore[<![ignoreSectContents]]>Ignore]
 [<![ignoreSectContents]]>Ignore]
 ...[<![ignoreSectContents]]>Ignore]
```

Where

- `<![` marks the start of the ignored section's contents.
- *Ignore* (p. 94) indicates the beginning and end of an included section nested in an ignored section. Syntax: *[Char[Char]...[Char]]*
- *ignoreSectContents* (p. 95) defines an ignored section's contents. Syntax: *Ignore [<![ignoreSectContents]]> Ignore][<![ignore SectContents]]> Ignore]...[<![ignoreSectContents]]> Ignore]*
- *]]>* marks the end of the ignored section's contents.

Notes

ignoreSectContents is a component of the ignoreSect and ignoreSectContents productions.

Use the ignoreSectContents production only within external document type definitions (DTDs).

For more information, see the Notes section of the conditionalSect production.

Example

The following example from the XML specification shows an included and ignored section with another included section nested in the ignored section:

```
<!ENTITY % draft 'INCLUDE' >
<!ENTITY % final 'IGNORE' >

<![%draft;[
<!ELEMENT book (comments*, title, body, supplements?)>
]]>
<![%final;[
<!ELEMENT book (title, body, supplements?)>
]]>
```

Related Productions

conditionalSect (p. 50), extSubsetDecl (p. 88), Ignore (p. 94), ignoreSect (p. 94), includeSect (p. 97), S (p. 124)

includeSect [62]   Included Section

Purpose
Indicates an included section.

EBNF Syntax
```
includeSect ::= '<![' S? 'INCLUDE' S?
'[' extSubsetDecl ']]>'
```

Standard Syntax
```
<![[ ... ]INCLUDE[ ... ][[extSubsetDecl]]>
```

Where
- `<![` marks the start of the character data section.
- *S* (p. 124) represents one or more whitespace characters: spaces, carriage returns, line feeds, or tabs. Syntax: *{[#x20|#x9|#xD|#xA][#x20| #x9|#xD|#xA]...[#x20|#x9|#xD|#xA]}*
- *INCLUDE* is an uppercase-only reserved keyword indicating that the character data section should be included in XML processing.
- *[* marks the start of the external subset declaration.
- *;* marks the end of the external subset declaration.
- *extSubsetDecl* (p. 88) declares external subset markup, conditions, and/or parameter-entity references. Syntax: *[markupdecl| conditionalSect|PEReference|[...]][markupdecl| conditionalSect|PEReference|[...]]...[markupdecl| conditionalSect|PEReference|[...]]*
- *]]>* marks the end of the character data section.

Notes
includeSect is a component of the conditionalSect production.

Use the includeSect production only within external document type definitions (DTDs).

For more information, see the Notes section of the conditionalSect production.

You can include appropriate parts of the extSubsetDecl in the included section.

Example
The following is a small included section:

```
<![ INCLUDE [
<!ELEMENT histate (#PCDATA)>
]]>
```

XML Syntax

Related Productions

conditionalSect (p. 50), extSubsetDecl (p. 88), Ignore (p. 94), ignoreSect (p. 94), ignoreSectContents (p. 95), S (p. 124)

Letter [84]   Letter

Purpose
Specifies a letter of the current alphabet.

EBNF Syntax
```
Letter ::= BaseChar | Ideographic
```

Standard Syntax
```
#xnnnn
```

Where

- *BaseChar* (p. 34) represents an alphabetic character. Syntax: *#xnnnn*
- *Ideographic* (p. 91) represents an ideogram, a symbol that represents another character, a word, or other object. Syntax: *#xnnnn*

Notes
Letter is a component of the Name and NameChar productions.

According to the XML 1.0 (Second Edition) recommendation (http://www.w3.org/TR/REC-xml), "A letter consists of an alphabetic or syllabic base character or an ideographic character."

Related Productions

BaseChar (p. 34), Char (p. 41), CharRef (p. 43), CombiningChar (p. 47), Digit (p. 60), EntityRef (p. 77), Extender (p. 84), Ideographic (p. 91), Name (p. 102), NameChar (p. 104), PEReference (p. 115), Reference (p. 123)

markupdecl [29]   Markup Declaration

Purpose
Declares markup of elements, attribute lists, entities, or notation within parameter entities.

EBNF Syntax
```
markupdecl ::= elementdecl | AttlistDecl
   | EntityDecl | NotationDecl | PI
   | Comment
```

Standard Syntax
```
elementdecl|AttlistDecl|EntityDecl|NotationDecl
   |PI|Comment
```

Where

- *elementdecl* (p. 66) declares an element and its content. Syntax: {<*!ELEMENT[* ... *]Name[* ... *]contentspec}[* ... *]{>}*
- *AttlistDecl* (p. 29) declares an element's attribute list. Syntax: <*!ATTLIST [* ... *]Name [AttDef[AttDef[...AttDef]]][* ... *]>*
- *EntityDecl* (p. 74) declares a general or parameter entity. Syntax: *GEDecl|PEDecl*
- *NotationDecl* (p. 110) declares a notation name. Syntax: <*!NOTATION [* ... *]Name[* ... *]{ExternalID|PublicID}[* ... *]>*
- *PI* (p. 117) specifies a process to be performed within a target application. Syntax: <*?PITarget [[* ... *][Char[Char]...[Char]]?>*
- *Comment* (p. 49) indicates a nonprinting, nonparsed comment. Syntax: <*!--[[Char]|[-Char][[Char]|[-Char]]...[[Char]|[-Char]]]-->*

Notes

markupdecl is a component of the doctypedecl and extSubsetDecl productions.

Use the markupdecl production only within document type definitions (DTDs).

Parameter entities are processed first, resulting in replacement text being placed in the markup declarations. Then the declarations are processed.

A parameter entity can contain an element-type declaration, attribute-list declaration, entity declaration, or notation declaration.

For an XML document to be valid, the complete markup declaration must be nested within the PEReference replacement text.

For an XML document to be well formed, it does not need a DTD. However, if a DTD exists, PEReferences can only be placed within the brackets ([and]) in the DOCTYPE declaration in the internal subset (the part of the DTD that is located within the source document). PEReferences cannot be placed within markup declarations in the internal subset.

PEReferences are allowed within markup declarations in external subsets (the part of a DTD that is stored in a separate document, completely outside the source document) and external parameter entities.

Nonvalidating XML processors can ignore PEReferences, because they are not required to process external subsets.

Internal subsets are higher in precedence than external subsets.

You can use conditional sections within external subsets but not within internal subsets.

Do not include one dash (-) or two dashes in a comment; dashes are reserved for the start and end of the comment.

XML Syntax

Examples

See the AttlistDecl, Comment, elementdecl, EntityDecl, NotationDecl, and PI productions.

Related Productions

AttlistDecl (p. 29), Comment (p. 49), doctypedecl (p. 61), elementdecl (p. 66), EntityDecl (p. 74), extSubsetDecl (p. 88), markupdecl (p. 98), NotationDecl (p. 110), PEReference (p. 115), PI (p. 117)

Misc [27]   Miscellaneous

Purpose

Indicates miscellaneous information in an XML document or prolog.

EBNF Syntax

    Misc ::= Comment | PI | S

Standard Syntax

    Comment|PI|[...]

Where

- Comment (p. 49) indicates a nonprinting, nonparsed comment. Syntax:
  `<!--[[Char]|[-Char][[Char]|[-Char]]...[[Char]|[-Char]]]-->`
- PI (p. 117) specifies a process to be performed within a target application. Syntax: `<?PITarget [[ ... ][Char[Char]...[Char]]?>`
- S (p. 124) represents one or more whitespace characters: spaces, carriage returns, line feeds, or tabs. Syntax: `{[#x20|#x9|#xD|#xA][#x20|#x9|#xD|#xA]...[#x20|#x9|#xD|#xA]}`

Notes

Misc is a component of the document and prolog productions.

Do not include one dash (-) or two dashes in a comment; dashes are reserved for the start and end of the comment.

This production helps to identify the current document, including the version of XML that was used to create it.

Although Misc enables you to add miscellaneous content — comments, processing instructions, and whitespace — to the document and prolog productions, do so carefully. Being careful helps links to work properly and XML processors to interpret XML statements correctly.

Examples

The following comment, which is part of miscellaneous information, marks the start of an element definition:

    <!--defining <para> paragraph element and attributes-->

The following is probably the most commonly used processing instruction (PI):

```
<?xml version="1.0"?>
```

● — **NOTE** —

The XML declaration is not within the `Misc` component. However, `version=` `"1.0"` is.

These examples show varying amounts of whitespace within the same comment line:

```
<!--defining <para> paragraph element-->
<!--defining      <para>      paragraph element-->
```

Related Productions

Comment (p. 49), doctypedecl (p. 61), document (p. 63), EncodingDecl (p. 71), Eq (p. 82), PI (p. 117), prolog (p. 119), S (p. 124), SDDecl (p. 126), VersionInfo (p. 135), VersionNum (p. 136), XMLDecl (p. 137)

Mixed [51]   Mixed Element Content

Purpose

Indicates mixed element content consisting of character data and, optionally, child elements.

EBNF Syntax

```
Mixed ::= '(' S? '#PCDATA' (S? '|' S? Name)*
    S? ')*' | '(' S? '#PCDATA' S? ')'
```

Standard Syntax

```
([ ... ]#PCDATA[[ ... ][ ... ]Name]
[[ ... ][ ... ]Name][[ ... ][ .. ]Name]]
[ ... ])*|([ ... ]#PCDATA[ ... ])
```

Where

- *(* marks the start of the names on the list.
- *S* (p. 124) represents one or more whitespace characters: spaces, carriage returns, line feeds, or tabs. Syntax: `{[#x20|#x9|#xD|#xA][#x20|` `#x9|#xD|#xA]...[#x20|#x9|#xD|#xA]}`
- *#PCDATA* is an uppercase-only reserved keyword indicating that the specified element contains parsed character data.
- | is a character that separates one name from the next.
- *Name* (p. 102) specifies a valid XML child-element name. Syntax: `#xnnnn` `[#xnnnn][_][:][#xnnnn]|[0|1|2|3|4|5|6|7|8|9][.]|[-][#xnnnn]` `[#xnnnn]...[#xnnnn]`
- *)* marks the end of the names on the list.

Notes

Mixed is a component of the contentspec production.

Mixed element content defines the content of an element as character data and optional element content.

Mixed declarations allow elements to contain both character data and child elements, and enable a document to be valid.

#PCDATA must be present as one of the components; this distinguishes Mixed declarations from simple-choice declarations.

For an XML document to be valid, any PEReference replacement text must be nested completely within its content particle in one of the following productions: choice, Mixed, or seq.

For an XML document to be valid, any PEReference replacement text cannot be empty and its first or last nonblank characters should not be a pipe (|) or ,) character combination.

You cannot declare the same element type more than once in an XML document. However, you can declare attributes and entities more than once.

Mixed declarations cannot be nested in other declarations.

Example

The following example shows an element with character data and a child element:

```
<?xml version="1.0"?>
<DOCTYPE mixedtext[>
<!ELEMENT mixedtext (#PCDATA|bold)>
<mixedtext>I want to get your <bold>attention
</bold>.</mixedtext>
```

Related Productions

choice (p. 46), contentspec (p. 53), Name (p. 102), PEReference (p. 115), S (p. 124), seq (p. 127)

Name [5]   Name

Purpose

Specifies a valid XML name.

EBNF Syntax

```
Name ::= (Letter | '_' | ':' ) (NameChar)*
```

Standard Syntax

```
[Letter|_|:][[NameChar][NameChar]...[NameChar]]
```

Where

- `Letter` (p. 98) represents either an alphabetic character or an *ideogram*, a symbol that represents another character, a word, or other object. Syntax: #*xnnnn*
- `NameChar` (p. 104) specifies one character in a name. Syntax: `Letter|` `Digit|.|-|_|:|CombiningChar|Extender`

Notes

Name is a data type used by the `AttDef`, `AttlistDecl`, `Attr`, `Attribute`, `AttrTerm`, `cp`, `doctypedecl`, `elementdecl`, `EmptyElemTag`, `EntityRef`, `ETag`, `GEDecl`, `IdLoc`, `Locator`, `Mixed`, `Names`, `NDataDecl`, `NodeType`, `NotationDecl`, `NotationType`, `PEDecl`, `PEReference`, `PITarget`, `Query`, `STag`, and `Val` productions.

A `Name` must begin with a letter or underscore character (except the upper-case or lowercase letters `X`, `M`, or `L`, which are reserved) unlike a `Nmtoken`, which can begin with any letter, digit, or valid character.

Each `Name` in an XML document must be unique.

It is a good idea not to use a colon (`:`) in a `Name`; the colon is reserved for namespaces, which is a method of making like names unique. However, XML processors are required to accept the colon as a name character. Currently, namespaces use colons to differentiate names (for example, *oil:fluid* and *consume:fluid*, whereby the name *fluid* is no longer unique when the two documents are combined).

● NOTE

For more information on namespaces, read the W3C Namespaces Recommendation at `http://www.w3.org/TR/REC-xml-names/`.

Example

Name can appear in almost any context in an XML document. For examples, look under the productions listed in the first paragraph under Notes.

Related Productions

`AttDef` (p. 28), `AttlistDecl` (p. 29), `Attribute` (p. 31), `CombiningChar` (p. 47), `cp` (p. 55), `Digit` (p. 60), `doctypedecl` (p. 61), `elementdecl` (p. 66), `EmptyElemTag` (p. 68), `EntityRef` (p. 77), `ETag` (p. 83), `Extender` (p. 84), `GEDecl` (p. 89), `Letter` (p. 98), `Mixed` (p. 101), `Names` (p. 105), `NDataDecl` (p. 106), `Nmtoken` (p. 107), `Nmtokens` (p. 108), `NotationDecl` (p. 110), `NotationType` (p. 111), `PEDecl` (p. 112), `PEReference` (p. 115), `PITarget` (p. 118), `S` (p. 124), `STag` (p. 129)

XML Syntax

NameChar [4]   Name Character

Purpose

Specifies one character in a name.

EBNF Syntax

```
NameChar ::= Letter | Digit | '.' | '-'
       | '_' | ':'  | CombiningChar | Extender
```

Standard Syntax

```
Letter|Digit|.|-|_|:|CombiningChar|Extender
```

Where

- *Letter* (p. 98) represents either an alphabetic character or an *ideogram*, a symbol that represents another character, a word, or other object. Syntax: #*xnnnn*
- *Digit* (p. 60) is a number. Valid values: 0, 1, 2, 3, 4, 5, 6, 7, 8, 9
- . -, _, and : are valid characters.
- *CombiningChar* (p. 47) specifies a character that combines with letters of the alphabet and other characters to denote special pronunciation or meaning. Syntax: #*xnnnn*
- *Extender* (p. 84) inserts an extender symbol. Syntax: #*xnnnn*

Notes

NameChar is a component of the Name and Nmtoken productions.

A name character can be a letter, digit, or valid character, including a syllabic base character, combining character, or ideographic character.

A *syllabic base character* represents a syllable rather than a single letter.

A Name production must begin with a letter or underscore character (except the uppercase or lowercase letters X, M, or L, which are reserved).

A Nmtoken production can begin with any letter, digit, or valid character.

It is a good idea not to use a colon (:) in a name; the colon is reserved for namespaces, which is a method of making like names unique. However, XML processors are required to accept the colon as a name character. Currently, namespaces use colons to differentiate names (for example, *oil:fluid* and *consume:fluid*, whereby the name *fluid* is no longer unique when the two documents are combined).

Each Name or Nmtoken in an XML document must be unique.

Related Productions

CombiningChar (p. 47), Digit (p. 60), Extender (p. 84), Letter (p. 98), Name (p. 102), Names (p. 105), Nmtoken (p. 107), Nmtokens (p. 108), S (p. 124)

Names [6]

Names

Purpose
Lists one or more valid XML names.

EBNF Syntax

```
Names ::= Name (S Name)*
```

Standard Syntax

```
Name[[ ... ]Name][[ ... ]Name]...[[ ... ]Name]
```

Where

- *Name* (p. 102) specifies a valid XML name in the list. Syntax: *#xnnnn
  [#xnnnn][_][:][#xnnnn]|[0|1|2|3|4|5|6|7|8|9][.]|[-][#xnnnn]
  [#xnnnn]...[#xnnnn]*
- *S* (p. 124) represents one or more whitespace characters — spaces, carriage returns, line feeds, or tabs — between the names in the list. Syntax:
  {[#x20|#x9|#xD|#xA][#x20|#x9|#xD|#xA]...[#x20|#x9|#xD|#xA]}

Notes
A Name production must begin with a letter or underscore character (except the uppercase or lowercase letters X, M, or L, which are reserved), unlike a Nmtoken, which can begin with any letter, digit, or valid character.

Each Name in an XML document must be unique.

It is a good idea not to use a colon (:) in a name; the colon is reserved for namespaces, which is a method of making like names unique. However, XML processors are required to accept the colon as a name character. Currently, namespaces use colons to differentiate names (for example, *oil:fluid* and *consume:fluid*, whereby the name *fluid* is no longer unique when the two documents are combined).

Example
The following example presents a list of names:

```
COBOL  BASIC  RPG  ADA  C
```

Related Productions
AttDef (p. 28), AttlistDecl (p. 29), Attribute (p. 31), CombiningChar (p. 47), cp (p. 55), Digit (p. 60), doctypedecl (p. 61), elementdecl (p. 66), EmptyElemTag (p. 68), EntityRef (p. 77), ETag (p. 83), Extender (p. 84), GEDecl (p. 89), Letter (p. 98), Mixed (p. 101), Name (p. 102), NDataDecl (p. 106), Nmtoken (p. 107), Nmtokens (p. 108), NotationDecl (p. 110), NotationType (p. 111), PEDecl (p. 112), PEReference (p. 115), PITarget (p. 118), S (p. 124), STag (p. 129)

XML Syntax

NDataDecl [76]   Unparsed External Entity Declaration

Purpose
Declares an unparsed external entity.

EBNF Syntax
```
NDataDecl ::= S 'NDATA' S Name
```

Standard Syntax
```
[ ... ]NDATA[ ... ]Name
```

Where
- S (p. 124) represents one or more whitespace characters: spaces, carriage returns, line feeds, or tabs. Syntax: {[#x20|#x9|#xD|#xA][#x20| #x9|#xD|#xA]...[#x20|#x9|#xD|#xA]}
- NDATA (notation data) is an uppercase-only reserved keyword that indicates that unparsed external nonmarkup data follows.
- Name (p. 102) specifies a valid XML unparsed external entity name. Syntax: #xnnnn [#xnnnn][_][:][#xnnnn]|[0|1|2|3|4|5|6|7|8|9] [.]|[-][#xnnnn][#xnnnn]...[#xnnnn]

Notes
NDataDecl is a component of the EntityDef production.

An *unparsed entity* contains unparsed data (for example, GIF graphic files), which may or may not be valid and have not been processed through an XML parser. An unparsed entity has a named notation, which the XML processor sends to the target application.

An *external entity* has its content stored in a separate file, completely outside the XML document. An unparsed external entity has an NDataDecl declaration. All other external entities are parsed.

For an XML document to be valid, Name must match one of the declared names of the notation type.

Example
This example from the Extensible Markup Language recommendation includes an unparsed external entity declaration:

```
<!ENTITY hatch-pic
         SYSTEM "../grafix/OpenHatch.GIF"
         NDATA gif >
```

Related Productions
EntityDef (p. 76), Name (p. 102), NDataDecl (p. 106), S (p. 124)

XML Syntax

Nmtoken [7]   Name Token

Purpose
Specifies a valid XML name token.

EBNF Syntax
```
Nmtoken ::= (NameChar)+
```

Standard Syntax
NameChar[[NameChar]...[NameChar]]

Where
- *NameChar* (p. 104) specifies one character in a name. Syntax: *Letter|Digit|.|-|_|:|CombiningChar|Extender*

Notes
Nmtoken is a component of the Enumeration and Nmtokens productions.

An Nmtoken can begin with any letter, digit, or valid character, unlike a Name, which must begin with a letter or underscore character.

The NMTOKEN attribute under the TokenizedType production must conform to the Nmtoken production.

Each Nmtoken in an XML document must be unique.

Example
See the Nmtokens production.

Related Productions
CombiningChar (p. 47), Digit (p. 60), Enumeration (p. 81), Extender (p. 84), Letter (p. 98), Name (p. 102), Names (p. 105), Nmtokens (p. 108), S (p. 124), TokenizedType (p. 134)

Related Attribute
NMTOKEN (p. 107)

NMTOKEN   Name Token Attribute

Purpose
Indicates that a valid XML name token follows.

EBNF Syntax
See the TokenizedType production (p. 134).

Standard Syntax
See the TokenizedType production.

Notes

NMTOKEN is an uppercase-only reserved keyword indicating that the defined attribute is a name token.

A Nmtoken can begin with any letter, digit, or valid character, unlike a Name, which must begin with a letter or underscore character.

The NMTOKEN attribute must conform to the Nmtoken production.

Each Nmtoken in an XML document must be unique.

For more information, see the Notes section of the TokenizedType production, which is a component of the AttType production.

Related Productions

AttType (p. 32), Name (p. 102), Names (p. 105), Nmtoken (p. 107), Nmtokens (p. 108), TokenizedType (p. 134)

Related Attributes

ENTITIES (p. 73), ENTITY (p. 73), ID (p. 91), IDREF (p. 92), IDREFS (p. 93), NMTOKENS (p. 109)

Nmtokens [8]   Name Tokens

Purpose
Specifies one or more valid XML name tokens.

EBNF Syntax

```
Nmtokens ::= Nmtoken (S Nmtoken)*
```

Standard Syntax

```
Nmtoken[[[ ... ]Nmtoken][[ ... ]Nmtoken]
   ...[[ ... ]Nmtoken]]
```

Where

- *Nmtoken* (p. 107) specifies a valid XML name token. Syntax:
  NameChar[[NameChar]...[NameChar]]
- *S* (p. 124) represents one or more whitespace characters: spaces, carriage returns, line feeds, or tabs. Syntax: *{[#x20|#x9|#xD|#xA][#x20| #x9|#xD|#xA]...[#x20|#x9|#xD|#xA]}*

Notes

A Nmtoken can begin with any letter, digit, or valid character, unlike a Name, which must begin with a letter or underscore character.

The NMTOKENS attribute under the TokenizedType production must conform to the Nmtokens production.

Each Nmtoken in an XML document must be unique.

Example

The following example is an enumerated list of name tokens:

```
(1st | 2nd | 3rd | 4th)
```

Related Productions

CombiningChar (p. 47), Digit (p. 60), Enumeration (p. 81), Extender (p. 84), Letter (p. 98), Name (p. 102), Names (p. 105), Nmtoken (p. 107), S (p. 124), TokenizedType (p. 134)

Related Attribute

NMTOKENS (p. 109)

NMTOKENS — Identifier Cross-Reference Attribute List

Purpose

Specifies a list of valid XML name tokens.

EBNF Syntax

See the TokenizedType production (p. 134).

Standard Syntax

See the TokenizedType production.

Notes

NMTOKENS is an uppercase-only reserved keyword indicating that a list of NMTOKENs follows.

A Nmtoken can begin with any letter, digit, or valid character, unlike a Name, which must begin with a letter or underscore character.

The NMTOKENS attribute under the TokenizedType production must conform to the Nmtokens production.

Each Nmtoken in an XML document must be unique.

For more information, see the Notes section of the TokenizedType production, which is a component of the AttType production.

Related Productions

AttType (p. 32), Name (p. 102), Names (p. 105), Nmtoken (p. 107), Nmtokens (p. 108), TokenizedType (p. 134)

Related Attributes

ENTITIES (p. 73), ENTITY (p. 73), ID (p. 91), IDREF (p. 92), IDREFS (p. 93), NMTOKEN (p. 107)

NotationDecl [82]   Notation Declaration

Purpose

Declares a notation name.

EBNF Syntax

```
NotationDecl ::= '<!NOTATION' S Name S (ExternalID
   | PublicID) S? '>'
```

Standard Syntax

```
<!NOTATION[ ... ]Name[ ... ]{ExternalID
   |PublicID}[ ... ]>
```

Where

- *<!NOTATION* is an uppercase-only reserved keyword that marks the start of the notation declaration.
- *S* (p. 124) represents one or more whitespace characters: spaces, carriage returns, line feeds, or tabs. Syntax: {[#x20|#x9|#xD|#xA][#x20| #x9|#xD|#xA]...[#x20|#x9|#xD|#xA]}
- *Name* (p. 102) specifies a valid XML notation name. Syntax: #xnnnn [#xnnnn][_][:][#xnnnn]|[0|1|2|3|4|5|6|7|8|9][.]|[-][#xnnnn] [#xnnnn]...[#xnnnn]
- *ExternalID* (p. 84) names a parsed external entity. Syntax: SYSTEM[...] SystemLiteral|PUBLIC[...]PubidLiteral[...]SystemLiteral
- *PublicID* (p. 122) resolves an external identifier into a system identifier. Syntax: PUBLIC[...]PubidLiteral
- *>* marks the end of the notation declaration.

Notes

NotationDecl is a component of the markupdecl production.

Notation defines the elements of a body of knowledge by using a formalized set of symbols or an alphabet. Braille, musical notes, and even computer file formats are types of notation. In XML, a notation names the format of an unparsed entity or an element that contains a notation attribute, or names the target application of a processing instruction.

A notation declaration names the notation itself, so that the notation can appear in entity declarations, attribute list declarations, attribute specifications, and some external identifiers.

A name in a notation declaration must be unique.

Example

The notation in this DTD segment indicates that the artmagic program stored on the network supports four types of common graphic files (gif, tif, jpg, and bmp). The filetype attribute lists the same file types.

```
<!NOTATION gif SYSTEM "artmagic.exe">
<!NOTATION tif SYSTEM "artmagic.exe">
<!NOTATION jpg SYSTEM "artmagic.exe">
<!NOTATION bmp SYSTEM "artmagic.exe">
<!ELEMENT  pix EMPTY>
<!ATTLIST  pix
   url      CDATA              #REQUIRED
   filetype NOTATION
            ( gif | tif | jpg | bmp ) "gif"
   align    (left | center | right)
```

Related Productions

ExternalID (p. 84), markupdecl (p. 98), Name (p. 102), PublicID (p. 122), S (p. 124)

NotationType [58]   Notation Names

XML Syntax

Purpose

Lists all the possible names of a notation type.

EBNF Syntax

```
NotationType ::= 'NOTATION' S '(' S? Name (S? '|'
                 S? Name)* S? ')'
```

Standard Syntax

```
NOTATION[ ... ]([ ... ]Name[[ ... ][ ... ]Name]
[[ ... ][ ... ]Name]...[[ ... ][ ... ]Name]][ ... ])
```

Where

- *NOTATION* is an uppercase-only reserved keyword indicating that a list of notation names follows.
- *S* (p. 124) represents one or more whitespace characters: spaces, carriage returns, line feeds, or tabs. Syntax: {[#x20|#x9|#xD|#xA][#x20|#x9|#xD|#xA]...[#x20|#x9|#xD|#xA]}
- *(* marks the start of the names on the list.
- Name (p. 102) specifies a valid XML notation-type name. Syntax: #xnnnn [#xnnnn][_][:][#xnnnn]|[0|1|2|3|4|5|6|7|8|9][.]|[-][#xnnnn] [#xnnnn]...[#xnnnn]
- *|* is a character that separates one name from the next.
- *)* marks the end of the names on the list.

Notes

NotationType is a component of the EnumeratedType production.

Notation defines the elements of a body of knowledge by using a formalized set of symbols or an alphabet. Braille, musical notes, and even computer file formats are types of notation. In XML, a notation names the format of an unparsed entity or an element that contains a notation attribute, or names the target application of a processing instruction.

For an XML document to be valid, each notation attribute type must match a declared notation name, only one notation should be associated with one element type, and empty elements should not include any notation.

Examples

The notation in this DTD segment indicates that the artmagic program stored on the network supports four types of common graphic files (gif, tif, jpg, and bmp). The filetype attribute lists the same file types.

```
<!NOTATION gif SYSTEM "artmagic.exe">
<!NOTATION tif SYSTEM "artmagic.exe">
<!NOTATION jpg SYSTEM "artmagic.exe">
<!NOTATION bmp SYSTEM "artmagic.exe">
<!ELEMENT  pix EMPTY>
<!ATTLIST  pix
    url        CDATA              #REQUIRED
    filetype   NOTATION
         ( gif | tif | jpg | bmp ) "gif"
    align      (left | center | right)
```

The following example presents a list of name tokens:

```
NOTATION   (CGM  |  TIF  |  JPG  |  GIF)
```

Related Productions

EnumeratedType (p. 80), Name (p. 102), S (p. 124)

PEDecl [72] | Parameter Entity Declaration

Purpose

Declares a parameter entity (PE).

EBNF Syntax

```
PEDecl ::= '<!ENTITY' S '%' S Name S PEDef S? '>'
```

Standard Syntax

```
<!ENTITY[ ... ]%[ ... ]Name[ ... ]PEDef[ ... ]>
```

Where

- `<!ENTITY` marks the beginning of a parameter-entity declaration.
- `S` (p. 124) represents one or more whitespace characters: spaces, carriage returns, line feeds, or tabs. Syntax: {[#x20|#x9|#xD|#xA][#x20|#x9|#xD|#xA]...[#x20|#x9|#xD|#xA]}
- `%` indicates a parameter-entity reference.

- *Name* (p. 102) specifies a valid XML parameter-entity name. Syntax:
  #xnnnn [#xnnnn][_][:][#xnnnn]|[0|1|2|3|4|5|6|7|8|9][.]|[-]
  [#xnnnn][#xnnnn]...[#xnnnn]
- *PEDef* (p. 114) prepares a parameter-entity definition. Syntax:
  EntityValue|ExternalID
- > marks the end of a parameter-entity declaration.

Notes

PEDecl is a component of the EntityDecl production.

A *parsed entity* contains parsed data, which is replacement text and which has been processed through an XML parser. A parsed entity has a name and is called by an entity reference.

An *internal entity* has its content stored completely within the DTD. An internal entity is a parsed EntityValue. Its content is declared within the current XML document. Any other entity is an external entity.

An *external entity* has its content stored in a separate file, completely outside the XML document. An unparsed external entity has an NDataDecl declaration. All other external entities are parsed.

A *parameter entity* (PE) is a variable that is named within markup in the prolog of a document, document type definition (DTD), or the document instance. A parameter entity is parsed, is preceded by a percent symbol (%), and is ended with a semicolon (;). Valid parameter-entity categories are internal parsed parameter and external parsed parameter. In other words, no unparsed parameter entities exist.

For a document to be well formed, internal parsed parameter entities must be syntactically correct, and external parameter entities must be syntactically correct.

Examples

The following example shows the parameter-entity declaration within the HTML INPUT element declaration:

```
<!ENTITY % InputType
"(TEXT | PASSWORD | CHECKBOX |
  RADIO | SUBMIT | RESET |
  FILE | HIDDEN | IMAGE | BUTTON)"
>
```

The following example shows an external parameter entity for the Full Latin 1 character entity set and the related entity reference:

```
<!ENTITY % HTMLlat1 PUBLIC
"-//W3C//ENTITIES Full Latin 1//EN//HTML">

%HTMLlat1;
```

XML Syntax

Related Productions

EntityDecl (p. 74), EntityDef (p. 76), EntityValue (p. 79), ExternalID (p. 84), GEDecl (p. 89), markupdecl (p. 98), Name (p. 102), NDataDecl (p. 106), PEDef (p. 114), S (p. 124)

PEDef [74]   Parameter-Entity Definition

Purpose

Defines a parameter entity (PE).

EBNF Syntax

    PEDef ::= EntityValue | ExternalID

Standard Syntax

    EntityValue|ExternalID

Where

- *EntityValue* (p. 79) specifies the value of an internal entity. Syntax: *{"[^%&"]|'[^%&']}[|PEReference|Reference][|PEReference| Reference]...[|PEReference|Reference]{"|'}*
- *ExternalID* (p. 84) names a parsed external entity. Syntax: *SYSTEM[...] SystemLiteral|PUBLIC[...]PubidLiteral[...]SystemLiteral*

Notes

PEDef is a component of the PEDecl production.

A *parsed entity* contains parsed data, which is replacement text and which has been processed through an XML parser. A parsed entity has a name and is called by an entity reference.

An *internal entity* has its content stored completely within the DTD. An internal entity is a parsed EntityValue. Its content is declared within the current XML document. Any other entity is an external entity.

An *external entity* has its content stored in a separate file, completely outside the XML document. An unparsed external entity has an NDataDecl declaration. All other external entities are parsed.

A *parameter entity* (PE) is a variable that is named within markup in the prolog of a document, document type definition (DTD), or the document instance. A parameter entity is parsed, is preceded by a percent symbol (%), and is ended with a semicolon (;). Valid parameter-entity categories are internal parsed parameter and external parsed parameter. In other words, no unparsed parameter entities exist.

For a document to be well formed, internal parsed parameter entities must be syntactically correct, and external parameter entities must be syntactically correct. The ampersand (&) is reserved; to specify an ampersand within character data, use the entity &.

Examples

The following example shows the parameter-entity declaration within the HTML INPUT element declaration:

```
<!ENTITY % InputType
"(TEXT | PASSWORD | CHECKBOX |
  RADIO | SUBMIT | RESET |
  FILE | HIDDEN | IMAGE | BUTTON)"
>
```

The following example shows an external parameter entity for the Full Latin 1 character entity set and the related entity reference:

```
<!ENTITY % HTMLlat1 PUBLIC
"-//W3C//ENTITIES Full Latin 1//EN//HTML">
%HTMLlat1;
```

Related Productions

EntityDecl (p. 74), EntityDef (p. 76), EntityValue (p. 79), ExternalID (p. 84), GEDecl (p. 89), markupdecl (p. 98), Name (p. 102), NDataDecl (p. 106), PEDecl (p. 112), S (p. 124)

PEReference [69]   **Parameter-Entity Reference**

Purpose

Names a parameter-entity reference.

EBNF Syntax

```
PEReference ::= '%' Name ';'
```

Standard Syntax

```
%Name;
```

Where

- % indicates a parameter-entity reference.
- *Name* (p. 102) specifies a valid XML parameter-entity reference name. Syntax: #xnnnn [#xnnnn][_][:][#xnnnn] | [0|1|2|3|4|5|6|7|8|9] [.] | [-] [#xnnnn] [#xnnnn]...[#xnnnn]
- ; indicates the end of the parameter-entity reference.

Notes

PEReference is a component of the doctypedecl, EntityValue, and extSubsetDecl productions.

An entity always has content, and most entities have a name.

Character references and entities begin with a variety of characters, but all end with a semicolon (;):

- Decimal character references start with the &# characters and are defined using the CharRef production.
- Hexadecimal character references start with the &#x characters and are defined using the CharRef production.
- Parsed general entities start with an ampersand (&) and are defined using the EntityRef production.
- Parameter-entity references start with a percent sign (%) and are defined using the PEReference production.

For an XML document to be well formed, it does not need a DTD. However, if it has an internal DTD subset without any occurrence of the PEReference production, the entity reference name must match the same name in an entity declaration. In addition, the entity reference name does not need to declare amp, lt, gt, apos, or quot. You must declare the entity before you refer to it. Otherwise all PEReference occurrences must appear only in the DTD.

For a nonstand-alone XML document with an external subset (the part of a DTD that is stored in a separate document, completely outside the source document) or external parameter entities to be compatible with SGML, it should declare amp with the && character reference, lt with &<, gt with >, apos with ', or quot with ".

For an XML document to be valid, the complete markup declaration must be nested within the PEReference replacement text.

PEReferences are allowed within markup declarations in external subsets and external parameter entities. However, PEReferences are not recognized as contents of ignored conditional sections or within comments, literals, or processing instructions.

For an XML document to be well formed, it does not need a DTD. However, if a DTD exists, PEReferences can only be placed within the brackets ([and]) in the doctype declaration in the internal subset (the part of the DTD that is located within the source document). PEReferences cannot be placed within markup declarations.

Nonvalidating XML processors can ignore PEReferences, because they are not required to process external subsets.

Examples

The following example shows an external parameter entity for the Full Latin 1 character entity set and the related parameter-entity reference:

```
<!ENTITY % HTMLlat1 PUBLIC
"-//W3C//ENTITIES Full Latin 1//EN//HTML">
%HTMLlat1;
```

The following example declares the `mixedtext` element, which can contain both data and two parameter-entity references:

```
<!ELEMENT mixedtext (#PCDATA|%typeface;|%pointsize;)>
```

Related Productions

AttValue (p. 33), BaseChar (p. 34), Char (p. 41), CharRef (p. 43), CombiningChar (p. 47), content (p. 52), Digit (p. 60), doctypedecl (p. 61), EntityRef (p. 77), EntityValue (p. 79), Extender (p. 84), extSubsetDecl (p. 88), Ideographic (p. 91), Letter (p. 98), Name (p. 102), Reference (p. 123)

PI [16]	**Processing Instruction**

Purpose

Specifies a process to be performed within a target application.

EBNF Syntax

```
PI ::= '<?' PITarget (S (Char* - (Char* '?>' Char*)))? '?>'
```

Standard Syntax

```
<?PITarget [[ ... ][Char[Char]...[Char]]?>
```

Where

- *<?* marks the start of a processing instruction.
- *PITarget* (p. 118) names a processing instruction's target application. Syntax: *Name*
- *S* (p. 124) represents one or more whitespace characters: spaces, carriage returns, line feeds, or tabs. Syntax: { [#x20 | #x9 | #xD | #xA] [#x20 | #x9 | #xD | #xA] ... [#x20 | #x9 | #xD | #xA] }
- *Char* (p. 41) specifies one legal character. Syntax: #xnnnn [n [n]]
- *?>* marks the end of a processing instruction.

Notes

PI is a component of the content, markupdecl, and Misc productions.

Processing instructions state how XML elements are processed by target applications.

A PI always starts with the name of an application associated with the instruction. When naming a target application, it's a good idea to use a notation name, which has an associated URI. The name is the PI target (PITarget)

The XMLDecl production is a processing instruction.

When naming a target application, do not start the name with the uppercase or lowercase letters X, M, or L, which are reserved, unless you are declaring an XML document.

XML Syntax

XML does not consider a PI to be character data; an XML processor sends the PI directly to the target application for processing.

For an XML document to be well formed, all elements must be nested properly: All tags, elements, comments, processing instructions, character references, and entity references must be completely enclosed within one entity.

Do not use the ?> character combination within the processing instruction; ?> marks the end of the processing instruction.

Do not use parameter entity references within processing instructions.

Examples

The following is probably the most commonly used processing instruction:

```
<?xml version="1.0"?>
```

The following processing instruction indicates that the target application, wizstil, is programmed to understand text and foreground-color styling commands:

```
<?wizstil text black foreground gray?>
```

Related Productions

Char (p. 41), content (p. 52), markupdecl (p. 98), Misc (p. 100), Name (p. 102), PITarget (p. 118), S (p. 124), XMLDecl (p. 137)

PITarget [17]　　　Processing-Instruction Target

Purpose

Names the target application for a processing instruction.

EBNF Syntax

```
PITarget ::= Name - (('X' | 'x') ('M' | 'm')
    ('L' | 'l'))
```

Standard Syntax

```
Name
```

Where

* Name (p. 102) specifies a valid XML target-application name. Syntax:
  #xnnnn [#xnnnn][_][:][#xnnnn]|[0|1|2|3|4|5|6|7|8|9][.]|[-]
  [#xnnnn][#xnnnn]...[#xnnnn]

Notes

PITarget is a component of the PI production.

When naming a target application, do not start the name with the uppercase or lowercase letters X, M, and L, which are reserved.

Example

The following, which is probably the most commonly used processing instruction, states that an XML processor is the target application:

```
<?xml version="1.0"?>
```

The following processing instruction indicates that the target application, wizstil, is programmed to understand text and foreground-color styling commands:

```
<?wizstil text black foreground gray?>
```

Related Productions

Char (p. 41), Name (p. 102), PI (p. 117), S (p. 124)

prolog [22]   Prolog

Purpose

Describes an XML document.

EBNF Syntax

```
prolog ::= XMLDecl? Misc* (doctypedecl Misc*)?
```

Standard Syntax

```
[XMLDecl][[Misc][Misc]...[Misc]][doctypedecl[[Misc]
[Misc]...[Misc]]]
```

Where

- *XMLDecl* (p. 137) identifies an XML document as consisting of XML text and specifies the XML version, encoding, and stand-alone information. Syntax: *<?xml VersionInfo [EncodingDecl][SDDecl][...]?>*
- *Misc* (p. 100) indicates miscellaneous information. Syntax: Comment|PI| [...]
- *doctypedecl* (p. 61) declares an XML document type. Syntax: *<!DOCTYPE[...]Name[[...]ExternalID][...][[markupdecl| PEReference|[...]][markupdecl|PEReference|[...]... [[markupdecl|PEReference|[...]][...]>*

Notes

prolog is a component of the document production.

prolog is part of the XML declaration that defines an XML document.

prolog is the XML counterpart to the HTML HEADER section; the prolog describes the XML document very generally.

The XML declaration must occur first in the prolog, and the document type declaration must precede any start tags in an XML document.

XML Syntax

Although Misc enables you to add miscellaneous content — comments, processing instructions, and whitespace — to the prolog element, use good syntax. Being careful helps links to work properly and XML processors to interpret XML statements correctly.

Examples

The following example is an entire valid, self-contained XML document with an internal DTD subset declared in a four-line prolog:

```
<?xml version="1.0"?>
<!DOCTYPE endstate[>
<!ELEMENT endstate (#PCDATA)>
]>
<endstate>Goodbye, cruel world!</endstate>
```

The following example is a two-line prolog that refers to an external DTD subset:

```
<?xml version="1.0"?>
<!DOCTYPE endstate SYSTEM "goodbye.dtd">
<endstate>Goodbye, cruel world!</endstate>
```

Related Productions

Comment (p. 49), doctypedecl (p. 61), document (p. 63), EncodingDecl (p. 71), Eq (p. 82), Misc (p. 100), PI (p. 117), S (p. 124), SDDecl (p. 126), VersionInfo (p. 135), VersionNum (p. 136), XMLDecl (p. 137)

PubidChar [13]   Public Identifier Character

Purpose

Specifies a public identifier character within a public identifier literal.

EBNF Syntax

```
PubidChar ::= #x20 | #xD | #xA | [a-zA-Z0-9]
   | [-'()+,./:=?;!*#@$_%]
```

Standard Syntax

```
#x20|#xD|#xA|[a-z|A-Z|0-9]|[-|'|(|)|+
   |,|.|/|:|=|?|;|!|*|#||$|_|%]
```

Where

- *#x20* (Unicode code *#x0020*) inserts a space, which is the equivalent of pressing the spacebar.
- *#xD* (Unicode code *#x000D*) inserts a carriage return (CR). This control character moves the cursor to the beginning of the next line.

- #xA (Unicode code #x000A) inserts a line feed (LF). This control character moves the cursor to the next line below its present position. For more information about Unicode characters, see Chapter 1, "Introducing XML" and Appendix A, "Unicode Characters and Character Sets" (p. 757).
- a-z and A-Z represent lowercase and uppercase letters of the current alphabet.
- 0-9 are numbers from 0 to 9.
- -, ', (,), +, ,, ., /, :, =, ?, ;, !, *, #, @, $, _, and % are supported characters.

Notes

PubidChar is a component of the PubidLiteral production.

Related Productions

AttValue (p. 33), EntityDef (p. 76), EntityValue (p. 79), PEDef (p. 114), PEReference (p. 115), PubidLiteral (p. 121), Reference (p. 123), SystemLiteral (p. 131)

PubidLiteral [12]	**Public Identifier Literal**

Purpose

Names a public identifier literal.

EBNF Syntax

```
PubidLiteral ::= '"' PubidChar* '"'
    | "'" (PubidChar - "'")* "'"
```

Standard Syntax

{"|'}[[PubidChar][PubidChar]...[PubidChar]]{"|'}

Where

- PubidChar (p. 120) specifies public identifier characters. Syntax:
  #x20|#xD|#xA|[a-z|A-Z|0-9]|[-|'|(|)|+|,|.|/|:|=|?|;|!|*|#|$|_|%]

Notes

PubidLiteral is a component of the ExternalID and PublicID productions.

A literal such as PubidLiteral replaces the current value of an entity or attribute.

If you enclose a production, string, element, or other object within single quote marks, do not use single quote marks within the quoted object; if you enclose a production, string, element, or other object within quotation marks, do not use quotation marks within the quoted object.

Do not mix single quote marks and quotation marks; the quote marks at the beginning and end of a quoted object must match.

XML Syntax

Example

The following example shows an external parameter entity for the Full Latin 1 character entity set and the related general entity:

```
<!ENTITY % HTMLlat1 PUBLIC
"-//W3C//ENTITIES Full Latin 1//EN//HTML">
%HTMLlat1;
```

Related Productions

AttValue (p. 33), EntityDef (p. 76), EntityValue (p. 79), ExternalID (p. 84), PEDef (p. 114), PEReference (p. 115), PubidChar (p. 120), PublicID (p. 122), Reference (p. 123), SystemLiteral (p. 131)

PublicID [83]   External Identifier

Purpose

Resolves an external identifier into a system identifier.

EBNF Syntax

```
PublicID ::= 'PUBLIC' S PubidLiteral
```

Standard Syntax

```
PUBLIC[ ... ]PubidLiteral
```

Where

- *PUBLIC* is an uppercase-only reserved keyword indicating that a public identifier follows.
- *S* (p. 124) represents one or more whitespace characters: spaces, carriage returns, line feeds, or tabs. Syntax: {*[#x20|#x9|#xD|#xA][#x20| #x9|#xD|#xA]...[#x20|#x9|#xD|#xA]*}
- *PubidLiteral* (p. 121) names a public identifier literal. Syntax: {"|'} *[[PubidChar][PubidChar]...[PubidChar]]*{"|'}

Notes

PublicID is a component of the NotationDecl production.

All system identifiers are URIs.

Notation defines the elements of a body of knowledge by using a formalized set of symbols or an alphabet. Braille, musical notes, and even computer file formats are types of notation. In XML, a notation names the format of an unparsed entity or an element that contains a notation attribute, or names the target application of a processing instruction.

A notation declaration names the notation itself so that the notation can appear in entity declarations, attribute list declarations, attribute specifications, and in some external identifiers.

Example

The following example shows an external parameter entity for the Full Latin 1 character entity set and the related general entity:

```
<!ENTITY % HTMLlat1 PUBLIC
"-//W3C//ENTITIES Full Latin 1//EN//HTML">
%HTMLlat1;
```

Related Productions

ExternalID (p. 84), markupdecl (p. 98), NotationDecl (p. 110), PublicID (p. 122), S (p. 124)

Reference [67]   Reference

Purpose

Names an entity reference or character reference.

EBNF Syntax

```
Reference ::= EntityRef | CharRef
```

Standard Syntax

```
EntityRef|CharRef
```

Where

- *EntityRef* (p. 77) specifies an entity reference, a named general entity's content. Syntax: &*Name*;
- *CharRef* (p. 43) specifies a legal hexadecimal or decimal character code from the ISO/IEC 10646 character set. Syntax: &#{*dec_num[dec_num [...dec_num]]*};|&#x{*hex_num[hex_num[...hex_num]]*};

Notes

Reference is a component of the AttValue, content, and EntityValue productions.

An entity always has content, and most entities have a name.

Character references and entities begin with a variety of characters, but all end with a semicolon (;):

- Decimal character references start with the &# characters and are defined using the CharRef production.
- Hexadecimal character references start with the &#x characters and are defined using the CharRef production.
- Parsed general entities start with an ampersand (&) and are defined using the EntityRef production.
- Parameter-entity references start with a percent sign (%) and are defined using the PEReference production.

XML Syntax

Examples

The following are examples of entity references:

```
&copyright;
&editdate;
```

The following are examples of character references:

```
&#251;
&#x628;&#x631;&#x627;&#x64a;
```

Related Productions

AttValue (p. 33), BaseChar (p. 34), Char (p. 41), CharRef (p. 43), CombiningChar (p. 47), content (p. 52), Digit (p. 60), EntityRef (p. 77), EntityValue (p. 79), Extender (p. 84), Ideographic (p. 91), Letter (p. 98), Name (p. 102), PEReference (p. 115)

S [3]　　　　　　　　　　　　　　　　　Whitespace

Purpose

Inserts whitespace in an XML document.

EBNF Syntax

```
S ::= (#x20 | #x9 | #xD | #xA)+
```

Standard Syntax

```
{[#x20|#x9|#xD|#xA][#x20|#x9|#xD
 |#xA]...[#x20|#x9|#xD|#xA]}
```

Where

- #x20 (Unicode code #x0020) inserts a space, which is the equivalent of pressing the spacebar.
- #x9 (Unicode code #x0009) inserts a tab (HT). This control character moves the cursor to the next tab stop.
- #xD (Unicode code #x000D) inserts a carriage return (CR). This control character moves the cursor to the beginning of the next line.
- #xA (Unicode code #x000A) inserts a line feed (LF). This control character moves the cursor to the next line below its present position. For a complete list of supported base characters, see Appendix A, "Unicode Characters and Character Sets" (p. 757). For more information about Unicode characters, see Chapter 2, "Introducing DTDs" (p. 669).

Notes

S is a component of the AttDef, AttlistDecl, choice, DefaultDecl, doctypedecl, elementdecl, EmptyElemTag, EncodingDecl, Enumeration, ETag, ExternalID, extSubsetDecl, GEDecl, ignoreSect, includeSect, Misc, Mixed, Names, NDataDecl, Nmtokens, NotationDecl, NotationType, PEDecl, PI, PublicID, SDDecl, seq, STag, TextDecl, VersionInfo, and XMLDecl productions.

The S production is a part of the XML specification. Do not use S in DTDs and XML documents. Instead, use xml:space or style-sheet styles to control whitespace. Whitespace consists of one or more space characters, carriage returns, line feeds, or tabs — all regarded by XML as nonmarkup text.

An XML processor passes *all* nonmarkup characters to the target application. A validating XML processor passes the characters and also reports to the application on the whitespace characters within the content of elements.

A validating XML processor should differentiate whitespace from other element content and should disregard the amount of whitespace inserted between other objects in content.

Use whitespace to separate and align elements and attributes in a DTD and to format text in an output document.

Be aware that in some languages, whitespace separates some characters and words. However, in XML, this is not considered whitespace.

You can use the xml:space attribute, which is analogous to the HTML <PRE> element, to control all whitespace in the XML document. If you use the xml:space attribute and you want a valid document, you must declare xml:space as an enumerated type with a choice of only two values: default and preserve. The default value allows a target application to set its own whitespace values, and preserve keeps the whitespace values in the document, assuming that the application supports xml:space. For example:

```
<!ATTLIST PRE_TYPE   xml:space   (default|preserve)
   'preserve'>
```

xml:space applies to all the whitespace in a document, unless you insert another xml:space attribute.

The presence or absence of an xml:space attribute has no effect on the well-formedness or validity of an XML document.

By default, the root element does not address whitespace handling. However, you can specify a whitespace attribute in the root element.

Different computer platforms handle line ends differently. For example, Windows issues a carriage-return/line-feed combination at the end of a line, MacOS issues a carriage return, and UNIX issues a line feed. To address this incompatibility, an XML processor issues one line-end control character, a #xA line-feed control character, at the end of a line.

Example

This example shows varying amounts of whitespace within the same line:

```
<!--defining <para> paragraph element-->
<!--defining      <para>      paragraph element-->
```

XML Syntax

Related Productions

AttDef (p. 28), AttlistDecl (p. 29), choice (p. 46), DefaultDecl (p. 58), doctypedecl (p. 61), elementdecl (p. 66), EmptyElemTag (p. 68), EncodingDecl (p. 71), Enumeration (p. 81), ETag (p. 83), ExternalID (p. 84), extSubsetDecl (p. 88), GEDecl (p. 89), ignoreSect (p. 94), includeSect (p. 97), Misc (p. 100), Mixed (p. 101), Names (p. 105), NDataDecl (p. 106), Nmtokens (p. 108), NotationDecl (p. 110), NotationType (p. 111), PEDecl (p. 112), PI (p. 117), PublicID (p. 122), SDDecl (p. 126), seq (p. 127), STag (p. 129), TextDecl (p. 132), VersionInfo (p. 135), XMLDecl (p. 137)

Related Attribute

xml:space (p. 140)

XML Syntax

SDDecl [32]   Stand-Alone Document Declaration

Purpose

Declares whether the current document contains an internal subset or refers to an external subset.

EBNF Syntax

```
SDDecl ::= S 'standalone' Eq (("'" ('yes' | 'no') "'")
           | '"' ('yes' | 'no') '"'))
```

Standard Syntax

```
[ ... ]standalone={"|'}yes|no{"|'}
```

Where

- *S* (p. 124) represents one or more whitespace characters: spaces, carriage returns, line feeds, or tabs. Syntax: {[#x20|#x9|#xD|#xA][#x20|#x9|#xD|#xA]...[#x20|#x9|#xD|#xA]}
- *standalone* is a reserved keyword indicating that a stand-alone declaration follows.
- *Eq* (p. 82) indicates an equal sign (=) preceded and followed by one or more spaces in an expression. Syntax: =
- *yes* indicates that no external markup declarations are associated with the current XML document; that is, the document does not use a DTD or the DTD is included in the internal subset (the part of the DTD that is located within the source document); the document "stands alone."
- *no* indicates that external markup declarations may be associated with the current XML document. This is the default if any external markup declarations are associated with the document.

Notes

SDDecl is a component of the XMLDecl production.

A markup declaration referred to in a stand-alone declaration is located in either an external subset (the part of a DTD that is stored in a separate document, completely outside the source document), specified in the DTD, or contained within an external parameter entity specified in the internal subset (the part of the DTD that is located within the source document).

According to the XML 1.0 (Second Edition) Review Version (http://www.w3.org/TR/REC-xml), "An external markup declaration is defined as a markup declaration occurring in the external subset or in a parameter entity (external or internal, the latter being included because non-validating processors are not required to read them)."A stand-alone declaration refers to external declarations, not external entities.

The presence or absence of a stand-alone declaration has no effect on the well-formedness or validity of an XML document.

If no external subset declarations (see extSubsetDecls) are associated with an XML document, an XML processor ignores the stand-alone declaration.

For an XML document to be valid, standalone must equal no if extSubsetDecls declare any of the following:

- Attributes with default values
- Entities (but not including &, ', >, <, and ")

Do not mix single quote marks and quotation marks; the quote marks at the beginning and end of the stand-alone declaration's value must match.

Example

The following example declares a stand-alone document:

```
<?xml version="1.0" standalone="yes"?>
```

Related Productions

Eq (p. 82), extSubsetDecl (p. 88), S (p. 124), XMLDecl (p. 137)

---

seq [50]   Sequence List

Purpose

Forces a user to use child elements in a specific order in a document.

EBNF Syntax

```
seq ::= '(' S? cp ( S? ',' S? cp )* S? ')'
```

Standard Syntax

```
([ ... ]cp[[ ... ],[ ... ]cp][[ ... ],[ ... ]cp]
...[[ ... ],[ ... ]cp][ ... ])
```

XML Syntax

Where

- *(* marks the start of the names on the list.
- *S* (p. 124) represents one or more whitespace characters: spaces, carriage returns, line feeds, or tabs. Syntax: { *[#x20 | #x9 | #xD | #xA] [#x20 | #x9 | #xD | #xA] ... [#x20 | #x9 | #xD | #xA]* }
- *cp* (p. 55) specifies the content-particle grammar in a list of child elements. Syntax: *{Name | choice | seq} [? | * | +]*
- *,* is a character that separates one element from the next and indicates a specific sequence of element use.
- *)* marks the end of the names on the list.

Notes

seq is a component of the children and cp productions.

Content models consist of content particles (CPs), which are names of child element types, as well as choice lists and sequence lists, which are, in turn, other content particles. This allows you to write very complex element-type declarations, which must be matched exactly during processing. Of course, the more complex a declaration, the more chances for errors exist in processing an XML document.

Use the following EBNF symbols to control the number of times that a child element can appear in a document:

- ? indicates that an element can occur up to one time but does not have to occur at all.
- * indicates that an element can occur an unlimited number of times.
- + indicates that an element *must* occur one or more times.

If the ?, *, or + character is not present, the element occurs once.

For an XML document to be valid, any PEReference replacement text must be nested completely within its content particle in one of the following productions: choice, Mixed, or seq (p. 127).

For an XML document to be valid, any PEReference replacement text cannot be empty and its first or last nonblank characters should not be a pipe (|) or ,) character combination.

For more information, see the Notes sections of the elementdecl and contentspec productions.

Example

The following example declares the longdoc element, which includes a sequence of three elements, which must be selected in the order in which they are declared:

```
<!ELEMENT longdoc (intro, body, index)>
```

XML Syntax

Related Productions

children (p. 44), choice (p. 46), contentspec (p. 53), cp (p. 55), elementdecl (p. 66), Mixed (p. 101), Name (p. 102), PEReference (p. 115), S (p. 124)

STag [40]   Start Tag

Purpose

Defines a start tag for an element.

EBNF Syntax

```
STag ::= '<' Name (S Attribute)* S? '>'
```

Standard Syntax

```
<Name[[[ ... ]Attribute][[ ... ]Attribute]
 ...[[ ... ]Attribute]]][ ... ]>
```

Where

- < marks the beginning of the start tag.
- Name (p. 102) specifies a valid XML element-type name. Syntax: #xnnnn [#xnnnn][_][:][#xnnnn]|[0|1|2|3|4|5|6|7|8|9][.]|[-][#xnnnn][#xnnnn]...[#xnnnn]
- S (p. 124) represents one or more whitespace characters: spaces, carriage returns, line feeds, or tabs. Syntax: {[#x20|#x9|#xD|#xA][#x20|#x9|#xD|#xA]...[#x20|#x9|#xD|#xA]}
- Attribute (p. 31) names and gives a value to an attribute. Syntax: Name[...]=[...]AttValue
- > marks the end of the start tag.

Notes

STag is a component of the element production.

An end tag (ETag) indicates the end of content.

The element-type name for the start tag must match that for the end tag.

Every non-empty element with a start tag must also have an end tag. Empty elements either follow the syntax of the EmptyElemTag production or have a start tag (with or without attributes) immediately followed by an end tag. Requiring an end tag for every start tag is a departure from HTML 4.0 (and older versions), in which some end tags are optional and some are omitted altogether. Because XHTML is a subset of XML, it follows XML rules.

Each attribute within an element-type contains two components: a name and a value.

For an XML document to be well formed, each attribute under an element, regardless of whether it has content, must be unique. However, the value of an attribute does not have to be unique and the order of attributes within a start tag is not important.

For an XML document to be well formed, all elements must be nested properly: all tags, elements, comments, processing instructions, character references, and entity references must be completely enclosed within one entity.

For an XML document to be valid, each of its attributes must have been declared and must match the declared type.

For an XML document to be well formed, it does not need a DTD. However, if a DTD exists, the attribute values of the document must be within the internal subset (the part of the DTD that is located within the source document) and not refer to external entities.

A less-than symbol (<) is reserved; it indicates the start of markup, among other things. To specify a less-than symbol within character data, use the entity <.

Examples

The following example is an entire valid, self-contained XML document with one start tag:

```
<?xml version="1.0"?>
<!DOCTYPE endstate[>
<!ELEMENT endstate (#PCDATA)>
]>
<endstate>Goodbye, cruel world!</endstate>
```

The following example is a start tag with two unique attributes:

```
<hithere align="left" id="abc">
</hithere>
```

The following example shows two versions of an empty element:

```
<image align="left" id="bighome" src="bighouse.GIF"></image>

<image align="left" id="bighome" src="bighouse.GIF"/>
```

Related Productions

Attribute (p. 31), content (p. 52), element (p. 64), EmptyElemTag (p. 68), Eq (p. 82), ETag (p. 83)

StringType [55]   String Type

Purpose

Indicates that an attribute type is a character data string.

EBNF Syntax

```
StringType ::= 'CDATA'
```

Standard Syntax

CDATA

Where

- CDATA is an uppercase-only reserved keyword indicating that the attribute type is character data only.

Notes

StringType is a component of the AttType production.

StringType is composed of any literal string.

Do not confuse CDATA with the CData production.

An attribute type allows you to ensure that proper and valid data are entered in an XML document.

Attributes are included within start tags and empty-element tags, not end tags.

For an XML document to be well formed, it does not need a DTD. Whether or not a DTD exists, you do not need to define any attribute types.

For an XML document to be valid, each attribute must be declared in a DTD associated with the document.

An XML processor must normalize minimized attribute values before sending them to the target application.

Example

The following example shows a string attribute type:

```
name   CDATA   #IMPLIED
```

Related Productions

AttType (p. 32), EnumeratedType (p. 80), TokenizedType (p. 134)

SystemLiteral [11]   System Literal

Purpose

Specifies the URI of an external identifier.

EBNF Syntax

```
SystemLiteral ::= ('"' [^"]* '"') | ("'" [^']* "'")
```

Standard Syntax

```
{"|'}URI{"|'}
```

XML Syntax

Where

- *URI* is a Uniform Resource Identifier, an Internet address, which is either an absolute Uniform Resource Locator (URL) or a Uniform Resource Name (URN), known as a system identifier.

Notes

SystemLiteral is a component of the ExternalID production.

A system literal is a URI, which identifies the content of an external entity. This is known as the *system identifier*.

A literal such as System Literal replaces the current value of an entity or attribute.

EntityValue supports entity references, which do not require a preceding # symbol. Each entity reference replaces one character.

An error occurs if an XPointer's fragment identifier (starting with #) is included in SystemLiteral.

If you enclose a production, string, element, or other object within single quote marks, do not use single quote marks within the quoted object; if you enclose a production, string, element, or other object within quotation marks, do not use quotation marks within the quoted object.

Within character data, you can use the apostrophe (') or quotation mark (") characters to indicate quote marks.

Do not mix single quote marks and quotation marks; the quote marks at the beginning and end of a quoted object must match.

Example

The following example shows an external ID:

```
<!ENTITY copyright SYSTEM
    "http://www.myfiles.com/copyright.txt">
```

Related Productions

AttValue (p. 33), EntityDef (p. 76), EntityValue (p. 79), ExternalID (p. 84), PEDef (p. 114), PEReference (p. 115), PubidChar (p. 120), PubidLiteral (p. 121), Reference (p. 123)

TextDecl [77]   Text Declaration

Purpose

Provides the version and encoding information about an external subset or external parameter entity.

EBNF Syntax

```
TextDecl ::= '<?xml' VersionInfo? EncodingDecl S? '?>'
```

XML Syntax

Standard Syntax

```
<?xml[VersionInfo] EncodingDecl[ ... ]?>
```

Where

- `<?xml` marks the start of the text declaration.
- `VersionInfo` (p. 135) names the XML version in which the document is written. Syntax: `[ ... ]version={"|'}VersionNum{"|'}`
- `EncodingDecl` (p. 71) declares the document's encoding name. Syntax: `[ ... ]encoding = {"|'}EncName{"|'}`
- `S` (p. 124) represents one or more whitespace characters: spaces, carriage returns, line feeds, or tabs. Syntax: `{[#x20|#x9|#xD|#xA][#x20| #x9|#xD|#xA]...[#x20|#x9|#xD|#xA]}`
- `?>` marks the end of the text declaration.

Notes

`TextDecl` is a component of the `extParsedEnt` and `extSubset` productions.

A text declaration is a literal and is *not* a reference to a parsed entity.

The text declaration is a stripped-down version of a document's opening XML declaration.

A text declaration appears only at the beginning of an external parsed entity. If a text declaration appears elsewhere in an external parsed entity, a fatal error occurs.

If an external parsed entity uses an encoding that is *not* UTF-8 or UTF-16, it must contain an opening `TextDecl` that includes an `EncodingDecl`.

Examples

The following example shows the reference to an external subset, quotes.dtd, in the source document, and some additional lines:

```
<?xml version="1.0"?>
<!DOCTYPE test SYSTEM "quotes.dtd">
```

The following example could be a very small external parsed entity named endstate.dtd:

```
<?xml version="1.0" encoding="UTF-8"?>
<!DOCTYPE endstate[>
<!ELEMENT endstate (#PCDATA)>
]>
```

Related Productions

`EncodingDecl` (p. 71), `extParsedEnt` (p. 86), `extSubset` (p. 87), `S` (p. 124), `VersionInfo` (p. 135)

TokenizedType [56]   Tokenized Type

Purpose

Indicates that an attribute type is a tokenized set.

EBNF Syntax

```
TokenizedType ::= 'ID'  |  'IDREF'  |  'IDREFS'  |  'ENTITY'
                 |  'ENTITIES'  |  'NMTOKEN'  |  'NMTOKENS'
```

Standard Syntax

```
ID | IDREF | IDREFS | ENTITY | ENTITIES | NMTOKEN | NMTOKENS
```

Where

- *ID* (p. 91) is an uppercase-only reserved keyword indicating that the defined attribute is an identifier.
- *IDREF* (p. 92) is an uppercase-only reserved keyword indicating that the defined attribute is an identifier cross-reference.
- *IDREFS* (p. 93) is an uppercase-only reserved keyword indicating that a list of *ID* cross-references follows.
- *ENTITY* (p. 73) is an uppercase-only reserved keyword indicating that the defined attribute is an entity.
- *ENTITIES* (p. 73) is an uppercase-only reserved keyword indicating that a list of *ENTITYs* follows.
- *NMTOKEN* (p. 107) is an uppercase-only reserved keyword indicating that the defined attribute is a name token. (See also the Nmtoken production on p. 107.)
- *NMTOKENS* (p. 109) is an uppercase-only reserved keyword indicating that a list of NMTOKENs follows. (See also the Nmtokens production on p. 108.)

Notes

TokenizedType is a component of the AttType production.

A *tokenized set* is a character data string with some constraints.

An attribute type allows you to ensure that proper and valid data is entered in an XML document.

Attributes are included within start tags and empty-element tags, not end tags.

For an XML document to be well formed, it does not need a DTD. Whether or not a DTD exists, you do not need to define any attribute types.

For an XML document to be valid, each attribute must be declared in a DTD associated with the document.

The ID and IDREF attribute types enable complex linking and optional extended pointers. For more information, refer to "XLink Language" (p. 145) and "XPointer Language" (p. 165) in Part I, and Chapter 6, "Adding Links and Pointers to an XML Document" (p. 733).

XML Syntax

Some nonvalidating XML processors assume that the default attribute type is ID. This allows a well-formed document to use identifiers for complex linking.

For an XML document to be valid and compatible with SGML, each element type can have only one ID attribute type.

For an XML document to be valid, the following attribute types must follow the rules and constraints controlling particular XML elements:

- ID, IDREF, and ENTITY must conform to the Name production.
- IDREFS and ENTITIES must conform to the Names production.
- NMTOKEN must conform to the Nmtoken production.
- NMTOKENS must conform to the Nmtokens production.

For an XML document to be valid, each ID name must be unique.

For an XML document to be valid, each ID must have a default value of #IMPLIED or #REQUIRED.

For an XML document to be valid, each IDREF name must match the value of an ID.

For an XML document to be valid, each ENTITY must be an unparsed entity declared in the DTD.

An XML processor must normalize minimized attribute values before sending them to the target application.

Example

The following example shows a tokenized type of attribute:

```
id    ID    #REQUIRED
```

Related Productions

AttType (p. 32), EnumeratedType (p. 80), Name (p. 102), Names (p. 105), Nmtoken (p. 107), Nmtokens (p. 108), StringType (p. 130)

Related Attributes

ENTITIES (p. 73), ENTITY (p. 73), ID (p. 91), IDREF (p. 92), IDREFS (p. 93), NMTOKEN (p. 107), NMTOKENS (p. 109)

VersionInfo [24]   XML Version Information

Purpose

Provides the XML version in which the document is written.

EBNF Syntax

```
VersionInfo ::= S 'version' Eq ("'" VersionNum "'"
  | '"' VersionNum '"')
```

Standard Syntax

```
[ ... ]version = {"|'}VersionNum{"|'}
```

Where

- *S* (p. 124) represents one or more whitespace characters: spaces, carriage returns, line feeds, or tabs. Syntax: {*[#x20|#x9|#xD|#xA][#x20| #x9|#xD|#xA]...[#x20|#x9|#xD|#xA]*}
- *version* is a string indicating that the version number follows.
- *Eq* (p. 82) indicates an equal sign (=) preceded and followed by one or more spaces in an expression. Syntax: =
- *VersionNum* (p. 136) represents the XML version number. Syntax: {*[a-z|A-z|0-9|_|.|:]|-[[a-z|A-z|0-9|_|.|:]|-]...[[a-z|A-z|0-9|_|.|:]|-]*}

Notes

VersionInfo is a component of the TextDecl and XMLDecl productions.

VersionInfo states the version number for the XML specification supporting the current document.

Do not mix single quote marks and quotation marks; the quote marks at the beginning and end of a quoted object must match.

For more information, see the Notes section of the XMLDecl production.

Examples

The following example declares an XML document:

```
<?xml version="1.0"?>
```

The following example declares a stand-alone document:

```
<?xml version="1.0" standalone="yes"?>
```

Related Productions

Comment (p. 49), doctypedecl (p. 61), document (p. 63), EncodingDecl (p. 71), Eq (p. 82), Misc (p. 100), PI (p. 117), prolog (p. 119), S (p. 124), SDDecl (p. 126), TextDecl (p. 132), VersionNum (p. 136), XMLDecl (p. 137)

VersionNum [26]   XML Version Number

Purpose

Represents the XML version number.

EBNF Syntax

```
VersionNum ::= ([a-zA-Z0-9_.:] | '-')+
```

Standard Syntax

```
{[a-z|A-Z|0-9|_|.|:]|-[[a-z|A-Z|0-9|_|.|:]|-]
...[[a-z|A-Z|0-9|_|.|:]|-]}
```

Where

- *a-z* and *A-Z* represent lowercase and uppercase letters of the alphabet.
- *0-9* are numbers from 0 to 9.
- *_*, *.*, and *:* are supported characters.
- *-* is a trailing character.

Notes

VersionNum is a component of the VersionInfo production.

Inserting the version number in an XML document specifies that the document conforms to a particular XML standard.

Examples

The following example declares an XML document:

```
<?xml version="1.0"?>
```

The following example declares a stand-alone document:

```
<?xml version="1.0" standalone="yes"?>
```

Related Productions

Comment (p. 49), doctypedecl (p. 61), document (p. 63), EncodingDecl (p. 71), Eq (p. 82), Misc (p. 100), PI (p. 117), prolog (p. 119), S (p. 124), SDDecl (p. 126), VersionInfo (p. 135), VersionNum (p. 136), XMLDecl (p. 137)

XMLDecl [23]   XML Declaration

Purpose

Identifies a document as consisting of XML text and specifies the XML version, encoding, and stand-alone information.

EBNF Syntax

```
XMLDecl ::= '<?xml' VersionInfo EncodingDecl?
SDDecl? S? '?>'
```

Standard Syntax

```
<?xml VersionInfo [EncodingDecl][SDDecl][ ... ]?>
```

Where

- *<?xml* are reserved characters that mark the start of the XML document type declaration.
- *VersionInfo* (p. 135) names the XML version in which the document is written. Syntax: *[...]version={"|'}VersionNum{"|'}*

- *EncodingDecl* (p. 71) declares the document's encoding name. Syntax: *[...]encoding = {"|'}EncName{"|'}*
- *SDDecl* (p. 126) declares whether the current document contains an internal subset or refers to an external subset. Syntax: *[...] standalone={"|'}yes|no{"|'}*
- *S* (p. 124) represents one or more whitespace characters: spaces, carriage returns, line feeds, or tabs. Syntax: *{[#x20|#x9|#xD|#xA][#x20| #x9|#xD|#xA]...[#x20|#x9|#xD|#xA]}*
- *?>* marks the end of the XML document type declaration.

Notes

XMLDecl is a component of the prolog production.

Use the XMLDecl production only within document type definitions (DTDs).

An XML declaration identifies an XML document, states the XML version that supports it, and can include the encoding declaration (using the EncodingDecl production) and stand-alone declaration (using the SDDecl production).

XMLDecl is a processing instruction.

Although an XML declaration is not required, you should begin an XML document with it.

If an XML declaration were required, SGML and HTML documents created before XML would not be well formed. However, an optional XML declaration allows many of these documents to be well formed without additional editing.

Examples

The following example declares an XML document:

```
<?xml version="1.0"?>
```

The following example declares a stand-alone document:

```
<?xml version="1.0" standalone="yes"?>
```

The following example declares an XML document and its encoding:

```
<?xml version="1.0" encoding='UTF-8'?>
```

Related Productions

Comment (p. 49), doctypedecl (p. 61), document (p. 63), EncodingDecl (p. 71), Eq (p. 82), Misc (p. 100), PI (p. 117), prolog (p. 119), S (p. 124), SDDecl (p. 126), VersionInfo (p. 135), VersionNum (p. 136)

xml:lang   Language Code

Purpose

Instructs XML to process the referred-to XML language code in which selected character data are written.

Standard Syntax

```
<element xml:lang=code>language_text</element>
```

Where

- `<element` is the start tag containing the element type.
- `xml:lang` is the processing instruction specifying that one or more language codes follows.
- `code` is the language code, country code, and/or subcode.
- `>` is the end of the start tag.
- `language_text` is the text output in the selected language.
- `</element>` is the end tag containing the element type and end-tag delimiters.

Notes

You can use the xml:lang attribute with any XML production to declare a language used as character data and attribute values in an XML document. IETF_RFC_1766 (ftp://ftp.isi.edu/in-notes/rfc1766.txt) lists supported values.

The language named in the xml:lang attribute is in effect until the next xml:lang attribute is declared.

Language codes and country codes are case-insensitive. Although this is not required, the language code is usually expressed in lowercase and the country code is usually expressed in uppercase.

The previous version of XML 1.0 included productions that are now obsolete in XML 1.0 (Second Edition). The deleted productions are: LanguageID, Langcode, ISO639Code, IanaCode, UserCode, and Subcode. Use xml:lang to specify language codes and subcodes and country codes.

XML Syntax

●—NOTE————————————————————————

To find an IANA language identifier, go to the Internet Assigned Numbers Authority (IANA) at http://www.iana.org/.

Examples

This example illustrates the xml:lang attribute and the IANA uk language code:

```
<para xml:lang="i-BS_4730">I'm speaking in
   proper English.</para>
```

This example illustrates the xml:lang attribute and the ISO 639 en (English) language code:

```
<para xml:lang="en">I'm speaking in English.</para>
```

This example illustrates the xml:lang attribute with an added US subcode:

```
<para xml:lang="en-US">I'm speaking in English.</para>
```

This example illustrates the xml:lang attribute and a user-defined language code:

```
<para xml:lang="x-uk_eng">I'm speaking
   in proper English.</para>
```

xml:space   Whitespace

Purpose
Controls the whitespace in an XML document.

Standard Syntax
```
xml:space    (default|preserve)
```

Where
- *xml:space* is the processing instruction specifying that a whitespace value follows.
- *default* allows a target application to set its own whitespace values.
- *preserve* keeps the whitespace values in the document.

Notes
xml:space applies to all the whitespace in a document, unless you insert another xml:space attribute.

An XML processor that does not support xml:space ignores the xml:space setting.

You can use the xml:space attribute, which is analogous to the HTML <PRE> element, to control all whitespace (spaces, tabs, and blank lines) in the XML document. If you use the xml:space attribute and you want a valid document, you must declare xml:space as an enumerated type with a choice of only two values: default and/or preserve. The default value allows a target application to set its own whitespace values, and preserve keeps the whitespace values in the document, assuming that the application supports xml:space. For example:

```
<!ATTLIST PRE_TYPE   xml:space   (default|preserve)
   'preserve'>
```

By default, the root element does not address whitespace handling. However, you can specify a whitespace attribute in the root element.

Different computer platforms handle line ends differently. For example, Windows issues a carriage-return/line-feed combination at the end of a line, MacOS issues a carriage return, and UNIX issues a line feed. To address this incompatibility, an XML processor issues one line-end control character, a #xA line-feed control character, at the end of a line.

The S production is a part of the XML specification. Do not use S in DTDs and XML documents. Instead, use xml:space or styles to add whitespace.

The presence or absence of an xml:space attribute has no effect on the well-formedness or validity of an XML document.

Examples

The following example shows an attribute list with its element, choices, and default value:

```
<!ATTLIST PRE_TYPE   xml:space   (default|preserve)
   'preserve'>
```

Related Production

S (p. 124)

---

xml-stylesheet   Style Sheet

Purpose

Instructs the XML processor to use the referred-to style sheet.

EBNF Syntax

```
[1] StyleSheetPI     ::= '<?xml-stylesheet'
                         (S PseudoAtt)* S? '?>'
[2] PseudoAtt        ::= Name S? '=' S? PseudoAttValue
[3] PseudoAttValue   ::= ('"' ([^'<&] | CharRef
                         | PredefEntityRef)* '"'
                         | ("'" ([^"<&]| CharRef
                         | PredefEntityRef)* "'")
                         - (Char* '?>' Char*)
[4] PredefEntityRef  ::= '&amp;' | '&lt;' | '&gt;'
                         | '&quot;' | '&apos;'
```

Standard Syntax

```
<?xml-stylesheet [ ... ]
  [PseudoAtt[PseudoAtt[PseudoAtt]]]
  [ ... ]?>


  Name [ ... ] = [ ... ] PseudoAttValue
```

XML Syntax

```
{"|'} [[^'<&]|[^"<&]] | CharRef
| [PredefEntityRef[PredefEntityRef
[...PredefEntityRef]]] {'|"}
- [Char[Char[Char]]] ?> [Char[Char[Char]]]
```

& | < | > | " | '

Where

- `<?xml-stylesheet` is a reserved keyword indicating that the attached document is a style sheet.
- `S` (p. 124) represents one or more whitespace characters: spaces, carriage returns, line feeds, or tabs. Syntax: `{[#x20|#x9|#xD|#xA][#x20| #x9|#xD|#xA]...[#x20|#x9|#xD|#xA]}`
- `PseudoAtt` names and gives a value to a pseudo-attribute in the same way as XML's `Attribute` production (p. 31). Syntax: `Name[ ... ]= [ ... ]PseudoAttValue`
- `Name` (p. 102) specifies a valid XML attribute name. Syntax: `#xnnnn [#xnnnn][_][:][#xnnnn]|[0|1|2|3|4|5|6|7|8|9][.]|[-][#xnnnn] [#xnnnn]...[#xnnnn]`
- `PseudoAttValue` (see above) states the value of an attribute in about the same way as XML's `AttValue` production (p. 33). Syntax: `{"|'} [[^'<&]|[^"<&]] | CharRef | [PredefEntityRef[PredefEntityRef [...PredefEntityRef]]] {'|"} - [Char[Char[Char]]] ?> [Char[Char[Char]]]`
- `CharRef` (p. 43) specifies a legal hexadecimal or decimal character code from the ISO/IEC 10646 character set. Syntax: `&#{dec_num[dec_num [...dec_num]]};|&#x{hex_num[hex_num[...hex_num]]};`
- `PredefEntityRef` (see above) enables you to select from five predefined entity references. Syntax: `&amp; | &lt; | &gt; | &quot; | &apos;`
- `Char` (p. 41) specifies one legal character. Syntax: `#xnnnn[n[n]]`

Notes

The `xml-stylesheet` processing instruction works in the same way as the HTML `<LINK REL="stylesheet">` statement. However, if an alternate style sheet is specified, the counterpart HTML statement reads `<LINK REL= "alternate stylesheet">`.

In the `xml-stylesheet` processing instruction, you cannot refer to entities that are not previously defined.

The predefined pseudo-attributes (`PseudoAtt`) are specified as follows:

```
href     CDATA    #REQUIRED
type     CDATA    #REQUIRED
title    CDATA    #IMPLIED
media    CDATA    #IMPLIED
```

```
charset     CDATA    #IMPLIED
alternate   (yes|no) "no"
```

where:

- *href* specifies a URI for a link to an external style sheet document or a style sheet embedded in the current document. External links to a style sheet are processed before links specified by *xml-stylesheet* processing instructions.
- *type* specifies a type name of the link, for information within the current document.
- *title* specifies a title name of the external style-sheet document.
- *media* indicates the type of destination.
- *charset* names the source of the character set of the data referred to by the href attribute.
- *alternate* indicates whether an alternate style sheet is used for the current document *(yes)*. The default value of no indicates that no alternate style sheet is used for the current document.

For more information about cascading style sheets, refer to *XHTML In Plain English*, also written by Sandra E. Eddy and published by IDG Books Worldwide. For more information about XPath, XSLT, and XSL, refer to "XPath Language" (p. 181), "XSLT Component" (p. 319), and "XSL Style Sheet Syntax" (p. 369), and Chapter 7, "Styling Documents with XSL" (p. 745).

Examples

The following examples appear in the document entitled "Associating Style Sheets with XML Documents" (http://www.w3.org/TR/xml-stylesheet):

```
<?xml-stylesheet alternate="yes" title="compact"
   href="small-base.css" type="text/css"?>
<?xml-stylesheet alternate="yes" title="compact"
   href="small-extras.css" type="text/css"?>
<?xml-stylesheet alternate="yes" title="big print"
   href="bigprint.css" type="text/css"?>
<?xml-stylesheet href="common.css" type="text/css"?>
```

XML Syntax

XLink Language

The attributes and link types in this section enable you to write XLinks, which in conjunction with XPointers establish hyperlinks in XML documents. The XLink candidate recommendation (http://www.w3.org/TR/xlink/) defines two general types of links:

- *Simple links*, which are analogous to the a and img elements in HTML. Simple links allow you to jump from a local location in the current document to a remote destination in the current document or in another document. Simple links always move in one direction. All simple links are *local links*, which are part of the link resource and local only.

- *Extended links*, which enable you to define one or more links to any combination of local or remote destinations. Using extended links, you can jump from any link to another link. You can identify the content associated with a particular link so that if the content changes but the identifier remains the same, you can still access the link. Extended links can be local or remote. A *remote* link specifies the location of the link.

●—**NOTE**————————————————————————————

World Wide Web Consortium (W3C) candidate recommendations are not final recommendations, so you can expect changes in these documents. Before you include XLinks in your XML documents, be sure to check the latest XLink documents at the W3C home page, `http://www.w3.org/`.

actuate	**Traversal Actuation Attribute**

Purpose

Specifies the way in which the linking resource is retrieved.

EBNF Syntax (declared in an attribute list)

```
xlink:actuate S (onLoad|onRequest|other|none)
   S #IMPLIED
```

Syntax (used in an XML document)

```
xlink:actuate={'|"}onLoad|onRequest|other
   |none{'|"}
```

Where

- `xlink` is a required namespace prefix.
- `actuate` is a keyword that indicates that an actuate value follows.
- `S` (p. 124) represents one or more whitespace characters: spaces, carriage returns, line feeds, or tabs. Syntax: `{[#x20|#x9|#xD|#xA] [#x20|#x9|#xD|#xA]...[#x20|#x9|#xD|#xA]}`
- `onLoad` retrieves the specified linking resource as soon as the resource containing the local link loads.
- `onRequest` retrieves the specified linking resource when the user or program explicitly requests it by triggering an event.
- `other` indicates that actuate does not control the traversal behavior. Other markup in the link may aid an application traversing to the ending resource.
- `none` indicates that actuate and other markup do not control traversal behavior.
- `#IMPLIED` is an uppercase-only reserved keyword indicating that the defined attribute *may* be supplied. For more information, see the `DefaultDecl` production (p. 58).

Notes

- `actuate` is a global attribute for almost any namespace — predefined or newly defined by an XML document developer — as long as elements are declared as XLink elements.
- Both `actuate` and `show` are known as behavior attributes.
- The `actuate` attribute is optional for the `simple` and `arc` link types.
- Link processing applications do not have to be programmed to implement `actuate` and `show` in a particular way.

Related Attributes

href (p. 150), role (p. 153), show (p. 155), title (p. 157), xlink (p. 161)

Related Link Types

arc (p. 147), simple (p. 156)

---

arc   Arc XLink Type

Purpose

Indicates the path of a link transversal including directional information.

Syntax

See the type attribute (p. 160).

Notes

- An element that is defined as an arc link type can have any content except for title link type elements. The title link type is an important child of the arc link type.
- An element that is defined as an arc link type must have an element that is defined as an extended link type; otherwise, XLink does not recognize the arc-type element.
- When an element that is defined as an arc link type has several to resources, traversal may be controlled by an application — not a future XLink specification.
- The from and to attributes, which are known as the traversal attributes, specify the traversal between a starting and ending resource.
- If no arc-type elements are embedded in an extended link, XLink is programmed to assume that the omitted from and to values for the extended link are all the role values in the extended link.
- Within a particular extended link, an arc with a missing value for one of its from or to attributes is not traversed. This is interpreted as standing for all the labels within that link.
- The type attribute is required for the arc link type.
- The actuate, arcrole, from, role, show, title, and to attributes are optional for the arc link type.
- An extended link can contain any number of the following declared link-type elements: arc, locator, resource, and title.
- The arc, locator, resource, and title link types are important child types of the extended link type. Although other link types can be embedded within extended, they are not significant to extended.
- If an arc type element has anything other than an extended-type element for its parent, then the arc type element has no XLink-specified meaning.

Related Attributes

actuate (p. 146), from (p. 149), role (p. 153), show (p. 155), title (p. 157), to (p. 158), type (p. 160)

XLink Language

Related Link Types
extended (p. 148), title (p. 157)

arcrole	Remote-Link-Content ArcRole Attribute

Purpose
Specifies the role of arc content.

EBNF Syntax (declared in an attribute list)
```
xlink:arcrole S CDATA S #IMPLIED|#FIXED S "fixed-uri"
```

Syntax (used in an XML document)
```
xlink:role={'|"}URI{'|"}
```

Where
- xlink is a required namespace prefix.
- arcrole is a keyword that indicates that an arcrole value follows.
- CDATA is a placeholder for content data — in this case, a *URI* or local file name.
- #IMPLIED is an uppercase-only reserved keyword indicating that the defined attribute may be supplied. For more information, see the DefaultDecl production (p. 58).
- #FIXED is an uppercase-only reserved keyword indicating that the defined attribute must always have the default attribute value.
- *fixed-uri* a placeholder for where a URI would go if the CDATA is #FIXED instead of #IMPLIED.
- *URI* is the user-provided URI.

Notes
- The arcrole attribute contains a URI that identifies some resource that describes the property. This resource can contain information about the author, creation or edit date, comments, and even documentation of the link, for those who will edit the link in the future.
- The value of the arcrole attribute must be a URI. If no value is supplied, then no role values will be inferred.
- The URI referenced in arcrole identifies a resource that describes the intended property.

extended	Extended XLink Type

Purpose
Associates a random number of resources which may be a combination of remote and local.

Syntax

See the `type` attribute (p. 160).

Notes

- An extended link can contain any number of the following declared link-type elements: `arc`, `locator`, `resource`, and `title`.
- If an extended link contains one `locator` or one `resource` element or none at all, it cannot be traversed.
- A `simple` link can be embedded within an `extended` link. The embedded link does not have to have an XLink affiliation to the `extended` link.
- An extended link can be used as a `simple` link, as long as it has one local resource and one remote resource.
- An extended link can be embedded within another `extended` link. The embedded link does not have to have an XLink affiliation to the `extended` link.
- The `type` attribute is required for the extended link type.
- The `role` and `title` attributes are optional for the extended link type.
- The `arc`, `locator`, `resource`, and `title` link types are important child types of the extended link type. Although other link types can be embedded within `extended`, they are not significant to `extended`.
- If `extended` contains a resource link type, the link is local. Otherwise, the link is remote.
- The only kind of link that is able to have inbound and third-party arcs are extended-links.

Related Attributes

role (p. 153), title (p. 157), type (p. 160)

Related Link Types

arc (p. 147), extended (p. 148), locator (p. 152), resource (p. 153), simple (p. 156), title (p. 157)

from	From Attribute

Purpose

Specifies the starting point of an arc link.

EBNF Syntax (declared in an attribute list)

```
xlink:from S NMTOKEN S #IMPLIED
```

Syntax (used in an XML document)

```
xlink:from={'|"}from_URI{'|"}
```

Where

- `xlink` is a required namespace prefix.
- `from` is a keyword that indicates that a `from` URI follows.

- S (p. 124) represents one or more whitespace characters: spaces, carriage returns, line feeds, or tabs. Syntax: `{[#x20|#x9|#xD|#xA][#x20|#x9| #xD|#xA]...[#x20|#x9|#xD|#xA]}`
- `NMTOKEN` (p. 107) specifies a valid XML-name-token role value.
- `#IMPLIED` is an uppercase-only reserved keyword indicating that the defined attribute *may* be supplied. For more information, see the `DefaultDecl` production (p. 58).
- *from_URI* is the URI of from.

Notes

- According to the XLink candidate recommendation (`http://www.w3. org/TR/xlink/`), "the from attribute defines resources from which traversal can be initiated, that is, starting resources."
- from is a global attribute for almost any namespace — predefined or newly defined by an XML document developer — as long as elements are declared as XLink elements.
- The from and to attributes, which are known as the traversal attributes, specify the traversal between a starting and ending resource. The starting resource is the *from* portion of a linking resource, and the ending resource is the *to* portion.
- The value of a from or to attribute must be the same as the local portion of a role attribute of an element that is defined as either a locator or resource link. The locator-link or resource-link element must be embedded within the same extended-link element as the arc-link element.
- The from attribute is optional for the arc-link type. If the from value is not supplied, the starting resource is all the role values for elements that are defined as locator-link types embedded within the same extended-link element as the arc-link element.
- The NMTOKEN value of a from attribute must correspond with the NMTOKEN value of a label attribute for a locator or resource element.

Related Attributes
role (p. 153), to (p. 158)

Related Link Type
arc (p. 147)

---

href Remote-Resource-Locator Attribute

Purpose
Specifies a remote resource locator.

EBNF Syntax (declared in an attribute list)
```
xlink:href S CDATA S {#IMPLIED|#REQUIRED}
```

Syntax (used in an XML document)

```
xlink:href={'|"}URI_name{'|"}
```

Where

- xlink is a required namespace prefix.
- href is a keyword that indicates that a URI follows.
- S (p. 124) represents one or more whitespace characters: spaces, carriage returns, line feeds, or tabs. Syntax: {[#x20|#x9|#xD|#xA][#x20| #x9|#xD|#xA]...[#x20|#x9|#xD|#xA]}
- CDATA represents character data; that is, any text that is not markup.
- #IMPLIED is an uppercase-only reserved keyword indicating that the defined attribute *may* be supplied. For more information, see the DefaultDecl production (p. 58).
- #REQUIRED is an uppercase-only reserved keyword indicating that the defined attribute *must* be supplied. For more information, see the DefaultDecl production (p. 58).
- URI_name is the name of a URI.

Notes

- href is a global attribute for almost any namespace — predefined or newly defined by an XML document developer — as long as elements are declared as XLink elements.
- The href attribute shows the target URI and/or extended pointers of the link element.
- The href attribute is required (#REQUIRED) for the locator link type and optional (#IMPLIED) for the simple link type.

Related Attributes

actuate (p. 146), role (p. 153), show (p. 155), title (p. 157), xlink (p. 161)

Related Link Type

locator (p. 152), simple (p. 156)

label   label Attribute

Purpose

Specifies the label of a locator or resource type XLink.

EBNF Syntax (declared in an attribute list)

```
xlink:label S NMTOKEN S #IMPLIED
```

Syntax (used in an XML document)

```
xlink:label={'|"}label_name{'|"}
```

Where

- xlink is a required namespace prefix.
- label is a keyword that indicates an identifier.

XLink Language

- S (p. 124) represents one or more whitespace characters: spaces, carriage returns, line feeds, or tabs. Syntax: {[#x20|#x9|#xD|#xA][#x20|#x9|#xD|#xA]...[#x20|#x9|#xD|#xA]}
- NMTOKEN (p. 107) specifies a valid XML-name-token role value.
- #IMPLIED is an uppercase-only reserved keyword indicating that the defined attribute may be supplied. For more information, see the DefaultDecl production (p. 58).
- *label_name* is the name of the label.

Notes

- The label, from and to attributes, which are known as the traversal attributes, specify the traversal between a starting and ending resource. The starting resource is the from portion of a linking resource, and the ending resource is the to portion. The label attribute corresponds with a locator or resource-type element.
- The NMTOKEN value of a from or to attribute must be the same as the value of a label attribute.

locator   Locator XLink Type

Purpose
Indicates a remote resource for a link.

Syntax
See the type attribute (p. 160).

Notes

- A *locator* is an address or identifier that specifies the remote target of a link.
- An element that is defined as a locator link type can have any content except for title link type elements. The title link type is an important child of the locator link type.
- An element that is defined as a locator link type is not a link if an explicit link is not made between it and a resource.
- The type and href attributes are required for the locator link type.
- The role, label, and title attributes are optional for the locator link type.
- Several locators that have the same role value are separate and unique.
- An extended link can contain any number of the following declared link-type elements: arc, locator, resource, and title.
- If an extended link contains one locator or one resource element or none at all, it cannot be traversed.
- The arc, locator, resource, and title link types are important child types of the extended link type. Although other link types can be embedded within extended, they are not significant to extended.

Related Attributes
href (p. 150), role (p. 153), title (p. 157), type (p. 160)

Related Link Type
resource (p. 153)

resource   Resource XLink Type

Purpose
Indicates a local resource for a link.

Syntax
See the type attribute (p. 160).

Notes
- A *resource* is an address or identifier that specifies the local target of a link.
- An element that is defined as a resource link type can have any content or no content.
- When resource is a starting point for a link, you should have some content to ensure that a user can traverse the link.
- The type attribute is required for the resource link type.
- The role and title attributes are optional for the resource link type.
- An extended link can contain any number of the following declared link-type elements: arc, locator, resource, and title.
- If an extended link contains one locator or resource elements or none, it cannot be traversed.
- The arc, locator, resource, and title link types are important child types of the extended link type. Although other link types can be embedded within extended, they are not significant to extended.
- If extended contains a resource link type, the link is local. Otherwise, the link is remote.

Related Attributes
role (p. 153), title (p. 157), type (p. 160)

Related Link Type
locator (p. 152)

role   Remote-Link-Content Role Attribute

Purpose
Specifies the role of link content.

XLink Language

EBNF Syntax (declared in an attribute list)

```
xlink:role SCDATA S#IMPLIED | #FIXED "fixed-uri"
```

Syntax (used in an XML document)

```
xlink:role={'|"}URI{'|"}
```

Where

- xlink is a required namespace prefix.
- role is a keyword that indicates that a role value follows.
- CDATA represents character data; that is, any text that is not markup.
- #IMPLIED is an uppercase-only reserved keyword indicating that the defined attribute *may* be supplied. For more information, see the DefaultDecl production (p. 58).
- #FIXED is an uppercase-only reserved keyword indicating that the defined attribute must always have the default attribute value.
- *fixed-uri* is the URI if the role is fixed.
- *URI* is the value of the user-provided URI.

Notes

- The role attribute contains a URI that identifies some resource that describes the property. This resource can contain information about the author, creation or edit date, comments, and even documentation of the link, for those who will edit the link in the future.
- role is a global attribute for almost any namespace — predefined or newly defined by an XML document developer — as long as elements are declared as XLink elements.
- Both the role and title attributes, which are known as the semantic attributes, describe the sum and substance of the resource. The role attribute is supposed to be readable by a computer application, and the title attribute should be readable by humans.
- The role attribute is optional for the simple, extended, locator, arc, and resource link types.
- The role value must be a qualified name from the XML namespace.
- If the from value is not supplied for the arc link type, the starting resource is all the role values for elements that are defined as locator link types embedded within the same extended-link element as the arc-link element.
- If the to value is not supplied for the arc link type, the ending resource is all the role values for elements that are defined as locator link types embedded within the same extended-link element as the arc-link element.
- If no arc-type elements are embedded in an extended link, XLink is programmed to assume that the omitted from and to values for the extended link are all the role values in the extended link.
- Several locators that have the same role value are separate and unique.
- When an extended link is entirely remote, you must create an *external linkset* (list of references to extended links) so that the link can be located. To do this, the role attribute must be set to a value of

prefix:external-linkset, where *prefix* is the name of a namespace declaration (such as xlink). The *linkbase* (the document that contains the external linkset) must be an XML document.

- An external linkset can refer to a linkbase that refers to another external linkset, which in turn can refer to another linkbase, and so forth.

Related Attributes
actuate (p. 146), href (p. 150), show (p. 155), title (p. 157), xlink (p. 161)

Related Link Types
arc (p. 147), locator (p. 152), resource (p. 153), simple (p. 156)

show	Show-Link-Resource Attribute

Purpose
Indicates how a link resource is displayed onscreen.

EBNF Syntax (declared in an attribute list)
```
xlink:show S (new|replace|embed|none|other)
   S #IMPLIED
```

Syntax (used in an XML document)
```
xlink:show={'|"}new|replace|embed|none)
   |other{'|"}
```

Where
- xlink is a required namespace prefix.
- show is a keyword that indicates that a show value follows.
- S (p. 124) represents one or more whitespace characters: spaces, carriage returns, line feeds, or tabs. Syntax: {[#x20|#x9|#xD|#xA][#x20|#x9|#xD|#xA]...[#x20|#x9|#xD|#xA]}
- new creates a new link resource without replacing the current resource.
- replace replaces the current resource with the new link resource at the location at which traversal originated.
- embed embeds the new link resource in the current resource at the location at which traversal originated.
- none indicates that actuate and other markup do not control traversal behavior.
- other indicates that actuate does not control the traversal behavior. Other markup in the link may aid an application traversing to the ending resource.
- #IMPLIED is an uppercase-only reserved keyword indicating that the defined attribute *may* be supplied. For more information, see the DefaultDecl production (p. 58).

XLink Language

Notes

- show is a global attribute for almost any namespace — predefined or newly defined by an XML document developer — as long as elements are declared as XLink elements.
- show defines the display behavior of a link.
- Both show and actuate are known as behavior attributes.
- The show attribute is optional for the simple and arc link types.
- Link processing applications do not have to be programmed in a particular way to implement actuate and show.

Related Attributes

actuate (p. 146), href (p. 150), role (p. 153), title (p. 157), xlink (p. 161)

Related Link Types

arc (p. 147), simple (p. 156)

---

simple	Simple XLink Type

Purpose

Indicates a link that associates one local resource and one remote resource.

Syntax

See the type attribute (p. 160).

Notes

- A simple link has a local resource, which means that the link is local, and a remote resource. According to the XLink candidate recommendation (http://www.w3.org/TR/xlink/), a "simple link element combines the basic functions of a linking element, a locator element, and an arc element."
- An element that is defined as a simple link type can have any content or no content. The simple link and its content make up the local resource.
- If a simple-type element has embedded link elements of any type, XLink does not recognize the relationship.
- The type attribute is required for the simple link type.
- The actuate, arcrole, href, role, show, and title attributes are optional for the simple link type. The href, role, and title attributes actually come from the simple element's implicit locator-type element. The actuate and show attributes come from the simple element's implicit arc-type element.
- Within a particular simple link, an href attribute with a missing value is not traversed.
- A simple link can be embedded within an extended link. The simple link does not have to have an XLink affiliation to the extended link.
- An extended link can be used as a simple link, as long as it has one local resource and one remote resource.

XLink Language

Related Attributes

actuate (p. 146), href (p. 150), role (p. 153), show (p. 155), type (p. 160)

Related Link Types

arc (p. 147), extended (p. 148), locator (p. 152)

title	Title XLink Type

Purpose

Provides title information with a link.

Syntax

See the type attribute (p. 160).

Notes

- According to the XLink candidate recommendation (http://www.w3.org/TR/xlink/), elements that are defined as title link types "are useful, for example, for cases where human-readable label information needs further element markup, or where multiple titles are necessary for internationalization purposes."
- An element that is defined as a title link type can have any content.
- If a title-type element has embedded link elements of any type, XLink does not recognize the relationship.
- The type attribute is required for the title link type.
- An extended link can contain any number of the following declared link-type elements: arc, locator, resource, and title, which are all important child types of extended.

Related Attributes

title (p. 157), type (p. 160)

Related Link Type

extended (p. 148)

title	Remote-Link-Content Title Attribute

Purpose

Specifies the title of a link resource.

EBNF Syntax (declared in an attribute list)

```
xlink:title S CDATA S #IMPLIED
```

Syntax (used in an XML document)

```
xlink:title={'|"}title_value{'|"}
```

XLink Language

Where

- xlink is a required namespace prefix.
- title is a keyword that indicates that a title value follows.
- S (p. 124) represents one or more whitespace characters: spaces, carriage returns, line feeds, or tabs. Syntax: {[#x20|#x9|#xD|#xA][#x20| #x9|#xD|#xA]...[#x20|#x9|#xD|#xA]}
- CDATA represents character data; that is, any text that is not markup.
- #IMPLIED is an uppercase-only reserved keyword indicating that the defined attribute *may* be supplied. For more information, see the DefaultDecl production (p. 58).
- *title_value* is the value of the title.

Notes

- title is a global attribute for almost any namespace — predefined or newly defined by an XML document developer — as long as elements are declared as XLink elements.
- Both the title and role attributes, which are known as the semantic attributes, describe the sum and substance of the resource. The title attribute should be readable by humans, and the role attribute is supposed to be readable by a computer application.
- The title is a displayed caption for the link.
- The title attribute is optional for the simple, extended, locator, arc, and resource link types.
- XLink does not require an application to use a title in a particular way.

Related Attributes
actuate (p. 146), href (p. 150), role (p. 153), show (p. 155), xlink (p. 161)

Related Link Types
arc (p. 147), extended (p. 148), locator (p. 152), resource (p. 153), simple (p. 156)

to   To Attribute

Purpose
Specifies the end point of an arc link.

EBNF Syntax (declared in an attribute list)
```
xlink:to S NMTOKEN S #IMPLIED
```

Syntax (used in an XML document)
```
xlink:to={'|"}to_URI{'|"}
```

Where

- xlink is a required namespace prefix.
- to is a keyword that indicates that a to URI follows.
- S (p. 124) represents one or more whitespace characters: spaces, carriage returns, line feeds, or tabs. Syntax: {[#x20|#x9|#xD|#xA][#x20|#x9|#xD|#xA]...[#x20|#x9|#xD|#xA]}
- NMTOKEN (p. 107) specifies a valid XML-name-token role value.
- #IMPLIED is an uppercase-only reserved keyword indicating that the defined attribute *may* be supplied. For more information, see the DefaultDecl production (p. 58).
- *to_URI* is the URI of to.

Notes

- According to the XLink candidate recommendation (http://www.w3.org/TR/xlink/), "the to attribute defines resources that can be traversed to, that is, ending resources."
- to is a global attribute for almost any namespace — predefined or newly defined by an XML document developer — as long as elements are declared as XLink elements.
- The from and to attributes, which are known as the traversal attributes, specify the traversal between a starting and ending resource. The starting resource is the *from* portion of a linking resource, and the ending resource is the *to* portion.
- The value of a from or to attribute must be the same as the local portion of a role attribute of an element that is defined as either a locator or resource link. The locator-link or resource-link element must be embedded within the same extended-link element as the arc-link element.
- The to attribute is optional for the arc link type. If the to value is not supplied, the ending resource is all the role values for elements that are defined as locator link types embedded within the same extended-link element as the arc-link element.
- The NMTOKEN value of a to attribute must correspond with the NMTOKEN value of a label attribute for a locator or resource element.

Related Attribute

to (p. 158)

Related Link Type

arc (p. 147)

XLink Language

type   Link Type Attribute

Purpose
Specifies a link type.

EBNF Syntax (declared in an attribute list)
```
xlink:type S (simple|extended|locator|arc
  |resource|title|none)
  S {(#FIXED S {'|"}simple|extended|locator|arc
  |resource|title{'|"})|#REQUIRED}
```

Syntax (used in an XML document that includes a non-XLink namespace)
```
xlink:type={'|"}simple|extended|locator
  |arc|resource|title|none{'|"}
```

Where
- xlink is a required namespace prefix.
- type is a keyword that indicates that a link type follows.
- S (p. 124) represents one or more whitespace characters: spaces, carriage returns, line feeds, or tabs. Syntax: {[#x20|#x9|#xD|#xA][#x20| #x9|#xD|#xA]...[#x20|#x9|#xD|#xA]}
- simple (p. 156) is a keyword that indicates that a simple link type declaration or value for the element follows.
- extended (p. 148) is a keyword that indicates that an extended link type declaration or value for the element follows.
- locator (p. 152) is a keyword that indicates that a locator link type declaration or value for the element follows.
- arc (p. 147) is a keyword that indicates that an arc link type declaration or value for the element follows.
- resource (p. 153) is a keyword that indicates that a resource link type declaration or value for the element follows.
- title (p. 157) is a keyword that indicates that a title link type declaration or value for the element follows.
- none indicates that the type attribute for the element has no XLink significance, attributes, or content.
- #FIXED is an uppercase-only reserved keyword indicating that the defined attribute *must* always have the default attribute value. For more information, see the DefaultDecl production (p. 58).
- #REQUIRED is an uppercase-only reserved keyword indicating that the defined attribute *must* be supplied. For more information, see the DefaultDecl production (p. 58).

Notes
- type is a global attribute for almost any namespace — predefined or newly defined by an XML document developer — as long as elements are declared as XLink elements.

- The type attribute is required for the simple, extended, locator, arc, resource, and title link types.
- A value of none combined with another link type indicates that the element is sometimes used as a link and sometimes is not.
- The optional title attribute is a displayed caption for the link. XLink does not require an application to use a title in a particular way.

Related Attributes
actuate (p. 146), href (p. 150), role (p. 153), show (p. 155), xlink (p. 161)

Related Link Types
arc (p. 147), extended (p. 148), locator (p. 152), resource (p. 153), simple (p. 156), title (p. 157)

---

xlink	XLink Link Processing

Purpose
Signals that a namespace URI or link attribute and attribute value follows.

Standard Syntax
```
[xmlns:]xlink:namespace
  |(actuate|from|href|label|role|show|title
  |to|type)
```

Where
- xmlns is a reserved keyword that indicates the XML namespace used by a document.
- xlink is a reserved keyword that indicates that an XLink attribute and attribute value follows.
- actuate (p. 146) is an attribute that actuates link traversal.
- from (p. 149) is an attribute that specifies the starting point of an arc link.
- href (p. 150) is an attribute that specifies a remote resource locator.
- label (p. 151) is an attribute that specifies the label name of a locator or resource-type.
- role (p. 153) is an attribute that specifies the role of link content.
- show (p. 155) is an attribute that indicates how a link resource is displayed onscreen.
- title (p. 157) is an attribute that specifies the title of a link resource.
- to (p. 158) is an attribute that specifies the end point of an arc link.
- type (p. 160) is an attribute that specifies a link type.

Notes
- A simple link has just one locator, included in the linking element.

XLink Language

- According to the XLink candidate recommendation (http://www.w3.org/TR/xlink/), arc "provides context for application behavior. The arc construct is intended to provide an explicit model for the relationship between two locators. The arc construct is the correct construct to associate XLink and non-XLink related traversal information."
- You can include any type of content in a link. However, the document must conform to its DTD.
- Use an extended link group to accumulate a list of related links. Use an extended link document element to specify each document in the list.
- You can express a link in two ways: either within a start tag and an end tag in a document or as a declaration in a DTD.

Related Attributes

actuate (p. 146), href (p. 150), role (p. 153), show (p. 155), title (p. 157)

Related Link Types

arc (p. 187), extended (p. 148), locator (p. 152), resource (p. 153), simple (p. 156), title (p. 157)

XLink Language

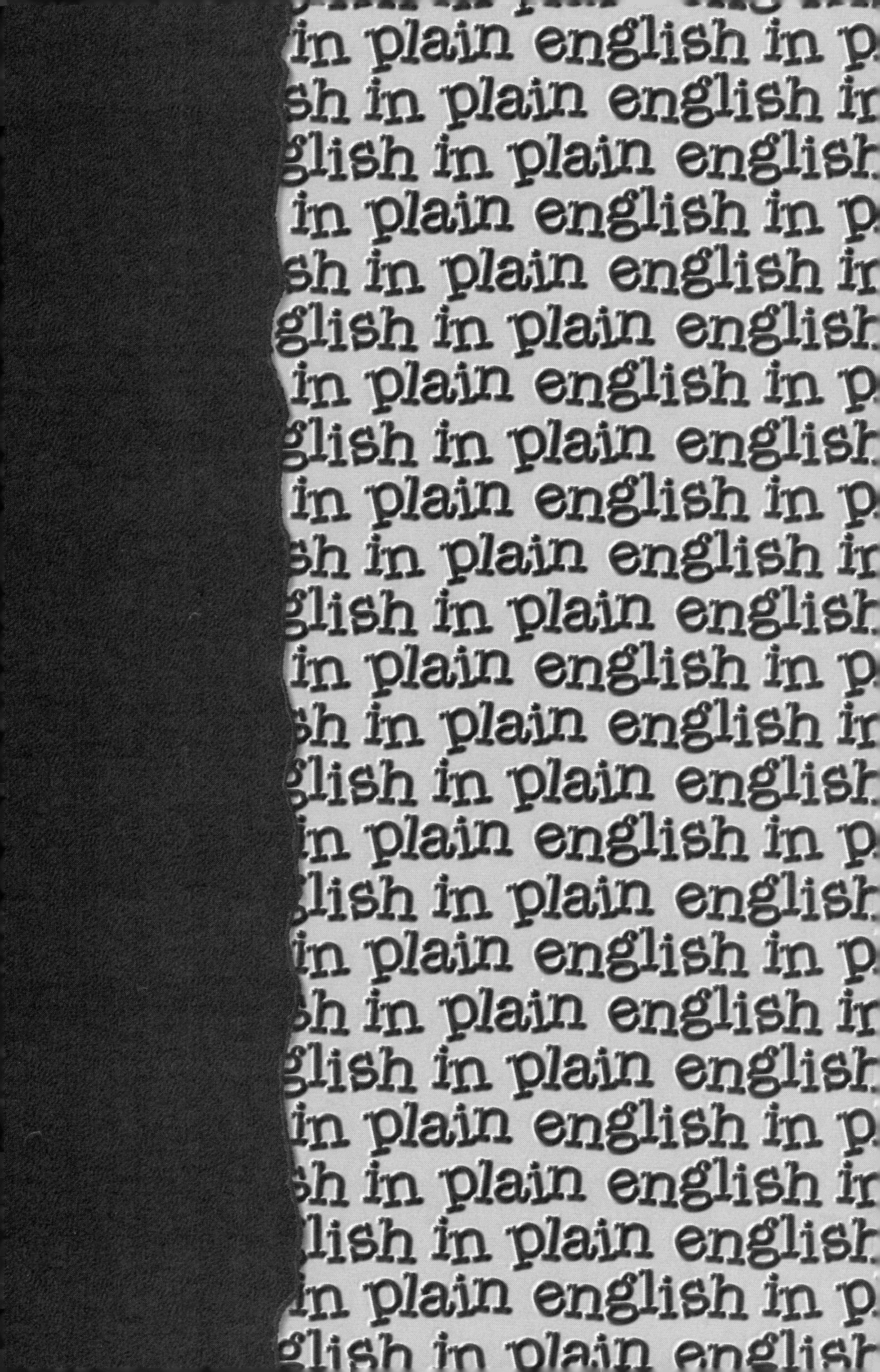

XPointer Language

The productions and functions in this chapter enable you to create XPointers (extended pointers), which pinpoint the location of XLink hyperlinks or other objects within a document. As pointed out in the "XLink Language" reference section, XML supports two types of links: *simple* and *extended*. Simple links are analogous to HTML links, and extended links enable you to jump from any link to any other link. Within extended links, you can use XPointers to pinpoint a location even further along a document chain. For example, you can find the seventh child of the third child of the fifth element within a document. XPointers use a series of location terms to point to and locate a particular link. A *location term* simply refers to an absolute, relative, or string-match location in a document. The first location term in an XPointer is usually absolute. The start of an extended pointer is signaled by the *fragment identifier* delimiter, a pound-sign symbol (#). The characters following the fragment identifier are the actual extended pointer.

More information about XPointer, now a candidate recommendation, is available at the W3C Web site (http://www.w3.org/TR/xptr).

●—NOTE

XPointers support Unicode — specifically the UTF-8 encoding. However, some Unicode characters are not allowed in a URI. For example, to insert a left-angle (<) or ampersand (&) in an XPointer, use the characters < and &, respectively. So, when testing an XPointer and getting strange results, try to precede characters with %*HH* (where *HH* indicates two hexadecimal digits).

ChildSeq	**Child Sequence**

Purpose

Locates a target element by navigating through the integer values for child elements.

EBNF Syntax

```
ChildSeq ::= '/1' ('/' [0-9]*)*| Name ('/' [0-9]*)+
```

Standard Syntax

```
/1 (/[0-9[0-9[...0-9]]])[(/[0-9[0-9[...0-9]]])
   (.../[0-9[0-9[...0-9]]])]
   | Name (/ [0-9[0-9[...0-9]]])
   [(/ [0-9[0-9[...0-9]]])[...(/ [0-9[0-9[...0-9]]])]]
```

Where

- /1 represents the document or root element.
- / is a delimiter that precedes an integer.
- 0-9 are numbers from 0 to 9.
- Name (p. 102) specifies a valid XML attribute name. Syntax: #x*nnnn* [#x*nnnn*][_][:][#x*nnnn*]|[0|1|2|3|4|5|6|7|8|9][.]|[-] [#x*nnnn*][#x*nnnn*]...[#x*nnnn*]

Notes

- ChildSeq is a component of the XPointer production.
- According to the XPointer candidate recommendation, "the child sequence form of addressing locates an element by stepwise navigation using a sequence of integers separated by slashes."
- For example, a child sequence finds the root element by providing the root's name or using the /1 string.
- An XPointer begins with the name of a scheme and includes an expression within parentheses.
- An XPointer that is not valid or that includes incorrect information can result in three types of errors: a syntax error, a resource error, or a sub-resource error. A *syntax error* results from an XPointer with a string that does not match the specified syntax. A *resource error* results from an XPointer with a missing or incorrectly-formed resource. A *sub-resource error* results from an XPointer with a missing or incorrectly formed sub-resource.

Related Productions
XPointer (p. 176), Name (p. 102), FullXPtr (p. 167)

end-point()	End-Point Function

Purpose
Returns the locations of the end-point type.

EBNF Syntax
```
point end-point( point_2 )
```

Standard Syntax
```
point end-point( point_2 )
```

Where
- point is a set of locations returned by the function.
- end-point is a function-name keyword.
- point_2 is one or more locations to be evaluated.

Notes
- The returned location-set contains every end point of each location in the evaluated location-set.
- XPointer defines two new location types, point and range, which are used to address non-node locations.
- According to the XPointer recommendation (www.w3.org/TR/xptr), a location of type point is defined by a node called the *container node* and a non-negative integer called the index.
- It is possible to navigate with respective boundaries of range locations using the start-point and end-point functions.

FullXPtr	Full XPointer

Purpose
Identifies the XPointer parts that make up a full XPointer.

EBNF Syntax
```
FullXPtr ::= XPtrPart (S? XPtrPart)*
```

Standard Syntax
```
XPtrPart (XPtrPart)
```

Where
- FullXPtr is the keyword that identifies information for a full XPointer.
- XPtrPart is a keyword that identifies the XPtrPart.

- S (p. 124) represents one or more whitespace characters: spaces, carriage returns, line feeds, or tabs. Syntax: {[#x20|#x9|#xD|#xA][#x20|#x9|#xD|#xA]...[#x20|#x9|#xD|#xA]}

Notes

- FullXPtr is part of the XPointer production.
- A full-form means of identifying an XPointer consists of one or more XPointer parts or XPtrPart. These parts may optionally be separated by a whitespace.
- Each XPtrPart starts with a scheme name followed by an expression in parentheses.
- Due to the inability to avoid conflicts in the naming of schemes, the only allowed scheme name in this version of XPointer is "xpointer."
- The "xpointer" scheme expression gives access to nodes within a set of XML documents and non-node locations.
- CDATA sections and entities are not accessible via a scheme.
- The two other means of identifying XPointers are short forms — ChildSeq or "child sequences" and Name or "bare names."

here()   Here Function

Purpose
Returns a location-set with one location.

EBNF Syntax
```
location-set here()
```

Standard Syntax
```
location-set here()
```

Where

- location-set is the location returned by the function.
- here is a function-name keyword.

Notes

- The returned location is an element, of the element type. The element contains the XPointer as either text or the value of an attribute.
- If the specified XPointer is not part of an XML document, the processor issues a syntax error.

NodeType   Node Type

Purpose
Identifies a specific node location type.

EBNF Syntax

```
NodeType ::= 'comment' | 'text'
  | 'processing-instruction' | 'node' | 'point'
  | 'range'
```

Standard Syntax

comment | text | processing-instruction | node | point | range

Where

- comment specifies an XML comment. (For more information about comments in XML, see the Comment production on page 49.)
- text specifies text within the XML element or CData sections (p. 37).
- processing-instruction specifies an XML processing instruction. (For more information about processing instructions, see the PI production on page 117)
- node names a particular node.
- point specifies a location preceding a character or node or succeeding a node in an XML document.
- range specifies a DOM-like range with a start point and an end point within a single XML document.

Notes

- A *node* is a point of connection in a tree structure of elements or documents. An *XPointer location* is an individual point in a document, a range, or an XPath node. An XPath location is always a node.
- To learn how an XPointer is processed in order to find a target, read Section 3.2, "Evaluation Content Initialization in the XML Pointer Language (XPointer)" working draft (http://www.w3.org/TR/xptr).
- The NodeType production enables XPointer extensions to XPath. For more information on XPath, refer to "XPointer Language" (p. 165).
- XPath has the following main functions within XPointer: locating node subsets, filtering axis output, and distinguishing between parts of documents that are nodes and those that are not.
- point enables the XPointer [ ] operator to select from several ranges.
- A *container node* (a specific node for a point location type) and an *index* (a 0 or positive integer) should combine to define a point location type.
- When a container node can have child nodes, the index refers to the child nodes. This is a *node-point*. A node-point can range from zero to the number of child nodes. A zero index specifies a point immediately before any child nodes. An index with a value of x specifies the point immediately after the xth child node.
- When a container node cannot have child nodes, the index refers to the characters within the value of the node's string. This is a *character-point*. A character-point can range from zero to the number of the characters in the node's string. A zero index specifies a point immediately before the first character. An index with a value of x specifies the point immediately after the xth character in the string.

- According to the XPointer working draft, "The axes of a point location are defined as follows: A point location has no children. A character-point has no preceding or following siblings. A node-point's siblings are the children of the container node that are before or after the node-point."
- A range contains all the markup and content within the start point and the end point.
- The start and end points of a range that is not a node type of element, text, or root must be the same node type.
- A range that starts and ends at the same point is known as a *collapsed range*.
- If both the starting and ending positions are both character-points, and the container nodes of those points are identical, the value of the string between the two points is the number of characters between. If one position is not a character-point, the value of the string between the two points is the number of characters in text nodes between. Use the start-point() and end-point() functions to travel between the two points.
- According to the XPointer working draft, "The axes of a range location are the axes of its starting position."
- A *covering range* completely encloses a location. To learn about covering ranges, refer to the XPointer working draft (http://www.w3.org/TR/xptr).

Related Productions
Comment (p. 49), PI (p. 117).

---

origin()   Origin Function

Purpose
Returns a location-set with one location for an out-of-line link.

EBNF Syntax
```
location-set origin()
```

Standard Syntax
```
location-set origin()
```

Where
- location-set is one location returned by the function.
- origin is a function-name keyword.

Notes
- If you use origin() in a locator that contains a URI with a remote target or traversal is not possible, the processor issues a resource error.
- For more information about out-of-line links, refer to "XLink Language" (p. 145).

- origin() allows XPointers to be used in applications.
- The origin() function will only return a usable location-set.

range() — Range Function

Purpose
Returns ranges for each location in the specified location-set.

EBNF Syntax
```
location-set range( location-set )
```

Standard Syntax
```
location-set range( location-set_2 )
```

Where
- location-set is a set of locations returned by the function.
- range is a function-name keyword.
- location-set_2 is one or more locations to be evaluated.

Note
- Each location in the range is added to the returned location-set.

range-inside() — Range-Inside Function

Purpose
Returns ranges within the contents of the resulting location-set.

EBNF Syntax
```
location-set range-inside( location-set )
```

Standard Syntax
```
location-set range-inside( location-set_2 )
```

Where
- location-set is a set of locations returned by the function.
- range-inside is a function-name keyword.
- location-set_2 is one or more locations to be evaluated.

Notes
- Each location in the range is added to the returned location-set.
- If a location is not a range location, that location becomes the container location of the start and end points and its index is 0. If the end point is a character point, its index is the length of the location string. If the end point is not a character point, its value is the number of children of the location.

XPointer Language

range-to()　　　　　　　　　　　　Range-To Function

Purpose
Returns the range for each location in the expression.

EBNF Syntax
```
location-set range-to(expression)
```

Standard Syntax
```
location-set start-point(expression)
```

Where
- `location-set` is a set of ranges returned by the function.
- `range-to` is a function-name keyword.
- `expression` contains information about the location range to be evaluated by the expression.

Notes
- This example of range-to() would select a range starting at the beginning of an element and ending at another element for each "edit." (This example would be for using empty elements such as <EDBEGIN /> for "edit begin" and <EDEND /> for "edit end".)

```
xpointer(descendant::REVST/range-to(following::REVEND[1]))
```

- In the above example, XPath would not allow for functions to immediately follow the slash. Only XPointer would.

Scheme　　　　　　　　　　　　　　　　Scheme

Purpose
Identifies the notation used to express the XPointer.

EBNF Syntax
```
Scheme ::= QName - 'xpointer'
```

Standard Syntax
```
QName - xpointer
```

Where
- `QName` is a qualified scheme name that names nodes defined in the XML namespace.
- `xpointer` is an all-lowercase reserved keyword that names nodes that are compatible with XPath.

Notes
- Scheme is a component of the `XPtrPart` production.

- Naming the scheme enables a processor to interpret the XML document properly and to ignore schemes that it is not programmed to understand.
- The `xpointer` reserved keyword indicates that the scheme is compatible with XPath's access to nodes in the XML information set. The exceptions are CDATA sections and entities.
- Reserving specific scheme names enables future versions of XPointer and other related technologies to be identified explicitly.
- Enclose scheme names within quotation marks or single quote marks.

Related Production

XPtrPart (p. 177).

SchemeSpecificExpr   Scheme-Specific Expression

Purpose

Instructs an XML processor on how to interpret a named non-`xpointer` scheme.

EBNF Syntax

```
SchemeSpecificExpr ::= StringWithBalancedParens
```

Standard Syntax

```
StringWithBalancedParens
```

Where

- `StringWithBalancedParens` (p. 175) ensures that a string is enclosed within a pair of parentheses.

Notes

- `SchemeSpecificExpr` is a component of the `XPtrPart` production.
- For a document to be valid, the closed parenthesis at the end of the `XPtrPart` production must be preceded by an open parenthesis at the beginning of the location specifier.
- If the `SchemeSpecificExpr` production includes a parenthesis character within or outside a literal, it must be preceded by a circumflex (^).
- If `SchemeSpecificExp` contains a circumflex (^) in a literal, it must be preceded by another circumflex.

Related Productions

XPtrPart (p. 177), `StringWithBalancedParens` (p. 175)

start-point()   Start-Point Function

Purpose

Returns the locations of the start-point type.

EBNF Syntax

```
location-set start-point( location-set )
```

Standard Syntax

```
location-set start-point( location-set_2 )
```

Where

- location-set is a set of locations returned by the function.
- start-point is a function-name keyword.
- location-set_2 is one or more locations to be evaluated.

Note

- The returned location-set contains every start point of each location in the evaluated location-set.

---

string-range()   String-Range Function

Purpose

Returns a range location for each string match that does not overlap.

EBNF Syntax

```
location-set string-range( location-set string
    number? number?)
```

Standard Syntax

```
location-set string-range( location-set_2 string
    [number_1] [number_2])
```

Where

- location-set is a set of locations returned by the function.
- string-range is a function-name keyword.
- location-set_2 is one or more locations to be evaluated.
- string is a group of characters enclosed within quotation marks or single quote marks that might match location-set_2.
- number_1 represents the start of a range. The default value is 1.
- number_2 represents the number of characters to be evaluated within the range. The default value is the total number of characters in the range.

Note

- string-range regards several adjacent whitespace characters as one space.

| **StringWithBalancedParens** | **String with Matched Parentheses** |

Purpose
Ensures that a string is enclosed within a pair of parentheses.

EBNF Syntax
```
StringWithBalancedParens ::=
    [^()]* ('(' StringWithBalancedParens
    ')' [^()]*)*
```

Standard Syntax
```
[^()][^()][...^()]
    (( StringWithBalancedParens )
    [^()][^()][...^()]
    (( StringWithBalancedParens )
    [^()][^()][...^()]
    ...(( StringWithBalancedParens )
    [^()][^()][...^()])))
```

Where
- ^, (, and) are characters *not* to be included in the production.
- StringWithBalancedParens is an embedded string.

Notes
- StringWithBalanceParentheses is a component of the Scheme SpecificExpr and StringWithBalanceParentheses productions.
- For a document to be valid, the closed parenthesis at the end of the XPtrPart production must be preceded by an open parenthesis at the beginning of the location specifier.
- If the SchemeSpecificExpr production includes a parenthesis character within or outside a literal, it must be preceded by a circumflex (^).
- If SchemeSpecificExp contains a circumflex (^) in a literal, it must be preceded by another circumflex.

Related Productions
XPtrPart (p. 177), SchemeSpecificExpr (p. 173)

| **unique()** | **Unique Function** |

Purpose
Returns true only if a location-set contains one location.

EBNF Syntax
```
unique()
```

Standard Syntax

```
unique()
```

Where

- unique is a function-name keyword.

Note

- unique() is a predicate function. A *predicate* ratifies a statement. This enables a developer to automate procedures that are run only if a location-set contains just one location and otherwise ignored.

XPointer   XPointer

Purpose

Designates a fully formed XPointer.

EBNF Syntax

```
XPointer ::= Name | ChildSeq | FullXPtr
```

Standard Syntax

```
Name | ChildSeq | FullXPtr
```

Where

- Name (p. 102) is a keyword that specifies a short-form XPointer called a "bare name."
- ChildSeq (p. 166) is a keyword that indicates a short-form XPointer called a "child sequence."
- FullXPtr (p. 167) is a keyword that specifies one or more XPointer parts or XPtrPart.

Notes

- There are three ways of addressing an XPointer, the full form (the method for this entry) and two short forms: ChildSeq (child sequences) and Name (bare names).
- A full-form means of identifying an XPointer consists of one or more XPointer parts or XPtrPart. These parts may optionally be separated by a whitespace.
- Each XPtrPart starts with a scheme name followed by an expression in parentheses.
- Due to the inability to avoid conflicts in the naming of schemes, the only allowed scheme name in this version of XPointer is "xpointer."
- The "xpointer" scheme expression gives access to nodes within a set of XML documents and non-node locations.
- CDATA sections and entities are not accessible via a scheme.

XPtrExpr   XPointer Expression

Purpose
Instructs an XML processor how to interpret the xpointer scheme.

EBNF Syntax
```
XPtrExpr ::= Expr | RangeExpr
```

Standard Syntax
```
Expr | RangeExpr
```

Where
- Expr is an XPath-supported expression. See the Expr production (p. 194) in the XPath recommendation.
- RangeExpr specifies a range of XPath expressions.

Notes
- XPtrExpr is a component of the XPtrPart production.
- The only valid XPath XPointer expressions are those that return a set of nodes.

Related Production
XPtrPart (p. 177)

XPtrPart   XPointer Part

Purpose
Locates a target element by specifying part of a full XPointer or FullXPtr.

EBNF Syntax
```
XPtrPart ::= 'xpointer' '(' XPtrExpr ')'
    | Scheme '(' SchemeSpecificExpr ')'
```

Standard Syntax
```
xpointer (XPtrExpr)
    | Scheme (SchemeSpecificExpr)
```

Where
- xpointer is an all-lowercase reserved keyword that names nodes that are compatible with XPath.
- XPtrExpr (p. 177) is a valid expression that instructs an XML processor how to interpret the xpointer scheme.
- Scheme (p. 172) is a valid scheme name.
- SchemeSpecificExpr (p. 173) is a valid expression that instructs an XML processor how to interpret a named non-xpointer scheme.

XPointer Language

Notes

- XPtrPart is a component of the FullXPtr production.
- XPtrPart is the core component of one of the three ways of expressing an XPointer, a FullXPtr or full XPointer. The other two XPointers are short-form: ChildSeq (child sequences) and Name (bare names).
- More than one XPtrPart can be included in a FullXPtr.
- An XML processor evaluates multiple XPtrParts from left to right. When a processor cannot interpret one XPtrPart, it should be programmed to move on to the next. If a processor cannot interpret any XPtrParts, an error message is issued.
- An XPtrPart begins with the name of a scheme and includes an expression within parentheses.
- Reserving specific scheme names enables future versions of XPointer and other related technologies to be identified explicitly; however, the only scheme name allowed in this version is xpointer.
- For a document to be valid, the close parenthesis at the end of the XPtrPart production must be preceded by an open parenthesis at the beginning of the location specifier.
- If the SchemeSpecificExpr production includes a parenthesis character within or outside a literal, it must be preceded by a circumflex (^).
- If SchemeSpecificExp contains a circumflex (^) in a literal, it must be preceded by another circumflex.
- Names must be enclosed within quotation marks or single quote marks.
- An XPointer that is not valid or includes incorrect information can result in three types of errors: a syntax error, a resource error, or a sub-resource error. A *syntax error* results from an XPointer with an invalid string. A *resource error* results from an XPointer with a missing or incorrect resource. A *sub-resource error* results from an XPointer with a missing or incorrect sub-resource.

Related Productions

ChildSeq (p. 166), Name (p. 102), Scheme (p. 172), SchemeSpecificExpr (p. 173), FullXPtr (p. 167), XPtrExpr (p. 177)

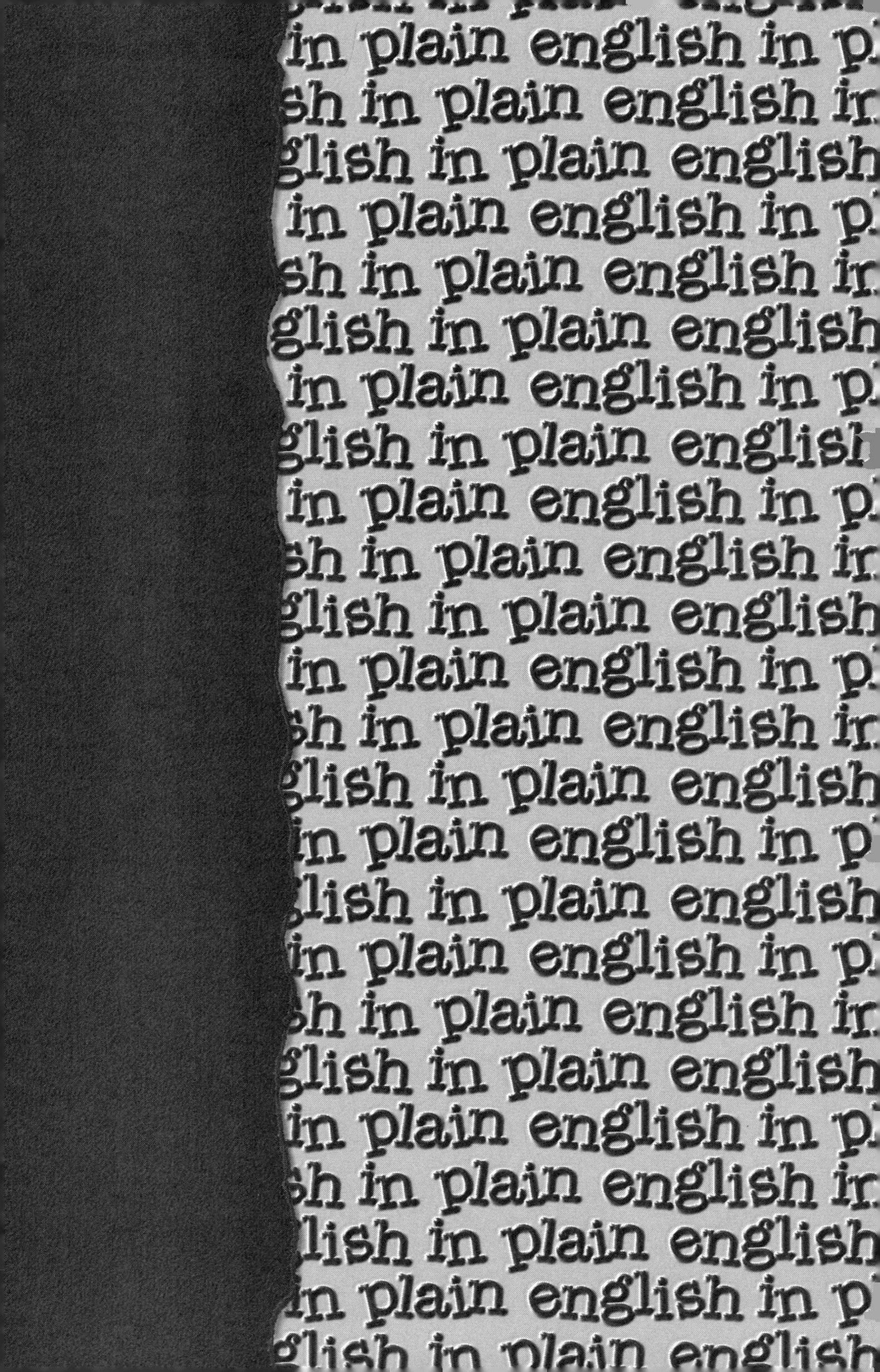
in plain english

XPath Language

The XPath language supports both Extended Pointers, or XPointers (see "XPointer Language" [p. 165]) and XSL Transformations, or XSLT (see "XSLT Component" [p. 319]).

The productions in this section enable you to build expressions to reference parts of an XML document in different ways. XPath expressions find node-sets, numbers, booleans, or strings. When used with XPointers, XPath finds particular objects in XML documents so that users can link to them. When used with XSLT, XPath finds objects in XML documents so that they can be transformed into other XML documents.

The XPath functions in this section enable you to convert the found objects in several ways. XPath functions can convert almost any object type to another: numbers to booleans, booleans to numbers, strings to numbers or booleans, node-sets to strings or booleans, and so forth.

AbbreviatedAbsolute LocationPath [10]

Abbreviated Absolute Location Path

Purpose

Abbreviates an absolute location path.

EBNF Syntax

```
AbbreviatedAbsoluteLocationPath ::=
    '//' RelativeLocationPath
```

Standard Syntax

```
//RelativeLocationPath
```

Where

- `//` are characters that represent `/descendant-or-self::node()/`.
- `RelativeLocationPath` (p. 219) specifies a series of relative steps to a location in a target document.

Notes

- `AbbreviatedAbsoluteLocationPath` is a component of `Absolute LocationPath`.
- `AbbreviatedAbsoluteLocationPath` abbreviates the `Absolute LocationPath` production.
- Use `//` in conjunction with `Abbreviated Step` (`.`).
- An absolute location path starts with a slash (/) and is followed by a series of optional relative location steps. The starting slash indicates the root node of the target document. A processor selects the nodes for all subsequent relative location steps by using their relationships to the root node.

Related Productions

`AbbreviatedAbsoluteLocationPath` (p. 182), `AbbreviatedRelative LocationPath` (p. 183), `AbsoluteLocationPath` (p. 184), `Expr` (p. 194), `LocationPath` (p. 203), `RelativeLocationPath` (p. 219)

AbbreviatedAxisSpecifier [13] — Abbreviated Axis Specifier

Purpose

Abbreviates an axis specifier.

EBNF Syntax

```
AbbreviatedAxisSpecifier ::= '@'?
```

Standard Syntax

```
[@]
```

Where

- @ is a character that represents attribute:: (that is, AbbreviatedAxisSpecifier (p. 182).

Notes

- AbbreviatedAxisSpecifer is a component of the AxisSpecifier production.
- AbbreviatedAxisSpecifier abbreviates the AxisSpecifier production.

Related Productions

AbbreviatedAbsoluteLocationPath (p. 182), AbbreviatedRelative LocationPath (p. 183), AbbreviatedStep (p. 184), AxisName (p. 187), AxisSpecifier (p. 188), NodeTest (p. 208), Predicate (p. 216), RelativeLocationPath (p. 219), Step (p. 221)

AbbreviatedRelative LocationPath [11] — Abbreviated Relative Location Path

Purpose

Abbreviates a relative location path.

EBNF Syntax

```
AbbreviatedRelativeLocationPath ::=
   RelativeLocationPath '//' Step
```

Standard Syntax

```
RelativeLocationPath//Step
```

Where

- RelativeLocationPath (p. 219) specifies a series of relative steps to a location in a target document.
- // are characters that represent /descendant-or-self::node()/.
- Step (p. 221) specifies the contents of a location step.

Notes

- AbbreviatedRelativeLocationPath is a component of the Relative LocationPath production.
- AbbreviatedRelativeLocationPath abbreviates the Relative LocationPath production.
- Use // in conjunction with Abbreviated Step (.).

Related Productions

AbbreviatedAbsoluteLocationPath (p. 182), AbbreviatedAxis Specifier (p. 182), AbbreviatedStep (p. 184), RelativeLocationPath (p. 219), Step (p. 221)

AbbreviatedStep [12]   Abbreviated Step

Purpose
Abbreviates a step.

EBNF Syntax
```
AbbreviatedStep ::= '.'
```

Standard Syntax
.

Where
- A location step of . is a character that represents self::node().

Notes
- AbbreviatedStep is a component of the Step production.
- AbbreviatedStep abbreviates the Step production.
- Use . in conjunction with // (/descendant-or-self::node()/), which instructs the processor to select all the elements of the context node for the defined element.

Related Productions
AbbreviatedAbsoluteLocationPath (p. 182), AbbreviatedAxisSpecifier (p. 182), AbbreviatedRelativeLocationPath (p. 183), AxisName (p. 187), AxisSpecifier (p. 188), NodeTest (p. 208), Predicate (p. 216), RelativeLocationPath (p. 219), Step (p. 221)

AbsoluteLocationPath [2]   Absolute Location Path

Purpose
Specifies an absolute step and an optional series of relative steps to a location in a target document.

EBNF Syntax
```
AbsoluteLocationPath ::= '/' RelativeLocationPath?
   | AbbreviatedAbsoluteLocationPath
```

Standard Syntax
```
/[RelativeLocationPath]
   |AbbreviatedAbsoluteLocationPath
```

Where
- / is a character that indicates the separation between one location step and another.
- RelativeLocationPath (p. 219) specifies a series of relative steps to a location in a target document.

- AbbreviatedAbsoluteLocationPath (p. 182) abbreviates an absolute location path.

Notes

- AbsoluteLocationPath is a component of the LocationPath production.
- A location step has an *axis* (which shows the tree relationship between the nodes selected by the location step and the context node), a *node test* (which specifies the node type and expanded-name of the selected node), and optional *predicates* (which filter the selected nodes set to a greater extent using arbitrary expressions).
- For examples of unabbreviated location paths, see Section 2, Location Paths, in the XPath recommendation (http://www.w3.org/TR/xpath).

Related Productions

AbbreviatedAbsoluteLocationPath (p. 182), AbbreviatedRelative LocationPath (p. 183), LocationPath (p. 203), RelativeLocationPath (p. 219), Step (p. 221).

AdditiveExpr [25]   Additive Expression

Purpose

Acts on one or more expressions through addition or subtraction.

EBNF Syntax

```
AdditiveExpr ::= MultiplicativeExpr
    | AdditiveExpr '+' MultiplicativeExpr
    | AdditiveExpr '-' MultiplicativeExpr
```

Standard Syntax

```
MultiplicativeExpr
    | AdditiveExpr + MultiplicativeExpr
    | AdditiveExpr - MultiplicativeExpr
```

Where

- MultiplicativeExpr (p. 204) acts on one or more expressions through multiplication or division or finding a modulus.
- AdditiveExpr (p. 185) acts on one or more expressions through addition or subtraction.
- + is the addition operator.
- – is the subtraction operator.

Notes

- AdditiveExpr is a component of the RelationalExpr production.
- Because the minus sign (–) is not only the subtraction operator but can also be included in names, it's a good idea to precede and follow the – subtraction operator with at least one space.

Related Productions

AdditiveExpr (p. 185), AndExpr (p. 186), Digits (p. 192), EqualityExpr (p. 192), Expr (p. 194), ExprToken (p. 194), ExprWhitespace (p. 196), FilterExpr (p. 197), FunctionName (p. 199), Literal (p. 202), MultiplicativeExpr (p. 204), MultiplyOperator (p. 205), NameTest (p. 207), NodeType (p. 208), Number (p. 210), Operator (p. 212), OperatorName (p. 213), OrExpr (p. 214), PathExpr (p. 215), PrimaryExpr (p. 217), RelationalExpr (p. 218), UnaryExpr (p. 228), UnionExpr (p. 228), VariableReference (p. 229)

AndExpr [22]   And Expression

Purpose

Evaluates two operands to find if *both* are true or false.

EBNF Syntax

```
AndExpr ::= EqualityExpr
    | AndExpr 'and' EqualityExpr
```

Standard Syntax

```
EqualityExpr | AndExpr and EqualityExpr
```

Where

- EqualityExpr (p. 192) compares two operands for equality or nonequality.
- AndExpr (p. 186) evaluates two operands to find if *both* are true or false.
- and is a reserved keyword that represents the and logical expression.

Notes

- AndExpr is a component of the OrExpr production.
- In an and expression, XPath evaluates each operand and returns a value of true or false. If the value of *both* operands is true, the value of the entire expression is true.
- The order of precedence for logical and mathematical operators is as follows: <=, <, >=, and > (highest); = and != (next highest); and; and or (lowest).

Related Productions

AdditiveExpr (p. 185), Digits (p. 192), EqualityExpr (p. 192), Expr (p. 194), ExprToken (p. 194), ExprWhitespace (p. 196), FilterExpr (p. 197), FunctionName (p. 199), Literal (p. 202), MultiplicativeExpr (p. 204), MultiplyOperator (p. 205), NameTest (p. 207), NodeType (p. 208), Number (p. 210), Operator (p. 212), OperatorName (p. 213), OrExpr (p. 214), PathExpr (p. 215), PrimaryExpr (p. 217), RelationalExpr (p. 218), UnaryExpr (p. 228), UnionExpr (p. 228), VariableReference (p. 229)

Argument [17]

Argument

Purpose
Represents an argument.

EBNF Syntax

```
Argument ::= Expr
```

Standard Syntax

```
Expr
```

Where
- Expr (p. 194) indicates an expression.

Note
- Argument is a component of the FunctionCall production.

Related Productions
Expr (p. 194), FunctionCall (p. 198), FunctionName (p. 199), Literal (p. 202), Number (p. 210), OrExpr (p. 214), PrimaryExpr (p. 217), VariableReference (p. 229)

AxisName [6]

Axis Name

Purpose
Gives a predefined axis name to the current context node.

EBNF Syntax

```
AxisName ::= 'ancestor' | 'ancestor-or-self'
    | 'attribute' | 'child' | 'descendant'
    | 'descendant-or-self' | 'following'
    | 'following-sibling' | 'namespace' | 'parent'
    | 'preceding' | 'preceding-sibling' | 'self'
```

Standard Syntax

```
ancestor | ancestor-or-self
    | attribute | child | descendant
    | descendant-or-self | following
    | following-sibling | namespace | parent
    | preceding | preceding-sibling | self
```

Where
- ancestor is a parent, grandparent, or other forebear of a particular context node. The ancestor axis always includes the root node unless the context node is the root node.

- ancestor-or-self is a parent, grandparent, or other forebear of a particular context node *or* the current context node. The ancestor-or-self axis will always contain the root node.
- attribute contains all attributes of the context node, which must be an element (to have any attributes).
- child is a successor to a particular context node. The child axis includes the children of the context node.
- descendant is a child, grandchild, or other offspring of a particular context node. The descendant axis never contains attribute or namespace nodes.
- descendant-or-self is a child, grandchild, or other offspring of a particular context node *and* the current context node.
- a following axis contains all nodes related or not, processed properly after the context node is processed. The following axis does not include descendants, attribute nodes, or namespace nodes.
- the following-sibling axis contains all the following siblings of the context node If the context node is an attribute node or namespace node, the following-sibling axis is vacant.
- namespace contains all namespace nodes of the context node, which must be an element (to have any namespaces).
- parent is a forebear to a particular context node, if that source has a parent.
- preceding is any node, related or not, processed properly before a particular context node is processed. The preceding axis does not include descendant nodes, attribute nodes, or namespace nodes.
- preceding-sibling is any node having the same parent as the context node and processed properly before the named node is processed. If the context node is an attribute node or namespace node, the preceding-sibling axis is vacant. In prior versions of XPointer, this was known as psibling.
- self is the current context node.

Notes

- AxisName is a component of the AxisSpecifier and ExprToken productions.
- The ancestor, descendant, following, preceding, and self axes contain all the nodes in a document.

Related Productions

AbbreviatedAxisSpecifier (p. 182), AbbreviatedStep (p. 184), AxisSpecifier (p. 188), NodeTest (p. 208), Predicate (p. 216), Step (p. 221).

AxisSpecifier [5]   Axis Specifier

Purpose

Specifies an axis name and a predefined specifier.

EBNF Syntax

```
AxisSpecifier ::= AxisName '::'
  | AbbreviatedAxisSpecifier
```

Standard Syntax

```
AxisName ::  | AbbreviatedAxisSpecifier
```

Where

- AxisName (p. 187) names an axis of the current context node.
- :: are characters that separate an axis name and node test.
- AbbreviatedAxisSpecifier (p. 182) abbreviates an axis specifier.

Notes

- AxisSpecifier is a component of the Step production.
- Every axis has a principal node type, which varies depending on the axis name and specifier. If an axis can contain one or more elements, the principal node type is element. This is the default for all types of axis except for attribute and namespace. If the AxisName is attribute, the principal node type is attribute. If the AxisName is namespace, the principal node type is namespace.

Related Productions

AbbreviatedAxisSpecifier (p. 182), AbbreviatedStep (p. 184), AxisName (p. 187), NodeTest (p. 208), Predicate (p. 216), Step (p. 221).

boolean()   boolean Function

Purpose

Returns an argument that has been converted to a boolean.

EBNF Syntax

```
boolean boolean(object)
```

Standard Syntax

```
boolean boolean(object)
```

Where

- *boolean* is the boolean returned by the function.
- boolean is a function-name keyword.
- *object* is a node-set, number, string, or another object evaluated by the function.

Notes

- If a node-set is empty, the value of the returned boolean is false. All other node-sets return a value of true.
- If a number is positive zero, negative zero, or NaN, the value of the returned boolean is false. All other numbers return a value of true.

- If a string has a length of zero, the value of the returned boolean is false. All other strings return a value of true.
- If the argument is not a node-set, number, or string, boolean() returns a value based on that argument type.

Related Functions

false() (p. 197), lang() (p. 201), not() (p. 210), true() (p. 227).

ceiling()   Ceiling Function

Purpose

Returns the lowest integer closest to negative infinity that is not less than the argument (in parentheses).

EBNF Syntax

    number_r ceiling(number)

Standard Syntax

    number_r ceiling(number)

Where

- *number_r* is the number returned by the function.
- ceiling is a function-name keyword.
- *number* represents the argument's number.

Related Functions

floor() (p. 198), number() (p. 211), round() (p. 220), sum() (p. 226)

concat()   Concatenate Function

Purpose

Returns a concatenation of the strings in an argument.

EBNF Syntax

    string_r concat(string_1, string_2, string_3*)

Standard Syntax

    string_r concat(string_1, string_2,
      [string_3, string_4, ... string_n])

Where

- *string* is a string returned by the function.
- concat is a function-name keyword.
- *string_1, string_2, string_3, string_4,* and *string_n* each represent one of the strings concatenated by the function.

Related Functions
contains() (p. 191), normalize-space() (p. 209), starts-with() (p. 221),
string() (p. 222), string-length() (p. 223), substring() (p. 224),
substring-after() (p. 225), substring-before() (p. 225), translate()
(p. 226)

contains()   Contains Function

Purpose
Returns true or false depending on whether one argument string contains the
other argument string.

EBNF Syntax
```
boolean contains(string_1, string_2)
```

Standard Syntax
```
true|false contains(string_1, string_2)
```

Where
- *boolean* is a true or false value returned by the function.
- contains is a function-name keyword.
- *string_1* and *string_2* represent each of the strings evaluated by
  the function.
- true is a boolean value returned if *string_1* contains *string_2*.
- false is a boolean value returned if *string_1* does not contain
  string_2.

Related Functions
concat() (p. 190), normalize-space() (p. 209), starts-with() (p. 221),
string() (p. 222), string-length() (p. 223), substring() (p. 224),
substring-after() (p. 225), substring-before() (p. 225), translate()
(p. 226)

Related Functions
boolean() (p. 189), false() (p. 197), lang() (p. 201), not() (p. 210), true()
(p. 227)

count()   Count Function

Purpose
Returns a count of the number of nodes in the argument's node-set.

EBNF Syntax
```
number count(node-set)
```

Standard Syntax

```
number count(node-set)
```

Where

- *number* is a number returned by the function.
- count is a function-name keyword.
- *node-set* represents the argument's node-set.

Related Functions

id() (p. 200), last() (p. 201), local-name() (p. 203), name() (p. 206), namespace-uri() (p. 206), position() (p. 216)

Digits [31]   Digits

Purpose

Specifies one or more digits.

EBNF Syntax

```
Digits ::= [0-9]+
```

Standard Syntax

```
0-9 [0-9]... [0-9]
```

Where

0-9 represents a number from 0 to 9.

Notes

- Digits is a component of the Number production.
- Digits represents digits supported by the Unicode Organization. See Appendix A, "Unicode Characters and Character Sets" (p. ___).

Related Productions

AdditiveExpr (p. 185), AndExpr (p. 186), EqualityExpr (p. 192), Expr (p. 194), ExprToken (p. 194), ExprWhitespace (p. 196), FilterExpr (p. 197), FunctionName (p. 199), Literal (p. 202), MultiplicativeExpr (p. 204), MultiplyOperator (p. 205), NameTest (p. 207), NodeType (p. 208), Number (p. 210), Operator (p. 212), OperatorName (p. 213), OrExpr (p. 214), PathExpr (p. 215), PrimaryExpr (p. 217), RelationalExpr (p. 218), UnaryExpr (p. 228), UnionExpr (p. 228), VariableReference (p. 229)

EqualityExpr [23]   Equality Expression

Purpose

Compares two operands for equality or nonequality.

EBNF Syntax

```
EqualityExpr ::= RelationalExpr
    | EqualityExpr '=' RelationalExpr
    | EqualityExpr '!=' RelationalExpr
```

Standard Syntax

```
RelationalExpr
    | EqualityExpr = RelationalExpr
    | EqualityExpr != RelationalExpr
```

Where

- RelationalExpr (p. 218) tests the relationship of one expression to another.
- EqualityExpr (p. 192) compares two operands for equality or nonequality.
- = is a character that indicates equal-to.
- != are characters that indicate not-equal-to.

Notes

- EqualityExpr is a component of the AndExpr production.
- The EqualityExpr production evaluates the results of two operands in an expression.
- EqualityExpr checks whether or not operands are node-sets using the following operators: =, !=, <=, <, >=, and >. If two node-sets are found and each has a string value, the resulting value is true. If one operand is a node-set and the other is a number, EqualityExpr uses the number() function to convert the string value of the node-set and then compares the results with the number for a true condition. If one operand is a node-set and the other is a boolean, EqualityExpr uses the boolean() function to convert the string value of the node-set and then compares the results with the boolean for a true condition.
- When both operands are not node-sets and the operator is either = or !=, EqualityExpr converts at least one operand to a boolean (using the boolean() function), number (using the number() function), or string (using the string() function). Then, using the = and != operators, EqualityExpr checks whether the operands are equal (that is, both true or both false). String operands are equal only if they are identical.
- When both operands are not node-sets and the operator is <=, <, >=, or >, EqualityExpr converts both operands to numbers and compares them for true or false conditions using the appropriate operator.
- The order of precedence for logical and mathematical operators is as follows: <=, <, >=, and > (highest); = and != (next highest); and; and or (lowest).

Related Productions

AdditiveExpr (p. 185), AndExpr (p. 186), Digits (p. 192), EqualityExpr (p. 192), Expr (p. 194), ExprToken (p. 194), ExprWhitespace (p. 196), FilterExpr (p. 197), FunctionName (p. 199), Literal (p. 202),

MultiplicativeExpr (p. 204), MultiplyOperator (p. 205), NameTest
(p. 207), NodeType (p. 208), Number (p. 210), Operator (p. 212), OperatorName
(p. 213), OrExpr (p. 214), PathExpr (p. 215), PrimaryExpr (p. 217),
RelationalExpr (p. 217), UnaryExpr (p. 228), UnionExpr (p. 228),
VariableReference (p. 229)

Related Functions

boolean() (p. 189), number() (p. 211), string() (p. 222)

Expr [14]   Expression

Purpose
Indicates an expression.

EBNF Syntax

```
Expr ::= OrExpr
```

Standard Syntax

```
OrExpr
```

Where

* OrExpr (p. 214) evaluates two operands to find if *each* is true or false.

Note

* Expr is a component of the Argument, PredicateExpr, and PrimaryExpr
  productions.

Related Productions

AdditiveExpr (p. 185), AndExpr (p. 186), Argument (p. 187), Digits
(p. 192), EqualityExpr (p. 192), ExprToken (p. 194), ExprWhitespace
(p. 196), FilterExpr (p. 197), FunctionCall (p. 198), FunctionName
(p. 199), Literal (p. 202), MultiplicativeExpr (p. 204), Multiply
Operator (p. 205), NameTest (p. 207), NodeType (p. 208), Number (p. 210),
Operator (p. 212), OperatorName (p. 213), OrExpr (p. 214), PathExpr
(p. 215), PrimaryExpr (p. 217), RelationalExpr (p. 218), UnaryExpr
(p. 228), UnionExpr (p. 228), VariableReference (p. 229)

ExprToken [28]   Expression Token

Purpose
Tokenizes an expression character by character or name by name.

EBNF Syntax

```
ExprToken ::= '(' | ')' | '[' | ']' | '.'
          | '..' | '@' | ',' | '::' | NameTest
          | NodeType | Operator | FunctionName
```

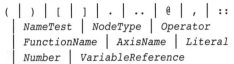

```
| AxisName | Literal | Number
| VariableReference
```

Standard Syntax

```
( | ) | [ | ] | . | .. | @ | , | ::
| NameTest | NodeType | Operator
| FunctionName | AxisName | Literal
| Number | VariableReference
```

Where

- (marks the start of an arguments list.
-) marks the end of an arguments list.
- [is a character that starts a predicate.
-] is a character that ends a predicate.
- . is a character that represents self::node() (that is, Abbreviated Step [p. 184]).
- .. are characters that represent parent::node().
- @ is a character that represents attribute:: (that is, Abbreviated AxisSpecifier (p. 182).
- , is a character that separates arguments.
- :: are characters that separate an axis name and node test.
- NameTest (p. 207) checks on a namespace name collection or a specific node name.
- NodeType (p. 208) identifies a specific node type or number.
- Operator (p. 212) provides a list of mathematical and logical operators.
- FunctionName (p. 199) provides a QName for a function.
- AxisName (p. 187) names an axis of the current context node.
- Literal (p. 202) represents a literal, a string within quotation marks or single quote marks.
- Number (p. 210) represents a number made up of one or more digits.
- VariableReference (p. 229) specifies the qualified name of a variable reference.

Notes

- A *token* is a basic unit that cannot be further broken down. In XML, a token is a reserved word, operator, entity, symbol, punctuation mark, or variable name.
- The XPath recommendation (http://www.w3.org/TR/xpath) states the following: "For readability, whitespace may be used in expressions even though not explicitly allowed by the grammar: ExprWhitespace may be freely added within patterns before or after any ExprToken."
- The XPath recommendation also states that "When tokenizing, the longest possible token is always returned."
- If a preceding token is not @, ::, (, [, ,, or an Operator, then * is a MultiplyOperator and NCName is an OperatorName.
- If (follows NCName (either immediately or after ExprWhitespace), the token is either NodeType or FunctionName.

- If :: follows NCName (either immediately or after ExprWhitespace), the token is AxisName.
- If the preceding two bullets are not true, the token *cannot* be Multiply Operator, OperatorName, NodeType, FunctionName, or AxisName.

Related Productions

AdditiveExpr (p. 185), AndExpr (p. 186), AxisName (p. 187), Digits (p. 192), EqualityExpr (p. 192), Expr (p. 194), ExprWhitespace (p. 196), FilterExpr (p. 197), FunctionName (p. 199), Literal (p. 202), MultiplicativeExpr (p. 204), MultiplyOperator (p. 205), NameTest (p. 207), NodeType (p. 208), Number (p. 210), Operator (p. 212), OperatorName (p. 213), OrExpr (p. 214), PathExpr (p. 215), PrimaryExpr (p. 217), RelationalExpr (p. 218), UnaryExpr (p. 228), UnionExpr (p. 228), VariableReference (p. 229)

ExprWhitespace [39]   Expression Whitespace

Purpose

Inserts whitespace into an expression.

EBNF Syntax

```
ExprWhitespace ::= S
```

Standard Syntax

```
[ ... ]
```

Where

- S (p. 124) represents one or more whitespace characters: spaces, carriage returns, line feeds, or tabs. Syntax: {[#x20|#x9|#xD|#xA][#x20|#x9| #xD|#xA]...[#x20|#x9|#xD|#xA]}

Note

- The XPath recommendation (http://www.w3.org/TR/xpath) states the following: "For readability, whitespace may be used in expressions even though not explicitly allowed by the grammar: ExprWhitespace may be freely added within patterns before or after any ExprToken."

Related Productions

AdditiveExpr (p. 185), AndExpr (p. 186), Digits (p. 192), EqualityExpr (p. 192), Expr (p. 194), ExprToken (p. 194), FilterExpr (p. 197), FunctionName (p. 199), Literal (p. 202), MultiplicativeExpr (p. 204), MultiplyOperator (p. 205), NameTest (p. 207), NodeType (p. 208), Number (p. 210), Operator (p. 212), OperatorName (p. 213), OrExpr (p. 214), PathExpr (p. 215), PrimaryExpr (p. 217), RelationalExpr (p. 218), S (p. 124), UnaryExpr (p. 228), UnionExpr (p. 228), VariableReference (p. 229), xml:space (p. 140)

false()   False Function

Purpose
Returns a value of false.

EBNF Syntax
```
boolean false()
```

Standard Syntax
```
boolean false()
```

Where
- *boolean* is the false boolean returned by the function.
- false is a function-name keyword.

Related Functions
boolean() (p. 189), lang() (p. 201), not() (p. 210), true() (p. 227)

FilterExpr [20]   Filter Expression

Purpose
Filters a primary expression or a combination of another filter expression and a predicate to achieve desired results.

EBNF Syntax
```
FilterExpr ::= PrimaryExpr | FilterExpr Predicate
```

Standard Syntax
```
PrimaryExpr | FilterExpr Predicate
```

Where
- PrimaryExpr (p. 217) symbolizes a primary expression.
- FilterExpr (p. 197) filters a primary expression or a combination of another filter expression and a predicate to achieve desired results.
- Predicate (p. 216) inserts a predicate expression that filters nodes in a location path.

Notes
- FilterExpr is a component of the PathExpr production.
- According to the XPath recommendation (http://www.w3.org/TR/xpath), "predicates are used to filter expressions in the same way that they are used in location paths. It is an error if the expression to be filtered does not evaluate to a node-set. The predicate filters the node-set with respect to the child axis."

Related Productions

AdditiveExpr (p. 185), AndExpr (p. 186), Digits (p. 192), EqualityExpr
(p. 192), Expr (p. 194), ExprToken (p. 194), ExprWhitespace (p. 196),
FilterExpr (p. 197), FunctionName (p. 199), Literal (p. 202),
MultiplicativeExpr (p. 204), MultiplyOperator (p. 205), NameTest
(p. 207), NodeType (p. 208), Number (p. 210), Operator (p. 212), Operator
Name (p. 213), OrExpr (p. 214), PathExpr (p. 215), Predicate (p. 216),
PrimaryExpr (p. 217), RelationalExpr (p. 218), UnaryExpr (p. 228),
UnionExpr (p. 228), VariableReference (p. 229)

floor()   Floor Function

Purpose
Returns the highest integer.

EBNF Syntax

```
number_r floor(number)
```

Standard Syntax

```
number_r floor(number)
```

Where

- *number_r* is the number returned by the function.
- floor is a function-name keyword.
- *number* represents the argument's number.

Notes

- floor() returns the number that is closest to positive infinity.
- The returned number must not be greater than the argument.

Related Functions

ceiling() (p. 190), number() (p. 211), round() (p. 220), sum() (p. 226)

FunctionCall [16]   Function Call

Purpose
Evaluates and processes an expression and calls a function.

EBNF Syntax

```
FunctionCall ::= FunctionName '(' ( Argument
   (',' Argument )* )? ')'
```

Standard Syntax

```
FunctionName ( [ Argument [, Argument [, Argument
   [, Argument ]]]] )
```

Where

- FunctionName (p. 199) provides a QName for a function.
- (marks the start of the arguments list.
- Argument (p. 187) represents an argument.
- , is a character that separates arguments.
-) marks the end of the arguments list.

Notes

- FunctionCall is a component of the PrimaryExpr production.
- The XPath recommendation (http://www.w3.org/TR/xpath) states that "a FunctionCall expression is evaluated by using the FunctionName to identify a function in the expression evaluation context function library, evaluating each of the Arguments, converting each argument to the type required by the function, and finally calling the function, passing it the converted arguments."
- The FunctionCall expression makes the function's result its own result.
- If a function converts an argument to a boolean, it behaves as though it is the boolean( ) function.
- If a function converts an argument to a number, it behaves as though it is the number( ) function.
- If a function converts an argument to a string, it behaves as though it is the string( ) function.
- A function cannot convert an argument that is not a node-set to a node-set.

Related Productions

Argument (p. 187), Expr (p. 194), FunctionName (p. 199), Literal (p. 202), Number (p. 210), OrExpr (p. 214), PrimaryExpr (p. 217), VariableReference (p. 229)

Related Functions

boolean( ) (p. 189), number( ) (p. 211), string( ) (p. 222)

FunctionName [35]   Function Name

Purpose

Provides a QName for a function.

EBNF Syntax

```
FunctionName ::= QName - NodeType
```

Standard Syntax

```
QName
```

Where

- QName creates a qualified name.
- NodeType (p. 208) must be absent from the function name.

Note

- FunctionName is a component of the ExprToken and FunctionCall productions.

Related Productions

AdditiveExpr (p. 185), AndExpr (p. 186), Digits (p. 192), EqualityExpr (p. 192), Expr (p. 194), ExprToken (p. 194), ExprWhitespace (p. 196), FilterExpr (p. 197), Literal (p. 202), MultiplicativeExpr (p. 204), MultiplyOperator (p. 205), NameTest (p. 207), NodeType (p. 208), Number (p. 210), Operator (p. 212), OperatorName (p. 213), OrExpr (p. 214), PathExpr (p. 215), PrimaryExpr (p. 217), RelationalExpr (p. 218), UnaryExpr (p. 228), UnionExpr (p. 228), VariableReference (p. 229)

id() ID Function

Purpose

Returns selected elements by the value of their ID.

EBNF Syntax

```
node-set id(object)
```

Standard Syntax

```
node-set id(object)
```

Where

- *node-set* represents the returned node-set.
- id is a function-name keyword.
- *object* is the string value of the requested ID.

Notes

- According to the XPath recommendation (http://www.w3.org/TR/xpath), "An element node may have a unique identifier (id). This is the value of the attribute that is declared in the DTD as type ID. No two elements in a document may have the same unique ID."
- When the id() function's argument is a node-set, the result of the function is the combination of checking id against the string value of each of the nodes in the node-set. When the id() function's argument is anything but a node-set, the function converts the argument to a string in the same way that the string() function converts an object to a string.

Related Functions

count() (p. 191), last() (p. 201), local-name() (p. 203), name() (p. 206), namespace-uri() (p. 206), position() (p. 216), string() (p. 222)

lang()   Language Function

Purpose
Returns a boolean after evaluating the context-node language and xml:lang attribute of the context node.

EBNF Syntax
```
boolean lang(string)
```

Standard Syntax
```
boolean lang(string)
```

Where
- *boolean* is the boolean returned by the function.
- lang is a function-name keyword.
- *string* is a string evaluated by the function.

Notes
- If the context-node language or sublanguage is the same as that of *string*, lang() returns a value of true.
- If the context node has no xml:lang attribute, lang() evaluates the xml:lang attribute of the closest ancestor.
- If lang() cannot find an appropriate xml:lang attribute, it returns a value of false.
- The lang() function is case-insensitive and ignores suffixes beginning with -.

Related Functions
boolean() (p. 189), ceiling() (p. 190), false() (p. 197), floor() (p. 198), not() (p. 210), number() (p. 211), round() (p. 220), sum() (p. 226), true() (p. 227)

last()   Last Function

Purpose
Returns a number that equals the context size.

EBNF Syntax
```
number last()
```

Standard Syntax
```
number last()
```

Where

- *number* is a number returned by the function.
- last is a function-name keyword.

Related Functions

count() (p. 191), id() (p. 200), local-name() (p. 203), name() (p. 206), namespace-uri() (p. 206), position() (p. 216)

Literal [29]   Literal

Purpose

Represents a literal, a string within quotation marks or single quote marks.

EBNF Syntax

```
Literal ::= '"' ["^"]* '"' | """ ["^']* """
```

Standard Syntax

```
{"|'}literal{"|'}
```

Where

- literal represents a literal, a string within quotation marks or single quote marks.

Notes

- Literal is a component of the ExprToken and PrimaryExpr productions.
- If you enclose a string within single quote marks, do not use single quote marks within the quoted object; if you enclose a string within quotation marks, do not use quotation marks within the quoted object. Within character data, you can use the apostrophe (') or quotation mark (") entities to indicate quote marks.
- If a quotation mark is included in a string, enclose the string within single quote marks; if a single quote mark is included in a string, enclose the string within quotation marks.
- Do not mix single quote marks and quotation marks; the quote marks at the beginning and end of a quoted object must match.

Related Productions

AdditiveExpr (p. 185), AndExpr (p. 186), Digits (p. 192), EqualityExpr (p. 192), Expr (p. 194), ExprToken (p. 194), ExprWhitespace (p. 196), FilterExpr (p. 197), FunctionName (p. 199), MultiplicativeExpr (p. 204), MultiplyOperator (p. 205), NameTest (p. 207), NodeType (p. 208), Number (p. 210), Operator (p. 212), OperatorName (p. 213), OrExpr (p. 214), PathExpr (p. 215), PrimaryExpr (p. 217), RelationalExpr (p. 218), UnaryExpr (p. 228), UnionExpr (p. 228), VariableReference (p. 229)

local-name()   Local Name Function

Purpose

Returns the local part of the expanded-name of the first node in the
argument's node-set.

EBNF Syntax

```
string local-name(node-set?)
```

Standard Syntax

```
string local-name([node-set])
```

Where

- *string* is a string returned by the function.
- local-name is a function-name keyword.
- *node-set* represents the argument's node-set.

Notes

- If the argument's node-set is blank or does not have an expanded-name,
  local-name() returns an empty string.
- A missing argument results in a node-set containing the context
  node only.
- The strings returned for the local-name() and name() functions are
  the same except for element nodes and attribute nodes.

Related Functions

count() (p. 191), id() (p. 200), last() (p. 201), name() (p. 206),
namespace-uri() (p. 206), position() (p. 216)

LocationPath [1]   Location Path

Purpose

Specifies a series of absolute and relative steps to a location in a target
document.

EBNF Syntax

```
LocationPath ::= RelativeLocationPath
    | AbsoluteLocationPath
```

Standard Syntax

```
RelativeLocationPath | AbsoluteLocationPath
```

Where

- RelativeLocationPath (p. 219) specifies a series of relative steps to a
  location in a target document.

XPath Language

- AbsoluteLocationPath (p. 184) specifies a series of absolute steps to a location in a target document.

Notes

- LocationPath is a component of the PathExpr production.
- A LocationPath is a type of Expr.
- A relative location path consists of one or more location steps ordered from left to right. Each step, which is separated from the next by a slash (/), selects a nodes set relative to a *context node* (which indicates the ongoing framework of nodes and nodes sets in the target document).
- An absolute location path starts with a slash (/) and is followed by a series of optional relative location steps. The starting slash indicates the root node of the target document. The processor selects nodes for all subsequent relative location steps by utilizing their relationships to the root node.
- A location step has an *axis* (which shows the tree relationship between the selected node and the context node), a *node test* (which names the node type and expanded qualifier name, with a prefix, of the selected node), and optional *predicates* (which filter the selected nodes set to a greater extent).

Related Productions

AbsoluteLocationPath (p. 184), RelativeLocationPath (p. 219)

MultiplicativeExpr [26]   Multiplicative Expression

Purpose

Acts on one or more expressions through multiplication, division, or finding a modulus.

EBNF Syntax

```
MultiplicativeExpr ::= UnaryExpr
    | MultiplicativeExpr MultiplyOperator UnaryExpr
    | MultiplicativeExpr 'div' UnaryExpr
    | MultiplicativeExpr 'mod' UnaryExpr
```

Standard Syntax

```
UnaryExpr
    | MultiplicativeExpr MultiplyOperator UnaryExpr
    | MultiplicativeExpr div UnaryExpr
    | MultiplicativeExpr mod UnaryExpr
```

Where

- UnaryExpr (p. 228) negates an expression.
- MultiplyOperator (p. 205) inserts a * multiplication operator.

- div is a reserved keyword that represents the division operator.
- mod is a reserved keyword that represents the modulus operator.

Notes

- MultiplicativeExpr is a component of the AdditiveExpr.
- The XPath div operator performs floating-point division as defined in IEEE 754.
- The XPath mod operator returns a remainder from a shortened division (for example, 7 mod 3 returns 1.

Related Productions

AdditiveExpr (p. 185), AndExpr (p. 186), Digits (p. 192), EqualityExpr (p. 192), Expr (p. 194), ExprToken (p. 194), ExprWhitespace (p. 196), FilterExpr (p. 197), FunctionName (p. 199), Literal (p. 202), MultiplicativeExpr (p. 204), MultiplyOperator (p. 205), NameTest (p. 207), NodeType (p. 208), Number (p. 210), Operator (p. 212), OperatorName (p. 213), OrExpr (p. 214), PathExpr (p. 215), PrimaryExpr (p. 217), RelationalExpr (p. 218), UnaryExpr (p. 228), UnionExpr (p. 228), VariableReference (p. 229)

MultiplyOperator [34]   Multiply Operator

Purpose

Inserts a multiply operator.

EBNF Syntax

```
MultiplyOperator ::= '*'
```

Standard Syntax

```
*
```

Where

- * is a character that indicates multiplication.

Note

- MultiplyOperator is a component of the MultiplicativeExpr and Operator productions.

Related Productions

AdditiveExpr (p. 185), AndExpr (p. 186), Digits (p. 192), EqualityExpr (p. 192), Expr (p. 194), ExprToken (p. 194), ExprWhitespace (p. 196), FilterExpr (p. 197), FunctionName (p. 199), Literal (p. 202), MultiplicativeExpr (p. 204), NameTest (p. 207), NodeType (p. 208), Number (p. 210), Operator (p. 212), OperatorName (p. 213), OrExpr (p. 214), PathExpr (p. 215), PrimaryExpr (p. 217), RelationalExpr (p. 218), UnaryExpr (p. 228), UnionExpr (p. 228), VariableReference (p. 229)

name() — Name Function

Purpose

Returns a QName representing the expanded-name of the first node in the argument node-set.

EBNF Syntax

```
string name(node-set?)
```

Standard Syntax

```
string name([node-set])
```

Where

- *string* is a string returned by the function.
- name is a function-name keyword.
- *node-set* represents the argument's node-set.

Notes

- To ensure that the QName is that in the source XML document, include the original prefix in the node-set information.
- The target node with the expanded-name must have an associated namespace declaration.
- If the argument's node-set is blank or does not have an expanded-name, name() returns an empty string.
- A missing argument results in a node-set containing the context node only.
- The strings returned for the local-name() and name() functions are the same except for element nodes and attribute nodes.

Related Functions

count() (p. 191), id() (p. 200), last() (p. 201), local-name() (p. 203), namespace-uri() (p. 206), position() (p. 216)

namespace-uri() — Namespace URI Function

Purpose

Returns the namespace URI of the expanded-name of the first node in the argument node-set.

EBNF Syntax

```
namespace-uri(node-set?)
```

Standard Syntax

```
namespace-uri([node-set])
```

Where

- *string* is a string returned by the function.

- `namespace-uri` is a function-name keyword.
- *node-set* represents the argument's node-set.

Notes

- If the argument's node-set is blank, does not have an expanded-name, or the namespace URI is null, `namespace-uri( )` returns an empty string.
- A missing argument results in a node-set containing the context node only.

Related Functions

`count( )` (p. 191), `id( )` (p. 200), `last( )` (p. 201), `local-name( )` (p. 203), `name( )` (p. 206), `position( )` (p. 216)

NameTest [37]   Name Test

Purpose

Checks on a namespace name collection or a specific node name.

EBNF Syntax

    NameTest ::= '*' | NCName ':' '*' | QName

Standard Syntax

    * | NCName: * | QName

Where

- `*` is a wildcard character.
- `NCName` provides a name for a collection of namespace names.
- `:` is a delimiting character that separates an `NCName` and a `*` wildcard character.
- `QName` creates a qualified name.

Notes

- `NameTest` is a component of the `ExprToken` and `NodeTest` productions.
- In prior versions of XPath, `NameTest` was known as `WildcardName`.
- If `NCName` or `QName` has a namespace prefix without a corresponding namespace declaration, the processor issues an error message.

Related Productions

`AdditiveExpr` (p. 185), `AndExpr` (p. 186), `Digits` (p. 192), `EqualityExpr` (p. 192), `Expr` (p. 194), `ExprToken` (p. 194), `ExprWhitespace` (p. 196), `FilterExpr` (p. 197), `FunctionName` (p. 199), `Literal` (p. 202), `MultiplicativeExpr` (p. 204), `MultiplyOperator` (p. 205), `NodeType` (p. 208), `Number` (p. 210), `Operator` (p. 212), `OperatorName` (p. 213), `OrExpr` (p. 214), `PathExpr` (p. 215), `PrimaryExpr` (p. 217), `RelationalExpr` (p. 218), `UnaryExpr` (p. 228), `UnionExpr` (p. 228), `VariableReference` (p. 229)

XPath Language

NodeTest [7]   Node Test

Purpose

Checks on a node for type and the expanded name of the location-step nodes set.

EBNF Syntax

```
NodeTest ::= NameTest | NodeType '(' ')'
    | 'processing-instruction' '(' Literal ')'
```

Standard Syntax

```
NameTest | NodeType()
    | processing-instruction( Literal )
```

Where

- `NameTest` (p. 207) checks on a namespace name collection or a specific node name.
- `NodeType` (p. 208) identifies a specific node type or number.
- `(` marks the start of the arguments or literals list.
- `)` marks the end of the arguments or literals list.
- `processing-instruction` is a reserved keyword that specifies XML processing instructions. For more information about processing instructions, refer to the `PI` production (p. 117).
- `Literal` (p. 202) represents a literal, a string within quotation marks or single quote marks.

Notes

- `NodeTest` is a component of the `Step` production.
- Every axis has a principal node type, which varies depending on the axis name and specifier. If an axis can contain one or more elements, the principal node type is element. This is the default for all types of axis except for `attribute` and `namespace`. If the `AxisName` is `attribute`, the principal node type is attribute. If the `AxisName` is `namespace`, the principal node type is namespace.
- You can use the `*` wildcard character to indicate any node of the principal node type.

Related Productions

`AbbreviatedStep` (p. 184), `AbbreviatedAxisSpecifier` (p. 182), `AxisName` (p. 187), `AxisSpecifier` (p. 188), `Literal` (p. 202), `NameTest` (p. 207), `NodeType` (p. 208), `Predicate` (p. 216), `Step` (p. 221)

NodeType [38]   Node Type

Purpose

Identifies a specific node type or number.

EBNF Syntax

```
NodeType ::= 'comment' | 'text'
    | 'processing-instruction' | 'node'
```

Standard Syntax

```
comment | text | processing-instruction | node
```

Where

- comment is a reserved keyword that indicates a nonprinting, nonparsed comment. This keyword was formerly known as #comment.
- text is a reserved keyword that specifies text within the XML element or CDATA sections. This keyword was formerly known as #text.
- processing-instruction is a reserved keyword that specifies XML processing instructions. This keyword was formerly known as #pi.
- node is a reserved keyword that indicates a node.

Note

- NodeType is a component of the ExprToken, NodeTest, and NodeType productions.

Related Productions

AdditiveExpr (p. 185), AndExpr (p. 186), Digits (p. 192), EqualityExpr (p. 192), Expr (p. 194), ExprToken (p. 194), ExprWhitespace (p. 196), FilterExpr (p. 197), FunctionName (p. 199), Literal (p. 202), MultiplicativeExpr (p. 204), MultiplyOperator (p. 205), NameTest (p. 207), Number (p. 210), Operator (p. 212), OperatorName (p. 213), OrExpr (p. 214), PathExpr (p. 215), PrimaryExpr (p. 217), RelationalExpr (p. 218), UnaryExpr (p. 228), UnionExpr (p. 228), VariableReference (p. 229)

normalize-space()   Normalize Space Function

Purpose

Returns an argument with excess whitespace stripped out.

EBNF Syntax

```
string normalize-space(string?)
```

Standard Syntax

```
string_r normalize-space([string])
```

Where

- string_r is the string returned by the function.
- normalize-space is a function-name keyword.
- string represents the string evaluated by the function.

Notes

- The normalize-space() function replaces instances of two or more spaces with one space.
- XPath whitespace characters are the same as those supported by the XML S production: #x20 (Unicode code #x0020), #x9 (Unicode code #x0009), #xD (Unicode code #x000D), and #xA (Unicode code #x000A). #x20 inserts a space, which is the equivalent of pressing the spacebar. #x9, which inserts a tab (HT), moves the cursor to the next tab stop. #xD, which inserts a carriage return (CR), moves the cursor to the beginning of the next line. #xA, which inserts a line feed (LF), moves the cursor to the next line below its present position.
- For a complete list of supported base characters, see Appendix A, "Unicode Characters and Character Sets" (p. 757). For more information about Unicode characters, see Chapter 2, "Introducing DTDs" (p. 669).

Related Production

S (p. 124).

Related Functions

concat() (p. 190), contains() (p. 191), starts-with() (p. 221), string() (p. 222), string-length() (p. 223), substring() (p. 224), substring-after() (p. 225), substring-before() (p. 225), translate() (p. 226)

not()   Not Function

Purpose

Returns a value of true if the argument is false and false if the argument is true.

EBNF Syntax

```
boolean _r not(boolean)
```

Where

- *boolean_r* is the boolean returned by the function.
- not is a function-name keyword.
- *boolean* represents the boolean evaluated by the function.

Related Functions

boolean() (p. 189), false() (p. 197), lang() (p. 201), true() (p. 227)

Number [30]   Number

Purpose

Represents a floating-point number made up of one or more digits.

EBNF Syntax

```
Number ::= Digits ('.' Digits?)? | '.' Digits
```

Standard Syntax

```
Digits [.Digits] |.Digits
```

Where

- Digits (p. 192) specifies one or more digits.
- . is a character that represents self::node() (that is, Abbreviated Step [p. 184]).

Notes

- Number is a component of the ExprToken and PrimaryExpr productions.
- According to the XPath recommendation (http://www.w3.org/TR/xpath), a "number can have any double-precision 64-bit format IEEE 754 value. These include a special 'Not-a-Number' value, positive and negative infinity, and positive and negative zero."
- Not-a-Number is also known as NaN.
- XPath numeric operators convert their operands to numbers in the same way that the number() function converts its operands.

Related Productions

AdditiveExpr (p. 185), AndExpr (p. 186), Digits (p. 192), EqualityExpr (p. 192), Expr (p. 194), ExprToken (p. 194), ExprWhitespace (p. 196), FilterExpr (p. 197), FunctionName (p. 199), Literal (p. 202), MultiplicativeExpr (p. 204), MultiplyOperator (p. 205), NameTest (p. 207), NodeType (p. 208), Operator (p. 212), OperatorName (p. 213), OrExpr (p. 214), PathExpr (p. 215), PrimaryExpr (p. 217), RelationalExpr (p. 218), UnaryExpr (p. 228), UnionExpr (p. 228), VariableReference (p. 229)

Related Function

number() (p. 211).

number() | Number Function

Purpose

Returns an argument that has been converted to a number.

EBNF Syntax

```
number number(object?)
```

Standard Syntax

```
number number([object])
```

Where

- *number* is the number returned by the function.
- number is a function-name keyword.

- *object* is a node-set, boolean, string, or another object evaluated by the function.

Notes

- number() converts a node-set argument to a string in the same way that the string() function works.
- number() converts a boolean true to 1 and a boolean false to 0.
- number() converts a string consisting of a number followed by white-space to a number following the XPath Number production and rounded using IEEE 754 rules. This type of string can also include a minus sign and can be preceded by whitespace. All other strings are converted to NaN (Not-a-Number).
- If the argument is not a node-set, boolean, or string, number() returns a value based on that argument type.
- A missing argument results in a node-set containing the context node only.
- Do not use number() to convert language-specific formats under an XML element.
- The use of number() must agree with the Number production.

Related Production

Number (p. 210).

Related Functions

ceiling() (p. 190), floor() (p. 198), round() (p. 220), string() (p. 222), sum() (p. 226)

Operator [32]   Operator

Purpose

Provides a list of mathematical and logical operators.

EBNF Syntax

```
Operator ::= OperatorName | MultiplyOperator
   | '/' | '//' | '|' | '+' | '-'
   | '=' | '!=' | '<' | '<=' | '>' | '>='
```

Standard Syntax

```
OperatorName | MultiplyOperator | / | // | | | + | -
   | = | != | < | <= | > | >=
```

Where

- OperatorName (p. 213) names a mathematical or logical operator.
- MultiplyOperator (p. 205) inserts a * multiplication operator.
- / is a character that indicates the separation between one location step and another.

- // are characters that represent /descendant-or-self::node()/.
- | is a character that separates one expression from the next and indicates a choice of expression use.
- + is the addition operator.
- - is the subtraction operator.
- = is a character that indicates equal-to.
- != are characters that indicate not-equal-to.
- < is a character that indicates less-than.
- <= are characters that indicate less-than or equal-to.
- > is a character that indicates greater-than.
- >= are characters that indicate greater-than or equal-to.

Note

- Operator is a component of the ExprToken production.

Related Productions

AdditiveExpr (p. 185), AndExpr (p. 186), Digits (p. 192), EqualityExpr (p. 192), Expr (p. 194), ExprToken (p. 194), ExprWhitespace (p. 196), FilterExpr (p. 197), FunctionName (p. 199), Literal (p. 202), MultiplicativeExpr (p. 204), MultiplyOperator (p. 205), NameTest (p. 207), NodeType (p. 208), Number (p. 210), OperatorName (p. 213), OrExpr (p. 214), PathExpr (p. 215), PrimaryExpr (p. 217), RelationalExpr (p. 218), UnaryExpr (p. 228), UnionExpr (p. 228), VariableReference (p. 229)

OperatorName [33]   Operator Name

Purpose

Names a logical or mathematical operator.

EBNF Syntax

```
OperatorName ::= 'and' | 'or' | 'mod' | 'div'
```

Standard Syntax

```
and | or | mod | div
```

Where

- and is a reserved keyword that represents the and logical expression.
- or is a reserved keyword that represents the or logical expression.
- mod is a reserved keyword that represents the modulus operator.
- div is a reserved keyword that represents the division operator.

Notes

- OperatorName is a component of the Operator production.
- In an or expression, XPath evaluates each operand and returns a value of true or false. If the value of *either* operand is true, the value of the entire expression is true.

- In an and expression, XPath evaluates each operand and returns a value of true or false. If the value of *both* operands is true, the value of the entire expression is true.
- The XPath div operator performs floating-point division as defined in IEEE 754.
- The XPath mod operator returns a remainder from a shortened division (for example, 7 mod 3 returns 1).

Related Productions

AdditiveExpr (p. 185), AndExpr (p. 186), Digits (p. 192), EqualityExpr (p. 192), Expr (p. 194), ExprToken (p. 194), ExprWhitespace (p. 196), FilterExpr (p. 197), FunctionName (p. 199), Literal (p. 202), MultiplicativeExpr (p. 204), MultiplyOperator (p. 205), NameTest (p. 207), NodeType (p. 208), Number (p. 210), Operator (p. 212), OrExpr (p. 214), PathExpr (p. 215), PrimaryExpr (p. 217), RelationalExpr (p. 218), UnaryExpr (p. 228), UnionExpr (p. 228), VariableReference (p. 229)

OrExpr [21]   Or Expression

Purpose

Evaluates two operands to find if *each* is true or false.

EBNF Syntax

```
OrExpr ::= AndExpr | OrExpr 'or' AndExpr
```

Standard Syntax

```
AndExpr | OrExpr or AndExpr
```

Where

- AndExpr (p. 186) evaluates two operands to find if *both* are true or false.
- OrExpr (p. 214) evaluates two operands to find if *each* is true or false.
- or is a reserved keyword that represents the or logical expression.

Notes

- OrExpr is a component of the Expr production.
- In an or expression, XPath evaluates each operand and returns a value of true or false. If the value of *either* operand is true, the value of the entire expression is true.
- The order of precedence for logical and mathematical operators is as follows: <=, <, >=, and > (highest); = and != (next highest); and; and or (lowest).

Related Productions

AdditiveExpr (p. 185), AndExpr (p. 186), Digits (p. 192), EqualityExpr (p. 192), Expr (p. 194), ExprToken (p. 194), ExprWhitespace (p. 196), FilterExpr (p. 197), FunctionName (p. 199), Literal (p. 202), MultiplicativeExpr (p. 204), MultiplyOperator (p. 205), NameTest (p. 207),

NodeType (p. 208), Number (p. 210), Operator (p. 212), OperatorName (p. 213), PathExpr (p. 215), PrimaryExpr (p. 217), RelationalExpr (p. 218), UnaryExpr (p. 228), UnionExpr (p. 228), VariableReference (p. 229)

PathExpr [19]   Location Path Expression

Purpose
Creates a path by composing a location path and a filter expression, or vice-versa.

EBNF Syntax
```
PathExpr ::= LocationPath | FilterExpr
    | FilterExpr '/' RelativeLocationPath
    | FilterExpr '//' RelativeLocationPath
```

Standard Syntax
```
LocationPath | FilterExpr
    | FilterExpr / RelativeLocationPath
    | FilterExpr // RelativeLocationPath
```

Where
- LocationPath (p. 203) specifies a series of absolute and relative steps to a location in a target document.
- FilterExpr (p. 197) filters a primary expression or a combination of another filter expression and a predicate to achieve desired results.
- RelativeLocationPath (p. 219) specifies a series of relative steps to a location in a target document.
- / is a character that indicates the separation between one location step and another.
- // are characters that represent /descendant-or-self::node()/.

Note
- PathExpr is a component of the UnionExpr production.

Related Productions
AdditiveExpr (p. 185), AndExpr (p. 186), Digits (p. 192), EqualityExpr (p. 192), Expr (p. 194), ExprToken (p. 194), ExprWhitespace (p. 196), FilterExpr (p. 197), FunctionName (p. 199), Literal (p. 202), LocationPath (p. 203), MultiplicativeExpr (p. 204), MultiplyOperator (p. 205), NameTest (p. 207), NodeType (p. 208), Number (p. 210), Operator (p. 212), OperatorName (p. 213), OrExpr (p. 214), PrimaryExpr (p. 217), RelationalExpr (p. 218), RelativeLocationPath (p. 219), UnaryExpr (p. 228), UnionExpr (p. 228), VariableReference (p. 229)

position()   Position Function

Purpose
Returns a number that equals the context position.

EBNF Syntax
```
number position()
```

Standard Syntax
```
number position()
```

Where
- *number* is a number returned by the function.
- position is a function-name keyword.

Related Functions
count() (p. 191), id() (p. 200), last() (p. 201), local-name() (p. 203), name() (p. 206), namespace-uri() (p. 206)

Predicate [8]   Predicate

Purpose
Inserts a predicate expression that filters nodes in a location path.

EBNF Syntax
```
Predicate ::= '[' PredicateExpr ']'
```

Standard Syntax
```
[ PredicateExpr ]
```

Where
- [is a character that starts a predicate.
- PredicateExpr (p. 217) represents a predicate expression, which filters one or more nodes in a location path.
-] is a character that ends a predicate.

Notes
- Predicate is a component of the FilterExpr and Step productions.
- According to the XPath recommendation (http://www.w3.org/TR/xpath), "predicates are used to filter expressions in the same way that they are used in location paths. It is an error if the expression to be filtered does not evaluate to a node-set. The Predicate filters the node-set with respect to the child axis."

Related Productions

AbbreviatedStep (p. 184), AbbreviatedAxisSpecifier (p. 182), AxisName (p. 187), AxisSpecifier (p. 188), NodeTest (p. 208), PredicateExpr (p. 217), Step (p. 221).

PredicateExpr [9]   Name

Purpose

Represents a predicate expression, which filters one or more nodes in a location path.

EBNF Syntax

```
PredicateExpr ::= Expr
```

Standard Syntax

```
Expr
```

Where

* Expr (p. 194) indicates an expression.

Note

* PredicateExpr is a component of the Predicate production.

Related Productions

Expr (p. 194), Predicate (p. 216)

PrimaryExpr [15]   Primary Expression

Purpose

Symbolizes a primary expression.

EBNF Syntax

```
PrimaryExpr ::= VariableReference | '(' Expr ')'
    | Literal | Number | FunctionCall
```

Standard Syntax

```
VariableReference | (Expr)
    | Literal | Number | FunctionCall
```

Where

* VariableReference (p. 229) specifies the QName of a variable reference.
* (marks the start of the expression.
* Expr (p. 194) indicates an expression.
*) marks the end of the expression.

- Literal (p. 202) represents a literal, a string within quotation marks or single quote marks.
- Number (p. 210) represents a number made up of one or more digits.
- FunctionCall (p. 198) evaluates and processes an expression and calls a function.

Note

- PrimaryExpr is a component of the FilterExpr production.

Related Productions

AdditiveExpr (p. 185), AndExpr (p. 186), Digits (p. 192), EqualityExpr (p. 192), Expr (p. 194), ExprToken (p. 194), ExprWhitespace (p. 196), FilterExpr (p. 197), FunctionCall (p. 198), FunctionName (p. 199), Literal (p. 202), MultiplicativeExpr (p. 204), MultiplyOperator (p. 205), NameTest (p. 207), NodeType (p. 208), Number (p. 210), Operator (p. 212), OperatorName (p. 213), OrExpr (p. 214), PathExpr (p. 215), RelationalExpr (p. 218), UnaryExpr (p. 228), UnionExpr (p. 228), VariableReference (p. 229)

RelationalExpr [24]   Relational Expression

Purpose

Tests the relationship of one expression to another.

EBNF Syntax

```
RelationalExpr ::= AdditiveExpr
    | RelationalExpr '<' AdditiveExpr
    | RelationalExpr '>' AdditiveExpr
    | RelationalExpr '<=' AdditiveExpr
    | RelationalExpr '>=' AdditiveExpr
```

Standard Syntax

```
AdditiveExpr
    | RelationalExpr < AdditiveExpr
    | RelationalExpr > AdditiveExpr
    | RelationalExpr <= AdditiveExpr
    | RelationalExpr >= AdditiveExpr
```

Where

- AdditiveExpr (p. 185) acts on one or more expressions through addition or subtraction.
- < is a character that indicates less-than.
- > is a character that indicates greater-than.
- <= are characters that indicate less-than or equal-to.
- >= are characters that indicate greater-than or equal-to.

Notes

- RelationalExpr is a component of the EqualityExpr production.
- The order of precedence for logical and mathematical operators is as follows: <=, <, >=, and > (highest); = and != (next highest); and; and or (lowest).

Related Productions

AdditiveExpr (p. 185), AndExpr (p. 186), Digits (p. 192), EqualityExpr (p. 192), Expr (p. 194), ExprToken (p. 194), ExprWhitespace (p. 196), FilterExpr (p. 197), FunctionName (p. 199), Literal (p. 202), MultiplicativeExpr (p. 204), MultiplyOperator (p. 205), NameTest (p. 207), NodeType (p. 208), Number (p. 210), Operator (p. 212), OperatorName (p. 213), OrExpr (p. 214), PathExpr (p. 215), PrimaryExpr (p. 217), RelationalExpr (p. 218), UnaryExpr (p. 228), UnionExpr (p. 228), VariableReference (p. 229)

RelativeLocationPath [3]   Relative Location Path

Purpose

Specifies a series of relative steps to a location in a target document.

EBNF Syntax

```
RelativeLocationPath ::= Step
    | RelativeLocationPath '/' Step
    | AbbreviatedRelativeLocationPath
```

Standard Syntax

```
Step | RelativeLocationPath / Step
    | AbbreviatedRelativeLocationPath
```

Where

- Step (p. 221) specifies the contents of a location step.
- RelativeLocationPath (p. 219) specifies a series of relative steps to a location in a target document.
- / is a character that indicates the separation between one location step and another.
- AbbreviatedRelativeLocationPath (p. 183) abbreviates a relative location path.

Notes

- RelativeLocationPath is a component of the Abbreviated AbsoluteLocationPath, AbbreviatedRelativeLocationPath, AbsoluteLocationPath, LocationPath, PathExpr, and RelativeLocationPath productions.

- A relative location path consists of one or more location steps ordered from left to right. Each step, which is separated from the next by a slash (/), selects a nodes set relative to a *context node* (which indicates the ongoing framework of nodes and nodes sets in the target document).
- A location step has an *axis* (which shows the tree relationship between the selected node and the context node), a *node test* (which names the node type and expanded qualifier name, with a prefix, of the selected node), and optional *predicates* (which filter the selected nodes set to a greater extent).
- For examples of unabbreviated location paths, see Section 2, Location Paths, in the XPath recommendation (http://www.w3.org/TR/xpath).

Related Productions

AbbreviatedAbsoluteLocationPath (p. 182), AbbreviatedRelative
LocationPath (p. 183), AbsoluteLocationPath (p. 184), LocationPath
(p. 203), RelativeLocationPath (p. 219), Step (p. 221)

round()   Round Function

Purpose

Returns a rounded integer that is closest in value to the argument.

EBNF Syntax

number_r round(*number*)

Standard Syntax

number_r round(*number*)

Where

- *number_r* is the number returned by the function.
- round is a function-name keyword.
- *number* represents the argument's number.

Notes

- If two numbers have the same value, round() returns the number that is closest to positive infinity.
- If the argument is NaN (Not-a-Number), round() returns a value of NaN.
- If the argument is positive infinity, negative infinity, positive zero, or negative zero, round() returns the same value (positive infinity, negative infinity, positive zero, or negative zero, respectively).
- If the argument is less than zero but greater than or equal to -0.5, round() returns a value of negative zero.
- For the prior two bulleted items, the XPath recommendation (http://www.w3.org/TR/xpath) states that "the result of calling the round function is not the same as the result of adding 0.5 and then calling the floor function."

Related Functions
ceiling() (p. 190), floor() (p. 198), number() (p. 211), round() (p. 220), substring() (p. 224), sum() (p. 226)

starts-with()   Starts With Function

Purpose
Returns true or false depending on whether one argument string starts with the other argument string.

EBNF Syntax
```
boolean starts-with(string_1, string_2)
```

Standard Syntax
```
true|false starts-with(string_1, string_2)
```

Where
- *boolean* is a true or false value returned by the function.
- starts-with is a function-name keyword.
- *string_1* and *string_2* represent each of the strings evaluated by the function.
- true is a boolean value returned if *string_1* starts with *string_2*.
- false is a boolean value returned if *string_1* in the argument does not start with *string_2*.

Related Functions
concat() (p. 190), contains() (p. 191), normalize-space() (p. 209), string() (p. 222), string-length() (p. 223), substring() (p. 224), substring-after() (p. 225), substring-before() (p. 225), translate() (p. 226).

Step [4]   Step

Purpose
Specifies the contents of a location step.

EBNF Syntax
```
Step ::= AxisSpecifier NodeTest Predicate*
       | AbbreviatedStep
```

Standard Syntax
```
AxisSpecifier NodeTest
    [Predicate  [ Predicate  [... Predicate]]]
    | AbbreviatedStep
```

XPath Language

Where

- AxisSpecifier (p. 188) specifies an axis name and a predefined specifier.
- NodeTest (p. 208) checks on the node type and the expanded name of the location-step nodes set.
- Predicate (p. 216) inserts a predicate expression that filters nodes in a location path.
- AbbreviatedStep (p. 184) abbreviates a step.

Notes

- Step is a component of the AbbreviatedRelativeLocationPath and RelativeLocationPath production.
- A location step has an *axis* (which shows the tree relationship between the selected node and the context node), a *node test* (which names the node type and expanded qualifier name, with a prefix, of the selected node), and optional *predicates* (which filter the selected nodes set to a greater extent).

Related Productions

AbbreviatedStep (p. 184), AbbreviatedAxisSpecifier (p. 182), AxisName (p. 187), AxisSpecifier (p. 188), NodeTest (p. 208), Predicate (p. 216)

---

string() | String Function

Purpose

Returns a string converted from an object.

EBNF Syntax

```
string string(object?)
```

Standard Syntax

```
string string([object])
```

Where

- *string* is a string returned by the function.
- string is a function-name keyword.
- *object* is a node-set, number, boolean, or another object.

Notes

- If the argument is a node-set, string() returns the string value of the expanded-name of the first node in the node-set.
- If the argument is a blank node-set, string() returns an empty string.
- If the argument is a NaN (Not-a-Number), string() returns a string with the value of NaN.
- If the argument is either negative or positive zero, string() returns a string with the value of 0.

- If the argument is positive infinity, string() returns a string with the value of Infinity.
- If the argument is negative infinity, string() returns a string with the value of -Infinity.
- If the argument is a boolean true value, string() returns a string with the value of true.
- If the argument is a boolean false value, string() returns a string with the value of false.
- If the argument is a positive integer, string() returns a number (see the Number production) with no leading zeroes and no decimal point.
- If the argument is a negative integer, string() returns a number (see the Number production) preceded by a minus sign (-), with no leading zeroes and no decimal point.
- If the argument is a positive floating-point number, string() returns a number (see the Number production) with a decimal point. At least one digit, which may be a leading zero, precedes the decimal point, and at least one digit follows the decimal point.
- If the argument is a negative floating-point number, string() returns a number (see the Number production) with a decimal point and with a preceding minus sign (-). At least one digit, which may be a leading zero, precedes the decimal point, and at least one digit follows the decimal point.
- If the argument is not a node-set, boolean, or number, string() returns a value based on that argument type.
- A missing argument results in a node-set containing the context node only.
- To format a number, use the format-number() function (p. 322) and xsl:number element (p. 348), both in XSLT (see "XSLT Component", which starts on p. 319).

Related Production

Number (p. 210)

Related Functions

concat() (p. 190), contains() (p. 191), normalize-space() (p. 209), starts-with() (p. 221), string-length() (p. 223), substring() (p. 224), substring-after() (p. 225), substring-before() (p. 225), translate() (p. 226)

string-length()   String Length Function

Purpose

Returns the number of characters in the argument's string.

EBNF Syntax

```
number string-length(string?)
```

Standard Syntax

```
number string-length([string])
```

Where

- *number* is the number returned by the function.
- string-length is a function-name keyword.
- *string* represents the string evaluated by the function.

Note

- A missing argument results in a string value for the context node.

Related Functions

concat() (p. 190), contains() (p. 191), normalize-space() (p. 209), starts-with() (p. 221), string() (p. 222), substring() (p. 224), substring-after() (p. 225), substring-before() (p. 225), translate() (p. 226)

substring()   Substring Function

Purpose

Returns the part of the first argument string starting at the character position specified by the second argument number and ending after the number of characters specified by the third argument number.

EBNF Syntax

```
string_r substring(string, number_1, number_2?)
```

Standard Syntax

```
string_r substring(string, number_1, [number_2])
```

Where

- *string_r* is the substring returned by the function.
- substring is a function-name keyword.
- *string* represents the string evaluated by the function.
- *number_1* represents a starting character position.
- *number_2* provides the number of characters.

Notes

- If the third argument is not given, the substring ends at the end of the first argument string.
- The first character in the first argument string is at the position 1, the second character is 2 (the number of characters), and so forth. Note that most programming and scripting languages start counting at 0.
- If the second or third argument numbers are floating-point, substring() rounds the numbers in the same way that the round() function does.

Related Functions

concat() (p. 190), contains() (p. 191), normalize-space() (p. 209), round() (p. 220), starts-with() (p. 221), string() (p. 222), string-length() (p. 223), substring-after() (p. 225), substring-before() (p. 225), translate() (p. 226)

substring-after() — Substring After Function

Purpose

Returns the part of the first argument string after the initial occurrence of the second argument string in the first argument string.

EBNF Syntax

string_r substring-after(string_1, string_2)

Standard Syntax

string_r substring-after(string_1, string_2)

Where

- string_r is the substring returned by the function.
- substring-after is a function-name keyword.
- string_1 and string_2 represent the strings evaluated by the function.

Note

- If string_1 does not contain any part of string_2, substring-after() returns an empty string.

Related Functions

concat() (p. 190), contains() (p. 191), normalize-space() (p. 209), starts-with() (p. 221), string() (p. 222), string-length() (p. 223), substring() (p. 224), substring-before() (p. 225), translate() (p. 226)

substring-before() — Substring Before Function

Purpose

Returns the part of the first argument string before the initial occurrence of the second argument string in the first argument string.

EBNF Syntax

string_r substring-before(string_1, string_2)

Standard Syntax

string_r substring-before(string_1, string_2)

Where
- *string_r* is the substring returned by the function.
- substring-before is a function-name keyword.
- *string_1* and *string_2* represent the strings evaluated by the function.

Note
- If *string_1* does not contain any part of *string_2*, substring-before() returns an empty string.

Related Functions
concat() (p. 190), contains() (p. 191), normalize-space() (p. 209), starts-with() (p. 221), string() (p. 222), string-length() (p. 223), substring() (p. 224), substring-after() (p. 225), translate() (p. 226).

sum()   Sum Function

Purpose
Returns the sum of all nodes in a node-set.

EBNF Syntax
> *number* sum (*node-set*)

Standard Syntax
> *number* sum (*node-set*)

Where
- *number* is the number returned by the function.
- sum is a function-name keyword.
- *node-set* represents the argument's node-set.

Note
- sum() converts the string values of each node to a number before summing the nodes.

Related Functions
ceiling() (p. 190), floor() (p. 198), number() (p. 211), round() (p. 220)

translate()   Translate Function

Purpose
Returns an argument with translated characters.

EBNF Syntax
> *string_r* translate(*string_1*, *string_2*, *string_3*)

Standard Syntax

```
string_r translate(string_1, string_2, string_3)
```

Where

- *string* is the string returned by the function.
- translate is a function-name keyword.
- *string_1* represents the string to be translated.
- *string_2* represents the string that supplies source characters.
- *string_3* represents the string that supplies replacement characters.

Notes

- The main function of translate() is to change the case of characters. However, translate() does not work for all the Unicode character sets.
- translate() translates the characters in *string_1* by replacing characters in *string_2*, regardless of case, with those in *string_3*.
- If *string_2* and *string_3* have the same number of characters, translate() replaces *string_2* characters in *string_1* with characters in the same position in *string_3*.
- If *string_2* is longer than *string_3*, translate() removes the excess characters from *string_1*.
- If *string_3* is longer than *string_2*, translate() ignores the excess characters.
- If the same character is repeated in *string_2*, translate() uses the first character and ignores any remaining repeat characters.

Related Functions

concat() (p. 190), contains() (p. 191), normalize-space() (p. 209), starts-with() (p. 221), string() (p. 222), string-length() (p. 223), substring() (p. 224), substring-after() (p. 225), substring-before() (p. 225), translate() (p. 226)

true()   True Function

Purpose

Returns a value of true.

EBNF Syntax

```
boolean true()
```

Standard Syntax

```
boolean true()
```

Where

- *boolean* is the true boolean returned by the function.
- true is a function-name keyword.

Related Functions

boolean() (p. 189), false() (p. 197), lang() (p. 201), not() (p. 210)

XPath Language

XPath Language

UnaryExpr [27]   Unary Expression

Purpose
Negates an expression.

EBNF Syntax
```
UnaryExpr ::= UnionExpr | '-' UnaryExpr
```

Standard Syntax
```
UnionExpr | - UnaryExpr
```

Where
- UnionExpr (p. 228) unites a path expression or a path expression and another union expression.
- - is a unary minus character.
- UnaryExpr negates an expression.

Notes
- UnaryExpr is a component of the MultiplicativeExpr.
- The minus sign (-) serves two purposes: it is the subtraction operator and is unary minus. Unary minus changes the sign of a variable to a minus.

Related Productions
AdditiveExpr (p. 185), AndExpr (p. 186), Digits (p. 192), EqualityExpr (p. 192), Expr (p. 194), ExprToken (p. 194), ExprWhitespace (p. 196), FilterExpr (p. 197), FunctionName (p. 199), Literal (p. 202), MultiplicativeExpr (p. 204), MultiplyOperator (p. 205), NameTest (p. 207), NodeType (p. 208), Number (p. 210), Operator (p. 212), OperatorName (p. 213), OrExpr (p. 214), PathExpr (p. 215), PrimaryExpr (p. 217), RelationalExpr (p. 218), UnionExpr (p. 228), VariableReference (p. 229)

UnionExpr [18]   Union Expression

Purpose
Unites a path expression or a path expression and another union expression.

EBNF Syntax
```
UnionExpr ::= PathExpr | UnionExpr '|' PathExpr
```

Standard Syntax
```
PathExpr | UnionExpr | PathExpr
```

Where
- PathExpr (p. 215) creates a path by composing a location path, a filter expression, or a filter expression and a location path.

- | is a character that separates one expression from the next and indicates a choice of expression use.
- UnionExpr unites a path expression or a path expression and another union expression.

Note

- UnionExpr is a component of the UnaryExpr production.

Related Productions

AdditiveExpr (p. 185), AndExpr (p. 186), Digits (p. 192), EqualityExpr (p. 192), Expr (p. 194), ExprToken (p. 194), ExprWhitespace (p. 196), FilterExpr (p. 197), FunctionName (p. 199), Literal (p. 202), MultiplicativeExpr (p. 204), MultiplyOperator (p. 205), NameTest (p. 207), NodeType (p. 208), Number (p. 210), Operator (p. 212), Operator Name (p. 213), OrExpr (p. 214), PathExpr (p. 215), PrimaryExpr (p. 217), RelationalExpr (p. 218), UnaryExpr (p. 228), VariableReference (p. 229)

VariableReference [36]   Variable Reference

Purpose

Specifies the qualified name of a variable reference.

EBNF Syntax

```
VariableReference ::= '$' QName
```

Standard Syntax

$QName

Where

- $ is a character indicating a variable reference.
- QName creates a qualified name.

Note

- VariableReference is a component of the ExprToken and PrimaryExpr productions.

Related Productions

AdditiveExpr (p. 185), AndExpr (p. 186), Digits (p. 192), EqualityExpr (p. 192), Expr (p. 194), ExprToken (p. 194), ExprWhitespace (p. 196), FilterExpr (p. 197), FunctionName (p. 199), Literal (p. 202), MultiplicativeExpr (p. 204), MultiplyOperator (p. 205), NameTest (p. 207), NodeType (p. 208), Number (p. 210), Operator (p. 212), Operator Name (p. 213), OrExpr (p. 214), PathExpr (p. 215), PrimaryExpr (p. 217), RelationalExpr (p. 218), UnaryExpr (p. 228), UnionExpr (p. 228)

Style Sheet Reference

Part II presents a comprehensive reference to XML's custom-made style sheet language, Extensible Stylesheet Language (XSL) and the XSL Transformations (XSLT) component. The XSL and XSLT sections are preceded by special tables of contents. If you know the task that you want to perform or style you want to apply but don't remember the property name, review the tasks in "Style Sheets in Plain English." and find the appropriate page in either reference section. On the other hand, if you know the property name but want to find it in Part II or Part III, browse through the alphabetical list in "XML A to Z." In addition, "Style Sheets by Category" enable you to look up styling properties by category type. Again, find the desired property by going to one of the cross-referenced pages. The three tables of contents also include references to

IN THIS PART

- Style Sheets in Plain English
- Style Sheets A to Z
- Style Sheets by Category
- XSLT Component
- XSL Style Sheet Syntax

Style Sheets in
Plain English

This section of the book is for those of you who know what style you want to apply to an XML document but may not remember the name of a particular production, element, function, or property. This part is composed of four columns. The left column lists tasks to be performed, which are organized alphabetically by the *italicized* keywords. The second column contains the name of the component with which you'll accomplish your goal. The third column lists the technology; and the last column provides page numbers for more information about each entry.

●—**NOTE**————————————————————————————

The CSS2 technology is not covered in this book. Any reference to CSS2 in this part of the book simply points out the origin of a particular style. To learn more about cascading style sheets and specific style sheet properties, refer to *XHTML In Plain English*, also written by Sandra E. Eddy and published by IDG Books Worldwide.

If you want to...	Use this production or element	Technology	Page(s)
indicate an *absolute length* ending with an absolute unit of measure name	`AbsoluteLength`	XSL	371
represent an *absolute numeric value*	`AbsoluteNumeric`	XSL	371
set an *absolute position* for a block-level container	`absolute-position`	XSL	372
represent an *absolute unit of measure name*	`AbsoluteUnitName`	XSL	372
return the *absolute value* of the argument	`abs()`	XSL	370
apply styles to an element when a user *activates* it	`:active`	CSS2	
act on one or more expressions through *addition or subtraction*	`AdditiveExpr`	XSL	374
adjust line height for subscript or superscript characters	`line-height-shift-adjustment`	XSL	539
automatically insert content *after* the content of an element	`:after`	CSS2	
specify the number of characters *after* the hyphenation character	`hyphenation-push-character-count`	XSL	519
declare that a namespace URI is an *alias* for another namespace URI	`xsl:namespace-alias`	XSLT	347
align the last line of selected text	`text-align-last`	XSL	626

If you want to...	Use this production or element	Technology	Page(s)
align selected text horizontally	`text-align`	CSS2, XSL	625, 750
precisely *align elements*	`alignment-adjust`	XSL	375
align leaders for several `fo:leaders`	`leader-alignment`	XSL	532
define how an object is *aligned* with the parent object	`baseline-identifier`	XSL	387
configure the *alignment* in a block-progression-dimension of children in a reference area	`display-align`	XSL	454
define the *alignment* of two or more areas in a block-progression-dimension	`relative-align`	XSL	591
allow hyphenation	`hyphenate`	XSL	516
represent one or more *alphabetic characters or digits*	`AlphaOrDigits`	XSL	376
set an *alternate properties set* for formatting	`fo:multi-property-set`	XSL	480, 754
include *another XSLT style sheet*	`xsl:include`	XSLT	345
apply template rule override in imported style sheet	`xsl:apply-imports`	XSLT	329
apply template rules to all the children of the current node	`xsl:apply-templates`	XSLT	330, 748
represent an *argument*	`Argument`	XSL	376
adjust the font *aspect value* so it's legible no matter its size	`font-size-adjust`	CSS2, XSL	487

Continued

If you want to...	Use this production or element	Technology	Page(s)
specify whether the background image is *attached* to the background of the page	`background-attachment`	CSS2, XSL	380
specify and name an *attribute set*	`xsl:attribute-set`	XSLT	332
create *attributes* for elements produced by `xsl:element`	`xsl:attribute`	XSLT	331, 752
sound an *auditory cue* before and/or after an element	`cue`	CSS2, XSL	449
sound an *auditory cue* *after* an element	`cue-after`	CSS2, XSL	450
sound an *auditory cue* *before* an element	`cue-before`	CSS2, XSL	451
select some node sets for *automatically processing*	`xsl:for-each`	XSLT	342
indicate whether the first `fo:multi-case` formatting object is *automatically restored* when the `fo:multi-switch` formatting object is concealed by an ancestor	`auto-restore`	XSL	377
return true or false depending on whether a function-*available* is named	`function-available()`	XSLT	323
use an *axis specifier*, *child*, or *attribute* to create a pattern	`ChildOrAttribute AxisSpecifier`	XSLT	320
specify the *azimuth* location (in a 360-degree left-to-right arc) of a sound file	`azimuth`	CSS2, XSL	377

If you want to...	Use this production or element	Technology	Page(s)
specify a *background color* for the current document or document part	background-color	CSS2, XSL	381
specify a *background image* for the current document or document part	background-image	CSS2, XSL	382
specify whether the *background image* is fixed or follows the page as the user scrolls through	background-attachment	CSS2, XSL	380
cause a *background-image repeat* a number of times	background-repeat	CSS2, XSL	386
specify a starting position for a *background image*	background-position	CSS2, XSL	383
play a *background sound* while speaking an element's content	play-during	CSS2, XSL	582
move the selected *baseline* of a selection away from the default baseline location toward superscript or subscript	baseline-shift	XSL	388
set the height of the text line from *baseline-to-baseline*	line-height	CSS2, XSL	538
automatically insert content *before* the content of an element	:before	CSS2	
specify the number of characters *before* the hyphenation character	hyphenation-remain-character-count	XSL	520
override *bidirectionality writing direction* for an inline script	fo:bidi-override	XSL	465

Continued

If you want to...	Use this production or element	Technology	Page(s)
make a *blank page master* eligible for selection	blank-or-not-blank	XSL	389
blink text	text-decoration	CSS2, XSL	628, 754
create a *block-level box*	fo:block-container	XSL	467
format *block-level selections*	fo:block	XSL	466, 748
specify an area's *block progression dimension* for block-level and replaced-elements areas	block-progression-dimension	XSL	390
return the *body-start* value for a list	body-start()	XSL	391
set *bold* or light font weight	font-weight	CSS2, XSL	491, 750
set all *border colors*	border-color	CSS2, XSL	406
set all *border properties*	border	CSS2, XSL	392
set all *border styles*	border-style	CSS2, XSL	426
control all *border widths*	border-width	CSS2, XSL	432
specify the distance between *borders* of adjacent cells	border-separation	XSL	421
set the color of the *bottom-border* of a box	border-bottom-color	CSS2, XSL	402
set *bottom-border properties*	border-bottom	CSS2, XSL	400
style the *bottom-border* of a box	border-bottom-style	CSS2, XSL	403
set the width of the *bottom-border* of a box	border-bottom-width	CSS2, XSL	404
control or size the *bottom margin*	margin-bottom	CSS2, XSL	543, 752
control an element's *bottom offset position*	bottom	CSS2, XSL	434
control or size the *bottom padding* of an element	padding-bottom	CSS2, XSL	566

If you want to...	Use this production or element	Technology	Page(s)
break a page after the current element	page-break-after	CSS2, XSL	572
break a page before the current element	page-break-before	CSS2, XSL	573
avoid a page *break* inside the current element	page-break-inside	CSS2, XSL	574
set a *bullet type* preceding list items	list-style-type	CSS2	
evaluate and process an expression and *call a function*	FunctionCall	XSL	511
call a template by name	xsl:call-template	XSLT	334, 752
specify a *caption's* position and alignment within a table	caption-side	CSS2, XSL	437
control *case* of selected text	text-transform	CSS2, XSL	631
contain content for a table *cell*	fo:table-cell	XSL	505, 753
create *cells* around locations with no visible content	empty-cells	CSS2, XSL	457
contain properties for table-column *cells*	fo:table-column	XSL	506, 752
specify a Unicode *character*	character	XSL	439
indicate whether a *character* is a space or letter	treat-as-word-space	XSL	633
indicate a *character* mapped to a glyph	fo:character	XSL	467
specify a *character set* in an external style sheet	@charset	CSS2	
choose the first xsl:when condition that is true	xsl:choose	XSLT	335, 753
define the *clipping* (visible) area of a box	clip	CSS2, XSL	440

Continued

If you want to...	Use this production or element	Technology	Page(s)
collapse (hide) or separate a table-cell border	border-collapse	CSS2, XSL	405
return a system *color*	system-color()	XSL	622
specify the *color* of document text	color	CSS2, XSL	441
set the *color* of the ending edge of a block or inline area border	border-end-color	XSL	408
set the *color* of the leading edge of a block or inline area border	border-before-color	XSL	397
set the *color* of the left border of a box	border-left-color	CSS2, XSL	413
set the *color* of the right border of a box	border-right-color	XSL	418
specify the page-background *color*	background-color	CSS2, XSL	381
return an RGB *color*	rgb()	XSL	596
set the *color* of the starting edge of a block or inline area border	border-start-color	XSL	422
set the *color* of the top border of a box	border-top-color	CSS2, XSL	429
set the *color* of the trailing edge of a block or inline area border	border-after-color	XSL	393
identify an RGB hexadecimal *color code*	Color	XSL	443
declare an ICC *Color Profile* for a style sheet	fo:color-profile	XSL	468
return a specific color from the ICC *Color Profile*	icc-color()	XSL	521
specify the name of a *color profile*	color-profile-name	XSL	443
set all outline *colors*	outline-color	CSS2	
set *colors* of all borders	border-color	CSS2, XSL	406
contain properties for cells in a table *column*	fo:table-column	XSL	506, 752

If you want to...	Use this production or element	Technology	Page(s)
set a *column gap* between columns in the current box	column-gap	XSL	444
set the first *column number* in a table-cell span	column-number	XSL	445, 750
set the *column width* in the column-number property	column-width	XSL	446
specify the number of *columns* in the current box	column-count	XSL	444
start a *comment*	*/	CSS2	
end a *comment*	/*	CSS2	
create a *comment node* in the result tree	xsl:comment	XSLT	336
select a *condensed or expanded* font	font-stretch	CSS2, XSL	448
generate *content* before or after the current element	content	CSS2	
set the *content height* of an object	content-height	XSL	446
define the *content type* of an element	content-type	XSL	447
set the content width of an object	content-width	XSL	448
create a single component out of *contiguous flow objects*	fo:flow	XSL	471
copy a result tree fragment into the same result tree	xsl:copy-of	XSLT	337
copy the current node and its namespace nodes	xsl:copy	XSLT	336
specify the number of *columns* in the current box	column-count	XSL	444

Continued

If you want to...	Use this production or element	Technology	Page(s)
increment one or more named *counters*	counter-increment	CSS2	
reset one or more named *counters*	counter-reset	CSS2	
specify a *country code* from RFC-1766	country	XSL	448
set cross or *crop marks* for a page box	marks	CSS2	
specify a *cross-reference identifier*	ref-id	XSL	589
sound an auditory *cue* before and/or after an element	cue	CSS2, XSL	449
sound an auditory *cue* *after* an element	cue-after	CSS2, XSL	450
sound an auditory *cue* *before* an element	cue-before	CSS2, XSL	451
return a node set that contains the *current node*	current()	XSLT	321
specify the *cursor type* for the mouse pointer or other pointing device	cursor	CSS2	
specify a *decimal format*	xsl:decimal-format	XSLT	338
decorate or blink text lines	text-decoration	CSS2, XSL	628, 754
indicate the *destination* of a simple link in an external document	external-destination	XSL	462, 754
indicate the distance from the top of the page to the location of a *destination area*	destination-placement-offset	XSL	452
show *destination resource* areas	indicate-destination	XSL	523
specify the *destination resource* location	show-destination	XSL	604, 754
provide the XSLT-processor *developer's* name	xsl:vendor	XSLT	364

If you want to...	Use this production or element	Technology	Page(s)
specify one or more *digits*	`Digits`	XSL	452
represent one or more *digits or alphabetic characters*	`AlphaOrDigits`	XSL	376
set the *dimensions and orientation* of a page box	`size`	CSS2, XSL	605
specify the *direction* in which text is displayed or printed	`direction`	CSS2, XSL	453
set the *direction* in which text is written	`writing-mode`	XSL	645
display the current element in a particular way onscreen or printed	`display`	CSS2	
set the *distance* between the end of a list-item label start indent and a list item	`provisional-distance-between-starts`	XSL	586, 751
set the *distance* between the end of a list-item label and a list item	`provisional-label-separation`	XSL	587, 751
divide, multiply, or find a modulus for expressions	`MultiplicativeExpr`	XSL	554
return an XML *document* that is not the main document	`document()`	XSLT	321
generate up to five *document page regions*	`fo:simple-page-master`	XSL	501, 752
determine the *dominant baseline* again	`dominant-baseline`	XSL	455
create an *element* with a template for its attributes and child elements	`xsl:element`	XSLT	340
return true or false depending on whether an instruction *element* is named	`element-available()`	XSLT	322
specify *element height*	`height`	CSS2, XSL	514

Continued

If you want to...	Use this production or element	Technology	Page(s)
specify the *elevation* (from top to bottom) of sound from a sound file	elevation	CSS2, XSL	456
force a specific type of page at the *end* of the current pages' sequence	force-page-count	XSL	494
suppress a non-control character at the *end or start of a flow object*	suppress-at-line-break	XSL	621
set the *ending-edge color* of a block or inline area border	border-end-color	XSL	408
specify *ending-edge indention* of the current formatting object box	end-indent	XSL	457, 750
control or size *ending-edge padding*	padding-end	XSL	567
set the *ending-edge style* of a block or inline area border	border-end-style	XSL	409
set the *ending-edge width* of a block or inline area border	border-end-width	XSL	410
set the *ending indention* for the last line of the current paragraph	last-line-end-indent	XSL	531
indicate whether the current table cell *ends a table row*	ends-row	XSL	458
enhance text with lines or blinking	text-decoration	CSS2, XSL	628, 754
provide an NCName for an *enumeration token*	EnumerationToken	XSL	459
select a page-master depending on its odd or *even* position in the page sequence	odd-or-even	XSL	559
select an *expanded or condensed* font	font-stretch	CSS2, XSL	488

If you want to...	Use this production or element	Technology	Page(s)
indicate an *expression*	Expr	XSL	459
tokenize an *expression* *character* by character or name by name	ExprToken	XSL	460
insert whitespace in an *expression*	ExprWhitespace	XSL	461
specify the *extent* of the width or height of the box	extent	XSL	461
indicate the *external destination* of a simple link in an document	external-destination	XSL	462, 754
indicate an inline *external graphic*	fo:external-graphic	XSL	470, 750
fall back to a template when a particular condition is false	xsl:fallback	XSLT	341
specify a *family of voices* by name, family, or both	voice-family	CSS2, XSL	637
apply styles to a matching element that is the *first child* element of that element	:first-child	CSS2	
indicate the distance from the top of the page to the location of the *first destination area*	destination-placement-offset	XSL	452
style the *first letter* of a paragraph	:first-letter	CSS2	
indent the *first line*	text-indent	CSS2, XSL	629
format the *first line* of an fo:block	fo:initial-property-set	XSL	473, 750
style the *first line* of a paragraph	:first-line	CSS2	
style the *first-page-box* of a document	:first	CSS2	
set the *first-page number* in a page sequence	initial-page-number	XSL	524

Continued

If you want to...	Use this production or element	Technology	Page(s)
float an element right or left	float	CSS2, XSL	463
specifies which side of an element box may not be adjacent to a *floating box*	clear	CSS2, XSL	440
contain a *floating note*	fo:footnote	XSL	472
contain *floating object* content	fo:float	XSL	471
represent a *floating-point number*	FloatingPoint Number	XSL	463
represent an absolute or relative *floating-point number* in an expression	Numeric	XSL	558
name the current *flow*	flow-name	XSL	465
create a single component out of contiguous *flow objects*	fo:flow	XSL	471
format an *fo:block first line*	fo:initial-property-set	XSL	473, 750
apply styles to the *focused-on* element	:focus	CSS2	
align several *fo:leaders* formatting objects	leader-alignment	XSL	532
keep *following output* with selected output	keep-with-next	XSL	527
identify one *fo:marker* with another	marker-class-name	XSL	547
specify that certain *fo:markers* whose children are retrieved must have a marker-class-name	retrieve-class-name	XSL	595
toggle from one *fo:multi-case* to another	fo:multi-toggle	XSL	481
control *fo:multi-property-sets* used to format child flow objects	active-state	XSL	373, 754

If you want to...	Use this production or element	Technology	Page(s)
allow *fo:multi-toggle* objects to select fo:multi-case objects to switch with	case-name	XSL	438
provide a title for an *fo:multi-case* formatting object	case-title	XSL	438
nest displayed or hidden flow objects, depending on a *fo:multi-switch*	fo:multi-case	XSL	480
give an *fo:namespace identifier* to a formatting object	id	XSL	521
return a characteristic of a *font* defined by the computer system	system-font()	XSL	623
adjust the *font aspect value* so it's legible no matter its size	font-size-adjust	CSS2, XSL	487
specify up to six *font descriptor* values	@font-face	CSS2	
select a *font family* or name	font-family	CSS2, XSL	483
set all *font properties*	font	CSS2, XSL	482
set the *font size*	font-size	CSS2, XSL	486, 750
set all *font styles*	font-style	CSS2, XSL	489
specify a small-cap *font variant*	font-variant	CSS2, XSL	490
set bold or light *font weight*	font-weight	CSS2, XSL	491, 750
specify whether to omit table *footer* at a break	table-omit-footer-at-break	XSL	624
format the body of a *footnote*	fo:footnote-body	XSL	472
select some node sets *for automatic processing*	xsl:for-each	XSLT	342

Continued

If you want to...	Use this production or element	Technology	Page(s)
force a specific type of page at the end of the current sequence of pages	force-page-count	XSL	494
set a viewing after an fo:region-body	fo:region-after	XSL	495
set an *fo:region-body viewing area* at the end of an fo:region-body	fo:region-end	XSL	497
set an *fo:region-body viewing area* at the start of an fo:region-body	fo:region-start	XSL	497
set an *fo:region-body viewing area* before an fo:region-body	fo:region-before	XSL	496
specify a *foreground color* for document text	color	CSS2, XSL	441, 750
return a number as a *formatted string*	format-number()	XSLT	322
switch to one of several *formatting-object subtrees*	fo:multi-switch	XSL	481
point to the source document of a *formatting-object tree*	source-document	XSL	606
indicate the *fo:simple-link target resource*	internal-destination	XSL	526
return the inherited value of a property from an *fo:table-column*	from-table-column()	XSL	510
place a result tree *fragment* into the same result tree	xsl:copy-of	XSLT	337
return the value of a property *from the nearest-ancestor* formatting object	from-parent()	XSL	510
return true or false depending on whether a *function-available* is named	function-available()	XSLT	323

If you want to...	Use this production or element	Technology	Page(s)
provide a *function NCName*	FunctionName	XSL	512
group *global declarations* for a style sheet	fo:declarations	XSL	469
indicate a *glyph-mapped character*	fo:character	XSL	467
orient horizontally displayed *glyphs*	glyph-orientation-horizontal	XSL	512
orient vertically displayed *glyphs*	glyph-orientation-vertical	XSL	513
scale an external *graphic*	scaling	XSL	601
indicate an *href* for a link or graphic	href	XSL	515
specify whether to omit table *header* at a break	table-omit-header-at-break	XSL	624
specify element *height*	height	CSS2, XSL	514
determine the page *height*	page-height	XSL	575, 752
set the *height* of the text line from baseline to baseline	line-height	CSS2, XSL	538
specify the *height extent* of the box	extent	XSL	461
hide or separate a table-cell border	border-collapse	CSS2, XSL	405
return the *highest integer*	floor()	XSL	464
specify the initial *horizontal position* of a background image	background-position-horizontal	XSL	385
horizontally align selected text	text-align	CSS2, XSL	625, 750
horizontally align the last line of selected text	text-align-last	XSL	626
orient *horizontally displayed* text glyphs	glyph-orientation-horizontal	XSL	512

Continued

If you want to...	Use this production or element	Technology	Page(s)
apply styles to an element when a user *hovers* over it	:hover	CSS2	
specify a *hyphen character*	hyphenation-character	XSL	517
control the split of a *hyphenated word*	hyphenation-keep	XSL	517
allow *hyphenation*	hyphenate	XSL	516
specify the number of rows that can end with the *hyphenation character*	hyphenation-ladder-count	XSL	518
specify the number of characters after the *hyphenation character*	hyphenation-push-character-count	XSL	519
specify the number of characters before the *hyphenation character*	hyphenation-remain-character-count	XSL	520
declare an *ICC Color Profile* for a style sheet	fo:color-profile	XSL	468
return a specific color from the *ICC Color Profile*	icc-color()	XSL	521
specify a cross-reference *identifier*	ref-id	XSL	589
return a string *identifier* for a node in the first node-set	generate-id()	XSLT	324
locate a node with a pattern of *identifiers and keys*	IDKeyPattern	XSLT	324
evaluate an expression and return a template *if* it is true	xsl:if	XSLT	343, 753
set an *image* to be used as a bullet preceding a list	list-style-image	CSS2	
scale an external *image*	scaling	XSL	601
specify a page-background *image*	background-image	CSS2, XSL	382

If you want to...	Use this production or element	Technology	Page(s)
set a starting position for a background *image*	background-position	CSS2, XSL	383
import an XSLT style sheet	xsl:import	XSLT	344
import styles from an external style sheet	@import	CSS2	
include another XSLT style sheet	xsl:include	XSLT	345
indent the first line	text-indent	CSS2, XSL	629
specify *indention* at the ending edge of the current formatting object box	end-indent	XSL	457, 750
indicate destination resource areas	indicate-destination	XSL	523
specify the highest stress (*inflection*) level in a voice	stress	CSS2, XSL	620
set *inherited properties* for a formatting-objects group	fo:wrapper	XSL	508, 754
return the *inherited property value*	inherited-property-value()	XSL	523
create an *inline box*	fo:inline-container	XSL	474
indicate an *inline external graphic*	fo:external-graphic	XSL	470, 750
set an *inline object* with descendant data	fo:instream-foreign-object	XSL	475
set the *inline-progression-dimension* of block-level and replaced-element boxes	inline-progression-dimension	XSL	525
format selected *inline text* with a background or border	fo:inline	XSL	473
keep output produced by the current flow object together	keep-together	XSL	526

Continued

If you want to...	Use this production or element	Technology	Page(s)
keep following output with selected output	keep-with-next	XSL	527
keep previous output with the selected output	keep-with-previous	XSL	528
return a node set matching a *key*	key()	XSLT	325
declare *keys* for the current document	xsl:key	XSLT	345
locate a node with a pattern of *keys and identifiers*	IDKeyPattern	XSLT	324
represent a reserved *keyword*	Keyword	XSL	529
include a *label and list-item body*	fo:list-item	XSL	478, 751
return the *label-end* value for a list	label-end()	XSL	530
apply styles to an element that matches a particular *language*	:lang	CSS2	
specify a *language code* from RFC-1766	language	XSL	530
set the *last-line indention* for the current paragraph	last-line-end-indent	XSL	531
specify a *layout* for a table	table-layout	CSS2, XSL	623, 752
contain all *layout masters* for a document	fo:layout-master-set	XSL	475
create a *leader* that connects two formatting objects	fo:leader	XSL	476
specify a maximum and minimum *leader length*	leader-length	XSL	533
specify a *leader pattern*	leader-pattern	XSL	533
specify *leader-pattern width*	leader-pattern-width	XSL	533
align *leaders* for several fo:leaders	leader-alignment	XSL	532

If you want to...	Use this production or element	Technology	Page(s)
set the *leading-edge color* of a block or inline area border	border-before-color	XSL	397
control or size *leading-edge padding*	padding-before	XSL	564
set the *leading-edge style* of a block or inline area border	border-before-style	XSL	398
set the *leading-edge width* of a block or inline area border	border-before-width	XSL	399
set the *left-border color* of a box	border-left-color	CSS2, XSL	413
set all *left-border properties*	border-left	CSS2, XSL	411
set the *left-border style*	border-left-style	CSS2, XSL	414
set *left-border width*	border-left-width	CSS2, XSL	415
control or size the *left margin*	margin-left	CSS2, XSL	544, 752
control an element's *left offset position*	left	CSS2, XSL	535
control or size *left padding*	padding-left	CSS2, XSL	568
set the *left-page-box style* of a document when working with double-sided pages	:left	CSS2	
set spacing between *letters*	letter-spacing	CSS2, XSL	535
set the *level* of a box in a stack of elements	z-index	CSS2, XSL	648
limit the pages in a page sequence	maximum-repeats	XSL	549

Continued

If you want to...	Use this production or element	Technology	Page(s)
indicate whether *line breaks* can occur before and after the current flow object	`suppress-at-line-break`	XSL	621
modify *line height* for subscript or superscript characters	`line-height-shift-adjustment`	XSL	539
specify the way in which a *linefeed* character is treated	`linefeed-treatment`	XSL	537
set a font's *line-spacing height above* the baseline	`font-height-override-before`	XSL	485
set a font's *line-spacing height below* the baseline	`font-height-override-after`	XSL	484
specify the number of *lines* that must be left at the bottom of a page	`orphans`	CSS2, XSL	561
set strategy for positioning adjacent *lines*	`line-stacking-strategy`	XSL	540
indicate a *link* or graphic href	`href`	XSL	515
contain a *list-item body*	`fo:list-item-body`	XSL	478, 751
set a *list-item image* to be used as a bullet preceding a list	`list-style-image`	CSS2	
include a *list-item label*	`fo:list-item-label`	XSL	479, 751
set the distance between the end of a *list-item label* start indent and a list item	`provisional-distance-between-starts`	XSL	586, 751
set the distance between the end of a *list-item label* and a list item	`provisional-label-separation`	XSL	587, 751
set a *list number or bullet type*	`list-style-type`	CSS2	
format a *list or list item*	`fo:list-block`	XSL	477, 751
control a *list style*	`list-style`	CSS2	
return a *list's* label-end value	`label-end()`	XSL	530

If you want to...	Use this production or element	Technology	Page(s)
specify a *list's position*	list-style-position	CSS2	
represent a *literal*	Literal	XSL	541
specify a set of *location path patterns*	Pattern	XSLT	326
specify a *location-path pattern*	LocationPath Pattern	XSLT	325
name a *logical* or mathematical operator	OperatorName	XSL	560
return the *lowest integer*	ceiling()	XSL	439
control a bottom *margin* or set its size	margin-bottom	CSS2, XSL	543, 752
control left *margin* or set its size	margin-left	CSS2, XSL	544, 752
control the right *margin* or set its size	margin-right	CSS2, XSL	545, 752
control top *margin* or set its size	margin-top	CSS2, XSL	546, 752
control or size all *margins*	margin	CSS2, XSL	542
create and specify the distance between a *marker box's* borders and the associated principal box	marker-offset	CSS2	
specify that certain fo:markers whose children are retrieved must have a *marker-class-name*	retrieve-class-name	XSL	595
name a page *master*	master-name	XSL	547, 752
name a logical or *mathematical* operator	OperatorName	XSL	560
list *mathematical operators*	Operator	XSL	559
return the *maximum* of two numeric arguments	max()	XSL	548
specify a *maximum and minimum* leader length	leader-length	XSL	533

Continued

If you want to...	Use this production or element	Technology	Page(s)
specify the *maximum height* of an element	max-height	CSS2, XSL	548
specify the *maximum width* of an element	max-width	CSS2, XSL	550
specify different styles for different types of *media output*	@media	CSS2	
send a *message template* from the XSLT processor	xsl:message	XSLT	346
set a viewing area in the *middle* of an fo:region-body	fo:region-body	XSL	496
return the *minimum* of two numeric arguments	min()	XSL	552
specify the *minimum height* of an element	min-height	CSS2, XSL	552
specify the *minimum width* of an element	min-width	CSS2, XSL	553
find a *modulus*, multiply, or divide expressions	MultiplicativeExpr	XSL	554
switch between *multiple properties*	fo:multi-properties	XSL	480, 754
multiply, divide, or find a modulus for expressions	MultiplicativeExpr	XSL	554
insert a *multiply operator*	MultiplyOperator	XSL	555
name or identify the current region	region-name	XSL	590
provide a function *NCName*	FunctionName	XSL	512
return the value of a property from the *nearest-ancestor* formatting object	from-nearest-specified-value()	XSL	509
negate an expression	UnaryExpr	XSL	633
produce a template based on *no true condition*	xsl:otherwise	XSLT	350, 753
contain a floating *note*	fo:footnote	XSL	472
format and insert a *number* in the result tree	xsl:number	XSLT	348, 751

If you want to...	Use this production or element	Technology	Page(s)
represent a *number*	Number	XSL	555
return a *number* as a formatted string	format-number()	XSLT	322
represent an absolute or relative floating-point *number* in an expression	Numeric	XSL	558
set a relative *number*	RelativeNumeric	XSL	593
indicate the *number* of the current page	fo:page-number	XSL	492
specify the *number* of the first column in a table-cell span	column-number	XSL	445, 753
set the *number* of the first page number in a page sequence	initial-page-number	XSL	524
specify the *number of lines* left at the top of a page	widows	CSS2, XSL	641
set a *number type* preceding list items	list-style-type	CSS2	
define how user agent should "speak" *numbers*	speak-numeral	CSS2, XSL	615
select a page-master depending on its *odd* or even position in the page sequence	odd-or-even	XSL	559
insert a multiply *operator*	MultiplyOperator	XSL	555
specify whether to *omit table footer* at a break	table-omit-footer-at-break	XSL	624
specify whether to *omit table header* at a break	table-omit-header-at-break	XSL	624
name a logical or mathematical *operator*	OperatorName	XSL	560
list mathematical *operators*	Operator	XSL	559
orient and set page-box dimensions	size	CSS2, XSL	605

Continued

If you want to...	Use this production or element	Technology	Page(s)
orient horizontally displayed text glyphs	glyph-orientation-horizontal	XSL	512
orient a selection with its box	reference-orientation	XSL	588
orient vertically displayed text glyphs	glyph-orientation-vertical	XSL	513
specify the *orphan lines* that must be left at the bottom of a page	orphans	CSS2, XSL	561
set all *outline colors*	outline-color	CSS2	
set all *outline properties*	outline	CSS2	
set all *outline styles*	outline-style	CSS2	
control all *outline widths*	outline-width	CSS2	
create result-tree *output*	xsl:output	XSLT	351
specify whether and how the contents of a box *overflow*	overflow	CSS2, XSL	561
override a template rule in an imported style sheet	xsl:apply-imports	XSLT	329
specify a user style to *override* an author's style rule or vice-versa	!important	CSS2	
override bidirectionality writing direction for an inline script	fo:bidi-override	XSL	465
control or size all *padding*	padding	CSS2, XSL	562
control or size bottom *padding*	padding-bottom	CSS2, XSL	566
control or size ending-edge *padding*	padding-end	XSL	567
control or set leading-edge *padding*	padding-before	XSL	564
control or size left *padding*	padding-left	CSS2, XSL	568
control or size right *padding*	padding-right	CSS2, XSL	569
control or size starting-edge *padding*	padding-start	XSL	570

If you want to...	Use this production or element	Technology	Page(s)
control or size top *padding*	padding-top	CSS2, XSL	571
control or size trailing-edge *padding*	padding-after	XSL	564
specify the *page-background color*	background-color	CSS2, XSL	381
specify whether the background image is fixed or scrolls in the *page-background*	background-attachment	CSS2, XSL	380
specify a *page-background image*	background-image	CSS2, XSL	382
set the *page-background image position*	background-position	CSS2, XSL	383
specify one or more *page-background properties*	background	CSS2, XSL	379
set dimensions, orientation, and margins of a *page-box*	@page	CSS2	
size *page-box dimensions and orientation*	size	CSS2, XSL	605
insert a *page break after* a particular flow object appears	break-after	XSL	435
insert a *page break after* the current element	page-break-after	CSS2, XSL	572
insert a *page break before* the current flow object appears	break-before	XSL	436
insert a *page break before* the current element	page-break-before	CSS2, XSL	573
avoids a *page break inside* the current element	page-break-inside	CSS2, XSL	574
specify the *page-foreground color*	color	CSS2, XSL	411, 750
determine the *page height*	page-height	XSL	575, 752
name a *page master*	master-name	XSL	547, 752

Continued

If you want to...	Use this production or element	Technology	Page(s)
lay out a set of pages from a single *page master*	`fo:single-page-master-reference`	XSL	502
select a *page-master* depending on its odd or even position in the page sequence	`odd-or-even`	XSL	559
select a *page-master* depending on its position in the page sequence	`page-position`	XSL	575, 752
name a *page-master* that is used if certain conditions are true	`fo:conditional-page-master-reference`	XSL	469
set the *page-masters* used to produce a page sequence	`fo:page-sequence-master`	XSL	494
indicate the *page number*	`fo:page-number`	XSL	492
set the first *page number* in a page sequence	`initial-page-number`	XSL	524
give the *page-number citation*	`fo:page-number-citation`	XSL	492
set a *page-sequence boundary*	`retrieve-boundary`	XSL	594
produce a *page sequence* of recurring occurrences of alternate page masters	`fo:repeatable-page-master-alternatives`	XSL	498
produce a *page sequence* of recurring occurrences of a particular page master	`fo:repeatable-page-master-reference`	XSL	499
set *page-sequence* page masters	`fo:page-sequence-master`	XSL	494
name a *page type* on which the current element should appear	`page`	CSS2	
specify the *page width*	`page-width`	XSL	576
format a set of *pages*	`fo:page-sequence`	XSL	493
limit the *pages* in a page sequence	`maximum-repeats`	XSL	549
provide *parameters* for templates	`xsl:with-param`	XSLT	366

If you want to...	Use this production or element	Technology	Page(s)
return the value of a property from a *parent* formatting object	`from-parent()`	XSL	510
specify a *pattern* for a leader	`leader-pattern`	XSL	533
set the *pattern* for a rule	`rule-style`	XSL	599
construct a *pattern* from a mix of axis specifier, child, attribute, or separator	`ChildOrAttribute AxisSpecifier`	XSLT	320
locate a node with a *pattern of identifiers and keys*	`IDKeyPattern`	XSLT	324
specify a *pattern of location paths*	`LocationPath Pattern`	XSLT	325
specify a *pattern of steps* to locate a node	`StepPattern`	XSLT	328
specify a set of location path *patterns*	`Pattern`	XSLT	326
specify a *pattern of relative paths* to locate a node	`RelativePath Pattern`	XSLT	327
pause after and/or before speaking an element	`pause`	CSS2, XSL	577
pause after speaking an element	`pause-after`	CSS2, XSL	578
pause before speaking an element	`pause-before`	CSS2, XSL	579
symbolize a number followed by a *percent-sign symbol*	`Percent`	XSL	580
set the *pitch* of a speaking-voice	`pitch`	CSS2, XSL	580
vary the *pitch range* of a speaking voice	`pitch-range`	CSS2, XSL	581
play a background sound while speaking an element's content	`play-during`	CSS2, XSL	582

Continued

If you want to...	Use this production or element	Technology	Page(s)
set the *point size*	`font-size`	CSS2, XSL	486, 750
position the current element	`position`	CSS2, XSL	583
specify a starting *position* for a background image	`background-position`	CSS2, XSL	383
select a page-master depending on its *position* in the page sequence	`page-position`	XSL	575, 752
set the *precedence* of regions in a simple-page-master	`precedence`	XSL	584
preserve whitespace in a list of elements	`xsl:preserve-space`	XSLT	354
keep *previous output* with selected output	`keep-with-previous`	XSL	528
symbolize a *primary expression*	`PrimaryExpr`	XSL	585
create a *processing-instruction node*	`xsl:processing-instruction`	XSLT	354
switch between multiple *properties*	`fo:multi-properties`	XSL	480, 754
set an alternate *properties set* for formatting	`fo:multi-property-set`	XSL	480, 754
find a *property value*	`merge-property-values()`	XSL	551, 754
return the inherited *property value*	`inherited-property-value()`	XSL	523
find the *proportional factor units* of the proportional measure	`proportional-column-width()`	XSL	585
define how *punctuation* is spoken	`speak-punctuation`	CSS2, XSL	615
specify pairs of *quotation marks* that open and close a quotation	`quotes`	CSS2	
vary the *range* of pitch for a voice	`pitch-range`	CSS2, XSL	581

If you want to...	Use this production or element	Technology	Page(s)
produce a page sequence of *recurring* occurrences of alternate page masters	`fo:repeatable-page-master-alternatives`	XSL	498
produce a page sequence of *recurring* occurrences of a particular page master	`fo:repeatable-page-master-reference`	XSL	499
name or identify the current *region*	`region-name`	XSL	590
generate up to five document page *regions*	`fo:simple-page-master`	XSL	501, 752
set the precedence of *regions* in a simple-page-master	`precedence`	XSL	584
indicate a *relative length* and name a unit of measure	`RelativeLength`	XSL	592
set a *relative number*	`RelativeNumeric`	XSL	593
specify a pattern of *relative paths* to locate a node	`RelativePath Pattern`	XSLT	327
determine the relative position of an object to other objects	`relative-position`	XSL	591
represent the *relative unit of measure*	`RelativeUnitName`	XSL	593
specify your own color-profile *rendering intent*	`rendering-intent`	XSL	594
cause a page-background image to *repeat* a number of times	`background-repeat`	CSS2, XSL	386
repeat the table-column property	`number-columns-repeated`	XSL	556
represent a *reserved keyword*	`Keyword`	XSL	529

Continued

If you want to...	Use this production or element	Technology	Page(s)
indicate whether the first fo:multi-case is *restored* when fo:multi-switch is concealed by ancestor	auto-restore	XSL	377
create *result-tree output*	xsl:output	XSLT	351
retrieve the position of a retrieve-marker	retrieve-position	XSL	595
specify an *RFC-1766 country code*	country	XSL	448
specify an *RFC-1766 language code*	language	XSL	530
return an *RGB color*	rgb()	XSL	596
identify an *RGB hexadecimal color code*	Color	XSL	443
specify the *richness* of a voice	richness	CSS2, XSL	597
set the *right-border color* of a box	border-right-color	XSL	418
set all *right-border properties*	border-right	CSS2, XSL	416
set the *right-border style* of a box	border-right-style	XSL	419
set the *right-border width* of a box	border-right-width	CSS2, XSL	420
control the *right margin* or set its size	margin-right	CSS2, XSL	545, 752
control an element's *right offset position*	right	CSS2, XSL	597
control or size *right padding*	padding-right	CSS2, XSL	569
set the *right-page-box style* of a document	:right	CSS2	
specify the *role* of a formatting object for alternate document processors	role	XSL	598
indicate the *root node* of the current XSL result tree	fo:root	XSL	500

If you want to...	Use this production or element	Technology	Page(s)
return a *rounded integer* that is closest in value to the argument	round()	XSL	599
contain properties for table *rows*	fo:table-row	XSL	507, 753
contain properties for *rows* in a table footer	fo:table-footer	XSL	506
contain properties for *rows* in a table header	fo:table-header	XSL	507
set a *rule* pattern	rule-style	XSL	599
set a *rule* thickness	rule-thickness	XSL	600
produce *running headers or footers* with fo:retrieve-marker	fo:marker	XSL	479
produce *running headers or footers* with fo:-marker	fo:retrieve-marker	XSL	499
scale an external graphic	scaling	XSL	601
define a preference when *scaling* bitmapped graphics	scaling-method	XSL	602
name a *script* for parts of an XML document	script	XSL	603
format a *set of pages*	fo:page-sequence	XSL	493
set an alternate *set of properties* for formatting	fo:multi-property-set	XSL	480, 754
apply one or more *shadow effects* to text	text-shadow	CSS2, XSL	630
shift the baseline of a sentence away from the default location toward superscript or subscript	baseline-shift	XSL	388
indicate the start of a *simple link*	fo:simple-link	XSL	500, 754
lay out a set of pages from a *single page-master*	fo:single-page-master-reference	XSL	502
size and orient a page-box	size	CSS2, XSL	605

Continued

If you want to...	Use this production or element	Technology	Page(s)
set a *small-cap font variant*	font-variant	CSS2, XSL	490
sort selected nodes	xsl:sort	XSLT	355
play a background *sound* while speaking an element's content	play-during	CSS2, XSL	582
point to the *source* document of a formatting-object tree	source-document	XSL	606
indicate a *source file* for a link or graphic	src	XSL	617, 750
space a cell border from adjacent table borders	border-spacing	XSL	422
insert *space after* the flow-object area	space-after	XSL	607
insert *space at the end* of an inline flow-object area	space-end	XSL	609
insert *space at the start* of an inline flow-object area	space-start	XSL	610
insert *space before* the flow-object area	space-before	XSL	608, 750
treat *spaces* and whitespace characters	space-treatment	XSL	611
set *spacing between words*	word-spacing	CSS2, XSL	643
span a number of table columns	number-columns-spanned	XSL	557
span a number of table rows	number-rows-spanned	XSL	557
span columns in a multi-column area	span	XSL	612
define how user agent should *speak* numbers	speak-numeral	CSS2, XSL	615
define how user agent should *speak* punctuation	speak-punctuation	CSS2, XSL	615
speak text	speak	CSS2, XSL	613

If you want to...	Use this production or element	Technology	Page(s)
pause after and/or before *speaking* an element	pause	CSS2, XSL	577
pause after *speaking* an element	pause-after	CSS2, XSL	578
pause before *speaking* an element	pause-before	CSS2, XSL	579
control the *speaking rate*	speech-rate	CSS2, XSL	616
set the pitch of a *speaking* voice	pitch	CSS2, XSL	580
specify indention at the starting edge of the current formatting object box	start-indent	XSL	618, 750
set the *stack level* of the current box in a stack of elements	z-index	CSS2, XSL	648
set strategy for *stacking* adjacent lines	line-stacking-strategy	XSL	540
set the *starting-edge color* of a block or inline area border	border-start-color	XSL	422
control or size *starting-edge padding*	padding-start	XSL	570
set the *starting-edge style* of a block or inline area border	border-start-style	XSL	424
set the *starting-edge width* of a block or inline area border	border-start-width	XSL	425
indicate the *starting state* of the fo:multi-case formatting object	starting-state	XSL	619
indicate whether the current table cell *starts a table row*	starts-row	XSL	619
set the *static content* for one or more regions	fo:static-content	XSL	502

Continued

If you want to...	Use this production or element	Technology	Page(s)
specify a pattern of *steps* to locate a node	StepPattern	XSLT	328
specify the highest *stress* (inflection) level in a voice	stress	CSS2, XSL	620
select a *stretched or condensed font*	font-stretch	CSS2, XSL	488
indicate whether *strikethrough* characters are drawn over spaces	score-spaces	XSL	602
represent a *string*	Literal	XSL	541
return a *string identifier* for a node in the first node-set	generate-id()	XSLT	324
strip whitespace from a list of elements	xsl:strip-space	XSLT	357
style the bottom-border of a box	border-bottom-style	CSS2, XSL	403
style the ending edge of a block or inline area border	border-end-style	XSL	409
style the leading edge of a block or inline area border	border-before-style	XSL	398
style the right border of a box	border-right-style	XSL	419
style the starting edge of a block or inline area border	border-start-style	XSL	424
style the top border of a box	border-top-style	CSS2, XSL	430
style the trailing edge of a block or inline area border	border-after-style	XSL	395
indicate an XSL *style sheet synonym*	xsl:transform	XSLT	361
set all outline *styles*	outline-style	CSS2	
adjust *subscript or superscript* line height	line-height-shift-adjustment	XSL	539

If you want to...	Use this production or element	Technology	Page(s)
switch between two or more properties	`fo:multi-properties`	XSL	480, 754
switch to a particular `fo:multi-case` formatting object	`switch-to`	XSL	621
switch to one of several formatting-object subtrees	`fo:multi-switch`	XSL	481
indicate a *synonym* of an XSL style sheet	`xsl:transform`	XSLT	361
return a *system color*	`system-color()`	XSL	622
return an object that indicates the value of the *system properties*	`system-property()`	XSLT	328
format a particular *table*	`fo:table`	XSL	583, 752
format a particular *table and caption*	`fo:table-and-caption`	XSL	504
format a particular *table body*	`fo:table-body`	XSL	504, 752
apply block-level formats to a *table caption*	`fo:table-caption`	XSL	505
contain content for a *table cell*	`fo:table-cell`	XSL	505, 753
set a *table-cell border collapse* or separation	`border-collapse`	CSS2, XSL	405
specify *table-cell border spacing* from adjacent cells	`border-spacing`	CSS2, XSL	422
specify *table-cell headers* are spoken	`speak-header`	CSS2, XSL	614
contain properties for cells in a *table column*	`fo:table-column`	XSL	506, 752
repeat the *table-column property*	`number-columns-repeated`	XSL	556
span a number of *table columns*	`number-columns-spanned`	XSL	557
span *table columns* in a multi-column area	`span`	XSL	612

Continued

If you want to...	Use this production or element	Technology	Page(s)
contain properties for *table-footer rows*	fo:table-footer	XSL	506
specify whether to omit *table footer* at a break	table-omit-footer-at-break	XSL	624
specify whether to omit *table header* at a break	table-omit-header-at-break	XSL	624
contain properties for *table-header rows*	fo:table-header	XSL	507
specify a *table layout*	table-layout	CSS2, XSL	623, 752
contain properties for *table rows*	fo:table-row	XSL	507, 753
span a number of *table rows*	number-rows-spanned	XSL	557
indicate the fo:simple-link *target resource*	internal-destination	XSL	526
call a *template* by name	xsl:call-template	XSLT	334, 752
specify a *template rule*	xsl:template	XSLT	358, 748
speak *text*	speak	CSS2, XSL	613
set horizontal *text alignment*	text-align	CSS2, XSL	625, 750
set *text color* for a document	color	CSS2, XSL	441, 750
specify *text direction*	direction	CSS2, XSL	453
specify one or more *text enhancements*	font-style	CSS2, XSL	489
set *text indention* of the first line	text-indent	CSS2, XSL	629
set *text-line height* from baseline to baseline	line-height	CSS2, XSL	538
create a *text node* in a template	xsl:text	XSLT	360
apply one or more *text shadow effects*	text-shadow	CSS2, XSL	630
set the *thickness* of a rule	rule-thickness	XSL	600

If you want to...	Use this production or element	Technology	Page(s)
associate a *title* with a given document	fo:title	XSL	508
toggle from one fo:multi-case to another	fo:multi-toggle	XSL	481
tokenize an expression character by character or name by name	ExprToken	XSL	460
set all *top-border properties*	border-top	CSS2, XSL	427
set the *top-border color* of a box	border-top-color	XSL	429
set the *top-border style* of a box	border-top-style	XSL	430
set the *top-border width* of a box	border-top-width	CSS2, XSL	432
control or size the *top margin*	margin-top	CSS2, XSL	546, 752
control an element's *top offset position*	top	CSS2, XSL	632
control or size *top padding*	padding-top	CSS2, XSL	571
set *top-to-bottom alignment* of the element	vertical-align	CSS2, XSL	635
set the *trailing-edge color* of a block or inline area border	border-after-color	XSL	393
control or size *trailing-edge padding*	padding-after	XSL	564
set the *trailing-edge style* of a block or inline area border	border-after-style	XSL	395
set the *trailing-edge width* of a block or inline area border	border-after-width	XSL	396
treat a linefeed character in a certain way	linefeed-treatment	XSL	537
treat spaces and whitespace characters	space-treatment	XSL	611

Continued

If you want to...	Use this production or element	Technology	Page(s)
specify one or more *typefaces*	font-family	CSS2, XSL	483
embed or override the *Unicode bidirectional algorithm* for the current element	unicode-bidi	CSS2, XSL	634
specify a *Unicode character*	character	XSL	439
represent an absolute *unit of measure*	AbsoluteUnitName	XSL	372
represent the relative *unit of measure*	RelativeUnitName	XSL	593
return the URI of the *unparsed entity* with the same name as the context node	unparsed-entity-uri	XSLT	329
apply styles to an *unvisited link*	:link	CSS2	
provide the XSLT-processor vendor's *URL*	xsl:vendor-url	XSLT	365
specify a *user style* to override an author's style rule or vice-versa	!important	CSS2	
generate text using the *value of* an expression	xsl:value-of	XSLT	362, 752
set a *variable value*	xsl:variable	XSLT	363, 754
set a *variable's default value*	xsl:param	XSLT	353
vary small-cap font characteristics	font-variant	CSS2, XSL	490
provide the XSLT-processor *vendor's name*	xsl:vendor	XSLT	364
provide the XSLT-processor *vendor's URL*	xsl:vendor-url	XSLT	365
provide the XSLT-processor *version*	xsl:version	XSLT	365
set the *vertical alignment*	vertical-align	CSS2, XSL	635

If you want to...	Use this production or element	Technology	Page(s)
specify the initial *vertical position* of a background image	background-position-vertical	XSL	385
orient *vertically displayed* text glyphs	glyph-orientation-vertical	XSL	513
set a *viewing area after* a fo:region-body	fo:region-after	XSL	495
set a *viewing area at the end* of a fo:region-body	fo:region-end	XSL	497
set a *viewing area at the start* of a fo:region-body	fo:region-start	XSL	497
set a *viewing area before* a fo:region-body	fo:region-before	XSL	496
set a *viewing area in the middle* of a fo:region-body	fo:region-body	XSL	496
specify whether a box for an element is *visible* or invisible	visibility	CSS2, XSL	636
define the *visible area* of a box	clip	CSS2, XSL	440
apply styles to a *visited link*	:visited	CSS2	
specify the richness of a *voice*	richness	CSS2, XSL	597
select a *voice family* or name	voice-family	CSS2, XSL	637
specify the median *volume* of a waveform file	volume	CSS2, XSL	638
test *when* a condition is true	xsl:when	XSLT	365, 753
control how *whitespace* is handled	white-space	CSS2, XSL	639
insert *whitespace* in an expression	ExprWhitespace	XSL	461

Continued

If you want to...	Use this production or element	Technology	Page(s)
ignore contiguous *whitespace* characters	`white-space-collapse`	XSL	640
treat spaces and *whitespace characters*	`space-treatment`	XSL	611
specify the number of *widow* paragraph-lines at the top of a page	`widows`	CSS2, XSL	641
set an element's *width*	`width`	CSS2, XSL	642
specify the page *width*	`page-width`	XSL	576
set the *width* of the bottom border of a box	`border-bottom-width`	CSS2, XSL	404
set the *width* of the column in the column-number property	`column-width`	XSL	446
set the *width* of the ending edge of a block or inline area border	`border-end-width`	XSL	410
specify the *width* of the leader pattern	`leader-pattern-width`	XSL	533
set the *width* of the leading edge of a block or inline area border	`border-before-width`	XSL	399
set the *width* of the right border	`border-right-width`	CSS2, XSL	420
set the *width* of the starting edge of a block or inline area border	`border-start-width`	XSL	425
set the *width* of the top border of a box	`border-top-width`	CSS2, XSL	432
set the *width* of the trailing edge of a block or inline area border	`border-after-width`	XSL	396
specify the *width extent* of the box	`extent`	XSL	461
control all outline *widths*	`outline-width`	CSS2	
set *word spacing*	`word-spacing`	CSS2, XSL	643

If you want to...	Use this production or element	Technology	Page(s)
wrap inherited properties for a group of formatting-objects	`fo:wrapper`	XSL	508, 754
wrap lines in a box	`wrap-option`	XSL	644
set the *writing direction* for text	`writing-mode`	XSL	645
process the *XML language code* for character data	`xml:lang`	XSL	647
create attributes for elements produced by *xsl:element*	`xsl:attribute`	XSLT	331, 752
import an *XSLT style sheet*	`xsl:import`	XSLT	344
indicate an *XSL style sheet*	`xsl:stylesheet`	XSLT	357
indicate an *XSL style sheet synonym*	`xsl:transform`	XSLT	361
choose the first *xsl:when condition* that is true	`xsl:choose`	XSLT	335, 753

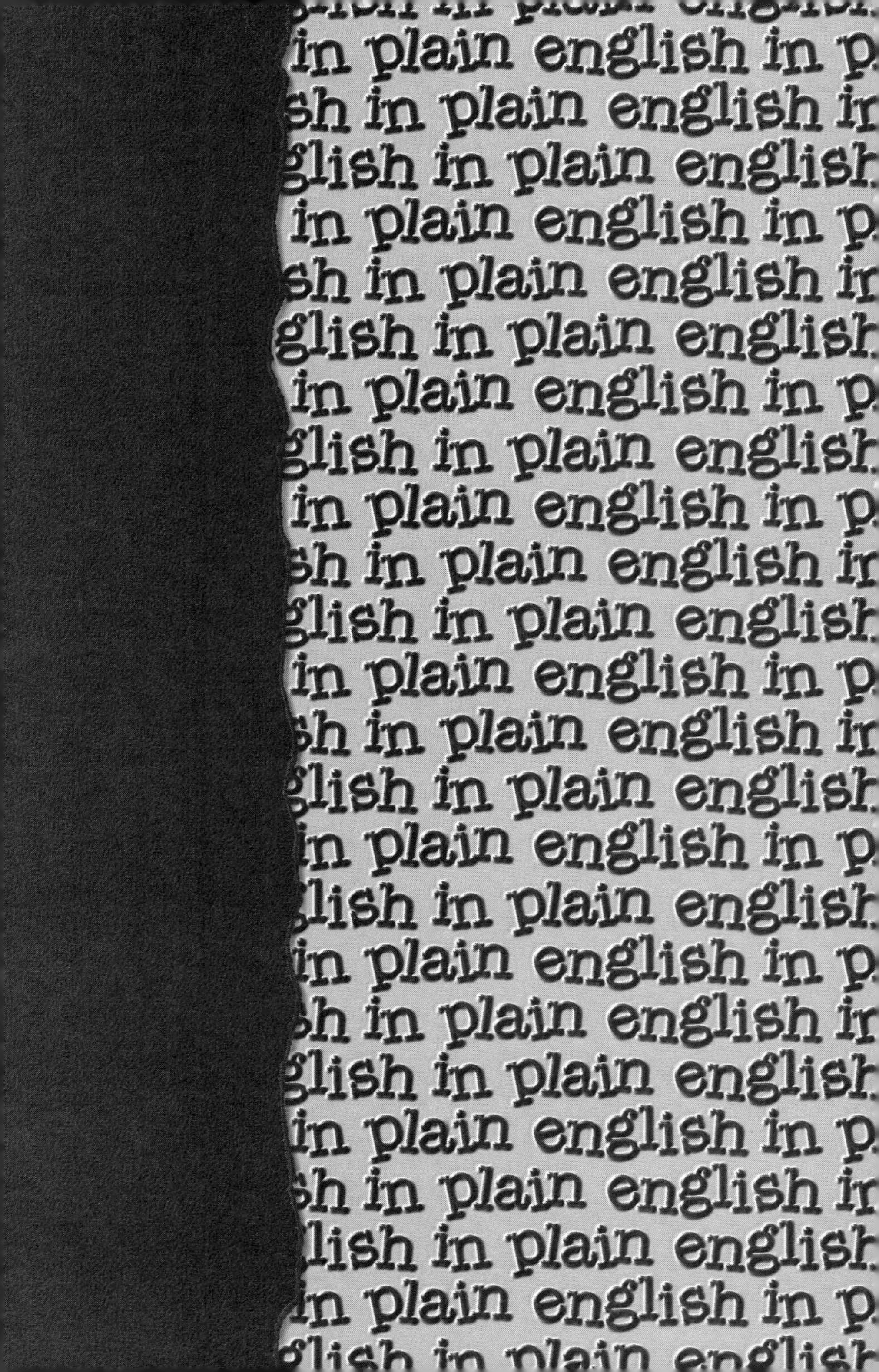
in plain english

Style Sheets A to Z

This reference is a table of the at-rules, properties, selectors, productions, and attributes covered comprehensively in "XSLT Component" (see page 319), and "XSL Style Sheet Syntax" (see page 369). The following table is an alphabetically arranged master list of CSS2 at-rules, properties, selectors, and descriptors; XSLT functions, expressions and elements; and XSL formatting objects, properties, and expressions, productions and attributes; as well as the pages on which they appear in Part 2, "Style Sheet Reference," and Part 3, "XML Tutorial."

● **NOTE**

The CSS2 technology is not covered in this book. Any reference to CSS2 in this part of the book simply points out the origin of a particular styling property. To learn more about cascading style sheets and specific style-sheet properties, refer to *XHTML In Plain English*, also written by Sandra E. Eddy and published by IDG Books Worldwide.

Element	Technology	Page(s)
*/	CSS2	
/*	CSS2	
|	CSS2	
~	CSS2	
=	CSS2	
abs()	XSL	370
AbsoluteLength	XSL	371
AbsoluteNumeric	XSL	371
absolute-position	XSL	372
AbsoluteUnitName	XSL	372
:active	CSS2	
active-state	XSL	373, 754
AdditiveExpr	XSL	374
:after	CSS2	
alignment-adjust	XSL	375
AlphaOrDigits	XSL	376
Argument	XSL	376
auto-restore	XSL	377
azimuth	CSS2	
azimuth	XSL	377
background	CSS2	
background	XSL	379
background-attachment	CSS2	
background-attachment	XSL	380
background-color	CSS2	
background-color	XSL	381
background-image	CSS2	

Element	Technology	Page(s)
background-image	XSL	382
background-position	CSS2	
background-position	XSL	383
background-position-horizontal	XSL	385
background-position-vertical	XSL	385
background-repeat	CSS2	
background-repeat	XSL	386
baseline-identifier	XSL	387
baseline-shift	XSL	388
:before	CSS2	
blank-or-not-blank	XSL	389
block-progression-dimension	XSL	390
body-start()	XSL	391
border	CSS2	
border	XSL	392
border-after-color	XSL	393
border-after-style	XSL	395
border-after-width	XSL	396
border-before-color	XSL	397
border-before-style	XSL	398
border-before-width	XSL	399
border-bottom	CSS2	
border-bottom	XSL	400
border-bottom-color	CSS2	
border-bottom-color	XSL	402
border-bottom-style	CSS2	
border-bottom-style	XSL	403
border-bottom-width	CSS2	
border-bottom-width	XSL	404
border-collapse	CSS2	
border-collapse	XSL	405
border-color	CSS2	
border-color	XSL	406

Continued

Style Sheets A to Z

Element	Technology	Page(s)
border-end-color	XSL	408
border-end-style	XSL	409
border-end-width	XSL	410
border-left	CSS2	
border-left	XSL	411
border-left-color	CSS2	
border-left-color	XSL	413
border-left-style	CSS2	
border-left-style	XSL	414
border-left-width	CSS2	
border-left-width	XSL	415
border-right	CSS2	
border-right	XSL	416
border-right-color	CSS2	
border-right-color	XSL	418
border-right-style	CSS2	
border-right-style	XSL	419
border-right-width	CSS2	
border-right-width	XSL	420
border-separation	XSL	421
border-spacing	CSS2	
border-spacing	XSL	422
border-start-color	XSL	422
border-start-style	XSL	424
border-start-width	XSL	425
border-style	CSS2	
border-style	XSL	426
border-top	CSS2	
border-top	XSL	427
border-top-color	CSS2	
border-top-color	XSL	429
border-top-style	CSS2	
border-top-style	XSL	430
border-top-width	CSS2	

Element	Technology	Page(s)
border-top-width	XSL	432
border-width	CSS2	
border-width	XSL	432
bottom	CSS2	
bottom	XSL	434
break-after	XSL	435
break-before	XSL	436
caption-side	CSS2	
caption-side	XSL	437
case-name	XSL	438
case-title	XSL	438
ceiling()	XSL	439
character	XSL	439
@charset	CSS2	
ChildOrAttributeAxisSpecifier*	XSLT	320
clear	CSS2	
clear	XSL	440
clip	CSS2	
clip	XSL	440
color	CSS2	
color	XSL	441, 750
Color	XSL	443
color-profile-name	XSL	443
column-count	XSL	444
column-gap	XSL	444
column-number	XSL	445, 753
column-width	XSL	446
content	CSS2	
content-height	XSL	446
content-type	XSL	447
content-width	XSL	448
counter-increment	CSS2	
counter-reset	CSS2	

Continued

Style Sheets A to Z

Element	Technology	Page(s)
country	XSL	448
cue	CSS2	
cue	XSL	449
cue-after	CSS2	
cue-after	XSL	450
cue-before	CSS2	
cue-before	XSL	451
current()	XSLT	321
cursor	CSS2	
destination-placement-offset	XSL	452
Digits	XSL	452
direction	CSS2	
direction	XSL	453
display	CSS2	
display-align	XSL	454
document()	XSLT	321
dominant-baseline	XSL	455
element-available()	XSLT	322
elevation	CSS2	
elevation	XSL	456
empty-cells	CSS2	
empty-cells	XSL	457
end-indent	XSL	457, 750
ends-row	XSL	458
EnumerationToken	XSL	459
Expr	XSL	459
ExprToken	XSL	460
ExprWhitespace	XSL	461
extent	XSL	461
external-destination	XSL	462, 754
:first	CSS2	
:first-child	CSS2	
:first-letter	CSS2	
:first-line	CSS2	

Style Sheets A to Z

Element	Technology	Page(s)
float	CSS2	
float	XSL	463
FloatingPointNumber	XSL	463
floor()	XSL	464
flow-name	XSL	465
fo:bidi-override	XSL	465
fo:block	XSL	466, 748
fo:block-container	XSL	467
fo:character	XSL	467
fo:color-profile	XSL	468
fo:conditional-page-master-reference	XSL	469
:focus	CSS2	
fo:declarations	XSL	469
fo:external-graphic	XSL	470, 750
fo:float	XSL	471
fo:flow	XSL	471
fo:footnote	XSL	472
fo:footnote-body	XSL	472
fo:initial-property-set	XSL	473, 750
fo:inline	XSL	473
fo:inline-container	XSL	474
fo:instream-foreign-object	XSL	475
fo:layout-master-set	XSL	475
fo:leader	XSL	476
fo:list-block	XSL	477, 751
fo:list-item	XSL	478, 751
fo:list-item-body	XSL	478, 751
fo:list-item-label	XSL	479, 751
fo:marker	XSL	479
fo:multi-case	XSL	480
fo:multi-properties	XSL	480, 754
fo:multi-property-set	XSL	480, 754

Continued

Element	Technology	Page(s)
fo:multi-switch	XSL	481
fo:multi-toggle	XSL	481
font	CSS2	
font	XSL	482
@font-face	CSS2	
font-family	CSS2	
font-family	XSL	483
font-height-override-after	XSL	484
font-height-override-before	XSL	485
font-size	CSS2	
font-size	XSL	486, 750
font-size-adjust	CSS2	
font-size-adjust	XSL	487
font-stretch	CSS2	
font-stretch	XSL	488
font-style	CSS2	
font-style	XSL	489
font-variant	CSS2	
font-variant	XSL	490
font-weight	CSS2	
font-weight	XSL	491, 750
fo:page-number	XSL	492
fo:page-number-citation	XSL	492
fo:page-sequence	XSL	493
fo:page-sequence-master	XSL	494
fo:region-after	XSL	495
fo:region-before	XSL	496
fo:region-body	XSL	496
fo:region-end	XSL	497
fo:region-start	XSL	497
fo:repeatable-page-master-alternatives	XSL	498
fo:repeatable-page-master-reference	XSL	499
fo:retrieve-marker	XSL	499

Element	Technology	Page(s)
force-page-count	XSL	494
format-number()	XSLT	322
fo:root	XSL	500
fo:simple-link	XSL	500, 754
fo:simple-page-master	XSL	501, 752
fo:single-page-master-reference	XSL	502
fo:static-content	XSL	502
fo:table	XSL	503, 752
fo:table-and-caption	XSL	504
fo:table-body	XSL	504, 752
fo:table-caption	XSL	505
fo:table-cell	XSL	505, 753
fo:table-column	XSL	506, 752
fo:table-footer	XSL	506
fo:table-header	XSL	507
fo:table-row	XSL	507, 753
fo:title	XSL	508
fo:wrapper	XSL	508, 754
from-nearest-specified-value()	XSL	509
from-parent()	XSL	510
from-table-column()	XSL	510
function-available()	XSLT	323
FunctionCall	XSL	511
FunctionName	XSL	512
generate-id()	XSLT	324
glyph-orientation-horizontal	XSL	512
glyph-orientation-vertical	XSL	513
height	CSS2	
height	XSL	514
:hover	CSS2	
href	XSL	515

Style Sheets A to Z

Continued

Element	Technology	Page(s)
hyphenate	XSL	516
hyphenation-character	XSL	517
hyphenation-keep	XSL	517
hyphenation-ladder-count	XSL	518
hyphenation-push-character-count	XSL	519
hyphenation-remain-character-count	XSL	520
icc-color()	XSL	521
id	XSL	521
IdKeyPattern	XSLT	324
!important	CSS2	
indicate-destination	XSL	523
inherited-property-value()	XSL	523
initial-page-number	XSL	524
inline-progression-dimension	XSL	525
internal-destination	XSL	526
@import	CSS2	
keep-together	XSL	526
keep-with-next	XSL	527
keep-with-previous	XSL	528
key()	XSLT	325
Keyword	XSL	529
label-end()	XSL	530
:lang	CSS2	
language	XSL	530
last-line-end-indent	XSL	531
leader-alignment	XSL	532
leader-length	XSL	533
leader-pattern	XSL	533
leader-pattern-width	XSL	533
left	CSS2	
left	XSL	535
:left	CSS2	
letter-spacing	CSS2	

Style Sheets A to Z

Element	Technology	Page(s)
letter-spacing	XSL	535
linefeed-treatment	XSL	537
line-height	CSS2	
line-height	XSL	538
line-height-shift-adjustment	XSL	539
line-stacking-strategy	XSL	540
:link	CSS2	
list-style	CSS2	
list-style-image	CSS2	
list-style-position	CSS2	
list-style-type	CSS2	
Literal	XSL	541
LocationPathPattern*	XSLT	325
margin	CSS2	
margin	XSL	542
margin-bottom	CSS2	
margin-bottom	XSL	543, 752
margin-left	CSS2	
margin-left	XSL	544, 752
margin-right	CSS2	
margin-right	XSL	545, 752
margin-top	CSS2	
margin-top	XSL	546, 752
marker-class-name	XSL	547
marker-offset	CSS2	
marks	CSS2	
master-name	XSL	547, 752
max()	XSL	548
max-height	CSS2	
max-height	XSL	548
maximum-repeats	XSL	549
max-width	CSS2	

Style Sheets A to Z

Continued

Element	Technology	Page(s)
max-width	XSL	550
@media	CSS2	
merge-property-values()	XSL	551, 754
min()	XSL	552
min-height	CSS2	
min-height	XSL	552
min-width	CSS2	
min-width	XSL	553
MultiplicativeExpr	XSL	554
MultiplyOperator	XSL	555
Number	XSL	555
number-columns-repeated	XSL	556
number-columns-spanned	XSL	557
number-rows-spanned	XSL	557
Numeric	XSL	558
odd-or-even	XSL	559
Operator	XSL	559
OperatorName	XSL	560
orphans	CSS2	
orphans	XSL	561
outline	CSS2	
outline-color	CSS2	
outline-style	CSS2	
outline-width	CSS2	
overflow	CSS2	
overflow	XSL	561
padding	CSS2	
padding	XSL	562
padding-after	XSL	564
padding-before	XSL	564
padding-bottom	CSS2	
padding-bottom	XSL	566
padding-end	XSL	567
padding-left	CSS2	

Element	Technology	Page(s)
padding-left	XSL	568
padding-right	CSS2	
padding-right	XSL	569
padding-start	XSL	570
padding-top	CSS2	
padding-top	XSL	571
page	CSS2	
@page	CSS2	
page-break-after	CSS2	
page-break-after	XSL	572
page-break-before	CSS2	
page-break-before	XSL	573
page-break-inside	CSS2	
page-break-inside	XSL	574
page-height	XSL	575, 752
page-position	XSL	575, 752
page-width	XSL	576
Pattern*	XSLT	326
pause	CSS2	
pause	XSL	577
pause-after	CSS2	
pause-after	XSL	578
pause-before	CSS2	
pause-before	XSL	579
Percent	XSL	580
pitch	CSS2	
pitch	XSL	580
pitch-range	CSS2	
pitch-range	XSL	581
play-during	CSS2	
play-during	XSL	582
position	CSS2	
position	XSL	583

Continued

Style Sheets A to Z

Element	Technology	Page(s)
precedence	XSL	584
PrimaryExpr	XSL	585
proportional-column-width()	XSL	585
provisional-distance-between-starts	XSL	586, 751
provisional-label-separation	XSL	586, 751
quotes	CSS2	
reference-orientation	XSL	588
ref-id	XSL	589
region-name	XSL	590
relative-align	XSL	591
RelativeLength	XSL	592
RelativeNumeric	XSL	593
RelativePathPattern	XSLT	327
relative-position	XSL	591
RelativeUnitName	XSL	593
rendering-intent	XSL	594
retrieve-boundary	XSL	594
retrieve-class-name	XSL	595
retrieve-position	XSL	595
rgb()	XSL	596
richness	CSS2	
richness	XSL	597
right	XSL	597
right	CSS2	
:right	CSS2	
role	XSL	598
round()	XSL	599
rule-style	XSL	599
rule-thickness	XSL	600
scaling	XSL	601
scaling-method	XSL	602
score-spaces	XSL	602
script	XSL	603
show-destination	XSL	604, 754

Element	Technology	Page(s)
size	CSS2	
size	XSL	605
source-document	XSL	606
space-after	XSL	607
space-before	XSL	608, 750
space-end	XSL	609
space-start	XSL	610
space-treatment	XSL	611
span	XSL	612
speak	CSS2	
speak	XSL	613
speak-header	CSS2	
speak-header	XSL	614
speak-numeral	CSS2	
speak-numeral	XSL	615
speak-punctuation	CSS2	
speak-punctuation	XSL	615
speech-rate	CSS2	
speech-rate	XSL	616
src	XSL	617,750
start-indent	XSL	618
starting-state	XSL	619
starts-row	XSL	619
StepPattern	XSLT	328
stress	CSS2	
stress	XSL	620
suppress-at-line-break	XSL	621
switch-to	XSL	621
system-color()	XSL	622
system-font()	XSL	623
system-property()	XSLT	328
table-layout	CSS2	
table-layout	XSL	623, 752

Style Sheets A to Z

Continued

Element	Technology	Page(s)
table-omit-footer-at-break	XSL	624
table-omit-header-at-break	XSL	624
text-align	CSS2	
text-align	XSL	625, 750
text-align-last	XSL	626
text-decoration	CSS2	
text-decoration	XSL	628, 754
text-indent	CSS2	
text-indent	XSL	629
text-shadow	CSS2	
text-shadow	XSL	630
text-transform	CSS2	
text-transform	XSL	631
top	XSL	632
top	CSS2	
treat-as-word-space	XSL	633
UnaryExpr	XSL	633
unicode-bidi	CSS2	
unicode-bidi	XSL	634
unparsed-entity-uri()	XSLT	329
vertical-align	CSS2	
vertical-align	XSL	635
visibility	CSS2	
visibility	XSL	636
:visited	CSS2	
voice-family	CSS2	
voice-family	XSL	637
volume	CSS2	
volume	XSL	638
white-space	CSS2	
white-space	XSL	639
white-space-collapse	XSL	640
widows	CSS2	
widows	XSL	641

Style Sheets A to Z

Element	Technology	Page(s)
width	CSS2	
width	XSL	642
word-spacing	CSS2	
word-spacing	XSL	643
wrap-option	XSL	644
writing-mode	XSL	645
xml:lang	XSL	647
xsl:apply-imports	XSLT	329
xsl:apply-templates	XSLT	330, 748
xsl:attribute	XSLT	331, 752
xsl:attribute-set	XSLT	332
xsl:call-template	XSLT	334, 752
xsl:choose	XSLT	335, 753
xsl:comment	XSLT	336
xsl:copy	XSLT	336
xsl:copy-of	XSLT	337
xsl:decimal-format	XSLT	338
xsl:element	XSLT	340
xsl:fallback	XSLT	341
xsl:for-each	XSLT	342
xsl:if	XSLT	343, 753
xsl:import	XSLT	344
xsl:include	XSLT	345
xsl:key	XSLT	345
xsl:message	XSLT	346
xsl:namespace-alias	XSLT	347
xsl:number	XSLT	348, 751
xsl:otherwise	XSLT	350, 753
xsl:output	XSLT	351
xsl:param	XSLT	353
xsl:preserve-space	XSLT	354

Continued

Style Sheets A to Z

Element	Technology	Page(s)
xsl:processing-instruction	XSLT	354
xsl:sort	XSLT	355
xsl:strip-space	XSLT	357
xsl:stylesheet	XSLT	357, 748
xsl:template	XSLT	358, 748
xsl:text	XSLT	360
xsl:transform	XSLT	361
xsl:value-of	XSLT	362, 752
xsl:variable	XSLT	363, 754
xsl:vendor	XSLT	364
xsl:vendor-url	XSLT	365
xsl:version	XSLT	365
xsl:when	XSLT	365, 753
xsl:with-param	XSLT	366, 752
z-index	CSS2	
z-index	XSL	648

Style Sheets by Category

You can style XML documents using CSS2 properties, which are composed of both CSS1 and CSS2 properties, and the XSL language, which also uses components and productions from the XSLT component of XSL.

CSS1 and CSS2 properties fall into four categories:

- **Properties**, which are the largest category, enable you to assign properties to XHTML elements.

- **Pseudo-elements** enable you to specify particular styles for the first line or first letter of a paragraph and document content that occurs before and/or after the current document.

- **Pseudo-classes** enable you to categorize elements by hierarchy or by their current status.

- **At-rules** enable you to set overall default characteristics for a document.

●—NOTE

The CSS2 technology is not covered in this book. Any reference to CSS2 in this part of the book simply points out the origin of a particular styling property. To learn more about cascading style sheets and specific style-sheet properties, refer to *XHTML In Plain English*, also written by Sandra E. Eddy and published by IDG Books Worldwide.

The XSL language is composed of productions, properties, functions, and formatting objects:

- **Expressions** enable you to construct XSL productions.
- **Properties**, which are the largest category, enable you to assign properties to XML elements. Many of these properties originated in CSS1 or CSS2 or in DSSSL-O.
- **Functions** enable you to perform calculations on expressions.
- **Formatting objects** enable you to "flow" formatted elements into assigned areas in XML documents.

This reference contains four comprehensive tables of all the CSS1 and CSS2 properties, and presents four XSL tables and two tables for XSLT productions covered in this book. To learn more about a particular production, property, function, and so forth, refer to the page numbers shown in the second column of each table.

Cascading style sheets are covered in detail in *XHTML In Plain English*, also written by Sandra E. Eddy and published by IDG Books Worldwide. In this book, the reference sections "XSLT Component" (see page 319) and "XSL Style Sheet Syntax" (see page 369) are your references for XSLT and XSL. Learn how to use XSLT and XSL in Chapter 7, "Styling Documents with XSL" (see page 735).

Table CAT-1 lists CSS elements in their categories.

Table CAT-1 *CSS Elements*

Element	Category
@charset	At-Rule
@font-face	At-Rule
@import	At-Rule
@media	At-Rule
@page	At-Rule
*/	Property
=	Property

Element	Category
~	Property
|	Property
/*	Property
azimuth	Property
background	Property
background-attachment	Property
background-color	Property
background-image	Property
background-position	Property
background-repeat	Property
border	Property
border-bottom	Property
border-bottom-color	Property
border-bottom-style	Property
border-bottom-width	Property
border-collapse	Property
border-color	Property
border-left	Property
border-left-color	Property
border-left-style	Property
border-left-width	Property
border-right	Property
border-right-color	Property
border-right-style	Property
border-right-width	Property
border-spacing	Property
border-style	Property
border-top	Property
border-top-color	Property
border-top-style	Property
border-top-width	Property
border-width	Property

Continued

Table CAT-1 *Continued*

Element	Category
bottom	Property
caption-side	Property
clear	Property
clip	Property
color	Property
content	Property
counter-increment	Property
counter-reset	Property
cue	Property
cue-after	Property
cue-before	Property
cursor	Property
direction	Property
display	Property
elevation	Property
empty-cells	Property
float	Property
font	Property
font-family	Property
font-size	Property
font-size-adjust	Property
font-stretch	Property
font-style	Property
font-variant	Property
font-weight	Property
height	Property
!important	Property
letter-spacing	Property
line-height	Property
list-style	Property
list-style-image	Property
list-style-position	Property

Element	Category
list-style-type	Property
margin	Property
margin-bottom	Property
margin-left	Property
margin-right	Property
margin-top	Property
marker-offset	Property
marks	Property
max-height	Property
max-width	Property
min-height	Property
min-width	Property
orphans	Property
outline	Property
outline-color	Property
outline-style	Property
outline-width	Property
overflow	Property
padding	Property
padding-bottom	Property
padding-left	Property
padding-right	Property
padding-top	Property
page	Property
page-break-after	Property
page-break-before	Property
page-break-inside	Property
pause	Property
pause-after	Property
pause-before	Property
pitch	Property
pitch-range	Property

Continued

Table CAT-1 *Continued*

Element	Category
play-during	Property
position	Property
quotes	Property
richness	Property
size	Property
speak	Property
speak-header	Property
speak-numeral	Property
speak-punctuation	Property
speech-rate	Property
stress	Property
table-layout	Property
text-align	Property
text-decoration	Property
text-indent	Property
text-shadow	Property
text-transform	Property
unicode-bidi	Property
vertical-align	Property
visibility	Property
voice-family	Property
volume	Property
white-space	Property
widows	Property
width	Property
word-spacing	Property
z-index	Property
:active	Pseudo-Class
:first	Pseudo-Class
:first-child	Pseudo-Class
:focus	Pseudo-Class
:hover	Pseudo-Class

Element	Category
:lang	Pseudo-Class
:left	Pseudo-Class
:link	Pseudo-Class
:right	Pseudo-Class
:visited	Pseudo-Class
:after	Pseudo-Element
:before	Pseudo-Element
:first-letter	Pseudo-Element
:first-line	Pseudo-Element

Table CAT-2 lists XSL expressions.

Table CAT-2   *XSL Expressions*

Production	Page(s)
AbsoluteLength	371
AbsoluteNumeric	371
AbsoluteUnitName	372
AdditiveExpr	374
AlphaOrDigits	376
Argument	376
Color	443
Digits	452
EnumerationToken	459
Expr	459
ExprToken	460
ExprWhitespace	461
FloatingPointNumber	463
FunctionCall	511
FunctionName	512
Keyword	529
Literal	541

Continued

Table CAT-2 *Continued*

Production	Page(s)
MultiplicativeExpr	554
MultiplyOperator	555
Number	555
Numeric	558
Operator	559
OperatorName	560
Percent	580
PrimaryExpr	585
RelativeLength	592
RelativeNumeric	593
RelativeUnitName	593
UnaryExpr	633

Table CAT-3 lists XSL properties.

Table CAT-3 *XSL Properties*

Properties	Located on These Page(s)
absolute-position	372
active-state	373, 754
alignment-adjust	375
auto-restore	377
azimuth	377
background	379
background-attachment	380
background-color	381
background-image	382
background-position	383
background-position-horizontal	385
background-position-vertical	385
background-repeat	386
baseline-identifier	387
baseline-shift	388

Properties	Located on These Page(s)
blank-or-not-blank	389
block-progression-dimension	390
border	392
border-after-color	393
border-after-style	395
border-after-width	396
border-before-color	397
border-before-style	398
border-before-width	399
border-bottom	400
border-bottom-color	402
border-bottom-style	403
border-bottom-width	404
border-collapse	405
border-color	406
border-end-color	408
border-end-style	409
border-end-width	410
border-left	411
border-left-color	413
border-left-style	414
border-left-width	415
border-right	416
border-right-color	418
border-right-style	419
border-right-width	420
border-separation	421
border-spacing	422
border-start-color	422
border-start-style	424
border-start-width	425
border-style	426

Continued

Table CAT-3 *Continued*

Properties	Located on These Page(s)
border-top	427
border-top-color	429
border-top-style	430
border-top-width	432
border-width	432
bottom	434
break-after	435
break-before	436
caption-side	437
case-name	438
case-title	438
character	439
clear	440
clip	440
color	441, 750
color-profile-name	443
column-count	444
column-gap	444
column-number	445, 753
column-width	446
content-height	446
content-type	447
content-width	448
country	448
cue	449
cue-after	450
cue-before	451
destination-placement-offset	452
direction	453
display-align	454
dominant-baseline	455
elevation	456

Properties	Located on These Page(s)
empty-cells	457
end-indent	457, 750
ends-row	458
extent	461
external-destination	462, 754
float	463
flow-name	465
font	482
font-family	483
font-height-override-after	484
font-height-override-before	485
font-size	486, 750
font-size-adjust	487
font-stretch	488
font-style	489
font-variant	490
font-weight	491, 750
force-page-count	494
glyph-orientation-horizontal	512
glyph-orientation-vertical	513
height	514
href	515
hyphenate	516
hyphenation-character	517
hyphenation-keep	517
hyphenation-ladder-count	518
hyphenation-push-character-count	519
hyphenation-remain-character-count	520
id	521

Continued

Table CAT-3 *Continued*

Properties	Located on These Page(s)
indicate-destination	523
initial-page-number	524
inline-progression-dimension	525
internal-destination	526
keep-together	526
keep-with-next	527
keep-with-previous	528
language	530
last-line-end-indent	531
leader-alignment	532
leader-length	533
leader-pattern	533
leader-pattern-width	533
left	535
letter-spacing	535
linefeed-treatment	537
line-height	538
line-height-shift-adjustment	539
line-stacking-strategy	540
margin	542
margin-bottom	543, 752
margin-left	544, 752
margin-right	545, 752
margin-top	543 752
marker-class-name	547
master-name	547, 752
max-height	548
maximum-repeats	549
max-width	550
min-height	552
min-width	553

Properties	Located on These Page(s)
number-columns-repeated	556
number-columns-spanned	557
number-rows-spanned	557
odd-or-even	559
orphans	561
overflow	561
padding	562
padding-after	564
padding-before	564
padding-bottom	566
padding-end	567
padding-left	568
padding-right	569
padding-start	570
padding-top	571
page-break-after	572
page-break-before	573
page-break-inside	574
page-height	575, 752
page-position	575, 752
page-width	576
pause	577
pause-after	578
pause-before	579
pitch	580
pitch-range	581
play-during	582
position	583
precedence	584
provisional-distance-between-starts	586, 751
provisional-label-separation	587, 751
reference-orientation	588

Continued

Table CAT-3 *Continued*

Properties	Located on These Page(s)
ref-id	589
region-name	590
relative-align	591
relative-position	591
rendering-intent	594
retrieve-boundary	594
retrieve-class-name	595
retrieve-position	595
richness	597
right	597
role	598
rule-style	599
rule-thickness	600
scaling	601
scaling-method	602
score-spaces	602
script	603
show-destination	604, 754
size	605
source-document	606
space-after	607
space-before	608, 750
space-end	609
space-start	610
space-treatment	611
span	612
speak	613
speak-header	614
speak-numeral	615
speak-punctuation	615
speech-rate	616
src	617, 750

Properties	Located on These Page(s)
start-indent	618, 750
starting-state	619
starts-row	619
stress	620
suppress-at-line-break	621
switch-to	621
table-layout	623, 752
table-omit-footer-at-break	624
table-omit-header-at-break	624
text-align	625, 750
text-align-last	626
text-decoration	628, 754
text-indent	630
text-shadow	631
text-transform	631
top	632
treat-as-word-space	633
unicode-bidi	634
vertical-align	635
visibility	636
voice-family	637
volume	638
white-space	639
white-space-collapse	640
widows	641
width	642
word-spacing	643
wrap-option	644
writing-mode	645
xml:lang	647
z-index	648

Table CAT-4 lists XSL functions.

Table CAT-4 *XSL Functions*

Function	Located on These Page(s)
abs()	370
body-start()	391
ceiling()	439
floor()	464
from-nearest-specified-value()	509
from-parent()	510
from-table-column()	510
icc-color()	521
inherited-property-value()	523
label-end()	530
max()	548
merge-property-values()	551, 754
min()	552
proportional-column-width()	585
rgb()	596
round()	599
system-color()	622
system-font()	623

Table CAT-5 lists XSL formatting objects.

Table CAT-5 *XSL Formatting Objects*

Formatting Object	Page(s)
fo:bidi-override	465
fo:block	466, 748
fo:block-container	467
fo:character	467
fo:color-profile	468
fo:conditional-page-master-reference	469
fo:declarations	469

Formatting Object	Page(s)
fo:external-graphic	470, 750
fo:float	471
fo:flow	471
fo:footnote	472
fo:footnote-body	472
fo:initial-property-set	473, 750
fo:inline	473
fo:inline-container	474
fo:instream-foreign-object	475
fo:layout-master-set	475
fo:leader	476
fo:list-block	477, 751
fo:list-item	478, 751
fo:list-item-body	478, 751
fo:list-item-label	479, 751
fo:marker	479
fo:multi-case	480
fo:multi-properties	480, 754
fo:multi-property-set	480, 754
fo:multi-switch	481
fo:multi-toggle	481
fo:page-number	492
fo:page-number-citation	492
fo:page-sequence	493
fo:page-sequence-master	494
fo:region-after	495
fo:region-before	496
fo:region-body	496
fo:region-end	497
fo:region-start	497
fo:repeatable-page-master-alternatives	498
fo:repeatable-page-master-reference	499

Continued

Table CAT-5 *Continued*

Formatting Object	Page(s)
fo:retrieve-marker	499
fo:root	500
fo:simple-link	500, 754
fo:simple-page-master	501, 752
fo:single-page-master-reference	502
fo:static-content	502
fo:table	503, 752
fo:table-and-caption	504
fo:table-body	504, 752
fo:table-caption	505
fo:table-cell	505, 753
fo:table-column	506, 752
fo:table-footer	506
fo:table-header	507
fo:table-row	507, 753
fo:title	508
fo:wrapper	508, 754

Table CAT-6 lists XSLT expressions and elements.

Table CAT-6 *XSLT Expressions and Elements*

Expression/Element	Page(s)
ChildOrAttributeAxisSpecifier	320
IdKeyPattern	324
LocationPathPattern	325
Pattern	326
RelativePathPattern	327
StepPattern	328
xsl:apply-imports	329
xsl:apply-templates	330, 748
xsl:attribute	331, 752
xsl:attribute-set	332

Expression/Element	Page(s)
xsl:call-template	334, 752
xsl:choose	335, 753
xsl:comment	336
xsl:copy	336
xsl:copy-of	337
xsl:decimal-format	338
xsl:element	340
xsl:fallback	341
xsl:for-each	342
xsl:if	343, 753
xsl:import	344
xsl:include	345
xsl:key	345
xsl:message	346
xsl:namespace-alias	347
xsl:number	348, 751
xsl:otherwise	350 753
xsl:output	351
xsl:param	353
xsl:preserve-space	354
xsl:processing-instruction	354
xsl:sort	355
xsl:strip-space	357
xsl:stylesheet	357, 748
xsl:template	358, 748
xsl:text	360
xsl:transform	361
xsl:value-of	362, 752
xsl:variable	363, 754

Continued

Table CAT-6 *Continued*

Expression/Element	Page(s)
xsl:vendor	364
xsl:vendor-url	365
xsl:version	365
xsl:when	365
xsl:with-param	366

Table CAT-7 lists XSLT functions.

Table CAT-7 *XSLT Functions*

Function	Page(s)
current()	321
document()	321
element-available()	322
format-number()	322
function-available()	323
generate-id()	324
key()	325
system-property()	328
unparsed-entity-uri()	329

XSLT Component

Because XML is strictly markup, it is nor formatted by nature. XSL and other style sheet languages supported by XML enable a document creator or editor to format an XML document's component pages, paragraphs, and selected text. By attaching a single style sheet to all XML documents, a business can ensure an identical official style for an entire document archive and its component parts — using the same colors, fonts, font sizes, whitespace, indentations, line spacing, and margins. Professional page designers can distribute style sheet templates with predefined table, heading, and body text formats and alignments, text enhancements, and page background colors. Then an XML developer can attach the template and work only on marking up the context of a document's content; the formats and enhancements are predefined by the style sheet.

Extensible Stylesheet Language (XSL) incorporates features from other style sheet languages, such as CSS2, into a language specifically created for XML documents. XSL documents are constructed in the same way as XML documents; once you have learned how to use XML, you are well on your way to creating properly constructed XSL documents.

XSL Transformations (XSLT) is a language meant to be used with XSL. XSLT exists to transform XML documents into other XML documents using different vocabularies. While XSLT wasn't meant to be used as a total general-purpose XML transformation language, it was designed to be used independently of XSL. XSLT was also designed, however, primarily for transformations one would need to do when working with XSL.

ChildOrAttribute AxisSpecifier [6]	**Child or Attribute Axis Specifier**

Purpose
Provides an abbreviated axis specifier, child, attribute, or separator.

EBNF Syntax
```
ChildOrAttributeAxisSpecifier ::=
    AbbreviatedAxisSpecifier
    | ('child' | 'attribute') '::'
```

Standard Syntax
```
AbbreviatedAxisSpecifier
    | child | attribute ::
```

Where
- AbbreviatedAxisSpecifier (p. 182) abbreviates an axis specifier, which specifies an axis name and a predefined specifier.
- child is a successor to a particular context node. The child axis includes the children of the context node.
- attribute contains all attributes of the context node, which must be an element (to have any attributes).
- :: are characters that separate an axis name and node test.

Notes
- ChildOrAttributeAxisSpecifier is a component of the StepPattern pattern.
- ChildOrAttributeAxisSpecifier is a pattern. A *pattern* names one or more input element types in the *source tree*, which contains all the elements defined in the XML document's DTD.

Related Productions
AbbreviatedAxisSpecifier (p. 182), AxisSpecifier (p. 188), IdKeyPattern (p. 324), LocationPathPattern (p. 325), Pattern (p. 326), RelativePathPattern (p. 327), StepPattern (p. 328)

current() | Current-Node Function

Purpose
Returns a node-set that contains the current node, which is the only node in the set.

EBNF Syntax
```
node-set current()
```

Standard Syntax
```
node-set current()
```

Where
- node-set represents the returned node-set.
- current is a function-name keyword.

Note
- Do not use the current() function in a pattern.

Example
The following example is from the XSLT recommendation (http://www.w3.org/TR/xslt):

```
<xsl:value-of select="current()"/>
```

document() | Document Function

Purpose
Returns an XML document that is not the main document.

EBNF Syntax
```
node-set document(object, node-set?)
```

Standard Syntax
```
node-set document(object[, node-set])
```

Where
- node-set represents the returned node-set.
- document is a function-name keyword.
- object is the requested document.
- node-set represents the argument's node-set.

Example
The following example is from the XSLT recommendation (http://www.w3.org/TR/xslt):

```
generate-id(document("foo.xml"))
  =generate-id(document("foo.xml"))
```

XSLT Component

element-available() Element-Available Function

Purpose

Returns true or false depending on whether an instruction element is named.

EBNF Syntax

```
boolean element-available(string)
```

Standard Syntax

```
boolean element-available(string)
```

Where

- boolean is the boolean returned by the function.
- element-available is a function-name keyword.
- string is a QName of an element.

Notes

- Use element-available() with the xsl:choose and xsl:if element.
- element-available() returns a boolean value of true if the QName is the name of an instruction element.
- According to the XSLT recommendation (http://www.w3.org/TR/xslt), "A QName is expanded into an expanded-name using the namespace declarations in scope for the expression."
- If the XSLT processor does not have an implementation of a particular extension element available, then the element-available function must return false for the name of the element.

Related Elements

xsl:choose (p. 335), xsl:if (p. 343)

Related Function

function-available() (p. 323)

format-number() Format-Number Function

Purpose

Returns a number as a formatted string.

EBNF Syntax

```
string_r format-number(number, string_1, string_2?)
```

Standard Syntax

```
string_r format-number(number, string_1[, string_2])
```

Where
- string_r is the string returned by the function.
- format-number is a function-name keyword.
- *number* is a number evaluated and converted to a string by the function.
- *string_1* is a pattern string used in the conversion by the function.
- *string_2* is the QName of a decimal format used in the conversion by the function.

Note
- Do not use the currency sign (#x00A4) in *string_1*.
- The decimal format name must be a QName.

function-available() Function-Available Function

Purpose
Returns true or false depending on whether a function in the function library is named.

EBNF Syntax
```
boolean function-available(string)
```

Standard Syntax
```
boolean function-available(string)
```

Where
- *boolean* is the boolean returned by the function.
- function-available is a function-name keyword.
- *string* is a QName of a function.

Notes
- Use function-available() with the xsl:choose and xsl:if elements.
- function-available() returns a boolean value of true if the QName is the name of a function in the function library.
- According to the XSLT recommendation (http://www.w3.org/TR/xslt), "A QName is expanded into an expanded-name using the namespace declarations in scope for the expression."

Related Elements
xsl:choose (p. 335), xsl:if (p. 343)

Related Function
element-available() (p. 322)

XSLT Component

generate-id()   Generate Node ID Function

Purpose
Returns a string identifier for the node in the first node-set in the document.

EBNF Syntax
```
string_r generate-id(node-set?)
```

Standard Syntax
```
string_r generate-id([node-set])
```

Where
- *string_r* is the string returned by the function.
- generate-id is a function-name keyword.
- *node-set* represents the argument's node-set.

Notes
- The returned identifier must be a valid XML name; it must start with an alphabetic character and contain only ASCII alphanumeric characters.
- According to the XSLT recommendation (http://www.w3.org/TR/xslt), "If there is no such system property, the empty string should be returned."
- Whenever this function generates an identifier, it must *always* generate the same identifier for each node.

IdKeyPattern [3]   ID Key Pattern

Purpose
Specifies a pattern of identifiers and keys to locate a node.

EBNF Syntax
```
IdKeyPattern ::= 'id' '(' Literal ')'
    | 'key' '(' Literal ',' Literal ')'
```

Standard Syntax
```
id (Literal) |key (Literal, Literal)
```

Where
- id is a reserved keyword that indicates that an identifier pattern follows.
- key is a reserved keyword that indicates that a key pattern follows.
- (marks the start of an arguments list.
- Literal (p. 541) represents a literal, a string within quotation marks or single quote marks.

- , is a character that separates literals.
-) marks the end of an arguments list.

Note

- IdKeyPattern is a pattern. A *pattern* names one or more input element types in the *source tree*, which contains all the elements defined in the XML document's DTD.

Related Productions

ChildOrAttributeAxisSpecifier (p. 230), LocationPathPattern (p. 325), Pattern (p. 326), RelativePathPattern (p. 327), StepPattern (p. 328)

key()   Key Function

Purpose

Returns a node-set that matches a key.

EBNF Syntax

```
node-set key(string, object)
```

Standard Syntax

```
node-set key(string, object)
```

Where

- *node-set* represents the returned node-set.
- key is a function-name keyword.
- *string* is the name of the key evaluated by the function.
- *object* is the string value of the requested key.

Notes

- The key() function is similar to the XPath id() function.
- If *object* is a node-set, the processor applies the key() function to the string value of each of the nodes in the node-set.
- If *object* is not a node-set, the *string* argument is converted to a string in the same way that the string() function works.

Example

The following example is from the XSLT recommendation (http://www.w3.org/TR/xslt):

```
<xsl:key name="idkey" match="div" use=@id" />
```

LocationPathPattern [2]   Location Path Pattern

Purpose

Specifies a pattern of location paths to locate a node.

EBNF Syntax

```
LocationPathPattern ::= '/' RelativePathPattern?
    | IdKeyPattern (('/' | '//')
    RelativePathPattern)?
```

Standard Syntax

```
/[RelativePathPattern]
    | IdKeyPattern{/|//}
    [RelativePathPattern]
```

Where

- RelativePathPattern (p. 327) specifies a pattern of relative paths to locate a node.
- IdKeyPattern (p. 324) specifies a pattern of identifiers and keys to locate a node.
- / is a character that indicates the separation between one location step and another.
- // are characters that represent /descendant-or-self::node()/.

Note

- LocationPathPattern is a pattern. A *pattern* names one or more input element types in the *source tree*, which contains all the elements defined in the XML document's DTD.

Related Productions

ChildOrAttributeAxisSpecifier (p. 320), IdKeyPattern (p. 324), Pattern (p. 326), RelativePathPattern (p. 327), StepPattern (p. 328)

Pattern [1]   Pattern

Purpose

Specifies a set of location path patterns.

EBNF Syntax

```
Pattern ::= LocationPathPattern
    | Pattern '|' LocationPathPattern
```

Standard Syntax

```
LocationPathPattern | Pattern | LocationPathPattern
```

Where

- LocationPathPattern (p. 325) specifies a pattern of location paths to locate a node.
- | is a character that separates one expression from the next and indicates a choice of expression use.
- Pattern (p. 326) specifies a set of location path patterns.

Notes

- Pattern is a pattern. A *pattern* names one or more input element types in the *source tree*, which contains all the elements defined in the XML document's DTD.

Related Productions

ChildOrAttributeAxisSpecifier (p. 320), IdKeyPattern (p. 324), LocationPathPattern (p. 325), RelativePathPattern (p. 327), StepPattern (p. 328)

RelativePathPattern [4]	Relative Path Pattern

Purpose

Specifies a pattern of relative paths to locate a node.

EBNF Syntax

```
RelativePathPattern ::= StepPattern
    | RelativePathPattern '/' StepPattern
    | RelativePathPattern '//' StepPattern
```

Standard Syntax

```
StepPattern
    | RelativePathPattern/StepPattern
    | RelativePathPattern//StepPattern
```

Where

- StepPattern (p. 328) specifies a pattern of steps to locate a node
- RelativePathPattern specifies a pattern of relative paths to locate a node.
- / is a character that indicates the separation between one location step and another.
- // are characters that represent /descendant-or-self::node()/.

Notes

- RelativePathPattern is a pattern. A *pattern* names one or more input element types in the *source tree*, which contains all the elements defined in the XML document's DTD.

Related Productions

ChildOrAttributeAxisSpecifier (p. 320), IdKeyPattern (p. 324), LocationPathPattern (p. 325), Pattern (p. 326), StepPattern (p. 328)

XSLT Component

StepPattern [5]   Step Pattern

Purpose
Specifies a pattern of steps to locate a node.

EBNF Syntax
```
StepPattern ::= ChildOrAttributeAxisSpecifier NodeTest
    Predicate*
```

Standard Syntax
```
ChildOrAttributeAxisSpecifier NodeTest
    [Predicate [Predicate [...Predicate]]]
```

Where
- ChildOrAttributeAxisSpecifier (p. 320) provides an abbreviated axis specifier, child, attribute, or separator.
- NodeTest (p. 208) checks on the node type and the expanded name of the location-step nodes set.
- Predicate (p. 216) inserts a predicate expression that filters nodes in a location path.

Note
- StepPattern is a pattern. A *pattern* names one or more input element types in the *source tree*, which contains all the elements defined in the XML document's DTD.

Related Productions
ChildOrAttributeAxisSpecifier (p. 320), IdKeyPattern (p. 324), LocationPathPattern (p. 325), Pattern (p. 326), RelativePathPattern (p. 327)

system-property()   System-Property Function

Purpose
Returns an object that indicates the value of the system properties.

EBNF Syntax
```
object system-property(string)
```

Standard Syntax
```
object system-property(string)
```

Where
- *object* is the returned string, which must be a QName.
- system-property is a function-name keyword.
- *string* represents the string evaluated by the function.

Notes

- System properties include the XSLT version (xsl:version), the vendor of the XSLT processor (xsl:vendor), and the vendor's URL (xsl:vendor-url).
- According to the XSLT recommendation (http://www.w3.org/TR/xslt), "A QName is expanded into an expanded-name using the namespace declarations in scope for the expression."
- According to the XSLT recommendation (http://www.w3.org/TR/xslt), "If there is no such system property, the empty string should be returned."

Related Elements

xsl:vendor (p. 364), xsl:vendor-url (p. 365), xsl-version (p. 365)

unparsed-entity-uri() — Unparsed-Entity URI Function

Purpose

Returns the URI of the unparsed entity with the same name as the context node.

EBNF Syntax

```
string_r unparsed-entity-uri(string)
```

Standard Syntax

```
string_r unparsed-entity-uri(string)
```

Where

- *string_r* is the string returned by the function.
- unparsed-entity-uri is a function-name keyword.
- *string* represents the string evaluated by the function.

Note

- The unparsed-entity-uri() function returns an empty string if there is no unparsed entity with the same name as the context node.

xsl:apply-imports — Override Imported Rule

Purpose

Instructs the processor to override a template rule in an imported style sheet.

EBNF Syntax

```
<xsl:apply-imports />
```

Standard Syntax

```
<xsl:apply-imports />
```

XSLT Component

Notes

- The xsl: prefix points to an element in the XSLT namespace.
- This element is in the instruction category.

Example

The following example is from the XSLT recommendation (http://www.w3. org/TR/xslt):

```
<xsl:import href="doc.xsl" />

<xsl:template match="example">
  <div style="border: solid red">
    <xsl:apply-imports />
  </div>
</xsl:template>
```

Related Elements

xsl:apply-templates (p. 330), xsl:attribute (p. 331), xsl:call-template (p. 334), xsl:choose (p. 335), xsl:comment (p. 336), xsl:copy (p. 336), xsl:copy-of (p. 337), xsl:element (p. 340), xsl:fallback (p. 341), xsl: for-each (p. 342), xsl:if (p. 343), xsl:message (p. 346), xsl:number (p. 348), xsl:processing-instruction (p. 354), xsl:text (p. 360), xsl:value-of (p. 362), xsl:variable (p. 363)

---

xsl:apply-templates	Apply Template Rules

Purpose

Applies template rules to all the children of the current node.

EBNF Syntax

```
<xsl:apply-templates select = node-set-expression
  mode = qname> (xsl:sort | xsl:with-param)*
</xsl:apply-templates>
```

Standard Syntax

```
<xsl:apply-templates select = node-set-expression
  mode = qname>
  [xsl:sort | xsl:with-param[ xsl:sort
  | xsl:with-param[... xsl:sort | xsl:with-param]]]
</xsl:apply-templates>
```

Where

- select is a keyword that indicates that node-set-expression follows.
- node-set-expression is an expression that selects one or more node-sets.

- mode is a keyword that indicates that a mode for the template follows.
- qname is the QName for a mode that differentiate between two matches.
- xsl:sort is a child element that sorts selected nodes.
- xsl:with-param is a child element that provides parameters for templates.

Notes

- The xsl: prefix points to an element in the XSLT namespace.
- This element is in the instruction category.
- xsl:sort is a child of xsl:apply-templates and xsl:for-each.

Example

The following example is from the XSLT recommendation (http://www.w3.org/TR/xslt):

```
<xsl:template name="apply-templates-copy-lang">
  <xsl:for-each select="@xml:lang">
    <xsl:copy/>
  </xsl:for-each>
  <xsl:apply-templates/>
</xsl:template>
```

Related Elements

xsl:apply-imports (p. 329), xsl:attribute (p. 331), xsl:call-template (p. 334), xsl:choose (p. 335), xsl:comment (p. 336), xsl:copy (p. 336), xsl:copy-of (p. 337), xsl:element (p. 340), xsl:fallback (p. 341), xsl:for-each (p. 342), xsl:if (p. 434), xsl:message (p. 346), xsl:number (p. 348), xsl:processing-instruction (p. 354), xsl:text (p. 360), xsl:value-of (p. 362), xsl:variable (p. 363)

xsl:attribute   Create Attribute

XSLT Component

Purpose

Creates attributes for elements produced by xsl:element.

EBNF Syntax

```
<xsl:attribute name = { qname }
  [namespace = { uri-reference }]>template_content
</xsl:attribute>
```

Standard Syntax

```
<xsl:attribute name = { qname }
  [namespace = { uri-reference }]>template_content
</xsl:attribute>
```

Where

- name is a required keyword indicating that a qname follows.
- *qname*, which is the expanded qualified name of the attribute, names the attribute-value template. *qname* can also be the xmlns string.
- namespace is a keyword indicating that a uri-reference follows.
- *uri-reference*, which is the name of the namespace, names the attribute-value template. If uri-reference is not provided, the XSL processor uses the qname value.
- *template_content* is the result of processing the element.

Notes

- The xsl: prefix points to an element in the XSLT namespace.
- This element is in the instruction category.
- A namespace is a set of unique names, defined in the DTD or elsewhere. In XML, a *qualified name* is comprised of two parts: an identifier and either a URI or element name, depending on whether it is external or internal, respectively.
- Elements are the only objects that can have attributes.
- You cannot create an attribute for an element after child elements have been declared.

Example

```
<xsl:attribute-set name="head4-style">
  <xsl:attribute name="font-size">10pt</xsl:attribute>
  <xsl:attribute name="font-style">italic
  </xsl:attribute>
  <xsl:attribute name="font-weight">bold
  </xsl:attribute>
</xsl:attribute-set>
```

Related Elements

xsl:apply-imports (p. 329), xsl:apply-templates (p. 330), xsl:call-template (p. 334), xsl:choose (p. 335), xsl:comment (p. 336), xsl:copy (p. 336), xsl:copy-of (p. 337), xsl:element (p. 340), xsl:fallback (p. 341), xsl:for-each (p. 342), xsl:if (p. 343), xsl:message (p. 346), xsl:number (p. 348), xsl:processing-instruction (p. 354), xsl:text (p. 360), xsl:value-of (p. 362), xsl:variable (p. 363)

xsl:attribute-set	Attribute Set Name

Purpose

Specifies and names an attribute set.

EBNF Syntax

```
<xsl:attribute-set name = { qname }
  use-attribute-sets = qnames>xsl:attribute*
</xsl:attribute-set>
```

Standard Syntax

```
<xsl:attribute-set name = { qname }
  use-attribute-sets = qnames>
  [xsl:attribute[ xsl:attribute[... xsl:attribute]]]
</xsl:attribute-set>
```

Where

- name is a required keyword indicating that a qname follows.
- *qname*, which is the expanded qualified name of the attribute, names the attribute-value template.
- use-attribute-sets is a keyword indicating that *qnames* for attribute sets follows.
- *qnames* names the attribute-value templates in the attribute set.
- xsl:attribute are the xsl:attribute elements that are the result of processing.

Notes

- The xsl: prefix points to an element in the XSLT namespace.
- This element is in the top-level category.
- A namespace is a set of unique names, defined in the DTD or elsewhere. In XML, a *qualified name* is comporised of two parts: an identifier and either a URI or element name, depending on whether it is external or internal, respectively.
- In the xsl:attribute-set, xsl:copy, and xsl:element elements, use the use-attribute-sets attribute to list names of attribute sets. Using use-attribute-sets is the same as adding individual xsl:attribute elements for each attribute in the attribute sets.

Example

```
<xsl:attribute-set name="head4-style">
  <xsl:attribute name="font-size">10pt</xsl:attribute>
  <xsl:attribute name="font-style">italic
  </xsl:attribute>
  <xsl:attribute name="font-weight">bold
  </xsl:attribute>
</xsl:attribute-set>
```

Related Elements

xsl:decimal-format (p. 338), xsl:include (p. 345), xsl:key (p. 345), xsl:namespace-alias (p. 347), xsl:output (p. 351), xsl:param (p. 353),

XSLT Component

xsl:preserve-space (p. 354), xsl:strip-space (p. 357), xsl:template (p. 358), xsl:variable (p. 363)

---

xsl:call-template   Call Template

Purpose
Calls a template by name.

EBNF Syntax
```
<xsl:call-template name = qname>xsl:with-param*
</xsl:call-template>
```

Standard Syntax
```
<xsl:call-template name = qname>[xsl:with-param
  [ xsl:with-param[... xsl:with-param]]]
</xsl:call-template>
```

Where
- name is a required keyword that indicates that a QName follows.
- qname is the expanded qualified name of the attribute.
- xsl:with-param is a child element that provides parameters for templates.

Notes
- The xsl: prefix points to an element in the XSLT namespace.
- This element is in the instruction category.
- According to the XSLT recommendation (http://www.w3.org/ TR/xslt), "If an xsl:template element has a name attribute it may, but need not, also have a match attribute."
- The XSLT recommendation also states, "Unlike xsl:apply-template, xsl:call-template does not change the current node or current node-list.

Example
The following example is a segment from the XSLT recommendation (http://www.w3.org/TR/xslt):

```
<xsl:template match="ol//ol/li">
  <xsl:call-template name="numbered-block">
    <xsl:with-param name="format">a. </xsl:with-param>
  </xsl:call-template>
</xsl:template>
```

Related Elements

xsl:apply-imports (p. 329), xsl:apply-templates (p. 330), xsl:attribute
(p. 331), xsl:choose (p. 335), xsl:comment (p. 336), xsl:copy (p. 336),
xsl:copy-of (p. 337), xsl:element (p. 340), xsl:fallback (p. 341),
xsl:for-each (p. 342), xsl:if (p. 343), xsl:message (p. 346), xsl:number
(p. 348), xsl:processing-instruction (p. 354), xsl:text (p. 360),
xsl:value-of (p. 362), xsl:variable (p. 363)

xsl:choose   Choose One Template

Purpose

Chooses the first xsl:when condition that is true from a set of alternatives.

EBNF Syntax

```
<xsl:choose>(xsl:when+, xsl:otherwise?)</xsl:choose>
```

Standard Syntax

```
<xsl:choose>
  xsl:when[ xsl:when[ xsl:when[... xsl:when]]]
  [, xsl:otherwise]
</xsl:choose>
```

Where

- xsl:when tests if a condition is true.
- xsl:otherwise produces a template based on no condition being true.

Notes

- The xsl: prefix points to an element in the XSLT namespace.
- This element is in the instruction category.
- xsl:choose and xsl:if are used in conditional processing.
- If no xsl:otherwise is included in an xsl:choose statement, no
  template is returned.

Related Elements

xsl:apply-imports (p. 329), xsl:apply-templates (p. 330), xsl:attribute
(p. 331), xsl:call-template (p. 334), xsl:choose (p. 335), xsl:comment
(p. 336), xsl:copy (p. 336), xsl:copy-of (p. 337), xsl:element (p. 340),
xsl:fallback (p. 341), xsl:for-each (p. 342), xsl:if (p. 343), xsl:message
(p. 346), xsl:number (p. 348), xsl:otherwise (p. 350), xsl:processing-
instruction (p. 354), xsl:text (p. 360), xsl:value-of (p. 362), xsl:variable
(p. 363)

XSLT Component

xsl:comment
Create Comment

Purpose
Creates a comment node in the result tree.

EBNF Syntax
```
<xsl:comment>template</xsl:comment>
```

Standard Syntax
```
<xsl:comment>template</xsl:comment>
```

Where
- *template* is the template for the comment-node string.

Notes
- The xsl: prefix points to an element in the XSLT namespace.
- This element is in the instruction category.
- Do not include the double-dash (- -) string in a comment or end a comment with the dash (-) string.

Example
```
<xsl:comment>The beginning of the PRINT section
</xsl:comment>
```

Related Elements
xsl:apply-imports (p. 329), xsl:apply-templates (p. 330), xsl:attribute (p. 331), xsl:call-template (p. 334), xsl:choose (p. 335), xsl:copy (p. 336), xsl:copy-of (p. 337), xsl:element (p. 340), xsl:fallback (p. 341), xsl:for-each (p. 342), xsl:if (p. 343), xsl:message (p. 346), xsl:number (p. 348), xsl:processing-instruction (p. 354), xsl:text (p. 360), xsl:value-of (p. 362), xsl:variable (p. 363)

xsl:copy
Copy Node

Purpose
Copies the current node and its namespace nodes.

EBNF Syntax
```
<xsl:copy [use-attribute-sets = qnames]>
template</xsl:copy>
```

Standard Syntax
```
<xsl:copy [use-attribute-sets = qnames]>
template</xsl:copy>
```

XSLT Component

Where

- use-attribute-sets is a keyword indicating that *qnames* for attribute sets follows.
- *qnames* names the attribute-value templates in the attribute set.
- *template* is the result of processing the element.

Notes

- The xsl: prefix points to an element in the XSLT namespace.
- This element is in the instruction category.
- When you copy the root node, the processor does not create another root node.
- The children and attributes of a copied node are not automatically copied.
- Use xsl:copy to copy a node-set to the result tree without automatically converting it to a string.
- In the xsl:attribute-set, xsl:copy, and xsl:element elements, use the use-attribute-sets attribute to list names of attribute sets. Using use-attribute-sets is the same as adding individual xsl:attribute elements for each attribute in the attribute sets. An alternate attribute to use-attribute-sets is xsl:use-attribute-sets, used only when copying element nodes.

Example

The following example is from the XSLT recommendation (http://www.w3. org/TR/xslt):

```
<xsl:template name="apply-templates-copy-lang">
 <xsl:for-each select="@xml:lang">
   <xsl:copy/>
 </xsl:for-each>
 <xsl:apply-templates/>
</xsl:template>
```

Related Elements

xsl:apply-imports (p. 329), xsl:apply-templates (p. 330), xsl:attribute (p. 331), xsl:call-template (p. 334), xsl:choose (p. 335), xsl:comment (p. 336), xsl:copy-of (p. 337), xsl:element (p. 340), xsl:fallback (p. 341), xsl:for-each (p. 342), xsl:if (p. 343), xsl:message (p. 346), xsl:number (p. 348), xsl:processing-instruction (p. 354), xsl:text (p. 360), xsl:value-of (p. 362), xsl:variable (p. 363)

xsl:copy-of   Copy Fragment

Purpose

Places a fragment of a result tree into the same result tree.

XSLT Component

EBNF Syntax

```
<xsl:copy-of select = expression />
```

Standard Syntax

```
<xsl:copy-of select = expression />
```

Where

• select is a keyword that indicates that *expression* follows.
• *expression* is an expression that selects one or more nodes.

Notes

• The xsl: prefix points to an element in the XSLT namespace.
• This element is in the instruction category.
• The difference between xsl:copy-of and xsl:value-of is that xsl:value-of converts a result tree fragment into a string and xsl:copy-of does not.

Related Elements

xsl:apply-imports (p. 329), xsl:apply-templates (p. 330), xsl:attribute (p. 331), xsl:call-template (p. 334), xsl:choose (p. 335), xsl:comment (p. 336), xsl:copy (p. 336), xsl:element (p. 340), xsl:fallback (p. 341), xsl:for-each (p. 342), xsl:if (p. 343), xsl:message (p. 346), xsl:number (p. 348), xsl:processing-instruction (p. 354), xsl:text (p. 360), xsl:value-of (p. 362), xsl:variable (p. 363)

xsl:decimal-format   Decimal Format

Purpose

Specifies a decimal format.

EBNF Syntax

```
<xsl:decimal-format name = qname
  decimal-separator = ds_char
  grouping-separator = gs_char infinity = i_string
  minus-sign = m_char NaN = NaN_string
  percent = per_char per-mille = p_char
  zero-digit = z-char digit = d_char
  pattern-separator = p_char />
```

Standard Syntax

```
<xsl:decimal-format name = qname
  decimal-separator = ds_char
  grouping-separator = gs_char infinity = i_string
  minus-sign = m_char NaN = NaN_string
  percent = per_char per-mille = p_char
```

```
zero-digit = z-char digit = d_char
pattern-separator = p_char />
```

Where

- name is a required keyword indicating that a qname follows.
- qname, which is the expanded qualified name of the element, names the decimal format.
- decimal-separator is a keyword that indicates that a decimal-separator character follows.
- ds_char represents a decimal-separator character. The default is a period (.).
- grouping-separator is a keyword that indicates that a grouping-separator character follows. Grouping separators are the characters that separate groups of digits.
- gs_char is the character used for a grouping-separator. For the United States, the default grouping-separator is a comma.
- infinity is a keyword that indicates that a character that represents that infinity follows.
- i_string is the character used to represent infinity. The default is Infinity.
- minus-sign is a keyword that indicates that a character that represents a minus sign follows.
- m_char is the character used to represent a minus sign. The default is #x2D, the hyphen.
- NaN is a keyword that indicates that a character that represents a Not-a-Number value follows.
- NaN_string is the string used to represent NaN. The default is NaN.
- percent is a keyword that indicates that a character that represents a percent sign follows.
- per_char is the string used to represent the percent sign. The default is %.
- per-mille is a keyword that indicates that a character that represents the per-mille symbol follows.
- p_char is the character used to represent the per-mille sign. The default is #x2030.
- zero-digit is a keyword that indicates that a character that represents a zero digit follows.
- z-char is the character used to represent zero. The default is 0.
- digit is a keyword that indicates that a character that represents a formatting digit follows.
- d_char is the character used to represent a formatting digit. The default is #.
- pattern-separator is a keyword that indicates that a character that represents a pattern-separator character follows.
- p_char is the character used to represent a pattern separator. The default is ;.

Notes

- The xsl: prefix points to an element in the XSLT namespace.
- xsl:decimal-format and the format-number() function are related and work together.
- This element is in the top-level category.

Related Elements

xsl:attribute-set (p. 332), xsl:include (p. 345), xsl:key (p. 345), xsl:namespace-alias (p. 347), xsl:output (p. 351), xsl:param (p. 353), xsl:preserve-space (p. 354), xsl:strip-space (p. 357), xsl:template (p. 358), xsl:variable (p. 363)

xsl:element	**Create Element**

Purpose

Creates an element with a template for its attributes and child elements.

EBNF Syntax

```
<xsl:element name = { qname }
  [namespace = { uri-reference }]
  use-attribute-sets = qnames>template_content
</xsl:element>
```

Standard Syntax

```
<xsl:element name = { qname }
  [namespace = { uri-reference }]
  use-attribute-sets = qnames>template_content
</xsl:element>
```

Where

- name is a required keyword indicating that a qname follows.
- qname, which is the expanded qualified name of the element, names the attribute-value template.
- namespace is a keyword indicating that a uri-reference follows.
- uri-reference, which is the name of the namespace, names the attribute-value template. If uri-reference is not provided, the XSL processor uses the qname value.
- use-attribute-sets is a keyword indicating that qnames for attribute sets follows.
- qnames names the attribute-value templates in the attribute set.
- template_content is the result of processing the element.

Notes

- The xsl: prefix points to an element in the XSLT namespace.
- This element is in the instruction category.

- A namespace is a set of unique names, defined in the DTD or elsewhere. In XML, a *qualified name* is comporised of two parts: an identifier and either a URI or element name, depending on whether it is external or internal, respectively.
- In the xsl:attribute-set, xsl:copy, and xsl:element elements, use the use-attribute-sets attribute to list names of attribute sets. Using use-attribute-sets is the same as adding individual xsl:attribute elements for each attribute in the attribute sets. An alternate attribute to use-attribute-sets is xsl:use-attribute-sets used only when copying element nodes.
- The xsl:client element allows an element to be created with a computed name.
- An error occurs if the string is not a syntactically legal URI reference.

Related Elements

xsl:apply-imports (p. 329), xsl:apply-templates (p. 330), xsl:attribute (p. 331), xsl:call-template (p. 334), xsl:choose (p. 335), xsl:comment (p. 336), xsl:copy (p. 336), xsl:copy-of (p. 337), xsl:fallback (p. 341), xsl:for-each (p. 342), xsl:if (p. 343), xsl:message (p. 346), xsl:number (p. 348), xsl:processing-instruction (p. 354), xsl:text (p. 360), xsl:value-of (p. 362), xsl:variable (p. 363)

xsl:fallback   Fallback

Purpose
Falls back to a template when a particular condition is false.

EBNF Syntax
```
xsl:fallback>template</xsl:fallback>
```

Standard Syntax
```
xsl:fallback>template</xsl:fallback>
```

Where
- *template* is the result of processing the element.

Notes
- The xsl: prefix points to an element in the XSLT namespace.
- This element is in the instruction category.
- When an XSLT processor runs xsl:fallback for most elements, no template results. However, when an XSLT processor runs xsl:fallback for an instruction element that has children, each child must also be instantiated in sequence.

XSLT Component

Related Elements

xsl:apply-imports (p. 329), xsl:apply-templates (p. 330), xsl:attribute (p. 331), xsl:call-template (p. 334), xsl:choose (p. 335), xsl:comment (p. 336), xsl:copy (p. 336), xsl:copy-of (p. 337), xsl:element (p. 340), xsl:for-each (p. 342), xsl:if (p. 343), xsl:message (p. 346), xsl:number (p. 348), xsl:processing-instruction (p. 354), xsl:text (p. 360), xsl:value-of (p. 362), xsl:variable (p. 363)

xsl:for-each	Repeat For Each

Purpose

Selects some node-sets for automatic processing.

EBNF Syntax

```
<xsl:for-each select = node-set-expression>
  (xsl:sort* template)</xsl:for-each>
```

Standard Syntax

```
<xsl:for-each select = node-set-expression>
  ([xsl:sort[ xsl:sort[... xsl:sort]]] template)
</xsl:for-each>
```

Where

- select is a keyword that indicates that *node-string-expression* follows.
- *node-string-expression* is an expression that selects one or more nodes.
- xsl:sort is an element that sorts nodes.
- *template* is the result of processing the element.

Notes

- The xsl: prefix points to an element in the XSLT namespace.
- This element is in the instruction category.
- xsl:sort is a child of xsl:apply-templates and xsl:for-each.

Example

The following example is from the XSLT recommendation (http://www.w3.org/TR/xslt):

```
<xsl:template name="apply-templates-copy-lang">
  <xsl:for-each select="@xml:lang">
    <xsl:copy/>
  </xsl:for-each>
  <xsl:apply-templates/>
</xsl:template>
```

Related Elements

xsl:apply-imports (p. 329), xsl:apply-templates (p. 330), xsl:attribute
(p. 331), xsl:call-template (p. 334), xsl:choose (p. 335), xsl:comment
(p. 336), xsl:copy (p. 336), xsl:copy-of (p. 337), xsl:element (p. 340),
xsl:fallback (p. 341), xsl:if (p. 343), xsl:message (p. 346), xsl:number
(p. 348), xsl:processing-instruction (p. 354), xsl:text (p. 360),
xsl:value-of (p. 362), xsl:variable (p. 363)

xsl:if   If-Then

Purpose
Evaluates an expression and returns a template based on true and false
conditions.

EBNF Syntax
```
<xsl:if test = boolean-expression>template</xsl:if>
```

Standard Syntax
```
<xsl:if test = boolean-expression>template</xsl:if>
```

Where
- test is a keyword that indicates that *boolean-expression* follows.
- *boolean-expression* is an expression that tests a node for true or false
  conditions.
- *template* is the result of processing the element.

Notes
- The xsl: prefix points to an element in the XSLT namespace.
- This element is in the instruction category.
- xsl:if and xsl:choose are used in conditional processing.
- If the result is true, then the content template is instantiated; otherwise,
  nothing is created.

Example
The following example is from the XSLT recommendation
(http://www.w3.org/TR/xslt):

```
<xsl:template match="namelist/name">
  <xsl:apply-templates/>
  <xsl:if test="not(position()=last())">, </xsl:if>
</xsl:template>
```

XSLT Component

Related Elements

xsl:apply-imports (p. 329), xsl:apply-templates (p. 330), xsl:attribute (p. 331), xsl:call-template (p. 334), xsl:choose (p. 335), xsl:comment (p. 336), xsl:copy (p. 336), xsl:copy-of (p. 337), xsl:element (p. 340), xsl:fallback (p. 341), xsl:for-each (p. 342), xsl:message (p. 346), xsl:number (p. 348), xsl:processing-instruction (p. 354), xsl:text (p. 360), xsl:value-of (p. 362), xsl:variable (p. 363)

xsl:import   Import XSL Style Sheet

Purpose

Imports an XSLT style sheet.

EBNF Syntax

```
<xsl:import href = uri />
```

Standard Syntax

```
<xsl:import href = uri />
```

Where

- href is a keyword that indicates that a URI follows.
- uri is the URI of the included style sheet.

Notes

- The xsl: prefix points to an element in the XSLT namespace.
- According to the XSLT recommendation (http://www.w3.org/TR/xslt), "importing a style sheet is the same as including it (xsl:include) except that definitions and template rules in the importing style sheet take precedence over template rules and definitions in the imported style sheet."
- The xsl:import element is only allowed as a top-level element.

Example

The following example is from the XSLT recommendation (http://www.w3.org/TR/xslt):

```
<xsl:import href="doc.xsl" />

<xsl:template match="example">
  <div style="border: solid red">
    <xsl:apply-imports />
  </div>
</xsl:template>
```

Related Element

xsl:apply-imports (p. 329)

xsl:include

Include XSLT Style Sheet

Purpose
Includes another XSLT style sheet.

EBNF Syntax
```
<xsl:include href = uri />
```

Standard Syntax
```
<xsl:include href = uri />
```

Where
- href is a keyword that indicates that a URI follows.
- uri is the URI of the included style sheet.

Notes
- The xsl: prefix points to an element in the XSLT namespace.
- This element is in the top-level category.

Related Elements
xsl:attribute-set (p. 332), xsl:decimal-format (p. 338), xsl:key (p. 345), xsl:namespace-alias (p. 347), xsl:output (p. 351), xsl:param (p. 353), xsl:preserve-space (p. 354), xsl:strip-space (p. 357), xsl:template (p. 358), xsl:variable (p. 363)

xsl:key

Declare Key

Purpose
Declares keys for the current document.

EBNF Syntax
```
<xsl:key name = qname match = pattern use = expression
/>
```

Standard Syntax
```
<xsl:key name = qname match = pattern use = expression
/>
```

Where
- name is a required keyword indicating that a qname follows.
- qname is the expanded qualified name of the key.
- match is a keyword indicating that a pattern to match follows.
- pattern is a pattern to match the key.
- use is a keyword indicating that an expression follows.
- expression is an expression that selects one or more nodes.

Notes

- The xsl: prefix points to an element in the XSLT namespace.
- A key is a cross-reference identifier, which contains the node that has the key, the key name, and the string value of the key.
- This element is in the top-level category.
- A namespace is a set of unique names, defined in the DTD or elsewhere. In XML, a *qualified name* is comporised of two parts: an identifier and either a URI or element name, depending on whether it is external or internal, respectively.

Example

The following example is from the XSLT recommendation (http://www.w3. org/TR/xslt):

```
<xsl:key name="idkey" match="div" use=@id" />
```

Related Elements

xsl:attribute-set (p. 332), xsl:decimal-format (p. 338), xsl:include (p. 345), xsl:namespace-alias (p. 347), xsl:output (p. 351), xsl:param (p. 353), xsl:preserve-space (p. 354), xsl:strip-space (p. 357), xsl:template (p. 358), xsl:variable (p. 363)

---

xsl:message	**XSLT Processor Message**

Purpose

Sends a message template dependent on the XSLT processor.

EBNF Syntax

```
<xsl:message terminate = "yes" | "no">template
</xsl:message>
```

Standard Syntax

```
<xsl:message terminate = "yes" | "no">template
</xsl:message>
```

Where

- terminate is a keyword that indicates that a yes or no value determining whether processing ends follows.
- yes is a keyword that indicates that processing ends.
- no is a keyword that indicates that processing continues.
- *template* is the result of processing the element.

Notes

- The xsl: prefix points to an element in the XSLT namespace.
- This element is in the instruction category.
- According to the XSLT recommendation, the message can appear in a message box or in a log file.

Example

The following example is from the XSLT recommendation (http://www.w3.
org/TR/xslt):

```
<xsl:template name="localized-message">
<xsl:param name="name" />
<xsl:message>
<xsl:value-of select="$messages/message[@name=$name]"
 />
</xsl:message>
</xsl:template>
```

Related Elements

xsl:apply-imports (p. 329), xsl:apply-templates (p. 330), xsl:attribute
(p. 331), xsl:call-template (p. 334), xsl:choose (p. 335), xsl:comment
(p. 336), xsl:copy (p. 336), xsl:copy-of (p. 337), xsl:element (p. 340),
xsl:fallback (p. 341), xsl:for-each (p. 342), xsl:if (p. 343), xsl:number
(p. 348), xsl:processing-instruction (p. 354), xsl:text (p. 360),
xsl:value-of (p. 362), xsl:variable (p. 363)

xsl:namespace-alias   Namespace URI Alias

Purpose

Declares that a namespace URI for the style sheet and result tree is an alias
for another namespace URI.

EBNF Syntax

```
<xsl:namespace-alias stylesheet-prefix = s_prefix
 | "#default" | result-prefix = r_prefix
 | "#default" />
```

Standard Syntax

```
<xsl:namespace-alias stylesheet-prefix = s_prefix
 | "#default" | result-prefix = r_prefix
 | "#default" />
```

Where

- stylesheet-prefix is a keyword that indicates that a style sheet prefix
  follows.
- s_prefix names a prefix that specifies the URI of the namespace named
  in the style sheet.
- "#default" is a keyword that indicates that the default namespace is
  used within the style sheet.
- result-prefix is a keyword that indicates that a result prefix follows.
- r_prefix names a prefix that specifies the URI of the namespace named
  in the result tree.

XSLT Component

Notes

- The xsl: prefix points to an element in the XSLT namespace.
- This element is in the top-level category.
- According to the XSLT recommendation (http://www.w3.org/TR/xslt), "If a namespace URI is declared to be an alias for multiple different namespace URIs, then the declaration with the highest import precedence is used."

Example

```
<xsl:namespace-alias style sheet-prefix="lxsl"
    result-prefix="xsl" />
```

Related Elements

xsl:attribute-set (p. 332), xsl:decimal-format (p. 338), xsl:include (p. 345), xsl:key (p. 345), xsl:output (p. 351), xsl:param (p. 353), xsl:preserve-space (p. 354), xsl:strip-space (p. 357), xsl:template (p. 358), xsl:variable (p. 363)

xsl:number	Formatted Number

Purpose

Formats and inserts a number in the result tree.

EBNF Syntax

```
<xsl:number level = "single" | "multiple" | "any"
    count = c_pattern from = f_pattern
    [value = number-expression]
    format = { string}
    [lang = { nmtoken }]
    [letter-value = { "alphabetic" | "traditional" }]
    grouping-separator = { char }
    grouping-size = { number } />
```

Standard Syntax

```
<xsl:number level = "single" | "multiple" | "any"
    count = pattern from = pattern
    [value = number-expression]
    format = { string }
    [lang = { nmtoken }]
    [letter-value = { "alphabetic" | "traditional" }]
    grouping-separator = { char }
    grouping-size = { number } />
```

Where

- `level` is a keyword that indicates that certain source-tree levels will be examined.
- `single` is a keyword that indicates that one source-tree level will be examined. This is the default.
- `multiple` is a keyword that indicates that all source-tree levels will be examined.
- `any` is a keyword that indicates that any source-tree level matching the count *c_pattern* will be examined.
- `count` is a keyword that indicates that a pattern follows.
- *c_pattern* is a value that sets the node count, depending on the value of `level`.
- `from` is a keyword that indicates that a pattern follows.
- *f_pattern* is a value that starts the node count at a particular location.
- `value` is a keyword that indicates that *number-expression* follows.
- *number-expression* is the expression to be evaluated.
- `format` is a keyword that indicates that a string type-attribute value follows.
- *string* is a string that sets the `type`-attribute value for an ordered list.
- `lang` is a keyword that indicates that a language name token follows.
- *nmtoken* specifies a valid XML name token. A name token can begin with any letter, digit, or valid character.
- `letter-value` is a keyword that indicates that alphabetic numbering in ordered lists will use one of two types of letter characters.
- `alphabetic` is a keyword that indicates that alphabetic numbering will start with a in English and some other letter in other languages.
- `traditional` is a keyword that indicates that alphabetic numbering will start with i in English and some other letter in other languages.
- `grouping-separator` is a keyword that indicates that a grouping-separator character follows. Grouping separators are the characters that separate groups of digits. The `grouping-separator` attribute and value work in conjunction with the `grouping-size` attribute and value.
- *char* is the character used for a grouping-separator. For the United States, the default grouping-separator is a comma.
- `grouping-size` is a keyword that indicates the number of digits in a group. The `grouping-size` attribute and value work in conjunction with the `grouping-separator` attribute and value.
- *number* represents the number of digits in a group For the United States, the default grouping-separator is 3.

Notes

- The `xsl:` prefix points to an element in the XSLT namespace.
- This element is in the instruction category.
- The `xsl:number` element evaluates number-expression and converts the resulting number as if it used the `number()` function. The number is changed to an integer, converted to a string, and stored in the result tree.

Example

The following example is from the XSLT recommendation (http://www.w3.
org/TR/xslt):

```
<xsl:template match="items">
 <xsl:for-each select="item">
  <xsl:sort select="." />
  <p>
   <xsl:number value="position()" format="1. " />
   <xsl:value-of select="." />
  </p>
 </xsl:for-each>
</xsl:template>
```

Related Elements

xsl:apply-imports (p. 329), xsl:apply-templates (p. 330), xsl:attribute
(p. 331), xsl:call-template (p. 334), xsl:choose (p. 335), xsl:comment
(p. 336), xsl:copy (p. 336), xsl:copy-of (p. 337), xsl:element (p. 340),
xsl:fallback (p. 341), xsl:for-each (p. 342), xsl:if (p. 343), xsl:message
(p. 346), xsl:processing-instruction (p. 354), xsl:text (p. 360),
xsl:value-of (p. 362), xsl:variable (p. 363)

xsl:otherwise	**No Conditions True**

Purpose

Produces a template based on no condition being true.

EBNF Syntax

```
<xsl:otherwise>template</xsl:otherwise>
```

Standard Syntax

```
<xsl:otherwise>template</xsl:otherwise>
```

Where

- template is the template that is returned when no condition is true
  in a series of xsl:when statements.

Notes

- The xsl: prefix points to an element in the XSLT namespace.
- If no xsl:otherwise is included in an xsl:choose statement, no
  template is returned.
- xsl:otherwise follows the xsl:when element.

Related Elements

xsl:choose (p. 335), xsl:when (p. 365)

xsl:output

Purpose

Creates result-tree output.

EBNF Syntax

```
<xsl:output method = "xml" | "html" | "text"
    | qname-but-not-ncname version = nmtoken
    encoding = e_string omit-xml-declaration = "yes"
    | "no" standalone = "yes" | "no"
    doctype-public = p_string doctype-system = d_string
    cdata-section-elements = qnames
    indent = "yes" | "no" media-type = m_string />
```

Standard Syntax

```
<xsl:output method = "xml" | "html" | "text"
    | qname-but-not-ncname version = nmtoken
    encoding = e_string omit-xml-declaration = "yes"
    | "no" standalone = "yes" | "no"
    doctype-public = p_string doctype-system = d_string
    cdata-section-elements = qnames
    indent = "yes" | "no" media-type = m_string />
```

Where

- method is a keyword that indicates the output method.
- xml is a QName keyword that designates the XML output method. This is sometimes the default.
- html is a QName keyword that designates the HTML output method. This is usually the default.
- text is a QName keyword that designates the text output method.
- qname-but-not-ncname is a expanded-name QName whose activities are not further described by the XSLT recommendation.
- version is a keyword that indicates that the output-method version follows.
- nmtoken specifies a valid XML name token. A name token can begin with any letter, digit, or valid character.
- encoding is a keyword that indicates that the character encoding follows.
- e_string is the character encoding. The value must range from #x21 to #x7E, a charset from IANA, RFC2278, or start with x-.
- omit-xml-declaration is a keyword that indicates whether the XSLT processor produces an XML declaration.
- yes is a keyword that indicates that the processor should produce an XML declaration.
- no is a keyword that indicates that the processor should not produce an XML declaration.

- standalone is a keyword that indicates whether the processor should declare that the document is standalone.
- yes is a keyword that indicates that the processor should declare a standalone document.
- no is a keyword that indicates that the processor should not declare a standalone document.
- doctype-public is a keyword that indicates that a public-identifier follows.
- *p_string* is a public-identifier string.
- doctype-system is a keyword that indicates that a system-identifier follows.
- *d_string* is a system-identifier string.
- cdata-section-elements is a keyword that indicates that a list of elements whose text nodes will be output using CDATA sections follows.
- *qnames* names the qualified names of elements output using CDATA sections.
- indent is a keyword that indicates whether the processor can add whitespace to the output result tree.
- yes is a keyword that indicates that the processor can add whitespace.
- no is a keyword that indicates that the processor cannot add whitespace.
- media-type indicates that a media (MIME) type for the output data follows.
- *m_string* is the name of the MIME type.

Notes

- The xsl: prefix points to an element in the XSLT namespace.
- This element is in the top-level category.
- A namespace is a set of unique names, defined in the DTD or elsewhere. In XML, a *qualified name* is comporised of two parts: an identifier and either a URI or element name, depending on whether it is external or internal, respectively.
- To send an XML declaration to output, use the xsl:output element, not xsl:processing-instruction.
- If media-type is text, add a charset parameter.
- A document can contain one or more xsl:output elements.
- The xsl:output element is only allowed as a top-level element.

Example

The following example is from the XSLT recommendation (http://www.w3.org/TR/xslt):

```
<xsl:output cdata-section-elements="example" />
```

Related Elements

xsl:attribute-set (p. 332), xsl:decimal-format (p. 338), xsl:include (p. 345), xsl:key (p. 345), xsl:namespace-alias (p. 347), xsl:param (p. 353), xsl:preserve-space (p. 354), xsl:strip-space (p. 357), xsl:template (p. 358), xsl:variable (p. 363)

xsl:param   Variable Default Value

Purpose

Sets a default value for a variable.

EBNF Syntax

```
<xsl:param name = qname select = expression>
   template</xsl:param>
```

Standard Syntax

```
<xsl:param name = qname select = expression>
   template</xsl:param>
```

Where

- name is a required keyword indicating that a qname follows.
- qname, which is the expanded qualified name of the attribute, names the attribute-value template.
- select is a keyword that indicates that expression follows.
- expression is an expression that selects one or more nodes.
- template is the result of processing the element.

Notes

- The xsl: prefix points to an element in the XSLT namespace.
- This element is in the top-level category.
- A namespace is a set of unique names, defined in the DTD or elsewhere. In XML, a *qualified name* is composed of two parts: an identifier and either a URI or element name, depending on whether it is external or internal, respectively.

Example

The following example is from the XSLT recommendation (http://www.w3.org/TR/xslt):

```
<xsl:param name="x" select="1"/>
<xsl:template name="foo">
<xsl:variable name="x" select="2"/>
</xsl:template>
```

Related Elements

xsl:attribute-set (p. 332), xsl:decimal-format (p. 338), xsl:include (p. 345), xsl:key (p. 345), xsl:namespace-alias (p. 347), xsl:output (p. 351), xsl:param (p. 353), xsl:preserve-space (p. 354), xsl:strip-space (p. 357), xsl:template (p. 358), xsl:variable (p. 363)

XSLT Component

xsl:preserve-space   Preserve Whitespace

Purpose
Preserves whitespace in a list of elements.

EBNF Syntax
```
<xsl:preserve-space elements = tokens />
```

Standard Syntax
```
<xsl:preserve-space elements = tokens />
```

Where
- elements is a keyword that indicates that the names of elements affected by xsl:preserve-space follow.
- tokens lists the names of elements.

Notes
- The xsl: prefix points to an element in the XSLT namespace.
- When xsl:preserve-space specifies a particular element, that element is added to the list for xsl:strip-space. When xsl:strip-space specifies a particular element, that element is added to the list for xsl:preserve-space.
- This element is in the top-level category.

Related Elements
xsl:attribute-set (p. 332), xsl:decimal-format (p. 338), xsl:include (p. 345), xsl:key (p. 345), xsl:namespace-alias (p. 347), xsl:output (p. 351), xsl:param (p. 353), xsl:preserve-space (p. 354), xsl:strip-space (p. 357), xsl:template (p. 358), xsl:variable (p. 363)

xsl:processing-instruction   Create Processing Instruction

Purpose
Creates a processing-instruction node.

EBNF Syntax
```
<xsl:processing-instruction name = { ncname }>
  processing-instruction_template
</xsl:processing-instruction>
```

Standard Syntax
```
<xsl:processing-instruction name = { ncname }>
  processing-instruction_template
</xsl:processing-instruction>
```

Where

- name is a keyword indicating that an *ncname* follows.
- *ncname* is a name for a collection of namespace names.
- *processing-instruction_template* represents a string that is both an NCName and a PITarget (p. 118).

Notes

- The xsl: prefix points to an element in the XSLT namespace.
- This element is in the instruction category.
- To send an XML declaration to output, use the xsl:output element, not xsl:processing-instruction.
- According to the XSLT recommendation (http://www.w3.org/TR/xslt), "The content of the xsl:processing-instruction element is a template for the string-value of the processing instruction node."

Related Elements

xsl:apply-imports (p. 329), xsl:apply-templates (p. 330), xsl:attribute (p. 331), xsl:call-template (p. 334), xsl:choose (p. 335), xsl:comment (p. 336), xsl:copy (p. 336), xsl:copy-of (p. 337), xsl:element (p. 340), xsl:fallback (p. 341), xsl:for-each (p. 342), xsl:if (p. 343), xsl:message (p. 346), xsl:number (p. 348), xsl:text (p. 360), xsl:value of (p. 362), xsl:variable (p. 363)

xsl:sort   Sort

XSLT Component

Purpose

Sorts selected nodes.

EBNF Syntax

```
<xsl:sort select = string-expression
    lang = { nmtoken } data-type = { "text" | "number"
    | qname-but-not-ncname } order = { "ascending"
    | "descending" } case-order = { "upper-first"
    | "lower-first" } />
```

Standard Syntax

```
<xsl:sort select = string-expression
    lang = { nmtoken } data-type = { "text" | "number"
    | qname-but-not-ncname } order = { "ascending"
    | "descending" } case-order = { "upper-first"
    | "lower-first" } />
```

Where

- select is a keyword that indicates that a string-expression follows.
- *string-expression* is an expression that selects one or more strings.
- lang is a keyword that indicates that a language name token follows.

- *nmtoken* specifies a valid XML name token. A name token can begin with any letter, digit, or valid character.
- data-type is a keyword that indicates that a data-type value follows.
- text is a keyword that indicates that sorting should occur by the language specified with the lang attribute.
- number is a keyword that indicates that the sort key should be converted to a number and sorting should be based on the current number system.
- *qname-but-not-ncname* is a expanded-name QName whose activities are not further described by the XSLT recommendation.
- order is a keyword that indicates that a sorting order follows.
- ascending is a keyword that indicates that sorting is in ascending order.
- descending is a keyword that indicates that sorting is in descending order.
- case-order is a keyword that indicates the order in which uppercase and lowercase characters are sorted.
- upper-first is a keyword that indicates that uppercase characters come before lowercase characters.
- lower-first is a keyword that indicates that lowercase characters come before uppercase characters.

Notes

- The xsl: prefix points to an element in the XSLT namespace.
- xsl:sort is a child of xsl:apply-templates and xsl:for-each.
- When converting a sort key to numbers, the processor should convert in the same way as the number() function.
- Regardless of the attribute values for xsl:sort, some processors sort differently from others.
- A namespace is a set of unique names, defined in the DTD or elsewhere. In XML, a *qualified name* is comprised of two parts: an identifier and either a URI or element name, depending on whether it is external or internal, respectively.

Example

The following example is from the XSLT recommendation (http://www.w3.org/TR/xslt):

```
<xsl:template match="items">
 <xsl:for-each select="item">
 <xsl:sort select="." />
 <p>
  <xsl:number value="position()" format="1. "/>
  <xsl:value-of select="." />
 </p>
 </xsl:for-each>
</xsl:template>
```

xsl:strip-space

Strip Whitespace

Purpose
Strips whitespace from a list of elements.

EBNF Syntax
```
<xsl:strip-space elements = tokens />
```

Standard Syntax
```
<xsl:strip-space elements = tokens />
```

Where
- elements is a keyword that indicates that the names of elements affected by xsl:strip-space follow.
- tokens lists the names of elements.

Notes
- The xsl: prefix points to an element in the XSLT namespace.
- When xsl:strip-space specifies a particular element, that element is added to the list for xsl:preserve-space. When xsl:preserve-space specifies a particular element, that element is added to the list for xsl:strip-space.
- This element is in the top-level category.

Related Elements
xsl:attribute-set (p. 332), xsl:decimal-format (p. 338), xsl:include (p. 345), xsl:key (p. 345), xsl:namespace-alias (p. 347), xsl:output (p. 351), xsl:param (p. 353), xsl:preserve-space (p. 354), xsl:template (p. 358), xsl:variable (p. 363)

xsl:stylesheet

XSL Style Sheet

Purpose
Indicates an XSL style sheet.

EBNF Syntax
```
<xsl:stylesheet version = number id = id
   extension-element-prefixes = e_tokens
   exclude-result-prefixes = er_tokens
   (xsl:import*, top-level-elements)
</xsl:stylesheet>
```

Standard Syntax
```
<xsl:stylesheet version = number id = id
   extension-element-prefixes = e_tokens
   exclude-result-prefixes = er_tokens
```

XSLT Component

```
([xsl:import[ xsl:import[... xsl:import]]],
top-level-elements)
</xsl:stylesheet>
```

Where

- version is a keyword that indicates that the XSLT version number follows.
- *number* specifies the XSLT version number. The current version number is 1.0. This is required.
- id is a keyword that indicates that an identifier follows.
- *id* is a style sheet identifier.
- extension-element-prefixes is a keyword indicating that one or more tokens representing extension element prefixes follow.
- *e_tokens* indicates a list of tokens representing prefixes for elements not in the official namespace.
- exclude-result-prefixes is a keyword indicating that one or more tokens representing excluded result prefixes follow.
- *er_tokens* indicates a list of tokens representing excluded result prefixes in the official namespace.
- xsl:import is an element that imports an XSLT style sheet.
- *top-level-elements* are child elements of the xsl:stylesheet element: xsl:attribute-set, xsl:decimal-format, xsl:include, xsl:key, xsl:namespace-alias, xsl:output, xsl:param, xsl:preserve-space, xsl:strip-space, xsl:template, and xsl:variable.

Notes

- The xsl: prefix points to an element in the XSLT namespace.
- You can use the xsl:transform element as a synonym for xsl:stylesheet.

Related Elements

xsl:attribute-set (p. 332), xsl:decimal-format (p. 338), xsl:include (p. 345), xsl:key (p. 345), xsl:namespace-alias (p. 347), xsl:output (p. 351), xsl:param (p. 353), xsl:preserve-space (p. 354), xsl:strip-space (p. 354), xsl:template (p. 358), xsl:transform (p. 361), xsl:variable (p. 363)

xsl:template	Template Rule

Purpose

Specifies a template rule.

EBNF Syntax

```
<xsl:template match = pattern name = n_qname
priority = number mode = m_qname>
(xsl:param*, template)
</xsl:template>
```

Standard Syntax

```
<xsl:template match = pattern name = n_qname
  priority = number mode = m_qname>
  [xsl:param[ xsl:param[... xsl:param]]], template
</xsl:template>
```

Where

- match is an attribute that is a pattern identifying the source node or nodes to which the rule applies.
- *pattern* is a pattern, which names one or more input element types that should match in the source tree.
- name is a keyword that indicates that a QName follows.
- *qname* is the expanded qualified name of the attribute.
- priority is a keyword that indicates that a priority number for the template follows.
- *number* sets the priority of the rule that contains the pattern.
- mode is a keyword that indicates that a mode for the template follows.
- *m_qname* is the QName for a mode that differentiates between two matches.
- xsl:param is a child element that sets a default value for a variable.
- *template* is the result of processing the element.

Notes

- The xsl: prefix points to an element in the XSLT namespace.
- This element is in the top-level category.
- A namespace is a set of unique names, defined in the DTD or elsewhere. In XML, a *qualified name* is composed of two parts: an identifier and either a URI or element name, depending on whether it is external or internal, respectively.
- The match attribute is required unless the xsl:template element has a name attribute.
- According to the XSLT recommendation (http://www.w3.org/TR/xslt), "It is an error for the value of the match attribute to contain a variable reference."

Example

The following example is from the XSLT recommendation (http://www.w3.org/TR/xslt):

```
<xsl:template name="apply-templates-copy-lang">
  <xsl:for-each select="@xml:lang">
    <xsl:copy/>
  </xsl:for-each>
  <xsl:apply-templates/>
</xsl:template>
```

XSLT Component

Related Elements

xsl:attribute-set (p. 332), xsl:decimal-format (p. 338), xsl:include
(p. 345), xsl:key (p. 345), xsl:namespace-alias (p. 347), xsl:output (p. 351),
xsl:param (p. 353), xsl:preserve-space (p. 354), xsl:strip-space (p. 357),
xsl:variable (p. 363)

xsl:text   Create Text

Purpose

Creates a text node in a template.

EBNF Syntax

```
<xsl:text disable-output-escaping = "yes" | "no">
  #PCDATA</xsl:text>
```

Standard Syntax

```
<xsl:text disable-output-escaping = "yes" | "no">
  #PCDATA</xsl:text>
```

Where

- disable-output-escaping is a keyword that indicates that certain symbols, such as ampersands (&), greater-than (>), less-than (<), and quotation marks (") can or cannot be used in the output of character data.
- yes is a keyword that indicates that no escaping of certain symbols is allowed during output.
- no is a keyword that indicates that escaping of certain symbols is allowed during output. This is the default.
- #PCDATA is the resulting character data.

Notes

- The xsl: prefix points to an element in the XSLT namespace.
- This element is in the instruction category.

Example

The following example is from the XSLT recommendation (http://www.w3.org/TR/xslt):

```
<xsl:template match="person">
  <p>
    <xsl:value-of select="@given-name"/>
    <xsl:text> </xsl:text>
    <xsl:value-of select="@family-name"/>
  </p>
</xsl:template>
```

XSLT Component

Related Elements

`xsl:apply-imports` (p. 329), `xsl:apply-templates` (p. 330), `xsl:attribute` (p. 331), `xsl:call-template` (p. 334), `xsl:choose` (p. 335), `xsl:comment` (p. 336), `xsl:copy` (p. 336), `xsl:copy-of` (p. 337), `xsl:element` (p. 340), `xsl:fallback` (p. 341), `xsl:for-each` (p. 342), `xsl:if` (p. 343), `xsl:message` (p. 346), `xsl:number` (p. 348), `xsl:processing-instruction` (p. 354), `xsl:value-of` (p. 362), `xsl:variable` (p. 363)

xsl:transform	**XSL Style Sheet Synonym**

Purpose

Indicates a synonym of an XSL style sheet.

EBNF Syntax

```
<xsl:stylesheet version = number id = id
  extension-element-prefixes = e_tokens
  exclude-result-prefixes = er_tokens
  (xsl:import*, top-level-elements)
</xsl:stylesheet>
```

Standard Syntax

```
<xsl:stylesheet version = number id = id
  extension-element-prefixes = e_tokens
  exclude-result-prefixes = er_tokens
  ([xsl:import[ xsl:import[... xsl:import]]],
  top-level-elements)
</xsl:stylesheet>
```

Where

- *version* is a keyword that indicates that the XSLT version number follows.
- *number* specifies the XSLT version number. The current version number is 1.0. This is required.
- *id* is a keyword that indicates that an identifier follows.
- *id* is a style sheet identifier.
- `extension-element-prefixes` is a keyword indicating that one or more tokens representing extension element prefixes follow.
- *e_tokens* indicates a list of tokens representing prefixes for elements not in the official namespace.
- `exclude-result-prefixes` is a keyword indicating that one or more tokens representing excluded result prefixes follow.
- *er_tokens* indicates a list of tokens representing excluded result prefixes in the official namespace.
- `xsl:import` is an element that imports an XSLT style sheet.

XSLT Component

- *top-level-elements* are child elements of the xsl:stylesheet element: xsl:attribute-set, xsl:decimal-format, xsl:include, xsl:key, xsl:namespace-alias, xsl:output, xsl:param, xsl:preserve-space, xsl:strip-space, xsl:template, and xsl:variable.

Notes

- The xsl: prefix points to an element in the XSLT namespace.
- You can use the xsl:transform element as a synonym for xsl:stylesheet.

Related Elements

xsl:attribute-set (p. 332), xsl:decimal-format (p. 338), xsl:include (p. 345), xsl:key (p. 345), xsl:namespace-alias (p. 347), xsl:output (p. 351), xsl:param (p. 353), xsl:preserve-space (p. 354), xsl:strip-space (p. 357), xsl:stylesheet (p. 357), xsl:template (p. 358), xsl:variable (p. 363)

xsl:value-of   Generate Text

Purpose

Generates text using an expression.

EBNF Syntax

```
<xsl:value-of select = string-expression
    disable-output-escaping = "yes" | "no" />
```

Standard Syntax

```
<xsl:value-of select = string-expression
    disable-output-escaping = "yes" | "no" />
```

Where

- select is a required keyword that indicates that *string-expression* follows.
- *string-expression* is an expression that is converted to a string as if it were using the string() function.
- disable-output-escaping is a keyword that indicates that certain symbols, such as ampersands (&), greater-than (>), less-than (<), and quotation marks (") can or cannot be used in the output of character data.
- yes is a keyword that indicates that no escaping of certain symbols is allowed during output.
- no is a keyword that indicates that escaping of certain symbols is allowed during output. This is the default.

Notes

- The xsl: prefix points to an element in the XSLT namespace.
- This element is in the instruction category.

XSLT Component

- The difference between xsl:copy-of and xsl:value-of is that xsl:value-of converts a result tree fragment into a string and xsl:copy-of does not.
- If you use *string-expression* within attribute values of elements that result in literals, enclose it within braces ({ }).
- If the string is empty, the processor will not create a text node.

Example

The following example is from the XSLT recommendation (http://www.w3.org/TR/xslt):

```
<xsl:template match="person">
  <p>
    <xsl:value-of select="@given-name"/>
    <xsl:text> </xsl:text>
    <xsl:value-of select="@family-name"/>
  </p>
</xsl:template>
```

Related Elements

xsl:apply-imports (p. 329), xsl:apply-templates (p. 330), xsl:attribute (p. 331), xsl:call-template (p. 334), xsl:choose (p. 335), xsl:comment (p. 336), xsl:copy (p. 336), xsl:copy-of (p. 337), xsl:element (p. 340), xsl:fallback (p. 341), xsl:for-each (p. 342), xsl:if (p. 343), xsl:message (p. 346), xsl:number (p. 348), xsl:processing-instruction (p. 354), xsl:text (p. 360), xsl:variable (p. 363)

xsl:variable   Variable Value

Purpose

Sets a value for a variable.

EBNF Syntax

```
<xsl:variable name = qname select = expression>
  template</xsl:variable>
```

Standard Syntax

```
<xsl:variable name = qname select = expression>
  template</xsl:variable>
```

Where

- name is a required keyword indicating that a qname follows.
- qname, which is the expanded qualified name of the attribute, names the attribute-value template.
- select is a keyword that indicates that *expression* follows.

- *expression* is an expression that selects one or more nodes.
- *template* is the result of processing the element.

Notes

- The xsl: prefix points to an element in the XSLT namespace.
- This element is in the instruction and top-level categories.
- A namespace is a set of unique names, defined in the DTD or elsewhere. In XML, a *qualified name* is composed of two parts: an identifier and either a URI or element name, depending on whether it is external or internal, respectively.

Example

The following example is from the XSLT recommendation (http://www.w3.org/TR/xslt):

```
xsl:variable name="para-font-size">12pt</xsl:variable>
```

Related Elements

xsl:apply-imports (p. 329), xsl:apply-templates (p. 330), xsl:attribute (p. 331), xsl:attribute-set (p. 332), xsl:call-template (p. 334), xsl:choose (p. 335), xsl:comment (p. 336), xsl:copy (p. 336), xsl:copy-of (p. 337), xsl:decimal-format (p. 338), xsl:element (p. 340), xsl:fallback (p. 341), xsl:for-each (p. 342), xsl:if (p. 343), xsl:include (p. 345), xsl:key (p. 345), xsl:message (p. 346), xsl:namespace-alias (p. 347), xsl:number (p. 348), xsl:output (p. 351), xsl:param (p. 353), xsl:preserve-space (p. 354), xsl:processing-instruction (p. 354), xsl:strip-space (p. 357), xsl:template (p. 358), xsl:text (p. 360), xsl:value-of (p. 362).

xsl:vendor	**Vendor**

XSLT Component

Purpose

Provides the name of the vendor that developed the XSLT processor.

Syntax

See the system-property() function.

Note

This element is a system property.

Related Elements

xsl:vendor-url (p. 365), xsl:version (p. 365)

Related Function

system-property() (p. 328)

xsl:vendor-url | Vendor URL

Purpose

Provides the URL for the vendor's company.

Syntax

See the system-property() function.

Note

This element is a system property.

Related Elements

xsl:vendor (p. 364), xsl:version (p. 365)

Related Function

system-property() (p. 328)

xsl:version | XSLT Version

Purpose

Provides the version of the XSLT processor.

Syntax

See the system-property() function.

Note

This element is a system property.

Related Elements

xsl:vendor (p. 364), xsl:vendor:url (p. 365)

Related Function

system-property() (p. 328)

xsl:when | Condition True

Purpose

Tests if a condition is true.

EBNF Syntax

```
<xsl:when test = boolean-expression>template
</xsl:when>
```

Standard Syntax

```
<xsl:when test = boolean-expression>template
</xsl:when>
```

XSLT Component

Where

- test is a keyword that indicates that *boolean-expression* follows.
- *boolean-expression* is an expression that tests a node for true or false conditions.
- *template* is the result of processing the element.

Notes

- The xsl: prefix points to an element in the XSLT namespace.
- The xsl:when element is a child of xsl:choose.
- The xsl:when element may be followed by an xsl:otherwise element.

Related Elements

xsl:choose (p. 355), xsl:otherwise (p. 350)

xsl:with-param	Pass Parameters

Purpose

Provides parameters for templates.

EBNF Syntax

```
<xsl:with-param name = qname select = expression>
  template</xsl:with-param>
```

Standard Syntax

```
<xsl:with-param name = qname select = expression>
  template</xsl:with-param>
```

Where

- name is a required keyword indicating that a qname follows.
- *qname*, which is the expanded qualified name of the attribute, names the attribute-value template.
- select is a keyword that indicates that *expression* follows.
- *expression* is an expression that selects one or more nodes.
- *template* is the result of processing the element.

Notes

- The xsl: prefix points to an element in the XSLT namespace.
- A namespace is a set of unique names, defined in the DTD or elsewhere. In XML, a *qualified name* is composed of two parts: an identifier and either a URI or element name, depending on whether it is external or internal, respectively.

Example

The following example is a segment from the XSLT recommendation (http://www.w3.org/TR/xslt):

```
<xsl:template match="ol//ol/li">
  <xsl:call-template name="numbered-block">
    <xsl:with-param name="format">a. </xsl:with-param>
  </xsl:call-template>
</xsl:template>
```

Related Elements

xsl:apply-templates (p. 330), xsl:call-template (p. 334)

XSL Style
Sheet Syntax

Extensible Style Sheet Language (XSL) is a work in progress. Specially developed to style XML documents, XSL is a two-part language; XSL both transforms and formats XML documents using the best properties from cascading style sheets (CSS1 and CSS2) and the online version of Document Style Semantics and Specification Language (DSSSL-O) and some properties developed specifically for XML documents.

XSL applies style properties to *formatting objects* — objects that fill a defined area in document output. Formatting objects come in three types — those that create areas; those that give information about areas, but do not create them; and items used in the creation of areas. The first two types are commonly known as *flow objects*; and the last is either an auxiliary object or a layout object.

Typical flow objects include any part of a document — from a specific character to a paragraph or a set of pages, graphics, or tables. When a parser interprets an XML document, the processor organizes flow objects into trees, which show specific ancestor-and-descendant relationships. When a flow-object tree is created, each flow object is assigned its own set of formatting characteristics.

Formats of parent flow objects can control the formats of child flow objects (that is the reason for the inherit keyword that you see throughout this section). Child flow objects can also have their own formats. The output of a formatted flow object "flows" into an *area*, which is a rectangle with a set height and width. In many ways, an area is analogous to a frame in a word-processing document — especially if you consider that a frame can include document elements as diverse as text and graphics.

This section lists XSL formatting objects, properties (most of which are closely related to CSS and DSSSL-O properties), and subsidiary functions. For more information about CSS, refer to *XHTML in Plain English*, also written by Sandra E. Eddy and published by IDG Books Worldwide.

To keep up to date with XSL, be sure to periodically browse the latest working draft and eventual recommendation at http://www. w3.org/TR/xsl/.

●—NOTE

World Wide Web Consortium (W3C) working drafts are not final recommendations, so you can expect changes in these documents. Before you use XSL, be sure to check the latest XSL documents at the W3C home page, http://www.w3.org/.

abs()   Absolute Function

Purpose
Returns the absolute value of the argument.

EBNF Syntax
```
number_r abs(number)
```

Standard Syntax
```
number_r abs(number)
```

Where
- *number_r* is the number returned by the function.
- *abs* is a function-name keyword.
- *number* represents the argument's number.

Note
- The absolute value can be either positive or negative. If it is negative, it is a negation of the argument.

Related Productions

ceiling() (p. 439), floor() (p. 464), max() (p. 548), min() (p. 552), round()
(p. 599)

AbsoluteLength [7]	**Absolute Length**

Purpose

Indicates an absolute length, which ends with the name of an absolute unit
of measure.

EBNF Syntax

```
AbsoluteLength ::= Number AbsoluteUnitName?
```

Standard Syntax

```
Number [AbsoluteUnitName]
```

Where

- Number (p. 555) represents a floating-point number made up of one or
  more digits.
- AbsoluteUnitName (p. 372) represents an absolute unit of measure.

Note

- AbsoluteLength is a component of the AbsoluteNumeric production.

Related Productions

AbsoluteNumeric (p. 371), AbsoluteUnitName (p. 372)

AbsoluteNumeric [6]	**Brief Description**

Purpose

Represents a number with an absolute value.

EBNF Syntax

```
AbsoluteNumeric ::= AbsoluteLength
```

Standard Syntax

```
AbsoluteLength
```

Where

- AbsoluteLength (p. 371) indicates an absolute length, which ends with
  the name of an absolute unit of measure.

Note

- AbsoluteNumeric is a component of the Numeric production.

XSL Style Sheet Syntax

Related Productions

AbsoluteLength (p. 371), AbsoluteUnitName (p. 372), Numeric (p. 558)

absolute-position
Absolute Position

Purpose

Specifies the absolute position of a fo:block-container

Syntax

```
absolute-position: auto|absolute|fixed|inheritWhere
```

- auto is a keyword that indicates there is no absolute-positioning restriction.
- absolute is a keyword that indicates the position of fo:block-container is specified by the XSL properties right, left, top, or bottom.
- fixed is a keyword that indicates that the position of fo:block-container is calculated based on the absolute model but that the area has some degree of being fixed.
- inherit is a keyword that indicates that this property takes the same computed value as its parent.

Notes

- The only objects using this property that may have page or column breaks are those whose absolute-position property is set to auto.
- If a property's absolute-position value (inherited or set) is set to either fixed or absolute, then any keep and break properties will be overlooked.
- The area generated as a result of using absolute-position with fo:block-container is actually a descendant of the page-area where the original area would have been placed if the original object's position had been specified using this property.

Related Properties

bottom (p. 434), left (p. 535), right (p. 597), top (p. 632)

AbsoluteUnitName [27]
Brief Description

Purpose

Represents an absolute unit of measure.

EBNF Syntax

```
AbsoluteUnitName ::= 'cm' | 'mm' | 'in' | 'pt'
    | 'pc' | 'px'
```

Standard Syntax

```
cm | mm | in | pt | pc | px
```

Where

- cm represents centimeters.
- mm represents millimeters.
- in represents inches.
- pt represents points.
- pc represents picas.
- px represents pixels.

Note

- AbsoluteUnitName represents part of an expression.
- AbsoluteUnitName is a component of the AbsoluteLength production.

Related Productions

AlphaOrDigits (p. 376), Color (p. 443), Digits (p. 452), EnumerationToken (p. 459), ExprToken (p. 460), ExprWhitespace (p. 461), FloatingPointNumber (p. 463), FunctionName (p. 512), Keyword (p. 529), Literal (p. 541), MultiplyOperator (p. 555), Number (p. 555), Operator (p. 559), OperatorName (p. 560), RelativeUnitName (p. 593)

active-state   Active State

Purpose

Determines which of the fo:multi-property-sets will be used to format the related (child flow) objects.

Syntax

active-state: link|visited|active|hover|focus

Where

- link is a fo:multi-property-set that applies when there is a fo: simple-link within a fo:multi-properties that has not yet been visited.
- visited is a fo:multi-property-set that applies when there is a fo:simple-link within a fo:multi-properties that has been visited.
- active is a fo:multi-property-set that applies when the area returned by a fo:multi-properties is being activated, like a link between the time a user presses on the mouse button and releases it.
- hover is a fo:multi-property-set that applies when the area returned by a fo:multi-properties has not been activated yet but is currently being hovered over.
- focus is a fo:multi-property-set that applies when the area returned by a fo:multi-properties has the current focus. For instance, if you are tabbing through links or form-fields, when you settle on one of these objects it usually has some indication that it is selected. This is the *focus*.

Note

- This property is in the links category.

Related Properties

auto-restore (p. 377), case-title (p. 438), destination-placement-offset (p. 452), external-destination (p. 462), indicate-destination (p. 523), internal-destination (p. 526), show-destination (p. 604), starting-state (p. 619), switch-to (p. 621)

AdditiveExpr [11]   Additive Expression

Purpose

Acts on one or more expressions through addition or subtraction.

EBNF Syntax

```
AdditiveExpr ::= MultiplicativeExpr
    | AdditiveExpr '+' MultiplicativeExpr
    | AdditiveExpr '-' MultiplicativeExpr
```

Standard Syntax

```
MultiplicativeExpr
    | AdditiveExpr + MultiplicativeExpr
    | AdditiveExpr - MultiplicativeExpr
```

Where

- MultiplicativeExpr (p. 554) acts on one or more expressions through multiplication or division or finding a modulus.
- AdditiveExpr (p. 374) acts on one or more expressions through addition or subtraction.
- + is the addition operator.
- - is the subtraction operator.

Notes

- AdditiveExpr is a component of the Expr production.
- AdditiveExpr has an identical purpose to that of XPath's AdditiveExpr.
- Because minus (–) is not only the subtraction operator but can also be included in names, it's a good idea to precede and succeed the — subtraction operator with at least one space.

Related Productions

AdditiveExpr (p. 374), Expr (p. 459), MultiplicativeExpr (p. 554)

alignment-adjust

Alignment Adjust

Purpose

Allows more precise alignments of elements.

Syntax

```
alignment-adjust: auto|percentage|length|inherit
```

Where

- auto is a keyword that tells the browser to automatically determine how to adjust the element based on the current baseline or baseline-identifier property.
- percentage is a value that when multiplied by the height of the area in question, computes the final value by which the alignment should be adjusted.
- length specifies how much an area's alignment should be adjusted.
- inherit is a keyword that indicates that this property takes the same computed value as its parent.

Notes

- This is an area alignment property.
- This property works well to better align elements that do not have a baseline-table or lack the optimal baseline in their existing baseline-table.
- A glyph's alignment-point is at the point where start edge of its pre-defined area and its baseline meet.
- The baseline of a glyph is identified by the baseline-identifier property.
- For other areas, the alignment-point is at the intersection start edge of the element's border rectangle and its baseline.
- If no baseline-identifier exists, the application or browser may use heuristics to determine what the missing baseline might be.
- The dominant-baseline may be used as a backup if no baseline-identifier exists.
- The height of an area used in conjunction with percentage may be defined by the height of a fo:external-graphic or fo:instream-foreign-object, the font-size of an fo:character, or the line-height for all other areas.
- A percentage of 0% or a length of 0cm makes the dominant-baseline the alignment point.

Related Properties

baseline-identifier (p. 387), baseline-shift (p. 388), display-align (p. 454), dominant-baseline (p. 455), relative-align (p. 591)

XSL Style Sheet Syntax

AlphaOrDigits [19]   Alphabetic Character or Digit

Purpose

Represents one or more alphabetic characters or decimal or hexadecimal numbers.

EBNF Syntax

```
AlphaOrDigits ::= [a-fA-F0-9]+
```

Standard Syntax

```
(a-f|A-F|0-9[a-f|A-F|0-9]...[a-f|A-F|0-9])
```

Where

- a-f and A-F represent alphabetic characters for a hexadecimal number.
- 0-9 are decimal numbers from 0 to 9.

Note

- AlphaOrDigits represents part of an expression.

Related Productions

AbsoluteUnitName (p. 372), AlphaOrDigits (p. 376), Color (p. 443), Digits (p. 452), EnumerationToken (p. 459), ExprToken (p. 460), ExprWhitespace (p. 461), FloatingPointNumber (p. 463), FunctionName (p. 512), Keyword (p. 529), Literal (p. 541), MultiplyOperator (p. 555), Number (p. 555), Operator (p. 559), OperatorName (p. 560), RelativeUnitName (p. 593)

Argument [4]   Argument

Purpose

Represents an argument.

EBNF Syntax

```
Argument ::= Expr
```

Standard Syntax

```
Expr
```

Where

- Expr (p. 459) indicates an expression.

Notes

- Argument is a component of the FunctionCall production.
- The XSL Argument production is identical to the XPath Argument production.

Related XPath Productions

Expr (p. 459), FunctionCall (p. 511)

auto-restore   Automatic Restore

Purpose

Indicates whether the first fo:multi-case formatting object is restored when the fo:multi-switch formatting object is concealed by an ancestor.

Syntax

```
auto-restore: yes|no
```

Where

- yes is a keyword that indicates that the first fo:multi-case is restored.
- no is a keyword that indicates that the current fo:multi-case remains. This is the default.

Notes

- This property is in the links category.
- By default, the characteristics of this property are inherited.

Related Properties

case-name (p. 438), case-title (p. 438), destination-placement-offset (p. 452), external-destination (p. 462), indicate-destination (p. 523), internal-destination (p. 526), show-destination (p. 604), starting-state (p. 619), switch-to (p. 621)

Related Formatting Object

fo:multi-switch (p. 481)

azimuth   Spatial Azimuth

Purpose

Specifies the left-to-right stereo speaker location of a sound file.

Syntax

```
azimuth: range_angle|((left-side|far-left|left
    |center-left|center|center-right|right|far-right
    |right-side)|behind)|leftwards|rightwards|inherit
```

Where

- *range_angle* is a specific angle in the arc in which stereo speakers are arranged. Valid values range from –360deg (degrees) to 360deg.
- left-side is a keyword that indicates that the sound is on the left side of the arc — at 270deg. If azimuth: left-side behind, the sound is at 270deg.
- far-left is a keyword that indicates that the sound is on the far left side of the arc — at 300deg. If azimuth: far-left behind, the sound is at 240deg.

- **left** is a keyword that indicates that the sound is on the left side — at 320deg. If **azimuth: left behind**, the sound is at 220deg.
- **center-left** is a keyword that indicates that the sound is to the left of center — at 340deg. If **azimuth: center-left behind**, the sound is at 200deg.
- **center** is a keyword that indicates that the sound is straight ahead — at 0deg. This is the default. If **azimuth: center behind**, the sound is straight behind — at 180deg.
- **center-right** is a keyword that indicates that the sound is to the right of center — at 20deg. If **azimuth: center-right behind**, the sound is at 160deg.
- **right** is a keyword that indicates that the sound is further right on the arc — at 40deg. If **azimuth: right behind**, the sound is at 140deg.
- **far-right** is a keyword that indicates that the sound is on the far right side of the arc — at 60deg. If **azimuth: far-right behind**, the sound is at 120deg.
- **right-side** is a keyword that indicates that the sound is on the right side of the arc — at 90deg. If **azimuth: right-side behind**, the sound is at 90deg.
- **behind** is a keyword that indicates that the sound is moved 90 degrees — in conjunction with the **left-side**, **far-left**, **left**, **center-left**, **center**, **center-right**, **right**, **far-right**, and **right-side** keywords.
- **leftwards** is a keyword that indicates that the sound is moved 20 degrees to the left, or counterclockwise from the current position.
- **rightwards** is a keyword that indicates that the sound is moved 20 degrees to the right, or clockwise from the current position.
- **inherit** is a keyword that indicates that this property takes the same computed value as its parent.

Notes

- This property is in the common-aural category.
- This property, which originated in CSS2, applies to all elements.
- By default, the characteristics of this property are inherited.

Related Properties

cue (p. 449), **cue-after** (p. 450), **cue-before** (p. 451), **elevation** (p. 456), **pause** (p. 577), **pause-after** (p. 578), **pause-before** (p. 579), **pitch** (p. 580), **pitch-range** (p. 581), **play-during** (p. 582), **richness** (p. 597), **speak** (p. 613), **speak-header** (p. 614), **speak-numeral** (p. 615), **speak-punctuation** (p. 615), **speech-rate** (p. 616), **stress** (p. 620), **voice-family** (p. 637), **volume** (p. 638)

Related Formatting Objects

fo:bidi-override (p. 465), **fo:block** (p. 466), **fo:external-graphic** (p. 470), **fo:footnote-body** (p. 472), **fo:initial-property-set** (p. 473), **fo:inline** (p. 473), **fo:instream-foreign-object** (p. 475), **fo:leader** (p. 476), **fo:list-block** (p. 477), **fo:list-item** (p. 478), **fo:page-number** (p. 492), **fo:page-number-citation** (p. 492), **fo:simple-link** (p. 500), **fo:table**

XSL Style Sheet Syntax

(p. 503), fo:table-and-caption (p. 504), fo:table-body (p. 504), fo:table-caption (p. 505), fo:table-cell (p. 505), fo:table-footer (p. 506), fo:table-header (p. 507), fo:table-row (p. 507)

background   Background Properties

Purpose
Specifies one, two, three, four, or five properties for the page background.

Syntax
```
background: [background-color_value]
    | [background-image_value]
    | [background-repeat_value]
    | [background-attachment_value]
    | [background-position_value]|inherit
```

Where
- *background-color_value* specifies the background color. For more information, see the background-color property (p. 381).
- *background-image_value* specifies the background image. For more information, see the background-image property (p. 382).
- *background-repeat_value* repeats a background image. For more information, see the background-repeat property (p. 386).
- *background-attachment_value* specifies whether the background image is fixed or scrolls. For more information, see the background-attachment property (p. 380).
- *background-position_value* specifies a starting position for a background image. For more information, see the background-position property (p. 383).
- inherit is a keyword that indicates that this property takes the same computed value as its parent.

Notes
- This property is in the common-border-padding-background category.
- This shortcut property originated in CSS1.
- Shortcut properties should be processed as follows: Set the "embedded" properties to their initial values; if the characteristics of the shortcut property are inherited, each "embedded" property should take the same computed value as its parent; if the characteristics of the shortcut property are not inherited, set each value; then the value of shorthand property overrides the counterpart value of the individual property.
- By default, the characteristics of this property are not inherited.

Example
```
p.image {background: url(pattern.gif) silver repeat fixed }
```

Related Properties

background properties (p. 379 – p. 387), border properties (p. 392 – p. 434), padding properties (p. 562 – p. 571)

Related Formatting Objects

fo:bidi-override (p. 465), fo:block (p. 466), fo:block-container (p. 467), fo:external-graphic (p. 470), fo:float (p. 471), fo:footnote (p. 472), fo:footnote-body (p. 472), fo:initial-property-set (p. 473), fo:inline (p. 473), fo:inline-container (p. 474), fo:instream-foreign-object (p. 475), fo:leader (p. 476), fo:list-block (p. 477), fo:list-item (p. 478), fo:page-number (p. 492), fo:page-number-citation (p. 492), fo:region-after (p. 495), fo:region-before (p. 496), fo:region-body (p. 496), fo:region-end (p. 497), fo:region-start (p. 497), fo:simple-link (p. 500), fo:table (p. 503), fo:table-and-caption (p. 504), fo:table-body (p. 504), fo:table-caption (p. 505), fo:table-cell (p. 505), fo:table-column (p. 506), fo:table-footer (p. 506), fo:table-header (p. 507), fo:table-row (p. 507)

---

background-attachment | Attach Background Image

Purpose

Specifies whether the background image is fixed or scrolls in the background of the page.

Syntax

```
background-attachment: scroll|fixed|inherit
```

Where

- scroll scrolls a background image as a user scrolls up or down the current page.
- fixed freezes the background image in place on the current page.
- inherit is a keyword that indicates that this property takes the same computed value as its parent.

Notes

- This property is in the common-border-padding-background category.
- This property, which originated in CSS1, applies to all elements.
- By default, the characteristics of this property are not inherited.

Example

```
body { background-image: url(pattern.gif); background-color: silver;
background-attachment: fixed }
```

Related Properties

background properties (p. 379 – p. 387), border properties (p. 392 – p. 434), padding properties (p. 562 – p. 571)

Related Formatting Objects

fo:bidi-override (p. 465), fo:block (p. 466), fo:block-container (p. 467), fo:external-graphic (p. 470), fo:float (p. 471), fo:footnote (p. 472), fo:footnote-body (p. 472), fo:initial-property-set (p. 473), fo:inline (p. 473), fo:inline-container (p. 474), fo:instream-foreign-object (p. 475), fo:leader (p. 476), fo:list-block (p. 477), fo:list-item (p. 478), fo:page-number (p. 492), fo:page-number-citation (p. 492), fo:region-after (p. 495), fo:region-before (p. 496), fo:region-body (p. 496), fo:region-end (p. 497), fo:region-start (p. 497), fo:simple-link (p. 500), fo:table (p. 503), fo:table-and-caption (p. 504), fo:table-body (p. 504), fo:table-caption (p. 505), fo:table-cell (p. 505), fo:table-column (p. 506), fo:table-footer (p. 506), fo:table-header (p. 507), fo:table-row (p. 507)

background-color   Background Color

Purpose

Specifies a background color for the current document or document part.

Syntax

```
background-color:
  (color-name|#rgb|#rrggbb|rgb(rrr,ggg,bbb)
  |rgb(rrr%,ggg%,bbb%))|transparent|inherit
```

Where

- *color-name* represents a foreground color by valid name (that is, Red (#FF0000), Maroon (#800000), Yellow (#FFFF00), Green (#008000), Lime (#00FF00), Teal (#008080), Olive (#808000), Aqua (#00FFFF), Blue (#0000FF), Navy (#000080), Purple (#800080), Fuchsia (#FF00FF), Black (#000000), Gray (#808080), White (#FFFFFF), and the default, Silver (#C0C0C0)). CSS2 adds the following colors: ActiveBorder, ActiveCaption, AppWorkspace, Background, ButtonFace, Button Highlight, ButtonShadow, ButtonText, CaptionText, GrayText, Highlight, HighlightText, InactiveBorder, InactiveCaption, InactiveCaptionText, InfoBackground, InfoText, Menu, MenuText, Scrollbar, ThreeDDarkShadow, ThreeDFace, ThreeDHighlight, ThreeDLightShadow, ThreeDShadow, Window, WindowFrame, and WindowText. All color names are case-insensitive.
- *#rgb* is a three-digit hexadecimal color code, where *r* represents the red attributes, from 0 to F; *g* represents the green attributes, from 0 to F; and *b* represents the blue attributes, from 0 to F.
- *#rrggbb* is a six-digit hexadecimal color code, where *rr* represents the red attributes, from 00 to FF; *gg* represents the green attributes, from 00 to FF; and *bb* represents the blue attributes, from 00 to FF.
- rgb(*rrr,ggg,bbb*) represents absolute red-green-blue values, each ranging from 000 to 255.

- rgb(*rrr.d%*, *ggg.e%*, *bbb.f%*) represents the relative red-green-blue values, each ranging from 0.0% to 100.0%. Note that 0.0% is equivalent to an absolute value of 000, and 100.0% is equivalent to 255.
- transparent represents no background color. This is the default.
- inherit is a keyword that indicates that this property takes the same computed value as its parent.

Notes

- This property is in the common-border-padding-background category.
- This property, which originated in CSS1, applies to all elements.
- By default, the characteristics of this property are not inherited.

Example

```
body { background-color: silver }
```

Related Properties

background properties (p. 379 – p. 387), border properties (p. 392 – p. 434), padding properties (p. 562 – p. 571)

Related Formatting Objects

fo:bidi-override (p. 465), fo:block (p. 466), fo:block-container (p. 467), fo:external-graphic (p. 470), fo:float (p. 471), fo:footnote (p. 472), fo:footnote-body (p. 472), fo:initial-property-set (p. 473), fo:inline (p. 473), fo:inline-container (p. 474), fo:instream-foreign-object (p. 475), fo:leader (p. 476), fo:list-block (p. 477), fo:list-item (p. 478), fo:page-number (p. 492), fo:page-number-citation (p. 492), fo:region-after (p. 495), fo:region-before (p. 496), fo:region-body (p. 496), fo:region-end (p. 497), fo:region-start (p. 497), fo:simple-link (p. 500), fo:table (p. 503), fo:table-and-caption (p. 504), fo:table-body (p. 504), fo:table-caption (p. 505), fo:table-cell (p. 505), fo:table-column (p. 506), fo:table-footer (p. 506), fo:table-header (p. 507), fo:table-row (p. 507)

background-image   Background Image

Purpose

Specifies a background image for the current document or document part.

Syntax

```
background-image: uri(uri_name)|none|inherit
```

Where

- uri is a reserved keyword that indicates that a URI will follow.
- *uri_name* names the URI of the image to be used for the background.
- none indicates no background image.
- inherit is a keyword that indicates that this property takes the same computed value as its parent.

Notes

- This property is in the common-border-padding-background category.
- This property, which originated in CSS1, applies to all elements.
- By default, the characteristics of this property are not inherited.

Example

```
onepage { background-image: url(pattern.gif); background-color: silver }
```

Related Properties

background properties (p. 379 – p. 387), border properties (p. 392 – p. 434), padding properties (p. 562 – p. 571)

Related Formatting Objects

fo:bidi-override (p. 465), fo:block (p. 466), fo:block-container (p. 467), fo:external-graphic (p. 470), fo:float (p. 471), fo:footnote (p. 472), fo:footnote-body (p. 472), fo:initial-property-set (p. 473), fo:inline (p. 473), fo:inline-container (p. 474), fo:instream-foreign-object (p. 475), fo:leader (p. 476), fo:list-block (p. 477), fo:list-item (p. 478), fo:page-number (p. 492), fo:page-number-citation (p. 492), fo:region-after (p. 495), fo:region-before (p. 496), fo:region-body (p. 496), fo:region-end (p. 497), fo:region-start (p. 497), fo:simple-link (p. 500), fo:table (p. 503), fo:table-and-caption (p. 504), fo:table-body (p. 504), fo:table-caption (p. 505), fo:table-cell (p. 505), fo:table-column (p. 506), fo:table-footer (p. 506), fo:table-header (p. 507), fo:table-row (p. 507)

---

background-position | Background Image Position

Purpose

Specifies a starting position for a background image.

Syntax

```
background-position: (([+|-]h_percent%
[[+|-]v_percent%])|(([+|-] h_length
[[+|-]v_length])|((top|center|bottom)
|(left|center|right))))|inherit
```

Where

- $h\_percent$ is a positive or negative value that is relative to the left-to-right position of the image. Follow each $h\_percent$ with a percentage sign (%).
- $v\_percent$ is a positive or negative value that is relative to the top-to-bottom position of the image. The default is 50%. Follow each $v\_percent$ with a percentage sign (%).
- h_length is a positive or negative value of the left-to-right position of the image away from the top-left corner. Follow each value with a two-letter abbreviation representing the unit of measure.

- *v_length* is a positive or negative value of the left-to-right position of the image away from the top-left corner. Follow each value with a two-letter abbreviation representing the unit of measure.
- top is a keyword that positions the background image in the top-to-bottom plane at the top of the current box's padding edge.
- center is a keyword that positions the background image in the top-to-bottom plane in the center of the current box.
- bottom is a keyword that positions the background image in the top-to-bottom plane at the bottom of the current box's padding edge.
- left is a keyword that positions the background image in the left-to-right plane at the left of the current box's padding edge.
- center is a keyword that positions the background image in the left-to-right plane in the center of the current box.
- right is a keyword that positions the background image in the left-to-right plane at the right of the current box's padding edge.
- inherit is a keyword that indicates that this property takes the same computed value as its parent.

Notes
- This property is in the common-border-padding-background category.
- This property originated in CSS1.
- By default, the characteristics of this property are not inherited.

Example
```
onepage { background-image: url(pattern.gif);
background-position: 50% 50%; background-color: silver }
```

Related Properties
background properties (p. 379 – p. 387), border properties (p. 392 – p. 434), padding properties (p. 562 – p. 571)

Related Formatting Objects
fo:bidi-override (p. 465), fo:block (p. 466), fo:block-container (p. 467), fo:external-graphic (p. 470), fo:float (p. 471), fo:footnote (p. 472), fo:footnote-body (p. 472), fo:initial-property-set (p. 473), fo:inline (p. 473), fo:inline-container (p. 474), fo:instream-foreign-object (p. 475), fo:leader (p. 476), fo:list-block (p. 477), fo:list-item (p. 478), fo:page-number (p. 492), fo:page-number-citation (p. 492), fo:region-after (p. 495), fo:region-before (p. 496), fo:region-body (p. 496), fo:region-end (p. 497), fo:region-start (p. 497), fo:simple-link (p. 500), fo:table (p. 503), fo:table-and-caption (p. 504), fo:table-body (p. 504), fo:table-caption (p. 505), fo:table-cell (p. 505), fo:table-column (p. 506), fo:table-footer (p. 506), fo:table-header (p. 507), fo:table-row (p. 507)

background-position-horizontal

Background Position - Horizontal

Purpose
Specifies the initial horizontal position of a background-image.

Syntax
background-position-horizontal: percentage|length|left|center|right|inherit

Where
- *percentage* is a percentage value (based on 100% of the area's width) that specifies the location of the background image.
- length specifies how far to the right of the left edge of the area that the background image will be placed.
- left is a keyword that means the same as 0%.
- right is a keyword that means the same as 100%.
- center is a keyword that means the same as 50%.
- inherit is a keyword that indicates that this property takes the same computed value as its parent.

Notes
- The default value of background-position-horizontal is 0%.
- This property is part of the Common Border, Padding, and Background group.
- background-position-horizontal pertains to all formatting objects that utilize the background property.

Related Properties
background properties (p. 379 – p. 387)

background-position-vertical

Background Position - Vertical

Purpose
Specifies the initial vertical position of a background-image.

Syntax
background-position-vertical: percentage|length|top|center|bottom|inherit

Where
- *percentage* is a percentage (based on 100% of the area's height from top-to-bottom) that specifies the location of the background image.
- *length* is a length value that specifies how far toward the bottom from the top-most point that the background image will be placed.
- top is a keyword that means the same as 0%.
- bottom is a keyword that means the same as 100%.

XSL Style Sheet Syntax

- center is a keyword that means the same as 50%.
- inherit is a keyword that indicates that this property takes the same computed value as its parent.

Notes

- The default value of background-position-vertical is 0%.
- This property is part of the Common Border, Padding, and Background group.
- background-position-vertical pertains to all formatting objects that utilize the background property.

Related Properties

background properties (p. 379 – p. 387)

background-repeat   Background Repeat

Purpose

Repeats a background image onscreen a particular number of times.

Syntax

```
background-repeat: repeat|repeat-x|repeat-y
  |no-repeat|inherit
```

Where

- repeat fills the page completely with the image.
- repeat-x fills the page with the image horizontally from the left edge to the right edge.
- repeat-y fills the page vertically from top to bottom.
- no-repeat does not repeat the image.
- inherit is a keyword that indicates that this property takes the same computed value as its parent.

Notes

- This property is in the common-border-padding-background category.
- This property, which originated in CSS1, applies to all elements.
- By default, the characteristics of this property are not inherited.

Example

```
bigpage { background-image: url(pattern.gif)
; background-repeat: repeat-x; background-color: teal }
```

Related Properties

background properties (p. 379 – p. 387), border properties (p. 392 – p. 434), and padding properties (p. 562 – p. 571)

XSL Style Sheet Syntax

Related Formatting Objects

fo:bidi-override (p. 465), fo:block (p. 466), fo:block-container (p. 467), fo:external-graphic (p. 470), fo:float (p. 471), fo:footnote (p. 472), fo:footnote-body (p. 472), fo:initial-property-set (p. 473), fo:inline (p. 473), fo:inline-container (p. 474), fo:instream-foreign-object (p. 475), fo:leader (p. 476), fo:list-block (p. 477), fo:list-item (p. 478), fo:page-number (p. 492), fo:page-number-citation (p. 492), fo:region-after (p. 495), fo:region-before (p. 496), fo:region-body (p. 496), fo:region-end (p. 497), fo:region-start (p. 497), fo:simple-link (p. 500), fo:table (p. 503), fo:table-and-caption (p. 504), fo:table-body (p. 504), fo:table-caption (p. 505), fo:table-cell (p. 505), fo:table-column (p. 506), fo:table-footer (p. 506), fo:table-header (p. 507), fo:table-row (p. 507)

baseline-identifier   Baseline Identifier

Purpose

Defines how an object is aligned with respect to its parent and determines the default alignment point, so it can be adjusted by other properties.

Syntax

```
baseline-identifier: baseline| before-edge
 | text-before-edge| middle| after-edge| text-after-edge|
ideographic| alphabetic
 | hanging| mathematical| inherit
```

Where

- baseline is a keyword that specifies that the alignment-point of the object is the dominant-baseline of the parent area.
- before-edge is a keyword that specifies that the alignment point of the object is the dominant-baseline before the edge of the parent area.
- text-before-edge is a keyword that specifies the alignment point of the object to be the baseline of any text before the edge of the parent area.
- middle is a keyword that specifies that the alignment point of the object should be aligned with the middle baseline of the parent area.
- text-after-edge is a keyword that specifies the alignment point of the object to be the baseline of any text after the edge of the parent area.
- ideographic is a keyword that defines alignment-point of the object to be aligned with the baseline for embedded ideographic or Indic characters of the parent area.
- alphabetic is a keyword that defines alignment-point of the object to be aligned with the baseline for some fonts' alphabetic characters within the parent area.
- hanging is a keyword that specifies that the alignment point of the object should be aligned with the hanging baseline of the parent area.

XSL Style Sheet Syntax

- `mathematical` is a keyword that specifies that the alignment point of the object should be aligned with the hanging baseline of the parent area.
- `inherit` is a keyword that indicates that this property takes the same computed value as its parent.

Notes

- This property is part of the Area Alignment property set.
- Western scripts tend to use an `alphabetic` baseline that touches at or near the bottom of capital letters.
- For the `fo:character` formatting object, the initial value of `baseline-identifier` is the `dominant-baseline` of the script to which the character belongs. If there is no way to tell what the script is, then the initial value becomes that of the `dominant-baseline` for the parent area.
- For areas that do not utilize `fo:character`, the default value for `baseline-identifier` is `baseline`.

Related Properties

`baseline-shift` (p. 388), `block-progression-dimension` (p. 390), `clip` (p. 440), `color` (p. 441), `direction` (p. 453), `font-height-override-after` (p. 484), `font-height-override-before` (p. 485), `glyph-orientation-horizontal` (p. 512), `glyph-orientation-vertical` (p. 513), `height` (p. 514), `href` (p. 515), `hyphenation-keep` (p. 517), `hyphenation-ladder-count` (p. 518), `id` (p. 521), `inline-progression-dimension` (p. 525), `last-line-end-indent` (p. 531), `linefeed-treatment` (p. 537), `line-height` (p. 538), `line-height-shift-adjustment` (p. 539), `line-stacking-strategy` (p. 540), `max-height` (p. 548), `max-width` (p. 550), `min-height` (p. 552), `min-width` (p. 553), `overflow` (p. 561), `provisional-distance-between-starts` (p. 586), `provisional-label-separation` (p. 587), `reference-orientation` (p. 588), `ref-id` (p. 589), `scaling` (p. 601), `score-spaces` (p. 602), `size` (p. 605), `space-treatment` (p. 611), `span` (p. 612), `text-align` (p. 625), `text-align-last` (p. 626), `text-indent` (p. 629), `unicode-bidi` (p. 634), `vertical-align` (p. 635), `visibility` (p. 636), `white-space` (p. 639), `white-space-collapse` (p. 640), `width` (p. 642), `wrap-option` (p. 644), `writing-mode` (p. 645), `z-index` (p. 648)

Related Formatting Objects

`fo:inline` (p. 473), `fo:leader` (p. 476)

baseline-shift   Baseline Shift

Purpose

Moves the selected baseline away from the default baseline location.

Syntax

```
baseline-shift: none|sub|super|length|inherit
```

Where

- none indicates no baseline shift. This is the default.
- sub is a keyword that indicates that the selected baseline be shifted below the current baseline.
- super is a keyword that indicates that the selected baseline be shifted above the current baseline.
- *length* is a positive value representing the amount of baseline shift. Follow *length* with a two-letter abbreviation representing the unit of measure.
- inherit is a keyword that indicates that this property takes the same computed value as its parent.

Notes

- This property is in the miscellaneous category.
- By default, the characteristics of this property are not inherited.

Related Properties

baseline-identifier (p. 387), block-progression-dimension (p. 390), clip (p. 440), color (p. 441), direction (p. 453), font-height-override-after (p. 484), font-height-override-before (p. 485), glyph-orientation-horizontal (p. 512), glyph-orientation-vertical (p. 513), height (p. 514), href (p. 515), hyphenation-keep (p. 517), hyphenation-ladder-count (p. 518), id (p. 521), inline-progression-dimension (p. 525), last-line-end-indent (p. 531), linefeed-treatment (p. 537), line-height (p. 538), line-height-shift-adjustment (p. 539), line-stacking-strategy (p. 540), max-height (p. 548), max-width (p. 550), min-height (p. 552), min-width (p. 553), overflow (p. 561), provisional-distance-between-starts (p. 586), provisional-label-separation (p. 587), reference-orientation (p. 588), ref-id (p. 589), scaling (p. 601), score-spaces (p. 602), size (p. 605), space-treatment (p. 611), span (p. 612), text-align (p. 625), text-align-last (p. 626), text-indent (p. 629), unicode-bidi (p. 634), vertical-align (p. 635), visibility (p. 636), white-space (p. 639), white-space-collapse (p. 640), width (p. 642), wrap-option (p. 644), writing-mode (p. 645), z-index (p. 648)

Related Formatting Objects

fo:inline (p. 473), fo:leader (p. 476)

blank-or-not-blank   Blank Page

XSL Style Sheet Syntax

Purpose

Makes a page-master eligible for selection depending on whether it is blank or filled.

Syntax

```
blank-or-not-blank: blank|nonblank|any|inherit
```

Where

- blank is a keyword that indicates that the page-master can be selected if a blank page is needed to end a page sequence with an odd or even page.
- nonblank is a keyword that indicates that the page-master can be selected if the current page is not a blank page in the page sequence.
- any is a keyword that indicates that the page-master can be selected if this page is either blank or nonblank within the page sequence. This is the default.
- inherit is a keyword that indicates that this property takes the same computed value as its parent.

Notes

- This property is in the pagination-and-layout category.
- This property applies to the fo:conditional-page-master-reference formatting object.
- By default, characteristics of this property are not inherited.

Related Properties

column-count (p. 444), column-gap (p. 444), extent (p. 461), flow-name (p. 465), force-page-count (p. 494), initial-page-number (p. 524), master-name (p. 547), maximum-repeats (p. 549), odd-or-even (p. 559), page-height (p. 575), page-position (p. 575), page-width (p. 576), precedence (p. 584), region-name (p. 590)

Related Formatting Object

fo:conditional-page-master-reference (p. 469)

block-progression-dimension	Block Progression Dimension

Purpose

Specifies an area's block progression dimension for block-level and replaced-elements areas.

Syntax

```
block-progression-dimension: length|percentage|auto
    |inherit
```

Where

- *length* is a positive value followed by a two-letter abbreviation representing the unit of measure.
- *percent* is a positive value that is relative to the size of the parent. Follow *percent* with a percentage sign (%).
- auto is a keyword that represents a value automatically calculated by the user's browser. This is the default.

- inherit is a keyword that indicates that this property takes the same computed value as its parent.

Notes

- This property is in the miscellaneous category.
- By default, the characteristics of this property are not inherited.

Related Properties

baseline-shift (p. 388), clip (p. 440), color (p. 441), direction (p. 453), font-height-override-after (p. 484), font-height-override-before (p. 485), glyph-orientation-horizontal (p. 512), glyph-orientation-vertical (p. 513), height (p. 514), href (p. 515), hyphenation-keep (p. 517), hyphenation-ladder-count (p. 518), id (p. 521), inline-progression-dimension (p. 525), last-line-end-indent (p. 531), linefeed-treatment (p. 537), line-height (p. 538), line-height-shift-adjustment (p. 539), line-stacking-strategy (p. 540), max-height (p. 548), max-width (p. 550), min-height (p. 552), min-width (p. 553), overflow (p. 561), provisional-distance-between-starts (p. 586), provisional-label-separation (p. 587), reference-orientation (p. 588), ref-id (p. 589), scaling (p. 601), score-spaces (p. 602), size (p. 605), space-treatment (p. 611), span (p. 612), text-align (p. 625), text-align-last (p. 626), text-indent (p. 629), unicode-bidi (p. 634), vertical-align (p. 635), visibility (p. 636), white-space (p. 639), white-space-collapse (p. 640), width (p. 642), wrap-option (p. 644), writing-mode (p. 645), z-index (p. 648)

Related Formatting Objects

fo:block-container (p. 467), fo:external-graphic (p. 470), fo:inline-container (p. 474), fo:instream-foreign-object (p. 475), fo:table (p. 503), fo:table-caption (p. 505), fo:table-cell (p. 505), fo:table-row (p. 507)

body-start() — Body-Start Function

Purpose

Returns the body-start value for a list.

EBNF Syntax

    number_r body-start()

Standard Syntax

    number_r body-start()

Where

- *number_r* is the number returned by the function.
- body-start is a function-name keyword.

Note

- If you use this function outside a list, it returns a body-start value.

Related Production
provisional-label-separation (p. 587)

Related Functions
from-nearest-specified-value() (p. 509), from-parent() (p. 510),
from-table-column() (p. 510), inherited-property-value() (p. 523),
label-end() (p. 530)

border	Border Properties

Purpose
Specifies the color, style, and/or width of all four borders of a box.

Syntax
```
border: ([border-width_value][ border-style_value]
  [ border-color_value])|inherit
```

Where
- *border-width_value* specifies the width of all four borders. For more information, see the border-width property (p. 432).
- *border-style_value* specifies the style of all four borders. For more information, see the border-style property (p. 426).
- *border-color_value* specifies the color of all four borders. For more information, see the border-color property (p. 406).
- inherit is a keyword that indicates that this property takes the same computed value as its parent.

Notes
- This property is in the common-border-padding-background category.
- This property originated in CSS1.
- This shortcut property specifies multiple properties for the four borders in the same way that you can individually set rules for the following properties: border-color, border-style, and border-width.
- There is no initial value for this property.
- By default, the characteristics of this property are not inherited.
- In CSS, you must specify the processing order for properties "embedded" in shortcut properties. In XML, "embedded" properties are explicitly defined as unordered. XSL has a specific order of preference: Properties that affect part of a whole are processed first; properties that affect the entire whole are processed last. Specifically, border properties are processed in the following four ranks: border (processed first); border-style, border-color, and border-width; border-top, border-bottom, border-right, and border-left; and border-*-* (processed last).

- Shortcut properties should be processed as follows: Set the "embedded" properties to their initial values; if the characteristics of the shortcut property are inherited, each "embedded" property should take the same computed value as its parent; if the characteristics of the shortcut property are not inherited, set each value; then, the value of shorthand property overrides the counterpart value of the individual property.

Example

```
s { border: red double medium }
```

Related Properties

background properties (p. 379, p. 387), border properties (p. 392 – p. 434), padding properties (p. 562 – p. 571)

Related Formatting Objects

fo:bidi-override (p. 465), fo:block (p. 466), fo:block-container (p. 467), fo:external-graphic (p. 470), fo:float (p. 471), fo:footnote (p. 472), fo:footnote-body (p. 472), fo:initial-property-set (p. 473), fo:inline (p. 473), fo:inline-container (p. 474), fo:instream-foreign-object (p. 475), fo:leader (p. 476), fo:list-block (p. 477), fo:list-item (p. 478), fo:page-number (p. 492), fo:page-number-citation (p. 492), fo:region-after (p. 495), fo:region-before (p. 496), fo:region-body (p. 496), fo:region-end (p. 497), fo:region-start (p. 497), fo:simple-link (p. 500), fo:table (p. 503), fo:table-and-caption (p. 504), fo:table-body (p. 504), fo:table-caption (p. 505), fo:table-cell (p. 505), fo:table-column (p. 506), fo:table-footer (p. 506), fo:table-header (p. 507), fo:table-row (p. 507)

border-after-color   Border Trailing-Edge Color

Purpose

Sets the color of the trailing edge of a block or inline area border.

Syntax

```
border-after-color: color-name_s|#rgb_s|#rrggbb_s
 |rgb(rrr_s,ggg_s,bbb_s)|rgb(rrr_s%,ggg_s%,bbb_s%)
 |inherit
```

Where

- *color-name_s* specifies the top-border color by valid name (that is, Red (#FF0000), Maroon (#800000), Yellow (#FFFF00), Green (#008000), Lime (#00FF00), Teal (#008080), Olive (#808000), Aqua (#00FFFF), Blue (#0000FF), Navy (#000080), Purple (#800080), Fuchsia (#FF00FF), Black (#000000), Gray (#808080), White (#FFFFFF), and the default, Silver (#C0C0C0)). CSS2 adds the following case-insensitive colors: ActiveBorder, ActiveCaption, AppWorkspace, Background, ButtonFace,

XSL Style Sheet Syntax

ButtonHighlight, ButtonShadow, ButtonText, CaptionText, GrayText, Highlight, HighlightText, InactiveBorder, InactiveCaption, InactiveCaptionText, InfoBackground, InfoText, Menu, MenuText, Scrollbar, ThreeDDarkShadow, ThreeDFace, ThreeDHighlight, ThreeDLightShadow, ThreeDShadow, Window, WindowFrame, and WindowText.

- *#rgb_s* represents a three-digit hexadecimal top-border color code, where *r* represents the red attributes, from 0 to F; *g* represents the green attributes, from 0 to F; and *b* represents the blue attributes, from 0 to F.

- *#rrggbb_s* represents a six-digit hexadecimal top-border color code, where *rr* represents the red attributes, from 00 to FF; *gg* represents the green attributes, from 00 to FF; and *bb* represents the blue attributes, from 00 to FF.

- rgb(*rrr_s,ggg_s,bbb_s*) represents absolute red-green-blue values for the top border. Each of the values ranges from 000 to 255.

- rgb(*rrr.d_s%, ggg.e_s%, bbb.f_s%*) represents the relative red-green-blue values for the top border, ranging from 0.0% to 100.0%. Note that 0.0% is equivalent to an absolute value of 000, and 100.0% is equivalent to 255.

- inherit is a keyword that indicates that this property takes the same computed value as its parent.

Notes

- This property is in the common-border-padding-background category.
- For more information about how this property works, see border-top-color in this section.
- By default, the characteristics of this property are not inherited.

Related Properties

background properties (p. 379 – p.387), border properties (p. 392 – p. 434), padding properties (p. 562 – p. 571)

Related Formatting Objects

fo:bidi-override (p. 465), fo:block (p. 466), fo:block-container (p. 467), fo:external-graphic (p. 470), fo:float (p. 471), fo:footnote (p. 472), fo:footnote-body (p. 472), fo:initial-property-set (p. 473), fo:inline (p. 473), fo:inline-container (p. 474), fo:instream-foreign-object (p. 475), fo:leader (p. 476), fo:list-block (p. 477), fo:list-item (p. 478), fo:page-number (p. 492), fo:page-number-citation (p. 492), fo:region-after (p. 495), fo:region-before (p. 496), fo:region-body (p. 496), fo:region-end (p. 497), fo:region-start (p. 497), fo:simple-link (p. 500), fo:table (p. 503), fo:table-and-caption (p. 504), fo:table-body (p. 504), fo:table-caption (p. 505), fo:table-cell (p. 505), fo:table-column (p. 506), fo:table-footer (p. 506), fo:table-header (p. 507), fo:table-row (p. 507)

border-after-style	Border Trailing-Edge Style

Purpose
Sets the style of the trailing edge of a block or inline area border.

Syntax
```
border-after-style:
none|hidden|dotted|dashed|solid|double|groove
|ridge|inset|outset|inherit
```

Where
- none is a keyword that indicates that the border is omitted. This overrides any border-width (p. ___) value.
- hidden is a keyword that indicates that the processor hides the border. When table-cell borders are involved, the values of border-collapse, border-spacing, and empty-cells properties may have an effect.
- dotted draws a dotted-line border over the element background.
- dashed draws a dashed-line border over the element background.
- solid draws a solid-line border over the element background.
- double draws a double-solid-line border over the element background.
- groove draws a three-dimensional grooved border over the element background. using the border-color or border-top-color value.
- ridge draws a three-dimensional ridged border over the element background using the border-color or border-top-color value.
- inset draws a three-dimensional inset over the element background using the border-color or border-top-color value.
- outset draws a three-dimensional outset over the element background using the border-color or border-top-color value.
- inherit is a keyword that indicates that this property takes the same computed value as its parent.

Notes
- This property is in the common-border-padding-background category.
- For more information about this property, see border-top-style (p. 430)
- In XSL, some processors may interpret values of dashed, dotted, double, groove, inset, outset, and ridge as solid.
- By default, the characteristics of this property are not inherited.

Related Properties
background properties (p. 379 – p. 387), border properties (p. 392 – p. 434), padding properties (p. 562 – p. 571)

XSL Style Sheet Syntax

Related Formatting Objects

fo:bidi-override (p. 465), fo:block (p. 466), fo:block-container (p. 467),
fo:external-graphic (p. 470), fo:float (p. 471), fo:footnote (p. 472),
fo:footnote-body (p. 472), fo:initial-property-set (p. 473), fo:inline
(p. 473), fo:inline-container (p. 474), fo:instream-foreign-object (p. 475),
fo:leader (p. 476), fo:list-block (p. 477), fo:list-item (p. 478),
fo:page-number (p. 492), fo:page-number-citation (p. 492), fo:region-after
(p. 495), fo:region-before (p. 496), fo:region-body (p. 496), fo:region-end
(p. 497), fo:region-start (p. 497), fo:simple-link (p. 500), fo:table (p. 503),
fo:table-and-caption (p. 504), fo:table-body (p. 504), fo:table-caption
(p. 505), fo:table-cell (p. 505), fo:table-column (p. 506), fo:table-footer
(p. 506), fo:table-header (p. 507), fo:table-row (p. 507)

border-after-width   Border Trailing-Edge Width

Purpose
Sets the width of the trailing edge of a block or inline area border.

Syntax
border-after-width: thin|medium|thick|*length*|inherit

Where
- thin is a narrower width than medium or thick.
- medium is wider than thin but narrower than thick.
- thick is wider than thin or medium.
- *length* is a positive value followed by a two-letter abbreviation representing the unit of measure.
- inherit is a keyword that indicates that this property takes the same computed value as its parent.

Notes
- This property is in the common-border-padding-background category.
- For more information about this property, see border-top-width (p. 642).
- By default, the characteristics of this property are not inherited.

Related Properties
background properties (p. 379 – p. 387), border properties (p. 392 – p. 434), and padding properties (p. 562 – p. 571)

Related Formatting Objects
fo:bidi-override (p. 465), fo:block (p. 466), fo:block-container (p. 467),
fo:external-graphic (p. 470), fo:float (p. 471), fo:footnote (p. 472),
fo:footnote-body (p. 472), fo:initial-property-set (p. 473), fo:inline
(p. 473), fo:inline-container (p. 474), fo:instream-foreign-object (p. 475),
fo:leader (p. 476), fo:list-block (p. 477), fo:list-item (p. 478), fo:page-number (p. 492), fo:page-number-citation (p. 492), fo:region-after (p. 495),

fo:region-before (p. 496), fo:region-body (p. 496), fo:region-end (p. 497),
fo:region-start (p. 497), fo:simple-link (p. 500), fo:table (p. 503),
fo:table-and-caption (p. 504), fo:table-body (p. 504), fo:table-caption
(p. 505), fo:table-cell (p. 505), fo:table-column (p. 506), fo:table-footer
(p. 506), fo:table-header (p. 507), fo:table-row (p. 507)

border-before-color	**Border Leading-Edge Color**

Purpose

Sets the color of the leading edge of a block or inline area border.

Syntax

```
border-before-color: color-name_s|#rgb_s|#rrggbb_s
|rgb(rrr_s,ggg_s,bbb_s)|rgb(rrr_s%,ggg_s%,bbb_s%)
|inherit
```

Where

- *color-name_s* specifies the top-border color by valid name (that is,
  Red (#FF0000), Maroon (#800000), Yellow (#FFFF00), Green (#008000),
  Lime (#00FF00), Teal (#008080), Olive (#808000), Aqua (#00FFFF),
  Blue (#0000FF), Navy (#000080), Purple (#800080), Fuchsia (#FF00FF),
  Black (#000000), Gray (#808080), White (#FFFFFF), and the default,
  Silver (#C0C0C0)). CSS2 adds the following case-insensitive colors:
  ActiveBorder, ActiveCaption, AppWorkspace, Background, ButtonFace,
  ButtonHighlight, ButtonShadow, ButtonText, CaptionText, GrayText,
  Highlight, HighlightText, InactiveBorder, InactiveCaption,
  InactiveCaptionText, InfoBackground, InfoText, Menu, MenuText,
  Scrollbar, ThreeDDarkShadow, ThreeDFace, ThreeDHighlight,
  ThreeDLightShadow, ThreeDShadow, Window, WindowFrame, and
  WindowText.
- *#rgb_s* represents a three-digit hexadecimal top-border color code,
  where *r* represents the red attributes, from 0 to F; *g* represents the green
  attributes, from 0 to F; and *b* represents the blue attributes, from 0 to F.
- *#rrggbb_s* represents a six-digit hexadecimal top-border color code,
  where *rr* represents the red attributes, from 00 to FF; *gg* represents the
  green attributes, from 00 to FF; and *bb* represents the blue attributes,
  from 00 to FF.
- rgb(*rrr_s,ggg_s,bbb_s*) represents absolute red-green-blue values for
  the top border. Each of the values ranges from 000 to 255.
- rgb(*rrr.d_s%, ggg.e_s%, bbb.f_s%*) represents the relative red-green-
  blue values for the top border, ranging from 0.0% to 100.0%. Note that
  0.0% is equivalent to an absolute value of 000, and 100.0% is equivalent
  to 255.
- inherit is a keyword that indicates that this property takes the same
  computed value as its parent.

XSL Style Sheet Syntax

Notes

- This property is in the common-border-padding-background category.
- For more information about how this property works, see border-top-color (p. 429).
- By default, the characteristics of this property are not inherited.

Related Properties

background properties (p. 379 – p. 387), border properties (p. 392 – p. 434), padding properties (p. 562 – p. 571)

Related Formatting Objects

fo:bidi-override (p. 465), fo:block (p. 466), fo:block-container (p. 467), fo:external-graphic (p. 470), fo:float (p. 471), fo:footnote (p. 472), fo:footnote-body (p. 472), fo:initial-property-set (p. 473), fo:inline (p. 473), fo:inline-container (p. 474), fo:instream-foreign-object (p. 475), fo:leader (p. 476), fo:list-block (p. 477), fo:list-item (p. 478), fo:page-number (p. 492), fo:page-number-citation (p. 492), fo:region-after (p. 495), fo:region-before (p. 496), fo:region-body (p. 496), fo:region-end (p. 497), fo:region-start (p. 497), fo:simple-link (p. 500), fo:table (p. 503), fo:table-and-caption (p. 504), fo:table-body (p. 504), fo:table-caption (p. 505), fo:table-cell (p. 505), fo:table-column (p. 506), fo:table-footer (p. 506), fo:table-header (p. 507), fo:table-row (p. 507)

border-before-style	Border Leading-Edge Style

Purpose

Sets the style of the leading edge of a block or inline area border.

Syntax

```
border-before-style:
    none|hidden|dotted|dashed|solid|double|groove
    |ridge|inset|outset|inherit
```

Where

- none is a keyword that indicates that the border is omitted. This overrides any border-width (p. 642) value.
- hidden is a keyword that indicates that the border is hidden. When table-cell borders are used, the values of border-collapse, border-spacing, and empty-cells properties may have an effect.
- dotted draws a dotted-line border over the element background.
- dashed draws a dashed-line border over the element background.
- solid draws a solid-line border over the element background.
- double draws a double-solid-line border over the element background.
- groove draws a three-dimensional grooved border over the element background using the border-color or border-top-color value.

- `ridge` draws a three-dimensional ridged border over the element background using the `border-color` or `border-top-color` value.
- `inset` draws a three-dimensional inset over the element background using the `border-color` or `border-top-color` value.
- `outset` draws a three-dimensional outset over the element background using the `border-color` or `border-top-color` value.
- `inherit` is a keyword that indicates that this property takes the same computed value as its parent.

Notes

- This property is in the common-border-padding-background category.
- For more information about this property, see `border-top-style` (p. 430).
- In XSL, some processors may interpret values of `dashed`, `dotted`, `double`, `groove`, `inset`, `outset`, and `ridge` as `solid`.
- By default, the characteristics of this property are not inherited.

Related Properties

background properties (p. 379 – p. 387), border properties (p. 392 – p. 434), padding properties (p. 562 – p. 571)

Related Formatting Objects

`fo:bidi-override` (p. 465), `fo:block` (p. 466), `fo:block-container` (p. 467), `fo:external-graphic` (p. 470), `fo:float` (p. 471), `fo:footnote` (p. 472), `fo:footnote-body` (p. 472), `fo:initial-property-set` (p. 473), `fo:inline` (p. 473), `fo:inline-container` (p. 474), `fo:instream-foreign-object` (p. 475), `fo:leader` (p. 476), `fo:list-block` (p. 477), `fo:list-item` (p. 478), `fo:page-number` (p. 492), `fo:page-number-citation` (p. 492), `fo:region-after` (p. 495), `fo:region-before` (p. 496), `fo:region-body` (p. 496), `fo:region-end` (p. 497), `fo:region-start` (p. 497), `fo:simple-link` (p. 500), `fo:table` (p. 503), `fo:table-and-caption` (p. 504), `fo:table-body` (p. 504), `fo:table-caption` (p. 505), `fo:table-cell` (p. 505), `fo:table-column` (p. 506), `fo:table-footer` (p. 506), `fo:table-header` (p. 507), `fo:table-row` (p. 507)

border-before-width | Border Leading-Edge Width

Purpose

Sets the width of the leading edge of a block or inline area border.

Syntax

```
border-before-width: thin|medium|thick|length|inherit
```

Where

- `thin` is a narrower width than `medium` or `thick`.
- `medium` is wider than `thin` but narrower than `thick`.
- `thick` is wider than `thin` or `medium`.

XSL Style Sheet Syntax

- *length* is a positive value followed by a two-letter abbreviation representing the unit of measure.
- inherit is a keyword that indicates that this property takes the same computed value as its parent.

Notes

- This property is in the common-border-padding-background category.
- For more information about this property, see border-top-width (p. 642).
- By default, the characteristics of this property are not inherited.

Related Properties

background properties (p. 379 – p. 387), border properties (p. 392 – p. 434), padding properties (p. 562 – p. 571)

Related Formatting Objects

fo:bidi-override (p. 465), fo:block (p. 466),fo:block-container (p. 467), fo:external-graphic (p. 470), fo:float (p. 471), fo:footnote (p. 472), fo:footnote-body (p. 472), fo:initial-property-set (p. 473), fo:inline (p. 473), fo:inline-container (p. 474), fo:instream-foreign-object (p. 475), fo:leader (p. 476), fo:list-block (p. 477), fo:list-item (p. 478), fo:page-number (p. 492), fo:page-number-citation (p. 492), fo:region-after (p. 495), fo:region-before (p. 496), fo:region-body (p. 496), fo:region-end (p. 497), fo:region-start (p. 497), fo:simple-link (p. 500), fo:table (p. 503), fo:table-and-caption (p. 504), fo:table-body (p. 504), fo:table-caption (p. 505), fo:table-cell (p. 505), fo:table-column (p. 506), fo:table-footer (p. 506), fo:table-header (p. 507), fo:table-row (p. 507)

border-bottom   Bottom Border Properties

Purpose

Specifies the color, style, and/or width of the bottom border of a box.

Syntax

```
border-bottom: ([border-bottom-width_value]
  [border-style_value] [border-color_value])
  |inherit
```

Where

- *border-bottom-width_value* specifies the border width. For more information, see the border-width property (p. 432).
- *border-style_value* specifies the border style. For more information, see the border-style property (p. 426).
- *border-color_value* specifies the border color. For more information, see the border-color property (p. 406).
- inherit is a keyword that indicates that this property takes the same computed value as its parent.

Notes

- This property is in the common-border-padding-background category.
- This property originated in CSS1.
- This shortcut property specifies multiple properties for a bottom border in the same way that you can individually set rules for the following properties: border-bottom-color, border-bottom-style, and border-bottom-width.
- There is no initial value for this property.
- By default, the characteristics of this property are not inherited.
- In CSS, you must specify the processing order for properties "embedded" in shortcut properties. In XML, "embedded" properties are explicitly defined as unordered. XSL has a specific order of preference: Properties that affect part of a whole are processed first; properties that affect the entire whole are processed last. Specifically, border properties are processed in the following four ranks: border (processed first); border-style, border-color, and border-width; border-top, border-bottom, border-right, and border-left; and border-*-* (processed last).
- Shortcut properties should be processed as follows: Set the "embedded" properties to their initial values; if the characteristics of the shortcut property are inherited, each "embedded" property should take the same computed value as its parent; if the characteristics of the shortcut property are not inherited, set each value; then the value of shorthand property overrides the counterpart value of the individual property.

Example

    img { border-bottom: black solid thick }

Related Properties

background properties (p. 379 – p. 387), border properties (p. 392 – p. 434), padding properties (p. 562 – p. 571)

Related Formatting Objects

fo:bidi-override (p. 465), fo:block (p. 466), fo:block-container (p. 467), fo:external-graphic (p. 470), fo:float (p. 471), fo:footnote (p. 472), fo:footnote-body (p. 472), fo:initial-property-set (p. 473), fo:inline (p. 473), fo:inline-container (p. 474), fo:instream-foreign-object (p. 475), fo:leader (p. 476), fo:list-block (p. 477), fo:list-item (p. 478), fo:page-number (p. 492), fo:page-number-citation (p. 492), fo:region-after (p. 495), fo:region-before (p. 496), fo:region-body (p. 496), fo:region-end (p. 497), fo:region-start (p. 497), fo:simple-link (p. 500), fo:table (p. 503), fo:table-and-caption (p. 504), fo:table-body (p. 504), fo:table-caption (p. 505), fo:table-cell (p. 505), fo:table-column (p. 506), fo:table-footer (p. 506), fo:table-header (p. 507), fo:table-row (p. 507)

border-bottom-color   Bottom Border Color

Purpose
Sets the color of the bottom border of a box.

Syntax
```
border-bottom-color: (color-name_b|#rgb_b|#rrggbb_b
|rgb (rrr_b,ggg_b,bbb_b)|rgb(rrr_b%,ggg_b%,bbb_b%))
|transparent|inherit
```

Where
- color-name_b represents the bottom-border color by valid name (that is, Red (#FF0000), Maroon (#800000), Yellow (#FFFF00), Green (#008000), Lime (#00FF00), Teal (#008080), Olive (#808000), Aqua (#00FFFF), Blue (#0000FF), Navy (#000080), Purple (#800080), Fuchsia (#FF00FF), Black (#000000), Gray (#808080), White (#FFFFFF), and the default, Silver (#C0C0C0)). CSS2 adds the following colors: ActiveBorder, ActiveCaption, AppWorkspace, Background, ButtonFace, ButtonHighlight, ButtonShadow, ButtonText, CaptionText, GrayText, Highlight, HighlightText, InactiveBorder, InactiveCaption, InactiveCaptionText, InfoBackground, InfoText, Menu, MenuText, Scrollbar, ThreeDDarkShadow, ThreeDFace, ThreeDHighlight, ThreeDLightShadow, ThreeDShadow, Window, WindowFrame, and WindowText. All color names are case-insensitive.
- #rgb_b represents a three-digit hexadecimal bottom-border color code, where r represents the red attributes, from 0 to F; g represents the green attributes, from 0 to F; and b represents the blue attributes, from 0 to F.
- #rrggbb_b represents a six-digit hexadecimal bottom-border color code, where rr represents the red attributes, from 00 to FF; gg represents the green attributes, from 00 to FF; and bb represents the blue attributes, from 00 to FF.
- rgb(rrr_b,ggg_b,bbb_b) represents absolute red-green-blue values for the bottom border. Each of the values ranges from 000 to 255.
- rgb(rrr.d_b%, ggg.e_b%, bbb.f_b%) represents the relative red-green-blue values for the bottom border, ranging from 0.0% to 100.0%. Note that 0.0% is equivalent to an absolute value of 000, and 100.0% is equivalent to 255.
- transparent is a keyword that indicates that the background is transparent.
- inherit is a keyword that indicates that this property takes the same computed value as its parent.

Notes
- This property is in the common-border-padding-background category.
- This property, which originated in CSS2, applies to all elements.
- By default, the characteristics of this property are not inherited.

Related Properties

background properties (p. 379 – p. 387), border properties (p. 392 – p. 434), padding properties (p. 562 – p. 571)

Related Formatting Objects

fo:bidi-override (p. 465), fo:block (p. 466), fo:block-container (p. 467), fo:external-graphic (p. 470), fo:float (p. 471), fo:footnote (p. 472), fo:footnote-body (p. 472), fo:initial-property-set (p. 473), fo:inline (p. 473), fo:inline-container (p. 474), fo:instream-foreign-object (p. 475), fo:leader (p. 476), fo:list-block (p. 477), fo:list-item (p. 477), fo:page-number (p. 492), fo:page-number-citation (p. 492), fo:region-after (p. 495), fo:region-before (p. 496), fo:region-body (p. 496), fo:region-end (p. 497), fo:region-start (p. 497), fo:simple-link (p. 500), fo:table (p. 503), fo:table-and-caption (p. 504), fo:table-body (p. 504), fo:table-caption (p. 505), fo:table-cell (p. 505), fo:table-column (p. 506), fo:table-footer (p. 506), fo:table-header (p. 507), fo:table-row (p. 507)

border-bottom-style | Bottom Border Style

Purpose

Formats the bottom border of a box.

Syntax

```
border-bottom-style:
  none|hidden|dotted|dashed|solid|double|groove
  |ridge|inset|outset|inherit
```

Where

- none is a keyword that indicates that the border is omitted. This overrides any border-width (p. 432) value.
- hidden is a keyword that indicates that the border is hidden. When table-cell borders are used, the values of border-collapse, border-spacing, and empty-cells properties may have an effect.
- dotted draws a dotted-line border over the element background.
- dashed draws a dashed-line border over the element background.
- solid draws a solid-line border over the element background.
- double draws a double-solid-line border over the element background.
- groove draws a three-dimensional grooved border over the element background using the border-color or border-top-color value.
- ridge draws a three-dimensional ridged border over the element background using the border-color or border-top-color value.
- inset draws a three-dimensional inset over the element background using the border-color or border-top-color value.
- outset draws a three-dimensional outset over the element background using the border-color or border-top-color value.

XSL Style Sheet Syntax

- inherit is a keyword that indicates that this property takes the same computed value as its parent.

Notes

- This property is in the common-border-padding-background category.
- This property originated in CSS2.
- In XSL, some processors may interpret values of dashed, dotted, double, groove, inset, outset, and ridge as solid.
- By default, the characteristics of this property are not inherited.

Related Properties

background properties (p. 379 – p. 387), border properties (p. 392 – p. 434), padding properties (p. 562 – p. 521)

Related Formatting Objects

fo:bidi-override (p. 465), fo:block (p. 466), fo:block-container (p. 467), fo:external-graphic (p. 470), fo:float (p. 471), fo:footnote (p. 472), fo:footnote-body (p. 472), fo:initial-property-set (p. 473), fo:inline (p. 473), fo:inline-container (p. 474), fo:instream-foreign-object (p. 475), fo:leader (p. 476), fo:list-block (p. 477), fo:list-item (p. 478), fo:page-number (p. 492), fo:page-number-citation (p. 492), fo:region-after (p. 495), fo:region-before (p. 496), fo:region-body (p. 496), fo:region-end (p. 497), fo:region-start (p. 497), fo:simple-link (p. 500), fo:table (p. 503), fo:table-and-caption (p. 504), fo:table-body (p. 504), fo:table-caption (p. 505), fo:table-cell (p. 505), fo:table-column (p. 506), fo:table-footer (p. 506), fo:table-header (p. 507), fo:table-row (p. 507)

border-bottom-width   Bottom Border Width

Purpose

Sets the width of the bottom border of a box.

Syntax

```
border-bottom-width: thin|medium|thick|length
  |inherit
```

Where

- thin is a narrower width than medium or thick.
- medium is wider than thin but narrower than thick.
- thick is wider than thin or medium.
- length is a positive value followed by a two-letter abbreviation representing the unit of measure.
- inherit is a keyword that indicates that this property takes the same computed value as its parent.

Notes

- This property is in the common-border-padding-background category.
- This property, which originated in CSS1, applies to all elements.
- By default, the characteristics of this property are not inherited.

Example

```
text { border-bottom-width: thick }
```

Related Properties

background properties (p. 379 – p. 387), border properties (p. 392 – p. 434), padding properties (p. 562 – p. 571)

Related Formatting Objects

fo:bidi-override (p. 465), fo:block (p. 466), fo:block-container (p. 467), fo:external-graphic (p. 470), fo:float (p. 471), fo:footnote (p. 472), fo:footnote-body (p. 472), fo:initial-property-set (p. 473), fo:inline (p. 473), fo:inline-container (p. 474), fo:instream-foreign-object (p. 475), fo:leader (p. 476), fo:list-block (p. 477), fo:list-item (p. 478), fo:page-number (p. 492), fo:page-number-citation (p. 492), fo:region-after (p. 495), fo:region-before (p. 496), fo:region-body (p. 496), fo:region-end (p. 497), fo:region-start (p. 497), fo:simple-link (p. 500), fo:table (p. 503), fo:table-and-caption (p. 504), fo:table-body (p. 504), fo:table-caption (p. 505), fo:table-cell (p. 505), fo:table-column (p. 506), fo:table-footer (p. 506), fo:table-header (p. 507), fo:table-row (p. 507)

---

border-collapse   Cell Border Collapse?

Purpose

Collapses (hides) or separates a table-cell border.

Syntax

```
border-collapse: collapse|separate|inherit
```

Where

- collapse is a keyword that indicates that a row or column is hidden within a table. This is the default.
- separate is a keyword that indicates that a cell has its own separate border.
- inherit is a keyword that indicates that this property takes the same computed value as its parent.

Notes

- This property is in the table category.
- This property, which originated in CSS2, applies to table and inline-table elements (such as the HTML TABLE element).
- By default, the characteristics of this property are inherited.

XSL Style Sheet Syntax

Related Properties

border-spacing (p. 422), caption-side (p. 437), column-number (p. 445), column-width (p. 446), empty-cells (p. 457), ends-row (p. 458), number-columns-repeated (p. 556), number-columns-spanned (p. 557), number-rows-spanned (p. 557), starts-row (p. 619), table-layout (p. 623), table-omit-footer-at-break (p. 624), table-omit-header-at-break (p. 624)

Related Formatting Object

fo:table (p. 503)

border-color   Border Color

Purpose

Sets colors of one, two, three, or four borders of a box.

Syntax

```
border-color: (color-name_t|#rgb_t|#rrggbb_t
  |rgb(rrr_t,ggg_t,bbb_t)|rgb(rrr_t%,ggg_t%,bbb_t%))
  (color-name_rt|#rgb_rt|#rrggbb_rt
  |rgb(rrr_r,ggg_r,bbb_r)|rgb(rrr_r%,ggg_r%,bbb_r%))
  (color-name_b|#rgb_b|#rrggbb_b
  |rgb(rrr_b,ggg_b,bbb_b) |rgb(rrr_b%,ggg_b%,bbb_b%))
  (color-name_l|#rgb_l|#rrggbb_l
  |rgb(rrr_l,ggg_l,bbb_l) |rgb(rrr_l%,ggg_l%,bbb_l%))
  |transparent|inherit
```

Where

- *color-name_t*, *color-name_r*, *color-name_b*, and *color-name_l* specify border colors for the top, right, bottom, and left borders by valid name (that is, Red (#FF0000), Maroon (#800000), Yellow (#FFFF00), Green (#008000), Lime (#00FF00), Teal (#008080), Olive (#808000), Aqua (#00FFFF), Blue (#0000FF), Navy (#000080), Purple (#800080), Fuchsia (#FF00FF), Black (#000000), Gray (#808080), White (#FFFFFF), and the default, Silver (#C0C0C0)). CSS2 adds the following colors: ActiveBorder, ActiveCaption, AppWorkspace, Background, ButtonFace, ButtonHighlight, ButtonShadow, ButtonText, CaptionText, GrayText, Highlight, HighlightText, InactiveBorder, InactiveCaption, InactiveCaptionText, InfoBackground, InfoText, Menu, MenuText, Scrollbar, ThreeDDarkShadow, ThreeDFace, ThreeDHighlight, ThreeDLightShadow, ThreeDShadow, Window, WindowFrame, and WindowText. All color names are case-insensitive.
- *#rgb_t*, *#rgb_r*, *#rgb_b*, and *#rgb_l* each represent a three-digit hexadecimal color code for the top, right, bottom, and left borders, where *r* represents the red attributes, from 0 to F; *g* represents the green attributes, from 0 to F; and *b* represents the blue attributes, from 0 to F.

- #rrggbb_t, #rrggbb_r, #rrggbb_b, and #rrggbb_l each represent a six-digit hexadecimal color code for the top, right, bottom, and left borders, where *rr* represents the red attributes, from 00 to FF; *gg* represents the green attributes, from 00 to FF; and *bb* represents the blue attributes, from 00 to FF.
- rgb(*rrr_t,ggg_t,bbb_t*), rgb(*rrr_rt,ggg_rt,bbb_r*), rgb(*rrr_b,ggg_b, bbb_b*), and rgb(*rrr_l,ggg_l,bbb_l*) each represent absolute red-green-blue values for the top, right, bottom, and left borders. Each of the values ranges from 000 to 255.
- rgb(*rrr.d_t%, ggg.e_t%, bbb.f_t%*), rgb(*rrr.d_r%, ggg.e_r%, bbb.f_r%*), rgb(*rrr.d_b%, ggg.e_b%, bbb.f_b%*), rgb(*rrr.d_l%, ggg.e_l%, bbb.f_l%*) each represent the relative red-green-blue values for the top, right, bottom, and left borders, each ranging from 0.0% to 100.0%. Note that 0.0% is equivalent to an absolute value of 000, and 100.0% is equivalent to 255.
- transparent is a keyword that indicates that the border is transparent.
- inherit is a keyword that indicates that this property takes the same computed value as its parent.

Notes

- This property is in the common-border-padding-background category.
- This shortcut property, which originated in CSS1, applies to all elements.
- By default, the characteristics of this property are not inherited.
- In CSS, you must specify the processing order for properties "embedded" in shortcut properties. In XML, "embedded" properties are explicitly defined as unordered. XSL has a specific order of preference: Properties that affect part of a whole are processed first; properties that affect the entire whole are processed last. Specifically, border properties are processed in the following four ranks: border (processed first); border-style, border-color, and border-width; border-top, border-bottom, border-right, and border-left; and border-*-* (processed last).
- Shortcut properties should be processed as follows: Set the "embedded" properties to their initial values; if the characteristics of the shortcut property are inherited, each "embedded" property should take the same computed value as its parent; if the characteristics of the shortcut property are not inherited, set each value; then the value of shorthand property overrides the counterpart value of the individual property.

Example

```
head4 { border-color: blue; border-width: thin }
```

Related Properties

background properties (p. 379 – p. 387), border properties (p. 392 – p. 434), padding properties (p. 562 – p. 571)

XSL Style Sheet Syntax

Related Formatting Objects

fo:bidi-override (p. 465), fo:block (p. 466), fo:block-container (p. 467), fo:external-graphic (p. 470), fo:float (p. 471), fo:footnote (p. 472), fo:footnote-body (p. 472), fo:initial-property-set (p. 473), fo:inline (p. 473), fo:inline-container (p. 474), fo:instream-foreign-object (p. 475), fo:leader (p. 476), fo:list-block (p. 477), fo:list-item (p. 478), fo:page-number (p. 492), fo:page-number-citation (p. 492), fo:region-after (p. 495), fo:region-before (p. 496), fo:region-body (p. 496), fo:region-end (p. 497), fo:region-start (p. 497), fo:simple-link (p. 500), fo:table (p. 503), fo:table-and-caption (p. 504), fo:table-body (p. 504), fo:table-caption (p. 505), fo:table-cell (p. 505), fo:table-column (p. 506), fo:table-footer (p. 506), fo:table-header (p. 507), fo:table-row (p. 507)

border-end-color | Border Ending-Edge Color

Purpose

Sets the color of the ending edge of a block or inline area border.

Syntax

```
border-end-color: color-name_s|#rgb_s|#rrggbb_s
|rgb(rrr_s,ggg_s,bbb_s)|rgb(rrr_s%,ggg_s%,bbb_s%)
|inherit
```

Where

- *color-name_s* specifies the top-border color by valid name (that is, Red (#FF0000), Maroon (#800000), Yellow (#FFFF00), Green (#008000), Lime (#00FF00), Teal (#008080), Olive (#808000), Aqua (#00FFFF), Blue (#0000FF), Navy (#000080), Purple (#800080), Fuchsia (#FF00FF), Black (#000000), Gray (#808080), White (#FFFFFF), and the default, Silver (#C0C0C0)). CSS2 adds the following case-insensitive colors: ActiveBorder, ActiveCaption, AppWorkspace, Background, ButtonFace, ButtonHighlight, ButtonShadow, ButtonText, CaptionText, GrayText, Highlight, HighlightText, InactiveBorder, InactiveCaption, InactiveCaptionText, InfoBackground, InfoText, Menu, MenuText, Scrollbar, ThreeDDarkShadow, ThreeDFace, ThreeDHighlight, ThreeDLightShadow, ThreeDShadow, Window, WindowFrame, and WindowText.

- *#rgb_s* represents a three-digit hexadecimal top-border color code, where *r* represents the red attributes, from 0 to F; *g* represents the green attributes, from 0 to F; and *b* represents the blue attributes, from 0 to F.

- *#rrggbb_s* represents a six-digit hexadecimal top-border color code, where *rr* represents the red attributes, from 00 to FF; *gg* represents the green attributes, from 00 to FF; and *bb* represents the blue attributes, from 00 to FF.

- rgb(*rrr_s,ggg_s,bbb_s*) represents absolute red-green-blue values for the top border. Each of the values ranges from 000 to 255.

- rgb(*rrr.d_s*%, *ggg.e_s*%, *bbb.f_s*%) represents the relative red-green-blue values for the top border, ranging from 0.0% to 100.0%. Note that 0.0% is equivalent to an absolute value of 000, and 100.0% is equivalent to 255.
- inherit is a keyword that indicates that this property takes the same computed value as its parent.

Notes

- This property is in the common-border-padding-background category.
- For more information about how this property works, see border-top-color (p. 429).
- By default, the characteristics of this property are not inherited.

Related Properties

background properties (p. 379 – p. 387), border properties (p. 392 – p. 434), padding properties (p. 562 – p. 571)

Related Formatting Objects

fo:bidi-override (p. 465), fo:block (p. 466), fo:block-container (p. 467), fo:external-graphic (p. 470), fo:float (p. 471), fo:footnote (p. 472), fo:footnote-body (p. 472), fo:initial-property-set (p. 473), fo:inline (p. 473), fo:inline-container (p. 474), fo:instream-foreign-object (p. 475), fo:leader (p. 476), fo:list-block (p. 477), fo:list-item (p. 478), fo:page-number (p. 492), fo:page-number-citation (p. 492), fo:region-after (p. 495), fo:region-before (p. 496), fo:region-body (p. 496), fo:region-end (p. 497), fo:region-start (p. 497), fo:simple-link (p. 500), fo:table (p. 503), fo:table-and-caption (p. 504), fo:table-body (p. 504), fo:table-caption (p. 505), fo:table-cell (p. 505), fo:table-column (p. 506), fo:table-footer (p. 506), fo:table-header (p. 507), fo:table-row (p. 507)

border-end-style   Border Ending-Edge Style

Purpose

Sets the style of the ending edge of a block or inline area border.

Syntax

```
border-end-style:
  none|hidden|dotted|dashed|solid|double|groove
  |ridge|inset|outset|inherit
```

Where

- none is a keyword that indicates that the border is omitted. This overrides any border-width (p. 642) value.
- hidden is a keyword that indicates that the border is hidden. When table-cell borders are used, the values of border-collapse, border-spacing, and empty-cells properties may have an effect.

- dotted draws a dotted-line border over the element background.
- dashed draws a dashed-line border over the element background.
- solid draws a solid-line border over the element background.
- double draws a double-solid-line border over the element background.
- groove draws a three-dimensional grooved border over the element background using the border-color or border-top-color value.
- ridge draws a three-dimensional ridged border over the element background using the border-color or border-top-color value.
- inset draws a three-dimensional inset over the element background using the border-color or border-top-color value.
- outset draws a three-dimensional outset over the element background using the border-color or border-top-color value.
- inherit is a keyword that indicates that this property takes the same computed value as its parent.

Notes

- This property is in the common-border-padding-background category.
- For more information about this property, see border-top-style (p. 430).
- In XSL, some processors may interpret values of dashed, dotted, double, groove, inset, outset, and ridge as solid.
- By default, the characteristics of this property are not inherited.

Related Properties

background properties (p. 379 - p. 387), border properties (p. 392 - p. 434), padding properties (p. 562 - p. 521)

Related Formatting Objects

fo:bidi-override (p. 465), fo:block (p. 466), fo:block-container (p. 467), fo:external-graphic (p. 470), fo:float (p. 471), fo:footnote (p. 472), fo:footnote-body (p. 472), fo:initial-property-set (p. 473), fo:inline (p. 473), fo:inline-container (p. 474), fo:instream-foreign-object (p. 475), fo:leader (p. 476), fo:list-block (p. 477), fo:list-item (p. 478), fo:page-number (p. 492), fo:page-number-citation (p. 492), fo:region-after (p. 495), fo:region-before (p. 496), fo:region-body (p. 496), fo:region-end (p. 497), fo:region-start (p. 497), fo:simple-link (p. 500), fo:table (p. 503), fo:table-and-caption (p. 504), fo:table-body (p. 504), fo:table-caption (p. 505), fo:table-cell (p. 505), fo:table-column (p. 506), fo:table-footer (p. 506), fo:table-header (p. 507), fo:table-row (p. 507)

border-end-width — Border Ending-Edge Width

Purpose

Sets the width of the ending edge of a block or inline area border.

Syntax

```
border-end-width: thin|medium|thick|length|inherit
```

Where

- thin is a narrower width than medium or thick.
- medium is wider than thin but narrower than thick.
- thick is wider than thin or medium.
- length is a positive value followed by a two-letter abbreviation representing the unit of measure.
- inherit is a keyword that indicates that this property takes the same computed value as its parent.

Notes

- This property is in the common-border-padding-background category.
- For more information about this property, see border-top-width (p. 642).
- By default, the characteristics of this property are not inherited.

Related Properties

background properties (p. 379 – p. 387), border properties (p. 392 – p. 434), padding properties (p. 582 – p. 571)

Related Formatting Objects

fo:bidi-override (p. 465), fo:block (p. 466), fo:block-container (p. 467), fo:external-graphic (p. 470), fo:float (p. 471), fo:footnote (p. 472), fo:footnote-body (p. 472), fo:initial-property-set (p. 473), fo:inline (p. 473), fo:inline-container (p. 474), fo:instream-foreign-object (p. 475), fo:leader (p. 476), fo:list-block (p. 477), fo:list-item (p. 478), fo:page-number (p. 492), fo:page-number-citation (p. 492), fo:region-after (p. 495), fo:region-before (p. 496), fo:region-body (p. 496), fo:region-end (p. 497), fo:region-start (p. 497), fo:simple-link (p. 500), fo:table (p. 503), fo:table-and-caption (p. 504), fo:table-body (p. 504), fo:table-caption (p. 505), fo:table-cell (p. 505), fo:table-column (p. 506), fo:table-footer (p. 506), fo:table-header (p. 507), fo:table-row (p. 507)

| **border-left** | Left Border Properties |

Purpose

Specifies the color, style, and/or width of the left border of a box.

Syntax

```
border-left: [ border-left-width_value]
   [ border-style_value] [ border-color_value]
   |inherit
```

Where

- *border-left-width_value* specifies the border width. For more information, see the border-width property (p. 432).
- *border-style_value* specifies the border style. For more information, see the border-style property (p. 426).
- *border-color_value* specifies the border color. For more information, see the border-color property (p. 406).
- inherit is a keyword that indicates that this property takes the same computed value as its parent.

Notes

- This property is in the common-border-padding-background category.
- This property originated in CSS1.
- This shortcut property specifies multiple properties for left borders in the same way that you can individually set rules for the following properties: border-left-color, border-left-style, and border-left-width.
- There is no initial value for this property.
- By default, the characteristics of this property are not inherited.
- border-left accepts only one style, in contrast to border-style, which accepts as many as four.
- In CSS, you must specify the processing order for properties "embedded" in shortcut properties. In XML, "embedded" properties are explicitly defined as unordered. XSL has a specific order of preference: Properties that affect part of a whole are processed first; properties that affect the entire whole are processed last. Specifically, border properties are processed in the following four ranks: border (processed first); border-style, border-color, and border-width; border-top, border-bottom, border-right, and border-left; and border-*-* (processed last).
- Shortcut properties should be processed as follows: Set the "embedded" properties to their initial values; if the characteristics of the shortcut property are inherited, each "embedded" property should take the same computed value as its parent; if the characteristics of the shortcut property are not inherited, set each value; then the value of shorthand property overrides the counterpart value of the individual property.

Example

```
ins { border-left: blue solid thin }
```

Related Properties

background properties (p. 379 – p. 387), border properties (p. 392 – p. 434), padding properties (p. 562 – p. 571)

Related Formatting Objects

fo:bidi-override (p. 465), fo:block (p. 466), fo:block-container (p. 467), fo:external-graphic (p. 470), fo:float (p. 471), fo:footnote (p. 472), fo:footnote-body (p. 472), fo:initial-property-set (p. 473), fo:inline (p. 473), fo:inline-container (p. 474), fo:instream-foreign-object (p. 475),

XSL Style Sheet Syntax

fo:leader (p. 476), fo:list-block (p. 477), fo:list-item (p. 478),
fo:page-number (p. 492), fo:page-number-citation (p. 492), fo:region-after
(p. 495), fo:region-before (p. 496), fo:region-body (p. 496), fo:region-end
(p. 497), fo:region-start (p. 497), fo:simple-link (p. 500), fo:table (p. 503),
fo:table-and-caption (p. 504), fo:table-body (p. 504), fo:table-caption
(p. 505), fo:table-cell (p. 505), fo:table-column (p. 506), fo:table-footer
(p. 506), fo:table-header (p. 507), fo:table-row (p. 507)

border-left-color   Left Border Color

Purpose

Sets the color of the left border of a box.

Syntax

```
border-left-color: color-name_l|#rgb_l|#rrggbb_l
 |rgb(rrr_l,ggg_l,bbb_l) |rgb(rrr_l%,ggg_l%,bbb_l%)
 |inherit
```

Where

- *color-name_l* specifies the left-border color by valid name (that is,
  Red (#FF0000), Maroon (#800000), Yellow (#FFFF00), Green (#008000),
  Lime (#00FF00), Teal (#008080), Olive (#808000), Aqua (#00FFFF),
  Blue (#0000FF), Navy (#000080), Purple (#800080), Fuchsia (#FF00FF),
  Black (#000000), Gray (#808080), White (#FFFFFF), and the default,
  Silver (#C0C0C0)). CSS2 adds the following case-insensitive colors:
  ActiveBorder, ActiveCaption, AppWorkspace, Background, ButtonFace,
  ButtonHighlight, ButtonShadow, ButtonText, CaptionText, GrayText,
  Highlight, HighlightText, InactiveBorder, InactiveCaption,
  InactiveCaptionText, InfoBackground, InfoText, Menu, MenuText,
  Scrollbar, ThreeDDarkShadow, ThreeDFace, ThreeDHighlight,
  ThreeDLightShadow, ThreeDShadow, Window, WindowFrame, and
  WindowText.
- *#rgb_l* represents a three-digit hexadecimal left-border color code,
  where *r* represents the red attributes, from 0 to F; *g* represents the green
  attributes, from 0 to F; and *b* represents the blue attributes, from 0 to F.
- *#rrggbb_l* represents a six-digit hexadecimal left-border color code,
  where *rr* represents the red attributes, from 00 to FF; *gg* represents the
  green attributes, from 00 to FF; and *bb* represents the blue attributes,
  from 00 to FF.
- rgb(*rrr_l,ggg_l,bbb_l*) represents absolute red-green-blue values for
  the left border. Each of the values ranges from 000 to 255.
- rgb(*rrr.d_l%, ggg.e_l%, bbb.f_l%*) represents the relative red-green-
  blue values for the left border, ranging from 0.0% to 100.0%. Note that
  0.0% is equivalent to an absolute value of 000, and 100.0% is equivalent
  to 255.

- inherit is a keyword that indicates that this property takes the same computed value as its parent.

Notes

- This property is in the common-border-padding-background category.
- This property, which originated in CSS2, applies to all elements.
- By default, the characteristics of this property are not inherited.

Related Properties

background properties (p. 379 – p. 387), border properties (p. 392 – p. 434), padding properties (p. 562 – p. 571)

Related Formatting Objects

fo:bidi-override (p. 465), fo:block (p. 466), fo:block-container (p. 467), fo:external-graphic (p. 470), fo:float (p. 471), fo:footnote (p. 472), fo:footnote-body (p. 472), fo:initial-property-set (p. 473), fo:inline (p. 473), fo:inline-container (p. 474), fo:instream-foreign-object (p. 475), fo:leader (p. 476), fo:list-block (p. 477), fo:list-item (p. 478), fo:page-number (p. 492), fo:page-number-citation (p. 492), fo:region-after (p. 495), fo:region-before (p. 496), fo:region-body (p. 496), fo:region-end (p. 497), fo:region-start (p. 497), fo:simple-link (p. 500), fo:table (p. 503), fo:table-and-caption (p. 504), fo:table-body (p. 504), fo:table-caption (p. 505), fo:table-cell (p. 505), fo:table-column (p. 506), fo:table-footer (p. 506), fo:table-header (p. 507), fo:table-row (p. 507)

border-left-style	**Left Border Style**

Purpose

Formats the left border of a box.

Syntax

border-left-style:
    none|hidden|dotted|dashed|solid|double|groove
    |ridge|inset|outset|inherit

Where

- none is a keyword that indicates that the border is omitted. This overrides any border-width (p. 642) value.
- hidden is a keyword that indicates that the border is hidden. When table-cell borders are used, the values of border-collapse, border-spacing, and empty-cells properties may have an effect.
- dotted draws a dotted-line border over the element background.
- dashed draws a dashed-line border over the element background.
- solid draws a solid-line border over the element background.
- double draws a double-solid-line border over the element background.

- groove draws a three-dimensional grooved border over the element background using the border-color or border-top-color value.
- ridge draws a three-dimensional ridged border over the element background using the border-color or border-top-color value.
- inset draws a three-dimensional inset over the element background using the border-color or border-top-color value.
- outset draws a three-dimensional outset over the element background using the border-color or border-top-color value.
- inherit is a keyword that indicates that this property takes the same computed value as its parent.

Notes

- This property is in the common-border-padding-background category.
- This property originated in CSS2.
- In XSL, some processors may interpret values of dashed, dotted, double, groove, inset, outset, and ridge as solid.
- By default, the characteristics of this property are not inherited.

Related Properties

background properties (p. 379 – p. 387), border properties (p. 392 – p. 434), padding properties (p. 562 – p. 571)

Related Formatting Objects

fo:bidi-override (p. 465), fo:block (p. 466), fo:block-container (p. 467), fo:external-graphic (p. 470), fo:float (p. 471), fo:footnote (p. 472), fo:footnote-body (p. 472), fo:initial-property-set (p. 473), fo:inline (p. 473), fo:inline-container (p. 474), fo:instream-foreign-object (p. 475), fo:leader (p. 476), fo:list-block (p. 477), fo:list-item (p. 478), fo:page-number (p. 492), fo:page-number-citation (p. 492), fo:region-after (p. 495), fo:region-before (p. 496), fo:region-body (p. 496), fo:region-end (p. 497), fo:region-start (p. 497), fo:simple-link (p. 500), fo:table (p. 503), fo:table-and-caption (p. 504), fo:table-body (p. 504), fo:table-caption (p. 505), fo:table-cell (p. 505), fo:table-column (p. 506), fo:table-footer (p. 507), fo:table-header (p. 507), fo:table-row (p. 507)

border-left-width   Left Border Width

Purpose

Sets the width of the left border of a box.

Syntax

```
border-left-width: thin|medium|thick|length|inherit
```

Where

- thin is a narrower width than medium or thick.
- medium is wider than thin but narrower than thick.
- thick is wider than thin or medium.

- *length* is a positive value followed by a two-letter abbreviation representing the unit of measure.
- inherit is a keyword that indicates that this property takes the same computed value as its parent.

Notes

- This property is in the common-border-padding-background category.
- This property, which originated in CSS1, applies to all elements.
- By default, the characteristics of this property are not inherited.

Example

    head1 { border-left-width: 0.25in }

Related Properties

background properties (p. 379 – p. 387), border properties (p. 392 – p. 434), and padding properties (p. 562 – p. 571)

Related Formatting Objects

fo:bidi-override (p. 465), fo:block (p. 466), fo:block-container (p. 467), fo:external-graphic (p. 470), fo:float (p. 471), fo:footnote (p. 472), fo:footnote-body (p. 472), fo:initial-property-set (p. 473), fo:inline (p. 473), fo:inline-container (p. 474), fo:instream-foreign-object (p. 475), fo:leader (p. 476), fo:list-block (p. 477), fo:list-item (p. 478), fo:page-number (p. 492), fo:page-number-citation (p. 492), fo:region-after (p. 495), fo:region-before (p. 496), fo:region-body (p. 496), fo:region-end (p. 497), fo:region-start (p. 497), fo:simple-link (p. 500), fo:table (p. 503), fo:table-and-caption (p. 504), fo:table-body (p. 504), fo:table-caption (p. 505), fo:table-cell (p. 505), fo:table-column (p. 506), fo:table-footer (p. 506), fo:table-header (p. 507), fo:table-row (p. 507)

border-right   Right Border Properties

Purpose

Specifies the color, style, and/or width of the right border of a box.

Syntax

    border-right: [border-right-width_value]
      [border-style_value] [border-color_value]
      |inherit

Where

- *border-right-width_value* specifies the border width. For more information, see the border-width property (p. 432).
- *border-style_value* specifies the border style. For more information, see the border-style property (p. 426).
- *border-color_value* specifies the border color. For more information, see the border-color property (p. 406).

- `inherit` is a keyword that indicates that this property takes the same computed value as its parent.

Notes

- This property is in the common-border-padding-background category.
- This property originated in CSS1.
- This shortcut property specifies multiple properties for right borders in the same way that you can individually set rules for the following properties: `border-right-color`, `border-right-style`, and `border-right-width`.
- There is no initial value for this property.
- By default, the characteristics of this property are not inherited.
- `border-right` accepts only one style, in contrast to `border-style`, which accepts as many as four.
- In CSS, you must specify the processing order for properties "embedded" in shortcut properties. In XML, "embedded" properties are explicitly defined as unordered. XSL has a specific order of preference: Properties that affect part of a whole are processed first; properties that affect the entire whole are processed last. Specifically, border properties are processed in the following four ranks: `border` (processed first); `border-style`, `border-color`, and `border-width`; `border-top`, `border-bottom`, `border-right`, and `border-left`; and `border-*-*` (processed last).
- Shortcut properties should be processed as follows: Set the "embedded" properties to their initial values; if the characteristics of the shortcut property are inherited, each "embedded" property should take the same computed value as its parent; if the characteristics of the shortcut property are not inherited, set each value; then the value of shorthand property overrides the counterpart value of the individual property.

Example

```
span { border-right: teal dotted medium }
```

Related Properties

background properties (p. 379 – p. 387), border properties (p. 392 – p. 434), padding properties (p. 562 – p. 571)

Related Formatting Objects

`fo:bidi-override` (p. 465), `fo:block` (p. 466), `fo:block-container` (p. 467), `fo:external-graphic` (p. 470), `fo:float` (p. 471), `fo:footnote` (p. 472), `fo:footnote-body` (p. 472), `fo:initial-property-set` (p. 473), `fo:inline` (p. 473), `fo:inline-container` (p. 474), `fo:instream-foreign-object` (p. 475), `fo:leader` (p. 476), `fo:list-block` (p. 477), `fo:list-item` (p. 478), `fo:page-number` (p. 492), `fo:page-number-citation` (p. 492), `fo:region-after` (p. 495), `fo:region-before` (p. 496), `fo:region-body` (p. 496), `fo:region-end` (p. 497), `fo:region-start` (p. 497), `fo:simple-link` (p. 500), `fo:table` (p. 503), `fo:table-and-caption` (p. 504), `fo:table-body` (p. 504), `fo:table-caption` (p. 505), `fo:table-cell` (p. 505), `fo:table-column` (p. 506), `fo:table-footer` (p. 506), `fo:table-header` (p. 507), `fo:table-row` (p. 507)

border-right-color	Right Border Color

Purpose

Sets the color of the right border of a box.

Syntax

```
border-right-color: color-name_r|#rgb_r|#rrggbb_r
   |rgb(rrr_r,ggg_r,bbb_r)|rgb(rrr_r%,ggg_r%,bbb_r%)
   |inherit
```

Where

- color-name_r specifies the right-border color by valid name (that is, Red (#FF0000), Maroon (#800000), Yellow (#FFFF00), Green (#008000), Lime (#00FF00), Teal (#008080), Olive (#808000), Aqua (#00FFFF), Blue (#0000FF), Navy (#000080), Purple (#800080), Fuchsia (#FF00FF), Black (#000000), Gray (#808080), White (#FFFFFF), and the default, Silver (#C0C0C0)). CSS2 adds the following case-insensitive colors: ActiveBorder, ActiveCaption, AppWorkspace, Background, ButtonFace, ButtonHighlight, ButtonShadow, ButtonText, CaptionText, GrayText, Highlight, HighlightText, InactiveBorder, InactiveCaption, InactiveCaptionText, InfoBackground, InfoText, Menu, MenuText, Scrollbar, ThreeDDarkShadow, ThreeDFace, ThreeDHighlight, ThreeDLightShadow, ThreeDShadow, Window, WindowFrame, and WindowText.

- #rgb_r represents a three-digit hexadecimal right-border color code, where r represents the red attributes, from 0 to F; g represents the green attributes, from 0 to F; and b represents the blue attributes, from 0 to F.

- #rrggbb_r represents a six-digit hexadecimal right-border color code, where rr represents the red attributes, from 00 to FF; gg represents the green attributes, from 00 to FF; and bb represents the blue attributes, from 00 to FF.

- rgb(rrr_r,ggg_r,bbb_r) represents absolute red-green-blue values for the right border. Each of the values ranges from 000 to 255.

- rgb(rrr.d_r%, ggg.e_r%, bbb.f_r%) represents the relative red-green-blue values for the right border, ranging from 0.0% to 100.0%. Note that 0.0% is equivalent to an absolute value of 000, and 100.0% is equivalent to 255.

- inherit is a keyword that indicates that this property takes the same computed value as its parent.

Notes

- This property is in the common-border-padding-background category.
- This property, which originated in CSS2, applies to all elements.
- By default, the characteristics of this property are not inherited.

Related Properties

background properties (p. 379 – p. 387), border properties (p. 392 – p. 434), padding properties (p. 562 – p. 571)

Related Formatting Objects

fo:bidi-override (p. 465), fo:block (p. 466), fo:block-container (p. 467), fo:external-graphic (p. 470), fo:float (p. 471), fo:footnote (p. 472), fo:footnote-body (p. 472), fo:initial-property-set (p. 473), fo:inline (p. 473), fo:inline-container (p. 474), fo:instream-foreign-object (p. 475), fo:leader (p. 476), fo:list-block (p. 477), fo:list-item (p. 478), fo:page-number (p. 492), fo:page-number-citation (p. 492), fo:region-after (p. 495), fo:region-before (p. 496), fo:region-body (p. 496), fo:region-end (p. 497), fo:region-start (p. 497), fo:simple-link (p. 500), fo:table (p. 503), fo:table-and-caption (p. 504), fo:table-body (p. 504), fo:table-caption (p. 505), fo:table-cell (p. 505), fo:table-column (p. 506), fo:table-footer (p. 506), fo:table-header (p. 507), fo:table-row (p. 507)

border-right-style   Right Border Style

Purpose

Formats the right border of a box.

Syntax

```
border-right-style:
  none|hidden|dotted|dashed|solid|double|groove
  |ridge|inset|outset|inherit
```

Where

- none omits a border. This overrides any border-width (p. 642) value.
- hidden omits a border. When table-cell borders are used, the values of border-collapse, border-spacing, and empty-cells properties may have an effect.
- dotted draws a dotted-line border over the element background.
- dashed draws a dashed-line border over the element background.
- solid draws a solid-line border over the element background.
- double draws a double-solid-line border over the element background.
- groove draws a three-dimensional grooved border over the element background using the border-color or border-right-color value.
- ridge draws a three-dimensional ridged border over the element background using the border-color or border-right-color value.
- inset draws a three-dimensional inset over the element background using the border-color or border-right-color value.
- outset draws a three-dimensional outset over the element background using the border-color or border-right-color value.
- inherit is a keyword that indicates that this property takes the same computed value as its parent.

XSL Style Sheet Syntax

Notes

- This property is in the common-border-padding-background category.
- This property originated in CSS2.
- In XSL, some processors may interpret values of dashed, dotted, double, groove, inset, outset, and ridge as solid.
- By default, the characteristics of this property are not inherited.

Related Properties

background properties (p. 379 – p. 387), border properties (p. 392 – p. 434), padding properties (p. 562 – p. 571)

Related Formatting Objects

fo:bidi-override (p. 465), fo:block (p. 466), fo:block-container (p. 467), fo:external-graphic (p. 470), fo:float (p. 471), fo:footnote (p. 472), fo:footnote-body (p. 472), fo:initial-property-set (p. 473), fo:inline (p. 473), fo:inline-container (p. 474), fo:instream-foreign-object (p. 475), fo:leader (p. 476), fo:list-block (p. 477), fo:list-item (p. 478), fo:page-number (p. 492), fo:page-number-citation (p. 492), fo:region-after (p. 495), fo:region-before (p. 496), fo:region-body (p. 496), fo:region-end (p. 497), fo:region-start (p. 497), fo:simple-link (p. 500), fo:table (p. 503), fo:table-and-caption (p. 504), fo:table-body (p. 504), fo:table-caption (p. 505), fo:table-cell (p. 505), fo:table-column (p. 506), fo:table-footer (p. 506), fo:table-header (p. 507), fo:table-row (p. 507)

---

border-right-width   Right Border Width

Purpose

Sets the width of the right border.

Syntax

```
border-right-width: thin|medium|thick|length|inherit
```

Where

- thin is a narrower width than medium or thick.
- medium is wider than thin but narrower than thick.
- thick is wider than thin or medium.
- length is a positive value followed by a two-letter abbreviation representing the unit of measure.
- inherit is a keyword that indicates that this property takes the same computed value as its parent.

Notes

- This property is in the common-border-padding-background category.
- This property, which originated in CSS1, applies to all elements.
- By default, the characteristics of this property are not inherited.

Example

```
longquote { border-right-width: 2pt }
```

Related Properties

background properties (p. 379 – p. 387), border properties (p. 392 – p. 434), padding properties (p. 562 – p. 571)

Related Formatting Objects

fo:bidi-override (p. 465), fo:block (p. 466), fo:block-container (p. 467), fo:external-graphic (p. 470), fo:float (p. 471), fo:footnote (p. 472), fo:footnote-body (p. 472), fo:initial-property-set (p. 473), fo:inline (p. 473), fo:inline-container (p. 474), fo:instream-foreign-object (p. 475), fo:leader (p. 476), fo:list-block (p. 477), fo:list-item (p. 478), fo:page-number (p. 492), fo:page-number-citation (p. 492), fo:region-after (p. 495), fo:region-before (p. 496), fo:region-body (p. 496), fo:region-end (p. 497), fo:region-start (p. 497), fo:simple-link (p. 500), fo:table (p. 503), fo:table-and-caption (p. 504), fo:table-body (p. 504), fo:table-caption (p. 505), fo:table-cell (p. 505), fo:table-column (p. 506), fo:table-footer (p. 506), fo:table-header (p. 507), fo:table-row (p. 507)

---

border-separation   Border Separation

Purpose

Specifies the distance between borders of adjacent cells.

Syntax

```
border-separation: length-bp-ip-direction | inherit
```

Where

- length-bp-ip-direction specifies the distance that separates adjacent cell borders (in the direction in which rows and columns stack).
- inherit is a keyword that indicates that this property takes the same computed value as its parent.

Notes

- This property is a table property.
- The row-stacking direction is given by the block-progression-direction of the table.
- The column-stacking direction is given by the inline-progression-direction of the table.
- Rows, columns, row groups, and column groups cannot have borders, only cells. The browser will ignore any border properties in those elements.

XSL Style Sheet Syntax

Related Properties

border-collapse (p. 405), caption-side (p. 437), column-number (p. 445), column-width (p. 446), empty-cells (p. 457), ends-row (p. 458), number-columns-repeated (p. 556), number-columns-spanned (p. 557), number-rows-spanned (p. 557), starts-row (p. 619), table-layout (p. 623), table-omit-footer-at-break (p. 624), table-omit-header-at-break (p. 624)

border-spacing — Cell Border Spacing

Purpose

Separates a cell border from adjacent borders.

Syntax

border-spacing: [*h_length*] [*v_length*]|inherit

Where

- *h_length* and *v_length* are positive horizontal-length and vertical-length cell-separation values followed by a two-letter abbreviation representing the unit of measure.
- inherit is a keyword that indicates that this property takes the same computed value as its parent.

Notes

- This property is in the table category.
- This property, which originated in CSS2, applies to table and inline-table elements (such as the HTML TABLE element).
- For more information about this property, see border-spacing (p. 422).
- By default, the characteristics of this element are inherited.

Related Properties

border-collapse (p. 405), caption-side (p. 437), column-number (p. 445), column-width (p. 446), empty-cells (p. 457), ends-row (p. 458), number-columns-repeated (p. 556), number-columns-spanned (p. 557), number-rows-spanned (p. 557), starts-row (p. 619), table-layout (p. 623), table-omit-footer-at-break (p. 624), table-omit-header-at-break (p. 624)

Related Formatting Object

fo:table (p. 503)

border-start-color — Border Starting-Edge Color

Purpose

Sets the color of the starting edge of a block or inline area border.

Syntax

```
border-start-color: color-name_s|#rgb_s|#rrggbb_s
|rgb(rrr_s,ggg_s,bbb_s)|rgb(rrr_s%,ggg_s%,bbb_s%)
|inherit
```

Where

- *color-name_s* specifies the top-border color by valid name (that is, Red (#FF0000), Maroon (#800000), Yellow (#FFFF00), Green (#008000), Lime (#00FF00), Teal (#008080), Olive (#808000), Aqua (#00FFFF), Blue (#0000FF), Navy (#000080), Purple (#800080), Fuchsia (#FF00FF), Black (#000000), Gray (#808080), White (#FFFFFF), and the default, Silver (#C0C0C0)). CSS2 adds the following case-insensitive colors: ActiveBorder, ActiveCaption, AppWorkspace, Background, ButtonFace, ButtonHighlight, ButtonShadow, ButtonText, CaptionText, GrayText, Highlight, HighlightText, InactiveBorder, InactiveCaption, InactiveCaptionText, InfoBackground, InfoText, Menu, MenuText, Scrollbar, ThreeDDarkShadow, ThreeDFace, ThreeDHighlight, ThreeDLightShadow, ThreeDShadow, Window, WindowFrame, and WindowText.
- *#rgb_s* represents a three-digit hexadecimal top-border color code, where *r* represents the red attributes, from 0 to F; *g* represents the green attributes, from 0 to F; and *b* represents the blue attributes, from 0 to F.
- *#rrggbb_s* represents a six-digit hexadecimal top-border color code, where *rr* represents the red attributes, from 00 to FF; *gg* represents the green attributes, from 00 to FF; and *bb* represents the blue attributes, from 00 to FF.
- rgb(*rrr_s,ggg_s,bbb_s*) represents absolute red-green-blue values for the top border. Each of the values ranges from 000 to 255.
- rgb(*rrr.d_s%, ggg.e_s%, bbb.f_s%*) represents the relative red-green-blue values for the top border, ranging from 0.0% to 100.0%. Note that 0.0% is equivalent to an absolute value of 000, and 100.0% is equivalent to 255.
- inherit is a keyword that indicates that this property takes the same computed value as its parent.

Notes

- This property is in the common-border-padding-background category.
- For more information about how this property works, see border-top-color (p. 429).
- By default, the characteristics of this property are not inherited.

Related Properties

background properties (p. 379 – p. 387), border properties (p. 392 – p. 434), and padding properties (p. 562 – p. 571)

XSL Style Sheet Syntax

Related Formatting Objects

fo:bidi-override (p. 465), fo:block (p. 466), fo:block-container (p. 467),
fo:external-graphic (p. 470), fo:float (p. 471), fo:footnote (p. 472),
fo:footnote-body (p. 472), fo:initial-property-set (p. 473), fo:inline
(p. 473), fo:inline-container (p. 474), fo:instream-foreign-object (p. 475),
fo:leader (p. 476), fo:list-block (p. 477), fo:list-item (p. 478),
fo:page-number (p. 492), fo:page-number-citation (p. 492), fo:region-after
(p. 495), fo:region-before (p. 496), fo:region-body (p. 496), fo:region-end
(p. 497), fo:region-start (p. 497), fo:simple-link (p. 500), fo:table (p. 503),
fo:table-and-caption (p. 504), fo:table-body (p. 504), fo:table-caption
(p. 505), fo:table-cell (p. 505), fo:table-column (p. 506), fo:table-footer
(p. 506), fo:table-header (p. 507), fo:table-row (p. 507)

---

border-start-style | Border Starting-Edge Style

Purpose

Sets the style of the starting edge of a block or inline area border.

Syntax

```
border-start-style:
  none|hidden|dotted|dashed|solid|double|groove
  |ridge|inset|outset|inherit
```

Where

- none is a keyword that indicates that the border is omitted. This overrides any border-width (p. 642) value.
- hidden is a keyword that indicates that the border is hidden. When table-cell borders are used, the values of border-collapse, border-spacing, and empty-cells properties may have an effect.
- dotted draws a dotted-line border over the element background.
- dashed draws a dashed-line border over the element background.
- solid draws a solid-line border over the element background.
- double draws a double-solid-line border over the element background.
- groove draws a three-dimensional grooved border over the element background using the border-color or border-top-color value.
- ridge draws a three-dimensional ridged border over the element background using the border-color or border-top-color value.
- inset draws a three-dimensional inset over the element background using the border-color or border-top-color value.
- outset draws a three-dimensional outset over the element background using the border-color or border-top-color value.
- inherit is a keyword that indicates that this property takes the same computed value as its parent.

Notes

- This property is in the common-border-padding-background category.
- For more information about this property, see `border-top-style` (p. 430).
- In XSL, some processors may interpret values of dashed, dotted, double, groove, inset, outset, and ridge as solid.
- By default, the characteristics of this property are not inherited.

Related Properties

background properties (p. 379 – p. 387), border properties (p. 392 – p. 434), padding properties (p. 562 – p. 571)

Related Formatting Objects

`fo:bidi-override` (p. 465), `fo:block` (p. 466), `fo:block-container` (p. 467), `fo:external-graphic` (p. 470), `fo:float` (p. 471), `fo:footnote` (p. 472), `fo:footnote-body` (p. 472), `fo:initial-property-set` (p. 473), `fo:inline` (p. 473), `fo:inline-container` (p. 474), `fo:instream-foreign-object` (p. 475), `fo:leader` (p. 475), `fo:list-block` (p. 477), `fo:list-item` (p. 478), `fo:page-number` (p. 492), `fo:page-number-citation` (p. 492), `fo:region-after` (p. 495), `fo:region-before` (p. 496), `fo:region-body` (p. 496), `fo:region-end` (p. 497), `fo:region-start` (p. 497), `fo:simple-link` (p. 500), `fo:table` (p. 503), `fo:table-and-caption` (p. 504), `fo:table-body` (p. 504), `fo:table-caption` (p. 505), `fo:table-cell` (p. 505), `fo:table-column` (p. 506), `fo:table-footer` (p. 506), `fo:table-header` (p. 507), `fo:table-row` (p. 507)

---

border-start-width | Border Starting-Edge Width

Purpose

Sets the width of the starting edge of a block or inline area border.

Syntax

```
border-start-width: thin|medium|thick|length|inherit
```

Where

- thin is a narrower width than medium or thick.
- medium is wider than thin but narrower than thick.
- thick is wider than thin or medium.
- *length* is a positive value followed by a two-letter abbreviation representing the unit of measure.
- inherit is a keyword that indicates that this property takes the same computed value as its parent.

Notes

- This property is in the common-border-padding-background category.
- For more information about this property, see `border-top-width` (p. 642).
- By default, the characteristics of this property are not inherited.

Related Properties

background properties (p. 379 – p. 387), border properties (p. 392 – p. 434),
padding properties (p. 562 – p. 571)

Related Formatting Objects

fo:bidi-override (p. 465), fo:block (p. 466), fo:block-container (p. 467),
fo:external-graphic (p. 470), fo:float (p. 471), fo:footnote (p. 472),
fo:footnote-body (p. 472), fo:initial-property-set (p. 473), fo:inline
(p. 473), fo:inline-container (p. 474), fo:instream-foreign-object (p. 425),
fo:leader (p. 476), fo:list-block (p. 477), fo:list-item (p. 478),
fo:page-number (p. 492), fo:page-number-citation (p. 492), fo:region-after
(p. 495), fo:region-before (p. 496), fo:region-body (p. 496), fo:region-end
(p. 497), fo:region-start (p. 497), fo:simple-link (p. 500), fo:table (p. 503),
fo:table-and-caption (p. 504), fo:table-body (p. 504), fo:table-caption
(p. 505), fo:table-cell (p. 505), fo:table-column (p. 506), fo:table-footer
(p. 506), fo:table-header (p. 507), fo:table-row (p. 507)

border-style	Border Style

Purpose

Formats one, two, three, or four borders of a box.

Syntax

```
border-style:
    ([none|hidden|dotted|dashed|solid|double|groove
    |ridge|inset|outset]
    [none|hidden|dotted|dashed|solid|double|groove
    |ridge|inset|outset]
    [none|hidden|dotted|dashed|solid|double|groove
    |ridge|inset|outset]
    [none|hidden|dotted|dashed|solid|double|groove
    |ridge|inset|outset])|inherit
```

Where

- none is a keyword that indicates that the border is omitted. This overrides any border-width (p. 642) value.
- hidden is a keyword that indicates that the border is hidden. When
  table-cell borders are used, the values of border-collapse, border-
  spacing, and empty-cells properties may have an effect.
- dotted draws a dotted-line border over the element background.
- dashed draws a dashed-line border over the element background.
- solid draws a solid-line border over the element background.
- double draws a double-solid-line border over the element background.
- groove draws a three-dimensional grooved border over the element
  background using the border-color or border-top-color value.

- ridge draws a three-dimensional ridged border over the element background using the border-color or border-top-color value.
- inset draws a three-dimensional inset over the element background using the border-color or border-top-color value.
- outset draws a three-dimensional outset over the element background using the border-color or border-top-color value.
- inherit is a keyword that indicates that this property takes the same computed value as its parent.

Notes

- This property is in the common-border-padding-background category.
- This property, which originated in CSS1, applies to all elements.
- In XSL, some processors may interpret values of dashed, dotted, double, groove, inset, outset, and ridge as solid.
- By default, the characteristics of this property are not inherited.

Example

```
head1 { border-style: inset outset }
```

Related Properties

background properties (p. 379 – p. 387), border properties (p. 392 – p. 434), padding properties (p. 562 – p. 571)

Related Formatting Objects

fo:bidi-override (p. 465), fo:block (p. 466), fo:block-container (p. 467), fo:external-graphic (p. 470), fo:float (p. 471), fo:footnote (p. 472), fo:footnote-body (p. 472), fo:initial-property-set (p. 473), fo:inline (p. 473), fo:inline-container (p. 474), fo:instream-foreign-object (p. 475), fo:leader (p. 476), fo:list-block (p. 477), fo:list-item (p. 478), fo:page-number (p. 492), fo:page-number-citation (p. 492), fo:region-after (p. 495), fo:region-before (p. 496), fo:region-body (p. 496), fo:region-end (p. 497), fo:region-start (p. 497), fo:simple-link (p. 500), fo:table (p. 503), fo:table-and-caption (p. 504), fo:table-body (p. 504), fo:table-caption (p. 505), fo:table-cell (p. 505), fo:table-column (p. 506), fo:table-footer (p. 506), fo:table-header (p. 507), fo:table-row (p. 507)

border-top Top Border Properties

XSL Style Sheet Syntax

Purpose

Specifies the color, style, and/or width of the top border of a box.

Syntax

```
border-top: [ border-top-width_value]
   [ border-style_value ] [ border-color_value]
   |inherit
```

Where

- *border-top-width_value* specifies the border width. For more information, see the border-top-width property (p. 432).
- *border-style_value* specifies the border style. For more information, see the border-style property (p. 426).
- *border-color_value* specifies the border color. For more information, see the border-color property (p. 406).
- inherit is a keyword that indicates that this property takes the same computed value as its parent.

Notes

- This property is in the common-border-padding-background category.
- This property originated in CSS1.
- This shortcut property specifies multiple properties for borders in the same way that you can individually set rules for the following properties: border-top-color, border-top-style, and border-top-width.
- There is no initial value for this property.
- By default, the characteristics of this property are not inherited.
- In CSS, you must specify the processing order for properties "embedded" in shortcut properties. In XML, "embedded" properties are explicitly defined as unordered. XSL has a specific order of preference: Properties that affect part of a whole are processed first; properties that affect the entire whole are processed last. Specifically, border properties are processed in the following four ranks: border (processed first); border-style, border-color, and border-width; border-top, border-bottom, border-right, and border-left; and border-*-* (processed last).
- Shortcut properties should be processed as follows: Set the "embedded" properties to their initial values; if the characteristics of the shortcut property are inherited, each "embedded" property should take the same computed value as its parent; if the characteristics of the shortcut property are not inherited, set each value; then the value of shorthand property overrides the counterpart value of the individual property.
- In CSS, you must specify the processing order for properties "embedded" in shortcut properties. In XML, "embedded" properties are explicitly defined as unordered. XSL has a specific order of preference: Properties that affect part of a whole are processed first; properties that affect the entire whole are processed last. Specifically, border properties are processed in the following four ranks: border (processed first); border-style, border-color, and border-width; border-top, border-bottom, border-right, and border-left; and border-*-* (processed last).

Example

```
para.intro { border-top: red dotted thin }
```

Related Properties

background properties (p. 379 – p. 387), border properties (p. 392 – p. 434), padding properties (p. 562 – p. 571)

Related Formatting Objects

fo:bidi-override (p. 465), fo:block (p. 466), fo:block-container (p. 467), fo:external-graphic (p. 470), fo:float (p. 471), fo:footnote (p. 472), fo:footnote-body (p. 472), fo:initial-property-set (p. 473), fo:inline (p. 473), fo:inline-container (p. 474), fo:instream-foreign-object (p. 475), fo:leader (p. 476), fo:list-block (p. 477), fo:list-item (p. 478), fo:page-number (p. 492), fo:page-number-citation (p. 495), fo:region-after (p. 496), fo:region-before (p. 496), fo:region-body (p. 496), fo:region-end (p. 497), fo:region-start (p. 497), fo:simple-link (p. 500), fo:table (p. 503), fo:table-and-caption (p. 504), fo:table-body (p. 504), fo:table-caption (p. 505), fo:table-cell (p. 505), fo:table-column (p. 506), fo:table-footer (p. 506), fo:table-header (p. 507), fo:table-row (p. 507)

---

border-top-color   Top Border Color

Purpose

Sets the color of the top border of a box.

Syntax

```
border-top-color: color-name_t|#rgb_t|#rrggbb_t
  |rgb(rrr_t,ggg_t,bbb_t)|rgb(rrr_t%,ggg_t%,bbb_t%)
  |inherit
```

Where

- *color-name_t* specifies the top-border color by valid name (that is, Red (#FF0000), Maroon (#800000), Yellow (#FFFF00), Green (#008000), Lime (#00FF00), Teal (#008080), Olive (#808000), Aqua (#00FFFF), Blue (#0000FF), Navy (#000080), Purple (#800080), Fuchsia (#FF00FF), Black (#000000), Gray (#808080), White (#FFFFFF), and the default, Silver (#C0C0C0)). CSS2 adds the following case-insensitive colors: ActiveBorder, ActiveCaption, AppWorkspace, Background, ButtonFace, ButtonHighlight, ButtonShadow, ButtonText, CaptionText, GrayText, Highlight, HighlightText, InactiveBorder, InactiveCaption, InactiveCaptionText, InfoBackground, InfoText, Menu, MenuText, Scrollbar, ThreeDDarkShadow, ThreeDFace, ThreeDHighlight, ThreeDLightShadow, ThreeDShadow, Window, WindowFrame, and WindowText.
- *#rgb_t* represents a three-digit hexadecimal top-border color code, where *r* represents the red attributes, from 0 to F; *g* represents the green attributes, from 0 to F; and *b* represents the blue attributes, from 0 to F.

- *#rrggbb_t* represents a six-digit hexadecimal top-border color code, where *rr* represents the red attributes, from 00 to FF; *gg* represents the green attributes, from 00 to FF; and *bb* represents the blue attributes, from 00 to FF.
- rgb(*rrr_t*,*ggg_t*,*bbb_t*) represents absolute red-green-blue values for the top border. Each of the values ranges from 000 to 255.
- rgb(*rrr.d_t%*, *ggg.e_t%*, *bbb.f_t%*) represents the relative red-green-blue values for the top border, ranging from 0.0% to 100.0%. Note that 0.0% is equivalent to an absolute value of 000, and 100.0% is equivalent to 255.
- inherit is a keyword that indicates that this property takes the same computed value as its parent.

Notes
- This property is in the common-border-padding-background category.
- This property, which originated in CSS2, applies to all elements.
- By default, the characteristics of this property are not inherited.

Related Properties
background properties (p. 379 – p. 387), border properties (p. 392 – p. 434), padding properties (p. 562 – p. 571)

Related Formatting Objects
fo:bidi-override (p. 465), fo:block (p. 466), fo:block-container (p. 469), fo:external-graphic (p. 470), fo:float (p. 471), fo:footnote (p. 472), fo:footnote-body (p. 472), fo:initial-property-set (p. 473), fo:inline (p. 473), fo:inline-container (p. 474), fo:instream-foreign-object (p. 475), fo:leader (p. 476), fo:list-block (p. 477), fo:list-item (p. 478), fo:page-number (p. 492), fo:page-number-citation (p. 492), fo:region-after (p. 495), fo:region-before (p. 496), fo:region-body (p. 496), fo:region-end (p. 497), fo:region-start (p. 497), fo:simple-link (p. 500), fo:table (p. 503), fo:table-and-caption (p. 504), fo:table-body (p. 504), fo:table-caption (p. 505), fo:table-cell (p. 505), fo:table-column (p. 506), fo:table-footer (p. 506), fo:table-header (p. 507), fo:table-row (p. 507)

border-top-style   Top Border Style

Purpose
Formats the top border of a box.

Syntax
```
border-top-style:
    none|hidden|dotted|dashed|solid|double|groove
    |ridge|inset|outset|inherit
```

Where

- none is a keyword that indicates that the border is omitted. This overrides any border-width (p. 642) value.
- hidden is a keyword that indicates that the border is hidden. When table-cell borders are used, the values of border-collapse, border-spacing, and empty-cells properties may have an effect.
- dotted draws a dotted-line border over the element background.
- dashed draws a dashed-line border over the element background.
- solid draws a solid-line border over the element background.
- double draws a double-solid-line border over the element background.
- groove draws a three-dimensional grooved border over the element background using the border-color or border-top-color value.
- ridge draws a three-dimensional ridged border over the element background using the border-color or border-top-color value.
- inset draws a three-dimensional inset over the element background using the border-color or border-top-color value.
- outset draws a three-dimensional outset over the element background using the border-color or border-top-color value.
- inherit is a keyword that indicates that this property takes the same computed value as its parent.

Notes

- This property is in the common-border-padding-background category.
- This property originated in CSS2.
- In XSL, some processors may interpret values of dashed, dotted, double, groove, inset, outset, and ridge as solid.
- By default, the characteristics of this property are not inherited.

Related Properties

background properties (p. 379 – p. 387), border properties (p. 392 – p. 434), padding properties (p. 562 – p. 571)

Related Formatting Objects

fo:bidi-override (p. 465), fo:block (p. 466), fo:block-container (p. 467), fo:external-graphic (p. 470), fo:float (p. 471), fo:footnote (p. 472), fo:footnote-body (p. 472), fo:initial-property-set (p. 473), fo:inline (p. 473), fo:inline-container (p. 474), fo:instream-foreign-object (p. 475), fo:leader (p. 476), fo:list-block (p. 477), fo:list-item (p. 478), fo:page-number (p. 492), fo:page-number-citation (p. 492), fo:region-after (p. 495), fo:region-before (p. 496), fo:region-body (p. 496), fo:region-end (p. 497), fo:region-start (p. 497), fo:simple-link (p. 500), fo:table (p. 503), fo:table-and-caption (p. 504), fo:table-body (p. 504), fo:table-caption (p. 505), fo:table-cell (p. 505), fo:table-column (p. 506), fo:table-footer (p. 506), fo:table-header (p. 507), fo:table-row (p. 507)

XSL Style Sheet Syntax

border-top-width   Top Border Width

Purpose
Sets the width of the top border of a box.

Syntax
```
border-top-width: thin|medium|thick|length|inherit
```

Where
- thin is a narrower width than medium or thick.
- medium is wider than thin but narrower than thick.
- thick is wider than thin or medium.
- length is a positive value followed by a two-letter abbreviation representing the unit of measure.
- inherit is a keyword that indicates that this property takes the same computed value as its parent.

Notes
- This property is in the common-border-padding-background category.
- This property, which originated in CSS1, applies to all elements.
- By default, the characteristics of this property are not inherited.

Example
```
bigquote { border-top-width: thin }
```

Related Properties
background properties (p. 379 – p. 387), border properties (p. 392 – p. 434), padding properties (p. 562 – p. 571)

Related Formatting Objects
fo:bidi-override (p. 465), fo:block (p. 466), fo:block-container (p. 467), fo:external-graphic (p. 470), fo:float (p. 471), fo:footnote (p. 472), fo:footnote-body (p. 472), fo:initial-property-set (p. 473), fo:inline (p. 473), fo:inline-container (p. 474), fo:instream-foreign-object (p. 475), fo:leader (p. 476), fo:list-block (p. 477), fo:list-item (p. 478), fo:page-number (p. 492), fo:page-number-citation (p. 492), fo:region-after (p. 495), fo:region-before (p. 496), fo:region-body (p. 496), fo:region-end (p. 497), fo:region-start (p. 497), fo:simple-link (p. 500), fo:table (p. 503), fo:table-and-caption (p. 504), fo:table-body (p. 504), fo:table-caption (p. 505), fo:table-cell (p. 505), fo:table-column (p. 506), fo:table-footer (p. 506), fo:table-header (p. 507), fo:table-row (p. 507)

border-width   Border Width

Purpose
Sets the width of one, two, three, or four borders of a box.

XSL Style Sheet Syntax

Syntax

```
border-width: [thin|medium|thick|length]
[thin|medium|thick|length][thin|medium|thick|length]
[thin|medium|thick|length]|inherit
```

Where

- thin is a narrower width than medium or thick.
- medium is wider than thin but narrower than thick. This is the default.
- thick is wider than thin or medium.
- length is a positive value followed by a two-letter abbreviation representing the unit of measure.
- inherit is a keyword that indicates that this property takes the same computed value as its parent.

Notes

- This property is in the common-border-padding-background category.
- This property, which originated in CSS1, applies to all elements.
- A border is outside the content of the page but within the page edges and within the top, left, right, and bottom margins.
- The shorthand property border-width is the equivalent of border-top-width, border-right -width, border-bottom -width, and/or border-left -width, in that order.
- By default, the characteristics of this property are not inherited.
- Shortcut properties should be processed as follows: Set the "embedded" properties to their initial values; if the characteristics of the shortcut property are inherited, each "embedded" property should take the same computed value as its parent; if the characteristics of the shortcut property are not inherited, set each value; then the value of shorthand property overrides the counterpart value of the individual property.
- In CSS, you must specify the processing order for properties "embedded" in shortcut properties. In XML, "embedded" properties are explicitly defined as unordered. XSL has a specific order of preference: Properties that affect part of a whole are processed first; properties that affect the entire whole are processed last. Specifically, border properties are processed in the following four ranks: border (processed first); border-style, border-color, and border-width; border-top, border-bottom, border-right, and border-left; and border-*-* (processed last).

Example

```
ul { border-width: thin }
```

Related Properties

background properties (p. 379 - p. 387), border properties (p. 392 - p. 434), and padding properties (p. 562 - p. 571)

XSL Style Sheet Syntax

Related Formatting Objects

fo:bidi-override (p. 465), fo:block (p. 466), fo:block-container (p. 467),
fo:external-graphic (p. 470), fo:float (p. 471), fo:footnote (p. 472),
fo:footnote-body (p. 472), fo:initial-property-set (p. 473), fo:inline
(p. 473), fo:inline-container (p. 474), fo:instream-foreign-object (p. 475),
fo:leader (p. 476), fo:list-block (p. 477), fo:list-item (p. 478),
fo:page-number (p. 492), fo:page-number-citation (p. 492), fo:region-after
(p. 495), fo:region-before (p. 496), fo:region-body (p. 496), fo:region-end
(p. 497), fo:region-start (p. 497), fo:simple-link (p. 500), fo:table (p. 503),
fo:table-and-caption (p. 504), fo:table-body (p. 504), fo:table-caption
(p. 505), fo:table-cell (p. 505), fo:table-column (p. 506), fo:table-footer
(p. 506), fo:table-header (p. 507), fo:table-row (p. 507)

bottom · Bottom Offset

Purpose

Controls the location of the bottom edge of a box from the bottom edge of
the block that contains the box.

Syntax

bottom: *length*|*percent*%|auto|inherit

Where

- *length* is a positive or negative value followed by a two-letter abbreviation representing the unit of measure.
- *percent* is a positive or negative value that is relative to the size of the image. Follow *percent* with a percentage sign (%).
- auto is a keyword that represents a value automatically calculated by the user's browser. This is the default.
- inherit is a keyword that indicates that this property takes the same computed value as its parent.

Notes

- This property is in the common-absolute-position category.
- This property originated in CSS2.
- The combination of top and bottom values overrides the current height of the content box.
- By default, the characteristics of this property are not inherited.

Related Properties

left (p. 353), position (p. 583), right (p. 597), top (p. 632)

Related Formatting Object

fo:block-container (p. 467)

break-after   Break After

Purpose
Indicates whether a page break is inserted after a particular flow object appears.

Syntax
```
break-after: auto|column|page|even-page
|odd-page|inherit
```

Where
- auto is a keyword that indicates that a page break is not forced after the page box is produced. Other properties that may affect auto are keep-with-next, keep-with previous, orphans, page-break-inside, and widows. This is the default.
- column is a keyword that indicates that a column break occurs after the page box for the current object is produced.
- page is a keyword that indicates that a page break occurs after the page box for the current object is produced.
- even-page is a keyword that indicates that a page break occurs after the page box for the current object is produced, and the next page will be an even-numbered page.
- odd-page is a keyword that indicates that a page break occurs after the page box for the current object is produced, and the next page will be an odd-numbered page.
- inherit is a keyword that indicates that this property takes the same computed value as its parent.

Notes
- This property is in the common-keeps-and-breaks category.
- The XSL working draft (http://www.w3.org/TR/xsl/) states that "all keep values are ordered from weakest (auto) to strongest (always) and break values are ordered from weakest (auto) to strongest (even/odd). In general, the strongest condition applies, with all breaks other than 'auto' being stronger than all keeps. Also, conflicting even-page/odd-page breaks behave as if they were 'page.'"
- The XSL break-after property is slightly related to the DSSSL-O break-after property.
- The break-after characteristic is not inherited.

Related Properties
break-before (p. 436), keep-with-next (p. 527), keep-with-previous (p. 528), page-break-after (p. 572), page-break-before (p. 573)

Related Formatting Objects
fo:list-block (p. 477), fo:list-item (p. 478), fo:table (p. 503)

break-before

Purpose

Indicates whether a page break is inserted before the current flow object appears.

Syntax

```
break-before: auto|column|page|even-page
  |odd-page|inherit
```

Where

- auto is a keyword that indicates that a page break is not forced before the page box is produced. Other properties that may affect auto are keep-with-next, keep-with previous, orphans, page-break-inside, and widows. This is the default.
- column is a keyword that indicates that the current object is placed in the top position in the current column.
- page is a keyword that indicates that the current object is placed in the top position on the current page.
- even-page is a keyword that indicates that the current object is placed in the top position on the next even-numbered page.
- odd-page is a keyword that indicates that the current object is placed in the top position on the next odd-numbered page.
- inherit is a keyword that indicates that this property takes the same computed value as its parent.

Notes

- This property is in the common-keeps-and-breaks category.
- The XSL working draft (http://www.w3.org/TR/xsl/) states that "all keep values are ordered from weakest (auto) to strongest (always) and break values are ordered from weakest (auto) to strongest (even/odd). In general, the strongest condition applies, with all breaks other than 'auto' being stronger than all keeps. Also, conflicting even-page/odd-page breaks behave as if they were 'page.'"
- The XSL break-before property is slightly related to the DSSSL-O break-before property.
- The break-before characteristic is not inherited.

Related Properties

break-after (p. 435), keep-with-next (p. 527), keep-with-previous (p. 528), page-break-after (p. 572), page-break-before (p. 573)

Related Formatting Objects

fo:list-block (p. 477), fo:list-item (p. 478), fo:table (p. 503)

caption-side   Table Caption Position

Purpose
Specifies the position and alignment of a table caption.

Syntax
```
caption-side: before|after|start|end|top|bottom|left
  |right|inherit
```

Where
- before is a keyword that indicates that the caption box is placed before the table box in the current block direction. This is an XSL-only value.
- after is a keyword that indicates that the caption box is placed after the table box in the current block direction. This is an XSL-only value.
- start is a keyword that indicates that the caption box is placed before the table box in the current inline direction. This is an XSL-only value.
- end is a keyword that indicates that the caption box is placed after the table box in the current inline direction. This is an XSL-only value.
- top is a keyword that indicates that the caption box is placed above the table box.
- bottom is a keyword that indicates that the caption box is placed below the table box.
- left is a keyword that indicates that the caption box is placed to the left of the table box.
- right is a keyword that indicates that the caption box is placed to the right of the table box.
- inherit is a keyword that indicates that this property takes the same computed value as its parent.

Notes
- This property is in the table category.
- This property, which originated in CSS2, applies to table-caption elements.
- For more information about this property, see border-top-style (p. 430).
- By default, the characteristics of this property are inherited.

Related Properties
border-collapse (p. 405), border-spacing (p. 422), column-number
(p. 445), column-width (p. 446), empty-cells (p. 457), ends-row (p. 458),
number-columns-repeated (p. 556), number-columns-spanned (p. 557),
number-rows-spanned (p. 557), starts-row (p. 619), table-layout (p. 623),
table-omit-footer-at-break (p. 624), table-omit-header-at-break (p. 624)

Related Formatting Object
fo:table-and-caption (p. 504)

case-name

Case Name

Purpose
Names a `fo:multi-case` formatting object.

Syntax
```
case-name: case_name
```

Where
- *case_name* is the unique name of a `fo:multi-case`.

Notes
- This property is in the links category.
- By default, the characteristics of this property are not inherited.

Related Properties
auto-restore (p. 377), case-title (p. 438), destination-placement-offset (p. 452), external-destination (p. 462), indicate-destination (p. 523), internal-destination (p. 526), show-destination (p. 604), starting-state (p. 619), switch-to (p. 621)

Related Formatting Object
fo:multi-case (p. 480)

case-title

Case Title

Purpose
Provides a title for a `fo:multi-case` formatting object.

Syntax
```
case-title: title_string
```

Where
- *title_string* is a title that effectively defines the fo:multi-case.

Notes
- This property is in the links category.
- By default, the characteristics of this property are not inherited.

Related Properties
auto-restore (p. 377), case-name (p. 438), destination-placement-offset (p. 452), external-destination (p. 462), indicate-destination (p. 523), internal-destination (p. 526), show-destination (p. 604), starting-state (p. 619), switch-to (p. 621)

Related Formatting Object
fo:multi-case (p. 480)

XSL Style Sheet Syntax

ceiling() — Ceiling Function

Purpose

Returns the lowest integer.

EBNF Syntax

```
number_r ceiling(number)
```

Standard Syntax

```
number_r ceiling(number)
```

Where

- *number_r* is the number returned by the function.
- ceiling is a function-name keyword.
- *number* represents the argument's number.

Notes

- ceiling() returns the number that is closest to negative infinity.
- The returned number must not be less than the argument.

Related XPath Functions

abs() (p. 370), floor() (p. 464), max() (p. 548), min() (p. 552), round() (p. 599)

character — Character

Purpose

Specifies a Unicode character.

Syntax

```
char: character
```

Where

- *character* is a character.

Notes

- This property is in the character category.
- By default this property is not inherited.

Related Properties

letter-spacing (p. 535), suppress-at-line-break (p. 621), text-decoration (p. 628), text-shadow (p. 630), text-transform (p. 631), word-spacing (p. 643)

clear   Clear Element

Purpose
Displays a floating element after the prior element is clear.

Syntax
```
clear: none|left|right|both|inherit
```

Where
- none does not wait for the margins to be clear; the element floats at the current alignment setting. This is the default.
- left floats an element below the bottom edge of left-floating boxes.
- right floats an element below the bottom edge of right-floating boxes.
- both floats an element below the bottom edges of all floating boxes.
- inherit is a keyword that indicates that this property takes the same computed value as its parent.

Notes
- This property is in the page-related category.
- This property, which originated in CSS1, applies only to block-level elements.
- By default, the characteristics of this property are not inherited.

Example
```
img.clearex.gif { clear: left }
```

Related Property
float (p. 463)

Related Formatting Object
fo:float (p. 471)

clip   Clipping Region

Purpose
Defines the clipping (visible) area of a box.

Syntax
```
clip: shape|auto|inherit
```

Where
- shape is the top, right, bottom, and left box offsets. For more information, see bottom (p. 434), left (p. 535), right (p. 597), and top (p. 632).
- auto is a keyword that represents the size and location of the box. This is the default.

- inherit is a keyword that indicates that this property takes the same computed value as its parent.

Notes

- This property is in the miscellaneous category.
- This property, which originated in CSS2, applies to block-level and re-placed elements.
- By default, characteristics of this property are not inherited.

Related Properties

baseline-shift (p. 388), block-progression-dimension (p. 390), color (p. 441), direction (p. 453), font-height-override-after (p. 484), font-height-override-before (p. 485), glyph-orientation-horizontal (p. 512), glyph-orientation-vertical (p. 513), height (p. 514), href (p. 515), hyphenation-keep (p. 517), hyphenation-ladder-count (p. 518), id (p. 521), in-line-progression-dimension (p. 525), last-line-end-indent (p. 531), linefeed-treatment (p. 537), line-height (p. 538), line-height-shift-adjust-ment (p. 539), line-stacking-strategy (p. 540), max-height (p. 548), max-width (p. 550), min-height (p. 552), min-width (p. 553), overflow (p. 561), provisional-distance-between-starts (p. 586), provisional-label-separation (p. 587), reference-orientation (p. 588), ref-id (p. 589), scaling (p. 601), score-spaces (p. 602), size (p. 605), space-treatment (p. 611), span (p. 612), text-align (p. 625), text-align-last (p. 626), text-indent (p. 629), unicode-bidi (p. 639), vertical-align (p. 635), visibility (p. 636), white-space (p. 639), white-space-collapse (p. 640), width (p. 642), wrap-option (p. 644), writing-mode (p. 645), z-index (p. 648)

Related Formatting Objects

fo:block-container (p. 467), fo:float (p. 471), fo:footnote (p. 472), fo:in-line-container (p. 474), fo:region-after (p. 495), fo:region-before (p. 496), fo:region-body (p. 496), fo:region-end (p. 497), fo:region-start (p. 497)

---

color	**Foreground Text Color**

Purpose

Specifies a color for the current element's document text.

Syntax

```
color: color-name|#rgb|#rrggbb|rgb(rrr,ggg,bbb)
  |rgb(rrr%,ggg%,bbb%)|inherit
```

Where

- color-name specifies a foreground color by valid name (that is, Red (#FF0000), Maroon (#800000), Yellow (#FFFF00), Green (#008000), Lime (#00FF00), Teal (#008080), Olive (#808000), Aqua (#00FFFF), Blue (#0000FF), Navy (#000080), Purple (#800080), Fuchsia (#FF00FF),

XSL Style Sheet Syntax

Black (#000000), Gray (#808080), White (#FFFFFF), and the default, Silver (#C0C0C0)). CSS2 adds the following case-insensitive colors: ActiveBorder, ActiveCaption, AppWorkspace, Background, ButtonFace, ButtonHighlight, ButtonShadow, ButtonText, CaptionText, GrayText, Highlight, HighlightText, InactiveBorder, InactiveCaption, InactiveCaptionText, InfoBackground, InfoText, Menu, MenuText, Scrollbar, ThreeDDarkShadow, ThreeDFace, ThreeDHighlight, ThreeDLightShadow, ThreeDShadow, Window, WindowFrame, and WindowText.

- *#rgb* is a three-digit hexadecimal color code, where *r* represents the red attributes, from 0 to F; *g* represents the green attributes, from 0 to F; and *b* represents the blue attributes, from 0 to F.
- *#rrggbb* is a six-digit hexadecimal color code, where *rr* represents the red attributes, from 00 to FF; *gg* represents the green attributes, from 00 to FF; and *bb* represents the blue attributes, from 00 to FF.
- rgb(*rrr,ggg,bbb*) represents absolute red-green-blue values, each ranging from 000 to 255.
- rgb(*rrr.d%, ggg.e%, bbb.f%*) represents the relative red-green-blue values, each ranging from 0.0% to 100.0%. Note that 0.0% is equivalent to an absolute value of 000, and 100.0% is equivalent to 255.
- inherit is a keyword that indicates that this property takes the same computed value as its parent.

Notes

- This property is in the miscellaneous category.
- This property, which originated in CSS1, applies to all elements.
- By default, the characteristics of this property are inherited.

Example

```
para.intro { color: teal; font-size: 10pt; font-style: italic }
```

Related Properties

baseline-shift (p. 388), block-progression-dimension (p. 390), clip (p. 440), direction (p. 453), font-height-override-after (p. 484), font-height-override-before (p. 485), glyph-orientation-horizontal (p. 512), glyph-orientation-vertical (p. 513), height (p. 514), href (p. 515), hyphenation-keep (p. 517), hyphenation-ladder-count (p. 518), id (p. 521), inline-progression-dimension (p. 525), last-line-end-indent (p. 531), linefeed-treatment (p. 537), line-height (p. 538), line-height-shift-adjustment (p. 539), line-stacking-strategy (p. 540), max-height (p. 548), max-width (p. 550), min-height (p. 552), min-width (p. 553), overflow (p. 561), provisional-distance-between-starts (p. 586), provisional-label-separation (p. 587), reference-orientation (p. 588), ref-id (p. 589), scaling (p. 601), score-spaces (p. 602), size (p. 605), space-treatment (p. 611), span (p. 612), text-align (p. 625), text-align-last (p. 626), text-indent (p. 629), unicode-bidi (p. 634), vertical-align (p. 635), visibility (p. 636), white-space (p. 639), white-space-collapse (p. 640), width (p. 642), wrap-option (p. 644), writing-mode (p. 645), z-index (p. 648)

Related Formatting Objects

fo:bidi-override (p. 465), fo:block (p. 466), fo:initial-property-set
(p. 473), fo:inline (p. 473), fo:leader (p. 476)

Color [18]   Color

Purpose
Identifies an RGB hexadecimal color code.

EBNF Syntax

    Color ::= '#' AlphaOrDigits

Standard Syntax

    #AlphaOrDigits

Where
- # indicates the start of an RGB hexadecimal color code.
- AlphaOrDigits (p. 376) represents one or more alphabetic characters or decimal or hexadecimal numbers.

Notes
- Color is a component of the PrimaryExpr production.
- Color represents part of an expression.

Related Productions
AbsoluteUnitName (p. 372), AlphaOrDigits (p. 376), Digits (p. 452),
EnumerationToken (p. 459), ExprToken (p. 460), ExprWhitespace (p. 461),
FloatingPointNumber (p. 463), FunctionName (p. 512), Keyword (p. 529),
Literal (p. 541), MultiplyOperator (p. 555), Number (p. 555), Operator
(p. 559), OperatorName (p. 560), PrimaryExpr (p. 585), RelativeUnitName
(p. 593)

color-profile-name   Color Profile Name

Purpose
Specifies the name of a color profile for internal reference.

Syntax

    color-profile-name: name | inherit

Where
- *name* specifies the color profile name.
- inherit is a keyword that indicates that this property takes the same computed value as its parent.

Notes

- This is a color-related property.
- This property works in conjunction with fo:color-profile.

column-count   Column Count

Purpose

Specifies the number of columns in the current box.

Syntax

```
column-count: integer|inherit
```

Where

- *integer* is a positive, non-zero integer. The initial value is 1.
- inherit is a keyword that indicates that this property takes the same computed value as its parent.

Notes

- This property is in the pagination-and-layout category.
- This property applies to the fo:body-region formatting object.
- If *integer* is negative or not an integer, the processor rounds the number to the closest integer greater than zero.
- An *integer* value greater than 1 indicates a multi-column area.
- By default, the characteristics of this property are inherited.

Related Properties

blank-or-not-blank (p. 389), column-gap (p. 444), extent (p. 461), flow-name (p. 465), force-page-count (p. 494), initial-page-number (p. 524), master-name (p. 547), maximum-repeats (p. 549), odd-or-even (p. 559), page-height (p. 575), page-position (p. 575), page-width (p. 576), precedence (p. 584), region-name (p. 590)

Related Formatting Object

fo:region-body (p. 496)

column-gap   Column Separation

Purpose

Specifies the amount of space between two columns in the current box.

Syntax

```
column-gap: length|inherit
```

Where

- *length* is a absolute length of the space between the columns. The default value is 12.0 points.

- inherit is a keyword that indicates that this property takes the same computed value as its parent.

Notes

- This property is in the pagination-and-layout category.
- The value of *length* can be either positive or 0.
- This property applies to the fo:body-region formatting object.
- By default, the characteristics of this property are not inherited.

Related Properties

blank-or-not-blank (p. 389), column-count (p. 444), extent (p. 461), flow-name (p. 465), force-page-count (p. 494), initial-page-number (p. 524), master-name (p. 547), maximum-repeats (p. 549), odd-or-even (p. 559), page-height (p. 575), page-position (p. 575), page-width (p. 576), precedence (p. 584), region-name (p. 590)

Related Formatting Object

fo:region-body (p. 496)

---

column-number   Column Number

Purpose

Specifies the number of the first column in a table-cell span.

Syntax

    column-number: *integer*

Where

- *integer* is a positive, non-zero integer.

Notes

- This property is in the table category.
- The default column-number for a table column is equal to the value of the prior table-column flow object plus 1. If no prior table column flow object exists, the default column-number value is 1, which represents the first column in the table.
- When a prior table row contains cells that span two or more rows, the table cells that follow use the column-number characteristic to clarify identification.
- The default column-number for a table cell is the current table-column number.
- The XSL column-number property is slightly related to the DSSSL-O column-number property.
- By default, the characteristics of this property are not inherited.

Related Properties

border-collapse (p. 405), border-spacing (p. 422), caption-side (p. 437),
column-width (p. 446), empty-cells (p. 457), ends-row (p. 458),
number-columns-repeated (p. 556), number-columns-spanned (p. 557),
number-rows-spanned (p. 557), starts-row (p. 619), table-layout (p. 623),
table-omit-footer-at-break (p. 624), table-omit-header-at-break (p. 624)

Related Formatting Objects

fo:table-cell (p. 505), fo:table-column (p. 506)

column-width — Column Width

Purpose

Sets the width of the column specified in the column-number property.

Syntax

```
column-width: length
```

Where

- *length* is the absolute width of the column.

Notes

- This property is in the table category.
- If number-columns-spanned is greater than 1, column-width is disregarded.
- The width of every column in the table must specified unless table-width="auto".
- By default, characteristics of this property are not inherited.

Related Properties

border-collapse (p. 405), border-spacing (p. 422), caption-side (p. 437),
column-number (p. 445), empty-cells (p. 457), ends-row (p. 458),
number-columns-repeated (p. 556), number-columns-spanned (p. 557),
number-rows-spanned (p. 557), starts-row (p. 619), table-layout (p. 623),
table-omit-footer-at-break (p. 624), table-omit-header-at-break (p. 624)

Related Formatting Object

fo:table-column (p. 506)

content-height — Content Height

Purpose

Specifies the content-height of a particular object.

Syntax

```
content-height: auto| length | percentage | inherit
```

Where

- auto is a keyword that specifies that the content-height should be the intrinsic content-height.
- *length* defines the absolute size for a content-height.
- percentage represents a scaling factor for the content-height.
- inherit is a keyword that indicates that this property takes the same computed value as its parent.

Notes

- This is an area-dimension property.
- The value of *length* implies a certain scaling factor to be applied to the content.
- An example of an object could be an external graphic.
- This property applies to fo:external-graphic and fo:instream-foreign-object.

Related Properties

block-progression-dimension (p. 390), content-width (p. 448), height (p. 514), inline-progression-dimension (p. 525), max-height (p. 548), max-width (p. 550), min-height (p. 552), min-width (p. 553), scaling (p. 601), scaling-method (p. 602), width (p. 642)

content-type   Content Type

Purpose

Specifies the type of content and allows the browser to choose an appropriate application to render the element.

Syntax

content-type: string| auto

Where

- *string* specifies the content-type by mime-type or namespace.
- auto is a keyword that doesn't specify the content-type and causes the user agent to discover other means of recognizing the element.

Notes

- This is a miscellaneous property.
- An example of mime-type use has the form "content-type:" followed by a mime-type. For example: content-type="content-type:xml/smil".
- An example of a namespace has the form "namespace-prefix:" followed by the declared namespace prefix. For example: content-type="namespace-prefix:smil". If there is no specified namespace prefix, then the content-type refers to the default namespace.
- The corresponding formatting objects are fo:external-graphic and fo:instream-foreign-object.

XSL Style Sheet Syntax

Related Properties

id (p. 521), provisional-label-separation (p. 587), provisional-distance-between-starts (p. 586), ref-id (p. 589), score-spaces (p. 602), src (p. 617), visibility (p. 636), z-index (p. 648)

content-width   Content Width

Purpose
Specifies width of content of a particular object.

Syntax
content-width: auto| *length* | *percentage* | inherit

Where

- auto is a keyword that specifies that the content-width should be the intrinsic content-width.
- *length* defines the absolute size for a content-width.
- *percentage* represents a scaling factor for the content-width.
- inherit is a keyword that indicates that this property takes the same computed value as its parent.

Notes

- This is an area dimension property.
- The value of *length* implies a certain scaling factor to be applied to the content.
- An example of an object could be an external graphic.
- This property applies to fo:external-graphic and fo:instream-foreign-object.

Related Properties

block-progression-dimension (p. 390), content-height (p. 446), height (p. 514), inline-progression-dimension (p. 525), max-height (p. 548), max-width (p. 550), min-height (p. 552), min-width (p. 553), scaling (p. 601), scaling-method (p. 602), width (p. 642)

country   Country Code

Purpose
Specifies a country code from RFC-1766.

Syntax
country: <u>none</u>|RFC_1766_*country_code*|inherit

Where

- none indicates no country code. This is the default.
- RFC_1766_*country_code* is a country code.

- inherit is a keyword that indicates that this property takes the same computed value as its parent.

Notes

- This property is in the common-hyphenation category.
- The country characteristic is part of the character, paragraph, and paragraph-break flow-objects classes.
- The XSL country property is related, but not closely, to the DSSSL-O country property.
- In XML, language codes and country codes are case-insensitive. Although it is not required, the language code is usually in lower case and the country code is usually in upper case.
- RFC_1766 is a subset of ISO 3166. You can find a list of ISO 3166 country codes at http://www.din.de/gremien/nas/nabd/iso3166ma/codlstp1.html.
- Use the XML Subcode element to specify language and country codes within XML documents.
- The country characteristic is inherited.
- For more information about country codes supported by XML, refer to Appendix B, "Country Codes" (p. 799).

Related Properties

hyphenate (p. 516), hyphenation-character (p. 517), hyphenation-push-character-count (p. 519), hyphenation-remain-character-count (p. 520), language (p. 530), script (p. 603), xml:lang (p. 647)

Related Formatting Object

fo:block (p. 466)

---

cue   Cue Element

Purpose

Sounds an auditory cue before and/or after an element.

Syntax

```
cue: (uri(b_uri_name)|none)(uri(a_uri_name)|none)
    |inherit
```

Where

- uri is a keyword that indicates that a URI name will follow.
- b_uri_name names the URI of the sound cue file that is sounded before the element.
- a_uri_name names the URI of the sound cue file that is sounded after the element.
- none indicates no sound cue.
- inherit is a keyword that indicates that this property takes the same computed value as its parent.

XSL Style Sheet Syntax

Notes

- This property is in the common-aural category.
- This property, which originated in CSS2, applies to all elements.
- By default, the characteristics of this property are not inherited.

Related Properties

azimuth (p. 377), cue-after (p. 450), cue-before (p. 451), elevation (p. 456), pause (p. 577), pause-after (p. 578), pause-before (p. 579), pitch (p. 580), pitch-range (p. 581), play-during (p. 582), richness (p. 597), speak (p. 613), speak-header (p. 614), speak-numeral (p. 615), speak-punctuation (p. 615), speech-rate (p. 616), stress (p. 620), voice-family (p. 637), volume (p. 638)

Related Formatting Objects

fo:bidi-override (p. 465), fo:block (p. 466), fo:external-graphic (p. 470), fo:footnote-body (p. 472), fo:initial-property-set (p. 473), fo:inline (p. 473), fo:instream-foreign-object (p. 475), fo:leader (p. 476), fo:list-block (p. 477), fo:list-item (p. 478), fo:page-number (p. 492), fo:page-number-citation (p. 492), fo:simple-link (p. 500), fo:table (p. 503), fo:table-and-caption (p. 504), fo:table-body (p. 504), fo:table-caption (p. 505), fo:table-cell (p. 505), fo:table-footer (p. 506), fo:table-header (p. 507), fo:table-row (p. 507)

cue-after · Cue After Element

Purpose

Sounds an auditory cue after an element.

Syntax

```
cue-after: uri(uri_name)|none|inherit
```

Where

- uri is a keyword that indicates that a URI name will follow.
- *uri_name* names the URI of the sound cue file.
- none indicates no sound cue. This is the default.
- inherit is a keyword that indicates that this property takes the same computed value as its parent.

Notes

- This property is in the common-aural category.
- By default, the characteristics of this property are not inherited.

Related Properties

azimuth (p. 377), cue (p. 449), cue-before (p. 451), elevation (p. 456), pause (p. 577), pause-after (p. 578), pause-before (p. 579), pitch (p. 580), pitch-range (p. 581), play-during (p. 582), richness (p. 597), speak (p. 613), speak-header (p. 614), speak-numeral (p. 615), speak-punctuation (p. 615), speech-rate (p. 616), stress (p. 620), voice-family (p. 637), volume (p. 638)

Related Formatting Objects

fo:bidi-override (p. 465), fo:block (p. 466), fo:block-character (p. 470), fo:external-graphic (p. 472), fo:footnote-body (p. 473), fo:initial-property-set (p. 473), fo:inline (p. 475), fo:instream-foreign-object (p. 476), fo:leader (p. 477), fo:list-block (p. 478), fo:list-item (p. 492), fo:page-number (p. 492), fo:page-number-citation (p. 500), fo:simple-link (p. 503), fo:table (p. 504), fo:table-and-caption (p. 504), fo:table-body (p. 505), fo:table-caption (p. 505), fo:table-cell (p. 506), fo:table-footer (p. 506), fo:table-header (p. 507), fo:table-row (p. 507)

cue-before | Cue Before Element

Purpose

Sounds an auditory cue before an element.

Syntax

cue-before: uri(*uri_name*)|none|inherit

Where

- uri is a keyword that indicates that a URI name will follow.
- *uri_name* names the URI of the sound cue file.
- none indicates no sound cue. This is the default.
- inherit is a keyword that indicates that this property takes the same computed value as its parent.

Notes

- This property is in the common-aural category.
- This property, which originated in CSS2, applies to all elements.
- By default, the characteristics of this property are not inherited.

Related Properties

azimuth (p. 377), cue (p. 449), cue-after (p. 450), elevation (p. 456), pause (p. 577), pause-after (p. 578), pause-before (p. 579), pitch (p. 580), pitch-range (p. 581), play-during (p. 582), richness (p. 597), speak (p. 613), speak-header (p. 614), speak-numeral (p. 615), speak-punctuation (p. 615), speech-rate (p. 616), stress (p. 620), voice-family (p. 637), volume (p. 638)

Related Formatting Objects

fo:bidi-override (p. 465), fo:block (p. 466), fo:external-graphic (p. 470), fo:footnote-body (p. 472), fo:initial-property-set (p. 473), fo:inline (p. 473), fo:instream-foreign-object (p. 475), fo:leader (p. 476), fo:list-block (p. 477), fo:list-item (p. 478), fo:page-number (p. 492), fo:page-number-citation (p. 492), fo:simple-link (p. 500), fo:table (p. 503), fo:table-and-caption (p. 504), fo:table-body (p. 504), fo:table-caption (p. 505), fo:table-cell (p. 505), fo:table-footer (p. 506), fo:table-header (p. 507), fo:table-row (p. 507)

destination-placement-offset

Destination Placement Offset

Purpose

Indicates the distance from the top of the page to the location of the first destination area.

Syntax

```
destination-placement-offset: length
```

Where

- `length` is a positive value followed by a two-letter abbreviation representing the unit of measure. The initial value is 0 point.

Notes

- This property is in the links category.
- If `length` reaches above the top of the document, the top of the document is the offset length.
- If `length` moves the first destination area below the page box, the offset length is adjusted so that the first destination area is in the page box.
- By default, the characteristics of this property are inherited.

Related Properties

auto-restore (p. 377), case-name (p. 438), case-title (p. 438), external-destination (p. 462), indicate-destination (p. 523), internal-destination (p. 526), show-destination (p. 604), starting-state (p. 619), switch-to (p. 621)

Related Formatting Object

fo:simple-link (p. 500)

Digits [17]

Digits

Purpose

Specifies one or more digits.

EBNF Syntax

```
Digits ::= [0-9]+
```

Standard Syntax

```
0-9 [0-9]... [0-9]
```

Where

0-9 represents a number from 0 to 9.

Notes

- `Digits` represents digits supported by the Unicode Organization. (See Appendix A, "Unicode Characters and Character Sets" (p. 757).
- `Digits` represents part of an expression.

Related Productions

`AbsoluteUnitName` (p. 372), `AlphaOrDigits` (p. 376), `Color` (p. 443), `EnumerationToken` (p. 459), `ExprToken` (p. 460), `ExprWhitespace` (p. 461), `FloatingPointNumber` (p. 463), `FunctionName` (p. 512), `Keyword` (p. 529), `Literal` (p. 541), `MultiplyOperator` (p. 555), `Number` (p. 555), `Operator` (p. 559), `OperatorName` (p. 560), `RelativeUnitName` (p. 593)

direction	**Text Direction**

Purpose

Specifies the direction in which text is displayed or printed.

Syntax

```
direction: ltr|rtl|inherit
```

Where

- `ltr` indicates that text is printed or displayed left to right. This is the default.
- `rtl` indicates that text is printed or displayed right to left.
- `inherit` is a keyword that indicates that this property takes the same computed value as its parent.

Notes

- This property is in the miscellaneous category.
- This property originated in CSS1.
- For more information about this property in XSL, refer to the XSL working draft (http://www.w3.org/TR/xsl/).
- By default, the characteristics of this property are inherited.

Related Properties

`baseline-shift` (p. 388), `block-progression-dimension` (p. 390), `clip` (p. 440), `color` (p. 441), `font-height-override-after` (p. 484), `font-height-override-before` (p. 485), `glyph-orientation-horizontal` (p. 512), `glyph-orientation-vertical` (p. 513), `height` (p. 514), `href` (p. 515), `hyphenation-keep` (p. 517), `hyphenation-ladder-count` (p. 518), `id` (p. 521), `inline-progression-dimension` (p. 525), `last-line-end-indent` (p. 531), `linefeed-treatment` (p. 537), `line-height` (p. 538), `line-height-shift-adjustment` (p. 539), `line-stacking-strategy` (p. 540), `max-height` (p. 548), `max-width` (p. 550), `min-height` (p. 552), `min-width` (p. 553), `overflow` (p. 561), `provisional-distance-between-starts` (p. 586), provisional-label-separation (p. 587), reference-orientation (p. 588), ref-id (p. 589), scaling (p. 601), score-spaces (p. 602), size (p. 605), space-treatment (p. 611), span (p. 612), text-align (p. 625), text-align-last (p. 626), text-indent (p. 629), unicode-bidi (p. 634), vertical-align (p. 635), visibility (p. 636), white-space (p. 639), white-space-collapse (p. 640), width (p. 642), wrap-option (p. 644), writing-mode (p. 645), z-index (p. 648)

Related Formatting Object

fo:bidi-override (p. 465)

display-align   Display Align

Purpose

Specifies the block-progression-direction alignment of reference-area children.

Syntax

```
display-align: auto|before|center|after|inherit
```

Where

- auto is a keyword that dictates if a relative-align property exists, it should be used. Otherwise, this value acts as if before has been chosen.
- before is a keyword that specifies the before-edge of a child area is placed coincident with the before-edge of the reference-area.
- center is a keyword that specifies that the child area should be placed at the same distance between the before-edge of the first-child area and reference-area and between the after-edge of the last-child area and the reference-area.
- after is a keyword that says the after-edge of the last-child area is placed coincident to the after-edge of the reference-area.
- inherit is a keyword that indicates that this property takes the same computed value as its parent.

Notes

- This is an area alignment property.
- This property is used with fo:table-cell, fo:region-body, fo:region-before, fo:region-after, fo:region-start, fo:region-end.
- The default value for this property is auto.

Related Properties

alignment-adjust (p. 375), baseline-identifier (p. 387), baseline-shift (p. 388), dominant-baseline (p. 455), relative-align (p. 591)

dominant-baseline   Dominant Baseline

Purpose

Re-determines the dominant-baseline and reestablishes the font-size used with the baseline-table.

Syntax

dominant-baseline: auto| autosense-script| nochange
 |reset-size|ideographic|alphabetic|hanging|mathematical|inherit

Where

- auto is a keyword that specifies that if this property occurs within a block-level formatting object, then the rules for autosense-script are used. Otherwise, the dominant-baseline and baseline-table stay the same as the parent area.
- autosense-script is a keyword that dictates the browser automatically detects the current font or script's baseline and changes to it.
- no-change is a keyword that says the dominant-baseline stays the same as that of the parent area.
- ideographic is a keyword that specifies the dominant-baseline gets set to the ideographic baseline.
- alphabetic is a keyword that dictates the dominant-baseline should be set to the alphabetic baseline.
- mathematical is a keyword that dictates the dominant-baseline should be set to the mathematical baseline.
- hanging is a keyword that dictates the dominant-baseline should be set to the hanging baseline.

Notes

- This is an area alignment property.
- The default value of this property is auto.
- If the character used to determine the baseline when the value is set to autosense-script does not exist, then the alphabetic baseline is used.
- This property can also be used to set the dominant-baseline when auto would produce an incorrect baseline specification.
- * If there is no baseline-table in the font being used, the User agent may use heuristics to determine the dominant-baseline.

Related Properties

alignment-adjust (p. 375), baseline-identifier (p. 387), baseline-shift (p. 388), display-align (p. 454), relative-align (p. 591)

XSL Style Sheet Syntax

elevation   Spatial Elevation

Purpose
Specifies the top-to-bottom stereo speaker location of a sound file.

Syntax
```
elevation: range_angle|below|level|above|higher|lower
|inherit
```

Where
- *range_angle* is a specific angle in the elevation in which stereo speakers are arranged. Valid values range from -90deg (degrees) to 90deg.
- below is a keyword that indicates that the sound is below level elevation — at -90deg.
- level is a keyword that indicates that the sound is approximately at the same level as the user — at 0deg. This is the default.
- above is a keyword that indicates that the sound is above level elevation — at 90deg.
- higher is a keyword that indicates that the sound is 10 degrees higher than the previous elevation.
- lower is a keyword that indicates that the sound is 10 degrees lower than the previous elevation.
- inherit is a keyword that indicates that this property takes the same computed value as its parent.

Notes
- This property is in the common-aural category.
- This property, which originated in CSS2, applies to all elements.
- By default, the characteristics of this property are inherited.

Related Properties
azimuth (p. 377), cue (p. 449), cue-after (p. 450), cue-before (p. 451), pause (p. 577), pause-after (p. 578), pause-before (p. 579), pitch (p. 580), pitch-range (p. 581), play-during (p. 582), richness (p. 597), speak (p. 613), speak-header (p. 614), speak-numeral (p. 615), speak-punctuation (p. 615), speech-rate (p. 616), stress (p. 620), voice-family (p. 637), volume (p. 638)

Related Formatting Objects
fo:bidi-override (p. 465), fo:block (p. 466), fo:external-graphic (p. 470), fo:footnote-body (p. 472), fo:initial-property-set (p. 473), fo:inline (p. 473), fo:instream-foreign-object (p. 475), fo:leader (p. 476), fo:list-block (p. 477), fo:list-item (p. 478), fo:page-number (p. 492), fo:page-number-citation (p. 492), fo:simple-link (p. 500), fo:table (p. 503), fo:table-and-caption (p. 504), fo:table-body (p. 504), fo:table-caption (p. 505), fo:table-cell (p. 505), fo:table-footer (p. 506), fo:table-header (p. 507), fo:table-row (p. 507)

empty-cells

Empty-Cell Borders

Purpose
Shows or hides borders around empty table cells.

Syntax
```
empty-cells: show|hide|inherit
```

Where
- show is a keyword that indicates that empty cells have borders.
- hide is a keyword that indicates that empty cells do not have borders.
- inherit is a keyword that indicates that this property takes the same computed value as its parent.

Notes
- This property is in the table category.
- This property, which originated in CSS2, applies to table-cell elements.
- If all the empty cells in a row have a value of empty-cells: hide and visibility: hidden, the implicit result is display: none.
- By default, the characteristics of this property are inherited.
- For more information about table cells and table-cell borders, refer to "Section 17.6" in the *Cascading Style Sheets, Level 2 CSS Specification* (http://www.w3.org/TR/REC-CSS2/).

Related Properties
border-collapse (p. 405), border-spacing (p. 422), caption-side (p. 437), column-number (p. 445), column-width (p. 446), ends-row (p. 458), number-columns-repeated (p. 556), number-columns-spanned (p. 557), number-rows-spanned (p. 557), starts-row (p. 619), table-layout (p. 623), table-omit-footer-at-break (p. 624), table-omit-header-at-break (p. 624)

Related Formatting Object
fo:table-cell (p. 505)

end-indent

End Indent

Purpose
Specifies indention at the ending edge of the current formatting object box.

Syntax
```
end-indent: length|inherit
```

Where
- length is an absolute length of the indention. The default value is 0 point.

- inherit is a keyword that indicates that this property takes the same computed value as its parent.

Notes

- This property is in the common-margins-block category.
- If the value of *length* is positive, the indention is a standard block indent; if the value of *length* is negative, the indention is an outdent.
- The XSL end-indent property is closely related to the DSSSL-O end-indent property.
- The end-indent characteristic is inherited.

Related Properties

margin properties (p. 542 - p. 546), space-after (p. 607), space-before (p. 608), start-indent (p. 618)

Related Formatting Objects

fo:block (p. 466), fo:block-container (p. 467), fo:external-graphic (p. 470), fo:float (p. 471), fo:footnote (p. 472), fo:footnote-body (p. 472), fo:inline (p. 473), fo:inline-container (p. 474), fo:instream-foreign-object (p. 475), fo:leader (p. 476), fo:list-block (p. 477), fo:list-item (p. 478), fo:page-number (p. 492), fo:page-number-citation (p. 492), fo:region-body (p. 496), fo:simple-link (p. 500), fo:simple-page-master (p. 501), fo:table (p. 503), fo:table-and-caption (p. 504)

---

ends-row   Ends Row?

Purpose

Indicates whether the current table cell ends a table row.

Syntax

ends-row: yes|<u>no</u>

Where

- yes is a keyword that indicates that the current cell ends the row.
- no is a keyword that indicates that the current cell does not end the row. This is the default value.

Notes

- This property is in the table category.
- The XSL ends-row property is somewhat related to the DSSSL-O ends-row? property.
- By default, characteristics of this property are not inherited.

Related Properties

border-collapse (p. 405), border-spacing (p. 422), caption-side (p. 437),
column-number (p. 445), column-width (p. 446), empty-cells (p. 457),
number-columns-repeated (p. 556), number-columns-spanned (p. 557),
number-rows-spanned (p. 557), starts-row (p. 619), table-layout (p. 623),
table-omit-footer-at-break (p. 624), table-omit-header-at-break (p. 624)

Related Formatting Object

fo:table-cell (p. 505)

EnumerationToken [26]   Enumeration Token

Purpose

Provides an NCName for an enumeration token.

EBNF Syntax

```
EnumerationToken ::= NCName
```

Standard Syntax

```
NCName
```

Where

- NCName represents a name from a collection of namespace names.

Notes

- EnumerationToken is a component of the ExprToken and PrimaryExpr
  productions.
- EnumerationToken represents part of an expression.

Related Productions

AbsoluteUnitName (p. 372), AlphaOrDigits (p. 376), Color (p. 443), Digits
(p. 452), ExprToken (p. 460), ExprWhitespace (p. 461), FloatingPointNumber
(p. 463), FunctionName (p. 512), Keyword (p. 529), Literal (p. 541),
MultiplyOperator (p. 555), Number (p. 555), Operator (p. 559), OperatorName
(p. 560), RelativeUnitName (p. 593)

Expr [1]   Expression

Purpose

Indicates an expression.

EBNF Syntax

```
Expr ::= AdditiveExpr
```

Standard Syntax

```
AdditiveExpr
```

XSL Style Sheet Syntax

Where

- AdditiveExpr (p. 374) acts on one or more expressions through addition or subtraction.

Notes

- Expr is a component of the PrimaryExpr production.
- The XSL Expr production is similar but not identical to the XPath Expr production.

Related Productions

AdditiveExpr (p. 374), PrimaryExpr (p. 585)

ExprToken [14]	**Expression Token**

Purpose

Tokenizes an expression character by character or name by name.

EBNF Syntax

```
ExprToken ::= '(' | ')' | '%' | Operator
    | FunctionName | EnumerationToken | Number
```

Standard Syntax

```
( | ) | % | Operator | FunctionName
    | EnumerationToken | Number
```

Where

- (marks the start of an arguments list.
-) marks the end of an arguments list.
- % starts a parameter-entity reference.
- Operator (p. 559) provides a list of mathematical operators.
- FunctionName (p. 512) provides an NCName for a function.
- EnumerationToken (p. 459) provides an NCName for an enumeration token.

Notes

- A *token* is a basic unit that cannot be further broken down. In XML, a token is a reserved word, operator, entity, symbol, punctuation mark, or variable name.
- ExprToken represents part of an expression.
- An NCName is a name for a collection of namespace names.

Related Productions

AbsoluteUnitName (p. 372), AlphaOrDigits (p. 376), Color (p. 443), Digits (p. 452), EnumerationToken (p. 459), ExprWhitespace (p. 461), FloatingPointNumber (p. 463), FunctionName (p. 512), Keyword (p. 529),

Literal (p. 541), MultiplyOperator (p. 555), Number (p. 555), Operator
(p. 559), OperatorName (p. 560), RelativeUnitName (p. 593)

ExprWhitespace [29]   Expression Whitespace

Purpose
Inserts whitespace in an expression.

EBNF Syntax
```
ExprWhitespace ::= S
```

Standard Syntax
```
[ ... ]
```

Where
- S (p. 124) represents one or more whitespace characters: spaces, car-
  riage returns, line feeds, or tabs. Syntax: {[#x20|#x9|#xD|#xA][#x20|
  #x9|#xD|#xA]...[#x20|#x9|#xD|#xA]}

Note
- The XPath recommendation (http://www.w3.org/TR/xpath) states the
  following: "For readability, whitespace may be used in expressions even
  though not explicitly allowed by the grammar: ExprWhitespace may be
  freely added within patterns before or after any ExprToken."
- ExprWhitespace represents part of an expression.

Related Productions
AbsoluteUnitName (p. 372), AlphaOrDigits (p. 376), Color (p. 443), Digits
(p. 452), EnumerationToken (p. 459), ExprToken (p. 460), FloatingPointNumber
(p. 463), FunctionName (p. 512), Keyword (p. 529), Literal (p. 541),
MultiplyOperator (p. 555), Number (p. 555), Operator (p. 559), OperatorName
(p. 560), RelativeUnitName (p. 593)

extent   Height or Width Extent

Purpose
Specifies the extent of the width of the horizontal part of the box or the
height of the vertical part of the box.

Syntax
```
extent: length|inherit
```

Where
- length is the absolute length of the horizontal part of the box or the
  height of the vertical part of the box.

- inherit is a keyword that indicates that this property takes the same computed value as its parent.

Notes

- This property is in the pagination-and-layout category.
- The value of *length* can be either positive or 0.
- This property applies to the fo:after-region, fo:before-region, fo:end-region, and fo:start-region formatting objects.
- By default, the characteristics of this property are not inherited.

Related Properties

blank-or-not-blank (p. 389), column-count (p. 444), column-gap (p. 444), flow-name (p. 465), force-page-count (p. 494), initial-page-number (p. 524), master-name (p. 547), maximum-repeats (p. 549), odd-or-even (p. 559), page-height (p. 575), page-position (p. 575), page-width (p. 576), precedence (p. 584), region-name (p. 590)

Related Formatting Objects

fo:region-after (p. 495), fo:region-before (p. 496), fo:region-end (p. 497), fo:region-start (p. 497)

external-destination   External Destination

Purpose

Indicates the destination or target resource of a simple link (fo:simple-link formatting object) in an external document.

Syntax

external-destination: *uri_name*

Where

- *uri_name* names the URI of the destination resource.

Notes

- This property is in the links category.
- A fragment identifier names the destination node. If there is no fragment identifier, the destination node is the root node.
- If both the external-destination and internal-destination properties are used for this link, internal-destination has precedence.
- By default, the characteristics of this property are not inherited.

Related Properties

auto-restore (p. 377), case-name (p. 438), case-title (p. 438), destination-placement-offset (p. 452), indicate-destination (p. 523), internal-destination (p. 526), show-destination (p. 604), starting-state (p. 619), switch-to (p. 621)

Related Formatting Object

fo:simple-link (p. 500)

float   Float Element

Purpose

Floats or inserts the element in the document.

Syntax

```
float: left|right|none|inherit
```

Where

- left floats the element on the left side and wraps text on its right side.
- right floats the element on the right side and wraps text on its left side.
- none displays the element as inserted on the page. This is the default.
- inherit is a keyword that indicates that this property takes the same computed value as its parent.

Notes

- This property is in the float-related category.
- This property, which originated in CSS1, applies to all but elements that are positioned and generated content.
- By default, the characteristics of this property are not inherited.
- For more information about the float property, see Section 9.5.1 in the *Cascading Style Sheets, Level 2 CSS Specification* (http://www.w3.org/TR/REC-CSS2/).

Example

```
img.float.gif { float: left }
```

Related Property

clear (p. 440)

Related Formatting Object

fo:float (p. 471)

FloatingPointNumber [16]   Floating Point Number

Purpose

Represents a floating-point number

EBNF Syntax

```
FloatingPointNumber ::= Digits ('.' Digits?)?
   | '.' Digits
```

Standard Syntax

```
Digits [(.[Digits])] | .Digits
```

Where

- `Digits` (p. 452) represents one or more numbers from 0 to 9.
- `.` is a decimal point.

Notes

- `FloatingPointNumber` represents part of an expression.
- A *floating-point number* is composed of one or more digits on either side of a decimal point.

Related Productions

`AbsoluteUnitName` (p. 372), `AlphaOrDigits` (p. 376), `Color` (p. 443), `Digits` (p. 452), `EnumerationToken` (p. 459), `ExprToken` (p. 460), `ExprWhitespace` (p. 461), `FunctionName` (p. 512), `Keyword` (p. 529), `Literal` (p. 541), `MultiplyOperator` (p. 555), `Number` (p. 555), `Operator` (p. 559), `OperatorName` (p. 560), `RelativeUnitName` (p. 593)

floor()   Floor Function

Purpose

Returns the highest integer.

EBNF Syntax

```
number_r floor(number)
```

Standard Syntax

```
number_r floor(number)
```

Where

- *number_r* is the number returned by the function.
- `floor` is a function-name keyword.
- *number* represents the argument's number.

Notes

- `floor()` returns the number that is closest to positive infinity.
- The returned number must not be greater than the argument.

Related XPath Functions

`abs()` (p. 370), `ceiling()` (p. 439), `max()` (p. 548), `min()` (p. 552), `round()` (p. 599)

flow-name

Flow Name

Purpose

Names the current flow.

Syntax

```
flow-name: flow_name
```

Where

* *flow_name* is the unique name of the current flow.

Notes

* This property is in the pagination-and-layout category.
* This property applies to the fo:flow and fo:static-content formatting objects.
* In XSL, you cannot give this property a value of inherit.
* By default, the characteristics of this property are not inherited.

Related Properties

blank-or-not-blank (p. 389), column-count (p. 444), column-gap (p. 444), extent (p. 461), force-page-count (p. 494), initial-page-number (p. 524), master-name (p. 547), maximum-repeats (p. 549), odd-or-even (p. 559), page-height (p. 575), page-position (p. 575), page-width (p. 576), precedence (p. 584), region-name (p. 590)

Related Formatting Objects

fo:flow (p. 471), fo:static-content (p. 502)

fo:bidi-override

Bidirectional Override
Formatting Object

Purpose

Overrides the bidirectionality writing direction for an inline script in a particular language.

Notes

* This formatting object is in the inline-level category.
* The following are inline formatting objects: fo:bidi-override, fo:character, fo:external-graphic, fo:inline, fo:inline-container, fo:instream-foreign-object, fo:leader, fo:multi-toggle, fo:page-number, fo:page-number-citation, and fo:simple-link.
* fo:bidi-override overrides a failed Unicode-bidi algorithm.

XSL Style Sheet Syntax

Related Formatting Objects

fo:character (p. 467), fo:external-graphic (p. 470), fo:initial-property-set (p. 473), fo:inline (p. 473), fo:inline-container p. 474), fo:instream-foreign-object (p. 475), fo:leader (p. 476), fo:multi-toggle (p. 481), fo:page-number (p. 492), fo:page-number-citation (p. 492), fo:simple-link (p. 500)

Related Properties

azimuth (p. 377), background properties (p. 379 - p. 389), border properties (p. 392 – p. 434), color (p. 441), cue (p. 449), cue-after (p. 450), cue-before (p. 451), direction (p. 453), elevation (p. 456), font properties (p. 482 - p. 492), id (p. 521), letter-spacing (p. 353), line-height (p. 538), line-height-shift-adjustment (p. 539), padding properties (p. 562 - p. 571), pause (p. 577), pause-after (p. 578), pause-before (p. 579), pitch (p. 580), pitch-range (p. 581), play-during (p. 582), richness (p. 587), score-spaces (p. 602), speak (p. 613), speak-header (p. 614), speak-numeral (p. 615), speak-punctuation (p. 615), speech-rate (p. 616), stress (p. 620), text-decoration (p. 628), text-shadow (p. 630), text-transform (p. 631), unicode-bidi (p. 634), voice-family (p. 637), volume (p. 638), word-spacing (p. 643)

fo:block	Block Formatting Object

Purpose

Formats paragraphs, captions, headings, and other block-level selections.

Notes

- This formatting object is in the block-level category.
- The following are regarded as block formatting objects: fo:block, fo:block-container, fo:list-block, fo:table, and fo:table-and-caption.
- fo:block returns one or more areas.

Related Formatting Object

fo:block-container (p. 467), fo:list-block (p. 477), fo:table (p. 503), fo:table-and-caption (p. 504).

Related Properties

azimuth (p. 377), background properties (p. 379 - p. 387), border properties (p. 392 – p. 434), color (p. 441), country (p. 448), cue (p. 449), cue-after (p. 650), cue-before (p. 451), elevation (p. 456), end-indent (p. 459), font properties (p. 482 - p. 492), hyphenate properties (p. 517 - p. 521), keep-together (p. 526), language (p. 530), last-line-end-indent (p. 531), linefeed-treatment (p. 537), line-height (p. 538), line-height-shift-adjustment (p. 539), line-stacking-strategy (p. 540), margin properties (p. 542 - p. 546), orphans (p. 561), padding properties (p. 562 - p. 571), page-break-inside (p. 574), pause (p. 577), pause-after (p. 578), pause-before (p. 579), pitch (p. 580), pitch-range (p. 581), play-during (p. 582), richness (p. 597), role (p. 598), script (p. 603), source-document (p. 606), space-after (p. 607), space-before (p. 608), space-treatment (p. 611), span (p. 612), speak (p. 613), speak-header (p. 614), speak-numeral (p. 615), speak-punctuation (p. 615), speech-rate (p. 616), start-indent (p. 618), stress (p. 620), text-align (p. 625), text-align-last (p. 626), text-indent (p. 629), visibility (p. 636), voice-family (p. 637), volume (p. 638), white-space (p. 639), white-space-collapse (p. 640), widows (p. 641), wrap-option (p. 644), writing-mode (p. 645), xml:lang (p. 647), z-index (p. 648)

fo:block-container — Block-Container Flow Object

Purpose
Creates a block-level box.

Notes
- This formatting object is in the block-level category.
- The following are regarded as block formatting objects: fo:block, fo:block-container, fo:list-block, fo:table, and fo:table-and-caption.
- fo:block-container returns one block area.

Formatting Object
fo:block (p. 466), fo:list-block (p. 477), fo:table (p. 503), fo:table-and-caption (p. 504).

Related Properties
background properties (p. 379 - p. 387), block-progression-dimension (p. 390), border properties (p. 392-p. 434), bottom (p. 434), clip (p. 440), end-indent (p. 457), left (p. 535), margin properties (p. 542 - p. 546), padding properties (p. 562 - p. 571), position (p. 583), right (p. 591), space-after (p. 607), space-before (p. 608), start-indent (p. 618), top (p. 632)

fo:character — Character Flow Object

Purpose
Indicates a character that is mapped to a glyph.

Notes
- This formatting object is in the inline-level category.
- The following are inline formatting objects: fo:bidi-override, fo:character, fo:external-graphic, fo:inline, fo:inline-container, fo:instream-foreign-object, fo:leader, fo:multi-toggle, fo:page-number, fo:page-number-citation, and fo:simple-link.
- A character is the smallest part of a document.

Related Formatting Objects

fo:bidi-override (p. 465), fo:external-graphic (p. 470), fo:initial-property-set (p. 473), fo:inline (p. 473), fo:inline-container (p. 474), fo:instream-foreign-object (p. 475), fo:leader (p. 476), fo:multi-toggle (p. 481), fo:page-number (p. 492), fo:page-number-citation (p. 492), fo:simple-link (p. 500)

Related Properties

azimuth (p. 377), background properties (p. 379 - p. 387), border properties (p. 392 - p. 434), character (p. 439), color (p. 441), cue (p. 449), cue-after (p. 450), cue-before (p. 451), elevation (p. 456), end-indent (p. 457), font properties (p. 482 - p. 492), glyph-orientation-horizontal (p. 512), glyph-orientation-vertical (p. 513), id (p. 521), letter-spacing (p. 535), line-height (p. 538), line-height-shift-adjustment (p. 539), margin properties (p. 542-p. 546), padding properties (p. 562-p. 571), pause (p. 577), pause-after (p. 578), pause-before (p. 579), pitch (p. 580), pitch-range (p. 581), play-during (p. 582), richness (p. 597), score-spaces (p. 602), space-after (p. 607), space-before (p. 608), speak (p. 613), speak-header (p. 614), speak-numeral (p. 615), speak-punctuation (p. 615), speech-rate (p. 616), start-indent (p. 618), stress (p. 620), suppress-at-line-break (p. 621), text-decoration (p. 628), text-shadow (p. 630), text-transform (p. 631), vertical-align (p. 635), voice-family (p. 637), volume (p. 638), word-spacing (p. 643)

fo:color-profile	Color Profile

Purpose

Declares an ICC Color Profile for a style sheet.

Notes

- This formatting object is in the pagination and layout category.
- The color-profile is referenced again using the color-profile-name property.
- The color-profile is identified by the URI specified in the src property.
- The color profile referenced in the src profile may be internally recognized or be an ICC Color Profile.
- When the color-profile is referenced via the icc-color function, the color value from the color-profile should be used, if available. However, if no color-profile exists, then the sRGB backup value should be used.
- This formatting object does not generate or return any areas.
- The src, color-profile-name, and rendering-intent properties may be used with this formatting object.

Related Formatting Objects

fo:conditional-page-master-reference (p. 469), fo:flow (p. 471),
fo:layout-master-set (p. 475), fo:page-sequence (p. 493),
fo:page-sequence-master (p. 494), fo:region-after (p. 495),
fo:region-before (p. 496), fo:region-body (p. 496), fo:region-end (p. 497),
fo:region-start (p. 497), fo:repeatable-page-master-alternatives
(p. 498), fo:repeatable-page-master-reference (p. 499), fo:root (p. 500),
fo:simple-page-master (p. 501), fo:static-content (p. 502), fo:title
(p. 508)

fo:conditional-page-master-reference	Conditional Page-Master

Purpose

Names a page-master that is used if certain conditions are true.

Notes

- This formatting object is in the pagination and layout category.
- fo:conditional-page-master-reference is a child of fo:repeatable-page-master-alternatives.
- fo:page-sequence uses fo:conditional-page-master to produce pages. However, fo:conditional-page-master-reference refers to the fo:simple-page-master with the same master-name.
- page-position, odd-or-even, and blank-or-not-blank set properties for the fo:simple-page-master.

Related Formatting Objects

fo:flow (p. 471), fo:layout-master-set (p. 475), fo:page-sequence
(p. 493), fo:page-sequence-master (p. 494), fo:region-after (p. 495),
fo:region-before (p. 496), fo:region-body (p. 496), fo:region-end (p. 497),
fo:region-start (p. 497), fo:repeatable-page-master-alternatives
(p. 498), fo:repeatable-page-master-reference (p. 499), fo:root (p. 500)
fo:simple-page-master (p. 501), fo:single-page-master-reference (p. 502),
fo:static-content (p. 502)

Related Properties

blank-or-not-blank (p. 389), id (p. 521), master-name (p. 547), odd-or-even
(p. 559), page-position (p. 575)

fo:declarations	Declarations

Purpose

Groups global declarations for a style sheet.

Notes

- This formatting object is in the pagination and layout category.

- This formatting object does not generate or return any areas.
- fo:color-profile is used in conjunction with this formatting object.

Related Formatting Objects

fo:color-profile (p. 468), fo:conditional-page-master-reference (p. 469),
fo:flow (p. 471), fo:layout-master-set (p. 475), fo:page-sequence (p. 493),
fo:page-sequence-master (p. 494), fo:region-after (p. 495), fo:region-before
(p. 496), fo:region-body (p. 496), fo:region-end (p. 497), fo:region-start
(p. 497), fo:repeatable-page-master-alternatives (p. 498),
fo:repeatable-page-master-reference (p. 499), fo:root (p. 500),
fo:simple-page-master (p. 501), fo:single-page-master-reference
(p. 502), fo:static-content (p. 502), fo:title (p. 508)

fo:external-graphic	**External Graphic Flow Object**

Purpose
Indicates an external graphic that is placed inline.

Notes

- This formatting object is in the inline-level category.
- The following are inline formatting objects: fo:bidi-override,
  fo:character, fo:external-graphic, fo:inline, fo:inline-container,
  fo:instream-foreign-object, fo:leader, fo:multi-toggle, fo:page-
  number, fo:page-number-citation, and fo:simple-link.
- An external graphic comes from an area outside the current formatting
  object tree.
- fo:external-graphic produces one inline area.

Related Formatting Objects

fo:bidi-override (p. 465), fo:character (p. 467), fo:initial-property-set
(p. 473), fo:inline (p. 473), fo:inline-container (p. 474),
fo:instream-foreign-object (p. 475), fo:leader (p. 476), fo:multi-toggle
(p. 481), fo:page-number (p. 492), fo:page-number-citation (p. 492),
fo:simple-link (p. 500)

Related Properties

azimuth (p. 377), background properties (p. 379 – p. 389), block-progression-
dimension (p. 390), border properties (p. 392 – p. 434), cue (p. 449), cue-after
(p. 450), cue-before (p. 451), elevation (p. 456), end-indent (p. 457), height
(p. 514), href (p. 515), id (p. 521), inline-progression-dimension (p. 525),
line-height (p. 538), line-height-shift-adjustment (p. 539), margin
properties (p. 542 - p. 546), max-height (p. 548), min-height (p. 552),
min-width (p. 553), padding properties (p. 562 - p. 571), pause (p. 577),
pause-after (p. 578), pause-before (p. 579), pitch (p. 580), pitch-range
(p. 581), play-during (p. 582), richness (p. 597), role (p. 598), scaling (p. 601),
source-document (p. 606), space-after (p. 607), space-before (p. 608),

speak (p. 613), speak-header (p. 614), speak-numeral (p. 615), speak-punctuation (p. 615), speech-rate (p. 616), start-indent (p. 618), stress (p. 620), vertical-align (p. 635), voice-family (p. 637), volume (p. 638), width (p. 642)

fo:float — Float-Content Flow Object

Purpose
Contains the content of a floating object.

Notes
- This formatting object is in the out-of-line category.
- A table, sidebar, or figure can be considered to be a floating object.

Related Formatting Objects
fo:footnote (p. 472), fo:footnote-body (p. 472)

Related Properties
background properties (p. 379 - p. 387), border properties (p. 392 - p. 434), clear (p. 440), clip (p. 440), end-indent (p. 457), float (p. 463), id (p. 521), margin properties (p. 542 - p. 546), max-height (p. 548), overflow (p. 561), padding properties (p. 562-p. 571), role (p. 578), source-document (p. 606), space-after (p. 607), space-before (p. 608), span (p. 612), start-indent (p. 618), visibility (p. 636), z-index (p. 648)

fo:flow — Flow Formatting Object

Purpose
Creates a single component out of contiguous flow objects.

Notes
- This formatting object is in the pagination and layout category.
- While creating one component out of several via concatenation, fo:flow does not produce an area.

Related Formatting Objects
fo:conditional-page-master-reference (p. 469), fo:layout-master-set (p. 425), fo:page-sequence (p. 493), fo:page-sequence-master (p. 494), fo:region-after (p. 495), fo:region-before (p. 496), fo:region-body (p. 496), fo:region-end (p. 497), fo:region-start (p. 497), fo:repeatable-page-master-alternatives (p. 498), fo:repeatable-page-master-reference (p. 499), fo:root (p. 500), fo:simple-page-master (p. 501), fo:single-page-master-reference (p. 502), fo:static-content (p. 502)

Related Properties
flow-name (p. 465), id (p. 521)

XSL Style Sheet Syntax

fo:footnote   Footnote Formatting Object

Purpose
Contains all the portions of a floating note.

Notes
- This formatting object is in the out-of-line category.
- fo:footnote produces two areas at the bottom of the page and places the footnote contents within.

Related Formatting Objects
fo:float (p. 471), fo:footnote-body (p. 472)

Related Properties
background properties (p. 379 – p. 387), border properties (p. 392 – p. 434), clip (p. 440), end-indent (p. 457), id (p. 521), margin properties (p. 542 – p. 546), max-height (p. 548), overflow (p. 561), padding properties (p. 562 – p. 571), role (p. 598), source-document (p. 606), space-after (p. 607), space-before (p. 608), span (p. 612), start-indent (p. 618), visibility (p. 636), z-index (p. 648)

fo:footnote-body   Footnote Body Properties

Purpose
Sets the formatting characteristics of a footnote citation.

Notes
- This formatting object is in the out-of-line category.
- fo:footnote-body produces one or more areas into which the citation is placed.

Related Formatting Objects
fo:float (p. 471), fo:footnote (p. 472)

Related Properties
azimuth (p. 377), background properties (p. 379 – p. 387), border properties (p. 392 – p. 439), cue (p. 449), cue-after (p. 450), cue-before (p. 451), elevation (p. 456), end-indent (p. 457), font properties (p. 482 – p. 492), id (p. 521), letter-spacing (p. 535), line-height (p. 538), line-height-shift-adjustment (p. 539), margin properties (p. 542 – p. 546), padding properties (p. 562 – p. 571), pause (p. 577), pause-after (p. 578), pause-before (p. 579), pitch (p. 580), pitch-range (p. 581), play-during (p. 582), richness (p. 597), role (p. 598), score-spaces (p. 602), source-document (p. 606), space-after (p. 607), space-before (p. 608), speak (p. 613), speak-header (p. 614), speak-numeral (p. 615), speak-punctuation (p. 615), speech-rate (p. 616), start-indent (p. 618), stress (p. 620), text-decoration (p. 628), text-shadow (p. 630),

text-transform (p. 631), vertical-align (p. 635), voice-family (p. 637), volume (p. 638), word-spacing (p. 643)

fo:initial-property-set   First-Line Block Properties

Purpose
Sets the formatting characteristics of the first line of a fo:block.

Notes
- This formatting object is in the inline-level category.
- fo:initial-property-set is similar to the CSS first-line pseudo-element.
- fo:initial-property-set does not produce an area.

Related Formatting Objects
fo:bidi-override (p. 465), fo:character (p. 467), fo:external-graphic (p. 470), fo:inline (p. 473), fo:inline-container p. 474), fo:instream-for-eign-object (p. 475), fo:leader (p. 476), fo:page-number (p. 492), fo:page-number-citation (p. 492)

Related Properties
azimuth (p. 377), background properties (p. 379 – p. 387), border properties (p. 392 – p. 434), color (p. 441), cue (p. 449), cue-after (p. 450), cue-before (p. 451), elevation (p. 456), font properties (p. 482 – p. 492), id (p. 521), letter-spacing (p. 535), line-height (p. 538), line-height-shift-adjustment (p. 539), padding properties (p. 562 - p. 571), pause (p. 577), pause-after (p. 578), pause-before (p. 579), pitch (p. 580), pitch-range (p. 581), play-during (p. 582), richness (p. 597), score-spaces (p. 602), speak (p. 613), speak-header (p. 614), speak-numeral (p. 615), speak-punctuation (p. 615), role (p. 598), source-document (p. 606), speech-rate (p. 616), stress (p. 620), text-decoration (p. 628), text-shadow (p. 630), text-transform (p. 631), voice-family (p. 637), volume (p. 638), word-spacing (p. 643)

fo:inline   Inline Formatting Object

Purpose
Formats selected inline text with a background or border.

Notes
- This formatting object is in the inline-level category.
- The following are inline formatting objects: fo:bidi-override, fo:character, fo:external-graphic, fo:inline, fo:inline-container, fo:instream-foreign-object, fo:leader, fo:multi-toggle, fo:page-number, fo:page-number-citation, and fo:simple-link.
- fo:inline returns one or more areas.

XSL Style Sheet Syntax

Related Formatting Objects

fo:bidi-override (p. 465), fo:character (p.467), fo:external-graphic
(p. 470), fo:initial-property-set (p. 473), fo:inline-container (p. 474),
fo:instream-foreign-object (p. 475), fo:leader (p. 476), fo:multi-toggle
(p. 481), fo:page-number (p. 492), fo:page-number-citation (p. 492),
fo:simple-link (p. 500)

Related Properties

azimuth (p. 377), background properties (p. 379 - p. 387), baseline-shift
(p. 388), border properties (p. 392 – p. 434), color (p. 441), cue (p. 449), cue-
after (p. 450), cue-before (p. 451), elevation (p. 456), end-indent (p. 457),
font properties (p. 482 – p. 492), id (p. 521), keep-together (p. 526), line-
height (p. 538), line-height-shift-adjustment (p. 539), margin properties
(p. 542 - p. 546), padding properties (p. 562 - p. 571), pause (p. 577), pause-
after (p. 578), pause-before (p. 579), pitch (p. 580), pitch-range (p. 581),
play-during (p. 582), richness (p. 597), role (p. 598), source-document
(p. 606), space-after (p. 607), space-before (p. 608), speak (p. 613), speak-
header (p. 614), speak-numeral (p. 615), speak-punctuation (p. 615), speech-
rate (p. 616), start-indent (p. 618), stress (p. 620), visibility (p. 636),
voice-family (p. 637), volume (p. 638), z-index (p. 648)

fo:inline-container   Inline Box

Purpose
Creates an inline box.

Notes
- This formatting object is in the inline-level category.
- The following are inline formatting objects: fo:bidi-override,
  fo:character, fo:external-graphic, fo:inline, fo:inline-container,
  fo:instream-foreign-object, fo:leader, fo:multi-toggle, fo:page-
  number, fo:page-number-citation, and fo:simple-link.
- fo:inline-container produces an inline area.

Related Formatting Objects

fo:bidi-override (p. 465), fo:character (p. 467), fo:external-graphic
(p. 470), fo:initial-property-set (p. 473), fo:inline (p. 473), fo:instream-
foreign-object (p. 475), fo:leader (p. 476), fo:multi-toggle (p. 481),
fo:page-number (p. 492), fo:page-number-citation (p. 492), fo:simple-link
(p. 500)

Related Properties

background properties (p. 379 – p. 387), block-progression-dimension (p.
390), border properties (p. 392 – p. 434), clip (p. 440), end-indent (p. 457),
height (p. 514), id (p. 521), inline-progression-dimension (p. 525), keep-
together (p. 526), line-height (p. 538), line-height-shift-adjustment
(p. 539), margin properties (p. 542 - p. 546), overflow (p. 561), padding

properties (p. 562 – p. 571), reference-orientation (p. 588), space-after (p. 607), space-before (p. 608), start-indent (p. 618), vertical-align (p. 635), width (p. 642), writing-mode (p. 645)

fo:instream-foreign-object   Instream-Graphic Flow Object

Purpose
Sets an inline graphic with descendant data.

Notes
- This formatting object is in the inline-level category.
- The following are inline formatting objects: fo:bidi-override, fo:character, fo:external-graphic, fo:inline, fo:inline-container, fo:instream-foreign-object, fo:leader, fo:multi-toggle, fo:page-number, fo:page-number-citation, and fo:simple-link.
- fo:instream-foreign-object produces one inline area.

Related Formatting Objects
fo:bidi-override (p. 465), fo:character (p. 467), fo:external-graphic (p. 470), fo:initial-property-set (p. 473), fo:inline (p. 473), fo:inline-container p. 474), fo:leader (p. 476), fo:multi-toggle (p. 481), fo:page-number (p. 492), fo:page-number-citation (p. 492), fo:simple-link (p. 500)

Related Properties
azimuth (p. 377), background properties (p. 379 – p. 387), block-progression-dimension (p. 390), border properties (p. 392 – p. 434), cue (p. 449), cue-after (p. 450), cue-before (p. 451), elevation (p. 456), end-indent (p. 457), height (p. 514), id (p. 521), inline-progression-dimension (p. 525), line-height (p. 538), line-height-shift-adjustment (p. 539), margin properties (p. 542 – p. 546), max-height (p. 548), max-width (p. 550), min-height (p. 552), min-width (p. 553), padding properties (p. 562 - p. 571), pause (p. 577), pause-after (p. 578), pause-before (p. 579), pitch (p. 580), pitch-range (p. 581), play-during (p. 582), richness (p. 597), role (p. 598), scaling (p. 601), source-document (p. 606), space-after (p. 607), space-before (p. 608), speak (p. 613), speak-header (p. 614), speak-numeral (p. 615), speak-punctuation (p. 615), speech-rate (p. 616), start-indent (p. 618), stress (p. 620), vertical-align (p. 635), voice-family (p. 637), volume (p. 638), width (p. 642)

fo:layout-master-set   Layout-Master-Set Container

Purpose
Contains all the layout masters for a single document.

Notes
- This formatting object is in the pagination and layout category.

- fo:root has two children: one fo:layout-master-set and one or more fo:page-sequences.
- The pagination and layout specifications, whose names include –master, are both embedded within the fo:layout-master-set.

Related Formatting Objects

fo:conditional-page-master-reference (p. 469), fo:flow (p. 471), fo:page-sequence (p. 493), fo:page-sequence-master (p. 494), fo:region-after (p. 495), fo:region-before (p. 496), fo:region-body (p. 496), fo:region-end (p. 497), fo:region-start (p. 497), fo:repeatable-page-master-alternatives (p. 498), fo:repeatable-page-master-reference (p. 499), fo:root (p. 500) fo:simple-page-master (p. 501), fo:single-page-master-reference (p. 502), fo:static-content (p. 502)

Related Property

id (p. 521)

---

fo:leader   Leader Formatting Object

Purpose

Creates a leader that connects two formatting objects.

Notes

- This formatting object is in the inline-level category.
- The following are inline formatting objects: fo:bidi-override, fo:character, fo:external-graphic, fo:inline, fo:inline-container, fo:instream-foreign-object, fo:leader, fo:multi-toggle, fo:page-number, fo:page-number-citation, and fo:simple-link.
- The XSL working draft (http://www.w3.org/TR/xsl/) states that the "fo:leader formatting object is often used in tables of contents to generate sequences of '.' glyphs that separate titles from page numbers, to create entry fields in fill-in-the-blank forms, and to create horizontal rules for use as separators."
- Leaders are limited to a single line.
- To have a leader fill the maximum width of a line, have the leader width at least as long as the width of the column.
- To make a leader a horizontal rule, embed fo:leader in an fo:block.

Related Formatting Objects

fo:bidi-override (p. 465), fo:character (p. 467), fo:external-graphic (p. 470), fo:initial-property-set (p. 473), fo:inline (p. 473), fo:inline-container (p. 474), fo:instream-foreign-object (p. 475), fo:multi-toggle (p. 481), fo:page-number (p. 492), fo:page-number-citation (p. 492), fo:simple-link (p. 500)

Related Properties

azimuth (p. 377), background properties (p. 379 – p. 387), baseline-shift
(p. 388), border properties (p. 392 – p. 434), color (p. 441), cue (p. 449), cue-after (p. 450), cue-before (p. 451), elevation (p. 456), end-indent (p. 457), font
properties (p. 482 – p. 492), id (p. 521), leader properties (p. 532 – p. 534),
letter-spacing (p. 535), line-height (p. 538), line-height-shift-adjustment
(p. 539), margin properties (p. 542 – p. 546), padding properties (p. 562 - p. 571),
pause (p. 577), pause-after (p. 578), pause-before (p. 579), pitch (p. 580),
pitch-range (p. 581), play-during (p. 582), richness (p. 597), role (p. 598),
rule-style (p. 599), rule-thickness (p. 600), source-document (p. 606), space-
after (p. 607), space-before (p. 608), speak (p. 613), speak-header (p. 614),
speak-numeral (p. 615), speak-punctuation (p. 615), speech-rate (p. 616),
start-indent (p. 618), stress (p. 620), text-shadow (p. 630), visibility
(p. 636), voice-family (p. 637), volume (p. 638), word-spacing (p. 643),
z-index (p. 648)

---

fo:list-block · List Block Flow Object

Purpose
Formats a list or list item.

Notes
- This formatting object is in the list category.
- The following are regarded as block formatting objects: fo:block,
  fo:block-container, fo:list-block, fo:table, and fo:table-and-
  caption.
- fo:list-block contains the entire list.
- one or more fo:list-items are children of fo:list-block.

Related Formatting Objects
fo:block (p. 466), fo:block-container (p. 467), fo:list-item (p. 478),
fo:list-item-body (p. 478), fo:list-item-label (p. 479), fo:table (p. 503),
fo:table-and-caption (p. 504)

Related Properties
azimuth (p. 377), background properties (p. 379 – p. 387), border properties
(p. 392 – p. 434), break-after (p. 435), break-before (p. 436), cue (p. 449),
cue-after (p. 450), cue-before (p. 451), elevation (p. 456), end-indent
(p. 457), id (p. 521), keep-together (p. 526), keep-with-next (p. 527), keep-
with-previous (p. 528), margin properties (p. 542-p. 546), padding properties
(p. 562-p. 571), page-break-after (p. 572), page-break-before (p. 573), pause
(p. 577), pause-after (p. 578), pause-before (p. 579), pitch (p. 580), pitch-
range (p. 581), play-during (p. 582), provisional-distance-between-starts
(p. 586), provisional-label-separation (p. 587), richness (p. 597), role
(p. 598), source-document (p. 606), space-after (p. 607), space-before
(p. 608), speak (p. 613), speak-header (p. 614), speak-numeral (p. 615),

speak-punctuation (p. 615), speech-rate (p. 616), start-indent (p. 618), stress (p. 620), voice-family (p. 637), volume (p. 638)

fo:list-item — List Item Formatting Object

Purpose
Includes a label and list-item body.

Notes
- This formatting object is in the list category.
- One or more fo:list-items are children of fo:list-block.

Related Formatting Objects
fo:list-block (p. 477), fo:list-item-body (p. 478), fo:list-item-label (p. 479)

Related Properties
azimuth (p. 377), background properties (p. 379 – p. 387), border properties (p. 392 – p. 434), break-after (p. 435), break-before (p. 436), cue (p. 449), cue-after (p. 450), cue-before (p. 451), elevation (p. 456), end-indent (p. 457), id (p. 521), keep-together (p. 526), keep-with-next (p. 527), keep-with-previous (p. 528), margin properties (p. 542 - p. 546), padding properties (p. 562 – p. 571), page-break-after (p. 572), page-break-before (p. 573), pause (p. 577), pause-after (p. 578), pause-before (p. 579), pitch (p. 580), pitch-range (p. 581), play-during (p. 582), richness (p. 597), role (p. 598), source-document (p. 606), space-after (p. 607), space-before (p. 608), speak (p. 613), speak-header (p. 614), speak-numeral (p. 615), speak-punctuation (p. 615), speech-rate (p. 616), start-indent (p. 618), stress (p. 620), voice-family (p. 637), volume (p. 638)

fo:list-item-body — List Item Body Formatting Object

Purpose
Contains a list-item body.

Notes
- This formatting object is in the list category.
- fo:list-item-body does not produce an area.

Related Formatting Objects
fo:list-block (p. 477), fo:list-item (p. 478), fo:list-item-label (p. 479)

Related Properties
id (p. 521), role (p. 598), source-document (p. 606)

fo:list-item-label

Purpose
Includes a list-item label.

Notes
- This formatting object is in the list category.
- A list-item label is a number, bullet, or other decoration.
- fo:list-item-label does not produce an area.

Related Formatting Objects
fo:list-block (p. 477), fo:list-item (p. 478), fo:list-item-body (p. 478)

Related Properties
id (p. 521), role (p. 598), source-document (p. 606)

fo:marker

Marker

Purpose
With fo:retrieve-marker, produces both running headers and running footers.

Notes
- This formatting object is in the other category.
- Examples of running headers and footers include dictionary headers showing first and last words defined on a page or headers showing a page's section and chapter titles.
- An fo:marker may only be used as a descendent of fo:flow.
- Any property values set on an fo:marker will not be inherited by child properties that are retrieved by fo:retrieve-marker.
- It is an error for two or more fo:markers to have the same marker-class-name value if they share the same parent.
- Contents of an fo:marker may include (#PCDATA|%inline;|%block;)*.
- An fo:marker may include any formatting objects that are allowed as a replacement for fo:retrieve-markers that retrieve the children of said fo:marker.
- While an fo:marker does not directly produce any areas, its children may be retrieved and formatted within an fo:static-content. However, it must use an fo:retrieve-marker whose retrieve-class-name value is identical to the marker-class-name of the fo:marker.

Related Formatting Objects
fo:retrieve-marker (p. 499), fo:wrapper (p. 508)

fo:multi-case — Display Nested Flow Objects

Purpose
Nests flow objects that are displayed or hidden, depending on its
fo:multi-switch.

Notes
- This formatting object is in the link and multi category.
- fo:multi-case is the child of fo:multi-switch.
- fo:multi-case does not produce an area.

Related Formatting Objects
fo:multi-properties (p. 480), fo:multi-property-set (p. 480),
fo:multi-switch (p. 481), fo:multi-toggle (p. 481), fo:simple-link (p. 500)

Related Properties
case-name (p. 438), case-title (p. 438), id (p. 521), starting-state (p. 619),
role (p. 598), source-document (p. 606)

fo:multi-properties — Multiple Properties Switch

Purpose
Switches between two or more properties.

Notes
- This formatting object is in the link and multi category.
- The following can be used with #PCDATA, block formatting objects, and
  inline formatting objects: fo:multi-properties, fo:multi-switch, and
  fo:wrapper.
- Use fo:multi-properties to change a color or enhancement.
- fo:multi-properties does not produce an area.

Related Formatting Objects
fo:multi-case (p. 480), fo:multi-property-set (p. 480), fo:multi-switch
(p. 481), fo:multi-toggle (p. 481), fo:simple-link (p. 500), fo:wrapper
(p. 508)

Related Properties
id (p. 521), role (p. 598), source-document (p. 606)

fo:multi-property-set — Alternate Properties Set

Purpose
Sets an alternate set of properties with which a selection is formatted.

Notes

- This formatting object is in the link and multi category.
- fo:multi-property-set does not produce an area.

Related Formatting Objects

fo:multi-case (p. 480), fo:multi-properties (p. 480), fo:multi-switch
(p. 481), fo:multi-toggle (p. 481), fo:simple-link (p. 500)

Related Property

id (p. 521)

fo:multi-switch   Formatting-Object Subtree Switch

Purpose

Switches to one of several formatting-object subtrees.

Notes

- This formatting object is in the link and multi category.
- The following can be used with #PCDATA, block formatting objects, and
  inline formatting objects: fo:multi-properties, fo:multi-switch, and
  fo:wrapper.
- fo:multi-case is the child of fo:multi-switch.
- fo:multi-switch can contain fo:multi-toggles.
- fo:multi-switch enables interactivity.
- fo:multi-switch does not produce an area.

Related Formatting Objects

fo:multi-case (p. 480), fo:multi-properties (p. 480), fo:multi-property-
set (p. 480), fo:multi-toggle (p. 481), fo:simple-link (p. 500), fo:wrapper
(p. 508)

Related Properties

auto-restore (p. 377), id (p. 521), role (p. 598), source-document (p. 606)

fo:multi-toggle   Multi-Case Toggle

Purpose

Toggles from one fo:multi-case to another.

Notes

- This formatting object is in the link and multi category.
- The following are inline formatting objects: fo:bidi-override,
  fo:character, fo:external-graphic, fo:inline, fo:inline-container,
  fo:instream-foreign-object, fo:leader, fo:multi-toggle, fo:page-
  number, fo:page-number-citation, and fo:simple-link.
- fo:multi-switch can contain fo:multi-toggles.

Related Formatting Objects

fo:bidi-override (p. 465), fo:character (p. 467), fo:external-graphic (p. 470), fo:inline (p. 473), fo:inline-container (p. 474), fo:instream-foreign-object (p. 475), fo:leader (p. 476), fo:multi-case (p. 480), fo:multi-properties (p. 480), fo:multi-property-set (p. 480), fo:multi-switch (p. 481), fo:page-number (p. 492), fo:page-number-citation (p. 492), fo:simple-link (p. 500)

Related Properties

id (p. 521), role (p. 598), source-document (p. 606), switch-to (p. 621)

font	Font Properties

Purpose

Specifies up to six properties for fonts.

Syntax

```
font: [[font-style_value]|[ font-variant_value]
   |[ font-weight_value ]| font-size_value
   [ /line-height_value ]
   | font-family_value]|caption|icon|menu
   |message-box|small-caption|status-bar|inherit
```

Where

- *font-style_value* specifies the font style. For more information, see the font-style property (p. 489).
- *font-variant_value* specifies the font variant. For more information, see the font-variant property (p. 490).
- *font-weight_value* specifies the font weight. For more information, see the font-weight property (p. 491).
- *font-size_value* specifies the font size. For more information, see the font-size property (p. 486).
- *line-height_value* specifies the line height. Be sure to precede the line-height_value with a slash (/). For more information, see the line-height property (p. 538).
- *font-family_value* specifies the font family. For more information, see the font-family property (p. 483).
- caption is a keyword that represents the font used for control captions. Typical *controls* are objects in forms and dialog boxes.
- icon is a keyword that represents the font used in icon labels.
- menu is a keyword that represents the font used in menus and menu lists.
- message-box is a keyword that represents the font used in dialog boxes.
- small-caption is a keyword that represents the font used to label smaller controls.

XSL Style Sheet Syntax

- status-bar is a keyword that represents the font used in the status bars at the bottom of windows.
- inherit is a keyword that indicates that this property takes the same computed value as its parent.

Notes

- This property is in the common-font category.
- This property originated in CSS1.
- This shortcut property specifies multiple properties for fonts in the same way that you can individually set rules for the following properties: font-size, font-style, font-variant, font-weight, and line-height.
- Shortcut properties should be processed as follows: Set the "embedded" properties to their initial values; if the characteristics of the shortcut property are inherited, each "embedded" property should take the same computed value as its parent; if the characteristics of the shortcut property are not inherited, set each value; then the value of shorthand property overrides the counterpart value of the individual property.
- By default, the characteristics of this property are inherited.

Example

```
para {font: small-caps/90% "times new roman", serif }
```

Related Properties

font-family (p. 483), font-size (p. 486), font-size-adjust (p. 487), font-stretch (p. 488), font-style (p. 489), font-variant (p. 490), font-weight (p. 491)

Related Formatting Objects

fo:bidi-override (p. 465), fo:block (p. 466), fo:footnote-body (p. 472), fo:initial-property-set (p. 473), fo:inline (p. 473), fo:leader (p. 476), fo:page-number (p. 492), fo:page-number-citation (p. 492)

font-family	Font Family

Purpose

Specifies one or more fonts by name, font family, or both.

Syntax

```
font-family:
  [["]family_name_1|serif
  |sans-serif|cursive|fantasy|monospace]
  [, ["]family_name_2["]]]|serif
  |sans-serif|cursive|fantasy|monospace]
  [..., ["]family_name_n["]]|serif
  |sans-serif|cursive|fantasy|monospace])|inherit
```

XSL Style Sheet Syntax

Where

- *family-name* is the name of a specific typeface.
- serif, sans-serif, cursive, fantasy, and monospace are the names of generic typefaces that might match one or more family names on a particular computer.
- inherit is a keyword that indicates that this property takes the same computed value as its parent.

Notes

- This property is in the common-font category.
- This property, which originated in CSS1, applies to all elements.
- This CSS property has a counterpart CSS descriptor.
- This property specifies a font by name and/or font family.
- By default, the characteristics of this property are inherited.

Example

```
bigpage { font-family: "Times New Roman", "Book Antigua", serif }
```

Related Properties

font (p. 482), font-size (p. 486), font-size-adjust (p. 487), font-stretch (p. 488), font-style (p. 489), font-variant (p. 490), font-weight (p. 491)

Related Formatting Objects

fo:bidi-override (p. 465), fo:block (p. 466), fo:footnote-body (p. 472), fo:initial-property-set (p. 473), fo:inline (p. 473), fo:leader (p. 476), fo:page-number (p. 492), fo:page-number-citation (p. 492)

font-height-override-after	Font Height Override Below Baseline

Purpose

Sets the line-spacing height of the font below the baseline.

Syntax

```
font-height-override-after: use-font-metrics|length
    |inherit
```

Where

- use-font-metrics is a keyword that indicates that this property uses the metrics of the current font to set the line-spacing height below the baseline.
- *length* is a positive value followed by a two-letter abbreviation representing the unit of measure.
- inherit is a keyword that indicates that this property takes the same computed value as its parent.

Notes

- This property is in the miscellaneous category.
- By default, the characteristics of this property are not inherited.

Related Properties

baseline-shift (p. 388), block-progression-dimension (p. 390), clip (p. 440), color (p. 441), direction (p. 453), font-height-override-before (p. 485), glyph-orientation-horizontal (p. 512), glyph-orientation-vertical (p. 513), height (p. 514), href (p. 515), hyphenation-keep (p. 517), hyphenation-ladder-count (p. 518), id (p. 521), inline-progression-dimension (p. 525), last-line-end-indent (p. 531), linefeed-treatment (p. 537), line-height (p. 538), line-height-shift-adjustment (p. 539), line-stacking-strategy (p. 540), max-height (p. 548), max-width (p. 550), min-height (p. 552), min-width (p. 553), overflow (p. 561), provisional-distance-between-starts (p. 586), provisional-label-separation (p. 587), reference-orientation (p. 588), ref-id (p. 589), scaling (p. 601), score-spaces (p. 602), size (p. 605), space-treatment (p. 611), span (p. 612), text-align (p. 625), text-align-last (p. 626), text-indent (p. 629), unicode-bidi (p. 634), vertical-align (p. 635), visibility (p. 636), white-space (p. 639), white-space-collapse (p. 640), width (p. 642), wrap-option (p. 644), writing-mode (p. 645), z-index (p. 648)

Related Formatting Object

fo:leader (p. 476)

font-height-override-before	Font Height Override Above Baseline

Purpose

Sets the line-spacing height of the font above the baseline.

Syntax

```
font-height-override-after: use-font-metrics|length
   |inherit
```

Where

- use-font-metrics is a keyword that indicates that this property uses the metrics of the current font to set the line-spacing height above the baseline.
- length is a positive value followed by a two-letter abbreviation representing the unit of measure.
- inherit is a keyword that indicates that this property takes the same computed value as its parent.

Notes

- This property is in the miscellaneous category.
- By default, the characteristics of this property are not inherited.

Related Properties

baseline-shift (p. 388), block-progression-dimension (p. 390), clip (p. 440), color (p. 441), direction (p. 453), font-height-override-after (p. 484), glyph-orientation-horizontal (p. 512), glyph-orientation-vertical (p. 513), height (p. 514), href (p. 515), hyphenation-keep (p. 517), hyphenation-ladder-count (p. 518), id (p. 521), inline-progression-dimension (p. 525), last-line-end-indent (p. 531), linefeed-treatment (p. 537), line-height (p. 538), line-height-shift-adjustment (p. 539), line-stacking-strategy (p. 540), max-height (p. 548), max-width (p. 550), min-height (p. 552), min-width (p. 553), overflow (p. 561), provisional-distance-between-starts (p. 586), provisional-label-separation (p. 587), reference-orientation (p. 588), ref-id (p. 589), scaling (p. 601), score-spaces (p. 602), size (p. 605), space-treatment (p. 611), span (p. 612), text-align (p. 625), text-align-last (p. 626), text-indent (p. 629), unicode-bidi (p. 634), vertical-align (p. 635), visibility (p. 636), white-space (p. 639), white-space-collapse (p. 640), width (p. 642), wrap-option (p. 644), writing-mode (p. 645), z-index (p. 648)

Related Formatting Object

fo:leader (p. 476)

font-size   Font Size

Purpose

Specifies an absolute or relative font size.

Syntax

```
font-size: length|percent%|(xx-small|x-small
  |small|medium|large|x-large|xx-large)
  |(larger|smaller)|inherit
```

Where

- *length* is a positive value followed by a two-letter abbreviation representing the unit of measure.
- *percent* is a positive value that is relative to the font size of the element immediately above the current element. Follow *percent* with a percentage sign (%).
- xx-small is a keyword that represents a font size that is 1.2 times smaller than x-small.
- x-small is a keyword that represents a font size that is 1.2 times larger than xx-small and 1.2 times smaller than small.
- small is a keyword that indicates a font size that is 1.2 times larger than x-small and 1.2 times smaller than medium.
- medium is a keyword that indicates a font size that is 1.2 times larger than xx-small and 1.2 times smaller than large.
- large is a keyword that indicates a font size that is 1.2 times larger than medium and 1.2 times smaller than x-large.

XSL Style Sheet Syntax

- x-large is a keyword that indicates a font size that is 1.2 times larger than large and 1.2 times smaller than xx-large.
- xx-large is a keyword that indicates a font size that is 1.2 times larger than x-large.
- larger is one size larger than the font of the parent element.
- smaller is one size smaller than the font of the parent element.
- inherit is a keyword that indicates that this property takes the same computed value as its parent.

Notes

- This property is in the common-font category.
- This property, which originated in CSS1, applies to all elements.
- This CSS property has a counterpart CSS descriptor.
- By default, the computed value of this property is inherited.

Example

```
head4 { font-size: 14pt }
head5 { font-size: 125% }
head6 { font-size: larger }
```

Related Properties

font (p. 482), font-family (p. 483), font-size-adjust (p. 487), font-stretch (p. 488), font-style (p. 489), font-variant (p. 490), font-weight (p. 491)

Related Formatting Objects

fo:bidi-override (p. 465), fo:block (p. 466), fo:footnote-body (p. 472), fo:initial-property-set (p. 473), fo:inline (p. 473), fo:leader (p. 476), fo:page-number (p. 492), fo:page-number-citation (p. 492)

font-size-adjust   Font Size Adjust

Purpose

Adjusts a font's aspect value.

Syntax

```
font-size-adjust: number|none|inherit
```

Where

- *number* represents an absolute numeric value of the aspect ratio.
- none is a keyword that indicates that the font's x-height is not preserved; it changes when the font size changes. This is the default.
- inherit is a keyword that indicates that this property takes the same computed value as its parent.

Notes

- This property is in the common-font category.
- This property, which originated in CSS2, applies to all elements.
- By default, the computed value of this property is inherited.

Related Properties

font (p. 482), font-family (p. 483), font-size (p. 486), font-stretch
(p. 488), font-style (p. 489), font-variant (p. 490), font-weight (p. 491)

Related Formatting Objects

fo:bidi-override (p. 465), fo:block (p. 466),fo:footnote-body (p. 472),
fo:initial-property-set (p. 473), fo:inline (p. 473), fo:leader (p. 476),
fo:page-number (p. 492), fo:page-number-citation (p. 492)

font-stretch   Stretched Font

Purpose

Selects a condensed or expanded version of a font.

Syntax

```
font-stretch: normal|wider|narrower
  |ultra-condensed|extra-condensed|condensed
  |semi-condensed|semi-expanded|expanded
  |extra-expanded|ultra-expanded|inherit
```

Where

- normal is a keyword that represents any variation that is not condensed
  and not expanded. This is the default.
- wider is a keyword that represents a variation that is the next wider
  stretch from the current stretch.
- narrower is a keyword that represents a variation that is the next narrower stretch from the current stretch.
- ultra-condensed is a keyword that represents the most condensed
  variation.
- extra-condensed is a keyword that represents a variation that is more
  condensed than condensed but less condensed than ultra-condensed.
- condensed is a keyword that represents a variation that is more condensed than semi-condensed but less condensed than extra-condensed.
- semi-condensed is a keyword that represents a variation that is more
  condensed than normal but less condensed than condensed.
- semi-expanded is a keyword that represents a variation that is more expanded than normal but less expanded than expanded.
- expanded is a keyword that represents a variation that is more expanded
  than semi-expanded but less expanded than extra-expanded.
- extra-expanded is a keyword that represents a variation that is more expanded than expanded but less expanded than ultra-expanded.

XSL Style Sheet Syntax

- ultra-expanded is a keyword that represents the most expanded variation.
- inherit is a keyword that indicates that this property takes the same computed value as its parent.

Notes

- This property is in the common-font category.
- This property, which originated in CSS2, applies to all elements.
- This CSS property has a counterpart CSS descriptor.
- By default, the characteristics of this property are inherited.

Related Properties

font (p. 482), font-family (p. 483), font-size (p. 486), font-size-adjust (p. 487), font-stretch (p. 488), font-style (p. 489), font-variant (p. 490), font-weight (p. 491)

Related Formatting Objects

fo:bidi-override (p. 465), fo:block (p. 466),fo:footnote-body (p. 472), fo:initial-property-set (p. 473), fo:inline (p. 473), fo:leader (p. 476), fo:page-number (p. 492), fo:page-number-citation (p. 492)

font-style | Font Style

Purpose

Specifies one or more text enhancements.

Syntax

```
font-style: normal|italic|oblique|backslant|inherit
```

Where

- normal is a keyword that indicates unitalicized text. This is the default.
- italic is a keyword that indicates italicized text.
- oblique is a keyword that indicates slightly italicized text.
- backslant is a keyword that indicates a font that is classified as having a backwards slant to it. This is an XSL value.
- inherit is a keyword that indicates that this property takes the same computed value as its parent.

Notes

- This property is in the common-font category.
- This property, which originated in CSS1, applies to all elements.
- This CSS property has a counterpart CSS descriptor.
- By default, the characteristics of this property are inherited.

Example

```
head2, head4 { font-style: italic; font-weight: bold}
```

Related Properties

font (p. 482), font-family (p. 483), font-size (p. 486), font-size-adjust (p. 487), font-stretch (p. 488), font-variant (p. 490), font-weight (p. 491)

Related Formatting Objects

fo:bidi-override (p. 465), fo:block (p. 466),fo:footnote-body (p. 472), fo:initial-property-set (p. 473), fo:inline (p. 473), fo:leader (p. 476), fo:page-number (p. 492), fo:page-number-citation (p. 492)

font-variant   Font Variations

Purpose

Specifies one or more font variations.

Syntax

font-variant: <u>normal</u>|small-caps|inherit

Where

- normal is a keyword that represents any variation that is not small caps. This is the default.
- small-caps is a keyword that represents a variation that is all uppercase characters that are smaller than the usual uppercase characters in a typeface.
- inherit is a keyword that indicates that this property takes the same computed value as its parent.

Notes

- This property is in the common-font category.
- This property, which originated in CSS1, applies to all elements.
- This CSS property has a counterpart CSS descriptor.
- By default, the characteristics of this property are inherited.

Example

para.note { font-variant: small-caps; font-weight: bolder }

Related Properties

font (p. 482), font-family (p. 483), font-size (p. 486), font-size-adjust (p. 487), font-stretch (p. 488), font-style (p. 489), font-weight (p. 491)

Related Formatting Objects

fo:bidi-override (p. 465), fo:block (p. 466),fo:footnote-body (p. 472), fo:initial-property-set (p. 473), fo:inline (p. 473), fo:leader (p. 476), fo:page-number (p. 492), fo:page-number-citation (p. 492)

XSL Style Sheet Syntax

font-weight   Bold Font

Purpose

Specifies the degree of boldness or lightness of a font.

Syntax

```
font-weight: normal|bold|bolder|lighter
     |100|200|300|400|500|600|700|800|900|inherit
```

Where

- normal is a keyword that indicates the standard non-bold, non-light weight of text. This is the default.
- bold is a keyword that indicates the standard boldface text.
- bolder is a keyword that indicates bolder than standard boldface. It can be the equivalent of ultra-bold or heavy text. This is a relative value.
- lighter is a keyword that indicates the equivalent of light text. This is a relative value.
- 100 is a keyword that indicates the lightest weight.
- 200 and 300 are keywords that indicate somewhere between light and normal weight.
- 400 is a keyword that is the equivalent of normal weight.
- 500 and 600 are keywords that indicate somewhere between normal and bold weight. 500 is the equivalent of a medium weight.
- 700 is a keyword that indicates the equivalent of bold weight.
- 800 and 900 are keywords that indicate bolder than bold weight.
- inherit is a keyword that indicates that this property takes the same computed value as its parent.

Notes

- This property is in the common-font category.
- This property, which originated in CSS1, applies to all elements.
- This CSS property has a counterpart CSS descriptor.
- By default, the characteristics of this property are inherited.

Example

```
para.warning { font-weight: 800 }
```

Related Properties

font (p. 482), font-family (p. 483), font-size (p. 486), font-size-adjust (p. 487), font-stretch (p. 488), font-style (p. 489), font-variant (p. 490)

XSL Style Sheet Syntax

Related Formatting Objects

fo:bidi-override (p. 465), fo:block (p. 466), fo:footnote-body (p. 472), fo:inline (p. 473), fo:leader (p. 476), fo:page-number (p. 492), fo:page-number-citation (p. 492)

fo:page-number	Page-Number Formatting Object

Purpose

Indicates the number of the current page.

Notes

- This formatting object is in the inline-level category.
- The following are inline formatting objects: fo:bidi-override, fo:character, fo:external-graphic, fo:inline, fo:inline-container, fo:instream-foreign-object, fo:leader, fo:multi-toggle, fo:page-number, fo:page-number-citation, and fo:simple-link.
- fo:page-number produces one inline area.

Related Formatting Objects

fo:bidi-override (p. 465), fo:character (p. 467), fo:external-graphic (p. 470), fo:initial-property-set (p. 473), fo:inline (p. 473), fo:inline-container (p. 474), fo:instream-foreign-object (p. 475), fo:leader (p. 476), fo:multi-toggle (p. 481), fo:page-number-citation (p. 492), fo:simple-link (p. 500)

Related Properties

azimuth (p. 377), background properties (p. 379 - p. 387), border properties (p. 392 – p. 434), cue (p. 449), cue-after (p. 450), cue-before (p. 451), elevation (p. 456), end-indent (p. 457), font properties (p. 482 – p. 492), id (p. 521), letter-spacing (p. 535), line-height (p. 538), line-height-shift-adjustment (p. 539), margin properties (p. 542 - p. 546), padding properties (p. 562 – p. 571), pause (p. 577), pause-after (p. 578), pause-before (p. 579), pitch (p. 580), pitch-range (p. 581), play-during (p. 582), richness (p. 597), role (p. 598), score-spaces (p. 602), source-document (p. 606), space-after (p. 607), space-before (p. 608), speak (p. 613), speak-header (p. 614), speak-numeral (p. 615), speak-punctuation (p. 615), speech-rate (p. 616), start-indent (p. 618), stress (p. 620), text-decoration (p. 628), text-shadow (p. 630), text-transform (p. 631), vertical-align (p. 635), voice-family (p. 637), volume (p. 638), word-spacing (p. 643)

fo:page-number-citation	Page-Number Citation

Purpose

Cites the number of the page containing the first box from a formatting object.

Notes

- This formatting object is in the inline-level category.
- The following are inline formatting objects: fo:bidi-override, fo:character, fo:external-graphic, fo:inline, fo:inline-container, fo:instream-foreign-object, fo:leader, fo:multi-toggle, fo:page-number, fo:page-number-citation, and fo:simple-link.
- fo:page-number-citation produces an inline area in the same way that fo:page-number does.

Related Formatting Objects

fo:bidi-override (p. 415), fo:character (p. 467), fo:external-graphic (p. 470), fo:initial-property-set (p. 473), fo:inline (p. 473), fo:inline-container (p. 474), fo:instream-foreign-object (p. 475), fo:leader (p. 476), fo:multi-toggle (p. 481), fo:page-number (p. 492), fo:simple-link (p. 500)

Related Properties

azimuth (p. 377), background properties (p. 379 – p. 387), border properties (p. 392 – p. 434), cue (p. 449), cue-after (p. 450), cue-before (p. 451), elevation (p. 456), end-indent (p. 457), font properties (p. 482 – p. 492), id (p. 521), letter-spacing (p. 535), line-height (p. 538), line-height-shift-adjustment (p. 539), margin properties (p. 542 – p. 546), padding properties (p. 562 – p. 571), pause (p. 577), pause-after (p. 578), pause-before (p. 579), pitch (p. 580), pitch-range (p. 581), play-during (p. 582), ref-id (p. 589), richness (p. 597), role (p. 598), score-spaces (p. 602), source-document (p. 606), space-after (p. 607), space-before (p. 608), speak (p. 613), speak-header (p. 614), speak-numeral (p. 615), speak-punctuation (p. 615), speech-rate (p. 616), start-indent (p. 618), stress (p. 620), text-decoration (p. 628), text-shadow (p. 630), text-transform (p. 631), vertical-align (p. 635), voice-family (p. 637), volume (p. 638), word-spacing (p. 643)

fo:page-sequence — Page-Sequence Formatting Object

Purpose

Formats a particular set of pages in a document.

Notes

- This formatting object is in the pagination and layout category.
- fo:root has two children: one fo:layout-master-set and one or more fo:page-sequences.
- *Flows*, which are the children of fo:page-sequences, supply page content.
- Page-sequence-masters describe one or more page-masters that produce sets of pages.

Related Formatting Objects

fo:conditional-page-master-reference (p. 569), fo:flow (p. 471), fo:layout-master-set (p. 475), fo:page-sequence-master (p. 494), fo:region-after (p. 495), fo:region-before (p. 496), fo:region-body (p. 496), fo:region-end (p. 497), fo:region-start (p. 497), fo:repeatable-page-master-alternatives (p. 498), fo:repeatable-page-master-reference (p. 499), fo-root (p. 500, fo:simple-page-master (p. 501), fo:single-page-master-reference (p. 502), fo:static-content (p. 502))

Related Properties

force-page-count (p. 494), id (p. 521), initial-page-number (p. 524), master-name (p. 547)

fo:page-sequence-master · Page-Sequence Master

Purpose

Sets the page-masters used to produce a page sequence.

Notes

- This formatting object is in the pagination and layout category.
- A fo:page-sequence-master specifies sequences of page-masters.

Related Formatting Objects

fo:conditional-page-master-reference (p. 469), fo:flow (p. 471), fo:layout-master-set (p. 425), fo:page-sequence (p. 493), fo:region-after (p. 495), fo:region-before (p. 496), fo:region-body (p. 496), fo:region-end (p. 497), fo:region-start (p. 497), fo:repeatable-page-master-alternatives (p. 498), fo:repeatable-page-master-reference (p. 499), fo:root (p. 500) fo:simple-page-master (p. 501), fo:single-page-master-reference (p. 502), fo:static-content (p. 502)

Related Properties

id (p. 521), master-name (p. 547)

force-page-count · Force Page Count

Purpose

Forces a specific type of page at the end of the current sequence of pages.

Syntax

force-page-count: even|odd|<u>no-force</u>|inherit

Where

- even is a keyword that indicates that the number of pages in the sequence end on an even-numbered page, even if it is blank.

- odd is a keyword that indicates that the number of pages in the sequence end on an odd-numbered page, even if it is blank.
- no-force is a keyword that indicates that the number of pages in the sequence end on the current last page. This is the default.
- inherit is a keyword that indicates that this property takes the same computed value as its parent.

Notes

- This property is in the pagination-and-layout category.
- By default, the characteristics of this property are not inherited.

Related Properties

blank-or-not-blank (p. 389), column-count (p. 444), column-gap (p. 444), extent (p. 461), flow-name (p. 465), initial-page-number (p. 524), master-name (p. 547), maximum-repeats (p. 549), odd-or-even (p. 559), page-height (p. 575), page-position (p. 575), page-width (p. 576), precedence (p. 584), region-name (p. 590)

Related Formatting Object

fo:page-sequence (p. 493)

fo:region-after — Region-After Region Body

Purpose

Sets a viewing area after the body of a defined region, fo:region-body.

Notes

- This formatting object is in the pagination and layout category.
- fo:region-after is analogous to the footer of a document.

Related Formatting Objects

fo:conditional-page-master-reference (p. 469), fo:flow (p. 471), fo:layout-master-set (p. 475), fo:page-sequence (p. 493), fo:page-sequence-master (p. 494), fo:region-before (p. 496), fo:region-body (p. 496), fo:region-end (p. 497), fo:region-start (p. 497), fo:repeatable-page-master-alternatives (p. 498), fo:repeatable-page-master-reference (p. 499), fo:root (p. 500), fo:simple-page-master (p. 501), fo:single-page-master-reference (p. 502), fo:static-content (p. 502)

Related Properties

background properties (p. 379 – p. 387), border properties (p. 392 – p. 434), clip (p. 440), extent (p. 461), id (p. 521), overflow (p. 561), padding properties (p. 562 – p. 571), precedence (p. 584), reference-orientation (p. 588), region-name (p. 590), vertical-align (p. 635), writing-mode (p. 645)

XSL Style Sheet Syntax

fo:region-before Region-Before Region Body

Purpose
Sets a viewing area before the body of a defined region, fo:region-body.

Notes
- This formatting object is in the pagination and layout category.
- The area before a region body is analogous to a document header.

Related Formatting Objects
fo:conditional-page-master-reference (p. 469), fo:flow (p. 471), fo:layout-master-set (p. 475), fo:page-sequence (p. 493), fo:page-sequence-master (p. 494), fo:region-after (p. 495), fo:region-body (p. 496), fo:region-end (p. 497), fo:region-start (p. 497), fo:repeatable-page-master-alternatives (p. 498), fo:repeatable-page-master-reference (p. 499), fo:root (p. 500), fo:simple-page-master (p. 501), fo:single-page-master-reference (p. 502), fo:static-content (p. 502)

Related Properties
background properties (p. 379 – p. 387), border properties (p. 392 – p. 434), clip (p. 440), extent (p. 461), id (p. 521), overflow (p. 561), padding properties (p. 562 – p. 571), precedence (p. 584), reference-orientation (p. 588), region-name (p. 590), vertical-align (p. 635), writing-mode (p. 645)

fo:region-body Region Body

Purpose
Sets a viewing area in the middle of a defined region.

Notes
- This formatting object is in the pagination and layout category.
- The overflow property determines how much of the region body is visible.
- fo:region-body is a child of fo:simple-page-master.

Related Formatting Objects
fo:conditional-page-master-reference (p. 469), fo:flow (p. 471), fo:layout-master-set (p. 475), fo:page-sequence (p. 493), fo:page-sequence-master (p. 494), fo:region-after (p. 495), fo:region-before (p. 496), fo:region-end (p. 497), fo:region-start (p. 497), fo:repeatable-page-master-alternatives (p. 498), fo:repeatable-page-master-reference (p. 499), fo-root (p. 500, fo:simple-page-master (p. 501), fo:single-page-master-reference (p. 502), fo:static-content (p. 502)

XSL Style Sheet Syntax

Related Properties

background properties (p. 379 – p. 387), border properties (p. 392 – p. 434), clip (p. 440), column-count (p. 444), column-gap (p. 444), end-indent (p. 457), id (p. 521), margin properties (p. 542 – p. 546), overflow (p. 561), padding properties (p. 562 - p. 571), reference-orientation (p. 588), region-name (p. 590), space-after (p. 607), space-before (p. 608), start-indent (p. 618), vertical-align (p. 635), writing-mode (p. 645)

fo:region-end   Region-Body End

Purpose

Sets a viewing area at the end of a region body.

Notes

- This formatting object is in the pagination and layout category.
- fo:region-end is analogous to a sidebar on the right side of a document page.

Related Formatting Objects

fo:conditional-page-master-reference (p. 469), fo:flow (p. 471), fo:layout-master-set (p. 475), fo:page-sequence (p. 493), fo:page-sequence-master (p. 494), fo:region-after (p. 495), fo:region-before (p. 496), fo:region-body (p. 496), fo:region-start (p. 497), fo:repeatable-page-master-alternatives (p. 498), fo:repeatable-page-master-reference (p. 499), fo-root (p. 500), fo:simple-page-master (p. 501), fo:single-page-master-reference (p. 502), fo:static-content (p. 502)

Related Properties

background properties (p. 379 – p. 387), border properties (p. 392 – p. 434), clip (p. 440), extent (p. 461), id (p. 521), overflow (p. 561), padding properties (p. 562 – p. 571), reference-orientation (p. 588), region-name (p. 590), vertical-align (p. 635), writing-mode (p. 645)

fo:region-start   Region-Body Start

Purpose

Sets a viewing area at the start of a region body.

Notes

- This formatting object is in the pagination and layout category.
- fo:region-start is analogous to a sidebar on the left side of a document page.

XSL Style Sheet Syntax

Related Formatting Objects

fo:conditional-page-master-reference (p. 469), fo:flow (p. 471),
fo:layout-master-set (p. 475), fo:page-sequence (p. 493), fo:page-se-
quence-master (p. 494), fo:region-after (p. 495), fo:region-before
(p. 496), fo:region-body (p. 496), fo:region-end (p. 497), fo:repeatable-
page-master-alternatives (p. 498), fo:repeatable-page-master-reference
(p. 499), fo-root (p. 500), fo:simple-page-master (p. 501), fo:single-page-
master-reference (p. 502), fo:static-content (p. 502)

Related Properties

background properties (p. 379 - p. 387), border properties(p. 392 - p. 394),
clip (p. 440), extent (p. 461), id (p. 521), overflow (p. 561), padding properties (p. 562 - p. 571), reference-orientation (p. 588), region-name (p. 590),
vertical-align (p. 635), writing-mode (p. 645)

---

fo:repeatable-page-master-alternatives

Repeatable Alternative Page-Masters

Purpose

Produces a sequence of pages composed of recurring occurrences of alternate
page-masters.

Notes

- This formatting object is in the pagination and layout category.
- fo:page-sequence uses fo:repeatable-page-master-alternatives
  to produce pages. However, an area is produced only when a condition
  is met.
- In a list of conditions, make sure that at least the last condition is true.
- fo:conditional-page-master-reference is a child of fo:repeatable-
  page-master-alternatives.
- Use maximum-repeats to limit the number of pages in a page sequence.

Related Formatting Objects

fo:conditional-page-master-reference (p. 469), fo:flow (p. 471),
fo:layout-master-set (p. 475), fo:page-sequence (p. 493), fo:page-se-
quence-master (p. 494), fo:region-after (p. 495), fo:region-before
(p. 496), fo:region-body (p. 496), fo:region-end (p. 497), fo:region-start
(p. 497), fo:repeatable-page-master-reference (p. 499), fo:root (p. 500),
fo:simple-page-master (p. 501), fo:single-page-master-reference (p. 502),
fo:static-content (p. 502),

Related Properties

id (p. 521), maximum-repeats (p. 549)

fo:repeatable-page-master-reference

Repeatable Page-Master Reference

Purpose

Produces a sequence of pages composed of recurring occurrences of a particular page-master.

Notes

- This formatting object is in the pagination and layout category.
- fo:page-sequence uses fo:repeatable-page-master-reference to produce pages.
- Use maximum-repeats to limit the number of pages in a page sequence.

Related Formatting Objects

fo:conditional-page-master-reference (p. 469), fo:flow (p. 471), fo:layout-master-set (p. 475), fo:page-sequence (p. 493), fo:page-sequence-master (p. 494), fo:region-after (p. 495), fo:region-before (p. 496), fo:region-body (p. 496), fo:region-end (p. 497), fo:region-start (p. 497), fo:repeatable-page-master-alternatives (p. 498), fo:root (p. 500), fo:simple-page-master (p. 501), fo:single-page-master-reference (p. 502), fo:static-content (p. 502)

Related Properties

id (p. 521), master-name (p. 547), maximum-repeats (p. 549)

fo:retrieve-marker

Retrieve Marker

Purpose

With fo:marker, produces both running headers and running footers.

Notes

- This formatting object is in the other category.
- Examples of running headers and footers include dictionary headers showing first and last words defined on a page or headers showing a page's section and chapter titles.
- An fo:retrieve-marker may only be used as the descendent of an fo:static-content.
- An fo:retrieve-marker does not itself generate any area because it is replaced by the children that it retrieves from fo:marker.
- When formatting the children of fo:marker, they are treated as if the properties and traits of fo:retrieve-marker were their own.
- Children of fo:marker are formatted as if they took the place of fo:retrieve-marker in the formatting tree.

XSL Style Sheet Syntax

- The properties retrieve-class-name, retrieve-position and retrieve-boundary are used in conjunction with this formatting object.

Related Formatting Objects

fo:marker (p. 479), fo:wrapper (p. 508)

---

fo:root   Result-Tree Root Node

Purpose

Indicates the root node of the current XSL result tree.

Notes

- This formatting object is in the pagination and layout category.
- fo:root has two children: one fo:layout-master-set and one or more fo:page-sequences.
- fo-root does not generate any areas. However, its fo:page-sequence child returns pages.

Related Formatting Objects

fo:conditional-page-master-reference (p. 469), fo:flow (p. 471), fo:layout-master-set (p. 475), fo:page-sequence (p. 493), fo:page-sequence-master (p. 494), fo:region-after (p. 495), fo:region-before (p. 496), fo:region-body (p. 496), fo:region-end (p. 497), fo:region-start (p. 497), fo:repeatable-page-master-alternatives (p. 498), fo:repeatable-page-master-reference (p. 499), fo:simple-page-master (p. 501), fo:single-page-master-reference (p. 502), fo:static-content (p. 502)

Related Property

id (p. 521)

---

fo:simple-link   Simple-Link Start

Purpose

Indicates the start of a simple link.

Notes

- This formatting object is in the link and multi category.
- The following are inline formatting objects: fo:bidi-override, fo:character, fo:external-graphic, fo:inline, fo:inline-container, fo:instream-foreign-object, fo:leader, fo:multi-toggle, fo:page-number, fo:page-number-citation, and fo:simple-link.
- fo:simple-link produces an inline area.

Related Formatting Objects

fo:bidi-override (p. 465), fo:character (p. 467), fo:external-graphic
(p. 470), fo:inline (p. 473), fo:inline-container (p. 474), fo:
instream-foreign-object (p. 475), fo:leader (p. 476), fo:multi-case
(p. 480), fo:multi-properties (p. 480), fo:multi-property-set (p. 480),
fo:multi-switch (p. 481), fo:multi-toggle (p. 481), fo:page-number
(p. 492), fo:page-number-citation (p. 492), fo:simple-link (p. 500)

Related Properties

azimuth (p. 377), background properties (p. 379 - p. 387), border properties
(p. 392 – p. 434), cue (p. 449), cue-after (p. 450), cue-before (p. 457),
destination-placement-offset (p. 452), elevation (p. 456), end-indent
(p. 457), external-destination (p. 462), id (p. 521), indicate-destination
(p. 523), internal-destination (p. 526), line-height (p. 538), line-height-
shift-adjustment (p. 539), margin properties (p. 542 – p. 546), padding properties (p. 562 – p. 571), pause (p. 577), pause-after (p. 578), pause-before
(p. 579), pitch (p. 580), pitch-range (p. 581), play-during (p. 582), richness
(p. 597), role (p. 598), show-destination (p. 604), source-document (p. 606),
space-after (p. 607), space-before (p. 608), speak (p. 673), speak-header
(p. 614), speak-numeral (p. 615), speak-punctuation (p. 615), speech-rate
(p. 616), start-indent (p. 618), stress (p. 620), vertical-align (p. 635),
voice-family (p. 637), volume (p. 638)

fo:simple-page-master	Simple Page-Master

Purpose

Generates up to five regions of a document page.

Notes

- This formatting object is in the pagination and layout category.
- fo:page-sequence uses fo:conditional-page-master to produce
  pages. However, fo:conditional-page-master-reference refers to
  the fo:simple-page-master with the same master-name.
- page-position, odd-or-even, and blank-or-not-blank set properties for
  the fo:simple-page-master.
- You can divide a page into as many as five regions: region-after, region-
  before, region-body, region-end, and region-start.
- When you use a page-master to produce a page, use page-height to set
  the height and page-width to set the width.

Related Formatting Objects

fo:conditional-page-master-reference (p. 469), fo:flow (p. 471),
fo:layout-master-set (p. 475), fo:page-sequence (p. 493),
fo:page-sequence-master (p. 494), fo:region-after (p. 495),
fo:region-before (p. 496), fo:region-body (p. 496), fo:region-end (p. 497),
fo:region-start (p. 497), fo:repeatable-page-master-alternatives (p. 498),

XSL Style Sheet Syntax

fo:repeatable-page-master-reference (p. 499), fo:root (p. 500), fo:single-page-master-reference (p. 502), fo:static-content (p. 502)

Related Properties

end-indent (p. 457), id (p. 521), margin properties (p. 542 – p. 546), master-name (p. 547), page-height (p. 575), page-width (p. 576), reference-orientation (p. 588), region-name (p. 590), size (p. 605), space-after (p. 607), space-before (p. 608), start-indent (p. 618), writing-mode (p. 645)

fo:single-page-master-reference	Page-Master Sequence

Purpose

Lays out a set of pages from a single page-master.

Note

- This formatting object is in the pagination and layout category.

Related Formatting Objects

fo:conditional-page-master-reference (p. 469), fo:flow (p. 471), fo:layout-master-set (p. 475), fo:page-sequence (p. 493), fo:page-sequence-master (p. 494), fo:region-after (p. 495), fo:region-before (p. 496), fo:region-body (p. 496), fo:region-end (p. 497), fo:region-start (p. 497), fo:repeatable-page-master-alternatives (p. 498), fo:repeatable-page-master-reference (p. 499),fo:root (p. 500), fo:simple-page-master (p. 501), fo:static-content (p. 502)

Related Properties

id (p. 521), master-name (p. 547)

fo:static-content	Static Content Formatting Object

Purpose

Sets the static content for one or more regions.

Notes

- This formatting object is in the pagination and layout category.
- Most often, *static content* refers to page headers and footers that are repeated for almost all the pages of a multiple-page document.
- Two types of flows are fo:static-content and fo:flow.
- When one component out of several is created via concatenation, fo:static-content does not produce an area.

Related Formatting Objects

fo:conditional-page-master-reference (p. 469), fo:flow (p. 471), fo:layout-master-set (p. 475), fo:page-sequence (p. 493), fo:page-sequence-master (p. 494), fo:region-after (p. 495), fo:region-before (p. 496), fo:region-body (p. 496), fo:region-end (p. 497), fo:region-start (p. 497), fo:repeatable-page-master-alternatives (p. 498), fo:repeatable-page-master-reference (p. 499), fo:root (p. 500), fo:simple-page-master (p. 501), fo:single-page-master-reference (p. 502)

Related Properties

flow-name (p. 465), id (p. 521)

fo:table	Table Flow Object

Purpose

Formats a particular table.

Notes

- This formatting object is in the table-formatting category.
- The following are regarded as block formatting objects: fo:block, fo:block-container, fo:list-block, fo:table, and fo:table-and-caption.
- fo:table formats a table in a row-wise way into a block area.
- A table is composed of one or more table body sections, an optional header, and an optional footer.

Related Formatting Objects

fo:block (p. 466), fo:block-container (p. 467), fo:list-block (p. 477), fo:table-and-caption (p. 504), fo:table-body (p. 504), fo:table-caption (p. 505), fo:table-cell (p. 505), fo:table-column (p. 506), fo:table-footer (p. 506), fo:table-header (p. 507), fo:table-row (p. 507)

Related Properties

azimuth (p. 377), background properties (p. 379 – p. 387), block-progression-dimension (p. 390), border properties (p. 392 – p. 434), break-after (p. 435), break-before (p. 436), cue (p. 449), cue-after (p. 450), cue-before (p. 451), elevation (p. 456), end-indent (p. 457), height (p. 514), id (p. 521), inline-progression-dimension (p. 525), keep-together (p. 526), keep-with-next (p. 527), keep-with-previous (p. 528), margin properties (p. 542 – p. 546), padding properties (p. 562 – p. 541), page-break-after (p. 572), page-break-before (p. 573), pause (p. 577), pause-after (p. 578), pause-before (p. 579), pitch (p. 580), pitch-range (p. 581), play-during (p. 582), richness (p. 597), role (p. 598), source-document (p. 606), space-after (p. 607), space-before (p. 608), speak (p. 613), speak-header (p. 614), speak-numeral (p. 615), speak-punctuation (p. 615), speech-rate (p. 616), start-indent (p. 618), stress (p. 620), table-layout (p. 623), table-omit-footer-at-break (p. 624), table-omit-header-at-break (p. 624), voice-family (p. 637), volume (p. 638), width (p. 642)

fo:table-and-caption | Table and Caption Flow Object

Purpose
Formats a particular table and its embedded caption.

Notes
- This formatting object is in the table-formatting category.
- The following are regarded as block formatting objects: fo:block, fo:block-container, fo:list-block, fo:table, and fo:table-and-caption.

Related Formatting Objects
fo:block (p. 466), fo:block-container (p. 467), fo:list-block (p. 477), fo:table (p. 503), fo:table-body (p. 504), fo:table-caption (p. 505), fo:table-cell (p. 505), fo:table-column (p. 506), fo:table-footer (p. 506), fo:table-header (p. 507), fo:table-row (p. 507)

Related Properties
azimuth (p. 377), background properties (p. 379 - p. 387), border properties (p. 392 - p. 434), caption-side (p. 437), cue (p. 449), cue-after (p. 450), cue-before (p. 451), elevation (p. 456), end-indent (p. 457), id (p. 521), keep-together (p. 526), margin properties (p. 542 - p. 546), space-after (p. 607), space-before (p. 608), start-indent (p. 618), padding properties (p. 562 - p. 571), pause (p. 577), pause-after (p. 578), pause-before (p. 579), pitch (p. 580), pitch-range (p. 581), play-during (p. 582), richness (p. 597), role (p. 598), source-document (p. 606), speak (p. 613), speak-header (p. 614), speak-numeral (p. 615), speak-punctuation (p. 615), speech-rate (p. 616), stress (p. 620), voice-family (p. 637), volume (p. 638)

fo:table-body | Table-Body Formatting Object

Purpose
Formats a particular table body.

Notes
- This formatting object is in the table-formatting category.
- fo:table-body does not produce an area.

Related Formatting Objects
fo:table (p. 503), fo:table-and-caption (p. 504), fo:table-caption (p. 505), fo:table-cell (p. 505), fo:table-column (p. 506), fo:table-footer (p. 506), fo:table-header (p. 507), fo:table-row (p. 507)

Related Properties
azimuth (p. 377), background properties (p. 379 – p. 387), border properties (p. 392 – p. 434), cue (p. 449), cue-after (p. 450), cue-before (p. 451),

elevation (p. 456), id (p. 521), padding properties (p. 562 - p. 571), pause (p. 577), pause-after (p. 578), pause-before (p. 579), pitch (p. 580), pitch-range (p. 581), play-during (p. 582), richness (p. 597), role (p. 598), source-document (p. 606)speak (p. 613), speak-header (p. 614), speak-numeral (p. 615), speak-punctuation (p. 615), speech-rate (p. 616), stress (p. 620), voice-family (p. 637), volume (p. 638)

fo:table-caption   Table-Caption Formatting Object

Purpose

Applies block-level formats to a table caption.

Notes

- This formatting object is in the table-formatting category.
- fo:table-caption produces an area.

Related Formatting Objects

fo:table (p. 503), fo:table-and-caption (p. 504), fo:table-body (p. 504), fo:table-cell (p. 505), fo:table-column (p. 506), fo:table-footer (p. 506), fo:table-header (p. 507), fo:table-row (p. 507)

Related Properties

azimuth (p. 377), background properties (p. 379 – p. 387), block-progression-dimension (p. 390), border properties (p. 392 – p. 434), cue (p. 449), cue-after (p. 450), cue-before (p. 451), elevation (p. 456), height (p. 514), id (p. 521), inline-progression-dimension (p. 525), keep-together (p. 526), padding properties (p. 562 – p. 571), pause (p. 577), pause-after (p. 578), pause-before (p. 579), pitch (p. 580), pitch-range (p. 581), play-during (p. 582), richness (p. 597), role (p. 598), source-document (p. 606), speak (p. 613), speak-header (p. 614), speak-numeral (p. 615), speak-punctuation (p. 615), speech-rate (p. 616), stress (p. 620), voice-family (p. 637), volume (p. 638), width (p. 642)

fo:table-cell   Table-Cell Formatting Object

Purpose

Contains content to be located in a particular table cell.

Notes

- This formatting object is in the table-formatting category.
- Row height determines the cell height.

Related Formatting Objects

fo:table (p. 503), fo:table-and-caption (p. 504), fo:table-body (p. 504), fo:table-caption (p. 505), fo:table-column (p. 506), fo:table-footer (p. 506), fo:table-header (p. 507), fo:table-row (p. 507)

Related Properties

azimuth (p. 377), background properties (p. 379 - p. 387), block-progression-dimension (p. 390), border properties (p. 392 - p. 434), column-number (p. 445), cue (p. 449), cue-after (p. 450), cue-before (p. 451), elevation (p. 456), empty-cells (p. 457), ends-row (p. 458), height (p. 514), id (p. 521), number-columns-spanned (p. 557), number-rows-spanned (p. 557), padding properties (p. 562-p. 571), pause (p. 577), pause-after (p. 578), pause-before (p. 579), pitch (p. 580), pitch-range (p. 581), play-during (p. 582), richness (p. 597), role (p. 598), source-document (p. 606), speak (p. 613), speak-header (p. 614), speak-numeral (p. 615), speak-punctuation (p. 615), speech-rate (p. 616), starts-row (p. 619), stress (p. 620), voice-family (p. 637), volume (p. 638)

fo:table-column — Table-Column Formatting Object

Purpose

Contains properties for cells in a particular table column.

Notes

- This formatting object is in the table-formatting category.
- fo:table-column does not produce an area.

Related Formatting Objects

fo:table (p. 503), fo:table-and-caption (p. 504), fo:table-body (p. 504), fo:table-caption (p. 505), fo:table-cell (p. 505), fo:table-footer (p. 506), fo:table-header (p. 507), fo:table-row (p. 507)

Related Properties

background properties (p. 379 – p. 387), border properties (p. 392 – p. 434), column-number (p. 445), column-width (p. 446), id (p. 521), number-columns-repeated (p. 556), number-columns-spanned (p. 557), padding properties (p. 562 – p. 571), visibility (p. 636)

fo:table-footer — Table-Footer Formatting Object

Purpose

Contains properties for rows in a table footer.

Notes

- This formatting object is in the table-formatting category.
- fo:table-footer does not produce an area.

Related Formatting Objects

fo:table (p. 503), fo:table-and-caption (p. 504), fo:table-body (p. 504), fo:table-caption (p. 505), fo:table-cell (p. 505), fo:table-column (p. 506), fo:table-header (p. 507), fo:table-row (p. 507)

XSL Style Sheet Syntax

Related Properties

azimuth (p. 377), background properties (p. 379 – p. 387), border properties
(p. 392 – p. 434), cue (p. 449), cue-after (p. 450), cue-before (p. 451), elevation (p. 456), id (p. 521), padding properties (p. 562 – p. 571), pause (p. 577),
pause-after (p. 578), pause-before (p. 579), pitch (p. 580), pitch-range
(p. 581), play-during (p. 582), richness (p. 597), role (p. 598), source-
document (p. 606), speak (p. 613), speak-header (p. 614), speak-numeral (p.
615), speak-punctuation (p. 615), speech-rate (p. 616), stress (p. 620),
voice-family (p. 637), volume (p. 638)

fo:table-header — Table-Header Formatting Object

Purpose

Contains properties for rows in a table header.

Notes

- This formatting object is in the table-formatting category.
- fo:table-header does not produce an area.

Related Formatting Objects

fo:table (p. 503), fo:table-and-caption (p. 504), fo:table-body (p. 504),
fo:table-caption (p. 505), fo:table-cell (p. 505), fo:table-column (p. 506),
fo:table-footer (p. 506), fo:table-row (p. 507)

Related Properties

azimuth (p. 377), background properties (p. 379 – p. 387), border properties
(p. 392 – p. 434), cue (p. 449), cue-after (p. 450), cue-before (p. 451), elevation (p. 456), id (p. 521), padding properties (p. 562 – p. 571), pause (p. 577),
pause-after (p. 578), pause-before (p. 579), pitch (p. 580), pitch-range
(p. 581), play-during (p. 582), richness (p. 597), role (p. 598), source-
document (p. 606)speak (p. 613), speak-header (p. 614), speak-numeral (p. 615),
speak-punctuation (p. 615), speech-rate (p. 616), stress (p. 620), voice-
family (p. 637), volume (p. 638)

fo:table-row — Table-Row Formatting Object

Purpose

Contains properties for table rows.

Notes

- This formatting object is in the table-formatting category.
- fo:table-row does not produce an area.

Related Formatting Objects

fo:table (p. 503), fo:table-and-caption (p. 504), fo:table-body (p. 504), fo:table-caption (p. 505), fo:table-cell (p. 505), fo:table-column (p. 506), fo:table-footer (p. 506), fo:table-header (p. 507)

Related Properties

azimuth (p. 377), background properties (p. 379 – p. 387), block-progression-dimension (p. 390), border properties (p. 392 - p. 434), cue (p. 449), cue-after (p. 450), cue-before (p. 451), elevation (p. 456), height (p. 514), id (p. 521), keep-together (p. 526), padding properties (p. 526 – p. 571), pause (p. 577), pause-after (p. 578), pause-before (p. 579), pitch (p. 580), pitch-range (p. 581), play-during (p. 582), richness (p. 597), role (p. 598), source-document (p. 606), speak (p. 613), speak-header (p. 614), speak-numeral (p. 615), speak-punctuation (p. 615), speech-rate (p. 616), stress (p. 620), voice-family (p. 637), volume (p. 638)

fo:title   Title

Purpose

Associates a title with a particular document.

Notes

- This formatting object is in the pagination and layout category
- fo:title returns the same sequence of areas that its flow children return.
- The returned flow children sequences of areas must be in the same order that the flow children occur.
- Contents of fo:title can include (#PCDATA|%inline;)*.

Related Formatting Objects

fo:color-profile (p. 468), fo:conditional-page-master-reference (p. 469), fo:flow (p. 471), fo:layout-master-set (p. 475), fo:page-sequence (p. 493), fo:page-sequence-master (p. 494), fo:region-after (p. 495), fo:region-before (p. 496), fo:region-body (p. 496), fo:region-end (p. 497), fo:region-start (p. 497), fo:repeatable-page-master-alternatives (p. 498), fo:repeatable-page-master-reference (p. 499), fo:root (p. 500), fo:simple-page-master (p. 501), fo:static-content (p. 502)

fo:wrapper   Formatting-Objects Wrapper

Purpose

Sets properties that are inherited by a group of formatting objects.

Notes

- The following can be used with #PCDATA, block formatting objects, and inline formatting objects: fo:multi-properties, fo:multi-switch, and fo:wrapper.
- fo:wrapper does not produce an area. However, its children may be able to produce an area.

Related Formatting Objects

fo:multi-properties (p. 480), fo:multi-switch (p. 481)

Related Property

id (p. 521)

---

from-nearest-specified-value()   Closest-Ancestor Function

Purpose

Returns the value of a property from the nearest-ancestor formatting object.

EBNF Syntax

    object from-nearest-specified-value(NCName)

Standard Syntax

    object from-nearest-specified-value(NCName)

Where

- *object* is the characteristic returned by the function.
- from-nearest-specified-value is a function-name keyword.
- *NCName* is a property name from the current namespace.

Notes

- If no ancestor matches *NCName*, the returned value is the initial value of the property.
- If *NCName* refers to a shortcut property, the shortcut is expanded into all its properties, each with its own value. Otherwise, an error message is issued.

Related Functions

body-start() (p. 391), from-parent() (p. 510), from-table-column() (p. 510), inherited-property-value (p. 523), label-end() (p. 530)

XSL Style Sheet Syntax

from-parent()   From-Parent Function

Purpose
Returns the value of a property from a parent formatting object.

EBNF Syntax
```
object from-parent(NCName)
```

Standard Syntax
```
object from-parent(NCName)
```

Where
- *object* is the characteristic returned by the function.
- from-parent is a function-name keyword.
- *NCName* is a property name from the current namespace.

Notes
- If no parent matches *NCName*, the returned value is the initial value of the property.
- If *NCName* refers to a shortcut property, the shortcut is expanded into all its properties, each with its own value. Otherwise, an error message is issued.

Related Functions
body-start() (p. 391), from-nearest-specified-value() (p. 509), from-table-column() (p. 510), inherited-property-value (p. 523), label-end() (p. 530)

from-table-column()   From Table-Column Function

Purpose
Returns the inherited value of a property from the fo:table-column with the matching column number.

EBNF Syntax
```
object from-table-column(NCName)
```

Standard Syntax
```
object from-table-column(NCName)
```

Where
- *object* is the characteristic returned by the function.
- from-table-column is a function-name keyword.
- *NCName* is a property name from the current namespace.

Notes

- If no table column matches *NCName*'s number-columns-spanned, the returned value is a span of 1.
- If you use this function for a formatting object that is not a fo:table-cell or a child of fo:table-cell, an error message is issued.

Related Formatting Objects

fo:table-cell (p. 505), fo:table-column (p. 506)

Related Property

number-columns-spanned (p. 557)

Related Functions

body-start() (p. 391), from-nearest-specified-value() (p. 509), from-parent() (p. 510), inherited-property-value (p. 523), label-end() (p. 530)

FunctionCall [3]   Function Call

Purpose

Evaluates and processes an expression and calls a function.

EBNF Syntax

```
FunctionCall ::= FunctionName '(' ( Argument
  ( ',' Argument )* )? ')'
```

Standard Syntax

```
FunctionName ( [ Argument [, Argument [, Argument
  [, Argument ]]]] )
```

Where

- FunctionName (p. 512) provides a QName for a function.
- (marks the start of the arguments list.
- Argument (p. 376) represents an argument.
- , is a character that separates arguments.
-) marks the end of the arguments list.

Notes

- FunctionCall is a component of the PrimaryExpr production.
- The XPath recommendation (http://www.w3.org/TR/xpath) states that "a FunctionCall expression is evaluated by using the FunctionName to identify a function in the expression evaluation context function library, evaluating each of the Arguments, converting each argument to the type required by the function, and finally calling the function, passing it the converted arguments."
- The FunctionCall expression makes the function's result its own result.
- If a function converts an argument to a Boolean, it behaves as though it is the boolean() function.

- If a function converts an argument to a number, it behaves as though it is the number() function.
- If a function converts an argument to a string, it behaves as though it is the string() function.
- A function cannot convert an argument that is not a node-set to a node-set.

Related Productions

Argument (p. 376), FunctionName (p. 512)

FunctionName [25]	**Function Name**

Purpose

Provides an NCName for a function.

EBNF Syntax

```
FunctionName ::= NCName
```

Standard Syntax

```
NCName
```

Where

- NCName creates a name for a collection of namespace names.

Note

- FunctionName is a component of the ExprToken and FunctionCall productions.
- FunctionName represents part of an expression.

Related Productions

AbsoluteUnitName (p. 372), AlphaOrDigits (p. 376), Color (p. 443), Digits (p. 452), EnumerationToken (p. 459), ExprToken (p. 460), ExprWhitespace (p. 461), FloatingPointNumber (p. 463), Keyword (p. 529), Literal (p. 541), MultiplyOperator (p. 555), Number (p. 555), Operator (p. 559), OperatorName (p. 560), RelativeUnitName (p. 593)

---

glyph-orientation-horizontal	**Horizontal Glyph Orientation**

Purpose

Changes the orientation of horizontally displayed text glyphs with the box in which it is located.

Syntax

```
glyph-orientation-horizontal: angle|inherit
```

Where

- *angle* specifies the angle at which the glyph is displayed. Valid values are -360, -270, -180, -90, 0, +90, +180, +270, and +360. The initial value is 0.
- inherit is a keyword that indicates that this property takes the same computed value as its parent.

Notes

- This property is in the miscellaneous category.
- By default, the characteristics of this property are inherited.

Related Properties

baseline-shift (p. 388), block-progression-dimension (p. 390), clip (p. 440), color (p. 441), direction (p. 453), font-height-override-after (p. 484), font-height-override-before (p. 485), glyph-orientation-vertical (p. 513), height (p. 514), href (p. 515), hyphenation-keep (p. 517), hyphenation-ladder-count (p. 518), id (p. 521), inline-progression-dimension (p. 525), last-line-end-indent (p. 531), linefeed-treatment (p. 537), line-height (p. 538), line-height-shift-adjustment (p. 539), line-stacking-strategy (p. 540), max-height (p. 548), max-width (p. 550), min-height (p. 552), min-width (p. 553), overflow (p. 561), provisional-distance-between-starts (p. 586), provisional-label-separation (p. 587), reference-orientation (p. 588), ref-id (p. 589), scaling (p. 601), score-spaces (p. 602), size (p. 605), space-treatment (p. 611), span (p. 612), text-align (p. 625), text-align-last (p. 626), text-indent (p. 629), unicode-bidi (p. 634), vertical-align (p. 635), visibility (p. 636), white-space (p. 639), white-space-collapse (p. 640), width (p. 642), wrap-option (p. 644), writing-mode (p. 645), z-index (p. 648)

glyph-orientation-vertical | Vertical Glyph Orientation

Purpose

Changes the orientation of vertically displayed text glyphs with the box in which it is located.

Syntax

glyph-orientation-horizontal: auto|*angle*|inherit

Where

- auto is a keyword that represents a value automatically calculated by the user's browser.
- *angle* specifies the angle at which the glyph is displayed. Valid values are –360, –270, –180, –90, 0, +90, +180, +270, and +360. The initial value is 0.

XSL Style Sheet Syntax

- inherit is a keyword that indicates that this property takes the same computed value as its parent.

Notes

- This property is in the miscellaneous category.
- By default, the characteristics of this property are inherited.

Related Properties

baseline-shift (p. 388), block-progression-dimension (p. 390), clip (p. 440), color (p. 441), direction (p. 453), font-height-override-after (p. 484), font-height-override-before (p. 485), glyph-orientation-horizontal (p. 512), height (p. 514), href (p. 515), hyphenation-keep (p. 517), hyphenation-ladder-count (p. 518), id (p. 521), inline-progression-dimension (p. 525), last-line-end-indent (p. 531), linefeed-treatment (p. 537), line-height (p. 538), line-height-shift-adjustment (p. 539), line-stacking-strategy (p. 540), max-height (p. 548), max-width (p. 550), min-height (p. 552), min-width (p. 553), overflow (p. 561), provisional-distance-between-starts (p. 586), provisional-label-separation (p. 587), reference-orientation (p. 588), ref-id (p. 589), scaling (p. 601), score-spaces (p. 602), size (p. 605), space-treatment (p. 611), span (p. 612), text-align (p. 625), text-align-last (p. 626), text-indent (p. 629), unicode-bidi (p. 634), vertical-align (p. 635), visibility (p. 636), white-space (p. 639), white-space-collapse (p. 640), width (p. 642), wrap-option (p. 644), writing-mode (p. 645), z-index (p. 648)

height   Element Height

Purpose

Specifies the height of the selected element.

Syntax

height: *length*|*percent*%|<u>auto</u>|inherit

Where

- *length* is a positive value followed by a two-letter abbreviation representing the unit of measure.
- *percent* is a positive value that is relative to the size of the image. Follow *percent* with a percentage sign (%).
- auto is a keyword that represents a value automatically calculated by the user's browser.

- inherit is a keyword that indicates that this property takes the same computed value as its parent.

Notes

- This property is in the miscellaneous category.
- This property, which originated in CSS1, applies to all elements but selected inline elements and individual or grouped table columns.
- By default, the characteristics of this property are not inherited.

Example

```
img.bigpics { height: 400px; width: 250px }
```

Related Properties

baseline-shift (p. 388), block-progression-dimension (p. 390), clip (p. 440), color (p. 441), direction (p. 453), font-height-override-after (p. 484), font-height-override-before (p. 485), glyph-orientation-horizontal (p. 512), glyph-orientation-vertical (p. 513), href (p. 515), hyphenation-keep (p. 517), hyphenation-ladder-count (p. 518), id (p. 521), in-line-progression-dimension (p. 525), last-line-end-indent (p. 531), linefeed-treatment (p. 537), line-height (p. 538), line-height-shift-adjustment (p. 539), line-stacking-strategy (p. 540), max-height (p. 548), max-width (p. 550), min-height (p. 552), min-width (p. 553), overflow (p. 561), provisional-distance-between-starts (p. 586), provisional-label-separation (p. 587), reference-orientation (p. 588), ref-id (p. 589), scaling (p. 601), score-spaces (p. 602), size (p. 605), space-treatment (p. 611), span (p. 612), text-align (p. 625), text-align-last (p. 626), text-indent (p. 629), unicode-bidi (p. 634), vertical-align (p. 635), visibility (p. 636), white-space (p. 639), white-space-collapse (p. 640), width (p. 642), wrap-option (p. 644), writing-mode (p. 645), z-index (p. 648)

Related Formatting Objects

fo:external-graphic (p. 470), fo:inline-container (p. 474), fo:instream-foreign-object (p. 475), fo:table (p. 503), fo:table-caption (p. 505), fo:table-cell (p. 505), fo:table-row (p. 507)

href	Link or Data URI

Purpose

Indicates the URI for a target link or a graphic file.

Syntax

```
href: uri_name|inherit
```

Where

- `uri_name` names the URI of the source document.
- `inherit` is a keyword that indicates that this property takes the same computed value as its parent.

Notes

- This property is in the miscellaneous category.
- By default, the characteristics of this property are not inherited.

Related Properties

`baseline-shift` (p. 388), `block-progression-dimension` (p. 390), `clip` (p. 440), `color` (p. 441), `direction` (p. 453), `font-height-override-after` (p. 484), `font-height-override-before` (p. 485), `glyph-orientation-horizontal` (p. 512), `glyph-orientation-vertical` (p. 513), `height` (p. 514), `hyphenation-keep` (p. 517), `hyphenation-ladder-count` (p. 518), `id` (p. 521), `inline-progression-dimension` (p. 525), `last-line-end-indent` (p. 531), `linefeed-treatment` (p. 537), `line-height` (p. 538), `line-height-shift-adjustment` (p. 539), `line-stacking-strategy` (p. 540), `max-height` (p. 548), `max-width` (p. 550), `min-height` (p. 552), `min-width` (p. 553), `overflow` (p. 561), `provisional-distance-between-starts` (p. 586), `provisional-label-separation` (p. 587), `reference-orientation` (p. 588), `ref-id` (p. 589), `scaling` (p. 601), `score-spaces` (p. 602), `size` (p. 605), `space-treatment` (p. 611), `span` (p. 612), `text-align` (p. 625), `text-align-last` (p. 626), `text-indent` (p. 629), `unicode-bidi` (p. 634), `vertical-align` (p. 635), `visibility` (p. 636), `white-space` (p. 639), `white-space-collapse` (p. 640), `width` (p. 642), `wrap-option` (p. 644), `writing-mode` (p. 645), `z-index` (p. 648)

Related Formatting Object

`fo:external-graphic` (p. 470)

---

hyphenate   Hyphenate?

Purpose

Indicates whether hyphenation is allowed.

Syntax

`hyphenate: false|true|inherit`

Where

- `false` indicates that the Boolean value of this expression is false (selected hyphenation is not allowed during the processing of the algorithm that creates line breaks). This is the default.
- `true` indicates that the Boolean value of this expression is true (selected hyphenation is allowed during the processing of the algorithm that creates line breaks).
- `inherit` is a keyword that indicates that this property takes the same computed value as its parent.

Notes

- This property is in the common-hyphenation category.
- The XSL hyphenate property is related to the DSSSL-O hyphenate? property.
- The hyphenate characteristic is inherited.

Related Properties

country (p. 448), hyphenation-character (p. 571), hyphenation-push-character-count (p. 519), hyphenation-remain-character-count (p. 520), language (p. 530), script (p. 603), xml:lang (p. 647)

Related Formatting Object

fo:block (p. 466)

hyphenation-character | Hyphenation Character

Purpose

Specifies a character that is displayed as a hyphen.

Syntax

```
hyphenation-character: character|inherit
```

Where

- *character* is a character. The initial value of *character* is u+2010.
- inherit is a keyword that indicates that this property takes the same computed value as its parent.

Notes

- This property is in the common-hyphenation category.
- The hyphenation-character characteristic is inherited.

Related Properties

country (p. 448), hyphenate (p. 516), hyphenation-push-character-count (p. 519), hyphenation-remain-character-count (p. 520), language (p. 530), script (p. 603), xml:lang (p. 647)

Related Formatting Object

fo:block (p. 466)

hyphenation-keep | Hyphenated-Word Location

Purpose

Sets the location of both parts of a hyphenated word.

Syntax

```
hyphenation-keep: none|column|page|spread|inherit
```

XSL Style Sheet Syntax

Where

- none indicates no hyphenation limits. This is the default.
- column keeps both parts of a hyphenated word within one column.
- page keeps both parts of a hyphenated word within one page.
- spread keeps both parts of a hyphenated word within a two-page spread.
- inherit is a keyword that indicates that this property takes the same computed value as its parent.

Notes

- This property is in the miscellaneous category.
- The XSL hyphenation-keep property is related to the DSSSL-O hyphenation-keep property.
- By default, the characteristics of this property are inherited.

Related Properties

baseline-shift (p. 388), block-progression-dimension (p. 390), clip (p. 440), color (p. 441), direction (p. 453), font-height-override-after (p. 484), font-height-override-before (p. 485), glyph-orientation-horizontal (p. 512), glyph-orientation-vertical (p. 513), height (p. 514), href (p. 515), hyphenation-ladder-count (p. 518), id (p. 521), inline-progression-dimension (p. 525), last-line-end-indent (p. 531), linefeed-treatment (p. 537), line-height (p. 538), line-height-shift-adjustment (p. 539), line-stacking-strategy (p. 540), max-height (p. 548), max-width (p. 550), min-height (p. 552), min-width (p. 553), overflow (p. 561), provisional-distance-between-starts (p. 586), provisional-label-separation (p. 587), reference-orientation (p. 588), ref-id (p. 589), scaling (p. 601), score-spaces (p. 602), size (p. 605), space-treatment (p. 611), span (p. 612), text-align (p. 625), text-align-last (p. 626), text-indent (p. 629), unicode-bidi (p. 634), vertical-align (p. 635), visibility (p. 636), white-space (p. 639), white-space-collapse (p. 640), width (p. 642), wrap-option (p. 644), writing-mode (p. 645), z-index (p. 648)

Related Formatting Object

fo:block (p. 466)

---

hyphenation-ladder-count   Hyphenation Ladder Count

Purpose

Specifies the maximum number of lines in a row that can end with the hyphenation character.

Syntax

hyphenation-ladder-count: <u>none</u>|*integer*|inherit

Where

- none indicates no hyphenation-ladder limits. This is the default.

XSL Style Sheet Syntax

- *integer* is a positive, non-zero integer.
- inherit is a keyword that indicates that this property takes the same computed value as its parent.

Notes

- This property is in the miscellaneous category.
- The XSL hyphenation-ladder-count property is related to the DSSSL-O hyphenation-ladder-count property.
- If *integer* has a value of 1 and the current line is hyphenated, the line above and the line below cannot be hyphenated.
- If *integer* has a value of 2 and the current line is hyphenated, the line above or the line below can be hyphenated. However, no more than two lines can be hyphenated in a row.
- By default, the characteristics of this property are inherited.

Related Properties

baseline-shift (p. 388), block-progression-dimension (p. 390), clip (p. 440), color (p. 441), direction (p. 453), font-height-override-after (p. 484), font-height-override-before (p. 485), glyph-orientation-horizontal (p. 512), glyph-orientation-vertical (p. 513), height (p. 514), href (p. 515), hyphenation-keep (p. 517), id (p. 521), inline-progression-dimension (p. 525), last-line-end-indent (p. 531), linefeed-treatment (p. 537), line-height (p. 538), line-height-shift-adjustment (p. 839), line-stacking-strategy (p. 540), max-height (p. 548), max-width (p. 550), min-height (p. 552), min-width (p. 553), overflow (p. 561), provisional-distance-between-starts (p. 586), provisional-label-separation (p. 587), reference-orientation (p. 588), ref-id (p. 589), scaling (p. 601), score-spaces (p. 602), size (p. 605), space-treatment (p. 611), span (p. 612), text-align (p. 625), text-align-last (p. 626), text-indent (p. 629), unicode-bidi (p. 634), vertical-align (p. 635), visibility (p. 636), white-space (p. 639), white-space-collapse (p. 640), width (p. 642), wrap-option (p. 644), writing-mode (p. 645), z-index (p. 648)

Related Formatting Object

fo:block (p. 466)

hyphenation-push-character-count	Post-Hyphenation Characters

Purpose

Specifies the minimum number of characters in a word *after* the hyphenation character.

Syntax

```
hyphenation-push-character-count: number|inherit
```

Where

- *number* represents a single positive number of characters past the hyphenation character. The initial value is 2.
- inherit is a keyword that indicates that this property takes the same computed value as its parent.

Notes

- This property is in the common-hyphenation category.
- If *number* is negative or not an integer, the processor rounds the number to the closest integer greater than zero.
- By default, the characteristics of this property are inherited.

Related Properties

country (p. 448), hyphenate (p. 516), hyphenation-character (p. 517), hyphenation-remain-character-count (p. 520), language (p. 530), script (p. 603), xml:lang (p. 647)

Related Formatting Object

fo:block (p. 466)

hyphenation-remain-character-count	Pre-Hyphenation Characters

Purpose

Specifies the minimum number of characters in a word *before* the hyphenation character.

Syntax

hyphenation-remain-character-count: *number*|inherit

Where

- *number* represents a single positive number of characters prior to the hyphenation character. The initial value is 2.
- inherit is a keyword that indicates that this property takes the same computed value as its parent.

Notes

- This property is in the common-hyphenation category.
- If number is negative or not an integer, the processor rounds the number to the closest integer greater than zero.
- By default, the characteristics of this property are inherited.

Related Properties

country (p. 448), hyphenate (p. 516), hyphenation-character (p. 517), hyphenation-push-character-count (p. 519), language (p. 530), script (p. 603), xml:lang (p. 647)

Related Formatting Object
fo:block (p. 466)

icc-color()   ICC Color Function

Purpose
Returns a color value from the ICC Color Profile.

EBNF Syntax
    color icc-color(number_1, number_2, number_3, NCName, number_4,
    number_5)

Standard Syntax
    color icc-color(number_1, number_2, number_3, NCName, number_4,
    number_5)

Where
- *color* is the ICC color value returned by the function
- icc-color is the function-name keyword.
- *number_1*, *number_2*, and *number_3* specify an sRGB fallback color
- *NCName* is a property name from the current namespace that specifies the color profile.
- *number_4* and *number_5* specify the ICC color value.

Notes
- This is a color function
- The RGB fallback color is used if no color profile is available.
- The color profile must have been declared in the fo:declarations formatting object in order to be called in this function.

Related Functions
rgb() (p. 596), system-color() (p. 622)

id   Identifier

Purpose
Gives a unique identifier to a formatting object within a fo:namespace formatting object.

Syntax
    id: identifier

Where
- *identifier* represents a unique identifier.

Notes

- This property is in the miscellaneous category.
- The initial value of this property is provided by a system algorithm.
- By default, the characteristics of this property are not inherited.

Related Properties

`baseline-shift` (p. 388), `block-progression-dimension` (p. 390), `clip` (p. 440), `color` (p. 441), `direction` (p. 453), `font-height-override-after` (p. 484), `font-height-override-before` (p. 485), `glyph-orientation-horizontal` (p. 512), `glyph-orientation-vertical` (p. 513), `height` (p. 514), `href` (p. 515), `hyphenation-keep` (p. 517), `hyphenation-ladder-count` (p. 518), `inline-progression-dimension` (p. 525), `last-line-end-indent` (p. 531), `linefeed-treatment` (p. 537), `line-height` (p. 538), `line-height-shift-adjustment` (p. 539), `line-stacking-strategy` (p. 540), `max-height` (p. 548), `max-width` (p. 550), `min-height` (p. 552), `min-width` (p. 553), `overflow` (p. 561), `provisional-distance-between-starts` (p. 586), `provisional-label-separation` (p. 587), `reference-orientation` (p. 588), `ref-id` (p. 589), `scaling` (p. 601), `score-spaces` (p. 602), `size` (p. 605), `space-treatment` (p. 611), `span` (p. 612), `text-align` (p. 625), `text-align-last` (p. 626), `text-indent` (p. 629), `unicode-bidi` (p. 634), `vertical-align` (p. 635), `visibility` (p. 636), `white-space` (p. 639), `white-space-collapse` (p. 640), `width` (p. 642), `wrap-option` (p. 644), `writing-mode` (p. 645), `z-index` (p. 648)

Related Formatting Objects

`fo:bidi-override` (p. 465), `fo:conditional-page-master-reference` (p. 469), `fo:external-graphic` (p. 470), `fo:float` (p. 471), `fo:flow` (p. 471), `fo:footnote` (p. 472), `fo:footnote-body` (p. 472), `fo:initial-property-set` (p. 473), `fo:inline` (p. 473), `fo:inline-container` (p. 474), `fo:instream-foreign-object` (p. 475), `fo:layout-master-set` (p. 475), `fo:leader` (p. 476), `fo:list-block` (p. 477), `fo:list-item` (p. 478), `fo:list-item-body` (p. 478), `fo:list-item-label` (p. 479), `fo:multi-case` (p. 480), `fo:multi-properties` (p. 480), `fo:multi-property-set` (p. 480), `fo:multi-switch` (p. 481), `fo:multi-toggle` (p. 481), `fo:page-number` (p. 492), `fo:page-number-citation` (p. 492), `fo:page-sequence` (p. 493), `fo:page-sequence-master` (p. 494), `fo:region-after` (p. 495), `fo:region-before` (p. 496), `fo:region-body` (p. 496), `fo:region-end` (p. 497), `fo:region-start` (p. 497), `fo:repeatable-page-master-alternatives` (p. 498), `fo:repeatable-page-master-reference` (p. 499), `fo:root` (p. 500), `fo:simple-link` (p. 500), `fo:simple-page-master` (p. 501), `fo:single-page-master-reference` (p. 502), `fo:static-content` (p. 502), `fo:table` (p. 503), `fo:table-and-caption` (p. 504), `fo:table-body` (p. 504), `fo:table-caption` (p. 505), `fo:table-cell` (p. 505), `fo:table-column` (p. 506), `fo:table-footer` (p. 506), `fo:table-header` (p. 507), `fo:table-row` (p. 507), `fo:wrapper` (p. 508)

indicate-destination   Indicate Destination?

Purpose
Specifies whether the areas that belong to the destination resource are shown.

Syntax
```
indicate-destination: yes|no
```

Where
- yes is a keyword that indicates that areas should be shown.
- no is a keyword that indicates that areas should not be shown. This is the default.

Notes
- This property is in the links category.
- By default, the characteristics of this property are not inherited.

Related Properties
auto-restore (p. 377), case-name (p. 438), case-title (p. 438), destination-placement-offset (p. 452), external-destination (p. 462), internal-destination (p. 526), show-destination (p. 604), starting-state (p. 619), switch-to (p. 621)

Related Formatting Object
fo:simple-link (p. 500)

inherited-property-value()   Inherited-Property-Value Function

Purpose
Returns the inherited value of a property.

EBNF Syntax
```
object inherited-property-value(NCName)
```

Standard Syntax
```
object inherited-property-value(NCName)
```

Where
- object is the characteristic returned by the function.
- inherited-property-value is a function-name keyword.
- NCName is a property name from the current namespace.

Note
- If the property is not an inherited property, an error message is issued.

XSL Style Sheet Syntax

Related Functions

body-start() (p. 391), from-nearest-specified-value() (p. 509), from-parent() (p. 510), from-table-column() (p. 510), label-end() (p. 530)

Related Formatting Objects

fo:external-graphic (p. 470), fo:footnote-body (p. 472), fo:inline-container (p. 474), fo:instream-foreign-object (p. 475), fo:page-number (p. 492), fo:page-number-citation (p. 492), fo:simple-link (p. 500)

initial-page-number	Initial Page Number

Purpose

Sets the number of the first page in the current sequence of pages.

Syntax

initial-page-number: auto|*integer*|inherit

Where

- auto is a keyword that represents a value automatically calculated by the user's browser. This is the default.
- *integer* indicates the explicit number of the first page in the current sequence of pages.
- inherit is a keyword that indicates that this property takes the same computed value as its parent.

Notes

- This property is in the pagination-and-layout category.
- If *integer* is negative or not an integer, the processor rounds the number to the closest integer greater than zero.
- The initial page number is 1 if the current sequence of pages is the first in the document. If the current sequence of pages is not the first in the document, the initial page number is one greater than the prior page number.
- By default, the characteristics of this property are not inherited.

Related Properties

blank-or-not-blank (p. 389), column-count (p. 444), column-gap (p. 444), extent (p. 461), flow-name (p. 465), force-page-count (p. 494), master-name (p. 547), maximum-repeats (p. 549), odd-or-even (p. 559), page-height (p. 575), page-position (p. 575), page-width (p. 576), precedence (p. 584), region-name (p. 590)

Related Formatting Object

fo:page-sequence (p. 493)

inline-progression-dimension	Inline Progression Dimension

Purpose

Sets the inline-progression-dimension of block-level and replaced-element boxes.

Syntax

```
inline-progression-dimension: length|percent|auto
   |inherit
```

Where

- *length* is a positive value followed by a two-letter abbreviation representing the unit of measure.
- *percent* is a positive value that is relative to the size of the box. Follow *percent* with a percentage sign (%).
- auto is a keyword that represents a value automatically calculated by the user's browser.
- inherit is a keyword that indicates that this property takes the same computed value as its parent.

Notes

- This property is in the miscellaneous category.
- Even if the value of this property is not auto, a browser may change the dimensions of the box.
- The value of this property is overridden when the line-height property is in effect for this box.
- By default, characteristics of this property are not inherited.

Related Properties

baseline-shift (p. 388), block-progression-dimension (p. 390), clip (p. 440), color (p. 441), direction (p. 453), font-height-override-after (p. 484), font-height-override-before (p. 485), glyph-orientation-horizontal (p. 512), glyph-orientation-vertical (p. 513), height (p. 514), href (p. 515), hyphenation-keep (p. 517), hyphenation-ladder-count (p. 518), id (p. 521), last-line-end-indent (p. 531), linefeed-treatment (p. 537), line-height (p. 538), line-height-shift-adjustment (p. 539), line-stacking-strategy (p. 540), max-height (p. 548), max-width (p. 550), min-height (p. 552), min-width (p. 553), overflow (p. 561), provisional-distance-between-starts (p. 586), provisional-label-separation (p. 587), reference-orientation (p. 589), ref-id (p. 589), scaling (p. 601), score-spaces (p. 602), size (p. 605), space-treatment (p. 611), span (p. 612), text-align (p. 625), text-align-last (p. 626), text-indent (p. 629), unicode-bidi (p. 634), vertical-align (p. 635), visibility (p. 636), white-space (p. 639), white-space-collapse (p. 640), width (p. 642), wrap-option (p. 644), writing-mode (p. 645), z-index (p. 648)

XSL Style Sheet Syntax

Related Formatting Objects

fo:external-graphic (p. 470), fo:inline-container (p. 474), fo:instream-foreign-object (p. 475), fo:table (p. 503), fo:table-caption (p. 505)

internal-destination — Internal Destination

Purpose

Indicates the destination or target resource of a simple link (fo:simple-link formatting object) in the current document.

Syntax

```
internal-destination: id_ref
```

Where

- *id_ref* names the identifier reference of the destination.

Notes

- This property is in the links category.
- If both the external-destination and internal-destination properties are used for this link, internal-destination has precedence.
- By default, the characteristics of this property are not inherited.

Related Properties

auto-restore (p. 377), case-name (p. 438), case-title (p. 438), destination-placement-offset (p. 452), external-destination (p. 462), indicate-destination (p. 523), show-destination (p. 604), starting-state (p. 619), switch-to (p. 621)

Related Formatting Object

fo:simple-link (p. 500)

keep-together — Keep Together

Purpose

Indicates whether output produced by the current flow object stays together.

Syntax

```
keep-together: auto|always|column|page|inherit
```

Where

- auto is a keyword that represents a value automatically calculated by the user's browser, so the break may or may not occur inside the box. This is the default.
- always is a keyword that indicates that no page, column, or region break can occur inside the box.

- column is a keyword that indicates that no break can occur within the column inside the box.
- page is a keyword that indicates that no break can occur within the page inside the box. However, a column break may occur.
- inherit is a keyword that indicates that this property takes the same computed value as its parent.

Notes

- This property is in the page-related category.
- The keep-together characteristic is part of the aligned-column, box, display-group, external-graphic, paragraph, rule, table, and table-part flow-objects classes.
- The XSL keep-together property is related to the DSSSL-O keep property.
- By default, the characteristics of this property are inherited.

Related Properties

orphans (p. 561), page-break-inside (p. 574), widows (p. 641)

Related Formatting Objects

fo:block (p. 466), fo:inline (p. 473), fo:inline-container (p. 474), fo:list-block (p. 477), fo:list-item (p. 478), fo:table (p. 503), fo:table-and-caption (p. 504), fo:table-caption (p. 505), fo:table-row (p. 507)

keep-with-next

Keep with Next?

Purpose

Indicates whether to keep the current flow object with the following one.

Syntax

keep-with-next: <u>auto</u>|always|column|page|inherit

Where

- auto is a keyword that indicates that the last box for the current object need not be next to the first box produced by the next formatting object. This is the default.
- always is a keyword that indicates that the last box for the current object must be next to the first box produced by the next formatting object.
- column is a keyword that indicates that the last box for the current object must be in the same column and page as the first box produced by the next formatting object.
- page is a keyword that indicates that the last box for the current object must be on the same page as the first box produced by the next formatting object but need not be in the same column.
- inherit is a keyword that indicates that this property takes the same computed value as its parent.

Notes

- This property is in the common-keeps-and-breaks category.
- The XSL working draft (http://www.w3.org/TR/xsl/) states that "all keep values are ordered from weakest (auto) to strongest (always) and break values are ordered from weakest (auto) to strongest (even/odd). In general, the strongest condition applies, with all breaks other than 'auto' being stronger than all keeps. Also, conflicting even-page/odd-page breaks behave as if they were 'page.'"
- The XSL keep-with-next property is slightly related to the DSSSL-O keep-with-next? property.
- The keep-with-next characteristic is not inherited.

Related Properties

break-after (p. 435), break-before (p. 436), keep-with-previous (p. 528), page-break-after (p. 572), page-break-before (p. 573)

Related Formatting Objects

fo:list-block (p. 477), fo:list-item (p. 478), fo:table (p. 503)

keep-with-previous   Keep with Previous?

Purpose

Indicates whether to keep the current flow object with the prior one.

Syntax

keep-with-previous: <u>auto</u>|always|column|page|inherit

Where

- auto is a keyword that indicates that the first box for the current object need not be next to the last box produced by the prior formatting object. This is the default.
- always is a keyword that indicates that the first box for the current object must be next to the last box produced by the prior formatting object.
- column is a keyword that indicates that the first box for the current object must be in the same column and page as the last box produced by the prior formatting object.
- page is a keyword that indicates that the first box for the current object must be on the same page as the last box produced by the prior formatting object but need not be in the same column.
- inherit is a keyword that indicates that this property takes the same computed value as its parent.

Notes

- This property is in the common-keeps-and-breaks category.
- The XSL working draft (http://www.w3.org/TR/xsl/) states that "all keep values are ordered from weakest (auto) to strongest (always) and break values are ordered from weakest (auto) to strongest (even/odd). In general, the strongest condition applies, with all breaks other than 'auto' being stronger than all keeps. Also, conflicting even-page/odd-page breaks behave as if they were 'page.'"
- The XSL keep-with-previous property is slightly related to the DSSSL-O keep-with-previous? property.
- The keep-with-previous characteristic is not inherited.

Related Properties

break-after (p. 435), break-before (p. 436), keep-with-next (p. 527), page-break-after (p. 572), page-break-before (p. 573)

Related Formatting Objects

fo:list-block (p. 477), fo:list-item (p. 478), fo:table (p. 503)

Keyword [24]   Keyword

Purpose

Represents a reserved keyword.

EBNF Syntax

```
Keyword ::= 'inherit'
```

Standard Syntax

```
inherit
```

Where

- inherit is a keyword that indicates that a property takes the same computed value as its parent.

Note

- Keyword represents part of an expression.

Related Productions

AbsoluteUnitName (p. 372), AlphaOrDigits (p. 376), Color (p. 443), Digits (p. 452), EnumerationToken (p. 459), ExprToken (p. 460), ExprWhitespace (p. 461), FloatingPointNumber (p. 463), FunctionName (p. 512), Literal (p. 541), MultiplyOperator (p. 555), Number (p. 555), Operator (p. 559), OperatorName (p. 560), RelativeUnitName (p. 593)

XSL Style Sheet Syntax

label-end()   List Label-End Function

Purpose
Returns the label-end value for a list.

EBNF Syntax
```
number_r label-end()
```

Standard Syntax
```
number_r label-end()
```

Where
- *number_r* is the number returned by the function.
- label-end is a function-name keyword.

Related Production
provisional-label-separation (p. 587)

Related Functions
body-start() (p. 391), from-nearest-specified-value() (p. 509), from-parent() (p. 510), from-table-column() (p. 510), inherited-property-value (p. 523), label-end() (p. 530)

language   Language Code

Purpose
Specifies a language code from RFC-1766.

Syntax
```
language: none|RFC-1766_language_code|inherit
```

Where
- none indicates no language code. This is the default.
- *RFC_1766_language_code* is a language code.
- inherit is a keyword that indicates that this property takes the same computed value as its parent.

Notes
- This property is in the common-hyphenation category.
- The language characteristic is part of the character, paragraph, and paragraph-break flow-objects classes.
- The XSL language property is related, but not closely, to the DSSSL-O language property.
- In XML, language codes and country codes are case-insensitive. Although it is not required, the language code is usually in lower case and the country code is usually in upper case.

- You can use the xml:lang attribute with any XML production to declare a language used as character data and attribute values in an XML document. IETF_RFC_1766 (ftp://ftp.isi.edu/in-notes/rfc1766.txt) lists supported values.
- Use the xml:lang attribute to specify language codes within XML documents.
- The language characteristic is inherited.
- For more information about language codes supported by XML, refer to Appendix C, "Language Codes" (p. 805).

Related Properties

country (p. 448), hyphenate (p. 516), hyphenation-character (p. 517), hyphenation-push-character-count (p. 519), hyphenation-remain-character-count (p. 580), script (p. 603), xml:lang (p. 647)

Related Formatting Object

fo:block (p. 466)

last-line-end-indent   Indent Last Line

Purpose

Sets the amount of ending indention for the last line of the current paragraph flow object.

Syntax

```
last-line-end-indent: length|percent|inherit
```

Where

- *length* is a positive or negative relative or absolute length. The default is 0 point.
- *percent* is a positive value that is relative to the size of the box. Follow *percent* with a percentage sign (%).
- inherit is a keyword that indicates that this property takes the same computed value as its parent.

Notes

- This property is in the miscellaneous category.
- The XSL last-line-end-indent property is related to the DSSSL-O last-line-end-indent property.
- By default, the characteristics of this property are inherited.

Related Properties

baseline-shift (p. 388), block-progression-dimension (p. 390), clip (p. 440), color (p. 441), direction (p. 453), font-height-override-after (p. 484), font-height-override-before (p. 485), glyph-orientation-horizontal (p. 512), glyph-orientation-vertical (p. 513), height (p. 514), href (p. 515), hyphenation-keep (p. 517), hyphenation-ladder-count (p. 518),

id (p. 521), inline-progression-dimension (p. 525), linefeed-treatment
(p. 537), line-height (p. 538), line-height-shift-adjustment (p. 539),
line-stacking-strategy (p. 540), max-height (p. 548), max-width (p. 550),
min-height (p. 552), min-width (p. 553), overflow (p. 561), provisional-
distance-between-starts (p. 586), provisional-label-separation (p. 587),
reference-orientation (p. 588), ref-id (p. 589), scaling (p. 601), score-
spaces (p. 602), size (p. 605), space-treatment (p. 611), span (p. 612),
text-align (p. 625), text-align-last (p. 626), text-indent (p. 629),
unicode-bidi (p. 634), vertical-align (p. 635), visibility (p. 636), white-
space (p. 639), white-space-collapse (p. 640), width (p. 642), wrap-option
(p. 644), writing-mode (p. 645), z-index (p. 648)

Related Formatting Object

fo:block (p. 466)

leader-alignment   Leader Alignment

Purpose

Indicates whether fo:leaders formatting objects with the same content and
values are aligned.

Syntax

leader-alignment: <u>none</u>|reference-area|page|inherit

Where

- none is a keyword that indicates that there is no leader alignment. This
  is the default.
- reference-area is a keyword that indicates that the leaders are aligned
  with the current reference area's starting edge.
- page is a keyword that indicates that the leaders are aligned with the
  current page's starting edge.
- inherit is a keyword that indicates that this property takes the same
  computed value as its parent.

Notes

- This property is in the rule-and-leader category.
- By default, characteristics of this property are inherited.

Related Properties

leader-length (p. 533), leader-pattern (p. 533), leader-pattern-width
(p. 533), rule-style (p. 599), rule-thickness (p. 600)

Related Formatting Object

fo:leader (p. 476)

leader-length   Leader Length

Purpose

Specifies a maximum and minimum leader length

Syntax

```
leader-length(.minimum=mn_length|.optimum=op_length
  |maximum=mx_length)|inherit
```

Where

- minimum is a keyword that precedes the minimum amount of width space of the leader length.
- *mn_length* is a positive value followed by a two-letter abbreviation representing the unit of measure or a percentage value with the width of the containing box at 100%. The initial value is 0 point.
- optimum is a keyword that precedes the ideal amount of width space of the leader length.
- *op_length* is a positive value followed by a two-letter abbreviation representing the unit of measure or a percentage value with the width of the containing box at 100%. The initial value is 12.0 points.
- maximum is a keyword that precedes the maximum amount of width space to be inserted after the flow-object area.
- *mx_length* is a positive value followed by a two-letter abbreviation representing the unit of measure or a percentage value with the width of the containing box at 100%. The initial value is 100%.
- inherit is a keyword that indicates that this property takes the same computed value as its parent.

Notes

- This property is in the rule-and-leader category.
- By default, the characteristics of this property are inherited.

Related Properties

leader-alignment (p. 532), leader-pattern (p. 533), leader-pattern-width (p. 533), rule-style (p. 599), rule-thickness (p. 600)

Related Formatting Object

fo:leader (p. 476)

leader-pattern   Leader Pattern

Purpose

Specifies a pattern for the leader.

Syntax

```
leader-pattern: space|rule|dots|use-content|inherit
```

Where

- space is a keyword that indicates that the leader is composed of spaces.
- rule is a keyword that indicates that the leader is composed of a horizontal rule.
- dots is a keyword that indicates that the leader is composed of dots.
- use-content is a keyword that indicates that the leader is composed of a pattern set by the fo:leader children.
- inherit is a keyword that indicates that this property takes the same computed value as its parent.

Notes

- This property is in the rule-and-leader category.
- If the leader is a horizontal rule, use the rule-thickness and rule-style properties to set rule attributes.
- By default, the characteristics of this property are inherited.

Related Properties

leader-alignment (p. 532), leader-length (p. 533), leader-pattern-width (p. 533), rule-style (p. 599), rule-thickness (p. 600)

Related Formatting Object

fo:leader (p. 476)

leader-pattern-width | Leader Pattern Width

Purpose

Specifies the width of the leader pattern.

Syntax

leader-pattern-width: use-font-metrics|*length*|inherit

Where

- use-font-metrics is a keyword that indicates that this property uses the metrics of the current font to set the leader pattern width.
- *length* is a positive value followed by a two-letter abbreviation representing the unit of measure.
- inherit is a keyword that indicates that this property takes the same computed value as its parent.

Notes

- This property is in the rule-and-leader category.
- The leader-width refers to the width of the box containing the leader.
- If the specified *length* is less than the use-font-metrics value, the leader uses the use-font-metrics value.
- By default, the characteristics of this property are inherited.

Related Properties

leader-alignment (p. 532), leader-length (p. 533), leader-pattern (p. 533), rule-style (p. 599), rule-thickness (p. 600)

Related Formatting Object

fo:leader (p. 476)

left   Left Offset

Purpose

Controls the location of the left edge of a box from the left edge of the block that contains the box.

Syntax

left: *length*|*percent*%|<u>auto</u>|inherit

Where

- *length* is a positive or negative value followed by a two-letter abbreviation representing the unit of measure.
- *percent* is a positive or negative value that is relative to the size of the image. Follow *percent* with a percentage sign (%).
- auto is a keyword that represents a value automatically calculated by the user's browser. This is the default.
- inherit is a keyword that indicates that this property takes the same computed value as its parent.

Notes

- This property is in the common-absolute-position category.
- This property, which originated in CSS2, applies to elements that are positioned.
- The combination of left and right values overrides the current width of the content box.
- By default, the characteristics of this property are not inherited.

Related Properties

bottom (p. 434), position (p. 583), right (p. 597), top (p. 632)

Related Formatting Object

fo:block-container (p. 467)

letter-spacing   Character Spacing

Purpose

Sets spacing between characters.

Syntax

```
letter-spacing: normal|[+|-]length
 |(space.minimum=npt,
 .optimum=npt, .maximum=npt,
 .conditionality=discard|retain,
 .precedence=force|integer)|inherit
```

Where

- normal is a keyword that represents the normal spacing between characters. This is the default.
- *length* is a positive or negative value followed by a two-letter abbreviation representing the unit of measure. *length* is usually an increase in the spacing between characters. When the *length* value is negative, spacing may decrease, depending on the browser.
- *space* is the value that determines width space for the selection.
- minimum is a keyword that precedes the minimum amount of width space to be inserted after the flow-object area. The initial value is 0 point.
- optimum is a keyword that precedes the ideal amount of width space to be inserted after the flow-object area. The initial value is 0 point.
- maximum is a keyword that precedes the maximum amount of width space to be inserted after the flow-object area. The initial value is 0 point.
- conditionality is a keyword that indicates whether the space is discarded (discard) or retained (retain) if it is the last space in the flow-object area.
- precedence is a keyword that indicates whether the space in the following flow-object area is merged with the space in the current one. A value of force prevents a merger. The integer value specifies the width of the merged width space.
- inherit is a keyword that indicates that this property takes the same computed value as its parent.

Notes

- This property is in the character category.
- This property, which originated in CSS1, applies to all elements.
- If you select normal, a browser can justify the selected text.
- Valid relative units of measure are em (the height of the current font), ex (the height of the letter *x* in the current font), and px (pixels, relative to the size of the window). Valid absolute units of measure are in (inches), cm (centimeters), mm (millimeters), pt (points), and pc (picas).
- By default, the characteristics of this property are inherited.

Example

```
para.emphasis { letter-spacing: 4mm; font-weight: bolder }
```

Related Properties

character (p. 439), suppress-at-line-break (p. 621), text-decoration (p. 628), text-shadow (p. 630), text-transform (p. 631), word-spacing (p. 643)

Related Formatting Objects

fo:bidi-override (p. 465), (p. 472), fo:initial-property-set (p. 473), fo:leader (p. 476), fo:page-number (p. 492), fo:page-number-citation (p. 492)

linefeed-treatment	Linefeed Treatment

Purpose

Specifies the way in which a linefeed character is treated.

Syntax

```
linefeed-treatment: preserve|treat-as-space|ignore
  |inherit
```

Where

- preserve is a keyword that indicates that a linefeed character is not treated in any particular way.
- treat-as-space is a keyword that indicates that a linefeed character is treated as a whitespace character. This is the default.
- ignore is a keyword that indicates that the linefeed character is discarded.
- inherit is a keyword that indicates that this property takes the same computed value as its parent.

Note

- This property is in the miscellaneous category.

Related Properties

baseline-shift (p. 388), block-progression-dimension (p. 390), clip (p. 440), color (p. 441), direction (p. 453), font-height-override-after (p. 484), font-height-override-before (p. 485), glyph-orientation-horizontal (p. 512), glyph-orientation-vertical (p. 513), height (p. 514), href (p. 515), hyphenation-keep (p. 517), hyphenation-ladder-count (p. 518), id (p. 521), inline-progression-dimension (p. 525), last-line-end-indent (p. 531), line-height (p. 538), line-height-shift-adjustment (p. 539), line-stacking-strategy (p. 540), max-height (p. 548), max-width (p. 550), min-height (p. 552), min-width (p. 553), overflow (p. 561), provisional-distance-between-starts (p. 586), provisional-label-separation (p. 587), reference-orientation (p. 588), ref-id (p. 589), scaling (p. 601), score-spaces (p. 602), size (p. 605), space-treatment (p. 611), span (p. 612), text-align (p. 625), text-align-last (p. 626), text-indent (p. 629), unicode-bidi (p. 634), vertical-align (p. 635), visibility (p. 636), white-space (p. 639), white-space-collapse (p. 640), width (p. 642), wrap-option (p. 644), writing-mode (p. 645), z-index (p. 648)

Related Formatting Object

fo:block (p. 466)

line-height	**Baseline Height**

Purpose
Specifies the height of the text line from baseline to baseline.

Syntax
```
line-height: normal|number|length|percent
|(space.minimum=npt, .optimum=npt, .maximum=npt,
|inherit
```

Where
- normal is a keyword that indicates the parent element's line height. The suggested numeric value for normal should range between 1.0 and 1.2.
- *number* is a number by which the current font size is multiplied to result in a new line height.
- *length* is a positive value followed by a two-letter abbreviation representing the unit of measure.
- *percent* is a positive value that is relative to the size of the line height. Follow *percent* with a percentage sign (%).
- space is a keyword that indicates that a sub-keyword — minimum, optimum, or maximum — follows. This is an XSL-only value.
- minimum is a keyword that precedes the minimum amount of line-height space to be set. This is an XSL-only value.
- optimum is a keyword that precedes the ideal amount of line-height space to be set. This is an XSL-only value.
- maximum is a keyword that precedes the maximum amount of line-height space to be set. This is an XSL-only value.
- inherit is a keyword that indicates that this property takes the same computed value as its parent.

Notes
- This property is in the miscellaneous category.
- This property originated in CSS1.
- Negative values are not valid.
- By default, the characteristics of this property are inherited.

Example
```
span { line-height: 110%; font-size: 12pt }
```

Related Properties
baseline-shift (p. 388), block-progression-dimension (p. 390), clip (p. 440), color (p. 441), direction (p. 453), font-height-override-after (p. 484), font-height-override-before (p. 485), glyph-orientation-horizontal (p. 512), glyph-orientation-vertical (p. 513), height (p. 514), href (p. 515), hyphenation-keep (p. 517), hyphenation-ladder-count (p. 518), id (p. 521), inline-progression-dimension (p. 525), last-line-end-indent (p. 531), linefeed-treatment (p. 537), line-height-shift-adjustment (p. 539),

line-stacking-strategy (p. 540), max-height (p. 548), max-width (p. 550), min-height (p. 552), min-width (p. 553), overflow (p. 561), provisional-distance-between-starts (p. 586), provisional-label-separation (p. 587), reference-orientation (p. 588), ref-id (p. 589), scaling (p. 611), score-spaces (p. 602), size (p. 605), space-treatment (p. 611), span (p. 612), text-align (p. 625), text-align-last (p. 626), text-indent (p. 629), unicode-bidi (p. 634), vertical-align (p. 635), visibility (p. 636), white-space (p. 639), white-space-collapse (p. 640), width (p. 642), wrap-option (p. 644), writing-mode (p. 645), z-index (p. 648)

Related Formatting Objects

fo:bidi-override (p. 465), fo:block (p. 466),fo:external-graphic (p. 470), fo:footnote-body (p. 472), fo:initial-property-set (p. 473), fo:inline (p. 473), fo:inline-container (p. 474), fo:instream-foreign-object (p. 475), fo:leader (p. 476), fo:page-number (p. 492), fo:page-number-citation (p. 492), fo:simple-link (p. 500)

line-height-shift-adjustment | Line Height Shift Adjustment?

Purpose

Indicates whether line height is modified for subscript or superscript characters.

Syntax

```
line-height-shift-adjustment: consider-shifts
|disregard-shifts|inherit
```

Where

- consider-shifts is a keyword that indicates that this property allows the shifting of the baseline for subscript and superscript characters to determine the calculation of line height.
- disregard-shifts is a keyword that indicates that this property calculates line height based on standard baseline-based characters only — not subscript and superscript characters.
- inherit is a keyword that indicates that this property takes the same computed value as its parent.

Notes

- This property is in the miscellaneous category.
- This property controls the spacing between lines of characters.
- By default, the characteristics of this property are inherited.

Related Properties

baseline-shift (p. 388), block-progression-dimension (p. 390), clip (p. 440), color (p. 441), direction (p. 453), font-height-override-after (p. 484), font-height-override-before (p. 485), glyph-orientation-horizontal (p. 512), glyph-orientation-vertical (p. 513), height (p. 514), href (p. 515), hyphenation-keep (p. 517), hyphenation-ladder-count (p. 518), id (p. 521), in-line-progression-dimension (p. 525), last-line-end-indent (p. 531), linefeed-treatment (p. 537), line-height (p. 538), line-stacking-strategy (p. 540), max-height (p. 548), max-width (p. 550), min-height (p. 552), min-width (p. 553), overflow (p. 561), provisional-distance-between-starts (p. 586), provisional-label-separation (p. 587), reference-orientation (p. 588), ref-id (p. 589), scaling (p. 601), score-spaces (p. 602), size (p. 605), space-treatment (p. 611), span (p. 612), text-align (p. 625), text-align-last (p. 626), text-indent (p. 629), unicode-bidi (p. 634), vertical-align (p. 635), visibility (p. 636), white-space (p. 639), white-space-collapse (p. 640), width (p. 642), wrap-option (p. 644), writing-mode (p. 645), z-index (p. 648)

Related Formatting Objects

fo:bidi-override (p. 465), fo:block (p. 466),fo:external-graphic (p. 470), fo:footnote-body (p. 472), fo:initial-property-set (p. 473), fo:inline (p. 473), fo:inline-container (p. 474), fo:instream-foreign-object (p. 475), fo:leader (p. 476), fo:page-number (p. 492), fo:page-number-citation (p. 492), fo:simple-link (p. 500)

line-stacking-strategy   Line Stacking Strategy

Purpose

Determines how contiguous lines are positioned in relationship to each other.

Syntax

```
line-stacking-strategy: line-height|font-height
  |max-height|inherit
```

Where

- line-height is a keyword that indicates that this property uses the specified line height and line positioning characteristics. This is the default.
- font-height is a keyword that indicates this property uses the font height characteristics and factors in the value of the font-height-override-after (p. 484) and font-height-override-before (p. 485) properties.
- max-height is a keyword that indicates that this property uses the vertical measurements of characters on the current line and factors in the value of the line-height-shift-adjustment (p. 539) property.
- inherit is a keyword that indicates that this property takes the same computed value as its parent.

Notes

- This property is in the miscellaneous category.
- By default, the characteristics of this property are inherited.

Related Properties

`baseline-shift` (p. 388), `block-progression-dimension` (p. 390), `clip` (p. 440), `color` (p. 441), `direction` (p. 453), `font-height-override-after` (p. 484), `font-height-override-before` (p. 485), `glyph-orientation-horizontal` (p. 512), `glyph-orientation-vertical` (p. 513), `height` (p. 514), `href` (p. 515), `hyphenation-keep` (p. 517), `hyphenation-ladder-count` (p. 518), `id` (p. 521), `in-line-progression-dimension` (p. 525), `last-line-end-indent` (p. 531), `linefeed-treatment` (p. 537), `line-height` (p. 538), `line-height-shift-adjustment` (p. 539), `max-height` (p. 548), `max-width` (p. 550), `min-height` (p. 552), `min-width` (p. 553), `overflow` (p. 561), `provisional-distance-between-starts` (p. 586), `provisional-label-separation` (p. 587), `reference-orientation` (p. 588), `ref-id` (p. 589), `scaling` (p. 601), `score-spaces` (p. 602), `size` (p. 605), `space-treatment` (p. 611), `span` (p. 612), `text-align` (p. 625), `text-align-last` (p. 626), `text-indent` (p. 629), `unicode-bidi` (p. 634), `vertical-align` (p. 635), `visibility` (p. 636), `white-space` (p. 639), `white-space-collapse` (p. 640), `width` (p. 642), `wrap-option` (p. 644), `writing-mode` (p. 645), `z-index` (p. 648)

Related Formatting Object

`fo:block` (p. 466)

Literal [20]   Literal

Purpose

Represents a *literal*, a string within quotation marks or single quote marks.

EBNF Syntax

```
Literal ::= '"' [^"]* '"' | "'" [^']* "'"
```

Standard Syntax

```
{"|'}literal{"|'}
```

Where

- `literal` represents a literal, a string within quotation marks or single quote marks.

Notes

- Literal is a component of the `ExprToken` and `PrimaryExpr` productions.
- Literal represents part of an expression.
- If you enclose a string within single quote marks, do not use single quote marks within the quoted object; if you enclose a string within quotation marks, do not use quotation marks within the quoted object. Within character data, you can use the apostrophe (') or quotation mark (") characters to indicate quote marks.
- If a quotation mark is included in a string, enclose the string within single quote marks; if a single quote mark is included in a string, enclose the string within quotation marks.

- Do not mix single quote marks and quotation marks; the quote marks at the beginning and end of a quoted object must match.

Related XPath Productions

AbsoluteUnitName (p. 372), AlphaOrDigits (p. 376), Color (p. 443), Digits (p. 452), EnumerationToken (p. 459), ExprToken (p. 460), ExprWhitespace (p. 461), FloatingPointNumber (p. 463), FunctionName (p. 512), Keyword (p. 529), MultiplyOperator (p. 555), Number (p. 555), Operator (p. 559), OperatorName (p. 560), RelativeUnitName (p. 593)

margin	Margins Characteristics

Purpose

Turns on or off one, two, three, or four margins or sets margin size of a box.

Syntax

```
margin: ([length_top|percent_top%|auto]
   [length_right|percent_right%|auto]
   [length_bottom|percent_bottom%|auto]
   [length_left|percent_left%|auto])|inherit
```

Where

- *length_top*, *length_right*, *length_bottom*, and *length_left* are positive or negative fixed values followed by a two-letter abbreviation representing the unit of measure.
- *percent_top*, *percent_right*, *percent_bottom*, and *percent_left* are positive values that are relative to the parent element's selected margins. Follow *percent* with a percentage sign (%).
- auto represents top-margin, right-margin, bottom-margin, and left-margin values automatically calculated by the user's browser.
- inherit is a keyword that indicates that this property takes the same computed value as its parent.

Notes

- This property is in the common-margins-block category.
- This property, which originated in CSS1, applies to all elements.
- Shortcut properties should be processed as follows: Set the "embedded" properties to their initial values; if the characteristics of the shortcut property are inherited, each "embedded" property should take the same computed value as its parent; if the characteristics of the shortcut property are not inherited, set each value; then the value of shorthand property overrides the counterpart value of the individual property.
- By default, the characteristics of this property are not inherited.

Example

```
bigpage {margin: 1in 1in 0.5in}
```

Related Properties

end-indent (p. 457), margin-bottom (p. 543), margin-left (p. 534), margin-right (p. 545), margin-top (p. 546), space-after (p. 607), space-before (p. 608), start-indent (p. 618)

Related Formatting Objects

fo:block (p. 466), fo:block-container (p. 467), fo:external-graphic (p. 470), fo:float (p. 471), fo:footnote (p. 472), fo:footnote-body (p. 472), fo:inline (p. 473), fo:inline-container (p. 474), fo:instream-foreign-object (p. 475), fo:leader (p. 476), fo:list-block (p. 477), fo:list-item (p. 478), fo:page-number (p. 492), fo:page-number-citation (p. 492), fo:region-body (p. 496), fo:simple-link (p. 500), fo:simple-page-master (p. 501), fo:table (p. 503), fo:table-and-caption (p. 504)

margin-bottom   Bottom Margin

Purpose

Turns on or off bottom margin and/or specifies bottom-margin size of a box.

Syntax

margin-bottom: 0|*length*|*percent*%|auto|inherit

Where

- 0 represents the parent element's current bottom margin. This is the default.
- *length* is a positive or negative value followed by a two-letter abbreviation representing the unit of measure.
- *percent* is a positive value that is relative to the parent element's bottom margin. Follow *percent* with a percentage sign (%).
- auto is a keyword that represents a value automatically calculated by the user's browser.
- inherit is a keyword that indicates that this property takes the same computed value as its parent.

Notes

- This property is in the common-margins-block category.
- This property, which originated in CSS1, applies to all elements.
- By default, the characteristics of this property are not inherited.

Example

bigpage { margin-bottom: 18pt }

Related Properties

end-indent (p. 457), margin (p. 542), margin-left (p. 544), margin-right (p. 545), margin-top (p. 546), space-after p. 607), space-before (p. 608), start-indent (p. 618)

Related Formatting Objects

fo:block (p. 466), fo:block-container (p. 467), fo:external-graphic
(p. 470), fo:float (p. 471), fo:footnote (p. 472), fo:footnote-body (p. 472),
fo:inline (p. 473), fo:inline-container (p. 474), fo:instream-foreign-ob-
ject (p. 475), fo:leader (p. 476), fo:list-block (p. 477), fo:list-item
(p. 478), fo:page-number (p. 492), fo:page-number-citation (p. 492), fo:re-
gion-body (p. 496), fo:simple-link (p. 500), fo:simple-page-master (p. 501),
fo:table (p. 503), fo:table-and-caption (p. 504)

margin-left   Left Margin

Purpose

Turns on or off left margins or sets left-margin size of a box.

Syntax

    margin-left: 0pt|*length*|*percent*%|auto|inherit

Where

- 0pt represents the parent element's current left margin, in points. This
  is the default.
- *percent* is a positive value that is relative to the parent element's left
  margin. Follow *percent* with a percentage sign (%).
- *length* is a positive or negative value followed by a two-letter abbreviation representing the unit of measure.
- auto is a keyword that represents a value automatically calculated by
  the user's browser.
- inherit is a keyword that indicates that this property takes the same
  computed value as its parent.

Notes

- This property is in the common-margins-block category.
- This property, which originated in CSS1, applies to all elements.
- By default, the characteristics of this property are not inherited.

Example

    bigpage { margin-right: 0.5in; margin-top: 1.0in;
    margin-bottom: 1.0in; margin-left: 0.5in }

Related Properties

end-indent (p. 457), margin (p. 542), margin-bottom (p. 543), margin-right
(p. 545), margin-top (p. 546), space-after p. 607), space-before (p. 608),
start-indent (p. 618)

Related Formatting Objects

fo:block (p. 466), fo:block-container (p. 467), fo:external-graphic (p.
470), fo:float (p. 471), fo:footnote (p. 472), fo:footnote-body (p. 472),

fo:inline (p. 473), fo:inline-container (p. 474), fo:instream-foreign-object (p. 475), fo:leader (p. 476), fo:list-block (p. 477), fo:list-item (p. 478), fo:page-number (p. 492), fo:page-number-citation (p. 492), fo:region-body (p. 496), fo:simple-link (p. 500), fo:simple-page-master (p. 501), fo:table (p. 503), fo:table-and-caption (p. 504)

margin-right	Right Margin

Purpose
Turns on or off the right margin and/or sets the right-margin size of a box.

Syntax
margin-right: 0pt|*length*|*percent*%|auto|inherit

Where
- 0 represents the parent element's current right margin, in points. This is the default.
- *percent* is a positive value that is relative to the parent element's right margin. Follow *percent* with a percentage sign (%).
- *length* is a positive or negative value followed by a two-letter abbreviation representing the unit of measure.
- auto is a keyword that represents a value automatically calculated by the user's browser.
- inherit is a keyword that indicates that this property takes the same computed value as its parent.

Notes
- This property is in the common-margins-block category.
- This property, which originated in CSS1, applies to all elements.
- By default, the characteristics of this property are not inherited.

Example
body { margin-right: 18pt; margin-top: 36pt
; margin-bottom: 18pt; margin-left: 18pt }

Related Properties
end-indent (p. 457), margin (p. 542), margin-bottom (p. 543), margin-left (p. 544), margin-top (p. 546), space-after p. 607), space-before (p. 608), start-indent (p. 618)

Related Formatting Objects
fo:block (p. 466), fo:block-container (p. 467), fo:external-graphic (p. 470), fo:float (p. 471), fo:footnote (p. 472), fo:footnote-body (p. 472), fo:inline (p. 473), fo:inline-container (p. 474), fo:instream-foreign-object (p. 475), fo:leader (p. 476), fo:list-block (p. 477), fo:list-item (p. 478), fo:page-number (p. 492), fo:page-number-citation (p. 492), fo:region-body (p. 496),

fo:simple-link (p. 500), fo:simple-page-master (p. 501), fo:table (p. 503),
fo:table-and-caption (p. 504)

margin-top	Top Margin

Purpose
Turns on or off top margins or sets top-margin size of a box.

Syntax
margin-top: <u>0</u>|*length*|*percent*%|auto|inherit

Where
- 0 represents the parent element's current top margin. This is the default.
- *percent* is a positive value that is relative to the parent element's top margin. Follow *percent* with a percentage sign (%).
- *length* is a positive or negative value followed by a two-letter abbreviation representing the unit of measure.
- auto is a keyword that represents a value automatically calculated by the user's browser.
- inherit is a keyword that indicates that this property takes the same computed value as its parent.

Notes
- This property is in the common-margins-block category.
- This property, which originated in CSS1, applies to all elements.
- By default, the characteristics of this property are not inherited.

Example
body { margin-top: 36pt }

Related Properties
end-indent (p. 457), margin (p. 542), margin-bottom (p. 543), margin-left (p. 544), margin-right (p. 545), space-after (p. 607), space-before (p. 608), start-indent (p. 618)

Related Formatting Objects
fo:block (p. 466), fo:block-container (p. 467), fo:external-graphic (p. 470), fo:float (p. 471), fo:footnote (p. 472), fo:footnote-body (p. 472), fo:inline (p. 473), fo:inline-container (p. 474), fo:instream-foreign-object (p. 475), fo:leader (p. 476), fo:list-block (p. 477), fo:list-item (p. 478), fo:page-number (p. 492), fo:page-number-citation (p. 492), fo:region-body (p. 496), fo:simple-link (p. 500), fo:simple-page-master (p. 501), fo:table (p. 503), fo:table-and-caption (p. 504)

marker-class-name · Marker Class Name

Purpose

Identifies the group name for multiple `fo:marker` formatting objects.

Syntax

```
marker-class-name: name
```

Where

- *name* specifies the `marker-class-name`.

Notes

- If *name* is empty or conflicting, an error will be reported and processing will continue.
- Each `fo:marker` within a group becomes a candidate to be retrieved by an `fo:retrieve-marker` that has the same `retrieve-class-name` as the `fo:marker marker-class-name`.

Related Properties

retrieve-boundary (p. 594), retrieve-class-name (p. 595), retrieve-position (p. 583)

master-name · Master Name

Purpose

Names the current page-master.

Syntax

```
master-name: master_name|inherit
```

Where

- *master_name* is the unique name of the current master.
- `inherit` is a keyword that indicates that this property takes the same computed value as its parent.

Notes

- This property is in the pagination-and-layout category.
- A master name cannot be empty.
- This property applies to the `fo:conditional-page-master-reference`, `fo:repeatable-page-master-reference`, `fo:simple-page-master`, and `fo:single-page-master-reference` formatting objects.
- By default, the characteristics of this property are not inherited.

Related Properties

blank-or-not-blank (p. 389), column-count (p. 444), column-gap (p. 444), extent (p. 461), flow-name (p. 465), force-page-count (p. 494), initial-page-number (p. 524), maximum-repeats (p. 549), odd-or-even (p. 559), page-height

XSL Style Sheet Syntax

(p. 575), page-position (p. 575), page-width (p. 576), precedence (p. 584), region-name (p. 590)

Related Formatting Objects

fo:conditional-page-master-reference (p. 469), fo:page-sequence (p. 493), fo:page-sequence-master (p. 494), fo:repeatable-page-master-reference (p. 499), fo:simple-page-master (p. 501), fo:single-page-master-reference (p. 502)

max()   Maximum Function

Purpose

Returns the maximum of two numeric arguments.

EBNF Syntax

    number_r max(number_1 , number_2)

Standard Syntax

    number_r max(number_1 , number_2)

Where

- *number_r* is the number returned by the function.
- max is a function-name keyword.
- *number_1* represents the first argument's number.
- *number_2* represents the second argument's number.

Related Productions

abs() (p. 370), ceiling() (p. 439), floor() (p. 464), min() (p. 552), round() (p. 599)

max-height   Maximum Element Height

Purpose

Specifies the maximum height of the selected element.

Syntax

    max-height: length|percent%|none|inherit

Where

- *length* is a positive value followed by a two-letter abbreviation representing the unit of measure.
- *percent* is a positive value that is relative to the size of the image. Follow *percent* with a percentage sign (%).
- none is a keyword that indicates that there is no maximum height. This is the default.

XSL Style Sheet Syntax

- inherit is a keyword that indicates that this property takes the same computed value as its parent.

Notes
- This property is in the miscellaneous category.
- This property originated in CSS2.
- By default, the characteristics of this property are not inherited.

Related Properties
baseline-shift (p. 388), block-progression-dimension (p. 390), clip (p. 440), color (p. 441), direction (p. 453), font-height-override-after (p. 484), font-height-override-before (p. 485), glyph-orientation-horizontal (p. 512), glyph-orientation-vertical (p. 513), height (p. 514), href (p. 515), hyphenation-keep (p. 517), hyphenation-ladder-count (p. 518), id (p. 521), inline-progression-dimension (p. 525), last-line-end-indent (p. 531), linefeed-treatment (p. 537), line-height (p. 538), line-height-shift-adjustment (p. 539), line-stacking-strategy (p. 540), max-width (p. 550), min-height (p. 552), min-width (p. 553), overflow (p. 561), provisional-distance-between-starts (p. 586), provisional-label-separation (p. 587), reference-orientation (p. 588), ref-id (p. 589), scaling (p. 601), score-spaces (p. 602), size (p. 605), space-treatment (p. 611), span (p. 612), text-align (p. 625), text-align-last (p. 626), text-indent (p. 629), unicode-bidi (p. 634), vertical-align (p. 635), visibility (p. 636), white-space (p. 639), white-space-collapse (p. 640), width (p. 642), wrap-option (p. 644), writing-mode (p. 645), z-index (p. 648)

Related Formatting Objects
fo:external-graphic (p. 470), fo:float (p. 471), fo:footnote (p. 472), fo:instream-foreign-object (p. 475)

maximum-repeats   Maximum Repeats

Purpose
Limits the number of pages in a page sequence within another page sequence.

Syntax
```
maximum-repeats: integer|no-limit|inherit
```

Where
- integer indicates the minimum number of pages in a page sequence within a page sequence.
- no-limit is a keyword that indicates that there is no limit to the number of pages in a page sequence within another page sequence.
- inherit is a keyword that indicates that this property takes the same computed value as its parent.

Notes

- This property is in the pagination-and-layout category.
- If *integer* is negative or not an integer, the processor rounds the number to the closest integer greater than zero.
- If *integer* equals 0 and maximum-repeats applies to fo:repeatable-page-master-reference, maximum-repeats is ignored.
- By default, characteristics of this property are not inherited.

Related Properties

blank-or-not-blank (p. 389), column-count (p. 444), column-gap (p. 444), extent (p. 461), flow-name (p. 465), force-page-count (p. 494), initial-page-number (p. 524), master-name (p. 547), odd-or-even (p. 559), page-height (p. 575), page-position (p. 575), page-width (p. 576), precedence (p. 584), region-name (p. 590)

Related Formatting Objects

fo:repeatable-page-master-alternatives (p. 498), fo:repeatable-page-master-reference (p. 499)

---

max-width · Maximum Element Width

Purpose

Specifies the maximum width of the selected element.

Syntax

```
max-width: length|percent%|none|inherit
```

Where

- *length* is a positive value followed by a two-letter abbreviation representing the unit of measure.
- *percent* is a positive value that is relative to the size of the image. Follow *percent* with a percentage sign (%).
- none is a keyword that indicates that there is no maximum width. This is the default.
- inherit is a keyword that indicates that this property takes the same computed value as its parent.

Notes

- This property is in the miscellaneous category.
- This property originated in CSS2.
- By default, the characteristics of this property are not inherited.

Related Properties

baseline-shift (p. 388), block-progression-dimension (p. 390), clip (p. 440), color (p. 441), direction (p. 453), font-height-override-after (p. 484), font-height-override-before (p. 485), glyph-orientation-horizontal (p. 512), glyph-orientation-vertical (p. 513), height (p. 514),

href (p. 515), hyphenation-keep (p. 517), hyphenation-ladder-count
(p. 518), id (p. 521), inline-progression-dimension (p. 525),
last-line-end-indent (p. 531), linefeed-treatment (p. 537),
line-height (p. 538), line-height-shift-adjustment (p. 539),
line-stacking-strategy (p. 340), max-height (p. 548), min-height
(p. 552), min-width (p. 553), overflow (p. 561), provisional-distance-between-starts (p. 586), provisional-label-separation (p. 587),
reference-orientation (p. 588), ref-id (p. 589), scaling (p. 601),
score-spaces (p. 602), size (p. 605), space-treatment (p. 611), span
(p. 612), text-align (p. 625), text-align-last (p. 626), text-indent
(p. 626), unicode-bidi (p. 634), vertical-align (p. 635), visibility
(p. 636), white-space (p. 639), white-space-collapse (p. 640), width
(p. 642), wrap-option (p. 644), writing-mode (p. 645), z-index (p. 648)

Related Formatting Object
fo:instream-foreign-object (p. 475)

merge-property-values() Merge Property Values

Purpose
Returns a value of the property whose name matches the argument.

EBNF Syntax
object merge-property-values(NCName)

Standard Syntax
object merge-property-values(*NCName*)

Where
- object is the value returned by the function.
- merge-property-values is a function-named keyword.
- *NCName* is the name of the property whose value we want.

Notes
- The value returned is that of the last fo:multiple-property-set. If no value exists, then the value of the parent fo:multi-properties is returned.
- If this function is used on any other formatting objects other than an fo:wrapper within an fo:multi-properties than it will cause an error.

Related Functions
body-start() (p. 391), from-nearest-specified-value() (p. 509),
from-parent() (p. 510), from-table-column() (p. 510), inherited-property-
value() (p. 523), label-end() (p. 530), proportional-column-width() (p. 585)

XSL Style Sheet Syntax

min() — Minimum Function

Purpose
Returns the minimum of two numeric arguments.

EBNF Syntax
```
number_r min(number_1 , number_2)
```

Standard Syntax
```
number_r min(number_1 , number_2)
```

Where
- *number_r* is the number returned by the function.
- min is a function-name keyword.
- *number_1* represents the first argument's number.
- *number_2* represents the second argument's number.

Related Productions
abs() (p. 370), ceiling() (p. 439), floor() (p. 464), max() (p. 548), round() (p. 599)

min-height — Minimum Element Height

Purpose
Specifies the minimum height of the selected element.

Syntax
```
min-width: length|percent%|inherit
```

Where
- *length* is a positive value followed by a two-letter abbreviation representing the unit of measure.
- *percent* is a positive value that is relative to the size of the image. Follow *percent* with a percentage sign (%).
- inherit is a keyword that indicates that this property takes the same computed value as its parent.

Notes
- This property is in the miscellaneous category.
- This property originated in CSS2.
- By default, the characteristics of this property are not inherited.

Related Properties
baseline-shift (p. 388), block-progression-dimension (p. 390), clip (p. 440), color (p. 441), direction (p. 453), font-height-override-after (p. 484), font-height-override-before (p. 485), glyph-orientation-horizontal (p. 512),

glyph-orientation-vertical (p. 513), height (p. 514), href (p. 515), hyphenation-keep (p. 517), hyphenation-ladder-count (p. 518), id (p. 521), inline-progression-dimension (p. 525), last-line-end-indent (p. 531), linefeed-treatment (p. 537), line-height (p. 538), line-height-shift-adjustment (p. 539), line-stacking-strategy (p. 540), max-height (p. 548), max-width (p. 550), min-width (p. 553), overflow (p. 561), provisional-distance-between-starts (p. 586), provisional-label-separation (p. 587), reference-orientation (p. 588), ref-id (p. 589), scaling (p. 601), score-spaces (p. 602), size (p. 605), space-treatment (p. 611), span (p. 612), text-align (p. 625), text-align-last (p. 626), text-indent (p. 629), unicode-bidi (p. 634), vertical-align (p. 635), visibility (p. 636), white-space (p. 639), white-space-collapse (p. 640), width (p. 642), wrap-option (p. 644), writing-mode (p. 645), z-index (p. 648)

Related Formatting Objects

fo:external-graphic (p. 470), fo:instream-foreign-object (p. 475)

min-width | Minimum Element Width

Purpose

Specifies the minimum width of the selected element.

Syntax

min-width: *length*|*percent*%|inherit

Where

- *length* is a positive value followed by a two-letter abbreviation representing the unit of measure.
- *percent* is a positive value that is relative to the size of the box. Follow *percent* with a percentage sign (%).
- inherit is a keyword that indicates that this property takes the same computed value as its parent.

Notes

- This property is in the miscellaneous category.
- This property originated in CSS2.
- By default, the characteristics of this property are not inherited.

Related Properties

baseline-shift (p. 388), block-progression-dimension (p. 390), clip (p. 440), color (p. 441), direction (p. 453), font-height-override-after (p. 484), font-height-override-before (p. 485), glyph-orientation-horizontal (p. 512), glyph-orientation-vertical (p. 513), height (p. 514), href (p. 515), hyphenation-keep (p. 517), hyphenation-ladder-count (p. 518), id (p. 521), inline-progression-dimension (p. 525), last-line-end-indent (p. 531), linefeed-treatment (p. 537), line-height (p. 538), line-height-shift-adjustment (p. 539), line-stacking-strategy (p. 540), max-height (p. 548), max-width (p. 560), min-height (p. 552), overflow (p. 561), provisional-distance-between-starts (p. 586), provisional-label-separation (p. 587), reference-orientation (p. 588), ref-id (p. 589), scaling (p. 601), score-spaces (p. 602), size (p. 605), space-treatment (p. 611), span (p. 612), text-align (p. 625), text-align-last (p. 626), text-indent (p. 629), unicode-bidi (p. 634), vertical-align (p. 635), visibility (p. 636), white-space (p. 639), white-space-collapse (p. 640), width (p. 642), wrap-option (p. 644), writing-mode (p. 645), z-index (p. 648)

Related Formatting Objects

fo:external-graphic (p. 470), fo:instream-foreign-object (p. 475)

MultiplicativeExpr [12]　　　Multiplicative Expression

Purpose

Acts on one or more expressions through multiplication, division, or finding a modulus.

EBNF Syntax

```
MultiplicativeExpr ::= UnaryExpr
  | MultiplicativeExpr MultiplyOperator UnaryExpr
  | MultiplicativeExpr 'div' UnaryExpr
  | MultiplicativeExpr 'mod' UnaryExpr
```

Standard Syntax

```
UnaryExpr
  | MultiplicativeExpr MultiplyOperator UnaryExpr
  | MultiplicativeExpr div UnaryExpr
  | MultiplicativeExpr mod UnaryExpr
```

Where

- UnaryExpr (p. 633) negates an expression.
- MultiplyOperator (p. 555) inserts a * multiplication operator.
- div is a reserved keyword that represents the division operator.
- mod is a reserved keyword that represents the modulus operator.

Notes

- MultiplicativeExpr is a component of the AdditiveExpr.
- MultiplicativeExpr is identical to the XPath MultiplicativeExpr.
- The div operator performs floating-point division as defined in IEEE 754.
- The mod operator is the same as the % operator in Java, JavaScript, and ECMAScript; its result is the remainder from a shortened division (for example, 7 mod 3 returns 1).

Related Productions

AdditiveExpr (p. 374), MultiplicativeExpr (p. 554), MultiplyOperator
(p. 555), UnaryExpr (p. 633)

MultiplyOperator [23]　　　　　　　　　　　　Multiply Operator

Purpose
Inserts a multiply operator.

EBNF Syntax

```
MultiplyOperator ::= '*'
```

Standard Syntax

```
*
```

Where
- * is a character that indicates multiplication.

Notes
- MultiplyOperator is a component of the MultiplicativeExpr and
  Operator productions.
- MultiplyOperator represents part of an expression.

Related XPath Productions

AbsoluteUnitName (p. 372), AlphaOrDigits (p. 376), Color (p. 443), Digits
(p. 452), EnumerationToken (p. 459), ExprToken (p. 460), ExprWhitespace
(p. 461), FloatingPointNumber (p. 463), FunctionName (p. 512), Keyword (p. 529),
Literal (p. 541), Number (p. 555), Operator (p. 559), OperatorName (p. 560),
RelativeUnitName (p. 593)

Number [15]　　　　　　　　　　　　　　　　　　Number

Purpose
Represents a floating-point number made up of one or more digits.

EBNF Syntax

```
Number ::= FloatingPointNumber
```

Standard Syntax

```
FloatingPointNumber
```

Where
- FloatingPointNumber (p. 463) represents a floating-point number.
- . is a character that represents a decimal point.

Notes

- Number is a component of the ExprToken and PrimaryExpr productions.
- Number represents part of an expression.
- According to the XPath recommendation (http://www.w3.org/TR/xpath), a "number can have any double-precision 64-bit format IEEE 754 value. These include a special 'Not-a-Number' value, positive and negative infinity, and positive and negative zero."
- Not-a-Number is also known as NaN.

Related Productions

AbsoluteUnitName (p. 372), AlphaOrDigits (p. 376), Color (p. 443), Digits (p. 452), EnumerationToken (p. 459), ExprToken (p. 460), ExprWhitespace (p. 461), FloatingPointNumber (p. 463), FunctionName (p. 512), Keyword (p. 529), Literal (p. 541), MultiplyOperator (p. 555), Operator (p. 559), OperatorName (p. 560), RelativeUnitName (p. 593)

number-columns-repeated — Number of Columns Repeated

Purpose

Sets the number of times the table-column property is repeated.

Syntax

```
number-columns-repeated: integer
```

Where

- integer is a positive, non-zero number indicating the columns spanned. The default value is 1.

Notes

- This property is in the table category.
- If integer is negative or not an integer, the processor rounds the number to the closest integer greater than zero.
- This property manages the HTML COLGROUP element.
- By default, characteristics of this property are not inherited.

Related Properties

border-collapse (p. 405), border-spacing (p. 422), caption-side (p. 437), column-number (p. 445), column-width (p. 446), empty-cells (p. 457), ends-row (p. 458), number-columns-spanned (p. 557), number-rows-spanned (p. 557), starts-row (p. 619), table-layout (p. 623), table-omit-footer-at-break (p. 624), table-omit-header-at-break (p. 624)

Related Formatting Object

fo:table-column (p. 506)

number-columns-spanned   Number of Spanned Columns

Purpose
Sets the number of columns spanned by one or more table cells.

Syntax
    number-columns-spanned: integer

Where
- *integer* is a positive, non-zero number indicating the columns spanned. The default value is 1.

Notes
- This property is in the table category.
- If *integer* is negative or not an integer, the processor rounds the number to the closest integer greater than zero.
- For the fo:table-column formatting object, number-columns-spanned indicates the number of columns that will inherit column attributes.
- For the fo:table-cell formatting object, number-columns-spanned indicates the number of columns spanned.
- By default, characteristics of this property are not inherited.

Related Properties
border-collapse (p. 405), border-spacing (p. 422), caption-side (p. 437), column-number (p. 445), column-width (p. 446), empty-cells (p. 457), ends-row (p. 458), number-columns-repeated (p. 556), number-rows-spanned (p. 557), starts-row (p. 619), table-layout (p. 623), table-omit-footer-at-break (p. 624), table-omit-header-at-break (p. 624)

Related Formatting Objects
fo:table-cell (p. 505), fo:table-column (p. 506)

number-rows-spanned   Number of Spanned Rows

Purpose
Sets the number of rows spanned by one or more table cells.

Syntax
    number-rows-spanned: integer

Where
- *integer* is a positive, non-zero number indicating the columns spanned. The default value is 1.

Notes
- This property is in the table category.

- If *integer* is negative or not an integer, the processor rounds the number to the closest integer greater than zero.
- For the fo:table-cell formatting object, number-rows-spanned indicates the number of rows spanned.
- By default, characteristics of this property are not inherited.

Related Properties

border-collapse (p. 405), border-spacing (p. 422), caption-side (p. 437), column-number (p. 445), column-width (p. 446), empty-cells (p. 457), ends-row (p. 458), number-columns-repeated (p. 556), number-columns-spanned (p. 557), starts-row (p. 619), table-layout (p. 623), table-omit-footer-at-break (p. 624), table-omit-header-at-break (p. 624)

Related Formatting Object

fo:table-cell (p. 505)

Numeric [5]   Expression Number

Purpose

Represents an absolute or relative floating-point number in an expression.

EBNF Syntax

    Numeric ::= AbsoluteNumeric | RelativeNumeric

Standard Syntax

    AbsoluteNumeric | RelativeNumeric

Where

- AbsoluteNumeric (p. 371) represents a number with an absolute value.
- RelativeNumeric (p. 593) represents a number with a value relative to one or more other values.

Notes

- Numeric is related to the XPath Number production.
- According to the XPath recommendation (http://www.w3.org/TR/xpath), a "number can have any double-precision 64-bit format IEEE 754 value. These include a special 'Not-a-Number' value, positive and negative infinity, and positive and negative zero."
- Not-a-Number is also known as NaN.

Related Productions

AbsoluteNumeric (p. 371), Number (p. 555), RelativeNumeric (p. 558)

odd-or-even   Odd or Even

Purpose
Makes a page-master eligible for selection depending on its odd or even position in the page sequence.

Syntax
```
odd-or-even: odd|even|any|inherit
```

Where
- odd is a keyword that indicates that the page-master can be selected if it is an odd page within the page sequence.
- even is a keyword that indicates that the page-master can be selected if it is an even page within the page sequence.
- any is a keyword that indicates that the page-master can be selected if this page is within the page sequence. This is the default.
- inherit is a keyword that indicates that this property takes the same computed value as its parent.

Notes
- This property is in the pagination-and-layout category.
- This property applies to the fo:conditional-page-master-reference formatting object.
- By default, characteristics of this property are not inherited.

Related Properties
blank-or-not-blank (p. 389), column-count (p. 444), column-gap (p. 444), extent (p. 461), flow-name (p. 465), force-page-count (p. 494), initial-page-number (p. 524), master-name (p. 547), maximum-repeats (p. 549), page-height (p. 575), page-position (p. 595), page-width (p. 576), precedence (p. 584), region-name (p. 590)

Related Formatting Object
fo:conditional-page-master-reference (p. 469)

Operator [21]   Operator

Purpose
Provides a list of mathematical operators.

EBNF Syntax
```
Operator ::= OperatorName | MultiplyOperator
     | '+' | '-'
```

Standard Syntax
```
OperatorName | MultiplyOperator | + | -
```

XSL Style Sheet Syntax

Where

- *OperatorName* (p. 560) names a mathematical or logical operator.
- *MultiplyOperator* (p. 555) inserts a * multiplication operator.
- + is the addition operator.
- – is the subtraction operator.

Notes

- Operator is a component of the ExprToken production.
- Operator represents part of an expression.
- The XPath Operator production also includes logical operators.

Related Productions

AbsoluteUnitName (p. 372), AlphaOrDigits (p. 376), Color (p. 443), Digits (p. 452), EnumerationToken (p. 459), ExprToken (p. 460), ExprWhitespace (p. 461), FloatingPointNumber (p. 463), FunctionName (p. 572), Keyword (p. 529), Literal (p. 541), MultiplyOperator (p. 555), Number (p. 555), OperatorName (p. 560), RelativeUnitName (p. 593)

OperatorName [22]   Operator Name

Purpose

Names a logical or mathematical operator.

EBNF Syntax

```
OperatorName ::= 'mod' | 'div'
```

Standard Syntax

```
mod | div
```

Where

- mod is a reserved keyword that represents the modulus operator.
- div is a reserved keyword that represents the division operator.

Notes

- OperatorName is a component of the Operator production.
- OperatorName represents part of an expression.
- The div operator performs floating-point division.
- The mod operator returns a remainder from a shortened division (for example, 7 mod 3 returns 1.

Related Productions

AbsoluteUnitName (p. 372), AlphaOrDigits (p. 376), Color (p. 443), Digits (p. 452), EnumerationToken (p. 459), ExprToken (p. 460), ExprWhitespace (p. 461), FloatingPointNumber (p. 463), FunctionName (p. 512), Keyword (p. 529), Literal (p. 541), MultiplyOperator (p. 555), Number (p. 555), Operator (p. 559), Relative UnitName (p. 593)

orphans | Orphans Paragraph Breaks

Purpose
Specifies the minimum number of paragraph-lines left at the bottom of a page.

Syntax
```
orphans: integer|inherit
```

Where
- *integer* indicates the minimum paragraph-lines (in the last paragraph on a page) that must remain at the bottom of a page when a page break is inserted within a paragraph. The default setting is 2 lines.
- inherit is a keyword that indicates that this property takes the same computed value as its parent.

Notes
- This property is in the page-related category.
- This property, which originated in CSS2, applies to block-level elements.
- By default, the characteristics of this property are inherited.

Related Properties
keep-together (p. 526), page-break-inside (p. 574), widows (p. 641)

Related Formatting Object
fo:block (p. 466)

overflow | Box Overflow?

Purpose
Specifies whether and how the contents of a box overflow.

Syntax
```
overflow: visible|hidden|scroll|auto|inherit
```

Where
- visible is a keyword that indicates that content can overflow its box. This is the default.
- hidden is a keyword that indicates that content cannot overflow its box; it is clipped.
- scroll is a keyword that indicates that indicates that content cannot overflow its box; it is clipped. A scrollbar always appears in the box.
- auto is a keyword that represents a value automatically calculated by the user's browser.
- inherit is a keyword that indicates that this property takes the same computed value as its parent.

XSL Style Sheet Syntax

Notes

- This property is in the miscellaneous category.
- This property originated in CSS2.
- Some browsers clip content even though overflow is set to visible.
- By default, characteristics of this property are not inherited.

Related Properties

baseline-shift (p. 388), block-progression-dimension (p. 390), clip (p. 440), color (p. 441), direction (p. 453), font-height-override-after (p. 484), font-height-override-before (p. 485), glyph-orientation-horizontal (p. 512), glyph-orientation-vertical (p. 513), height (p. 514), href (p. 515), hyphenation-keep (p. 517), hyphenation-ladder-count (p. 518), id (p. 521), inline-progression-dimension (p. 525), last-line-end-indent (p. 531), linefeed-treatment (p. 537), line-height (p. 538), line-height-shift-adjustment (p. 539), line-stacking-strategy (p. 540), max-height (p. 548), max-width (p. 550), min-height (p. 552), min-width (p. 553), provisional-distance-between-starts (p. 586), provisional-label-separation (p. 587), reference-orientation (p. 588), ref-id (p. 589), scaling (p. 601), score-spaces (p. 602), size (p. 605), space-treatment (p. 611), span (p. 612), text-align (p. 625), text-align-last (p. 626), text-indent (p. 629), unicode-bidi (p. 634), vertical-align (p. 635), visibility (p. 636), white-space (p. 639), white-space-collapse (p. 640), width (p. 642), wrap-option (p. 644), writing-mode (p. 645), z-index (p. 648)

Related Formatting Objects

fo:float (p. 471), fo:footnote (p. 472), fo:inline-container (p. 474), fo:region-after (p. 495), fo:region-before (p. 496), fo:region-body (p. 496), fo:region-end (p. 497), fo:region-start (p. 497)

---

padding	**Padding Characteristics**

Purpose

Turns on or off one, two, three, or four paddings or sets padding size of a box.

Syntax

```
padding: [length_top|percent_top%]
    [length_right|percent_right%]
    [length_bottom|percent_bottom%]
    [length_left|percent_left%]]|inherit
```

Where

- *length_top*, *length_right*, *length_bottom*, and *length_left* are positive fixed values each followed by a two-letter abbreviation representing the unit of measure.

- *percent_top*, *percent_right*, *percent_bottom*, and *percent_left* are positive values that are relative to the parent element's selected paddings. Follow *percent* with a percentage sign (%).
- inherit is a keyword that indicates that this property takes the same computed value as its parent.

Notes

- This property is in the common-border-padding-background category.
- This property, which originated in CSS1, applies to all elements.
- This shortcut property for padding-top, padding-right, padding-bottom, and padding-left (in that order) turns one, two, three, or four paddings on or off, or sets padding size (in the default unit of measure) as a percentage of the current width, or automatically by calculating a minimum amount.
- By default, the characteristics of this property are not inherited.
- Shortcut properties should be processed as follows: Set the "embedded" properties to their initial values; if the characteristics of the shortcut property are inherited, each "embedded" property should take the same computed value as its parent; if the characteristics of the shortcut property are not inherited, set each value; then, the value of shorthand property overrides the counterpart value of the individual property.

Example

```
para.special { padding: 6pt 4pt }
```

Related Properties

background properties (p. 379 – p. 387), border properties (p. 392 – p. 434), padding-after (p. 564), padding-before (p. 564), padding-bottom (p. 566), padding-end (p. 567), padding-left (p. 568), padding-right (p. 569), padding-start (p. 570), padding-top (p. 571)

Related Formatting Objects

fo:bidi-override (p. 465), fo:block (p. 466), fo:block-character (p. 467), fo:block-container (p. 470), fo:external-graphic (p. 471), fo:float (p. 472), fo:footnote (p. 472), fo:footnote-body (p. 473), fo:initial-property-set (p. 473), fo:inline (p. 474), fo:inline-container (p. 475), fo:instream-foreign-object (p. 476), fo:leader (p. 477), fo:list-block (p. 478), fo:list-item (p. 492), fo:page-number (p. 492), fo:page-number-citation (p. 492), fo:region-after (p. 495), fo:region-before (p. 496), fo:region-body (p. 496), fo:region-end (p. 497), fo:region-start (p. 497), fo:simple-link (p. 500), fo:table (p. 503), fo:table-and-caption (p. 504), fo:table-body (p. 504), fo:table-caption (p. 505), fo:table-cell (p. 505), fo:table-column (p. 506), fo:table-footer (p. 506), fo:table-header (p. 507), fo:table-row (p. 507)

XSL Style Sheet Syntax

padding-after   Trailing-Edge Padding

Purpose

Turns on or off trailing-edge padding or sets trailing-edge-padding size of a box.

Syntax

```
padding-after: 0pt|length|percent%|inherit
```

Where

- 0pt represents the parent element's current trailing-edge padding, in points.
- *percent* is a positive value that is relative to the parent element's trailing-edge padding. Follow *percent* with a percentage sign (%).
- *length* is a positive value followed by a two-letter abbreviation representing the unit of measure.
- inherit is a keyword that indicates that this property takes the same computed value as its parent.

Notes

- This property is in the common-border-padding-background category.
- By default, the characteristics of this property are not inherited.

Related Properties

background properties (p. 379 - p. 387), border properties (p. 392 - p. 434), padding (p. 562), padding-before (p. 564), padding-bottom (p. 566), padding-end (p. 567), padding-left (p. 568), padding-right (p. 569), padding-start (p. 570), padding-top (p. 571)

Related Formatting Objects

fo:bidi-override (p. 465), fo:block (p. 466), fo:block-container (p. 467), fo:external-graphic (p. 470), fo:float (p. 471), fo:footnote (p. 472), fo:footnote-body (p. 472), fo:initial-property-set (p. 473), fo:inline (p. 473), fo:inline-container (p. 474), fo:instream-foreign-object (p. 475), fo:leader (p. 476), fo:list-block (p. 477), fo:list-item (p. 478), fo:page-number (p. 492), fo:page-number-citation (p. 492), fo:region-after (p. 495), fo:region-before (p. 496), fo:region-body (p. 496), fo:region-end (p. 497), fo:region-start (p. 497), fo:simple-link (p. 500), fo:table (p. 503), fo:table-and-caption (p. 504), fo:table-body (p. 504), fo:table-caption (p. 505), fo:table-cell (p. 505), fo:table-column (p. 506), fo:table-footer (p. 506), fo:table-header (p. 507), fo:table-row (p. 507)

padding-before   Leading-Edge Padding

Purpose

Turns on or off leading-edge padding or sets leading-edge-padding size of a box.

Syntax

padding-before: <u>0pt</u>|*length*|*percent*%|inherit

Where

- 0pt represents the parent element's current leading-edge padding, in points.
- *percent* is a positive value that is relative to the parent element's leading-edge padding. Follow *percent* with a percentage sign (%).
- *length* is a positive value followed by a two-letter abbreviation representing the unit of measure.
- inherit is a keyword that indicates that this property takes the same computed value as its parent.

Notes

- This property is in the common-border-padding-background category.
- This property turns leading-edge padding on or off, or sets a padding size (in the default unit of measure) as a percentage of the current height, or automatically by calculating a minimum amount.
- Valid relative units of measure are em (the height of the current font), ex (the height of the letter x in the current font), and px (pixels, relative to the size of the window). Valid absolute units of measure are in (inches), cm (centimeters), mm (millimeters), pt (points), and pc (picas).
- Padding is outside the content of the page, within the page edges, and below margins and borders.
- By default, the characteristics of this property are not inherited.

Related Properties

background properties (p. 379 - p. 387), border properties (p. 392 - p. 434), padding (p. 362), padding-after (p. 564), padding-bottom (p. 566), padding-end (p. 567), padding-left (p. 568), padding-right (p. 569), padding-start (p. 570), padding-top (p. 571)

Related Formatting Objects

fo:bidi-override (p. 465), fo:block (p. 466), fo:block-container (p. 467), fo:external-graphic (p. 470), fo:float (p. 471), fo:footnote (p. 472), fo:footnote-body (p. 472), fo:initial-property-set (p. 473), fo:inline (p. 473), fo:inline-container (p. 474), fo:instream-foreign-object (p. 475), fo:leader (p. 476), fo:list-block (p. 477), fo:list-item (p. 478), fo:page-number (p. 492), fo:page-number-citation (p. 492), fo:region-after (p. 495), fo:region-before (p. 496), fo:region-body (p. 496), fo:region-end (p. 497), fo:region-start (p. 497), fo:simple-link (p. 500), fo:table (p. 503), fo:table-and-caption (p. 504), fo:table-body (p. 504), fo:table-caption (p. 505), fo:table-cell (p. 505), fo:table-column (p. 506), fo:table-footer (p. 506), fo:table-header (p. 507), fo:table-row (p. 507)

XSL Style Sheet Syntax

padding-bottom	Bottom Padding

Purpose
Turns on or off bottom padding and/or specifies bottom-padding size of a box.

Syntax
```
padding-bottom: 0pt|length|percent%|inherit
```

Where
- 0pt represents the parent element's current bottom padding, in points.
- *percent* is a positive value that is relative to the parent element's bottom padding. Follow *percent* with a percentage sign (%).
- *length* is a positive value followed by a two-letter abbreviation representing the unit of measure.
- inherit is a keyword that indicates that this property takes the same computed value as its parent.

Notes
- This property is in the common-border-padding-background category.
- This property, which originated in CSS1, applies to all elements.
- By default, the characteristics of this property are not inherited.

Example
```
bigpage { padding-bottom: 8pt }
```

Related Properties
background properties (p. 379 – p. 387), border properties (p. 392 – p. 434), padding (p. 562), padding-after (p. 564), padding-before (p. 564), padding-end (p. 567), padding-left (p. 568), padding-right (p. 569), padding-start (p. 570), padding-top (p. 571)

Related Formatting Objects
fo:bidi-override (p. 465), fo:block (p. 466), fo:block-container (p. 467), fo:external-graphic (p. 470), fo:float (p. 471), fo:footnote (p. 472), fo:footnote-body (p. 472), fo:initial-property-set (p. 473), fo:inline (p. 473), fo:inline-container (p. 474), fo:instream-foreign-object (p. 475), fo:leader (p. 476), fo:list-block (p. 477), fo:list-item (p. 478), fo:page-number (p. 492), fo:page-number-citation (p. 492), fo:region-after (p. 495), fo:region-before (p. 496), fo:region-body (p. 496), fo:region-end (p. 497), fo:region-start (p. 497), fo:simple-link (p. 500), fo:table (p. 503), fo:table-and-caption (p. 504), fo:table-body (p. 504), fo:table-caption (p. 505), fo:table-cell (p. 505), fo:table-column (p. 506), fo:table-footer (p. 506), fo:table-header (p. 507), fo:table-row (p. 507)

padding-end | Ending-Edge Padding

Purpose
Turns on or off ending-edge padding or sets ending-edge-padding size of a box.

Syntax
padding-end: <u>0pt</u>|*length*|*percent*%|inherit

Where
- 0pt represents the parent element's current ending-edge padding, in points.
- *percent* is a positive value that is relative to the parent element's ending-edge padding. Follow *percent* with a percentage sign (%).
- *length* is a positive value followed by a two-letter abbreviation representing the unit of measure.
- inherit is a keyword that indicates that this property takes the same computed value as its parent.

Notes
- This property is in the common-border-padding-background category.
- This property turns starting-edge padding on or off, or sets a padding size (in the default unit of measure) as a percentage of the current height, or automatically by calculating a minimum amount.
- Valid relative units of measure are em (the height of the current font), ex (the height of the letter *x* in the current font), and px (pixels, relative to the size of the window). Valid absolute units of measure are in (inches), cm (centimeters), mm (millimeters), pt (points), and pc (picas).
- Padding is outside the content of the page, within the page edges, and below margins and borders.
- By default, the characteristics of this property are not inherited.

Related Properties
background properties (p. 379 - p. 387), border properties (p. 392 - p. 434), padding (p. 562), padding-after (p. 564), padding-before (p. 564), padding-bottom (p. 566), padding-left (p. 568), padding-right (p. 569), padding-start (p. 570), padding-top (p. 571)

Related Formatting Objects
fo:bidi-override (p. 465), fo:block (p. 466), fo:block-container (p. 467), fo:external-graphic (p. 470), fo:float (p. 471), fo:footnote (p. 472), fo:footnote-body (p. 472), fo:initial-property-set (p. 473), fo:inline (p. 473), fo:inline-container (p. 474), fo:instream-foreign-object (p. 475), fo:leader (p. 476), fo:list-block (p. 477), fo:list-item (p. 478), fo:page-number (p. 492), fo:page-number-citation (p. 492), fo:region-after (p. 495), fo:region-before (p. 496), fo:region-body (p. 496), fo:region-end (p. 497), fo:region-start (p. 497), fo:simple-link (p. 500), fo:table (p. 503), fo:table-and-caption (p. 504), fo:table-body (p. 504), fo:table-cap-

tion (p. 505), fo:table-cell (p. 505), fo:table-column (p. 506), fo:table-footer (p. 506), fo:table-header (p. 507), fo:table-row (p. 507)

padding-left	Left Padding

Purpose
Turns on or off left padding or sets left-padding size of a box.

Syntax
padding-left: <u>0pt</u>|*length*|*percent*%|inherit

Where
- 0pt represents the parent element's current left padding, in points.
- *percent* is a positive value that is relative to the parent element's left padding. Follow *percent* with a percentage sign (%).
- *length* is a positive value followed by a two-letter abbreviation representing the unit of measure.
- inherit is a keyword that indicates that this property takes the same computed value as its parent.

Notes
- This property is in the common-border-padding-background category.
- This property, which originated in CSS1, applies to all elements.
- By default, the characteristics of this property are not inherited.

Example
bigpage { padding-right: 0.5in; padding-top: 0.25in;
padding-bottom: 0.5in; padding-left: 0.5in }

Related Properties
background properties (p. 379 - p. 387), border properties (p. 392 - p. 434), padding (p. 562), padding-after (p. 564), padding-before (p. 564), padding-bottom (p. 566), padding-end (p. 567), padding-right (p. 569), padding-start (p. 570), padding-top (p. 571)

Related Formatting Objects
fo:bidi-override (p. 465), fo:block (p. 466), fo:block-container (p. 467), fo:external-graphic (p. 470), fo:float (p. 471), fo:footnote (p. 472), fo:footnote-body (p. 472), fo:initial-property-set (p. 473), fo:inline (p. 473), fo:inline-container (p. 474), fo:instream-foreign-object (p. 475), fo:leader (p. 476), fo:list-block (p. 477), fo:list-item (p. 478), fo:page-number (p. 492), fo:page-number-citation (p. 492), fo:region-after (p. 495), fo:region-before (p. 496), fo:region-body (p. 496), fo:region-end (p. 497), fo:region-start (p. 497), fo:simple-link (p. 500), fo:table (p. 503), fo:table-and-caption (p. 504), fo:table-body (p. 504), fo:table-caption (p. 505), fo:table-cell (p. 505), fo:table-column (p. 506), fo:table-footer (p. 506), fo:table-header (p. 507), fo:table-row (p. 507)

padding-right   Right Padding

Purpose

Turns on or off the right padding and/or sets the right-padding size of a box.

Syntax

padding-right: 0|length|percent%|inherit

Where

- 0 represents the parent element's current right padding.
- percent is a positive value that is relative to the parent element's right padding. Follow percent with a percentage sign (%).
- length is a positive value followed by a two-letter abbreviation representing the unit of measure.
- inherit is a keyword that indicates that this property takes the same computed value as its parent.

Notes

- This property is in the common-border-padding-background category.
- This property, which originated in CSS1, applies to all elements.
- By default, the characteristics of this property are not inherited.

Example

bigpage { padding-right: 8pt; padding-top: 6pt;
padding-bottom: 4pt; padding-left: 8pt }

Related Properties

background properties (p. 379 - p. 387), border properties (p. 392 - p. 434), padding (p. 562), padding-after (p. 564), padding-before (p. 564), padding-bottom (p. 566), padding-end (p. 567), padding-left (p. 568), padding-start (p. 570), padding-top (p. 571)

Related Formatting Objects

fo:bidi-override (p. 465), fo:block (p. 466), fo:block-container (p. 467), fo:external-graphic (p. 470), fo:float (p. 471), fo:footnote (p. 472), fo:footnote-body (p. 472), fo:initial-property-set (p. 473), fo:inline (p. 473), fo:inline-container (p. 474), fo:instream-foreign-object (p. 475), fo:leader (p. 476), fo:list-block (p. 477), fo:list-item (p. 478), fo:page-number (p. 492), fo:page-number-citation (p. 492), fo:region-after (p. 495), fo:region-before (p. 496), fo:region-body (p. 496), fo:region-end (p. 497), fo:region-start (p. 497), fo:simple-link (p. 500), fo:table (p. 503), fo:table-and-caption (p. 504), fo:table-body (p. 504), fo:table-caption (p. 505), fo:table-cell (p. 505), fo:table-column (p. 506), fo:table-footer (p. 506), fo:table-header (p. 507), fo:table-row (p. 507)

XSL Style Sheet Syntax

padding-start

Starting-Edge Padding

Purpose

Turns on or off starting-edge padding or sets starting-edge-padding size of a box.

Syntax

padding-start: <u>0pt</u>|*length*|*percent*%|inherit

Where

- 0pt represents the parent element's current starting-edge padding, in points.
- *percent* is a positive value that is relative to the parent element's starting-edge padding. Follow *percent* with a percentage sign (%).
- *length* is a positive value followed by a two-letter abbreviation representing the unit of measure.
- inherit is a keyword that indicates that this property takes the same computed value as its parent.

Notes

- This property is in the common-border-padding-background category.
- This property turns starting-edge padding on or off, or sets a padding size (in the default unit of measure) as a percentage of the current height, or automatically by calculating a minimum amount.
- Valid relative units of measure are em (the height of the current font), ex (the height of the letter *x* in the current font), and px (pixels, relative to the size of the window). Valid absolute units of measure are in (inches), cm (centimeters), mm (millimeters), pt (points), and pc (picas).
- Padding is outside the content of the page, within the page edges, and below margins and borders.
- By default, the characteristics of this property are not inherited.

Related Properties

background properties (p. 379 – p. 387), border properties (p. 392 – p. 434), padding (p. 562), padding-after (p. 564), padding-before (p. 564), padding-bottom (p. 566), padding-end (p. 567), padding-left (p. 568), padding-right (p. 569), padding-top (p. 571)

Related Formatting Objects

fo:bidi-override (p. 465), fo:block (p. 466), fo:block-container (p. 467), fo:external-graphic (p. 470), fo:float (p. 471), fo:footnote (p. 472), fo:footnote-body (p. 472), fo:initial-property-set (p. 473), fo:inline (p. 473), fo:inline-container (p. 474), fo:instream-foreign-object (p. 475), fo:leader (p. 476), fo:list-block (p. 477), fo:list-item (p. 478), fo:page-number (p. 492), fo:page-number-citation (p. 492), fo:region-after (p. 495), fo:region-before (p. 496), fo:region-body (p. 496), fo:region-end (p. 497), fo:region-start (p. 497), fo:simple-link (p. 500), fo:table (p. 503), fo:table-and-caption (p. 504), fo:table-body (p. 504), fo:table-caption (p. 505), fo:table-cell (p. 505), fo:table-column (p. 506), fo:table-footer (p. 506), fo:table-header (p. 507), fo:table-row (p. 507)

padding-top   Top Padding

Purpose
Turns on or off top padding or sets top-padding size of a box.

Syntax
padding-top: <u>0pt</u>|*length*|*percent*%|inherit

Where
- 0pt represents the parent element's current top padding, in points.
- *percent* is a positive value that is relative to the parent element's top padding. Follow *percent* with a percentage sign (%).
- *length* is a positive value followed by a two-letter abbreviation representing the unit of measure.
- inherit is a keyword that indicates that this property takes the same computed value as its parent.

Notes
- This property is in the common-border-padding-background category.
- This property, which originated in CSS1, applies to all elements.
- By default, the characteristics of this property are not inherited.

Example
bigpage { padding-top: 6pt }

Related Properties
background properties (p. 379 – p. 387), border properties (p. 392 – p. 434), padding (p. 562), padding-after (p. 564), padding-before (p. 564), padding-bottom (p. 566), padding-end (p. 567), padding-left (p. 568), padding-right (p. 569), padding-start (p. 570)

Related Formatting Objects
fo:bidi-override (p. 465), fo:block (p. 466), fo:block-container (p. 467), fo:external-graphic (p. 470), fo:float (p. 471), fo:footnote (p. 472), fo:footnote-body (p. 472), fo:initial-property-set (p. 473), fo:inline (p. 473), fo:inline-container (p. 474), fo:instream-foreign-object (p. 475), fo:leader (p. 476), fo:list-block (p. 477), fo:list-item (p. 478), fo:page-number (p. 492), fo:page-number-citation (p. 492), fo:region-after (p. 495), fo:region-before (p. 496), fo:region-body (p. 496), fo:region-end (p. 497), fo:region-start (p. 497), fo:simple-link (p. 500), fo:table (p. 503), fo:table-and-caption (p. 504), fo:table-body (p. 504), fo:table-caption (p. 505), fo:table-cell (p. 505), fo:table-column (p. 506), fo:table-footer (p. 506), fo:table-header (p. 507), fo:table-row (p. 507)

page-break-after	Page Break After

Purpose

Inserts a page break after the current page box.

Syntax

```
page-break-after: auto|always|avoid|left|right|inherit
```

Where

- auto is a keyword that indicates that a page break is not forced or pre-vented after the page box is produced. This is the default. In XSL, auto is shorthand for break-after="auto" and keep-with-next="auto".
- always is a keyword that indicates that a page break always is inserted after the page box is produced. In XSL, always is shorthand for break-after="page" and keep-with-next="auto".
- avoid is a keyword that indicates that a page break is prevented after the page box is produced. In XSL, avoid is shorthand for break-after="auto" and keep-with-next="always".
- left is a keyword that indicates that after a page break occurs, the next page will be a left page. In XSL, left is shorthand for break-after="even-page" and keep-with-next="auto".
- right is a keyword that indicates that after a page break occurs, the next page will be a left page. In XSL, right is shorthand for break-after="odd-page" and keep-with-next="auto".
- inherit is a keyword that indicates that this property takes the same computed value as its parent.

Notes

- This property is in the common-keeps-and-breaks category.
- This property, which originated in CSS2, applies to block-level elements.
- The XSL working draft (http://www.w3.org/TR/xsl/) states that "all keep values are ordered from weakest (auto) to strongest (always) and break values are ordered from weakest (auto) to strongest (even/odd). In general, the strongest condition applies, with all breaks other than 'auto' being stronger than all keeps. Also, conflicting even-page/odd-page breaks behave as if they were 'page.'"
- The current page break is affected by the parent element's page-break-inside settings, the page-break-after settings of the prior element, and the page-break-before settings of the next element. The always, left, and right values have precedence over avoid when these page-break-inside, page-break-after, and page-break-before settings are not equal to auto.
- By default, characteristics of this property are not inherited.

Related Properties

break-after (p. 435), break-before (p. 436), keep-with-next (p. 527), keep-with-previous (p. 528), page-break-before (p. 573)

Related Formatting Objects

fo:list-block (p. 477), fo:list-item (p. 478), fo:table (p. 503)

page-break-before   Page Break Before

Purpose

Inserts a page break before the current page box.

Syntax

page-break-before: <u>auto</u>|always|avoid|left|right
  |inherit

Where

- auto is a keyword that indicates that a page break is not forced or prevented after the page box is produced. This is the default. In XSL, auto is shorthand for break-before="auto" and keep-with-previous="auto".
- always is a keyword that indicates that a page break is always inserted after the page box is produced. In XSL, auto is shorthand for break-before="page" and keep-with-previous="auto".
- avoid is a keyword that indicates that a page break is prevented after the page box is produced. In XSL, avoid is shorthand for break-before="auto" and keep-with-previous="always".
- left is a keyword that indicates that after a page break occurs, the next page will be a left page. In XSL, left is shorthand for break-before="even-page" and keep-with-previous="auto".
- right is a keyword that indicates that after a page break occurs, the next page will be a left page. In XSL, right is shorthand for break-before="odd-page" and keep-with-previous="auto".
- inherit is a keyword that indicates that this property takes the same computed value as its parent.

Notes

- This property is in the common-keeps-and-breaks category.
- This property, which originated in CSS2, applies to block-level elements.
- The XSL working draft (http://www.w3.org/TR/xsl/) states that "all keep values are ordered from weakest (auto) to strongest (always) and break values are ordered from weakest (auto) to strongest (even/odd). In general, the strongest condition applies, with all breaks other than 'auto' being stronger than all keeps. Also, conflicting even-page/odd-page breaks behave as if they were 'page.'"

XSL Style Sheet Syntax

- The current page break is affected by the parent element's page-break-inside settings, the page-break-after settings of the prior element, and the page-break-before settings of the next element. The always, left, and right values have precedence over avoid when these page-break-inside, page-break-after, and page-break-before settings are not equal to auto.
- By default, characteristics of this property are inherited.

Related Properties

break-after (p. 435), break-before (p. 436), keep-with-next (p. 527), keep-with-previous (p. 528), page-break-after (p. 572)

Related Formatting Objects

fo:list-block (p. 477), fo:list-item (p. 478), fo:table (p. 503)

page-break-inside   Page Break Inside

Purpose

Inserts a page break inside the current page box.

Syntax

    page-break-inside: avoid|auto|inherit

Where

- avoid is a keyword that indicates that a page break is prevented after the page box is produced.
- auto is a keyword that indicates that a page break is not forced or prevented after the page box is produced. This is the default.
- inherit is a keyword that indicates that this property takes the same computed value as its parent.

Notes

- This property is in the page-related category.
- This property, which originated in CSS2, applies to block-level elements.
- The current page break is affected by the parent element's page-break-inside settings, the page-break-after settings of the prior element, and the page-break-before settings of the next element. The always, left, and right values have precedence over avoid when these page-break-inside, page-break-after, and page-break-before settings are not equal to auto.
- By default, characteristics of this property are inherited.

Related Properties

keep-together (p. 526), orphans (p. 561), widows (p. 641)

Related Formatting Object
fo:block (p. 466)

page-height   Page Height

Purpose
Determines the page height, from the top edge to the bottom edge.

Syntax
    page-height: auto|indefinite|length|inherit

Where
- auto is a keyword that represents a value automatically calculated by the user's browser.
- indefinite is a keyword that indicates that page height is determined by the size of the laid-out page.
- length is an absolute height, in points. The default value varies, depending on the computer system.
- inherit is a keyword that indicates that this property takes the same computed value as its parent.

Notes
- This property is in the pagination-and-layout category.
- The XSL page-height property is related to the DSSSL-O page-height property.
- By default, characteristics of this property are not inherited.

Related Properties
blank-or-not-blank (p. 389), column-count (p. 444), column-gap (p. 444), extent (p. 461), flow-name (p. 465), force-page-count (p. 494), initial-page-number (p. 524), master-name (p. 547), maximum-repeats (p. 549), odd-or-even (p. 559), page-position (p. 575), page-width (p. 576), precedence (p. 584), region-name (p. 590)

Related Formatting Object
fo:simple-page-master (p. 501)

page-position   Page Position

Purpose
Makes a page-master eligible for selection depending on its position in the page sequence.

Syntax
    page-position: first|last|rest|any|inherit

Where

- first is a keyword that indicates that the page-master can be selected if this page is the first in the page sequence.
- last is a keyword that indicates that the page-master can be selected if this page is the last in the page sequence.
- rest is a keyword that indicates that the page-master can be selected if this page is is not the first or last in the page sequence.
- any is a keyword that indicates that the page-master can be selected if this page is within the page sequence. This is the default.
- inherit is a keyword that indicates that this property takes the same computed value as its parent.

Notes

- This property is in the pagination-and-layout category.
- This property applies to the fo:conditional-page-master-reference formatting object.
- By default, characteristics of this property are not inherited.

Related Properties

blank-or-not-blank (p. 389), column-count (p. 444), column-gap (p. 444), extent (p. 461), flow-name (p. 465), force-page-count (p. 464), initial-page-number (p. 524), master-name (p. 547), maximum-repeats (p. 549), odd-or-even (p. 559), page-height (p. 575), page-width (p. 576), precedence (p. 584), region-name (p. 590)

Related Formatting Object

fo:conditional-page-master-reference (p. 469)

---

page-width	Page Width

Purpose

Specifies the page width, from the left edge to the right edge.

Syntax

page-width: <u>auto</u>|indefinite|*length*|inherit

Where

- auto is a keyword that represents a value automatically calculated by the user's browser.
- indefinite is a keyword that indicates that page width is determined by the size of the laid-out page.
- *length* is an absolute height, in points. The default value varies, depending on the computer system.
- inherit is a keyword that indicates that this property takes the same computed value as its parent.

Notes

- This property is in the pagination-and-layout category.
- The XSL page-width property is related to the DSSSL-O page-width property.
- By default, characteristics of this property are not inherited.

Related Properties

blank-or-not-blank (p. 389), column-count (p. 444), column-gap (p. 444), extent (p. 461), flow-name (p. 465), force-page-count (p. 494), initial-page-number (p. 524), master-name (p. 547), maximum-repeats (p. 549), odd-or-even (p. 559), page-height (p. 575), page-position (p. 575), precedence (p. 584), region-name (p. 590)

Related Formatting Object

fo:simple-page-master (p. 501)

---

pause   Pause Speaking

Purpose

Pauses after and/or before an element is spoken.

Syntax

```
pause: [b_time| b_percentage][a_time| b_percentage]
    |inherit
```

Where

- *b_time* specifies the absolute pause, in seconds and milliseconds, before the element is spoken.
- *b_percentage* specifies the inverse percentage of the value of speech-rate (p. 616) before the element is spoken.
- *a_time* specifies the absolute pause, in seconds and milliseconds, after the element is spoken.
- *a_percentage* specifies the inverse percentage of the value of speech-rate after the element is spoken.
- inherit is a keyword that indicates that this property takes the same computed value as its parent.

Notes

- This property is in the common-aural category.
- This property, which originated in CSS2, applies to all elements.
- The *b_percentage* and *a_percentage* values are the inverse of the speech-rate value. So, if the speech-rate is 60 words per minute (1000 milliseconds), a pause of 100% is also 1000 milliseconds and a pause of 50% is a pause of 500 milliseconds.
- Any pauses are inserted between the content of the element and the content of cue-before or cue-after property.
- By default, the characteristics of this property are not inherited.

XSL Style Sheet Syntax

Related Properties

azimuth (p. 377), cue (p. 449), cue-after (p. 450), cue-before (p. 451), elevation (p. 456), pause-after (p. 578), pause-before (p. 579), pitch (p. 580), pitch-range (p. 581), play-during (p. 582), richness (p. 597), speak (p. 613), speak-header (p. 614), speak-numeral (p. 615), speak-punctuation (p. 615), speech-rate (p. 616), stress (p. 620), voice-family (p. 637), volume (p. 638)

Related Formatting Objects

fo:bidi-override (p. 465), fo:block (p. 466), fo:external-graphic (p. 470), fo:footnote-body (p. 472), fo:initial-property-set (p. 473), fo:inline (p. 473), fo:instream-foreign-object (p. 475), fo:leader (p. 476), fo:list-block (p. 477), fo:list-item (p. 478), fo:page-number (p. 492), fo:page-number-citation (p. 492), fo:simple-link (p. 500), fo:table (p. 503), fo:table-and-caption (p. 504), fo:table-body (p. 504), fo:table-caption (p. 505), fo:table-cell (p. 505), fo:table-footer (p. 506), fo:table-header (p. 507), fo:table-row (p. 507)

pause-after   Pause After

Purpose

Pauses after an element is spoken.

Syntax

```
pause-after: [time|percentage|inherit
```

Where

- *time* specifies the absolute pause, in seconds and milliseconds, after the element is spoken.
- *percentage* specifies the inverse percentage of the value of speech-rate (p. 616) after the element is spoken.
- inherit is a keyword that indicates that this property takes the same computed value as its parent.

Notes

- This property is in the common-aural category.
- This property, which originated in CSS2, applies to all elements.
- By default, the characteristics of this property are not inherited.

Related Properties

azimuth (p. 377), cue (p. 449), cue-after (p. 450), cue-before (p. 451), elevation (p. 456), pause (p. 577), pause-before (p. 579), pitch (p. 580), pitch-range (p. 581), play-during (p. 582), richness (p. 597), speak (p. 613), speak-header (p. 614), speak-numeral (p. 615), speak-punctuation (p. 615), speech-rate (p. 616), stress (p. 620), voice-family (p. 637), volume (p. 638)

Related Formatting Objects

fo:bidi-override (p. 465), fo:block (p. 466), fo:external-graphic (p. 470), fo:footnote-body (p. 472), fo:initial-property-set (p. 473), fo:inline (p. 473), fo:instream-foreign-object (p. 475), fo:leader (p. 476), fo:list-block (p. 477), fo:list-item (p. 478), fo:page-number (p. 492), fo:page-number-citation (p. 492), fo:simple-link (p. 500), fo:table (p. 503), fo:table-and-caption (p. 504), fo:table-body (p. 504), fo:table-caption (p. 505), fo:table-cell (p. 505), fo:table-footer (p. 506), fo:table-header (p. 507), fo:table-row (p. 507)

pause-before	Pause Before

Purpose

Pauses before an element is spoken.

Syntax

pause-before: [*time*|*percentage*|inherit]

Where

- *time* specifies the absolute pause, in seconds and milliseconds, after the element is spoken.
- *percentage* specifies the inverse percentage of the value of speech-rate (p. 616) after the element is spoken.
- inherit is a keyword that indicates that this property takes the same computed value as its parent.

Notes

- This property is in the common-aural category.
- This property, which originated in CSS2, applies to all elements.
- By default, the characteristics of this property are not inherited.

Related Properties

azimuth (p. 377), cue (p. 449), cue-after (p. 450), cue-before (p. 451), elevation (p. 456), pause (p. 577), pause-after (p. 578), pitch (p. 580), pitch-range (p. 581), play-during (p. 582), richness (p. 597), speak (p. 613), speak-header (p. 614), speak-numeral (p. 615), speak-punctuation (p. 615), speech-rate (p. 616), stress (p. 620), voice-family (p. 637), volume (p. 638)

Related Formatting Objects

fo:bidi-override (p. 465), fo:block (p. 466), fo:external-graphic (p. 470), fo:footnote-body (p. 472), fo:initial-property-set (p. 473), fo:inline (p. 473), fo:instream-foreign-object (p. 475), fo:leader (p. 476), fo:list-block (p. 477), fo:list-item (p. 478), fo:page-number (p. 492), fo:page-number-citation (p. 492), fo:simple-link (p. 500), fo:table (p. 503), fo:table-and-caption (p. 504), fo:table-body (p. 504), fo:table-caption (p. 505), fo:table-cell (p. 505), fo:table-footer (p. 506), fo:table-header (p. 507), fo:table-row (p. 507)

Percent [9]   Brief Description

Purpose

Symbolizes a number followed by a percent-sign symbol.

EBNF Syntax

```
Percent ::= Number '%'
```

Standard Syntax

```
Number%
```

Where

- Number (p. 55) represents a floating-point number made up of one or more digits.

Notes

- Percent is a component of the RelativeNumeric production.

Related Productions

Number (p. 555), RelativeNumeric (p. 568)

pitch   Pitch

Purpose

Sets the pitch of a speaking voice.

Syntax

```
pitch: frequency|x-low|low|medium|high|x-high|inherit
```

Where

- *frequency* represents an absolute pitch measured in hertz (Hz).
- x-low is a keyword that represents a pitch that is lower than low.
- low is a keyword that represents a pitch that is lower than medium but higher than x-low.
- medium is a keyword that represents a pitch that is lower than high but higher than low. This is the default.
- high is a keyword that represents a pitch that is lower than x-high but higher than medium.
- x-high is a keyword that represents a pitch that is higher than high.
- inherit is a keyword that indicates that this property takes the same computed value as its parent.

Notes

- This property is in the common-aural category.
- This property, which originated in CSS2, applies to all elements.
- By default, the characteristics of this property are inherited.

Related Properties

azimuth (p. 377), cue (p. 449), cue-after (p. 450), cue-before (p. 451), elevation (p. 456), pause (p. 577), pause-after (p. 578), pause-before (p. 579), pitch-range (p. 581), play-during (p. 582), richness (p. 597), speak (p. 613), speak-header (p. 614), speak-numeral (p. 615), speak-punctuation (p. 615), speech-rate (p. 616), stress (p. 620), voice-family (p. 637), volume (p. 638)

Related Formatting Objects

fo:bidi-override (p. 465), fo:block (p. 466), fo:external-graphic (p. 470), fo:footnote-body (p. 472), fo:initial-property-set (p. 473), fo:inline (p. 473), fo:instream-foreign-object (p. 475), fo:leader (p. 476), fo:list-block (p. 477), fo:list-item (p. 478), fo:page-number (p. 492), fo:page-number-citation (p. 492), fo:simple-link (p. 500), fo:table (p. 503), fo:table-and-caption (p. 504), fo:table-body (p. 504), fo:table-caption (p. 505), fo:table-cell (p. 505), fo:table-footer (p. 506), fo:table-header (p. 507), fo:table-row (p. 507)

pitch-range   Pitch Range

Purpose

Varies the range of pitch for a voice.

Syntax

    pitch-range: number | inherit

Where

- *number* represents a pitch variation. Valid values range from 0 (a relatively monotonous voice) to 100 (a relatively animated voice). The value of 50 represents a standard voice.
- inherit is a keyword that indicates that this property takes the same computed value as its parent.

Notes

- This property is in the common-aural category.
- This property, which originated in CSS2, applies to all elements.
- By default, the characteristics of this property are inherited.

Related Properties

azimuth (p. 377), cue (p. 449), cue-after (p. 450), cue-before (p. 451), elevation (p. 456), pause (p. 577), pause-after (p. 578), pause-before (p. 579), pitch (p. 580), play-during (p. 582), richness (p. 597), speak (p. 613), speak-header (p. 614), speak-numeral (p. 615), speak-punctuation (p. 615), speech-rate (p. 616), stress (p. 620), voice-family (p. 637), volume (p. 638)

Related Formatting Objects

fo:bidi-override (p. 465), fo:block (p. 466), fo:external-graphic (p. 470),
fo:footnote-body (p. 472), fo:initial-property-set (p. 473), fo:inline (p. 473),
fo:instream-foreign-object (p. 475), fo:leader (p. 476), fo:list-block (p. 477),
fo:list-item (p. 478), fo:page-number (p. 492), fo:page-number-citation (p. 492),
fo:simple-link (p. 500), fo:table (p. 503), fo:table-and-caption (p. 504),
fo:table-body (p. 504), fo:table-caption (p. 505), fo:table-cell (p. 505),
fo:table-footer (p. 506), fo:table-header (p. 507), fo:table-row (p. 507)

play-during   Play Background Sound

Purpose

Plays a sound while an element's content is spoken.

Syntax

```
play-during: uri(uri_name) [mix] [repeat]|auto|none
  |inherit
```

Where

- uri is a keyword that indicates that a URI name will follow.
- *uri_name* names the URI of the sound file.
- mix is a keyword that indicates that the parent element's sound continues to play and is mixed with the current element's sound.
- repeat is a keyword that indicates that the sound is repeated while the
  element is spoken. If repeat is absent, the sound file plays once and is
  clipped if it is longer than the element's "speak."
- auto is a keyword that represents a sound that has continued to play
  from the parent element. This is the default.
- none indicates no sound is played.
- inherit is a keyword that indicates that this property takes the same
  computed value as its parent. The sound is restarted when the current
  element is spoken.

Notes

- This property is in the common-aural category.
- This property, which originated in CSS2, applies to all elements.
- By default, the characteristics of this property are not inherited.

Related Properties

azimuth (p. 377), cue (p. 449), cue-after (p. 450), cue-before (p. 451), elevation
(p. 456), pause (p. 577), pause-after (p. 578), pause-before (p. 579), pitch
(p. 580), pitch-range (p. 581), richness (p. 597), speak (p. 613), speak-header
(p. 614), speak-numeral (p. 615), speak-punctuation (p. 615), speech-rate
(p. 616), stress (p. 620), voice-family (p. 637), volume (p. 638)

XSL Style Sheet Syntax

Related Formatting Objects

fo:bidi-override (p. 465), fo:block (p. 466), fo:external-graphic (p. 470), fo:footnote-body (p. 472), fo:initial-property-set (p. 473), fo:inline (p. 473), fo:instream-foreign-object (p. 475), fo:leader (p. 476), fo:list-block (p. 477), fo:list-item (p. 478), fo:page-number (p. 492), fo:page-number-citation (p. 492), fo:simple-link (p. 500), fo:table (p. 503), fo:table-and-caption (p. 504), fo:table-body (p. 504), fo:table-caption (p. 505), fo:table-cell (p. 505), fo:table-footer (p. 506), fo:table-header (p. 507), fo:table-row (p. 507)

position	Position Element

Purpose

Positions the current element in a particular way onscreen or in a printed format.

Syntax

position: static|relative|absolute|fixed|inherit

Where

- static places the box inline or block, depending on the current element. The processor ignores left and top properties. This is the default.
- relative places the box inline or block, depending on the current element. Then the processor offsets the box relative to the position that it would normally hold.
- absolute places the box according to its left, right, top, and bottom properties. An absolute box's margins cannot collapse and the layout of its sibling boxes are not affected.
- fixed places the box according to its left, right, top, and bottom properties and is fixed in reference to its page or *viewport* (a viewing area).
- inherit is a keyword that indicates that this property takes the same computed value as its parent.

Notes

- This property is in the common-absolute-position category.
- This property, which originated in CSS2, applies to all elements but not generated content (for example, :after and :before pseudo-elements).
- Elements with a position of static or relative only can have page breaks or column breaks.
- An element with a position of absolute or fixed creates a new reference-area. Then, it and its descendants fill that reference area. Page breaks, column breaks, and their keeps and breaks, as well as margins and space-before properties, are ignored within the area.

Related Common-Absolute-Position Properties
bottom (p. 434), left (p. 535), right (p. 597), top (p. 632)

Other Related Properties
break-after (p. 435), break-before (p. 436), clear (p. 440), float (p. 463), keep-with-next (p. 527), keep-with-previous (p. 528), page-break-after (p. 572), page-break-before (p. 573), space-before (p. 608)

Related Formatting Object
fo:block-container (p. 467)

---

precedence   Precedence

Purpose
Determines the precedence of the formatting-object regions that can reach into the corners of a simple-page-master.

Syntax
precedence: true|false|inherit

Where
- true is a keyword that indicates that the current region fills the area.
- false is a keyword that indicates that the current region does not fill the area.
- inherit is a keyword that indicates that this property takes the same computed value as its parent.

Notes
- This property is in the pagination-and-layout category.
- If adjacent regions currently have equal precedence, the after-region or before-region are considered to have a value of true, and the end-region or start-region are considered to have a value of false.
- By default, characteristics of this property are not inherited.

Related Properties
blank-or-not-blank (p. 389), column-count (p. 444), column-gap (p. 444), extent (p. 461), flow-name (p. 465), force-page-count (p. 494), initial-page-number (p. 524), master-name (p. 547), maximum-repeats (p. 549), odd-or-even (p. 559), page-height (p. 575), page-position (p. 575), page-width (p. 576), region-name (p. 590)

Related Formatting Objects
fo:region-after (p. 495), fo:region-before (p. 496)

PrimaryExpr [2]   Primary Expression

Purpose
Symbolizes a primary expression.

EBNF Syntax
```
PrimaryExpr ::= '(' Expr ')' | Numeric
    | Literal | Color | Keyword | EnumerationToken
    | FunctionCall
```

Standard Syntax
```
'(' Expr ')' | Numeric
    | Literal | Color | Keyword | EnumerationToken
    | FunctionCall
```

Where
- (marks the start of the expression.
- Expr (p. 459) indicates an expression.
-) marks the end of the expression.
- Literal (p. 541) represents a literal, a string within quotation marks or single quote marks.
- Color (p. 443) identifies an RGB hexadecimal color code.
- Keyword (p. 529) represents a reserved keyword.
- EnumerationToken (p. 459) provides an NCName for an enumeration token.
- FunctionCall (p. 511) evaluates and processes an expression and calls a function.

Notes
- PrimaryExpr is a component of the UnaryExpr production.
- The XSL PrimaryExpr production is similar but not identical to the XPath PrimaryExpr production.

Related Productions
Color (p. 443), Expr (p. 459), EnumerationToken (p. 459), FunctionName (p. 512), Literal (p. 541), Keyword (p. 529), UnaryExpr (p. 633)

proportional-column-width()   Proportional Column Width Function

Purpose
Returns the proportional factor units of proportional measure.

EBNF Syntax
```
number_r proportional-column-width(number)
```

XSL Style Sheet Syntax

Standard Syntax

number_r proportional-column-width(*number*)

Where

- *number_r* is the proportional factor unit returned.
- proportional-column-width is the function keyword.
- *number* is the proportional measurement.

Notes

- This is a property value function.
- The difference between the table-width and the sum of the column widths is the available proportional width.
- The unit of proportional measure equals the available proportional width, divided by the sum of proportional factors.
- If this function is used on any formatting object other than an fo:table-column, then it is an error.
- If the fixed table layout is not used in this function, then it will be considered an error.

Related Functions

body-start() (p. 391), from-nearest-specified-value() (p. 509), from-parent() (p. 510), from-table-column() (p. 510), inherited-property-value() (p. 523), label-end() (p. 530), merge-property-values() (p. 551)

provisional-distance-between-starts

Provisional Distance Between Starts

Purpose

Sets the length between the end of a start indent of list-item label and the beginning of the list item itself.

Syntax

provisional-distance-between-starts: *length*|inherit

Where

- *length* is the distance between the start indent and the item. The default value is 24.0 points.
- inherit is a keyword that indicates that this property takes the same computed value as its parent. This is a relative page-box size.

Notes

- This property is in the miscellaneous category.
- By default, the characteristics of this property are inherited.

Related Properties

baseline-shift (p. 388), block-progression-dimension (p. 390), clip (p. 440), color (p. 441), direction (p. 453), font-height-override-after (p. 484),

font-height-override-before (p. 485), glyph-orientation-horizontal
(p. 512), glyph-orientation-vertical (p. 513), height (p. 514), href (p. 515),
hyphenation-keep (p. 517), hyphenation-ladder-count (p. 518), id (p. 521),
inline-progression-dimension (p. 525), last-line-end-indent (p. 531), linefeed-treatment (p. 537), line-height (p. 538), line-height-shift-adjustment
(p. 539), line-stacking-strategy (p. 540), max-height (p. 548), max-width
(p. 550), min-height (p. 552), min-width (p. 553), overflow (p. 561), provisional-label-separation (p. 587), reference-orientation (p. 588), ref-id
(p. 589), scaling (p. 601), score-spaces (p. 602), size (p. 605), space-
treatment (p. 611), span (p. 612), text-align (p. 625), text-align-last
(p. 626), text-indent (p. 629), unicode-bidi (p. 634), vertical-align (p. 635),
visibility (p. 636), white-space (p. 639), white-space-collapse (p. 640),
width (p. 642), wrap-option (p. 644), writing-mode (p. 645), z-index (p. 648)

Related Formatting Object

fo:list-block (p. 477)

provisional-label-separation	Provisional Label Separation

Purpose

Sets the length between the end of a list-item label and the beginning of the
list item itself.

Syntax

provisional-label-separation: *length* | inherit

Where

- *length* is the distance between the label and the item. The default value
  is 6.0 points.
- inherit is a keyword that indicates that this property takes the same
  computed value as its parent. This is a relative page-box size.

Notes

- This property is in the miscellaneous category.
- By default, the characteristics of this property are inherited.

Related Properties

baseline-shift (p. 388), block-progression-dimension (p. 390), clip
(p. 440), color (p. 441), direction (p. 453), font-height-override-after
(p. 484), font-height-override-before (p. 485), glyph-orientation-
horizontal (p. 512), glyph-orientation-vertical (p. 513), height (p. 514),
href (p. 515), hyphenation-keep (p. 517), hyphenation-ladder-count (p. 518),
id (p. 521), inline-progression-dimension (p. 525), last-line-end-indent
(p. 531), linefeed-treatment (p. 537), line-height (p. 538), line-height-
shift-adjustment (p. 539), line-stacking-strategy (p. 540), max-height
(p. 548), max-width (p. 550), min-height (p. 552), min-width (p. 553),

overflow (p. 561), provisional-distance-between-starts (p. 586),
reference-orientation (p. 588), ref-id (p. 589), scaling (p. 601), score-
spaces (p. 602), size (p. 605), space-treatment (p. 611), span (p. 612), text-
align (p. 625), text-align-last (p. 626), text-indent (p. 629), unicode-bidi
(p. 634), vertical-align (p. 635), visibility (p. 636), white-space (p. 639),
white-space-collapse (p. 640), width (p. 642), wrap-option (p. 644),
writing-mode (p. 645), z-index (p. 648)

Related Formatting Object

fo:list-block (p. 477)

reference-orientation | Reference Orientation

Purpose

Changes the orientation of a selection with the box in which it is located.

Syntax

    reference-orientation: angle|inherit

Where

- angle specifies the angle at which the selection is displayed. Valid values are -270, -180, -90, 0, 90, 180, and 270. The initial value is 0.
- inherit is a keyword that indicates that this property takes the same
  computed value as its parent.

Notes

- This property is in the miscellaneous category.
- By default, the characteristics of this property are inherited.

Related Properties

baseline-shift (p. 388), block-progression-dimension (p. 390), clip (p. 440),
color (p. 441), direction (p. 453), font-height-override-after (p. 484), font-
height-override-before (p. 485), glyph-orientation-horizontal (p. 512), glyph-
orientation-vertical (p. 513), height (p. 514), href (p. 515), hyphenation-keep
(p. 517), hyphenation-ladder-count (p. 518), id (p. 521), inline-progression-dimension (p. 525), last-line-end-indent (p. 531), linefeed-treatment (p. 537),
line-height (p. 538), line-height-shift-adjustment (p. 539), line-stacking-
strategy (p. 540), max-height (p. 548), max-width (p. 550), min-height (p. 552),
min-width (p. 553), overflow (p. 561), provisional-distance-between-starts
(p. 586), provisional-label-separation (p. 587), ref-id (p. 589), scaling (p. 601),
score-spaces (p. 602), size (p. 605), space-treatment (p. 611), span (p. 612), text-
align (p. 625), text-align-last (p. 626), text-indent (p. 629), unicode-bidi
(p. 634), vertical-align (p. 635), visibility (p. 636), white-space (p. 639),
white-space-collapse (p. 640), width (p. 642), wrap-option (p. 644), writing-mode
(p. 645), z-index (p. 648)

Related Formatting Objects

fo:inline-container (p. 474), fo:region-after (p. 495), fo:region-before (p. 496), fo:region-body (p. 496), fo:region-end (p. 497), fo:region-start (p. 497), fo:simple-page-master (p. 501)

ref-id   Reference Identifier

Purpose

Specifies an identifier for a cross-reference.

Syntax

ref-id: *idref* | inherit

Where

- *idref* is a cross-reference identifier.
- inherit is a keyword that indicates that this property takes the same computed value as its parent.

Notes

- This property is in the miscellaneous category.
- By default, the characteristics of this property are not inherited.

Related Properties

baseline-shift (p. 388), block-progression-dimension (p. 390), clip (p. 440), color (p. 441), direction (p. 453), font-height-override-after (p. 484), font-height-override-before (p. 485), glyph-orientation-horizontal (p. 512), glyph-orientation-vertical (p. 513), height (p. 514), href (p. 515), hyphenation-keep (p. 517), hyphenation-ladder-count (p. 518), id (p. 521), inline-progression-dimension (p. 525), last-line-end-indent (p. 531), linefeed-treatment (p. 537), line-height (p. 538), line-height-shift-adjustment (p. 539), line-stacking-strategy (p. 540), max-height (p. 548), max-width (p. 550), min-height (p. 552), min-width (p. 553), overflow (p. 561), provisional-distance-between-starts (p. 586), provisional-label-separation (p. 587), reference-orientation (p. 588), scaling (p. 601), score-spaces (p. 602), size (p. 605), space-treatment (p. 611), span (p. 612), text-align (p. 625), text-align-last (p. 626), text-indent (p. 629), unicode-bidi (p. 634), vertical-align (p. 635), visibility (p. 636), white-space (p. 639), white-space-collapse (p. 640), width (p. 642), wrap-option (p. 644), writing-mode (p. 645), z-index (p. 648)

Related Formatting Object

fo:page-number-citation (p. 492)

XSL Style Sheet Syntax

| **region-name** | **Region Name** |

Purpose
Names or identifies the current region.

Syntax
```
region-name: xsl-region-body|xsl-region-start
  |xsl-region-end|xsl-region-before|xsl-region-after
  | region_name|inherit
```

Where
- xsl-region-body is a reserved keyword that provides a default name for the fo:region-body formatting object. You cannot use this name for any other type of formatting object.
- xsl-region-start is a reserved keyword that provides a default name for the fo:region-start formatting object. You cannot use this name for any other type of formatting object.
- xsl-region-end is a reserved keyword that provides a default name for the fo:region-end formatting object. You cannot use this name for any other type of formatting object.
- xsl-region-before is a reserved keyword that provides a default name for the fo:region-before formatting object. You cannot use this name for any other type of formatting object.
- xsl-region-after is a reserved keyword that provides a default name for the fo:region-after formatting object. You cannot use this name for any other type of formatting object.
- region_name is the unique name of the current region.
- inherit is a keyword that indicates that this property takes the same computed value as its parent.

Notes
- This property is in the pagination-and-layout category.
- This property applies to the fo:region-after, fo:region-before, fo:region-body, fo:region-end, and fo:region-start formatting objects.
- By default, the characteristics of this property are not inherited.

Related Properties
blank-or-not-blank (p. 389), column-count (p. 444), column-gap (p. 444), extent (p. 461), flow-name (p. 465), force-page-count (p. 464), initial-page-number (p. 524), master-name (p. 547), maximum-repeats (p. 549), odd-or-even (p. 559), page-height (p. 575), page-position (p. 575), page-width (p. 576), precedence (p. 584)

Related Formatting Objects

fo:region-after (p. 465), fo:region-before (p. 496), fo:region-body (p. 496), fo:region-end (p. 497), fo:region-start (p. 497), fo:simple-page-master (p. 501)

relative-align   Relative Align

Purpose

Specifies the alignment between two or more areas within a block-progression-dimension.

Syntax

    relative-align: before|baseline|inherit

Where

- before is a keyword that specifies that both before-edges of each area should be placed equidistant from each other.
- baseline is a keyword that specifies that each area should be spaced equidistant from each other based on their dominant baselines.
- inherit is a keyword that indicates that this property takes the same computed value as its parent.

Notes

- This is an area alignment property.
- If the display-align property applies to the formatting object using this relative-align, and the value is not auto, then this property is ignored.
- To relative-align with a "before" value of an fo:table-cell, the before-edge of the content-rectangle for the first child area in each row is placed at the same distance from the row grid.
- To relative-align with a "baseline" value of an fo:table-cell, the before-edge of the dominant-baseline for the first child area in each row is placed at the same distance from the row grid.

Related Properties

alignment-adjust (p. 375), baseline-identifier (p. 387), baseline-shift (p. 388), display-align (p. 454), dominant-baseline (p. 455)

relative-position   Relative Position

Purpose

Specifies the relative-position of an element.

Syntax

    relative-position: auto|static|relative|inherit

Where

- auto is a keyword that specifies there is no absolute positioning.
- static is a keyword that specifies that the area is normally stacked.
- relative is a keyword that specifies that the area's position is determined as if it were normally stacked; however, during rendering the area is offset relative to this position.
- inherit is a keyword that indicates that this property takes the same computed value as its parent.

Notes

- This is a layout-related property.
- For areas that break over a page boundary, only the content within the area on the page where the positioning was first defined is offset. The rest of the content within that area is clipped.
- This property pertains to all block-level and inline-level formatting objects.
- The default value for this property is static.

Related Properties

absolute-position (p. 372), direction (p. 453), letter-spacing (p. 535), reference-orientation (p. 588), text-decoration (p. 628), word-spacing (p. 643), writing-mode (p. 645)

RelativeLength [10]   Relative Length

Purpose

Indicates a relative length, which ends with the name of a relative unit of measure.

EBNF Syntax

    RelativeLength ::= Number RelativeUnitName

Standard Syntax

    Number RelativeUnitName

Where

- Number (p. 555) represents a floating-point number made up of one or more digits.
- RelativeUnitName (p. 593) represents a relative unit of measurement.

Note

- RelativeLength is a component of the RelativeNumeric production.

Related Productions

Number (p. 555), RelativeNumeric (p. 558), RelativeUnitName (p. 593)

RelativeNumeric [8]   Relative Numeric

Purpose

Represents a number with a value relative to one or more other values.

EBNF Syntax

```
RelativeNumeric ::= Percent | RelativeLength
```

Standard Syntax

```
Percent | RelativeLength
```

Where

- Percent (p. 580) represents a number followed by a percent sign.
- RelativeLength (p. 592) represents a number followed by the name of a relative unit of measure.

Notes

- RelativeNumeric is a component of the Numeric production.

Related Productions

Numeric (p. 558), Percent (p. 580), RelativeLength (p. 592)

RelativeUnitName [28]   Relative Unit Name

Purpose

Represents the relative unit of measure.

EBNF Syntax

```
'em'
```

Standard Syntax

```
em
```

Where

- em is the measurement of the current font height.

Note

- RelativeUnitName represents part of an expression.

Related Productions

AbsoluteUnitName (p. 372), AlphaOrDigits (p. 376), Color (p. 443), Digits (p. 452), EnumerationToken (p. 459), ExprToken (p. 460), ExprWhitespace (p. 461), FloatingPointNumber (p. 463), FunctionName (p. 512), Keyword (p. 529), Literal (p. 541), MultiplyOperator (p. 555), Number (p. 555), Operator (p. 559), OperatorName (p. 560)

XSL Style Sheet Syntax

rendering-intent   Rendering Intent

Purpose

Allows for the specification of a color profile rendering intent other than the default.

Syntax

```
rendering-intent: auto| perceptual| relative-colorimetric
  | saturation| absolute-colorimetric| inherit
```

Where

- auto is a keyword that commands the user agent to determine the best intent base on the content type.
- perceptual is a keyword that preserves the relationship between colors.
- relative-colorimetric is a keyword that leaves the colors within the gamut unchanged and converts colors outside the gamut to colors with the same lightness but that come just within the gamut.
- saturation is a keyword that keeps the relative saturation values of the original pixels and converts colors outside the gamut to ones just within the gamut with the same saturation.
- absolute-colorimetric is a keyword that disables whitepoint matching when converting colors.
- inherit is a keyword that indicates that this property takes the same computed value as its parent.

Notes

- This is a color property.
- absolute-colorimetric is generally not a recommended value.
- When using the perceptual value, pixel values originally within the gamut may be changed to avoid hue shifts or discontinuities and to preserve the overall appearance of a scene.
- rendering-intent is mostly applicable to color profiles that deal with CMYK color spaces.
- This property corresponds with the fo:color-profile formatting object.

Related Properties

color (p. 441), color-profile-name (p. 443)

retrieve-boundary   Retrieve Boundary

Purpose

Retrieves a boundary contained within an fo:marker.

Syntax

```
retrieve-boundary: page|page-sequence|document
```

Where

- page is a keyword that specifies children of an fo:marker whose parent generated or returned an area within the containing page may be retrieved by the fo:retrieve-marker.
- page-sequence is a keyword that specifies only children of fo:markers that are descendents of the fo:flow within the fo:page-sequnce can be retrieved by this fo:retrieved-marker.
- document is a keyword that says children of any fo:marker descendant of any fo:flow may be retrieved.

Notes

- This is a marker property.
- This property is used with fo:retrieve-marker.

Related Properties

marker-class-name (p. 547), retrieve-class-name (p. 495), retrieve-position (p. 583)

retrieve-class-name   Retrieve Class Name

Purpose

Specifies the name of a retrieve-class-marker.

Syntax

```
retrieve-class-name: name
```

Where

- name specifies the name of a retrieve-class-marker that matches a value of a marker-class-name for an fo:marker.

Notes

- This is a marker property.
- An fo:retrieve-marker must have the same retrieve-class-name as marker-class name of the fo:marker it wants to retrieve.

Related Properties

marker-class-name (p. 547), retrieve-boundary (p. 594), retrieve-position (p. 583)

retrieve-position   Retrieve Position

Purpose

Specifies a preference for an fo:retrieve-marker to retrieve children of an fo:marker.

XSL Style Sheet Syntax

Syntax

```
retrieve-position: first-starting-within-page
  | first-including-carryover| last-starting-within-page
  | last-ending-within-page
```

Where

- `first-starting-within-page` is a keyword that specifies a preference to retrieve children of an `fo:marker` that are within the current page, or whose "is-first" property is true.
- `first-including-carryover` is a keyword that specifies a preference to retrieve `fo:marker` children within the current page that precedes other areas attached to the same `fo:marker`.
- `last-starting-within-page` is a keyword that specifies a preference to retrieve children of an `fo:marker` within the current page and whose "is-last" property is true.
- `last-ending-within-page` is a keyword that specifies a preference for retrieving `fo:marker` children whose is-last property is true and that follows any area attached to the same `fo:marker`.

Notes

- This is a marker property.
- The default value of this property is `first-starting-within-page`.

Related Properties

marker-class-name (p. 547), retrieve-boundary (p. 594), retrieve-class-name (p. 595)

---

rgb()   RGB Color Function

Purpose

Returns an RGB color.

EBNF Syntax

```
color rgb(number_1 , number_2 , number_3)
```

Standard Syntax

```
color rgb(number_1 , number_2 , number_3)
```

Where

- `color` is the color returned by the function.
- `rgb` is a function-name keyword.
- `number_1` represents the first argument's number.
- `number_2` represents the second argument's number.
- `number_3` represents the third argument's number.

Related Function

system-color() (p. 622)

richness | Voice Richness

Purpose
Specifies the richness of a voice.

Syntax
```
richness: number|inherit
```

Where

- *number* represents a richness level. Valid values range from 0 (a softer, smoother voice) to 100 (a louder, harsher voice). The default value of 50 represents a standard richness level.
- inherit is a keyword that indicates that this property takes the same computed value as its parent.

Notes

- This property is in the common-aural category.
- This property, which originated in CSS2, applies to all elements.
- A richer voice carries in a larger room.
- By default, the characteristics of this property are inherited.

Related Properties
azimuth (p. 377), cue (p. 449), cue-after (p. 450), cue-before (p. 451), elevation (p. 456), pause (p. 577), pause-after (p. 578), pause-before (p. 579), pitch (p. 580), pitch-range (p. 581), play-during (p. 582), speak (p. 613), speak-header (p. 614), speak-numeral (p. 615), speak-punctuation (p. 615), speech-rate (p. 616), stress (p. 620), voice-family (p. 637), volume (p. 638)

Related Formatting Objects
fo:bidi-override (p. 465), fo:block (p. 466), fo:external-graphic (p. 470), fo:footnote-body (p. 472), fo:initial-property-set (p. 473), fo:inline (p. 473), fo:instream-foreign-object (p. 475), fo:leader (p. 476), fo:list-block (p. 477), fo:list-item (p. 478), fo:page-number (p. 492), fo:page-number-citation (p. 492), fo:simple-link (p. 500), fo:table (p. 503), fo:table-and-caption (p. 504), fo:table-body (p. 504), fo:table-caption (p. 505), fo:table-cell (p. 505), fo:table-footer (p. 506), fo:table-header (p. 507), fo:table-row (p. 507)

right | Right Offset

Purpose
Controls the location of the right edge of a box from the right edge of the block that contains the box.

Syntax
```
right: length|percent%|auto|inherit
```

XSL Style Sheet Syntax

Where

- *length* is a positive or negative value followed by a two-letter abbreviation representing the unit of measure.
- *percent* is a positive or negative value that is relative to the size of the image. Follow *percent* with a percentage sign (%).
- auto is a keyword that represents a value automatically calculated by the user's browser. This is the default.
- inherit is a keyword that indicates that this property takes the same computed value as its parent.

Notes

- This property is in the common-absolute-position category.
- This property, which originated in CSS2, applies to elements that are positioned.
- The combination of left and right values override the current width of the content box.
- By default, the characteristics of this property are not inherited.

Related Properties

bottom (p. 434), left (p. 535), position (p. 583), top (p. 632)

Related Formatting Object

fo:block-container (p. 467)

---

role   Role

Purpose

Specifies the role of a formatting object for alternate document processors.

EBNF Syntax

role: <string> | none | inherit

Standard Syntax

role: *string* | none | inherit

Where

- *string* is a string, such as the name of an element.
- none indicates no tag. This is the default.
- inherit is a keyword that indicates that this property takes the same computed value as its parent.

Notes

- Alternate document processors include speech synthesizing devices; Braille tactile feedback devices; paged Braille printing devices; handheld devices; printing devices and print-preview modes; projection devices and transparencies; color computer monitors; fixed-pitch teletypes, terminals, and some portable devices; and television monitors.

- This property can be used by fo:flow, fo:static-content, and their child formatting objects.
- By default, the characteristics of this property are not inherited.

Related Production
source-document (p. 606)

Related Formatting Object
fo:block (p. 466), fo:external-graphic (p. 470), fo:float (p. 471), fo:footnote (p. 472), fo:footnote-body (p. 472), fo:initial-property-set (p. 473), fo:inline (p. 473), fo:instream-foreign-object (p. 475), fo:leader (p. 476), fo:list-block (p. 477), fo:list-item (p. 478), fo:list-item-body (p. 478), fo:list-item-label (p. 479), fo:multi-case (p. 480), fo:multi-properties (p. 480), fo:multi-switch (p. 481), fo:multi-toggle (p. 481), fo:page-number (p. 492), fo:page-number-citation (p. 492), fo:simple-link (p. 500), fo:table (p. 503), fo:table-and-caption (p. 504), fo:table-body (p. 504), fo:table-caption (p. 505), fo:table-cell (p. 505), fo:table-footer (p. 506), fo:table-header (p. 507), fo:table-row (p. 507)

round() Round Function

Purpose
Returns a rounded integer that is closest in value to the argument.

EBNF Syntax
number_r round(number)

Standard Syntax
number_r round(number)

Where
- number_r is the number returned by the function.
- round is a function-name keyword.
- number represents the argument's number.

Note
- If two numbers have the same value, round() returns the number that is closest to positive infinity.

Related Functions
abs() (p. 370), ceiling() (p. 439), floor() (p. 464), max() (p. 548), min() (p. 552)

rule-style Rule Style

Purpose
Sets the pattern for the rule.

Syntax

```
rule-style: none|dotted|dashed|solid|double|groove
|ridge|inherit
```

Where

- none is a keyword that indicates that the rule is omitted.
- dotted draws a dotted-line rule.
- dashed draws a dashed-line rule.
- solid draws a solid-line rule. This is the default.
- double draws a double-solid-line rule.
- groove draws a three-dimensional grooved rule.
- ridge draws a three-dimensional ridged rule.
- inherit is a keyword that indicates that this property takes the same computed value as its parent.

Notes

- This property is in the rule-and-leader category.
- By default, the characteristics of this property are inherited.

Related Properties

leader-alignment (p. 532), leader-length (p. 533), leader-pattern (p. 533), leader-pattern-width (p. 533), rule-thickness (p. 600)

Related Formatting Object

fo:leader (p. 476)

rule-thickness   Rule Thickness

Purpose

Sets the thickness of a rule.

Syntax

```
rule-thickness: length
```

Where

- *length* is the thickness (height) of the rule. The default value is 1.0 points.

Notes

- This property is in the rule-and-leader category.
- This property applies only if leader-pattern: rule.
- By default, the characteristics of this property are inherited.

Related Properties

leader-alignment (p. 532), leader-length (p. 533), leader-pattern (p. 533), leader-pattern-width (p. 533), rule-style (p. 599)

Related Formatting Object
fo:leader (p. 476)

scaling	Scale

Purpose
Sets scaling of an external graphic.

Syntax
scaling: *number*|*two_number_list*|max|max-uniform|inherit

Where
- *number* represents a single number by which both the horizontal and vertical dimensions of the graphic are scaled. The initial value is 1.0.
- *two_number_list* represents a two-number list by which the graphic is scaled. The first number scales the horizontal dimension, and the second number scales the vertical dimension.
- max scales both the horizontal and vertical dimensions of the graphic to fill the maximum available space without necessarily keeping the dimensions in their original proportions.
- max-uniform scales both the horizontal and vertical dimensions of the graphic to fill the maximum available space while keeping the dimensions in their original proportions.
- inherit is a keyword that indicates that this property takes the same computed value as its parent.

Notes
- This property is in the miscellaneous category.
- The XSL scaling property is related to the DSSSL-O scale property.
- By default, the characteristics of this property are not inherited.

Related Properties
baseline-shift (p. 388), block-progression-dimension (p. 390), clip (p. 440), color (p. 441), direction (p. 453), font-height-override-after (p. 484), font-height-override-before (p. 485), glyph-orientation-horizontal (p. 512), glyph-orientation-vertical (p. 513), height (p. 514), href (p. 515), hyphenation-keep (p. 517), hyphenation-ladder-count (p. 518), id (p. 521), inline-progression-dimension (p. 525), last-line-end-indent (p. 531), linefeed-treatment (p. 537), line-height (p. 538), line-height-shift-adjustment (p. 539), line-stacking-strategy (p. 540), max-height (p. 548), max-width (p. 550), min-height (p. 552), min-width (p. 553), overflow (p. 561), provisional-distance-between-starts (p. 586), provisional-label-separation (p. 587), reference-orientation (p. 588), ref-id (p. 589), score-spaces (p. 602), size (p. 605), space-treatment (p. 611), span (p. 612), text-align (p. 625), text-align-last (p. 626), text-indent (p. 629), unicode-bidi (p. 634), vertical-align (p. 635), visibility (p. 636), white-space (p. 639), white-space-collapse (p. 640), width (p. 642), wrap-option (p. 644), writing-mode (p. 645), z-index (p. 648)

Related Formatting Objects
fo:external-graphic (p. 470), fo:instream-foreign-object (p. 475)

scaling-method   Scaling Method

Purpose
Specifies a scaling tradeoff when formatting bitmapped graphics.

Syntax
```
scaling-method: auto| integer-pixels| resample-any-method
   | inherit
```

Where
- auto is a keyword that dictates the user agent can choose either of these options.
- integer-pixels is a keyword that specifies the user agent should scale the image so that each pixel is scaled to the nearest integer number of device pixels that will yield a near-perfect image size based on the content-height and content-width.
- resample-any-method is a keyword that species the user agent should resample the image to provide an image that fills the size based on content-height and content-width using any sampling method it wants.
- inherit is a keyword that indicates that this property takes the same computed value as its parent.

Notes
- This is an area dimension property.
- This property applies to fo:external-object and fo:instream-foreign-object.
- The reason this property is so flexible is because it needs to allow for device limitation.

Related Properties
block-progression-dimension (p. 390), content-height (p. 446), content-width (p. 446), height (p. 514), inline-progression-dimension (p. 525), max-height (p. 548), max-width (p. 550), min-height (p. 552), min-width (p. 553), scaling (p. 601), width (p. 642)

score-spaces   Score Spaces?

Purpose
Indicates whether strikethrough characters are drawn over spaces.

Syntax
```
score-spaces?: false|true|inherit
```

Where

- `false` is a keyword that indicates that the Boolean value of this expression is false (strikethrough characters are drawn over characters only).
- `true` indicates that the Boolean value of this expression is true (strikethrough characters are drawn over both characters and spaces). This is the default.
- `inherit` is a keyword that indicates that this property takes the same computed value as its parent.

Notes

- This property is in the miscellaneous category.
- The XSL `score-spaces` property is related to the DSSSL-O `score-spaces` property.
- By default, the characteristics of this property are not inherited.

Related Properties

`baseline-shift` (p. 388), `block-progression-dimension` (p. 390), `clip` (p. 440), `color` (p. 441), `direction` (p. 453), `font-height-override-after` (p. 484), `font-height-override-before` (p. 485), `glyph-orientation-horizontal` (p. 512), `glyph-orientation-vertical` (p. 513), `height` (p. 514), `href` (p. 515), `hyphenation-keep` (p. 517), `hyphenation-ladder-count` (p. 518), `id` (p. 521), `inline-progression-dimension` (p. 525), `last-line-end-indent` (p. 531), `linefeed-treatment` (p. 537), `line-height` (p. 538), `line-height-shift-adjustment` (p. 539), `line-stacking-strategy` (p. 540), `max-height` (p. 548), `max-width` (p. 550), `min-height` (p. 552), `min-width` (p. 553), `overflow` (p. 561), `provisional-distance-between-starts` (p. 586), `provisional-label-separation` (p. 587), `reference-orientation` (p. 588), `ref-id` (p. 589), `scaling` (p. 601), `size` (p. 605), `space-treatment` (p. 611), `span` (p. 612), `text-align` (p. 625), `text-align-last` (p. 606), `text-indent` (p. 629), `unicode-bidi` (p. 634), `vertical-align` (p. 635), `visibility` (p. 636), `white-space` (p. 639), `white-space-collapse` (p. 640), `width` (p. 642), `wrap-option` (p. 644), `writing-mode` (p. 645), `z-index` (p. 648)

Related Formatting Objects

`fo:bidi-override` (p. 465), `fo:footnote-body` (p. 472), `fo:initial-property-set` (p. 473), `fo:page-number` (p. 492), `fo:page-number-citation` (p. 492)

script	Script Specifier

Purpose

Names a language or character-set-related script for composing selected lines in an XML document.

Syntax

```
script: none|auto|script_name|inherit
```

Where

- none is a keyword that indicates that no script has been named.
- auto is a keyword that represents a value that automatically matches the sheet on which the page box resides. This relative size is the default.
- *script_name* is the name of a script supported by ISO 15924.
- inherit is a keyword that indicates that this property takes the same computed value as its parent. This is a relative page-box size.

Notes

- This property is in the common-hyphenation category.
- According to the XSL working draft (http://www.w3.org/TR/xsl/), "the script is determined using codepoint ranges in the text of the document. This provides the automatic differentiation between Kanji, Katakana, Hiragana, and Romanji used in JIS-4051 and similar services in some other countries/languages."

Related Properties

country (p. 448), hyphenate (p. 516), hyphenation-character (p. 517), hyphenation-push-character-count (p. 519), hyphenation-remain-character-count (p. 520), language (p. 530), xml:lang (p. 647)

Related Formatting Object

fo:block (p. 466)

---

show-destination	**Show Destination**

Purpose

Specifies the location of the destination resource.

Syntax

```
show-destination: replace|new
```

Where

- replace is a keyword that indicates that the destination resource replaces the current view.
- new is a keyword that indicates that the destination resource is put in a new view.

Notes

- This property is in the links category.
- This property is related to the XLink show attribute.
- By default, the characteristics of this property are not inherited.

Related Properties

auto-restore (p. 377), case-name (p. 438), case-title (p. 438), destination-placement-offset (p. 452), external-destination (p. 462), indicate-destination (p. 523), internal-destination (p. 526), starting-state (p. 619), switch-to (p. 621)

Related Formatting Object

fo:simple-link (p. 500)

---

size   Page-Box Size

Purpose
Sets the dimensions and orientation of a page box.

Syntax
size: *w_length*| *h_length*|<u>auto</u>|portrait|landscape
|inherit

Where

- *w_length* is a positive, absolute page-box-width value followed by a two-letter abbreviation representing the unit of measure.
- *h_length* is a positive, absolute page-box-height value followed by a two-letter abbreviation representing the unit of measure.
- auto is a keyword that represents a value that automatically matches the sheet on which the page box resides. This relative size is the default.
- portrait is a keyword that makes the page-box long and narrow — with the same proportions as a standard letter. This is a relative page-box size.
- landscape is a keyword that makes the page-box short and wide — with the same proportions as a standard spreadsheet. This is a relative page-box size.
- inherit is a keyword that indicates that this property takes the same computed value as its parent. This is a relative page-box size.

Notes

- This property is in the miscellaneous category.
- This property originated in CSS2.
- Valid relative units of measure are em (the height of the current font), ex (the height of the letter *x* in the current font), and px (pixels, relative to the size of the window). Valid absolute units of measure are in (inches), cm (centimeters), mm (millimeters), pt (points), and pc (picas).
- In XSL, size is mapped to the page-height and page-width properties.
- By default, the characteristics of this property are not inherited.

Related Properties

baseline-shift (p. 388), block-progression-dimension (p. 390), clip (p. 440), color (p. 441), direction (p. 453), font-height-override-after (p. 484),

font-height-override-before (p. 485), glyph-orientation-horizontal (p. 512), glyph-orientation-vertical (p. 513), height (p. 514), href (p. 515), hyphenation-keep (p. 517), hyphenation-ladder-count (p. 578), id (p. 521), inline-progression-dimension (p. 525), last-line-end-indent (p. 531), line-feed-treatment (p. 537), line-height (p. 538), line-height-shift-adjustment (p. 539), line-stacking-strategy (p. 540), max-height (p. 548), max-width (p. 550), min-height (p. 552), min-width (p. 553), overflow (p. 561), page-height (p. 575), page-width (p. 576), provisional-distance-between-starts (p. 586), provisional-label-separation (p. 587), reference-orientation (p. 588), ref-id (p. 589), scaling (p. 601), score-spaces (p. 602), space-treatment (p. 611), span (p. 612), text-align (p. 625), text-align-last (p. 626), text-indent (p. 629), unicode-bidi (p. 634), vertical-align (p. 635), visibility (p. 636), white-space (p. 639), white-space-collapse (p. 640), width (p. 642), wrap-option (p. 649), writing-mode (p. 645), z-index (p. 648)

Related Formatting Objects

fo:simple-page-master (p. 501)

source-document — Source Document

Purpose

Points to the XML document that is the source of the current formatting-object tree.

EBNF Syntax

source-document: <uri>+ | none | inherit

Standard Syntax

source-document: uri_name[uri_name[...uri_name]]
| none | inherit

Where

- uri_name names the URI of the source document.
- none indicates no source document or one that is temporary or unknown. This is the default.
- inherit is a keyword that indicates that this property takes the same computed value as its parent.

Notes

- This property applies to the fo:root property.
- By default, the characteristics of this property are not inherited.

Related Property

role (p. 598)

Related Formatting Objects

fo:block (p. 466), fo:external-graphic (p. 470), fo:float (p. 471), fo:footnote
(p. 472), fo:footnote-body (p. 472), fo:initial-property-set (p. 473), fo:inline
(p. 473), fo:instream-foreign-object (p. 475), fo:leader (p. 476), fo:list-block
(p. 477), fo:list-item (p. 478), fo:list-item-body (p. 478), fo:list-item-label
(p. 479), fo:multi-case (p. 480), fo:multi-properties (p. 480), fo:multi-switch
(p. 481), fo:multi-toggle (p. 481), fo:page-number (p. 492), fo:page-number-ci-
tation (p. 492), fo:simple-link (p. 500), fo:table (p. 503), fo:table-and-
caption (p. 504), fo:table-caption (p. 505), fo:table-cell (p. 505), fo:table-
row (p. 507)

| space-after | Space After Flow Object |

Purpose

Inserts space after the flow-object area.

Syntax

```
space-after: (space.minimum=npt,
  .optimum=npt, .maximum=npt,
  .conditionality=discard|retain,
  .precedence=force|integer)
  |inherit
```

Where

- space is a keyword that indicates that a sub-keyword — minimum, optimum, or maximum — follows.
- minimum is a keyword that precedes the minimum amount of width space to be inserted after the flow-object area. The initial value is 0 point.
- optimum is a keyword that precedes the ideal amount of width space to be inserted after the flow-object area. The initial value is 0 point.
- maximum is a keyword that precedes the maximum amount of width space to be inserted after the flow-object area. The initial value is 0 point.
- conditionality is a keyword that indicates whether the space is dis-carded (discard) or retained (retain) if it is the last space in the flow-object area.
- precedence is a keyword that indicates whether the space in the follow-ing flow-object area is merged with the space in the current one. A value of force prevents a merger. The integer value specifies the width of the merged width space.
- inherit is a keyword that indicates that this property takes the same computed value as its parent.

Notes

- This property is in the common-margins-block category.

- If minimum is greater than optimum, the value of minimum takes the value of optimum.
- If maximum is less than optimum, the value of maximum takes the value of optimum.
- The XSL space-after property is related to the DSSSL-O space-after property.
- By default, the characteristics of this property are not inherited.

Related Properties

end-indent (p. 457), margin properties (p. 542-p. 546), space-before (p. 608), start-indent (p. 618)

Related Formatting Objects

fo:block (p. 466), fo:block-container (p. 467), fo:external-graphic (p. 470), fo:float (p. 471), fo:footnote (p. 472), fo:footnote-body (p. 472), fo:inline (p. 473), fo:inline-container (p. 474), fo:instream-foreign-object (p. 475), fo:leader (p. 476), fo:list-block (p. 477), fo:list-item (p. 478), fo:page-number (p. 492), fo:page-number-citation (p. 492), fo:region-body (p. 496), fo:simple-link (p. 500), fo:simple-page-master (p. 501), fo:table (p. 503), fo:table-and-caption (p. 504)

space-before — Space Before Flow Object

Purpose

Inserts space before the flow-object area.

Syntax

```
space-before: (space.minimum=npt,
    .optimum=npt, .maximum=npt,
    .conditionality=discard|retain,
    .precedence=force|integer)
    |inherit
```

Where

- minimum is a keyword that precedes the minimum amount of width space to be inserted before the flow-object area. The initial value is 0 point.
- optimum is a keyword that precedes the ideal amount of width space to be inserted before the flow-object area. The initial value is 0 point.
- maximum is a keyword that precedes the maximum amount of width space to be inserted before the flow-object area. The initial value is 0 point.
- conditionality is a keyword that indicates whether the space is discarded (discard) or retained (retain) if it is the first space in the flow-object area.

- precedence is a keyword that indicates whether the space in the preceding flow-object area is merged with the space in the current one. A value of force prevents a merger. The *integer* value specifies the width of the merged width space.
- inherit is a keyword that indicates that this property takes the same computed value as its parent.

Notes

- This property is in the common-margins-block category.
- If minimum is greater than optimum, the value of minimum takes the value of optimum.
- If maximum is less than optimum, the value of maximum takes the value of optimum.
- The XSL space-before property is related to the DSSSL-O space-before property.
- By default, characteristics of this property are not inherited.

Related Properties

end-indent (p. 457), margin properties (p. 542 - p. 546), space-after (p. 607), start-indent (p. 618)

Related Formatting Objects

fo:block (p. 466), fo:block-container (p. 467), fo:external-graphic (p. 470), fo:float (p. 471), fo:footnote (p. 472), fo:footnote-body (p. 472), fo:inline (p. 473), fo:inline-container (p. 474), fo:instream-foreign-object (p. 475), fo:leader (p. 476), fo:list-block (p. 477), fo:list-item (p. 478), fo:page-number (p. 492), fo:page-number-citation (p. 492), fo:region-body (p. 496), fo:simple-link (p. 500), fo:simple-page-master (p. 501), fo:table (p. 503), fo:table-and-caption (p. 504)

| space-end | Space End Flow Object |

Purpose

Inserts space at the end of an inline flow-object area.

Syntax

```
space-end: (space.minimum=npt,
   .optimum=npt, .maximum=npt,
   .conditionality=discard|retain,
   .precedence=force|integer)
   |inherit
```

Where

- minimum is a keyword that precedes the minimum amount of width space to be inserted after the flow-object area. The initial value is 0 point.

XSL Style Sheet Syntax

- optimum is a keyword that precedes the ideal amount of width space to be inserted after the flow-object area. The initial value is 0 point.
- maximum is a keyword that precedes the maximum amount of width space to be inserted after the flow-object area. The initial value is 0 point.
- conditionality is a keyword that indicates whether the space is discarded (discard) or retained (retain) if it is the last space in the flow-object area.
- precedence is a keyword that indicates whether the space in the following flow-object area is merged with the space in the current one. A value of force prevents a merger. The integer value specifies the width of the merged width space.
- inherit is a keyword that indicates that this property takes the same computed value as its parent.

Notes

- This property is in the common-margins-inline category.
- If minimum is greater than optimum, the value of minimum takes the value of optimum.
- If maximum is less than optimum, the value of maximum takes the value of optimum.
- The space-end characteristic is not inherited.

Related Property

space-start (p. 610)

| **space-start** | Space Start Flow Object |

Purpose

Inserts space at the start of an inline flow-object area.

Syntax

```
space-start: (space.minimum=npt,
  .optimum=npt, .maximum=npt,
  .conditionality=discard|retain,
  .precedence=force|integer)
  |inherit
```

Where

- minimum is a keyword that precedes the minimum amount of width space to be inserted after the flow-object area. The initial value is 0 point.
- optimum is a keyword that precedes the ideal amount of width space to be inserted after the flow-object area. The initial value is 0 point.

- `maximum` is a keyword that precedes the maximum amount of width space to be inserted after the flow-object area. The initial value is 0 point.
- `conditionality` is a keyword that indicates whether the space is discarded (`discard`) or retained (`retain`) if it is the last space in the flow-object area.
- `precedence` is a keyword that indicates whether the space in the following flow-object area is merged with the space in the current one. A value of `force` prevents a merger. The `integer` value specifies the width of the merged width space.
- `inherit` is a keyword that indicates that this property takes the same computed value as its parent.

Notes
- This property is in the common-margins-inline category.
- If `minimum` is greater than `optimum`, the value of `minimum` takes the value of `optimum`.
- If `maximum` is less than `optimum`, the value of `maximum` takes the value of `optimum`.
- The `space-start` characteristic is not inherited.

Related Property
space-end (p. 609)

---

space-treatment

Space Treatment

Purpose
Specifies the way in which spaces and whitespace characters are treated.

Syntax
```
space-treatment: ignore|preserve|inherit
```

Where
- `ignore` is a keyword that indicates that the space or whitespace character is discarded.
- `preserve` is a keyword that indicates that the space or whitespace character is not treated in any particular way.
- `inherit` is a keyword that indicates that this property takes the same computed value as its parent.

Notes
- This property is in the miscellaneous category.
- By default, the characteristics of this property are inherited.

Related Properties
baseline-shift (p. 388), block-progression-dimension (p. 390), clip (p. 440), color (p. 441), direction (p. 453), font-height-override-after (p. 484),

XSL Style Sheet Syntax

font-height-override-before (p. 485), glyph-orientation-horizontal (p. 512), glyph-orientation-vertical (p. 513), height (p. 514), href (p. 515), hyphenation-keep (p. 517), hyphenation-ladder-count (p. 518), id (p. 521), in-line-progression-dimension (p. 525), last-line-end-indent (p. 531), linefeed-treatment (p. 537), line-height (p. 538), line-height-shift-adjustment (p. 539), line-stacking-strategy (p. 540), max-height (p. 548), max-width (p. 550), min-height (p. 552), min-width (p. 553), overflow (p. 561), provisional-distance-between-starts (p. 586), provisional-label-separation (p. 587), reference-orientation (p. 588), ref-id (p. 589), scaling (p. 601), score-spaces (p. 602), size (p. 605), span (p. 612), text-align (p. 625), text-align-last (p. 626), text-indent (p. 629), unicode-bidi (p. 634), vertical-align (p. 635), visibility (p. 636), white-space (p. 639), white-space-collapse (p. 640), width (p. 642), wrap-option (p. 644), writing-mode (p. 644), z-index (p. 648)

Related Formatting Object

fo:block (p. 466)

span	Column Span

Purpose

Determines whether columns are spanned within a multi-column area.

Syntax

span: none|all|inherit

Where

- none indicates no column span. This is the default.
- all indicates a span of all columns.
- inherit is a keyword that indicates that this property takes the same computed value as its parent.

Notes

- This property is in the miscellaneous category.
- The XSL span property is related to the DSSSL-O span property.
- By default, the characteristics of this property are not inherited.

Related Properties

baseline-shift (p. 388), block-progression-dimension (p. 390), clip (p. 440), color (p. 441), direction (p. 453), font-height-override-after (p. 484), font-height-override-before (p. 485), glyph-orientation-horizontal (p. 512), glyph-orientation-vertical (p. 513), height (p. 514), href (p. 515), hyphen-ation-keep (p. 517), hyphenation-ladder-count (p. 518), id (p. 521), inline-progression-dimension (p. 525), last-line-end-indent (p. 531), linefeed-treatment (p. 537), line-height (p. 538), line-height-shift-adjustment (p. 539), line-stacking-strategy (p. 540), max-height (p. 548), max-width (p. 550), min-height (p. 552), min-width (p. 553), overflow (p. 561), provisional-distance-between-starts (p. 586), provisional-label-separation (p. 587), reference-orientation (p. 588), ref-id (p. 589), scaling (p. 681), score-spaces (p. 602), size (p. 605), space-treatment (p. 611), text-align (p. 602), text-align-last (p. 605), text-indent (p. 611), unicode-bidi (p. 634), vertical-align (p. 635), visibility (p. 636), white-space (p. 639), white-space-collapse (p. 640), width (p. 642), wrap-option (p. 644), writing-mode (p. 645), z-index (p. 648)

Related Formatting Objects

fo:block (p. 466), fo:float (p. 471), fo:footnote (p. 472)

speak	Speak?

Purpose

Specifies whether text is spoken.

Syntax

speak: _normal_|none|spell-out|inherit

Where

- normal is a keyword that indicates that the aural browser uses a set of rules to *speak* an element and its child elements. This is the default.
- none is a keyword that indicates that no speaking takes place.
- spell-out is a keyword that indicates that that the text is spelled out one letter at a time.
- inherit is a keyword that indicates that this property takes the same computed value as its parent.

Notes

- This property is in the common-aural category.
- This property, which originated in CSS2, applies to all elements.
- By default, the characteristics of this property are inherited, so if you do not want the current element to be spoken, be sure to turn off any speak characteristics of the parent element.

Related Properties

azimuth (p. 377), cue (p. 449), cue-after (p. 450), cue-before (p. 451), elevation (p. 456), pause (p. 577), pause-after (p. 578), pause-before (p. 579), pitch (p. 580), pitch-range (p. 581), play-during (p. 582), richness (p. 597), speak-header (p. 614), speak-numeral (p. 615), speak-punctuation (p. 615), speech-rate (p. 616), stress (p. 620), voice-family (p. 637), volume (p. 638)

Related Formatting Objects

fo:bidi-override (p. 465), fo:block (p. 466), fo:external-graphic (p. 470), fo:footnote-body (p. 472), fo:initial-property-set (p. 473), fo:inline (p. 473), fo:instream-foreign-object (p. 475), fo:leader (p. 476), fo:list-block (p. 477), fo:list-item (p. 478), fo:page-number (p. 492),

XSL Style Sheet Syntax

fo:page-number-citation (p. 492), fo:simple-link (p. 500), fo:table (p. 503), fo:table-and-caption (p. 504), fo:table-caption (p. 505), fo:table-cell (p. 505), fo:table-footer (p. 506), fo:table-header (p. 507), fo:table-row (p. 507)

speak-header	Speak Table Header

Purpose
Sets table-cell header "speak" characteristics.

Syntax
speak-header: once|always|inherit

Where
- once is a keyword that indicates that a table header (identified by a table header element such as the HTML TH element) is spoken the first time a cell in a particular set of cells is selected.
- always is a keyword that indicates that a table header is spoken every time a particular cell is selected.
- inherit is a keyword that indicates that this property takes the same computed value as its parent.

Notes
- This property is in the common-aural category.
- This property, which originated in CSS2, applies to elements that contain table header information.
- By default, the characteristics of this property are inherited.

Related Properties
azimuth (p. 377), cue (p. 449), cue-after (p. 450), cue-before (p. 451), elevation (p. 456), pause (p. 577), pause-after (p. 578), pause-before (p. 579), pitch (p. 580), pitch-range (p. 581), play-during (p. 582), richness (p. 597), speak (p. 613), speak-numeral (p. 615), speak-punctuation (p. 615), speech-rate (p. 616), stress (p. 620), voice-family (p. 637), volume (p. 638)

Related Formatting Objects
fo:bidi-override (p. 465), fo:block (p. 466), fo:external-graphic (p. 470), fo:footnote-body (p. 472), fo:initial-property-set (p. 473), fo:inline (p. 473), fo:instream-foreign-object (p. 475), fo:leader (p. 476), fo:list-block (p. 477), fo:list-item (p. 478), fo:page-number (p. 492), fo:page-number-citation (p. 492), fo:simple-link (p. 500), fo:table (p. 503), fo:table-and-caption (p. 504), fo:table-body (p. 504), fo:table-caption (p. 505), fo:table-cell (p. 505), fo:table-footer (p. 506), fo:table-header (p. 507), fo:table-row (p. 507)

speak-numeral   Speak-Numeral

Purpose
Controls how numerals are spoken in a document.

Syntax
```
speak-numeral: digits|continuous|inherit
```

Where
- digits is a keyword that indicates that numerals are spoken one digit at a time (for example, 561 would be spoken as *five six one*).
- continuous is a keyword that indicates that numerals are spoken as a whole (for example, 561 would spoken as *Five hundred and sixty-one*). This is the default.
- inherit is a keyword that indicates that this property takes the same computed value as its parent.

Notes
- This property is in the common-aural category.
- This property, which originated in CSS2, applies to all elements.
- By default, the characteristics of this property are inherited.

Related Properties
azimuth (p. 377), cue (p. 449), cue-after (p. 450), cue-before (p. 451), elevation (p. 456), pause (p. 577), pause-after (p. 578), pause-before (p. 579), pitch (p. 580), pitch-range (p. 581), play-during (p. 582), richness (p. 597), speak (p. 613), speak-header (p. 614), speak-punctuation (p. 615), speech-rate (p. 616), stress (p. 620), voice-family (p. 637), volume (p. 638)

Related Formatting Objects
fo:bidi-override (p. 465), fo:block (p. 466), fo:external-graphic (p. 470), fo:footnote-body (p. 472), fo:initial-property-set (p. 473), fo:inline (p. 473), fo:instream-foreign-object (p. 475), fo:leader (p. 476), fo:list-block (p. 477), fo:list-item (p. 478), fo:page-number (p. 492), fo:page-number-citation (p. 492), fo:simple-link (p. 500), fo:table (p. 503), fo:table-and-caption (p. 504), fo:table-body (p. 504), fo:table-caption (p. 505), fo:table-cell (p. 505), fo:table-footer (p. 506), fo:table-header (p. 507), fo:table-row (p. 507)

speak-punctuation   Speak Punctuation

Purpose
Controls how punctuation is spoken in a document.

Syntax
```
speak-punctuation: code|none|inherit
```

XSL Style Sheet Syntax

Where

- code is a keyword that indicates that punctuation is to be spoken.
- none is a keyword that indicates no spoken punctuation but the insertion of pauses to indicate particular types of punctuation. This is the default.
- inherit is a keyword that indicates that this property takes the same computed value as its parent.

Notes

- This property is in the common-aural category.
- This property, which originated in CSS2, applies to all elements.
- By default, the characteristics of this property are inherited.

Related Properties

azimuth (p. 377), cue (p. 449), cue-after (p. 450), cue-before (p. 451), elevation (p. 456), pause (p. 577), pause-after (p. 578), pause-before (p. 579), pitch (p. 580), pitch-range (p. 581), play-during (p. 582), richness (p. 597), speak (p. 613), speak-header (p. 614), speak-numeral (p. 615), speech-rate (p. 616), stress (p. 620), voice-family (p. 637), volume (p. 638)

Related Formatting Objects

fo:bidi-override (p. 465), fo:block (p. 466), fo:external-graphic (p. 470), fo:footnote-body (p. 472), fo:initial-property-set (p. 473), fo:inline (p. 473), fo:instream-foreign-object (p. 475), fo:leader (p. 476), fo:list-block (p. 477), fo:list-item (p. 478), fo:page-number (p. 492), fo:page-number-citation (p. 492), fo:simple-link (p. 500), fo:table (p. 503), fo:table-and-caption (p. 504), fo:table-body (p. 504), fo:table-caption (p. 505), fo:table-cell (p. 505), fo:table-footer (p. 506), fo:table-header (p. 507), fo:table-row (p. 507)

---

speech-rate	**Speech Rate**

Purpose

Controls the speaking rate.

Syntax

```
speech-rate: number|x-slow|slow|medium|fast|x-fast|
faster|slower|inherit
```

Where

- number represents an absolute rate of speech measured in words per minute.
- x-slow is a keyword that represents a speech rate of 80 words per minute.
- slow is a keyword that represents a speech rate of 120 words per minute.

- medium is a keyword that represents a speech rate of 180 to 200 words per minute. This is the default.
- fast is a keyword that represents a speech rate of 300 words per minute.
- x-fast is a keyword that represents a speech rate of 500 words per minute.
- faster is a keyword that increases the current speech rate by 40 words per minute.
- slower is a keyword that decreases the current speech rate by 40 words per minute.
- inherit is a keyword that indicates that this property takes the same computed value as its parent.

Notes

- This property is in the common-aural category.
- This property, which originated in CSS2, applies to all elements.
- By default, the characteristics of this property are inherited.

Related Properties

azimuth (p. 377), cue (p. 449), cue-after (p. 450), cue-before (p. 451), elevation (p. 456), pause (p. 577), pause-after (p. 578), pause-before (p. 579), pitch (p. 580), pitch-range (p. 581), play-during (p. 582), richness (p. 597), speak (p. 613), speak-header (p. 614), speak-numeral (p. 615), speak-punctuation (p. 615), stress (p. 620), voice-family (p. 637), volume (p. 638)

Related Formatting Objects

fo:bidi-override (p. 465), fo:block (p. 466), fo:external-graphic (p. 470), fo:footnote-body (p. 472), fo:initial-property-set (p. 473), fo:inline (p. 473), fo:instream-foreign-object (p. 475), fo:leader (p. 476), fo:list-block (p. 477), fo:list-item (p. 478), fo:page-number (p. 492), fo:page-number-citation (p. 492), fo:simple-link (p. 500), fo:table (p. 503), fo:table-and-caption (p. 504), fo:table-body (p. 504), fo:table-caption (p. 505), fo:table-cell (p. 505), fo:table-footer (p. 506), fo:table-header (p. 507), fo:table-row (p. 507)

src   Source

Purpose
Specifies the URI of an fo:external-graphic.

Syntax
```
src: uri|inherit
```

Where
- uri specifies the URI to an external resource.
- inherit is a keyword that indicates that this property takes the same computed value as its parent.

XSL Style Sheet Syntax

Note

• This is a miscellaneous property.

Related Properties

content-type (p. 447), id (p. 521), provisional-distance-between-starts (p. 586), provisional-label-separation (p. 587), ref-id (p. 589), score-spaces (p. 602), visibility (p. 636), z-index (p. 648)

start-indent	**Start Indent**

Purpose

Specifies indention at the starting edge of the current formatting object box.

Syntax

```
start-indent: length|inherit
```

Where

• *length* is an absolute length of the indention. The default value is 0 point.
• inherit is a keyword that indicates that this property takes the same computed value as its parent.

Notes

• This property is in the common-margins-block category.
• If the value of *length* is positive, the indention is a standard block indent; if the value of *length* is negative, the indention is an outdent.
• The XSL start-indent property is closely related to the DSSSL-O start-indent property.
• The start-indent characteristic is inherited.

Related Properties

end-indent (p. 547), margin properties (p. 542-p. 546), space-after p. 607), space-before (p. 608)

Related Formatting Objects

fo:block (p. 466), fo:block-container (p. 467), fo:external-graphic (p. 470), fo:float (p. 471), fo:footnote (p. 472), fo:footnote-body (p. 472), fo:inline (p. 473), fo:inline-container (p. 474), fo:instream-foreign-object (p. 475), fo:leader (p. 476), fo:list-block (p. 477), fo:list-item (p. 478), fo:page-number (p. 492), fo:page-number-citation (p. 492), fo:region-body (p. 496), fo:simple-link (p. 500), fo:simple-page-master (p. 501), fo:table (p. 503), fo:table-and-caption (p. 504)

starting-state   Starting State

Purpose
Indicates whether the fo:multi-case formatting object can be displayed first.

Syntax
```
starting-state: show|hide
```

Where
- show is a keyword that indicates that the content of fo:multi-case can be displayed first.
- hide is a keyword that indicates that the content of fo:multi-case cannot be displayed first..

Notes
- This property is in the links category.
- A value of show indicates that the parent fo:multi-switch chooses its first child.
- If no fo:multi-case appears, fo:multi-switch is hidden.
- By default, the characteristics of this property are not inherited.

Related Properties
auto-restore (p. 377), case-name (p. 438), case-title (p. 438), destination-placement-offset (p. 452), external-destination (p. 462), indicate-destination (p. 523), internal-destination (p. 526), show-destination (p. 604), switch-to (p. 621)

Related Formatting Object
fo:multi-case (p. 480)

starts-row   Starts Row?

Purpose
Indicates whether the current table cell starts a table row.

Syntax
```
starts-row: yes|no
```

Where
- yes is a keyword that indicates that the current cell starts the row.
- no is a keyword that indicates that the current cell starts the row. This is the default value.

Notes
- This property is in the table category.

- The XSL starts-row property is related to the DSSSL-O starts-row? property.
- By default, characteristics of this property are not inherited.

Related Properties

border-collapse (p. 405), border-spacing (p. 422), caption-side (p. 437), column-number (p. 445), column-width (p. 446), empty-cells (p. 547), ends-row (p. 458), number-columns-repeated (p. 556), number-columns-spanned (p. 557), number-rows-spanned (p. 557), table-layout (p. 623), table-omit-footer-at-break (p. 624), table-omit-header-at-break (p. 624)

Related Formatting Objects

fo:table-cell (p. 505)

stress   Voice Stress

Purpose

Specifies the highest level of inflection in a voice.

Syntax

```
stress: number|inherit
```

Where

- *number* represents an inflection level. Valid values range from 0 (a low level of inflection) to 100 (a high level). The default value of 50 represents a standard stress level.
- inherit is a keyword that indicates that this property takes the same computed value as its parent.

Notes

- This property is in the common-aural category.
- This property, which originated in CSS2, applies to all elements.
- The value of stress varies depending on the selected voice.
- By default, the characteristics of this property are inherited.

Related Properties

azimuth (p. 377), cue (p. 449), cue-after (p. 450), cue-before (p. 451), elevation (p. 456), pause (p. 577), pause-after (p. 578), pause-before (p. 579), pitch (p. 580), pitch-range (p. 581), play-during (p. 582), richness (p. 597), speak (p. 613), speak-header (p. 614), speak-numeral (p. 615), speak-punctuation (p. 615), speech-rate (p. 616), voice-family (p. 637), volume (p. 638)

Related Formatting Objects

fo:bidi-override (p. 465), fo:block (p. 466), fo:external-graphic (p. 470), fo:footnote-body (p. 472), fo:initial-property-set (p. 473), `fo:inline` (p. 473), `fo:instream-foreign-object` (p. 475), `fo:leader` (p. 476), `fo:list-block` (p. 477), `fo:list-item` (p. 478), `fo:page-number` (p. 492), `fo:page-number-citation` (p. 492), `fo:simple-link` (p. 500), `fo:table` (p. 503), `fo:table-and-caption` (p. 504), `fo:table-body` (p. 504), `fo:table-caption` (p. 505), `fo:table-cell` (p. 505), `fo:table-footer` (p. 506), `fo:table-header` (p. 507), `fo:table-row` (p. 507)

suppress-at-line-break — Suppress at End Of Line?

Purpose
Indicates whether a non-control character at the end of a line is printed or displayed.

Syntax
`suppress-at-line-break:` <u>`auto`</u>`|suppress|retain|inherit`

Where
- `auto` is a keyword that represents a value automatically calculated by the user's browser. This is the default.
- `suppress` is a keyword that indicates that the character is suppressed.
- `retain` is a keyword that indicates that the character is printed or displayed.
- `inherit` is a keyword that indicates that this property takes the same computed value as its parent.

Notes
- This property is in the character category.
- If the character is suppressed and the line is justified, the character is not considered in the measurement of justification.
- By default, the characteristics of this property are not inherited.

Related Properties
`character` (p. 439), `letter-spacing` (p. 535), `text-decoration` (p. 628), `text-shadow` (p. 630), `text-transform` (p. 631), `word-spacing` (p. 643)

switch-to — Switch to

Purpose
Switches to a particular `fo:multi-case` formatting object.

EBNF Syntax
`switch-to: xsl-preceding|xsl-following|xsl-any|case_name`
`[case-name]*`

Standard Syntax

```
switch-to: xsl-preceding|xsl-following
  |xsl-any|case_name[case_name_2[case_name_3
  [...case_name_n]]]
```

Where

- xsl-preceding is a keyword that indicates that the current fo:multi-case is replaced by the prior fo:multi-case sibling.
- xsl-following is a keyword that indicates that the current fo:multi-case is replaced by the following fo:multi-case sibling.
- xsl-any is a keyword that indicates that the user can choose any fo:multi-case.
- case_name, case_name_2, case_name_3, and case_name_n are the unique names of several instances of fo:multi-case.

Notes

- This property is in the links category.
- If the value is xsl-preceding and the current multi-case is the first sibling, xsl-preceding switches to the last fo:multi-case sibling.
- If the value is xsl-following and the current multi-case is the last sibling, xsl-preceding switches to the first fo:multi-case sibling.

Related Properties

auto-restore (p. 377), case-name (p. 438), case-title (p. 438), destination-placement-offset (p. 452), external-destination (p. 462), indicate-destination (p. 523), internal-destination (p. 526), show-destination (p. 604), starting-state (p. 619)

Related Formatting Object

fo:multi-toggle (p. 481)

system-color()   System-Color Function

Purpose

Returns the name of a color defined by the computer system.

EBNF Syntax

```
color system-color(NCName)
```

Standard Syntax

```
color system-color(NCName)
```

Where

- color is the color returned by the function.
- system-color is a function-name keyword.
- NCName is a name from a collection of namespace names.

Related Function
rgb() (p. 596)

system-font()   System-Font Function

Purpose
Returns a characteristic of a font defined by the computer system.

EBNF Syntax
```
object system-font(NCName_1 , NCName_2)
```

Standard Syntax
```
object system-font(NCName_1 [, NCName_2])
```

Where
- *object* is the characteristic returned by the function.
- system-font is a function-name keyword.
- *NCName_1* is a font name from the current namespace.
- *NCName_2* is a namespace-defined property that specifies the characteristic.

Note
- If you omit the *NCName_2* argument, the function returns the default value of the font's characteristic.

Example
```
system-font(para,font-family)
```

table-layout   Table Width Layout

Purpose
Specifies a layout for the cells, rows, and columns that make up a table.

Syntax
```
table-layout: auto|fixed|inherit
```

Where
- auto is a keyword that represents a value automatically calculated by the user's browser. This is the default.
- fixed is a keyword that indicates that the fixed table layout algorithm is used.
- inherit is a keyword that indicates that this property takes the same computed value as its parent.

Notes
- This property is in the table category.

- This property, which originated in CSS2, applies to table and inline-table elements (such as the HTML TABLE element).
- The fixed value usually results in a quickly-rendered table.
- By default, the characteristics of this property are not inherited.

Related Properties

border-collapse (p. 405), border-spacing (p. 422), caption-side (p. 437), column-number (p. 445), column-width (p. 446), empty-cells (p. 457), ends-row (p. 458), number-columns-repeated (p. 556), number-columns-spanned (p. 557), number-rows-spanned (p. 557), starts-row (p. 619), table-omit-footer-at-break (p. 624), table-omit-header-at-break (p. 624)

Related Formatting Object

fo:table (p. 503)

table-omit-footer-at-break   Table Omit Footer at Break?

Purpose

Specifies whether to omit the table footer at a column break or page break.

Syntax

```
table-omit-footer-at-break: yes|no
```

Where

- yes is a keyword that omits the footer.
- no is a keyword that does not omit the footer. This is the default value.

Notes

- This property is in the table category.
- By default, characteristics of this property are not inherited.

Related Properties

border-collapse (p. 405), border-spacing (p. 422), caption-side (p. 437), column-number (p. 445), column-width (p. 446), empty-cells (p. 457), ends-row (p. 458), number-columns-repeated (p. 556), number-columns-spanned (p. 557), number-rows-spanned (p. 557), starts-row (p. 619), table-layout (p. 623), table-omit-header-at-break (p. 624)

Related Formatting Object

fo:table (p. 503)

table-omit-header-at-break   Table Omit Header at Break?

Purpose

Specifies whether to omit the table header at a column break or page break.

Syntax

```
table-omit-header-at-break: yes|no
```

Where

- yes is a keyword that omits the header.
- no is a keyword that does not omit the header. This is the default.

Notes

- This property is in the table category.
- By default, characteristics of this property are not inherited.

Related Properties

border-collapse (p. 405), border-spacing (p. 422), caption-side (p. 437), column-number (p. 445), column-width (p. 446), empty-cells (p. 457), ends-row (p. 458), number-columns-repeated (p. 556), number-columns-spanned (p. 557), number-rows-spanned (p. 557), starts-row (p. 619), table-layout (p. 623), table-omit-footer-at-break (p. 624)

Related Formatting Object

fo:table (p. 503)

text-align | Horizontal Text Alignment

Purpose

Sets horizontal alignment of selected text.

Syntax

```
text-align: start|center|end|justify|inside|outside
 |left|right|align_string|inherit
```

Where

- start aligns text with the starting edge of the box. This is an XSL value.
- center centers text within the element between the left and right margins. The XSL working draft states that this is an XSL value (although it is also part of CSS2).
- end aligns text with the ending edge of the box. This is an XSL value.
- justify aligns text within the element with the both the left and right margins. The XSL working draft states that this is an XSL value (although it is also part of CSS2).
- inside aligns text with the edge of the page binding (if the page binding edge is on the starting side) or the ending edge (if the page binding edge is on the ending side). This is an XSL value.
- outside aligns text with the ending edge (if the page binding edge is on the starting side) or the edge of the page binding (if the page binding edge is on the ending side). This is an XSL value.

- left aligns text within the element with the left margin. This is the equivalent of text-align="start". The XSL working draft states that this is an XSL value (although it is also part of CSS2).
- right aligns text within the element with the right margin. This is the equivalent of text-align="end". The XSL working draft states that this is an XSL value (although it is also part of CSS2).
- align_string is a string with which table-column cells will align.
- inherit is a keyword that indicates that this property takes the same computed value as its parent.

Notes

- This property is in the miscellaneous category.
- This property, which originated in CSS1, applies to block-level elements.
- By default, the characteristics of this property are inherited.

Example

```
para.formal { text-align: justify }
```

Related Properties

baseline-shift (p. 388), block-progression-dimension (p. 390), clip (p. 440), color (p. 441), direction (p. 453), font-height-override-after (p. 484), font-height-override-before (p. 485), glyph-orientation-horizontal (p. 512), glyph-orientation-vertical (p. 513), height (p. 514), href (p. 515), hyphenation-keep (p. 517), hyphenation-ladder-count (p. 518), id (p. 521), inline-progression-dimension (p. 525), last-line-end-indent (p. 531), linefeed-treatment (p. 537), line-height (p. 538), line-height-shift-adjustment (p. 539), line-stacking-strategy (p. 540), max-height (p. 548), max-width (p. 550), min-height (p. 552), min-width (p. 553), overflow (p. 561), provisional-distance-between-starts (p. 586), provisional-label-separation (p. 587), reference-orientation (p. 588), ref-id (p. 589), scaling (p. 601), score-spaces (p. 602), size (p. 605), space-treatment (p. 611), span (p. 612), text-align-last (p. 626), text-indent (p. 629), unicode-bidi (p. 634), vertical-align (p. 635), visibility (p. 636), white-space (p. 689), white-space-collapse (p. 640), width (p. 642), wrap-option (p. 644), writing-mode (p. 645), z-index (p. 648)

Related Formatting Object

fo:block (p. 466)

---

text-align-last   Last-Line Text Alignment

Purpose

Sets horizontal alignment of the last line of selected text.

Syntax

```
text-align-last: relative|start|center|end|justify
|inside|outside|left|right|align_string|inherit
```

Where

- relative uses the value of text-align to determine last line alignment. If text-align="justify" the alignment of the last line is start. If text-align is not equal to "justify" the alignment of the last line is the value of text-align. This is an XSL value.
- start aligns text with the starting edge of the box. This is an XSL value.
- center centers text within the element between the left and right margins. The XSL working draft states that this is an XSL value (although it is also part of CSS2).
- end aligns text with the ending edge of the box. This is an XSL value.
- justify aligns text within the element with the both the left and right margins. The XSL working draft states that this is an XSL value (although it is also part of CSS2).
- inside aligns text with the edge of the page binding (if the page binding edge is on the starting side) or the ending edge (if the page binding edge is on the ending side). This is an XSL value.
- outside aligns text with the ending edge (if the page binding edge is on the starting side) or the edge of the page binding (if the page binding edge is on the ending side). This is an XSL value.
- left aligns text within the element with the left margin. This is the equivalent of text-align="start". The XSL working draft states that this is an XSL value (although it is also part of CSS2).
- right aligns text within the element with the right margin. This is the equivalent of text-align="end". The XSL working draft states that this is an XSL value (although it is also part of CSS2).
- align_string is a string with which table-column cells will align.
- inherit is a keyword that indicates that this property takes the same computed value as its parent.

Notes

- This property is in the miscellaneous category.

Related Properties

baseline-shift (p. 388), block-progression-dimension (p. 390), clip (p. 440), color (p. 441), direction (p. 453), font-height-override-after (p. 484), font-height-override-before (p. 485), glyph-orientation-horizontal (p. 512), glyph-orientation-vertical (p. 513), height (p. 514), href (p. 515), hyphenation-keep (p. 517), hyphenation-ladder-count (p. 518), id (p. 521), inline-progression-dimension (p. 525), last-line-end-indent (p. 531), linefeed-treatment (p. 537), line-height (p. 538), line-height-shift-adjustment (p. 539), line-stacking-strategy (p. 540), max-height (p. 548), max-width (p. 550), min-height (p. 552), min-width (p. 553), overflow (p. 561), provisional-distance-between-starts (p. 586), provisional-label-separation (p. 587), reference-orientation (p. 588), ref-id (p. 589), scaling (p. 601), score-spaces (p. 602), size (p. 605), space-treatment (p. 611), span (p. 612), text-align (p. 625), text-indent (p. 629), unicode-bidi (p. 634), vertical-align (p. 635), visibility (p. 636), white-space (p. 639), white-space-collapse (p. 640), width (p. 642), wrap-option (p. 644), writing-mode (p. 645), z-index (p. 648)

Related Formatting Objects

fo:block (p. 466)

text-decoration   Enhance Text

Purpose

Enhances text with lines or blinking.

Syntax

```
text-decoration: none|([underline][overline]
  [line-through][blink])|inherit
```

Where

- none does not decorate the selected text. This is the default.
- underline underlines the selected text.
- overline draws a line over the selected text.
- line-through strikes through the selected text.
- blink turns the display of selected text on and off.
- inherit is a keyword that indicates that this property takes the same computed value as its parent.

Notes

- This property is in the character category.
- This property, which originated in CSS1, applies to all elements..
- By default, the characteristics of this property are not inherited. However, the children of the current elements should have the same text-decoration properties.
- Although browsers should recognize blink, they may not "blink" the selected text.

Example

```
para.msg { text-decoration: underline }
```

Related Properties

character (p. 439), letter-spacing (p. 535), suppress-at-line-break (p. 621), text-shadow (p. 630), text-transform (p. 631), word-spacing (p. 643)

Related Formatting Objects

fo:bidi-override (p. 465), fo:footnote-body (p. 472), fo:initial-property-set (p. 473), fo:page-number (p. 492), fo:page-number-citation (p. 492)

text-indent   First-Line Indention

Purpose

Indents the first line of text.

Syntax

```
text-indent: length|percent%|inherit
```

Where

- *length* is a positive or negative value followed by a two-letter abbreviation representing the unit of measure. The initial value is 0 point.
- *percent* is a positive or negative value that is relative to the width of the parent element. Follow *percent* with a percentage sign (%).
- inherit is a keyword that indicates that this property takes the same computed value as its parent.

Notes

- This property is in the miscellaneous category.
- This property, which originated in CSS1, applies to block-level elements.
- By default, the characteristics of this property are inherited.

Example

```
para { text-indent: 0.5in }
```

Related Properties

baseline-shift (p. 388), block-progression-dimension (p. 390), clip (p. 440), color (p. 441), direction (p. 453), font-height-override-after (p. 484), font-height-override-before (p. 485), glyph-orientation-horizontal (p. 512), glyph-orientation-vertical (p. 513), height (p. 514), href (p. 515), hyphenation-keep (p. 517), hyphenation-ladder-count (p. 518), id (p. 521), inline-progression-dimension (p. 525), last-line-end-indent (p. 531), linefeed-treatment (p. 537), line-height (p. 538), line-height-shift-adjustment (p. 539), line-stacking-strategy (p. 540), max-height (p. 548), max-width (p. 550), min-height (p. 552), min-width (p. 553), overflow (p. 561), provisional-distance-between-starts (p. 586), provisional-label-separation (p. 587), reference-orientation (p. 588), ref-id (p. 589), scaling (p. 601), score-spaces (p. 602), size (p. 605), space-treatment (p. 611), span (p. 612), text-align (p. 625), text-align-last (p. 626), unicode-bidi (p. 634), vertical-align (p. 635), visibility (p. 636), white-space (p. 639), white-space-collapse (p. 640), width (p. 642), wrap-option (p. 644), writing-mode (p. 645), z-index (p. 648)

Related Formatting Objects

fo:block (p. 466)

XSL Style Sheet Syntax

text-shadow   Text Shadow

Purpose

Applies one or more shadow effects to text.

Syntax

```
text-shadow: none|([ color-name|#rgb|#rrggbb
|rgb(rrr,ggg,bbb)|rgb(rrr%,ggg%,bbb%)][ h_length]
[ v_length][ blur_length],)
([ color-name|#rgb|#rrggbb|rgb(rrr,ggg,bbb)
|rgb(rrr%,ggg%,bbb%)][ h_length][ v_length]
[ blur_length])|inherit
```

Where

- none is a keyword that indicates no text shadow. This is the default.
- *color-name* specifies a shadow color by valid name (that is, Red (#FF0000), Maroon (#800000), Yellow (#FFFF00), Green (#008000), Lime (#00FF00), Teal (#008080), Olive (#808000), Aqua (#00FFFF), Blue (#0000FF), Navy (#000080), Purple (#800080), Fuchsia (#FF00FF), Black (#000000), Gray (#808080), White (#FFFFFF), and the default, Silver (#C0C0C0)). CSS2 adds the following case-insensitive colors : ActiveBorder, ActiveCaption, AppWorkspace, Background, ButtonFace, ButtonHighlight, ButtonShadow, ButtonText, CaptionText, GrayText, Highlight, HighlightText, InactiveBorder, InactiveCaption, InactiveCaptionText, InfoBackground, InfoText, Menu, MenuText, Scrollbar, ThreeDDarkShadow, ThreeDFace, ThreeDHighlight, ThreeDLightShadow, ThreeDShadow, Window, WindowFrame, and WindowText. You can specify a color before or after length values.
- *#rgb* is a three-digit hexadecimal color code, where *r* represents the red attributes, from 0 to F; *g* represents the green attributes, from 0 to F; and *b* represents the blue attributes, from 0 to F. You can specify a color before or after length values.
- *#rrggbb* is a six-digit hexadecimal color code, where *rr* represents the red attributes, from 00 to FF; *gg* represents the green attributes, from 00 to FF; and *bb* represents the blue attributes, from 00 to FF. You can specify a color before or after length values.
- rgb(*rrr,ggg,bbb*) represents absolute red-green-blue values, each ranging from 000 to 255. You can specify a color before or after length values.
- rgb(*rrr.d%, ggg.e%, bbb.f%*) represents the relative red-green-blue values, each ranging from 0.0% to 100.0%. Note that 0.0% is equivalent to an absolute value of 000, and 100.0% is equivalent to 255. You can specify a color before or after length values.
- *h_length* is a positive or negative value for the horizontal distance between the shadow and the text. A positive value puts the shadow to the right of the text, and a negative value puts the shadow to the left of the

text. Follow the *h_length* value with a two-letter abbreviation representing the unit of measure.

- *v_length* is a positive or negative value for the vertical distance between the shadow and the text. A positive value puts the shadow below
the text, and a negative value puts the shadow above the text. Follow
the *v_length* value with a two-letter abbreviation representing the unit
of measure.
- *blur_length* is a positive or negative value of a blur effect on the
shadow. Follow the blur_length value with a two-letter abbreviation
representing the unit of measure.
- inherit is a keyword that indicates that this property takes the same
computed value as its parent.

Notes
- This property is in the character category.
- This property, which originated in CSS2, applies to all elements.
- By default, the characteristics of this property are not inherited.

Related Properties
character (p. 439), letter-spacing (p. 535), suppress-at-line-break (p. 621),
text-decoration (p. 628), text-transform (p. 631), word-spacing (p. 643)

Related Formatting Objects
fo:bidi-override (p. 465), fo:footnote-body (p. 472), fo:initial-
property-set (p. 473), fo:leader (p. 476), fo:page-number (p. 492),
fo:page-number-citation (p. 492)

text-transform   Change Case

Purpose
Changes case of the selected text.

Syntax
```
text-transform: capitalize|uppercase|lowercase
   |none|inherit
```

Where
- capitalize applies initial uppercase to the selected text.
- uppercase applies all uppercase to the selected text.
- lowercase applies all lowercase to the selected text.
- none turns off the value inherited from the parent. This is the default.
- inherit is a keyword that indicates that this property takes the same
computed value as its parent.

Notes
- This property is in the character category.
- This property, which originated in CSS1, applies to all elements.

- Because of internationalization, it is recommended that you not use this XSL property in XML documents.
- By default, the characteristics of this property are inherited.

Example

```
p.warn { text-transform: uppercase; font-weight: 900 }
```

Related Properties

character (p. 439), letter-spacing (p. 535), suppress-at-line-break (p. 621), text-decoration (p. 628), text-shadow (p. 630), word-spacing (p. 643)

Related Formatting Objects

fo:bidi-override (p. 465), fo:footnote-body (p. 472), fo:initial-property-set (p. 473), fo:page-number (p. 492), fo:page-number-citation (p. 492)

top   Top Offset

Purpose

Controls the location of the top edge of a box from the top edge of the block that contains the box.

Syntax

```
top: length|percent%|auto|inherit
```

Where

- *length* is a positive or negative value followed by a two-letter abbreviation representing the unit of measure.
- *percent* is a positive or negative value that is relative to the size of the image. Follow *percent* with a percentage sign (%).
- auto is a keyword that represents a value automatically calculated by the user's browser. This is the default.
- inherit is a keyword that indicates that this property takes the same computed value as its parent.

Notes

- This property is in the common-absolute-position category.
- This property, which originated in CSS2, applies to elements that are positioned.
- The combination of top and bottom values overrides the current height of the content box.
- By default, the characteristics of this property are not inherited.

Related Properties

bottom (p. 434), left (p. 535), position (p. 583), right (p. 597)

Related Formatting Object

fo:block-container (p. 467)

treat-as-word-space   Treat As Word Space

Purpose

Specifies if a character should be treated as a word-space or a normal character.

Syntax

    treat-as-word-space: auto|yes|no|inherit

Where

- auto is a keyword that specifies the value to be determined by the Unicode codepoint for the character.
- yes is a value that specifies the inline-progression-dimension of the character should be adjusted according to the word-spacing property.
- no is a value that specifies the character should not have a word-spacing adjustment applied.
- inherit is a keyword that indicates that this property takes the same computed value as its parent.

Notes

- This is a character property.
- The default value for this property is auto.
- This property pertains to fo:character.

Related Properties

character (p. 439), letter-spacing (p. 535), suppress-at-line-break (p. 621), text-decoration (p. 628), text-shadow (p. 630), text-transform (p. 631), word-spacing (p. 643)

UnaryExpr [13]   Unary Expression

Purpose

Negates an expression.

EBNF Syntax

    UnaryExpr ::= PrimaryExpr | '-' UnaryExpr

Standard Syntax

    PrimaryExpr | - UnaryExpr

Where

- PrimaryExpr (p. 585) symbolizes a primary expression.
- - is a unary minus character.
- UnaryExpr negates an expression.

XSL Style Sheet Syntax

Notes

- UnaryExpr is a component of the MultiplicativeExpr.
- UnaryExpr is related to the XPath UnaryExpr.
- The minus sign (-) serves two purposes: it is the subtraction operator and is unary minus. Unary minus changes the sign of a variable to a minus.

Related Productions

MultiplicativeExpr (p. 554), PrimaryExpr (p. 585), UnaryExpr (p. 633)

unicode-bidi   Unicode Bidirectional

Purpose

Instructs the Unicode bidirectional algorithm to open an additional level of embedding or to create an override for the current element.

Syntax

unicode-bidi: <u>normal</u>|embed|bidi-override|inherit

Where

- normal is a keyword that does not open a new embedding level. This is the default.
- embed is a keyword that opens a new embedding level for an inline level following the value of the direction property.
- bidi-override is a keyword that overrides reordering for an inline-level element or inline-level element nested within a block-level element following the value of the direction property.
- inherit is a keyword that indicates that this property takes the same computed value as its parent. Be careful about how you use this keyword for unicode-bidi.

Notes

- This property is in the miscellaneous category.
- This property originated in CSS2.
- By default, the characteristics of this property are not inherited.

Related Properties

baseline-shift (p. 388), block-progression-dimension (p. 390), clip (p. 440), color (p. 441), direction (p. 453), font-height-override-after (p. 484), font-height-override-before (p. 485), glyph-orientation-horizontal (p. 512), glyph-orientation-vertical (p. 513), height (p. 514), href (p. 515), hyphenation-keep (p. 517), hyphenation-ladder-count (p. 518), id (p. 521), inline-progression-dimension (p. 525), last-line-end-indent (p. 531), line-feed-treatment (p. 537), line-height (p. 538), line-height-shift-adjustment (p. 539), line-stacking-strategy (p. 540), max-height (p. 548), max-width (p. 550), min-height (p. 552), min-width (p. 553), overflow (p. 561),

provisional-distance-between-starts (p. 586), provisional-label-separation (p. 587), reference-orientation (p. 508), ref-id (p. 589), scaling
(p. 601), score-spaces (p. 602), size (p. 605), space-treatment (p. 611), span
(p. 612), text-align (p. 625), text-align-last (p. 626), text-indent (p. 629),
vertical-align (p. 635), visibility (p. 636), white-space (p. 639), white-
space-collapse (p. 640), width (p. 642), wrap-option (p. 644), writing-mode
(p. 645), z-index (p. 648)

Related Formatting Object

fo:bidi-override (p. 465)

vertical-align   Vertical Alignment

Purpose

Sets vertical alignment of the element.

Syntax

vertical-align: <u>baseline</u>|sub|super|top
|text-top|middle|bottom
|text-bottom|*percent*%|*length*|inherit

Where

- baseline vertically aligns the element with the baseline of the current
  element or the parent element if the current element has no baseline.
  This is the default.
- sub makes the element a subscript.
- super makes the element a superscript.
- top vertically aligns the top of the element with the top of the highest
  element on the current line.
- text-top vertically aligns the element with the top of the parent element's typeface.
- middle vertically aligns the element with the middle of the element,
  computed by starting with the baseline and adding half the x-height of
  the parent element's typeface.
- bottom vertically aligns the bottom of the element with the lowest element on the current line.
- text-bottom vertically aligns the bottom of the element with the bottom
  of the parent element's typeface.
- *percent* is a positive value that is relative to the element's height.
  Follow *percent* with a percentage sign (%).
- *length* is a positive value followed by a two-letter abbreviation representing the unit of measure.
- inherit is a keyword that indicates that this property takes the same
  computed value as its parent.

Notes

- This property is in the miscellaneous category.
- This property, which originated in CSS1, applies to inline-level and table-cell elements.
- By default, the characteristics of this property are not inherited.

Example

```
sub { vertical-align: text-bottom; color: red }
```

Related Properties

baseline-shift (p. 388), block-progression-dimension (p. 390), clip (p. 440), color (p. 441), direction (p. 453), font-height-override-after (p. 484), font-height-override-before (p. 485), glyph-orientation-horizontal (p. 512), glyph-orientation-vertical (p. 513), height (p. 514), href (p. 515), hyphenation-keep (p. 517), hyphenation-ladder-count (p. 518), id (p. 521), inline-progression-dimension (p. 525), last-line-end-indent (p. 531), linefeed-treatment (p. 537), line-height (p. 540), line-height-shift-adjustment (p. 548), line-stacking-strategy (p. 550), max-height (p. 548), max-width (p. 550), min-height (p. 552), min-width (p. 553), overflow (p. 561), provisional-distance-between-starts (p. 586), provisional-label-separation (p. 587), reference-orientation (p. 588), ref-id (p. 589), scaling (p. 601), score-spaces (p. 602), size (p. 605), space-treatment (p. 611), span (p. 612), text-align (p. 625), text-align-last (p. 626), text-indent (p. 629), unicode-bidi (p. 634), visibility (p. 636), white-space (p. 639), white-space-collapse (p. 640), width (p. 642), wrap-option (p. 644), writing-mode (p. 645), z-index (p. 648)

Related Formatting Objects

fo:external-graphic (p. 470), fo:footnote-body (p. 472), fo:inline-container (p. 474), fo:instream-foreign-object (p. 475), fo:page-number (p. 492), fo:page-number-citation (p. 492), fo:region-after (p. 495), fo:region-before (p. 496), fo:region-body (p. 496), fo:region-end (p. 497), fo:region-start (p. 497), fo:simple-link (p. 500)

visibility   Visible Box?

Purpose

Specifies whether a box in which an element resides is visible or invisible.

Syntax

```
visibility: visible|hidden|collapse|inherit
```

Where

- visible is a keyword that indicates that the box is visible. This is the default.
- hidden is a keyword that indicates that the box is invisible.
- collapse is a keyword that indicates that the box is invisible and may be collapsed.

- inherit is a keyword that indicates that this property takes the same computed value as its parent.

Notes

- This property is in the miscellaneous category.
- This property, which originated in CSS2, applies to all elements.
- By default, characteristics of this property are not inherited.

Related Properties

baseline-shift (p. 388), block-progression-dimension (p. 390), clip (p. 440), color (p. 441), direction (p. 453), font-height-override-after (p. 484), font-height-override-before (p. 485), glyph-orientation-horizontal (p. 512), glyph-orientation-vertical (p. 513), height (p. 514), href (p. 515), hyphenation-keep (p. 517), hyphenation-ladder-count (p. 518), id (p. 521), inline-progression-dimension (p. 525), last-line-end-indent (p. 531), linefeed-treatment (p. 537), line-height (p. 358), line-height-shift-adjustment (p. 539), line-stacking-strategy (p. 540), max-height (p. 548), max-width (p. 550), min-height (p. 552), min-width (p. 553), overflow (p. 561), provisional-distance-be-tween-starts (p. 586), provisional-label-separation (p. 587), reference-orientation (p. 588), ref-id (p. 589), scaling (p. 601), score-spaces (p. 602), size (p. 605), space-treatment (p. 611), span (p. 612), text-align (p. 625), text-align-last (p. 626), text-indent (p. 629), unicode-bidi (p. 634), vertical-align (p. 635), white-space (p. 639), white-space-collapse (p. 640), width (p. 642), wrap-option (p. 644), writing-mode (p. 645), z-index (p. 648)

Related Formatting Objects

fo:block (p. 466), fo:float (p. 471), fo:footnote (p. 472), fo:inline (p. 473), fo:leader (p. 476), fo:table-column (p. 506)

voice-family   Voice Family

Purpose

Specifies one or more voices by name, family, or both.

Syntax

```
voice-family: [voice_name_1|male|female|child]
[,voice_name_2|male|female|child]
[...,voice_name_n|male|female|child]|inherit
```

Where

- voice_name is the name of a specific voice.
- male is a keyword that indicates that a generic male voice will be used.
- female is a keyword that indicates that a generic female voice will be used.
- child is a keyword that indicates that a generic child voice will be used.
- inherit is a keyword that indicates that this property takes the same computed value as its parent.

Notes

- This property is in the common-aural category.
- This property, which originated in CSS2, applies to all elements.
- By default, the characteristics of this property are inherited.

Related Properties

azimuth (p. 377), cue (p. 449), cue-after (p. 450), cue-before (p. 451), elevation (p. 456), pause (p. 577), pause-after (p. 578), pause-before (p. 579), pitch (p. 580), pitch-range (p. 581), play-during (p. 582), richness (p. 597), speak (p. 613), speak-header (p. 614), speak-numeral (p. 615), speak-punctuation (p. 615), speech-rate (p. 616), stress (p. 620), volume (p. 638)

Related Formatting Objects

fo:bidi-override (p. 465), fo:block (p. 466), fo:external-graphic (p. 470), fo:footnote-body (p. 472), fo:initial-property-set (p. 473), fo:inline (p. 473), fo:instream-foreign-object (p. 475), fo:leader (p. 476), fo:list-block (p. 477), fo:list-item (p. 478), fo:page-number (p. 492), fo:page-number-citation (p. 492), fo:simple-link (p. 500), fo:table (p. 503), fo:table-and-caption (p. 504), fo:table-body (p. 504), fo:table-caption (p. 505), fo:table-cell (p. 505), fo:table-footer (p. 506), fo:table-header (p. 507), fo:table-row (p. 507)

volume — Median Waveform Volume

Purpose

Specifies the median volume of a waveform file.

Syntax

```
volume: number|percentage|silent|x-soft|soft|medium
  |loud|x-loud|inherit
```

Where

- *number* represents an audible volume level. Valid values range from 0 (the minimum level) to 100 (the maximum level).
- *percentage* is an audible volume level that is relative to the level inherited from the parent element. Follow *percent* with a percentage sign (%).
- silent is a keyword that represents no volume at all.
- x-soft is a keyword that represents an audible volume level of 0.
- soft is a keyword that represents an audible volume level of 25.
- medium is a keyword that represents an audible volume level of 50.
- loud is a keyword that represents an audible volume level of 75.
- x-loud is a keyword that represents an audible volume level of 100.
- inherit is a keyword that indicates that this property takes the same computed value as its parent.

Notes

- This property is in the common-aural category.

- This property, which originated in CSS2, applies to all elements.
- By default, the characteristics of this property are inherited.

Related Properties

azimuth (p. 377), cue (p. 449), cue-after (p. 450), cue-before (p. 451), elevation (p. 456), pause (p. 577), pause-after (p. 578), pause-before (p. 579), pitch (p. 580), pitch-range (p. 581), play-during (p. 582), richness (p. 597), speak (p. 613), speak-header (p. 614), speak-numeral (p. 615), speak-punctuation (p. 615), speech-rate (p. 616), stress (p. 620), voice-family (p. 637)

Related Formatting Objects

fo:bidi-override (p. 465), fo:block (p. 466), fo:external-graphic (p. 470), fo:footnote-body (p. 472), fo:initial-property-set (p. 473), fo:inline (p. 473), fo:instream-foreign-object (p. 475), fo:leader (p. 476), fo:list-item (p. 478), fo:page-number (p. 492), fo:page-number-citation (p. 492), fo:simple-link (p. 500), fo:table (p. 503), fo:table-and-caption (p. 504), fo:table-body (p. 504), fo:table-caption (p. 505), fo:table-cell (p. 505), fo:table-footer (p. 506), fo:table-header (p. 507), fo:list-block (p. 477), fo:table-row (p. 507)

white-space   White Space

Purpose

Turns on or off whitespace.

Syntax

white-space: <u>normal</u>|pre|nowrap|inherit

Where

- normal is a keyword that indicates no addition of whitespace to an element. This is the default.
- pre is a keyword that indicates that the element is treated as preformatted content in the same way that the HTML PRE element works.
- nowrap is a keyword that indicates no addition of whitespace and no wrapping of text except for that text controlled by a line-break element (such as HTML's BR).
- inherit is a keyword that indicates that this property takes the same computed value as its parent.

Notes

- This property is in the miscellaneous category.
- This property, which originated in CSS1, applies to block-level elements.
- By default, the characteristics of this property are inherited.

Example

head1 { white-space: pre }

XSL Style Sheet Syntax

Related Properties

baseline-shift (p. 388), block-progression-dimension (p. 390), clip (p. 440),
color (p. 441), direction (p. 453), font-height-override-after (p. 484), font-
height-override-before (p. 485), glyph-orientation-horizontal (p. 512),
glyph-orientation-vertical (p. 513), height (p. 514), href (p. 515), hyphenation-keep (p. 517), hyphenation-ladder-count (p. 518), id (p. 521), inline-
progression-dimension (p. 525), last-line-end-indent (p. 531), linefeed-
treatment (p. 537), line-height (p. 538), line-height-shift-adjustment (p. 539),
line-stacking-strategy (p. 540), max-height (p. 548), max-width (p. 550),
min-height (p. 552), min-width (p. 553), overflow (p. 561), provisional-
distance-between-starts (p. 586), provisional-label-separation (p. 587),
reference-orientation (p. 588), ref-id (p. 589), scaling (p. 601), score-spaces
(p. 602), size (p. 605), space-treatment (p. 611), span (p. 621), text-align
(p. 625), text-align-last (p. 626), text-indent (p. 629), unicode-bidi (p. 634),
vertical-align (p. 635), visibility (p. 636), white-space-collapse (p. 640),
width (p. 642), wrap-option (p. 644), writing-mode (p. 645), z-index (p. 648)

Related Formatting Object

fo:block (p. 466)

white-space-collapse   White Space Collapse

Purpose

Specifies the way in which contiguous whitespace characters are treated.

Syntax

white-space-collapse: false|<u>true</u>|inherit

Where

- false indicates that the Boolean value of this expression is false; the
  contiguous whitespace characters are not treated in any particular way.
- true indicates that the Boolean value of this expression is true; the contiguous whitespace characters are ignored when the whitespace does
  not have a value of linefeed-treatment="preserve" and the preceding
  character is a non-ignored whitespace character or the following character is a non-ignored preserved linefeed character. This is the default.
- inherit is a keyword that indicates that this property takes the same
  computed value as its parent.

Notes

- This property is in the miscellaneous category.
- By default, the characteristics of this property are inherited.

Related Properties

baseline-shift (p. 388), block-progression-dimension (p. 390), clip (p. 440),
color (p. 441), direction (p. 453), font-height-override-after (p. 484), font-
height-override-before (p. 485), glyph-orientation-horizontal (p. 512),

glyph-orientation-vertical (p. 513), height (p. 514), href (p. 515), hyphen-ation-keep (p. 517), hyphenation-ladder-count (p. 518), id (p. 521), inline-progression-dimension (p. 525), last-line-end-indent (p. 531), linefeed-treatment (p. 537), line-height (p. 538), line-height-shift-adjustment (p. 539), line-stacking-strategy (p. 540), max-height (p. 548), max-width (p. 550), min-height (p. 552), min-width (p. 553), overflow (p. 561), provisional-distance-between-starts (p. 586), provisional-label-separation (p. 587), reference-orientation (p. 588), ref-id (p. 589), scaling (p. 601), score-spaces (p. 602), size (p. 605), space-treatment (p. 611), span (p. 612), text-align (p. 625), text-align-last (p. 626), text-indent (p. 629), unicode-bidi (p. 634), vertical-align (p. 635), visibility (p. 636), white-space (p. 639), width (p. 642), wrap-option (p. 644), writing-mode (p. 645), z-index (p. 648)

Related Formatting Object

fo:block (p. 466)

widows | Widows Paragraph Breaks

Purpose

Specifies the minimum number of paragraph-lines left at the top of a page.

Syntax

widows: *integer*|inherit

Where

- *integer* indicates the minimum number of paragraph-lines (in the first paragraph on a page) that must remain at the top of a page when a page break is inserted within a paragraph. The default setting is two lines.
- inherit is a keyword that indicates that this property takes the same computed value as its parent.

Notes

- This property is in the page-related category.
- This property, which originated in CSS2, applies to block-level elements.
- By default, the characteristics of this property are inherited.

Related Properties

keep-together (p. 536), orphans (p. 561), page-break-inside (p. 574)

Related Formatting Object

fo:block (p. 466)

width	Element Width

Purpose
Specifies the width of the selected element.

Syntax
```
width: length|percent%|auto|inherit
```

Where
- *length* is a positive value followed by a two-letter abbreviation representing the unit of measure.
- *percent* is a positive value that is relative to the size of the image. Follow *percent* with a percentage sign (%).
- auto is a keyword that represents a value automatically calculated by the user's browser.
- inherit is a keyword that indicates that this property takes the same computed value as its parent.

Notes
- This property is in the miscellaneous category.
- This property, which originated in CSS1, applies to all elements but selected inline elements and individual or grouped table rows.
- By default, the characteristics of this property are not inherited.

Example
```
img.bigpics { width: 550px }
```

Related Properties
baseline-shift (p. 388), block-progression-dimension (p. 390), clip (p. 440), color (p. 441), direction (p. 453), font-height-override-after (p. 484), font-height-override-before (p. 485), glyph-orientation-horizontal (p. 512), glyph-orientation-vertical (p. 513), height (p. 514), href (p. 515), hyphenation-keep (p. 517), hyphenation-ladder-count (p. 518), id (p. 521), inline-progression-dimension (p. 525), last-line-end-indent (p. 531), linefeed-treatment (p. 537), line-height (p. 538), line-height-shift-adjustment (p. 539), line-stacking-strategy (p. 540), max-height (p. 548), max-width (p. 550), min-height (p. 552), min-width (p. 553), overflow (p. 561), provisional-distance-between-starts (p. 586), provisional-label-separation (p. 587), reference-orientation (p. 588), ref-id (p. 589), scaling (p. 601), score-spaces (p. 602), size (p. 605), space-treatment (p. 611), span (p. 612), text-align (p. 625), text-align-last (p. 626), text-indent (p. 629), unicode-bidi (p. 634), vertical-align (p. 635), visibility (p. 636), white-space (p. 639), white-space-collapse (p. 640), wrap-option (p. 644), writing-mode (p. 645), z-index (p. 648)

Related Formatting Objects
fo:external-graphic (p. 470) fo:inline-container (p. 474) fo:instream-foreign-object (p. 475) fo:table (p. 503), fo:table-caption (p. 505)

word-spacing	Word Spacing

Purpose

Sets spacing between words.

Syntax

```
word-spacing: normal|[+|-]length
  |(space.minimum=npt,
  .optimum=npt, .maximum=npt,
  .conditionality=discard|retain,
  .precedence=force|integer)|inherit
```

Where

- normal is a keyword that represents the normal spacing between words.
- length is a positive value followed by a two-letter abbreviation representing the unit of measure. length is usually an increase in the spacing between words but can be a decrease (a negative value) — depending on the browser.
- space is the value that determines width space for the selection.
- minimum is a keyword that precedes the minimum amount of width space to be inserted after the flow-object area. The initial value is 0 point.
- optimum is a keyword that precedes the ideal amount of width space to be inserted after the flow-object area. The initial value is 0 point.
- maximum is a keyword that precedes the maximum amount of width space to be inserted after the flow-object area. The initial value is 0 point.
- conditionality is a keyword that indicates whether the space is discarded (discard) or retained (retain) if it is the last space in the flow-object area.
- precedence is a keyword that indicates whether the space in the following flow-object area is merged with the space in the current one. A value of force prevents a merger. The integer value specifies the width of the merged width space.
- inherit is a keyword that indicates that this property takes the same computed value as its parent.

Notes

- This property is in the character category.
- This property, which originated in CSS1, applies to all elements.
- Valid relative units of measure are em (the height of the current font), ex (the height of the letter x in the current font), and px (pixels, relative to the size of the window). Valid absolute units of measure are in (inches), cm (centimeters), mm (millimeters), pt (points), and pc (picas).
- By default, the characteristics of this property are inherited.

XSL Style Sheet Syntax

Example

```
head1 { word-spacing: 2pt }
```

Related Properties

character (p. 439), letter-spacing (p. 535), suppress-at-line-break (p. 621), text-decoration (p. 628), text-shadow (p. 630), text-transform (p. 631)

Related Formatting Objects

fo:bidi-override (p. 465), fo:footnote-body (p. 472), fo:initial-property-set (p. 473), fo:leader (p. 476), fo:page-number (p. 492), fo:page-number-citation (p. 492)

wrap-option — Line-Wrap Option

Purpose

Specifies how line breaks occur in the box.

Syntax

```
wrap-option: nowrap|wrap|inherit
```

Where

- nowrap is a keyword that indicates no line wrapping within the box.
- wrap is a keyword that indicates line wrapping within the box whenever a line reaches the end of the box.
- inherit is a keyword that indicates that this property takes the same computed value as its parent.

Notes

- This property is in the miscellaneous category.
- The value of the overflow property affects the behavior of lines that reach the end of the box.
- By default, the characteristics of this property are inherited.

Related Properties

baseline-shift (p. 388), block-progression-dimension (p. 390), clip (p. 440), color (p. 441), direction (p. 453), font-height-override-after (p. 484), font-height-override-before (p. 485), glyph-orientation-horizontal (p. 512), glyph-orientation-vertical (p. 513), height (p. 514), href (p. 515), hyphenation-keep (p. 517), hyphenation-ladder-count (p. 518), id (p. 521), inline-progression-dimension (p. 525), last-line-end-indent (p. 531), linefeed-treatment (p. 537), line-height (p. 538), line-height-shift-adjustment (p. 539), line-stacking-strategy (p. 540), max-height (p. 548), max-width (p. 550), min-height (p. 552), min-width (p. 553), overflow (p. 561), provisional-distance-between-starts (p. 586), provisional-label-separation (p. 587), reference-orientation (p. 588), ref-id (p. 589), scaling (p. 601), score-spaces (p. 602), size (p. 605), space-treatment (p. 611), span (p. 612), text-align (p. 625), text-align-last (p. 626), text-indent (p. 629), unicode-bidi (p. 634), vertical-align (p. 635), visibility (p. 636), white-space (p. 369), white-space-collapse (p. 640), width (p. 642), writing-mode (p. 645), z-index (p. 648)

Related Formatting Object
fo:block (p. 466)

---

writing-mode   Writing Direction

Purpose
Sets the direction in which text is displayed or inlined.

Syntax
writing-mode: lr[-tb]|rl[-tb]|tb[-rl]|tb-lr|bt-lr
|bt-rl|lr-bt|rl-bt|lr-alternating-rl-bt
|lr-alternating-rl-tb|lr-inverting-rl-bt
|lr-inverting-rl-tb|tb-rl-in-rl-pairs|inherit

Where
- lr-tb (or lr) is a keyword that indicates the direction in which text is printed or displayed. Inline components and line text run from left to right; block components and lines run from top to bottom. This is the default.
- rl-tb (or rl) is a keyword that indicates the direction in which text is printed or displayed. Inline components and line text run from right to left; block components and lines run from top to bottom.
- tb-rl (or tb) is a keyword that indicates the direction in which text is printed or displayed. Inline components and line text run from top to bottom; block components and lines run from right to left.
- tb-lr is an additional internationalization keyword that indicates the direction in which text is printed or displayed. Inline components and line text run from top to bottom; block components run from left to right.
- bt-lr is an additional internationalization keyword that indicates the direction in which text is printed or displayed. Inline components and line text run from bottom to top; block components and lines run from left to right.
- bt-rl is an additional internationalization keyword that indicates the direction in which text is printed or displayed. Inline components and line text run from bottom to top; block components and lines run from right to left.
- lr-bt is an additional internationalization keyword that indicates the direction in which text is printed or displayed. Inline components and line text run from left to right; block components and lines run from bottom to top.
- rl-bt is an additional internationalization keyword that indicates the direction in which text is printed or displayed. Inline components and line text run from right to left; block components and lines run from bottom to top.

XSL Style Sheet Syntax

- lr-alternating-rl-bt is an additional internationalization keyword that indicates the direction in which text is printed or displayed. Inline components and line text alternate by running from left to right on one line and right to left on the next; block components and lines run from bottom to top.

- lr-alternating-rl-tb is an additional internationalization keyword that indicates the direction in which text is printed or displayed. Inline components and line text alternate by running from left to right on one line and right to left on the next; block components and lines run from top to bottom.

- lr-inverting-rl-bt is an additional internationalization keyword that indicates the direction in which text is printed or displayed. Inline components and line text alternate by running from left to right on one line and running an inverted right-to-left on the next; block components and lines run from bottom to top.

- lr-inverting-rl-tb is an additional internationalization keyword that indicates the direction in which text is printed or displayed. Inline components and line text alternate by running from left to right on one line and an inverted right-to-left on the next; block components and lines run from top to bottom.

- tb-rl-in-rl-pairs is an additional internationalization keyword that indicates the direction in which text is printed or displayed. Text is converted into two-character pairs that run from right to left, which then are piled from top to bottom. Lines and blocks run from right to left.

- inherit is a keyword that indicates that this property takes the same computed value as its parent.

Notes

- This property is in the miscellaneous category.
- The XSL writing-mode property is related to the DSSSL-O writing-mode property.
- By default, the characteristics of this property are inherited.

Related Properties

baseline-shift (p. 388), block-progression-dimension (p. 390), clip (p. 440), color (p. 441), direction (p. 453), font-height-override-after (p. 484), font-height-override-before (p. 485), glyph-orientation-horizontal (p. 512), glyph-orientation-vertical (p. 513), height (p. 514), href (p. 515), hyphenation-keep (p. 517), hyphenation-ladder-count (p. 518), id (p. 521), inline-progression-dimension (p. 525), last-line-end-indent (p. 531), linefeed-treatment (p. 537), line-height (p. 538), line-height-shift-adjustment (p. 539), line-stacking-strategy (p. 540), max-height (p. 548), max-width (p. 550), min-height (p. 552), min-width (p. 553), overflow (p. 561), provisional-distance-between-starts (p. 586), provisional-label-separation (p. 587), reference-orientation (p. 588), ref-id (p. 589), scaling (p. 601), score-spaces (p. 602), size (p. 605), space-treatment (p. 611), span (p. 612), text-align (p. 625), text-align-last (p. 626), text-indent (p. 629), unicode-bidi (p. 634), vertical-align (p. 635), visibility (p. 636), white-space (p. 640), white-space-collapse (p. 640), width (p. 642), wrap-option (p. 644), z-index (p. 648)

Related Formatting Objects

fo:block (p. 466), fo:inline-container (p. 474), fo:region-after (p. 495), fo:region-before (p. 496), fo:region-body (p. 496), fo:region-end (p. 497), fo:region-start (p. 497), fo:simple-page-master (p. 501)

xml:lang   Language Code

Purpose

Instructs XML to process the referred-to XML language code in which selected character data is written.

Standard Syntax

```
<element xml:lang=code>language_text</element>
```

Where

- `<element` is the start tag containing the element type.
- `xml:lang` is the processing instruction specifying that one or more language codes follow.
- `code` is the language code, country code, and/or subcode.
- `>` is the end of the start tag.
- `language_text` is the text output in the selected language.
- `</element>` is the end tag containing the element type and end-tag delimiters.

Notes

- This property is in the common-hyphenation category.
- For more information about this XML attribute, see xml:lang (p. 138).
- According to the XSL working draft (http://www.w3.org/TR/xsl/), "XSL treats xml:lang as a shorthand and uses it to set the country and language properties."

Example

```
<para xml:lang="en">I'm speaking in English.</para>
```

Related Properties

country (p. 448), hyphenate (p. 516), hyphenation-character (p. 517), hyphenation-push-character-count (p. 519), hyphenation-remain-character-count (p. 520), language (p. 530), script (p. 603)

Related Formatting Object

fo:block (p. 466)

XSL Style Sheet Syntax

z-index
Stack Level

Purpose

Sets the level of the current box in a stack of elements.

Syntax

z-index: <u>auto</u>|*integer*|inherit

Where

- auto is a keyword that represents a value automatically calculated by the user's browser. This is the default.
- *integer* indicates the number of the current box in the stack.
- inherit is a keyword that indicates that this property takes the same computed value as its parent.

Notes

- This property is in the miscellaneous category.
- This property, which originated in CSS2, applies to elements that are positioned.
- If there is no stack for the current box, the value of *integer* is 0.
- By default, the characteristics of this property are not inherited.

Related Properties

baseline-shift (p. 388), block-progression-dimension (p. 390), clip (p. 440), color (p. 441), direction (p. 453), font-height-override-after (p. 484), font-height-override-before (p. 485), glyph-orientation-horizontal (p. 512), glyph-orientation-vertical (p. 513), height (p. 514), href (p. 515), hyphenation-keep (p. 517), hyphenation-ladder-count (p. 518), id (p. 521), inline-progression-dimension (p. 525), last-line-end-indent (p. 531), linefeed-treatment (p. 537), line-height (p. 538), line-height-shift-adjustment (p. 539), line-stacking-strategy (p. 540), max-height (p. 548), max-width (p. 550), min-height (p. 552), min-width (p. 553), overflow (p. 561), provisional-distance-between-starts (p. 586), provisional-label-separation (p. 587), reference-orientation (p. 588), ref-id (p. 589), scaling (p. 601), score-spaces (p. 602), size (p. 605), space-treatment (p. 611), span (p. 612), text-align (p. 625), text-align-last (p. 626), text-indent (p. 629), unicode-bidi (p. 634), vertical-align (p. 635), visibility (p. 636), white-space (p. 639), white-space-collapse (p. 640), width (p. 642), wrap-option (p. 644), writing-mode (p. 645)

Related Formatting Objects

fo:block (p. 466) fo:float (p. 471) fo:footnote (p. 472) fo:inline (p. 473) fo:leader (p. 476)

XSL Style Sheet Syntax

III

XML Tutorial

Part III introduces you to XML — from the basics to advanced topics. The chapters in this part provide all the information you'll need to design and create accurate DTDs and robust XML documents. In this part, you'll learn about document structure — both defining that structure and constructing a document based on the structure. You'll also find out about elements, tags, attributes, and entities. You'll find out how to add special components to your documents and how to add XML links and pointers so that users can take full advantage of XML's hypertext features. Then you'll learn how to transform and style your documents. If you are completely new to XML, be sure to read through every chapter and test each example. If you are familiar with XML, browse the chapters to build your knowledge.

IN THIS PART

Chapter 1 Introducing XML

Chapter 2 Introducing DTDs

Chapter 3 Producing a DTD

Chapter 4 Constructing a Basic XML Document

Chapter 5 Using Custom XML Elements

Chapter 6 Adding Links and Pointers to an XML Document

Chapter 7 Styling Documents with XSL

Introducing XML

1

The Extensible Markup Language (XML) enables you to create custom markup languages. For example, if you work in a particular industry, you can incorporate technical terms into your new language. If you create most of your documents using the Standard Generalized Markup Language (SGML), you have a head start; because XML is a subset of SGML, you can convert those documents to XML. Then you can use the XLink (p. 145), XPointer (p. 165), and XPath (p. 181) languages to add simple and extended hypertext links, and post your documents to the World Wide Web.

● **NOTE**

The XML Industry Portal (http://www.xml.org/xmlorg_registry/ index.shtml) lists organizations that are working on XML specifications for their industries.

XML productions are written in *Extended Backus-Naur Form* (EBNF) notation. EBNF is the standard syntax that the XML recommendation uses to declare the element types and attributes that make up many programming and markup languages, including those discussed in this book. Before you start your first XML document or document type definition (DTD) or read through an existing custom-language definition, you should take the time to learn EBNF. Then you'll be able to better understand the XML and XML-related recommendations and working drafts.

● **CROSS-REFERENCE**

For more information about EBNF, see Appendix D, "EBNF Reference" (p. 809).

XML In Plain English explains XML at all levels; the book is tailor-made for those who create custom markup languages and for those who "code" XML documents by using text editors and word processors. However, those who use XML editors should know that underneath the documents shown on their desktops are the same XML statements and attributes that the custom-language developers see. Those who use word processors must save their XML documents in a text format.

All custom languages developed with XML syntax, and many XML documents using those languages, must be edited at the element-and-attribute level. For example, to tailor an XML document for a particular output, a person writing XML pages might find that adding XML statements directly to the document is faster and easier than working through menu commands and dialog boxes in an XML editor. Depending on what you want to accomplish and the features of the chosen application, you may want to use a word processor, text editor, or XML editor. Remember that XML is a very new language, so most applications that will help you write and edit XML documents are still being developed.

In addition to covering the basics of XML, custom-language development, and document creation, this chapter provides the background and history of XML and its relatives SGML, HTML, and XHTML; information about document structure; and an overview of writing an XML document.

The History of Hypertext

The interest in hypertext is a relatively recent development, spurred by the introduction and rapidly increasing popularity of the Web and its language, HTML. Hypertext enables a user to join individual chunks of text and multimedia — graphics, animation, audio, and video — into an informal network of information. In essence, by activating hypertext links, the user builds a series of documents that is tailored to his or her own needs.

The concept of hypertext is over 50 years old. In July 1945, Vannevar Bush wrote an article entitled "As We May Think" for *Atlantic Monthly*, in which he described a machine for "...browsing and making notes in an extensive online text and graphics system."

Theodor Holm (Ted) Nelson coined the terms *hypertext* and *hypermedia* (which encompass both text and multimedia) in 1960. He wrote the book *Computer Lib/Dream Machines* (originally published by Mindful Press in 1974 and republished in 1987 by Microsoft Press), which influenced the introduction of the Web. In the late 1970s, Nelson introduced Project Xanadu, which produced digital library and hypertext publishing systems — another pioneering effort that unfortunately did not reach fruition.

Although universities and other institutions experimented with hypertext during the 1960s and 1970s, the general public ignored it until Apple introduced Hypercard in 1987 and Apple and Microsoft developed their Mac and Windows Help systems, respectively, with which users can click hypertext terms to jump from one topic to another or open description boxes.

The World Wide Web demonstrates the true and best nature of hypertext. You can link to most pages on the Web by clicking hyperlinks on Web pages or by typing in their *Uniform Resource Locators* (URLs), or addresses, regardless of the server on which they reside — anywhere in the world. For example, you can start a session on the Web by viewing a document on one site, click a link to jump to a document in another site, go to the next site in yet another site, and so on, until you weave your way around the world several times in just a few minutes. Hypertext differentiates the Web from all other Internet resources, because it provides you with an alternative to the traditional method of reading printed or online pages — sequentially, line by line, from top to bottom, and page by page, until you reach the end of the document or the end of your attention span, whichever happens first.

The Web is a relatively new part of the Internet. In the late 1980s, researchers at the European Laboratory for Particle Physics (CERN) in Switzerland developed the Web to make their jobs easier; they wanted easy access to research documents that were networked at their laboratory. By 1990, they introduced a text-only browser and developed HyperText Markup Language (HTML). In 1991, they implemented the Web at CERN. They introduced the Web to the Internet community in 1992. Note that Hypertext Transport Protocol (http) is the protocol for *Web browsing*, the process of linking to specific addresses (URLs) on the Web.

The History of Markup Languages

A markup language combines text, graphics, and other multimedia links to parts of the current document, to other documents, and to other objects. *Markup* simply refers to the marks that editors make on manuscripts to be revised. Markup consists of *elements*, which define chunks of a document; *attributes*, which format or enhance those chunks; *entities*, which are one or more characters that represent a special character not found usually on your keyboard or are shortcuts to a chunk of text or even an entire document; and *notation*, which are sets of symbols or the characters that make up an alphabet. The non-markup part of a document is each element's contents — primarily text but also images.

The Extensible HyperText Markup Language (XHTML) is just the latest in a series of closely related markup languages, starting with SGML, extending through several generations of HTML elements, and continuing through XML.

SGML

Standard Generalized Markup Language (SGML) was made an International Standards Organization (ISO) standard in 1986. Because SGML is a standard, commercial organizations around the world use it for document publishing and distribution, and for custom markup-language creation. For example, HTML is SGML's most famous creation. SGML documents can contain text and multimedia elements, as well as headings of all levels, paragraphs, and a few formatted elements. Each SGML document has a *document type declaration*, which contains a document type definition (DTD). A DTD defines rules for document contents. In essence, a DTD specifies a markup language for one or more documents. For example, each version of HTML has been defined in a DTD.

HTML and XHTML

HTML developers designed the language to handle the Web's hypermedia functionality. Within a simple text document, the developer of an HTML document inserts an *element* that links one site on the Internet to another or describes the document to browsers, search indexes, computers, networks, and people. Several HTML versions have developed since HTML's inception; HTML 4.01 is the current version of the HTML standard.

●—NOTE

(For more details see http://www.w3.org/TR/html401/.) XHTML 1.0 is the successor to HTML (see "XHTML" below).

XML

Extensible markup language (XML) is a subset of SGML: XML is comprised of many SGML features, but is much less complex than SGML. As with SGML, you use XML to develop a markup language, with elements and attributes customized for your business or industry. After creating this language you can use XML — in the same way that you use HTML — to give structure and markup to documents.

Both XML and HTML support the Unicode Consortium's Universal Character Set (UCS), which not only includes special characters, including punctuation and mathematical symbols, but also adds foreign-language characters and alphabets, making XML an international standard. Note that these special characters and symbols are known as entities.

●—NOTE

XML and HTML support the use of *style sheets*, which help you to define the formatting structure and appearance of an entire large, complex document. However, whereas HTML has traditionally styled its own output in many ways, XML requires styles for formatted and enhanced output. (Of course, new versions of HTML and its successor XHTML strongly encourage you to use cascading style sheets to style documents.) In addition, XML goes beyond HTML by supporting the full version of Document Style Semantics and Specification Language (DSSSL) and cascading style sheets (CSS).

The style-sheet standard dedicated to "serving" XML is Extensible Stylesheet Language (XSL), which is based on DSSSL Online, a subset of DSSSL created specifically for electronic documents as well as CSS.

To learn more about CSS, refer to XHTML In Plain English, also by Sandra E. Eddy and published by IDG Books Worldwide. XSL is covered in "XSL Style Sheet Syntax" (p. 369) in Part II of this book and in Chapter 7, "Styling Documents with XSL" (p. 745), respectively. To keep up to date with XSL, which is now a recommendation, be sure to periodically browse the latest recommendation at `http://www.w3.org/TR/xsl/`. A new language, XSL Transformations (XSLT), works with XSL. Read about XSLT in "XSLT Component" (p. 319).

XML features and functions include the following:

- XML allows various types of document displays, not only for many computer platforms, but also for many other devices such as cell phones and handheld computers. Programmers can use any programming or scripting language to define documents.

- XML supports but does not require DTDs. If you use a DTD, tell XML parsers to process the document strictly following the rules set in the DTD.

- XML's supporting standards (XLink and XPointer) support more sophisticated linking than HTML does. In HTML and XML, you can link to a single URL. However, XML's standards support the use of several links simultaneously, as well as groups of links.

- XML's standards support printed and electronic documents and other output files in which the content and appearance are customized for different users.

- XML supports processing on either the client or the server computers. This allows developers to distribute and, optionally, save resources.

● NOTE

Currently, the XML 1.0 specification is set. However, the XLink and XPointer languages are still being developed and are in the Candidate Recommendation stage, which means that they have been reviewed by their technical communities. Both languages will probably change before the final recommendation.

XHTML

Currently, the World Wide Web Consortium (W3C), which is responsible for setting Web standards, has released the next HTML version, which is actually the first version of XHTML. XHTML is based on HTML 4.01 elements and attributes. XHTML is an *extensible* version of HTML: it *extends* HTML so that you can write custom elements and attributes using rules established in XML. Basically, it's HTML 4.01 in XML format. You can display XML data within an XHTML document and display XHTML data within an XML document because both XML and XHTML follow XML rules.

●—NOTE

For more information about present and future HTML versions, periodically go to W3C's HTML Activity page (http://www.w3.org/MarkUp/Activity/).

XHTML and XML

Because XHTML (and HTML) and XML are intertwined in so many ways, there are bound to be more similarities than differences.

The similarities

XHTML and XML documents essentially use the same structure of markup and character data. Once you have learned one of these languages, you are well on your way to understanding another.

XHTML and XML all support the Unicode Consortium's Universal Character Set (UCS), which not only includes special characters, including punctuation and mathematical symbols, but also adds foreign-language characters and alphabets, to make all three languages international standards.

●—CROSS-REFERENCE

For more information about inserting special characters in your XML documents, see "Inserting entities" (p. 705) in Chapter 4, "Constructing a Basic XML Document." For a list of supported characters, refer to Appendix A, "Unicode Characters and Character Sets" (p. 757).

The differences

XML and XHTML document processing differs. In general, XHTML documents are processed by some Web browsers and some XML parsers, and XML documents are processed by XML parsers — although Internet Explorer 5 has limited support for XML. Web browsers are designed to ignore many small HTML errors, such as missing punctuation or invalid construction of statements. Even if an XHTML document contains improperly coded markup, the browser will manage to create output — although it might not be formatted correctly. On the other hand, XML documents must follow XML standards stringently. If an XML document is coded badly, the errors may result in an end to processing and a flow of error messages. There is a major benefit to following the XML rules: Your documents will be more likely to endure future maintenance.

XML Document Structure

Early versions of HTML required an <HTML> element at the top and bottom of an HTML document. Within that were nested <HEAD> and <BODY> elements that defined the two main sections of the document. (In later HTML versions, these elements became optional.) XML documents follow the same general two-section format: The document *prolog* is at the head of the document, and the *instance* is the body. (Some XML developers say that the instance is the entire document, including the prolog.)

●─**CROSS-REFERENCE**────────────────────────

To learn about setting document structure and using the components described in this section, refer to Chapter 3, "Producing a DTD" (p. 681) and Chapter 4, "Constructing a Basic XML Document" (p. 699).

The document prolog

The prolog, which must precede any element but can be completely empty, can contain identifying information about an XML document, including an XML declaration (and the current XML version used for the document) and document type declaration. For example:

```
<?xml version="1.0"?>
<!DOCTYPE sampdoc [
<!ELEMENT greeting (#PCDATA)>
]>
```

The preceding example, which is an internal document type definition (DTD), could be the prolog for a well-formed document. (Learn about well-formed documents in the "Learning about XML Document Types" section starting on p. 670 in Chapter 2, "Introducing DTDs.")

An internal DTD is contained completely within its XML document. An external DTD, which is referred to from within one or more XML documents, is a completely separate document. In either case, a DTD sets all the rules about elements, attributes, and other document components. The following example refers to an external DTD:

```
<?xml version="1.0"?>
<!DOCTYPE sampdoc SYSTEM "sample.dtd">
```

You'll learn about DTDs in the following section as well as in Chapter 2, "Introducing DTDs" (p. 669) and Chapter 3, "Producing a DTD" (p. 681).

The prolog can also contain comments and other *processing instructions*, which tell the XML processor how to handle the statement enclosed within the <? and ?> delimiters.

The XML declaration can also include an *encoding declaration* (typically encoding="UTF-8"), which states the form of the Unicode characters, and a *standalone declaration*, which indicates whether the document is a standalone document (standalone="yes") or is associated with an external document (standalone="no"). Other encoding declarations are possible. The following XML declaration includes an encoding declaration and a standalone declaration:

```
<?xml version="1.0" encoding="UTF-8" standalone="yes"?>
```

The document type declaration

Many XML documents contain a document type (!DOCTYPE) declaration, which either includes a document type definition (DTD) contained inline to the document (see the following section) or has the option of referring to an external DTD. The document type declaration, which starts with the !DOCTYPE reserved keyword, declares the document type.

The document type definition

Document type definitions (DTDs) define elements and their attributes, entities, and notation. As the foundation of XML documents, DTDs enable a developer to create elements that set the structure and markup

1

of the content of an XML document. DTDs permit companies and departments to set standards for various types of documents, ranging from memoranda to reports to user and technical manuals.

For example, you can define custom elements to specify a rigid structure (such as an introduction, five chapters, and two appendices for a technical manual) or a more flexible structure (such as a letter's fixed name/address/date and its completely open body section). DTDs also enable you to create custom markup languages (that is, sets of custom elements) for particular industries and occupations. Perhaps the most well known XML-based markup language is Mathematical Markup Language (MathML). Other languages — most of which are still under development — include Spacecraft Markup Language (SML); BiblioML, for marking up bibliographic information; Customer Identity Markup Language (CIML) and Name and Address Markup Language (NAML), both of which are for customer relations; Geography Markup Language (GML); Legal XML; and Java Speech Markup Language (JSML). Research on markup languages is under way for industries and organizations ranging from accounting to workflow management.

●—**NOTE**——————————————————————————————

XML documents are made up of two types of components: markup and character data. Markup, which comprises the skeleton of the document, tells XML processors and browsers how to treat the content: how to store it and how it is organized. Markup consists of the prolog and the document type declaration, start tags, end tags, empty elements, comments, processing instructions, CDATA sections, and references to entities and characters. Markup represents the *logical structure* of the document. All of the non-markup content of a document is character data. The character data is what you will see on a printed or displayed page — the *physical structure* of the document. The combination of markup and character data is XML text.

Markup contains delimiters such as < and >, as well as reserved keywords such as !ELEMENT and !DOCTYPE and & (which delimits an entity). The presence or absence of delimiters and reserved keywords are the most important differences between markup and character data.

The document instance

The document instance includes the remaining part of the XML document — that is, everything but the prolog. (Remember that some XML developers say that the instance includes the entire document.)

The instance contains definitions of elements and attributes, as well as entities and content. As you learn about DTDs in the following chapters, you'll find out more about what makes up a document instance in DTDs. In other XML documents, the instance contains the actual contents of the document — the characters, paragraphs, pages, graphics, and whitespace that will make up the XML output.

Elements and tags

If you know about HTML elements, attributes, and tags, you are well on your way to understanding XML. However, if you are not familiar with HTML, you must note that elements and tags are *not* the same thing. An element begins with a *start tag* (the less-than < character, the element name, required and/or optional attributes and attribute values, and the greater-than (>) character) and ends with an *end tag*, which adds the slash (/) to the less-than and greater-than characters. Between the start tag and end tag are the element name, optional attributes, and other content. For example:

```
<text>This sentence is contained within the text element.
</text>
```

In HTML, some elements allow you to omit the end tag. However, in XML (and in XHTML), the end tag is *always* present. So, if you currently work with HTML documents but plan to convert to XML in the future, adding both required and optional end tags to your HTML documents is a good idea — for future compatibility with XML.

Empty elements

XML also provides *empty-element tags*, which are elements that have no current content. An empty-element tag refers to an object, such as an image or a line break that will be added to a document when it is output. Empty elements support two types of tag syntax: one is the same syntax that non-empty elements use (with a start tag and end tag), and the other is a syntax unique to empty-element tags:

```
<image />
```

or

```
<br />
```

Notice that the slash associated with a typical end tag appears at the end of the tag — preceded by a space. The empty-element syntax actually combines a start tag and end tag.

Empty elements usually have attributes. For example, if an image will be included in the document after it is processed, there must be a reference, such as a Uniform Resource Identifier (URI). For example:

```
<image src="flower.gif"/>
```

or

```
<image src="flower.gif"></image>
```

You can also have a start tag and an end tag with no future content:

```
<br></br>
```

Attributes

Attributes allow you to define properties or characteristics for elements. For example, you can start a numbered list with a particular value, or you can add an identifier to a graphic so that you can find it in a document — for linking purposes or to specify the start (or end) of an area to be formatted or enhanced. Elements with attributes look something like this:

```
<element option1="value1" option2="value2">
</element>
```

Notice that the start tag, within the less-than and greater-than symbols, includes all the attributes. For example:

```
<box border width="70" height="50"></box>
```

where

- < marks the beginning of the start tag.
- box is the element name.
- border is an attribute that turns on a border.
- width=70 is an attribute that sets the box width to 70 pixels.
- height=50 is an attribute that sets the box height to 50 pixels.
- > marks the completion of the start tag.
- < marks the beginning of the end tag.
- / is the important signal that differentiates this end tag from the start tag.
- box is the element name.
- > marks the completion of the end tag.

●─NOTE───

If an attribute has no set or optional values, define a default value in the DTD. For more information, see Chapter 2, "Introducing DTDs" (p. 669) and Chapter 3, "Producing a DTD" (p. 691).

You can nest XML elements within other elements, depending on how you define the elements in a DTD. For example:

```
<book><text><one>Watch this space!
</one></text></book>
```

The text element attribute size changes the size of the text to 12 points. The start and end bold (boldface) elements are nested within the text elements, and the ital (italics) elements are embedded within the bold elements. Notice that the nesting is completely symmetrical and does not overlap:

```
<book>          </book>
   <text>       </text>
      <one>  </one>
```

When creating an XML document, you should never overlap nested elements. Using the previous example, if you change the elements' layout to this:

```
<book><one><text>Watch this space!
</one></text></book>
```

and overlap nested elements:

```
<book>          </one>
   <one>        </text>
      <text>  </book>
```

processing of your document ends prematurely.

Entities

In XML, it is possible to insert a reference in a document to an *entity*, one or more characters from the ISO 10646 standard — up to and including an entire document — that will replace the reference. The characters that replace the reference are known as *replacement text*. Entity references and entities work like a word processor's search-and-replace function: the program searches for a word or phrase (the entity reference) and replaces it with another word or phrase (the entity).

If you use a particular technical term or a long name many times in a document, use an entity reference as a shortcut. For example, the entity reference wmc could represent The Widget Manufacturing Corporation, Inc.:

```
<!ENTITY wmc  "The Widget Manufacturing
              Corporation, Inc."
```

Then, when you specify wmc in a document:

```
<text>Buy from &wmc;--the world's best!<text>
```

the XML processor replaces it:

Buy from The Widget Manufacturing Corporation, Inc.--the world's best!

XML provides several types of entities:

- A *parsed entity*, which is parsed only if it is used in a document. A parsed entity can include both character data and markup.

- An *unparsed entity* will never be parsed.

- An *internal entity*, which is declared in the same document from which it is referenced.

- An *external entity* is in an external document and is referred to by using a URL.

- A *general entity*, which is named within the character data in an XML document.

- A *parameter entity* (PE) is named within DTD markup.

XML Output

XML elements control document structure and markup, but do not format documents. XML documents to be printed or displayed must have associated style sheets. Style sheets allow you to control the appearance of XML documents — when the documents are to be printed or displayed electronically. XML supports two types of style-sheet recommendations, cascading style sheets (CSS2) and Extensible Stylesheet Language (XSL).

Many people were introduced to CSS as they learned recent versions of HTML. CSS is a popular and easy-to-use styling language that sets rules to act on the element level. To write a rule, enter the element name (or *selector*) followed by a *declaration* (the name of the CSS2 property and a value). Note that many browsers still do not support CSS.

● NOTE

For more information about CSS1 and CSS2, refer to *XHTML In Plain English*, also written by Sandra E. Eddy and published by IDG Books Worldwide.

XSL, along with its component XSLT (see "XSLT Component" in Part II [p. 319]), allows writers and editors to write documents that format and enhance XML document output using Document Style Semantics and Specification Language (DSSSL) rules, which style SGML documents, and CSS properties. Construct XSL documents as you would develop XML documents; once you have learned how to use XML, you are well on your way to creating properly constructed XSL documents. XSL is comprised of two parts: a language that transforms XML documents and a vocabulary for specifying formats for XML documents. XSL processing starts with a source tree, which includes all the generations of elements and attributes in the document. XSL is currently a W3C working draft, which means that you can expect further changes to the language.

● CROSS-REFERENCE

For more information about XSL, refer to Chapter 7, "Styling Documents with XSL" (p. 745). In the reference section, XSL is covered in "XSL Style Sheet Syntax" (p. 369).

Introducing DTDs

In Chapter 1, you were introduced to document type
definitions (DTDs). In this chapter, you'll learn more
about DTDs, which define elements and their attributes,
entities, and notation. A DTD enables you to guide those
who develop XML documents. For example, you can control
the structure of a document by specifying which element a
document developer uses first, how many times the developer
can use a particular element in a document, and the order in
which the developer uses the elements. Using a DTD, you can
set initial values or ranges of values for attributes. In a DTD,
you can list entities that document developers can use as nick-
names for technical terms and long names, and you can name
special character sets to be used within documents.

This chapter also introduces the two types of XML
documents: well-formed and valid. In addition, you will learn
about the structure of a document and how the components
(elements, tags, attributes, entities, markup, character data)
fit together to form an accurate, well-organized document.

What Is a DTD?

A DTD, which is included or referred to in the document type declaration, defines all the rules for a named document type. In the DTD, you will define all the elements that control the document structure (the markup of content), and define some formats for the character data within the elements. If you do a good job, each of the documents using the same DTD will look almost identical. Then, if the DTD is well written and well organized, an XML processor, such as a parser within a browser, will be able to interpret the document's elements based on the definitions.

● **NOTE** ──────────────────────────────

The document type declaration is not the DTD; it *contains* the DTD. The document type definition, which is *always* known as the DTD, is the actual location of element, attribute, notation, and entity definitions.

In a way, using a `!DOCTYPE` declaration, introduced in Chapter 1, encourages the use of external DTDs because you are actually defining elements and other such components for a class of documents. External DTDs enable you to create the DTD in a separate document and refer to it from within multiple XML documents. This prevents associated documents from being gigantic (if your DTD consists of many lines). And, instead of editing every document when you change the central DTD, all you have to do is change the DTD. So, if your department or company produces sets of documents using document standards, DTDs are bound to make your life easier.

For many XML documents, a line starting with the `!DOCTYPE` reserved keyword specifies a particular type of document. For example, all memoranda fall into a single class of documents that look very similar, with *To*, *From*, and *Subject* headings at the top of the first page and content taking up the rest of the pages. So you could declare `to`, `from`, and `subject` elements as well as elements for one or more paragraph types for the content. Other document classes include user manuals, books, letters, reports, invoices, forms, and so on.

Learning About XML Document Types

XML supports two types of documents: well-formed and valid. Both types of documents produce appropriate XML output.

Well-formed documents

XML documents must be well-formed — at the very least. Well-formed documents must be well organized and are checked for accuracy by a nonvalidating XML parser or XML parsers running within some Web browsers. Well-formed documents must contain one root element under which all other elements are nested and meet other basic rules. In HTML and in XHTML, the root element is html. Because well-formed documents follow basic XML rules, all elements must have matching start tags and end tags. In HTML, the paragraph element (<P>) does not require an end tag: HTML browsers assume that the beginning of the next paragraph marks the end of the current paragraph. However, without a DTD, XML processors cannot figure out when elements end, how they are formatted, and so on. Therefore, start tags and end tags are necessary.

Well-formed documents must contain at least one root element:

```
<sayings>Money is the root of all evil.</sayings>
```

Thus, the following is not a well-formed document:

```
Money is the root of all evil.
```

Well-formed documents must nest child elements within the root element. For example:

```
<sayings>
<quote>Money is the root of all evil.</quote>
<quote>Money talks.</quote>
</sayings>
```

So, the following is not well-formed (because of the missing root element):

```
<quote>Money is the root of all evil.</quote>
<quote>Money talks.</quote>
```

nor is the following (because of a missing end tag and an improper end tag):

```
<sayings>
<quote>Money is the root of all evil.</quote>
<quote>Money talks.
<sayings>
```

Well-formed documents can use almost any XML production, including element and attribute declarations, in a standalone DTD.

Valid documents

Valid documents are well-formed documents that follow XML rules and go a step further: valid documents include DTDs. DTDs come in two flavors: internal and external. Valid XML documents include internal DTD subsets, external DTD subsets, or a combination of both.

An *internal DTD subset* is a DTD completely enclosed within the XML document whose elements, attributes, entities, and notation the DTD is defining or can be a reference to an external DTD file. *External DTD subsets* are XML documents that are used purely for defining elements, attributes, and so on that will be used in one or more "output" documents. Obviously, an internal DTD subset defines the components of one document — the one in which it is enclosed. You can use external DTD subsets to define the components of a set of documents: each document in the set refers to the external DTD file.

During processing, a validating XML processor creates a hierarchy of elements, with the root element, all its child and sibling elements, and the child, ancestor, and sibling elements of those child elements. Two XML features take advantage of this hierarchy:

- When you add extended links (XLinks) and extended pointers (XPointers) to a document, you can jump to particular generations of elements.

- When you style an XML document, style sheets use this hierarchy of elements to set styles for elements and their child elements.

DTDs also allow a company or department to set standards that control the structure and markup of each document, so that individual document creators don't have to develop or edit a particular document structure. It's already in the DTD.

XML element and attribute declarations belong in DTDs *only*. If a particular XML production is used in DTDs exclusively, you'll find a note to that effect in "XML Syntax" (p. 27) in Part I.

Understanding Internal and External Subsets

As you learned earlier in this chapter, DTDs are either internal DTD subsets or external DTD subsets. This section covers both types of subsets in greater detail.

Internal DTD subsets

Internal DTD subsets define all the non-character data components of the containing document. An internal DTD, which is located in the document prolog, starts after the !DOCTYPE declaration. The left bracket ([) signals the start of the DTD, and the end is marked with a right bracket and greater-than symbol (]>), followed immediately by the start of the content that will be output. For example:

```
<?xml version="1.0"?>
<!DOCTYPE doc [
<!ELEMENT doc (#PCDATA)>
]>
<doc>
This document contains its own DTD starting with the
left bracket and ending with the right bracket and
greater-than symbol.
</doc>
```

The DTD (the internal subset) is contained completely within the brackets. After the end of the sample DTD, the information to be output is contained within the <doc> start tag and the </doc> end tag. If you use components not defined in the DTD, a validating parser would display a message and possibly stop processing.

An internal DTD only defines elements for the document in which it is contained. You cannot use an internal DTD to specify the elements for a set of documents. So, if you must spend a great deal of time writing a long, complex DTD, using it for a single document would be a waste of your time. You should use an external DTD instead.

Why use an internal DTD at all?

- XML documents that do not fall into a standard document type may not need to use one of your standard external DTDs. If you know that a document will never be part of a document set, you may decide to use an internal DTD instead. Another example of a nonstandard document is one that contains many unique graphics that you will refer to using entity declarations.

- If you are dashing off a short document — even if it will eventually become part of a document set — the quick-and-dirty approach may be the best approach. In this situation, be prepared to edit the document later so that it will conform to one of your standard external DTDs.

- You can use a temporary internal DTD to validate a new XML document for the first time. Then, when the document is completely accurate and all its elements have been tested, you can replace the internal DTD with an external DTD.

External subsets

As you have already learned, you can use an internal DTD subset to define elements, attributes, entities, and other components for a particular document, or you can use an external DTD subset to define components for one or more documents. External DTDs enable entire sets of documents to share a single set of elements and other components, thereby enabling you to apply corporate or departmental standards and avoid having to plan and develop redundant DTDs.

If you use an external DTD subset, you call it from within an XML document by using a !DOCTYPE declaration with the option of a few variations:

```
<?xml version = "1.0" standalone="no"?>
<!DOCTYPE MANUAL SYSTEM
"/storage/manual.dtd"
```

or

```
<?xml version = "1.0"?>
<!DOCTYPE MANUAL PUBLIC
"http:/www/storage/manual.dtd"
```

The primary difference between the two sets of lines is the SYSTEM and PUBLIC keywords. SYSTEM indicates that the DTD is located on a local computer system or network. PUBLIC specifies that the DTD is stored in a folder or directory usually available to the public. Note the first example includes the standalone="no" component. This indicates that external DTDs may be associated with the current document. The value standalone="no" is the default if there is an external DTD. Therefore, you can consider standalone="no" a document comment.

Notice also that the !DOCTYPE line is very similar to that of an internal DTD subset. Since element declarations are in the external DTD, you don't have to include the brackets ([and]).

You can use external and internal DTDs together in a XML document. For example, if you are creating a document that generally conforms to a standard document type but has special sections that require additional elements, you can define those elements in an internal DTD:

```
<?xml version="1.0"?>
<DOCTYPE manual SYSTEM "document.dtd">

<?xml version="1.0"?>
<DOCTYPE manual SYSTEM "document.dtd" [
<!ENTITY % toc      SYSTEM "toc.dtd">
%toc;
<!ENTITY % intro    SYSTEM "intro.dtd">
%intro;
<!ENTITY % body     SYSTEM "body.dtd">
%body;
<!ENTITY % appendix SYSTEM "appendix.dtd">
%intro;
<!ENTITY % index    SYSTEM "index.dtd">
%index;
<!ELEMENT document (toc, intro, body,
                    appendix*, index)>
]>
```

The previous example shows the top of an XML document that refers to the document.dtd file and the first few lines of the DTD file itself. The document.dtd file contains parameter entity references to five DTDs that make up an entire document. Notice that the entities are declared before the root element. Remember that the internal DTD takes precedence over the external DTD.

Introducing Extended Backus-Naur Form

2

The XML 1.0 Recommendation uses Extended Backus-Naur Form (EBNF) notation to define the syntax for declaring element types, lists of attributes, entities, and so on. EBNF defines the standard syntax for DTDs and document markup. DTD notation enables you to specify components, valid values and ranges of values, and the location of particular elements in the hierarchy of declared elements. Before you declare your first XML element or write your first entity, you should take the time to learn EBNF.

EBNF is the International Standard ISO/IEC 14977: 1996 of the International Standardization Organization (ISO) and the International Electrotechnical Commission (IEC). EBNF syntax is the "official" standard used by developers of XML-based markup languages and for people learning about the productions and components that make up markup languages such as XML, its parent SGML, and its close relatives HTML and XHTML.

EBNF is known as a syntactic metalanguage, where *syntactic* means *of syntax* and *metalanguage* means data about language (just as metadata is data about data). Thus, EBNF is a syntax with which you can create languages.

You can use EBNF syntax to impose control over document creation. For example, you can require the use of specific elements, define attributes for those elements, limit the attribute values that can be entered, specify default attribute values, and set the order in which elements are used.

Among EBNF's unique terminology are three terms: *rule*, *production*, and *grammar*. A rule is a statement that defines a production. An entire set of productions is a grammar, which comprises every rule for a language. In addition, because EBNF is a technical syntax, it uses programming and mathematical terms such as *symbol*, *expression*, *operator*, and *operand*. EBNF uses special characters to delimit or connect components in XML documents. Each character has a unique meaning. For example, the less-than symbol (<) marks the beginning of components, such as declarations, start tags, and end tags. Quotation marks (") and single-quote marks (') mark the beginning and end of strings, and sets of parentheses (( )) group parts of expressions. Sets of brackets ([ ]) group optional ranges of characters or other components. Within statements, other characters connect components. For example, the pipe (|) connects components from which you can choose, or specifies the order in which elements can be used. EBNF enables a custom-language developer to specify whether certain characters are permitted as element values. Simply use the not symbol (^) to precede characters that are not allowed.

Each XML production follows this general syntax:

```
Symbol ::= expression
```

or

```
symbol ::= expression
```

Note that when inserting an XML rule in a document, you should not enter the symbol or `::=`; enter the expression only.

XML is a case-sensitive language; symbols that have an initial uppercase letter indicate a *regular expression* (a way of grouping characters or options); all other symbols are completely lowercase.

Most XML productions are composed of two or more components, which in most cases are other productions in the specification. This allows components used by two or more productions to be defined once — concisely and simply. As you continue through this chapter, you will see examples of the way in which XML declarations and other markup are constructed from individual components.

For more information about EBNF, read Appendix D, "EBNF Reference" (p. 799).

Reading a DTD

Perhaps the best way to learn about DTDs is to browse through the one for HTML. This enables you to understand the statements and symbols that make up a DTD. At first, this might seem to be a difficult task — almost like learning a new language — but you'll change your mind once you pick up a few basics. As you know, a DTD contains statements that specify rules for a markup language. The statements declare all the elements, attributes, entities, and so forth, that make up the language.

Perhaps the most important piece of a language is the element. An element declaration looks something like the following declaration for the HTML `table` element and its child elements, `caption`, `thead`, `tfoot`, `tbody`, `colgroup`, `col`, `tr`, `th`, and `td`:

```
<!ELEMENT TABLE   - -
   (CAPTION?, (COL*|COLGROUP*), THEAD?, TFOOT?, TBODY+)>
<!ELEMENT CAPTION  - - (%inline;)* -- table caption-->
<!ELEMENT THEAD    - O (TR)+       -- table header-->
<!ELEMENT TFOOT    - O (TR)+       -- table footer-->
<!ELEMENT TBODY    O O (TR)+       -- table body-->
```

```
<!ELEMENT COLGROUP - O (COL)*    -- table col. group-->
<!ELEMENT COL      - O EMPTY     -- table column -->
<!ELEMENT TR       - O (TH|TD)+  -- table row -->
<!ELEMENT (TH|TD)  - O (%flow;)* -- table header cell,
                                    table data cell
-->
```

Notice that each element declaration begins with the <! delimiter and the ELEMENT keyword. The - - and - O characters indicate that the start tag or end tag is either required (-) or not required (O). (Note that XML and XHTML end tags are always required for non-empty elements and special end tags are always required for empty elements, but HTML follows the rules in the HTML DTD.) Following that is a list of child elements, within parentheses. You'll also find child elements under the thead, tfoot, tbody, colgroup, and tr elements. Most of these children represent table rows (tr) and cells (th and td).

The EBNF notation uses certain characters to indicate how often an element can be used and in what order: A comma indicates that the listed components must be used in the order in which they appear. This means that the child element used immediately after the table element is caption. However, a question mark following an element (for example, caption) indicates that it is optional and can be used one time only. An asterisk indicates that an element, such as colgroup or col, can occur an unlimited number of times in a document. A plus sign, such as that following tbody, indicates that an element, such as tbody, *must* occur one or more times. However, the optional start tag and end tag for the tbody element show that a table must include a body, but the body does not have to be within <tbody> and </tbody> tags.

In the caption declaration, %inline; is a parameter entity (PE), which is a specific entity that occurs in DTDs. Remember that entities are shortcuts. The HTML DTD is loaded with PEs; without them, the DTD would be hundreds of pages long. The %inline; PE:

```
<!ENTITY % inline "#PCDATA | %fontstyle; | %phrase;
| %special; | %formctrl;">
```

states that inline elements (those that do not cause line breaks before or after) contain either *parsed character data* (#PCDATA) — which can include characters — other elements, or other entities.

Following almost all the element declarations is a comment, which starts with -- and ends with -->. An element declaration ends with the > delimiter.

Every element in the HTML DTD has a list of attributes. The
table element's attributes are as follows:

```
<!ATTLIST TABLE          -- table element --
%attrs;                  -- %coreattrs, %i18n, %events--
summary     %Text;    #IMPLIED -- speech output info--
width       %Length;  #IMPLIED -- table width--
border      %Pixels;  #IMPLIED -- table frame width--
frame       %TFrame;  #IMPLIED -- render frame parts--
rules       %TRules;  #IMPLIED -- row/col rulings--
cellspacing %Length;  #IMPLIED -- cell spacing--
cellpadding %Length;  #IMPLIED -- in-cell spacing--
%reserved;   -- reserved for possible future use --
datapagesize CDATA    #IMPLIED -- reserved --
  >
```

An attribute list, which begins with the <! delimiter and the
keyword ATTLIST and ends with the > delimiter, names the element
again. Notice the number of PEs (%attrs;, %coreattrs;, and so
forth). All these PEs are shortcuts that prevent the rapid expansion
of the DTD. The #IMPLIED keyword indicates that an attribute is
optional; you are not required to use it with the element. When you
see the #REQUIRED keyword next to a particular attribute, you must
use that attribute whenever you use the element.

This chapter just brushes the surface of DTD viewing and development. To learn more, continue to Chapter 3, "Producing a DTD."

Producing a DTD

3

In this chapter, you start to fill in the document prolog, the top part of any XML document instance, which is the entire document. The prolog includes the introduction to the document, or document type declaration (the DOCTYPE). The DOCTYPE points to an external or internal document type definition (DTD) that specifies the elements, attributes, entities, and notations for one or more XML documents.

This chapter shows you how to create a DTD, step by step. Suppose that you want to mark up a contacts database that contains several identification fields: the required first and last names and some optional information, such as the street address, city, state, ZIP code, one or more voice and fax telephone numbers, and fields that log record-creation and record-editing information.

Declaring an XML Document

The XML declaration is the first line in every XML document, whether the document is a DTD or a document that will appear on the Web. A typical XML declaration looks like this:

```
<?xml version = "1.0" standalone = "yes"?>
```

The entire line is a processing instruction that is enclosed within the processing-instruction <? and ?> delimiters. The line tells the XML processor how to interpret the rest of the lines in the document. In this case, the processing instruction states that this is an XML document and that it uses XML version 1.0, the current default. Thus, if you omit the version number from the processing instruction, an XML parser automatically processes the document against version 1.0 of the XML specification. XML supports other processing instructions, most of which refer the current document to an external document, such as an external style-sheet document.

The sample XML declaration also states that the current document is a standalone document with a completely enclosed internal DTD subset and no external DTD subset. So if all of the document's elements and attributes are defined completely within the document, the default value is standalone="yes". If an external DTD is declared in the document, the default value becomes standalone = "no".

Look at the following XML declaration:

```
<?xml version="1.0" encoding="UTF-8"?>
```

●─ CROSS-REFERENCE ────────────────────────

The XML declaration can include an encoding declaration (typically encoding="UTF-8") that states the supported Unicode character set for this document. For information about Unicode characters and character sets, refer to Appendix A, "Unicode Characters and Character Sets" (p. 757).

Although well-formed XML documents do not require an XML declaration, you should use one. Of course, valid XML documents require an XML declaration and must follow all other rules in the XML specification.

Referring to a DTD

After the XML declaration, the document prolog includes the document type declaration, which must precede the first start tag in an XML document. The document type declaration, which starts with the !DOCTYPE reserved keyword, either contains a complete internal DTD subset or refers to a separate external DTD subset. Both types of DTDs contain markup declarations that define XML elements, their attributes, values, and constraints, and can also define entities and notations.

In general, internal DTD subsets should be relatively short and contain few definitions; external DTD subsets can be longer and more complicated. For example, you can use an external DTD subset to define the root element and several generations of nested child elements and related attributes, as well as lists of entities. If you define elements with the same level of complexity in an internal DTD subset, its source document will be more difficult to review and maintain because it contains both the DTD and the information to be output. An internal DTD subset is contained within brackets ([and]) in its home document, whereas an external DTD subset is a separate document.

The internal DTD

As you know, an internal DTD subset is located within its source document. The DTD is composed of markup that can include elements, attributes, entities, and notation — all parts of an internal DTD subset — as well as references to external DTDs. When the DTD is completely located in the internal subset, the DTD is *local*. The source document contains both the DTD markup and the defined XML, which will be processed and output by the XML processor. It is best to use internal DTD subsets to define elements, attributes, notation, and entities for a single, unique XML document.

A !DOCTYPE declaration is required for an XML document to be valid; otherwise, the document is well-formed at best. Note that internal DTD subsets are higher in precedence than external DTD subsets. In other words, if an XML processor detects both types of DTD subsets in the same document, it processes the external subset first and then the internal subset. If all or part of the internal subset overrides information in the external subset, the internal subset takes precedence. Otherwise, the information in the external subset stands.

The external DTD

As you have learned in the previous chapter, an external DTD subset is the part of a DTD that is stored in a separate document, completely outside the source document. An external subset can be referred to by more than one XML document.

When your business or department sets standards for document output, produces many of the same type of document (such as corporate memos or letters), or creates long, complex documents (for example, user or technical manuals), it is a good idea to develop external DTD subsets. This way, one external DTD can define the elements, attributes, entities, and notation for sets of documents.

To refer to an external DTD subset from within an XML document, insert a uniform resource identifier (URI), which is the Internet address of the DTD, in the document type declaration. The URI can be an absolute address (an entire address such as `http://www.eddygrp.com/storage/entire.dtd`) or a relative address (a partial address such as `entire.dtd` or `/storage/entire.dtd`).

When you declare an external DTD subset, you can use the `SYSTEM` keyword or the `PUBLIC` keyword to indicate whether you can find the DTD file on a system (such as your local server or a small corporate network restricted to a relatively small population), or a public resource (for example, on a large industrial or governmental network accessible by a large population — including you).

Note that you can use an internal DTD subset temporarily to test an XML document; then, after successful testing, you can replace it with an external DTD subset.

●—**NOTE**—————————————————————————

If you don't need to produce a valid document, you need not associate it with a DTD. For example, you can use a nonvalidating XML processor on the document. A nonvalidating processor not only does not validate the document, but also is not even required to read an external DTD subset.

Defining the Root Element and Its Child Elements

Use the element declaration to list the root element and its first generation of descendant elements (that is, child elements). Generations of elements are similar to generations of human families: They include parents (that is, roots), ancestors (all elements above the parents), descendants (all elements below the parents), and children. In fact, several generations of descendant elements can exist. For example, the first generation (or child elements) is immediately under the root, the second generation (analogous to grandchildren) is under the first generation, the third generation (analogous to great-grandchildren) is under the second generation, and so on. The following example shows the definition of the root element, contacts, and its children (all within the parentheses):

```
<!ELEMENT contacts (name, address, city, state, zip,
   voice, fax, email, first_edit, update_edit, info)>
```

The element declaration starts with the uppercase keyword !ELEMENT, and each top-level element is separated from the next with a comma. The comma separator indicates that each element *must* appear in the order in which it was defined in the element declaration. However, you can separate all or some elements with pipe (|) symbols, which allow more latitude: each element may occur one or more times and can appear in any order. You can use a combination of commas and pipes to control strictly the use of some elements and more laxly the use of others. You can also place lists of elements, separated by pipes or commas, within parentheses. As the preceding declaration demonstrates, parentheses group like elements; in this case, they group all the first-generation child elements of the contacts element.

Adding Comments to Documents

Comments are an important part of XML documents — especially DTDs. Imagine what it would be like if you were a newly hired XML developer suddenly responsible for maintaining a complex, multipage company-wide DTD loaded with element declarations, many lists of attributes and values, and pages of entities. Without comments explaining the purpose of blocks of code, you could have problems interpreting the meanings of certain elements — not to mention many declarations and other statements.

You can identify XML comments by their delimiters: comments are preceded by the <!-- delimiters and followed by the --> delimiters. When XML processors interpret XML documents, comments should not appear in the output.

Because double hyphens (--) are reserved in comment delimiters, do not place them within the comment text. Embedded double hyphens may cause an XML processor to misinterpret the remaining part of a comment.

Continued

> You can insert comments almost anywhere in an XML document. However, there are important exceptions. Do not place comments at the very top of the document: the XML declaration must always be the first line in a document. Do not use comments within a character data section: an XML processor will interpret the comments and their delimiters as standard character data. In addition, do not embed comments within tags or in declarations. The XML recommendation states that embedded comments are invalid.
>
> Another way of clarifying an XML document is to use descriptive names for document components such as elements, attributes, and entities. For example, you can name the element that will contain the top-level heading text tophead, headingone, or even H1, which is identical to the name of HTML's top-level heading.

Specifying Element Occurrences

After you define the root element and list the top-level elements, you can use the following symbols to control the number of times that an element can appear in a record:

- ? indicates that an element can occur up to one time but does not have to occur at all.

- * indicates that an element (such as multiple telephone numbers) can occur an unlimited number of times.

- + indicates that an element (such as the restaurant name) *must* occur one or more times.

Now the element declaration looks like this:

```
<!ELEMENT contacts (name+, address*, city, state, zip,
  phone*, fax*, email*, first_edit, update_edit?,
  info*)>
```

Remember that using commas in an element declaration indicates that data must be entered in the exact order in which the elements appear. This type of list is known as a *sequence list*. To allow some data to be entered in any order (that is, a *choice list*), change some of the commas to pipe symbols (|):

```
<!ELEMENT contacts (name+, address*, city, state, zip,
  (phone|fax)*,email*, first_edit|update_edit?, info*)>
```

This now enables you to enter voice and fax telephone numbers in any order. However, you may not know which number is which.

Declaring Child Elements and Listing Their Children

After you list the child elements under their root elements, you can specify the contents of the elements immediately under the root element and list their own child elements, where necessary:

```
<!ELEMENT name                       (#PCDATA)>
<!ELEMENT address                    (#PCDATA)>
<!ELEMENT city                       (#PCDATA)>
<!ELEMENT state                      (#PCDATA)>
<!ELEMENT zip                        (#PCDATA)>
<!ELEMENT phone                      (#PCDATA)>
<!ELEMENT fax                        (#PCDATA)>
<!ELEMENT email                      (#PCDATA)>
<!ELEMENT first_edit    (first_date, first_editor)>
<!ELEMENT update_edit (update_date, update_editor)>
<!ELEMENT info                       (#PCDATA)>
```

#PCDATA represents parsed character data, which indicates non-markup data — that is, simply text.

● **NOTE**

#PCDATA can contain both elements and character data. All parsed character data is eventually parsed, and some may be modified by the parser.

Declaring an Empty Element

The EMPTY element specifies an element with no current content. No end tag exists; the start tag is simply a marker for future content, such as a graphic. So an empty element declaration for a graphic might look like this:

```
<!ELEMENT image (EMPTY)>
```

Continue defining elements and listing child elements until you have completed all the elements in the DTD.

Creating Attribute Lists and Values

You can define attributes in order to restrict or require input for an element. For example, for your contacts DTD, it's a good idea to set an initial value for the state element or to require that the zip code be filled in, to make future documents easier to fill in (for example, if most of the contacts work in the same state) or to ensure that certain fields be provided (for example, if you will use the contacts documents to fill in ground-mail form letters where the ZIP code must be used). Remember that you can always edit the DTD later to include additional options. The following example lists attributes for the image element.

```
<!ATTLIST image
          src       href        #REQUIRED
          alt       CDATA       #REQUIRED
          id        ID          #IMPLIED
          class     CDATA       #IMPLIED
          title     CDATA       #IMPLIED
          name      CDATA       #IMPLIED
>
```

Setting an attribute type

Attribute types control the values of particular attributes. For example, the CDATA type limits an attribute in two ways: the attribute must be a string, and it must contain character data. XML supports 10 attribute types in three categories: string, tokenized, and enumerated. The string type refers to an attribute that is a string. Tokenized types apply to *tokens*, which are basic units that cannot be broken down into smaller pieces. Tokens include reserved words, entities, operators, and variable names. The enumerated type is either a *notation* (a formalized set of symbols or an alphabet) or a list of notation values.

The CDATA Type

CDATA, the only string type, indicates that the attribute contains character data. This is the default attribute type. For example:

```
<!ATTLIST logo height CDATA #IMPLIED>)
```

In this case, the height attribute (for the logo element) will be expressed as a string (for example, "10" in the default unit of measure). Notice that the value of the string is enclosed within quotation marks. You also can enclose strings within single quote marks.

The ID type

The ID type, one of several tokenized types, is a unique identification value: no other attribute for this element type can have this particular value. In addition, an ID must be a valid XML name and it must have a default value of #IMPLIED or #REQUIRED, which you'll learn about in the following section. An example of the ID type is:

```
<!ATTLIST logo id ID #REQUIRED>
```

● CROSS-REFERENCE

You should almost always require an identifier for all elements — primarily to take advantage of XML's support for extended links and extended pointers. For more information about XLinks and XPointers, see "XLink Language" (p. 145) and "XPointer Language" (p. 165) in Part I. Also read through Chapter 6, "Adding Links and Pointers to an XML Document" (p. 733).

The IDREF and IDREFS types

The tokenized types IDREF and IDREFS are a cross-reference to one or more ID values that occur somewhere in the XML document. Both IDREF and IDREFS must be valid XML names. An attribute list with an IDREF type might look like this:

```
<!ATTLIST LABEL for IDREF #IMPLIED>
```

This example is for the for attribute of HTML 4.0's label element. The IDREFS type is a list of IDREF values. For example:

```
<!ATTLIST TH headers IDREFS #IMPLIED>
```

When you list IDREFS names in an XML document, separate each one with a space.

The ENTITY and ENTITIES types

Another set of tokenized types, ENTITY and ENTITIES, refers to one or more general entities. ENTITY refers to a single general entity. An example of the ENTITY type is:

```
<!ATTLIST logo src ENTITY #REQUIRED>
```

The src attribute refers to a URI in an entity declared elsewhere in the DTD. The ENTITIES type refers to a list of general entities, also declared in the DTD. For example:

```
<!ATTLIST pics src ENTITIES #REQUIRED>
```

In this case, ENTITIES indicates that there will be a list of pictures (pics), each separated by a space. Note that you do not precede the general entities with the & and ; delimiters.

The NMTOKEN and NMTOKENS types

The last set of tokenized attribute types is NMTOKEN and NMTOKENS, which refer to one or more valid XML name tokens. *Name tokens* are names that start with any letter, digit, or valid character. An example of an attribute list declaration for the NMTOKEN type is

```
<!ATTLIST macintosh model NMTOKEN #IMPLIED>
```

The model attribute of the macintosh element refers to a computer model name, which might contain both letters and numbers. The NMTOKENS type is a list of valid XML name tokens (in this case, a list of computer models), each separated by one space. For example:

```
<!ATTLIST macintosh models NMTOKENS #IMPLIED>
```

XML names and name tokens serve the same purpose. However, valid XML names must start with a letter or an underscore, and valid XML name tokens can start with any letter, digit, and many other characters. (Note that the XML specification also allows valid names to start with colons; however, the colon is reserved for future use.)

The NOTATION and enumerated NOTATION types

The enumerated attribute types, NOTATION and enumerated NOTATION, indicate that the attribute has one or more values specified by a notation declaration in the current DTD. For example:

```
<!ATTLIST audio play NOTATION #REQUIRED>
```

To use the enumerated version of NOTATION, enter the keyword NOTATION followed by notation values separated by the pipe symbol and enclosed within parentheses. For example:

```
<!ATTLIST audio play NOTATION (jp | ra) #REQUIRED>
```

● **NOTE**

Notation is a system of defining a means of communication using an authorized set of symbols or characters. It can identify Braille, musical notes, dance steps, and even computer file formats.

Making an attribute required or optional

The last item on an attribute list is the default declaration. This enables you to further control the attribute by making it required or optional; by setting a default value that is the only allowable value; by supplying one default value that can be changed; or by listing a set of valid values. In a default declaration, you can select from the following options:

- Use the #REQUIRED keyword to require that the XML document developer supply a value for a particular attribute.

- Use the #IMPLIED keyword to allow the XML document developer to decide whether to supply a value, accept the default value, or let the processing application choose a default value that may or may not be identical to the default value that you set in the DTD.

- Use the #FIXED keyword to fix a default value that you include in the attribute definition. If the XML document developer enters a value that is not the fixed value, the XML processor should issue a warning. If the developer does not enter a value, the processing application takes the default value.

- Supply a value. If the developer enters a value other than the one you entered in the DTD, the XML processor accepts that value. If the developer does not enter a value, the processing application uses the default value.

- Supply a set of valid values from which the developer can choose.

When you specify a value for an attribute, it cannot contain the less-than (<) symbol or the ampersand (&).

The XML specification includes certain rules for using the #REQUIRED and #IMPLIED keywords in XML documents. For instance, for an XML document to be valid, an attribute that is #REQUIRED must include the attribute name and an attribute value. If the XML document developer has not included a value for an #IMPLIED attribute, the XML parser must report on the missing value and continue processing.

Specifying Attribute Values

You can set a default attribute value in two ways: You can suggest the value or insist on it. The difference is the #FIXED keyword. Look at the following two examples:

```
<!ATTLIST  info  company  CDATA  "Acme">

<!ATTLIST  info  company  CDATA  #FIXED "Acme">
```

In the first example, although "Acme" is the default value for the company attribute, an XML document developer can override that value by typing a different company name. The second example forces the developer to accept the default company name. In both cases, however, if the company name is not entered, the XML processor uses the default value.

The value of an attribute can be an entity reference, which must be preceded by a hash (#) symbol. The entity reference cannot contain an ampersand symbol (&) (because the ampersand represents an entity-reference delimiter) or a less-than symbol (<) (because the less-than symbol indicates the beginning of a start tag or end tag). The attribute value must follow other rules of the attribute type and rules stated in the XML specification. For example, if the type is CDATA, the value must be treated as a string.

Keep in mind that when you use an attribute in an XML document, it is inserted completely within the start tag. If the element is not empty, the attribute looks something like this:

```
<table id="table1" height="30" width="60">
insert table contents here
</table>
```

However, if the element is empty, the attribute might look like this:

```
<image url="/pictures/sample1.gif />
```

Remember that the end-tag symbol is inserted at the end of the start tag. Also remember to insert a space before the last slash in the line.

Declaring Entities

An *entity* is an all-purpose term meaning a special character, specific text, or even a file such as a graphic. XML supports several types of entities: parsed and unparsed, external and internal, and general and parameter.

A parsed entity contains named replacement data that has been called by an entity reference and run through an XML parser. At the end of processing, the parsed data replaces the current contents of the entity. In contrast, an unparsed entity is not processed. It has a named notation (set of characters), which the XML processor sends to the target application.

As you might have guessed, the content of an internal entity is stored completely within the DTD; an internal entity is always parsed. An external entity has its content stored in a separate file, completely outside the XML document; an external entity is parsed or unparsed.

A general entity is a variable that is named within document instance text. A general entity is preceded by an ampersand (&) and other optional characters and is succeeded by a semicolon (;). Valid general entities can be internal parsed, external parsed, and external unparsed. General entities are comprised of the following subcategories:

- Parsed general entities, which start with the & character.
- Decimal character references, which start with the &# characters.
- Hexadecimal character references, which start with the &#x characters.

A parameter entity (PE) is a parsed variable that is named within document markup in the document prolog or document instance. A parameter entity is preceded by a percent symbol (%) and followed by a semicolon (;).

Parsed general entities

A parsed general entity contains replacement text that has been processed by an XML parser. The following example shows a general entity declaration:

```
<!ENTITY copyright "This document is copyrighted
 by The Eddy Group, Inc.">
```

Then, when you specify the &copyright; entity within a document, the XML processor replaces the entity with the text defined within the entity declaration.

XML reserves five general entities: &, ', >, <, and ", which represent the ampersand (&), apostrophe ('), greater-than symbol (>), less-than symbol (<), and quotation mark (").

Under some circumstances, you can declare an external entity. For example, if you work with lengthy documents, such as online books, you can "modularize" by declaring external pages, or even sections or chapters. Your home or index page can be a list of external entities that call individual documents. Then, when you edit pages at your site, you can simply replace one version of a page with a newer one. For example, the following entities are all stored on your local area network (LAN):

```
<!ELEMENT bigbook (#PCDATA)
<!ENTITY intro PUBLIC "intro.xml">
<!ENTITY chap1 PUBLIC "chap1-001.xml">
<!ENTITY chap2 PUBLIC "chap2-001.xml">
<!ENTITY chap3 PUBLIC "chap3-001.xml">
<!ENTITY chap4 PUBLIC "chap4-001.xml">
```

You can change them to:

```
<!ELEMENT bigbook (#PCDATA)
<!ENTITY intro PUBLIC "intro.rtf">
<!ENTITY chap1 PUBLIC "chap1-002. xml">
<!ENTITY chap2 PUBLIC "chap2-001. xml">
<!ENTITY chap3 PUBLIC "chap3-001. xml">
<!ENTITY chap4 PUBLIC "chap4-001. xml">
```

If the external entity is stored outside of your LAN, replace PUBLIC
with SYSTEM:

```
<!ELEMENT introduction (#PCDATA)
<!ENTITY introdoc SYSTEM "introdoc.xml">
```

Character and hexadecimal entities

You can declare character and hexadecimal references from the XML-
supported characters in the ISO/IEC 10646 character set. (The IEC is
the International Electrotechnical Commission.) To declare a character
reference, use the following syntax:

```
&#{0-9[0-9[...0-9]]};
```

Thus, you precede a character reference with the &# characters
and follow it with a semicolon (;). The character reference itself is
composed of a combination of the digits ranging from 0 to 9.

To declare a hexadecimal reference in the ISO/IEC 10646 character
set, use the following syntax:

```
&#x{0-9|a-f|A-F[0-9|a-f|A-F[...0-9|a-f|A-F]]};
```

This time, the hexadecimal reference is preceded by the &#x
characters. The character reference is composed of the digits ranging
from 0 to 9 and the letters (case-insensitive) ranging from A to F.

Parameter entities

Remember that a parameter entity is a parsed variable named within
declarations. A parameter entity, which is preceded by a percent symbol (%) and followed by a semicolon (;) works in about the same way
that a general parsed entity does: it can be a shortcut for a longer
string of markup contents. For example:

```
<!ENTITY % HTMLlat1 PUBLIC
"-//W3C//ENTITIES Full Latin 1//EN//HTML">
%HTMLlat1;
```

The preceding example shows an external parameter entity for the Full Latin 1 character entity set and the related general entity.

A parameter entity can group like elements together, as the following examples show:

```
<!ENTITY % InputType
"(TEXT | PASSWORD | CHECKBOX |
  RADIO | SUBMIT | RESET |
  FILE | HIDDEN | IMAGE | BUTTON)"
>
```

or

```
<!ENTITY % list "(UL | OL | DIR | MENU)">
```

Both examples show parameter entities used in the HTML standard. The first example groups input elements together under the name InputType, and the second example groups together list elements under the name list. Then, you can declare grouped child elements rather than a possibly lengthy list of individual elements.

If you declared a child element with children of its own:

```
<!ELEMENT record_info (create_date, edit_date, editor)
```

You can also group the two date elements in this way:

```
<!ENTITY % dates " (create_date | edit_date) "
```

and define the elements as follows:

```
<!ELEMENT record_info (%dates, editor)
```

External entities

Both general entities and PEs support external entities: To use an external entity in an XML document or a DTD, simply refer to a URI for a standalone file that contains one or more entity declarations. An external general entity refers to content that will be inserted in the non-DTD part of an XML document, whereas an external PE refers to markup that will be inserted in a DTD. Thus, you start with the !ENTITY keyword, add a valid XML name and an entity value, and complete the declaration with an external ID — either the SYSTEM or PUBLIC keyword followed by a system identifier or a public identifier, respectively.

Data entities

The XML specification supports the inclusion of unparsed external general entities in your documents. Unparsed external entities, also known as data entities, are truly external: they are produced by applications that have nothing to do with creating, editing, or processing XML. For example, you can declare a graphic, audio or video file, any format of word-processing document — anything that you don't intend the XML parser to process. Typically, these files are binary. Note that you can also use this type of declaration to import text (ASCII) files that would normally be parsed but that you don't want to parse in this case.

When you declare a data entity, you must include the NDATA keyword and the file type (such as gif, avi, pdf, doc, jpeg or jpg, mpeg, and so on). This example declares a GIF file called robin.gif:

```
<!ENTITY robin-pic
    SYSTEM "../grafix/robin.gif" NDATA gif >
```

As you know, you can usually place general-entity references anywhere in an XML document. The location of data entities is more restricted; they must be declared as element attributes, and the attribute type must be ENTITY or ENTITIES. For example, use the following declarations in a DTD for a document that contains illustrations of birds:

```
<!ELEMENT bird EMPTY>
<!ATTLIST bird url ENTITY #IMPLIED>
```

Then, insert the following line in the XML document:

```
<bird url="&robin-pic;"/>
```

Note the combined start tag and end tag for this empty-element line.

Now that you have learned about DTDs and how they are constructed, you can create your first XML document. To learn more, continue to Chapter 4, " Constructing a Basic XML Document."

Constructing a Basic XML Document

In this chapter, you learn how to create a basic XML document. In the previous two chapters, you learned about the document type definition (DTD), which defines the structure and markup of the document. But a DTD is meant to produce XML documents, not to provide the nonmarkup contents. However, as is the case with any foundation, you cannot ignore the DTD. You cannot expect to build a *valid* XML document without knowing its DTD completely.

Now, you will learn how to use the elements (both nonempty and empty), attributes, and entities declared in the DTD. As you know, the basic building block of an XML document is the element. As you have learned, an XML document must have at least one element, the root element, to be considered well formed.

If you have spent any time developing HTML documents, you are familiar with attributes that control the font of a particular element or define whether a specific piece of text should be bold, blue, or larger or smaller than the surrounding text. In this chapter, the discussion of attributes covers more than text formatting; you'll get a more general point of view.

You will also find out about how to add entities to your documents. Entities, which contain data, ranging from one character to an entire document to a complete file, are either parts of attributes or parts of elements.

Starting a Document

When you start constructing an XML document, you should have spent a great deal of time and effort planning and preparing. In fact, by the time you add content to a document, you should only have to think about the content and not think twice about the underlying structure of the document. If you structure the document (by writing the DTD) at the same time that you add content, the best you can hope for is that the document will be well-formed — due to the lack of initial planning. Whenever you create a valid XML document, you should have a clear idea of the contents of the completed DTD and should have tested it thoroughly before starting the XML document.

XML browsers are not programmed to be as forgiving as browsers that only read HTML. If you code the XML statements inaccurately, these mistakes will probably result in the browser showing the errors or even stopping altogether. Even if a well-formed document does produce good-looking output, it must follow a specific set of rules to be accurate. Throughout this chapter, you will learn more about the features of both well-formed and valid documents.

Declaring XML characteristics

Remember that the XML declaration is the first line in every XML document, whether the document is a DTD or a standard document with markup and content. The top line of any XML document should be an XML declaration that resembles one of the following four statements:

```
<?xml version="1.0"?>

<?xml version="1.0" standalone="no"?>

<?xml version="1.0" encoding="UTF-8"?>

<?xml version="1.0" standalone="yes"
  encoding="UTF-16"?>
```

Basically, the first declaration tells browsers that this is an XML document, and that the supported XML version is 1.0. This means that the XML document follows the rules in the XML 1.0 specification. Without the version information, some browsers may signal an error. The second, third, and fourth statements indicate whether the document has an internal DTD subset (standalone="yes") or refers to an external DTD subset (standalone="no"). The encoding information refers to the character set used in the document. To learn more about XML declarations, refer to Chapter 3, "Producing a DTD" (p. 681), and the XMLDecl production (p. 137).

4

Setting the document type and associating a DTD

Both DTDs and standard XML documents include a line that specifies the document type. DTDs are usually self-contained internal DTD subsets, but also can refer to external DTD subsets. For example, all the XML documents for a particular business may use the same basic set of element, attribute, and entity declarations. Then, each DTD developed for a specific set of documents can build on the base DTD by declaring additional elements, attributes, and entities.

As you know, an XML document can contain an internal DTD subset followed by a mix of markup and content. In that case, the document type declaration and its DTD will look something like this:

```
<?xml version="1.0" standalone="yes"?>
<!DOCTYPE manual [
<!ELEMENT manual (#PCDATA)>
]>
```

manual is the name of the root element, standalone="yes" indicates that no external DTD is associated with this document, and the internal DTD that declares the manual element starts with the [delimiter and ends with the]> delimiter.

When a document refers to an external DTD subset, its document type declaration resembles the following statement:

```
<!DOCTYPE manual SYSTEM "manual.dtd">
```

Once again, manual is the root element. However, the prior DTD is unnecessary; it is replaced by the reference to the external DTD subset, manual.dtd. The SYSTEM keyword indicates that the DTD is on the user's computer or on the local network to which the user's computer is attached.

●—**CROSS-REFERENCE**────────────────────

To learn more about document type declarations, refer to Chapter 3, "Producing a DTD" (p. 681), and the doctypedecl production (p. 61).

Building Document Structure

After you set up the document prolog, you're ready to add document content. This section covers all the bases of adding markup and character-data content.

Inserting elements, start tags, and end tags

Remember that when you create a DTD, you declare elements and define how to use those elements. Then, when you build a document based on the DTD, you will have to recall all the elements declared in the DTD and use the elements as directed in the DTD.

●—**NOTE**────────────────────────────────

The idea of trying to remember each element and its purpose — especially in a very long and complicated DTD — is the best impetus for adding numerous comments to each DTD that you develop. Without comments, the people responsible for maintaining the XML documents that you have created — perhaps a very long time ago — will not always know exactly how to use the declared elements or even what elements to use in particular situations. To learn about XML comments, refer to the Comment production (p. 49) in "XML Syntax" in Part I.

At the highest level of every XML document is the root element; all other elements are descended from this root element, either children of the root, grandchildren, or more distant descendants. The root element is often defined in the document type declaration. (For example, in <!DOCTYPE root1>, root1 is the root element.) Also remember that child elements are completely nested within parent elements; elements should never overlap. Lastly, when you start writing an element, you always need to finish it — each XML element *must* have both a start tag and an end tag.

Following is a repeat of an example from Chapter 1, "Introducing XML" (p. 653). There is a start tag, followed (in this case) by content, and an end tag.

```
<text>This sentence is contained within the text
element.</text>
```

Whenever a document is composed of multiple elements (and this is almost always the case), you will have to be careful about how the elements are nested. This becomes complicated as you add elements. Look at the following example of nesting:

```
<text>This <word>sentence </word> is contained within the
text element.</text>
```

Now, without seeing the DTD in which it is declared, it is hard to say whether text is a root element or a child element, but you know that the word element is a child element of text.

Using empty elements

As you know, empty elements contain no text content; they serve as containers or placeholders for future content. However, empty elements can have attributes, which might mark a particular location in a document or point to a file, such as a picture or a sound file, to be contained at the location of the empty element. In fact, if most empty elements did not have at least one attribute, which referred to a URI (Uniform Resource Identifier), they would have no purpose in life. To learn more about attributes, read the following section, "Adding attributes and attribute values."

You can insert empty elements in your documents in two ways: You can use start tags and end tags as you would with any nonempty element, or you can use a shortcut form that combines start tags and end tags into a single tag. Look at the following example:

```
<break />
```

The empty break element consists of a single start-tag/end-tag combination with no attributes. You might use <break> just as you would use the HTML br element — to insert a line break. You can also use an empty element without attributes to mark a section of the document.

In the following example, <image> is the empty element, which has separate start tags and end tags.

```
<listing>
   <rooms>6</rooms>
   <acreage>10</acreage>
   <image src="A349.jpg"></image>
<listing/>
```

This element contains no textual data but does have an attribute. You can also express image as follows:

```
<image src="A349.jpg" />
```

It is important to note that when you're using empty elements, both types of syntaxes work with attributes. One difference, however, is that people looking at the tags in the XML document will be able to immediately tell that an element is empty when you use the combined start-tag/end-tag syntax.

④ Adding attributes and attribute values

You have learned that you can find attributes in two places within a document, in start tags for nonempty elements and in start-tag/end-tag combinations for empty elements. As you learned in the "Creating Attribute Lists and Values" section (p. 687) of Chapter 3, attributes are pairs of names and values associated with an element. An attribute adds important information that refines its element. Sometimes, an attribute helps format or enhance an element for an end user; at other times, the information is completely invisible to the end user and is passed directly to another application.

> ●─**NOTE**───────────────────────
>
> Because you declare attributes in the DTD, you should be aware of all the declarations in the DTD before you add values to your elements. Adding an attribute to a document is easy; however, you may have problems if you don't remember exactly what to add.

In the following example, the attribute is in the correct location — within the start tag:

```
<text id="001">
This is one sentence.
</text>
```

An element can have more than one attribute. The only thing to remember is that each attribute must be followed by its value, enclosed within quotation marks or single quote marks. (When an XML processor issues warning messages or does not display certain attribute values, look for missing quotes.) For example:

```
<text id="001" author="Madeleine S." color="red" font="Times
New Roman" size="12pt">This is one sentence.
</text>
```

The above example also shows that it is possible to include so many attributes that content is not easily seen. In this case, you might want to reformat your code to make the XML document easier to read. For example:

```
<text
    id="001"
    author="Madeleine S."
    color="red">
    font="Times New Roman"
    size="12pt">
        This is one sentence.
</text>
```

The example shows how an element with many attributes might be organized in an XML document. The start tag begins in one column; each of the attributes is on its own line and indented from the start tag. The content is on the last line, separate from the attributes and followed by the end tag. You can format an XML document any way you want.

Inserting entities

As you learned in the "Declaring Entities" section (p. 692) of Chapter 3, entities are storage containers for information, ranging in size from a single character to an entire file. Remember that the XML specification supports the use of two basic categories of entities: general entities, which place character data in the content section of the document, and parameter entities (PEs), which can be internal or external and located in the DTD. General entities can be parsed or unparsed, whereas PEs are always parsed. In addition, XML supports two kinds of general entity: character and data. A character entity, which is parsed and either internal or external, represents special characters in a document. A data entity, which is unparsed and external, represents an imported non-XML file defined as binary.

Using general entities

The syntax of a general entity starts with an ampersand and ends with a semicolon. Take a look at the following internal general entity declaration, which is located within the current XML document — outside the internal DTD subset:

```
<!ENTITY name "Waterdogs Miss Madeleine">
<!ENTITY callname "Maddie">
```

Here is the entity reference, also outside the DTD:

```
<gooddog>
  <text>
    This Newfoundland's full name is &name;.
    We call her &callname;.
  </text>
</gooddog>
```

The following examples show how an external general entity works. Let's say that you have created the following XML statements:

```
<weather>
  <skies>Partly Cloudy</skies>
  <temp>40-50</temp>
  <precip>Rain</precip>
</weather>
```

After creating this information, assume that you save it on your local network in a file entitled weather.xml and store the file at http://www.joesweather.com/NewPaltz/weather.xml. You can declare the weather.xml file in a DTD using the following syntax:

```
<!ENTITY wthr SYSTEM
  "http://www.jweather.com/NewPaltz/wthr.xml"
```

In an XML document, refer to the entity as follows:

```
<MyWeather>
  <title>My Weather</title>
  &wthr;
</MyWeather>
```

Using character entities

Character entities are another type of general entity used to enter non-keyboard characters into an XML document. Say you're creating a cover letter in the English language and want to incorporate accented *es* into the word *resume* to make it *résumé*. Rather than omit the accented *es* or use a utility such as Windows Character Map to insert the accented *es* (which the processor or browser may misinterpret), you can declare entities for the character, as in this example:

```
<!ENTITY accent_e   "&#233;">
```

In a Web document, the character entity reference might look like this:

```
<p>
Enclosed is my r&#233;sum&#233;.
</p>
```

Remember that XHTML supports the entire Unicode character set. When you use a predefined entity name for the accented *e* (in this case, é), you can incorporate the accented *e*s into the word without declaring an entity. For example:

```
<p>
Enclosed is my r&eacute;sum&eacute;.
</p>
```

About Parameter Entities (PEs)

A parameter entity (PE) is a string that is named in the DTD only. A PE is always parsed because it is part of the document markup. Use a PE to enhance the current DTD by inserting a chunk of another DTD or by importing a DTD that is a standard either for your industry or the type of document on which you are working. For example, if you develop a document that combines a standard set of elements defined in your main DTD and elements declared especially for this document, use a PE to import the standard DTD. You could copy and paste, but this would unnecessarily increase the size of the current DTD. Using a PE to import the DTD limits the number of lines; the PE serves as a comment, too.

A PE's syntax differs slightly from that of a general entity. For example,

```
<!ENTITY % InputType
"(TEXT | PASSWORD | CHECKBOX | RADIO
    | SUBMIT | RESET | FILE | HIDDEN
    | IMAGE | BUTTON)"
>
```

When an HTML processor reads the % InputType entity in the input element declaration, it replaces % InputType with the list of 10 attributes. In other words, without the InputType entity, the number of lines in this very large element declaration would increase by 10.

Converting an HTML Document to XML

If you are planning to convert HTML documents to XML (actually making them XHTML documents), you have to determine your philosophy: Should you proceed in slow steps or go all out? Should you aim toward well-formed documents or valid documents? If you decide on valid documents, should you use the HTML DTD as a starting point or should you develop one or more DTDs? For some documents, the choice to use an XHTML DTD as a basis is tempting. The only real work might be to update or omit some attributes and make sure that there are matching end tags for every start tag. However, using the HTML DTD limits the benefits of converting to XML in the first place. In HTML, the content is held in tags that are not particularly descriptive. Custom XML tags allow you to organize content and search more easily for information about the content.

Considering DTDs

Obviously, if you decide that your XML documents should have a custom DTD, you will have to determine whether to write an external DTD for your entire document set, to write one internal DTD for each document, or to stop somewhere in the middle — combining one or two master DTDs for the document set and internal DTDs for other documents. For conversions of several HTML documents with the same general format and structure, it is easier to associate one external DTD with all the documents. For a single document, the choice is yours.

To keep up to date with the development of the XML and XHTML languages, periodically visit the HTML Activity page (http://www.w3.org/MarkUp/Activity/).

Allowing for style sheets

For most HTML documents — particularly those that are a few years old — document designers have not attached cascading style sheets but have relied on HTML elements for styling but not for document structure. To convert to XML and be able to properly send your documents to your users' computer screens or printers, you'll have to depend on either CSS2 or XSL.

● CROSS-REFERENCE ───────────────
For more information about CSS, refer to *XHTML In Plain English*, also by Sandra E. Eddy and published by IDG Books Worldwide. For more information about XSL and its component, XSLT, refer to "XSL Style Sheet Syntax" (p.369) and "XSLT Component" (p. 319) in Part II, as well as Chapter 7, "Styling Documents with XSL" (p. 745).

Declaring an XML document

At the beginning, every HTML document must become a well-formed XML document. First, change the top line of an HTML document to:

```
<?xml version="1.0"?>
```

Then edit the DOCTYPE line from:

```
<!DOCTYPE HTML PUBLIC "-//W3C//DTD HTML 4.0//EN">
<HTML>
```

to a document type declaration that starts something like this:

```
<!DOCTYPE manual [
<!ELEMENT manual (#PCDATA)>
]>
```

or a document type declaration that calls an external DTD subset:

```
<!DOCTYPE manual SYSTEM "manual.dtd">
```

● NOTE ───────────────
Keep in mind that most document type declarations with internal DTD subsets will include many more declarations than the declaration for the root element. A DTD will contain child-element declarations, attribute lists, entities, and sometimes notation.

Naming the root element

Selecting the root element for an HTML-to-XML conversion is the same process as selecting a root element for any XML document. Simply choose a root element that makes sense within the document. At first, you can remain with HTML's root, HTML, the <HTML> start tag, and the </HTML> end tag. Then, you might want to provide a more suitable root-element name.

Following XML rules

Then, go through each line of the document, keeping the following in mind:

- Some HTML elements do not require end tags. In XML, every start tag must have a matching end tag.

- All empty tags (elements used as placeholders for future contents) use the following syntax:
 (note the space between the element name and the slash) or <img src=" image.gif"/> (note that there is no space the attribute value and the slash) or a start-tag/end-tag combination.

- Although HTML child elements *should* be completely embedded within their parents' start tags and end tags, HTML browsers usually forgive errors. XML child elements *must* be entirely embedded within their parents' tags.

- HTML elements are not case-sensitive (although the unwritten standard for entering HTML elements is to use only uppercase letters). However, XML *is* case-sensitive, and elements must all be lowercase. XML parsers sense the differences among <Body>, <BODY>, and <boDy>, interpreting all three as separate tags.

● NOTE

One reason for the XML's case-sensitivity is that it supports Unicode. Each Unicode character — even uppercase and lowercase versions of what you might think of as the same character — is represented by a different code. For example, uppercase *A* is #x0041 and lowercase *a* is #x0061. When an XML parser processes a document, it evaluates each character or individual character code. XML keywords are also case-sensitive. Most XML keywords (such as #PCDATA and SYSTEM) must be rendered entirely in uppercase characters. On the other hand, reserved processing instructions (such as <?xml?> or <?xml-stylesheet?> must be rendered entirely in lowercase characters.

Converting attributes and attribute values

In XML documents, all attribute values must be enclosed within quotation marks or single quotes. However, that's just the beginning.

If you develop a DTD for your documents, you'll have to spend time declaring attributes and their values, requiring the use of certain attributes and making others optional. In HTML, each element has a set of predefined attributes that you select from but can't modify.

Typically, in older versions of HTML, many attributes were devoted to the presentation of an element in its electronic or printed format — its formats and enhancements. In XML, attributes tend to contain more information about the content associated with an element. In many cases, you will find yourself using most of the attribute information from the converted HTML document to help define the associated style sheet, deleting those attributes and their values from the converted XML document, and making sure that they are not included in the new DTD.

Another important use for XML attributes is for element identifiers. These attributes identify the location of specific elements, which makes it easy to create extended links and extended pointers.

Using entities

In HTML before the 4.0 version, entities are limited to character entities, which insert non-keyboard characters. In XML, this is one of several possibilities. If you are doing an HTML-to-XML conversion, look for other opportunities to use entities.

Whenever your document contains data that is subject to change, you can use general entities during the conversion. An example might be the copyright information placed on each page at a Web site. You might also define a general entity to use whenever your company name occurs in the document. Examine the HTML document that you are converting for opportunities to use general entities. In some instances, you can create a file of general entities to be plugged into each document you need to convert.

Use parameter entities to modify your DTD. One of the best uses for a parameter entity is to import a section of the DTD that is common to more than one of your documents. You might be involved in converting a large number of HTML documents that have the same structure. By using a parameter entity, you can define a single DTD and use it for multiple HTML-to-XML conversions. If the structure changes, converting is a simple matter of changing one DTD rather than several.

Now that you know the basics of creating an XML document, browse through Chapter 5, "Using Custom XML Elements," to learn about adding lists, tables, and forms to your documents.

in plain english in p
sh in plain english in
glish in plain english
in plain english in p
sh in plain english in
glish in plain english
in plain english in p
glish in plain english
in plain english in p
sh in plain english in
glish in plain english
in plain english in p
sh in plain english in
glish in plain english
in plain english in p
lish in plain english
in plain english in p
sh in plain english in
glish in plain english
in plain english in p
sh in plain english in
lish in plain english
in plain english in p
glish in plain english

Using Custom XML Elements

5

This chapter discusses elements that you can use to present document content using special formats. Here, you'll find out about lists, tables, and forms in your documents. All the components enable a designer to organize and present data. Note that this chapter covers the underlying structure of these custom elements rather than how they are styled for output.

In HTML, lists, tables, and forms have a specific structure that designers cannot easily modify. HTML presents elements that set the structure of certain types of these components. With XML, the structure of any of these components depends on the designer. The elements that you declare can either mimic those of HTML or can follow your own designs.

Using Lists

The two most popular lists in HTML are *ordered* and *unordered lists*. Ordered lists (made with the HTML OL element) are numbered and should be read (and possibly stepped through) from top to bottom; unordered lists (made with the HTML UL element) consist of bulleted items whose order in the list doesn't matter. Both ordered and unordered lists are composed of individual *list items*. In HTML, a list item, whether it's for an unordered or ordered list, is marked with the start tag <LI> and the optional end tag </LI>. In XML, if you declare a list-item element, it *must* include an end tag structure.

Another type of HTML list is the definition list (the DL element), which features paired list items: *definition terms* (the DT element) and *definition descriptions* (the DD element). A glossary of terms is a typical definition list.

Declaring ordered and unordered list elements

Essentially, to create a list, you must use the following structure: The beginning of the list is marked with a start tag followed by a number of list items and, at some point, an end tag to mark the end of the list. Translated into markup, this means that a list is an element containing a repeating child element. In a DTD, you can set up the element structure for a list as follows:

```
<!ELEMENT olist (item+)>
<!ELEMENT item (#PCDATA)>
```

with olist the parent list element and item the child list-item element.

You could use this structure for either ordered lists or unordered lists. The attributes declared for the lister element would control the item preceding a list item — a number or bullet. Obviously, declaring an attribute to add a preceding bullet to each list item would be much easier than declaring iterating numbers. In fact, numbering a list would probably involve some CSS or XSL styling, scripting, or programming.

Here is an example of an ordered list:

```
<olist>
  <item>Clean garage.</item>
  <item>Paint garage floor.</item>
  <item>Drive car into garage.</item>
  <item>Close garage door.</item>
</olist>
```

and the associated style sheet, which automatically numbers the list:

```
olist {display:block;
       margin-left: 30px;
       list-style-type: decimal;
       counter-reset: item}
olist item  {display: list-item; }
olist item {content: counter(item) ;
           counter-increment: item}
```

and an unordered list:

```
<ulist>
  <item>Prepare for dinner party.</item>
  <item>Clean garage.</item>
  <item>Sweep basement floor.</item>
  <item>Buy candles.</item>
  <item>Fix kitchen sink.</item>
  <item>Replace bathroom faucet gasket.</item>
</ulist>
```

and the associated style sheet:

```
ulist {display: block;
       margin-left: 30px;
       list-style-type: square}
ulist item  {display:list-item; }
```

●—NOTE

CSS is now in its second version (CSS2), so it is relatively stable, although neither version is completely supported by Web browsers or XML processors (especially not CSS2). When you want to use cascading style sheets to style your documents, be aware that many properties do not yet apply to XML documents. Be sure to spend plenty of time experimenting with various style properties and testing as many browsers as possible. For more information on cascading style sheets, see *XHTML In Plain English*, also by Sandra E. Eddy and published by IDG Books Worldwide.

Declaring definition-list elements

An HTML definition list consists of three elements: DL, DT, and DD. The DL element encloses the entire definition list, the DT element defines the term component, and the DD element describes that term.

To create a similar set of tags in XML, define an element and two child elements under it. In the following DTD segment, the child elements are required and appear in a particular order:

```
<!ELEMENT deflist (term,definition)+>
<!ELEMENT term (#PCDATA)>
<!ELEMENT definition (#PCDATA)>
```

Remember that the plus sign at the end of the first line indicates that one or more sets of child elements must be present in a document — but the sets must contain one of each of the term and definition elements. Without the plus sign, you would be limited to a single set of term and definition. That's hardly a definition list.

Nesting lists

In an HTML document, you can embed one list within another. In fact, you can nest several layers of ordered lists and unordered lists. Nesting a list in HTML is simple enough. Simply place a list completely within the start tags and end tags of another list. You can embed ordered lists within other ordered lists or within unordered lists, and you can nest unordered lists within both ordered and unordered lists.

Since you define list elements in XML and can declare additional elements to differentiate among list types, you can produce more readable nested listings. For example, think about creating an outline composed of nested lists. First, define a series of list elements as follows: the top-level list under which all other lists are nested is named nest1; the second, which is nested within nest1 lists, is nest2; the third, which is nested within nest2 lists, is nest3; and so on. Then, you style each list to indent it properly and to apply other distinctive formats and enhancements. Of course, this can work against you, too. When you create lists using different element names, you may have to make sure that you keep track of nesting levels. Every time you add or remove a nesting level or change the order of nesting, you have to edit the tags carefully.

Using Tables

Tables consist of rows and columns of data. The intersection of a row and a column, a *cell*, contains the actual data. Even though a table is flexible, it has a format that makes it easy to extract data as a row or a column but not as both a row and a column.

In HTML, you create a simple table by using five elements, each of which sets a distinctive table structure.

- The TABLE element defines a table.
- The TR element defines a single row in the table.
- The TH element defines a single heading cell. By default, a table heading is usually formatted in boldface. Under HTML rules, you must nest a TH element within a TR element.
- The TD element defines a single data cell. Under HTML rules, you must nest a TD element within a TR element.
- The CAPTION element specifies the title of a table. If a table contains a caption, the CAPTION element must be placed immediately after the start of the table.

In HTML, tables are *row-centric*: you add data one row at a time. This is great for people who look at data on a row-by-row basis, but not everyone does that. Some tables, like accountants' balance sheets, are based on a columnar layout; they are *column-centric*. Other tables, such as multiplication tables or the periodic table, are neutral; they are neither row-centric nor column-centric.

In XML, you can go your own way: You can define tables so that they are assembled on a row-by-row basis or on a column-by-column basis.

Declaring table elements

In XML, element declarations for a table could be as simple as this:

```
<!ELEMENT table (row+)>
<!ELEMENT row (cell+)>
<!ELEMENT cell (#PCDATA)>
```

This simple table is composed of one or more rows, each containing one or more cells. As usual, the cells contain the data. This table is little more than a series of lists. You can also define the table so that it is column-centric. Simply change the name of one element:

```
<!ELEMENT table (col+)>
<!ELEMENT col (cell+)>
<!ELEMENT cell (#PCDATA)>
```

Note that both tables and lists contain parent and child elements.

●—NOTE—————————————————————

Once all Web browsers support the use of CSS or XSL style sheets, you should use cascading style sheets to lay out pages. In the meantime, an alternative is to use tables to format your pages. Using tables can be a convenient way to format data and keep the data organized within the confines of row and column borders. For example, you can use a two-column table to create a page composed of a long narrow column of a given color and a long wide column of white. Or you can make sure that a graphic is located in the upper right corner of a page and that a link to corporate information stretches across the bottom of the page.

Building a simple table

To build a table, insert the table start tag and end tag and embed the child elements within. For example:

```
<register>Fred's Bank Account
  <label>
     <cell>Date</cell>
     <cell>Vendor</cell>
     <cell>Amount</cell>
     <cell>Description</cell>
  </label>
  <check>
     <cell>Sept. 9, 2001</cell>
     <cell>Moe's Car Service</cell>
     <cell>$1240.65</cell>
     <cell>Replace engine</cell>
  </check>
  <check>
     <cell>Sept. 10, 2001</cell>
     <cell>Dr. Joe Carson</cell>
     <cell>$500.00</cell>
     <cell>Money counseling</cell>
  </check>
</register>
```

This example table is a three-row, four-column table. The <register> start tag and </register> end tag mark the beginning and end of the table. The cells in the first row, which begins with the <label> start tag and ends with the </label> end tag, name the contents of the four columns. The remaining rows, starting with <check> and ending with </check>, display information about two checks. Each row is made up of four cells, marked with <cell> and </cell> tags.

A DTD for the register, label, check, and cell elements would look something like this:

```
<!ELEMENT register (label|check)+>
<!ELEMENT (label|check) (cell+)>
<!ELEMENT cell (#PCDATA)>
```

Sectioning a table

The previous example includes column labels. In many tables, the rows have labels, too. So, the top row of a table and its leftmost column usually indicate the type of content stored in the rest of the table. (A typical spreadsheet demonstrates the usual way to present column labels and row labels.) These labels are clues for those interpreting your data. If an individual doesn't know what the data means, he or she won't understand the table. However, this label information can get lost among the other data — especially if its format is the same as the format of the other rows or columns.

In HTML, the TH (table heading) element defines a table's label cells. You can enter information in the first one or two table rows to label each of the table's columns, or as first couple of columns to label each of the table's rows. The TD element (TD stands for table data) specifies all non-heading cells in a table. Both the TH and TD elements are child elements of the TR (table row) element.

Another piece of identifying information is the table caption, which is represented in HTML by the CAPTION element. A caption displays a table title or summary information.

The following example shows that a caption is optional but may only appear once — at the top of the table. Headings can be placed anywhere within the table but don't have to be used at all. At least one cell must occur within the table. So far the definition of elements for our table looks like this:

```
<!ELEMENT table (caption?, row+)>
<!ELEMENT row (heading*|cell+)>
<!ELEMENT caption (#PCDATA)>
<!ELEMENT heading (#PCDATA)>
<!ELEMENT cell (#PCDATA)>
```

Let's examine other table-sectioning methods. For example, some tables are longer than a single page. In this case, it makes sense to repeat information about columns at the top of each page. So you might add an element that contains this page-header information. You also can section tables by adding header and footer sections above and below the body. How you section a table depends on your requirements.

Organizing columns and rows

As you have learned, HTML tables are completely row-centric; an HTML table is a collection of rows. Remember that in XML, nothing prevents you from changing a table's orientation so that it is column-centric. From a design point of view, when you look at a table — whether it is created with HTML elements or XML elements — the data contained within is very easy to read when you look at it from either a row-wise or column-wise direction. Looking at the data that is not clearly row-centric or column-centric is more difficult because you may not be able to see how the data is organized.

One way to define columns is to use attributes. Look at the following example of an attribute declaration:

```
<!ATTLIST cell col (col1,col2,col3) #REQUIRED>
```

It is possible to define a different element for each column, but unless you always used the same number of columns, you'd always have to return to your DTD to add or subtract individual column elements.

You can also apply styles to a table to make it easier to read. For example, you can go the route of old computer printout paper, with its alternating stripes of light green and off white, by setting alternating colors for each column. Or you can experiment with various weights of borders or an easier-to-read typeface or point size.

Building an XML Database

XML databases should be highly structured documents with which you can control the organization of your information. Electronic databases are growing in popularity. For example, online catalog companies use electronic databases to compile information about customers and inventory, and individuals can gather information about contacts and organize it into easy-to-access files.

XML parsers not only produce standard Web pages but can also send processed information to intermediate applications for further processing. So XML developers can design fill-in forms where visitors to a Web site can enter information. With some programming, a parser can place the information into an XML document, which in turn can export to a database program.

When you design and create a DTD for a standard document (such as a memorandum or a computer manual), the ratio of elements to content is relatively low. For example, a single element can control a large amount of body text throughout a document. Creating a database DTD is an intense process. For every field in the database, there must be a corresponding element. Using a little forethought, you can convert the contents of a small database into a text (ASCII) file and then use a word processor to modify the text file into an accurate XML document. However, most e-commerce sites use object-oriented database programs to organize and manage collected data.

As the World Wide Web becomes more central to many enterprises, it becomes more important to use Internet-ready business applications for day-to-day business. These applications should provide the following features:

- They should support the standard file types for a given type of application. For example, database programs should support the .dbf file type and spreadsheets should support .xls and .wk* types.

- They should support some Web file types, such as .xml, .htm, .html, .shtml, and so on, depending on the type of application and its purpose. This makes it easier to convert word-processing documents, spreadsheets, and databases to Web pages and Web-based forms.

- They should incorporate various Web technologies, such as the ability to transfer files (such as Web pages) to and from servers. This means that the applications should be able to communicate with other applications.

- They should start supporting sophisticated technologies, such as scripting.

Databases have already become an important part of the Web. For example, any commercial site at which goods are sold should have one or more underlying databases, which include customer information as well as inventory information. The customer database produces lists of contacts for catalog mailings and e-mail contacts, and the inventory database allows for instantaneous checking for the availability of merchandise. Often, Web-based marketing sites ask prospective customers to enter information into fill-in forms. Then that information is exported into databases for later processing as mailing lists or contacts lists. Using XML, developers can not only declare elements to build a fill-in form but can also use parsers to transfer the output directly into the record. As with any other XML DTD, a fill-in form DTD can include elements that must be used in a particular order, attribute lists of valid values from which a choice is required, a set structure of root, child, and other descendant elements, and more.

●─NOTE─

Databases are made up of records, which are composed of fields. A field, which is the smallest unit of information, contains one piece of information, such as a first name or a ZIP code. A record is composed of a group of related fields. For example, a record can contain all the desired information about a customer, an employee, or an inventory item. Use forms, or input forms, to enter information into the records in a database. Forms should be formatted and arranged so that data entry is as easy as possible. Note that many forms are designed to include some, but not all, fields. For example, some fields contain the results of a calculation, which is performed after the information is entered into a record. Other forms are custom-made to enable only some parts of a record to be entered.

5

Declaring database elements

Planning, laying out, and creating a database DTD requires more effort than creating a new database using a program developed specifically for that purpose: For example, you won't have the help in automatically adding or defining fields that you would have if you were using a database program. However, once you have designed one database DTD, you probably can apply it to other similar types of DTDs.

Typically, each field in a database matches with an element in a database DTD. When you start compiling the list of potential elements, factor in the position of a particular element within the generations of elements. For example, in a database of name and address information, will you define a parent name element under which fall child elements for the first name, last name, and so on? Your other choice is to eliminate name altogether and just have one level of first-name, last-name, and middle-initial elements. You'll have to answer the same "generational" question about address elements and telephone elements. Your decision not only affects the way that the DTD is laid out but also the design of the database associated with the DTD. In addition, the way you specify generations might also affect the processing of output as well as the ease with which future developers understand the DTD's structure.

The top of a typical name-and-address DTD might look like this:

```
<?xml version="1.0" standalone="yes"?>
<!DOCTYPE customer [
<!ELEMENT customer (name+, address*,
    city+, state+, zip+, telephone*,
    fax?, email?)+>
]>
```

In this example, someone can enter any amount of information into each of the fields. However, a database — especially one whose fields you might export into another application — should contain a set number of fields.

When you declare the root element and first generation of child elements, allow for just one entry per element and use comma separators to set a specific order of entry. For example:

```
<!ELEMENT customer
    (name, address, city, state, zip,
    telephone, fax, email)+>
```

To keep tight control of the element structure, you should declare child elements for most child elements. For example, let's say that a database XML document is designed to send parsed output to a database with fields that are limited in size or type. Setting strict limitations in the DTD will help prevent future problems in fitting output to particular fields.

Here's a longer DTD for an inventory database:

```
<?xml version="1.0" standalone="yes"?>
<!DOCTYPE invent [
<!ELEMENT invent (name, itemno, dept, warehse, pdate,
    onhand)*>
    <!ELEMENT name (#PCDATA)>
    <!ATTLIST name
            id      ID      #REQUIRED>
    <!ELEMENT itemno (#PCDATA)>
    <!ATTLIST itemno
            id      ID      #REQUIRED>
    <!ELEMENT dept (#PCDATA)>
    <!ATTLIST dept
            name    (nails|bolts|tools)     "bolts"
            id      ID      #REQUIRED>
    <!ELEMENT warehse (#PCDATA)>
    <!ATTLIST warehse
            location (Miami|Erie|Troy)      "Troy"
            id      ID      #REQUIRED>
    <!ELEMENT pdate (year,month,day)>
    <!ATTLIST pdate
            id      ID      #REQUIRED>
      <!ELEMENT year
      <!ATTLIST year
            value   CDATA   #FIXED  "2001">
      <!ELEMENT month
      <!ELEMENT day
    <!ELEMENT onhand (#PCDATA)>
```

In the DTD, declare the root and list its child elements. Offer choices of department names and warehouse locations and a default value for each. Fix the year value to 2001. (Next year, change to 2002.)

●—NOTE —————————————————————————————

XML 1.0 supports very few data types—primarily parsed character data, names, and name tokens. On the other hand, database programs usually define several data types, including numerical, text, date, Boolean, and so on. This difference is probably DTD's main weakness. By definition, parsed character data encompasses letters, digits, and special characters, and there is no way to differentiate among character types. For now, you can declare lists of attribute values from which the individuals creating XML documents based on the DTD can choose. However, when the list gets too long, you may have to resort to the heavy use of comments and rely on the document developers to read the comments diligently.

Converting a database to an XML document

After you have completed a database DTD, create the database document. An XML document is a text (ASCII) document with no hidden formatting characters. So, even if you are working without a database program, you can move information into an XML document quite easily. First, edit the file containing the information to prepare it for conversion. Then save the file as a text file. You can now edit the text file, adding prolog lines, markup, and content, reflecting the DTD, until the file is an accurate XML document.

One of the best ways to ensure a smooth conversion operation is to prepare the material being moved. For example, if you want to move names and addresses that you have typed into a word-processing document, make sure that each field is separated from the next by a separator character and that each record is on a single line. Sometimes, you can convert the text as you edit into a table so that you can easily detect whether all fields are filled in. Another way to ensure that the information is properly prepared is to insert tabs, which add extra space between each field so that you can view it more easily. However, before you save the file, be sure to convert any tables back to text for an easier import.

When you move records from a database application — even if you convert the file to a text format — the first row may contain field labels and not the actual information. So be prepared to check the text file for accuracy and remove the field labels, unless you want to use them as titles — perhaps as the content of an element named `title`.

When you finally incorporate all the database information into the XML document, you will have to continue editing. For example, you may find that lines don't break the way you want them to, you may detect random characters and extra spaces that should have been removed earlier, and you will probably want to indent elements to show nesting. In addition, you will want to add attributes, entities, and other components to the document.

Creating a Form

If you are an experienced HTML developer, you already know that HTML 4.0 includes a variety of predefined elements and attributes for creating forms and making them work. These elements and attributes enable you to design and develop good-looking forms in HTML. Creating forms in XML will require the heavy use of CSS properties to turn on borders, change background and foreground colors, set margins, change typefaces and point sizes, and so on. (Remember that not all browsers and processors recognize style sheets.) The real purpose of a form is to gather information from visitors to your site and process it in some way. This means that you want to present easy-to-use forms that will attract people so that they will be happy to give you information. By using Active Server Pages (ASP) or CGI scripts and the HTTP protocol, you can send the supplied information to a server for further processing.

A form is a part of a document to which a user can insert information using a combination of typing, selecting items from lists, clicking on buttons, checking boxes, and so on. The HTML 4.0 specification says that "users generally 'complete' a form by modifying its controls, before submitting the form to an agent for processing." In HTML, use the FORM element to mark the start and end of a form.

XForms, which are being developed by the W3C, are the Web forms of the future. Among the planned features are support for many devices, including handheld computers, computer peripherals, and television. Using XForms, forms developers will be able to present a sophisticated user interface and address internationalization, and integrate with custom XML elements. Developers will also be able to write sophisticated scripts resulting in dynamic forms and to structure incoming data. To learn more about Web forms, periodically go to http://www.w3.org/MarkUp/Forms/.

Learning about controls

Controls are named components within forms. HTML 4.0 supports the following control types:

- The check box control type is a small square box that represents an on or off status. In HTML, specify a check box by using the INPUT element and the TYPE="CHECKBOX" attribute and value.

- The file select control type is a file-uploading control. In HTML, specify the file select control type by using the INPUT element and the TYPE="FILE" attribute and value.

- The hidden control type is a field that is not displayed on the form. It is typically used to transfer information between the client and the server, especially with the POST method (METHOD="POST"). In HTML, specify the hidden control type by using the INPUT element and the TYPE="HIDDEN" attribute and value.

- The menu control type is a list box or, sometimes, a pull-down menu. In HTML, specify the menu control type by using the SELECT element and either the OPTGROUP or OPTION element.

- The object control type is any type of multimedia object (image, video file, or sound file) within a form. In HTML, specify the object control type by using the OBJECT element. A multimedia object can also be located outside a form.

- The radio button control type is a small round button in a set of buttons from which you can select only one at a time. In HTML, specify a radio button by using the INPUT element and the TYPE="RADIO" attribute and value. Radio buttons are also known as option buttons in the Windows world.

- The reset button control type is a push (command) button that you click to clear a form. In HTML, specify a reset button by using the BUTTON element or the INPUT element and the TYPE="RESET" attribute and value.

- The submit button control type is a push (command) button that you click to submit a form. In HTML, specify a submit button by using the BUTTON element or the INPUT element and the TYPE="SUBMIT" attribute and value.

- A multiple-line text box control type has a defined height and width. In HTML, specify a multiple-line text box control type by using the TEXTAREA element.

- A single-line text box control type has just one line. You cannot set its height and width. In HTML, specify a single-line text box control type by using the INPUT element and the TYPE="TEXT" attribute and value.

Planning and designing a form

Before you create a form, you should plan and design it. As you know, forms are made up of controls. Designing a form layout is very similar to designing page layout for an entire document. You want to make sure that users enter information in a logical order and understand the meaning of each control. In addition, controls shouldn't be too far apart or too close together. Select easy-to-read fonts and don't vary point sizes too much. Let your eyes and those of colleagues be the judges.

Using the HTML model, create a form by inserting a start tag to mark the beginning of the form and an end tag to mark the end. Embed controls and optional text labels for those controls within the form tags. For guidance in declaring elements and attributes that are appropriate for forms, refer to the HTML 4.0 recommendation.

For forms developers using HTML, the INPUT element sets the type of user input: characters that are typed, buttons that are clicked, and boxes and buttons that are selected. (See the INPUT element and the attribute-list declarations on the facing page.) The last type of control, the list box, is controlled by the SELECT, OPTGROUP, and OPTION elements. (The SELECT, OPTGROUP, and OPTION element declarations are not shown in this book.)

In XML, you can declare elements similar to those that you use to create a form in HTML. However, you may have to incorporate some programming or scripts in order to submit the form and its information to the server. In HTML, use the METHOD attribute to specify the HTTP method by which the form is submitted to a server that contains a form-handling program. Your choices are METHOD="GET" and METHOD="POST". METHOD="GET" appends the submitted information to a newly created URI to which the form information is submitted. This URI is named by the ACTION attribute using an environment variable. The HTML 4.0 specification deprecates this method. METHOD="POST" specifies the form to be sent to a server. This method, which is recommended, is difficult to use according to some form experts.

Declaring form elements

Under the HTML model, the block-level FORM element marks the beginning and end of a form:

```
<!ELEMENT FORM - - (%block;|SCRIPT)+ -(FORM)>
```

The LABEL element provides information for an input control:

```
<!ELEMENT LABEL - - (%inline;)* -(LABEL)>
```

The INPUT element controls the type of input control: a one-line text box, a text box that contains a password, a check box, one radio button in a set, buttons that you click to submit the data or *reset* the form (remove the information), file selection, a hidden field, an image, or a button:

```
<!ENTITY % InputType
  "(TEXT | PASSWORD | CHECKBOX |
   RADIO | SUBMIT | RESET |
   FILE | HIDDEN | IMAGE | BUTTON)"

<!ELEMENT INPUT - O EMPTY>
```

Defining a form

A typical HTML form converted to XML would look something like this:

```
<form action="cgi-bin/form-example" method="post">
<para>Type your name:
   <input type="text" name="name" size="40"></para>
<para>Type your email address:
   <input type="text" name="email" size="30"></para>
<para>Type your password:
   <input type="hidden" name="pswd"
size="10"><maxlength="8"></para>
<para><input type="submit"><input type="reset"></para>
</form>
```

The FORM element specifies the processing action and method. Within the form, the first two controls are text boxes (<input type= "text">), the next is a password text box (<input type="password">), and the final two are submit (<input type="submit">) and reset buttons (<input type="reset">).

Processing a form

Once you have created a fill-in form, you have to provide a means of transferring the form information that a visitor to your site enters to an application that will process that information — perhaps load it into a database, send it to someone as an e-mail message, or reformat it for displaying on-line.

When a user clicks a submit button, a program or script should be activated. The browser with which the user is viewing the form transfers the information from the client computer to the URI specified in the ACTION attribute:

```
<FORM ACTION="http://x.com/cgi-bin/pgm123"
    METHOD="post">
```

The target resource is located on a server that is named x.com. The server takes over and searches for the pgm123 program in the cgi-bin folder. Furthermore, the server communicates by using the post method, which identifies the form and does not append it to the URI. Once the server locates pgm123, it transmits the information in the form to the program. The program then processes the information and sends a message back to the server.

In the example, remember that cgi-bin was a folder. It is also a reserved word for a folder that stores one or more cgi-bin programs. Applications that are categorized as cgi-bin use the Common Gateway Interface (CGI) protocol to create HTML in response to user requests. In addition, the program that you use to send a form from a client to a server uses the HyperText Transport Protocol (HTTP) as its transfer protocol. HTTP is programmed to understand the hypertext links in the documents that it transfers. In fact, you can use an HTTP script to process forms.

Learning about CGI

CGI is a platform-independent interface (a gateway) between a client and a server. A gateway can be written in any language that results in an executable file: C, C++, Perl, Python, and so on.

A CGI program runs when it is requested — in real time. This means that you can use the program to output up-to-date information immediately. CGI is executed on the server, so the client computer's resources are not used (as opposed to Java, which is executed on the client). When a user clicks a submit button, submission instructions trigger the CGI program. Two popular CGI sites are CGI Programming FAQ (http://htmlhelp.com/FAQ/cgifaq.html) and the Common Gateway Interface (http://hoohoo.ncsa.uiuc.edu/cgi/).

Learning about HTTP

HTTP is a protocol that allows client computers and server computers to communicate. Thus, if a browser program on a client computer requests a document from a program on the server, HTTP allows both events to occur. The markup language that you use to create the document is an important factor. For example, HTTP understands HTML and can interpret its elements, attributes, attribute values, and other document components and "explain" them to the server. Tim Berners-Lee, who is credited with developing the World Wide Web, also put HTTP into effect. To learn about HTTP, visit its home page (http://www.w3.org/Protocols/).

5

Adding Links and Pointers to an XML Document

6

If you are familiar with HTML and hypertext, you must know about hyperlinks. A hyperlink, or link, enables someone reading a document to jump to another part of the current document or another document to read more about a topic or study a completely different topic. XLinks (extended links) — in conjunction with XPointers (extended pointers) — establish links in XML documents. The W3C XLink working draft (http://www.w3.org/TR/xlink/) states that "a link is a relationship between two or more resources or portions of resources, made explicit by an XLink linking element." The XLink working draft defines two main categories of links: simple links and extended links. In this chapter, you'll get an overview of creating XML links using the XLink language and the XPointer language.

●─ **NOTE** ───────────────────────────────

Both XLink and XPointer are Candidate Recommendations. This means that they are still working drafts but have received a great deal of review. Therefore both XLink and XPointer are relatively stable technologies.

Calling the XLink Namespace

A *namespace* is a collection of valid element-type names and attribute names that has been defined by a standards organization and referred to with a URI. Linking to a namespace enables you to use a predefined set of names that are recognized by experts in a particular technical field.

To enable XLink, place the following declaration in a linking element:

```
xmlns:xlink="http://www.w3.org/1999/xlink">
```

The xmlns: keyword indicates that you will call the XLink namespace, which is located at the http://www.w3.org/1999/xlink URI.

About URIs

The URI, which is the centerpiece of a hyperlink, states the absolute or relative address of the resource that is the target of the link. An *absolute URI* starts with the name of an Internet protocol, such as http:, ftp:, gopher:, file:, mailto:, and so on. The next part of the syntax represents the *host name*, the actual address of the resource (such as www.eddygrp.com), which specifies (from left to right) the computer on which the server software is located, the registered name of the company or institution that owns the computer, and the domain of the computer.

The URI usually concludes with a filename (such as sample.xml, index.htm, or home.html). If you use extended links and extended pointers in your documents, that information is tacked onto the filename. The absolute URI is the complete name of a resource. A *relative URI* does not contain the complete Internet address. For example, if the current document and the document to which it links are located on the same computer, you don't need to enter an absolute URI. You can use the filename alone if the two documents share the same folder. You can add a folder name if the two documents are stored on the same drive in separate folders. If the two documents are stored on separate drives, add the drive name. The bottom line is that you should write URIs that ensure that the link works — that you can jump from the source document to the target.

●—**NOTE**

In HTML, URIs of both types can include *fragment identifiers*, which are pound-sign symbols (#) that match the value of the NAME attribute of the target resource's A element. Fragment identifiers are relatives of the connector that indicates the link-retrieval method for extended links as specified in the XLink language working draft. For more information about using fragment identifiers, read "Extended pointers" (p. 739), later in this chapter. In addition, refer to "XPointer Language" (p. 165) and "XPath Language" (p. 181) in Part I.

Simple Links and Extended Links

The XLink standard contains elements that enable you to write simple links and extended links, which in conjunction with XPointers (extended pointers) establish hyperlinks in XML documents.

Simple links

Simple links are analogous to the links formed by the A element in HTML. Insert a simple link in a document to be able to jump from its location in the local source document to a remote destination in either the same document or another document. Simple links always move in one direction, from the source location to the target location. This direction is known as *outbound*. Use one of the following two statements to indicate a simple link. Either use the xlink: keyword and a simple element name:

    xlink:simple

or an attribute and value:

    xlink:type="simple"

Simple links support the following attributes:

Name	Description	Required or Optional	Page
type	Specifies the type of link: simple, extended, locator, arc, resource, title, or none	#REQUIRED	160
href	Specifies the URI of a target resource	#IMPLIED	150
actuate	Actuates link traversal with or without a request	#IMPLIED	146

Continued

Name	Description	Required or Optional	Page
role	Specifies the role of link content	#IMPLIED	153
arcrole	Names a linkbase of potentially related linking elements that might help in locating both the starting resource and target link	#IMPLIED	148
show	Indicates how a link resource is displayed onscreen	#IMPLIED	155
title	Provides title information with a link	#IMPLIED	157

A simple link looks something like this:

```
<simple xlink:href="http://example.com/">
  Simple Link</simple>
```

or this:

```
<xlink:simple href="http://example.com/" role="test"
  title="Test Page">Simple Link Test</xlink:simple>
```

Another example of a simple link comes from the XLink candidate recommendation. The declaration is as follows:

```
<!-- studentlink = simple-type -->
<!ELEMENT studentlink ANY>
<!ATTLIST studentlink
  xlink:type    (simple)            #FIXED "simple"
  xlink:href    CDATA               #IMPLIED
  xlink:role    NMTOKEN             #FIXED "student"
  xlink:title   CDATA               #IMPLIED
  xlink:show    (new
                |replace
                |embed
                |undefined)         #FIXED "replace"
  xlink:actuate (onLoad
                |onRequest
                |undefined)         #FIXED "onRequest"
>
```

followed by a segment from an XML document:

```
...
<studentlink
  xlink:href="/students/patjones.xml"
  xlink:title="Info about Pat Jones">Pat</studentlink>
  is popular around the student union.
...
```

Read about simple links in Section 5.2, "Simple Links (Simple-Type Element)" in the XLink candidate recommendation.

●—**NOTE**————————————————————————————————

You would think that the href attribute must be required. After all, a link needs to refer to a target resource using a URI. However, the XLink working draft states, "It is not an error for a simple-type element to have no locator (href) attribute value. If a value is not provided, the link is simply untraversable."

Extended links

Extended links enable you to define many links in one or more XML documents. When you use extended links, you can jump from any link in any document to a link resource in any document. You can identify the content associated with a particular link so that if the content changes but the identifier remains the same, you can still access the link.

Extended links are composed of several link types: locator, arc, resource, title, or a combination of the above. The extended type (p. 148) indicates any number of links that are *inbound* (traversing from a remote location to a local starting resource), *outbound*, or *third-party* (traversing from one remote location to another). An extended link can contain any number of the following declared link-type elements: arc, locator, resource, and title.

- The locator (p. 152) type is an address or identifier that specifies the remote target resource of a link.

- The arc (p. 147) type indicates the beginning and end of a link. Via the from and to attributes, the beginning and end of the traversal between the links are specified.

- The resource (p. 153) type indicates a local resource for a link.

- The title (p. 157) type indicates that a title link type declaration or value for the element follows.

Use the xlink: keyword and one of the following element names to indicate a particular extended-link component:

```
xlink:extended
xlink:arc
xlink:locator
xlink:resource
xlink:title
```

or the following attributes and values:

```
xlink:type="extended"
xlink:type="arc"
xlink:type="locator"
xlink:type="resource"
xlink:type="title"
```

The arc, locator, resource, and title types are children of the extended type.

Extended links (and/or their child types) support the following attributes:

Name	Description (Support Link(s))	Required or Optional	Page
href	Specifies the URI of a target resource (locator)	#REQUIRED	150
type	Specifies the type of link: simple, extended, locator, arc, resource, title, or none (extended, locator, arc, resource, and title)	#REQUIRED	160
actuate	Actuates link traversal with or without a request (arc)	#IMPLIED	146
arcrole	Names a linkbase of potentially related linking elements that might help in locating both the starting resource and target link (arc)	#IMPLIED	148
from	Specifies the starting point of an arc link (arc)	#IMPLIED	149
label	Identifies the resources that form an arc (locator, resource)	#IMPLIED	151
role	Specifies the role of link content (extended, locator, and resource)	#IMPLIED	153
show	Indicates how a link resource is displayed onscreen (arc)	#IMPLIED	155
title	Provides title information with a link (extended, locator, arc, and resource)	#IMPLIED	157
to	Specifies the end point of an arc link (arc)	#IMPLIED	158

The following element and attribute-list declarations come from the XLink candidate recommendation:

```
<!ELEMENT courseload ((tooltip|person|course|gpa|go)*)>
<!ATTLIST courseload
  xmlns:xlink      CDATA       #FIXED
      "http://www.w3.org/1999/xlink
  xlink:type      (extended)   #FIXED "extended"
  xlink:role      CDATA        #IMPLIED
  xlink:title     CDATA        #IMPLIED>
```

The declarations apply to the following segments from an XML document, also from the XLink candidate recommendation:

```
<person
  xlink:href="students/patjones62.xml"
  xlink:label="student62"
  xlink:role="http://www.example.com/linkprops/student"
  xlink:title="Pat Jones" />

<go
  xlink:from="student62"
  xlink:to="PatJonesGPA"
  xlink:show="new"
  xlink:actuate="onRequest"
  xlink:title="Pat Jones's GPA" />

</courseload>
```

The href type states the target resources' URI. The label type identifies the arc. The title types provide titles for XML output. The from types specify the source resource, and the to types name the target resource. The actuate type sets the timing of the traversal.

Read more about extended links in Section 5.1, "Extended Links (Extended-Type Element)" in the XLink candidate recommendation.

Extended pointers

In this section, you'll learn about extended pointers (XPointers) and get a brief overview of the current version of the XPointer language, which is based on the XPath language. XPointers enable those using extended links to further pinpoint the location of their target resources by using such criteria as elements, attributes, attribute values, and other components within XML documents. Using a combination of extended links and extended pointers, you can even locate a span of components in a document. Simple links, which are analogous to HTML links, do not support extended pointers.

● **NOTE**

XPointer is in the Candidate Recommendation stage, which is the last working draft before the final recommendation is announced and released. To keep up to date with the progression of the XPointer language toward the final recommendation, go to the XPointer working draft (http://www.w3.org/TR/xptr).

The XML Path Language (XPath) is a recommendation. However, it's a good idea to visit its site (http://www.w3.org/TR/xpath) occasionally.

XPath axis-name keywords

The XPath language uses one of the following axis-name keywords to narrow the search for a link using an extended pointer. Supported axis-name keywords include:

Axis-Name Keyword	Description
ancestor	A parent, grandparent, or other forebear — including the root node — of a particular context node
ancestor-or-self	A parent, grandparent, or other forebear of a particular context node or the current context node
attribute	All attributes of the context node, which must be an element (to have any attributes)
child	A successor to a particular context node — including the children of the context node
descendant	A child, grandchild, or other offspring of a particular context node — not including attribute or namespace nodes
descendant-or-self	A child, grandchild, or other offspring of a particular context node or the current context node
following	Any node, related or not, processed properly after a particular context node is processed — not including descendant, attribute, or namespace nodes
following-sibling	Any node having the same parent as the context node and processed properly after the named node is processed
namespace	All namespace nodes of the context node, which must be an element (to have any namespaces)

Axis-Name Keyword	Description
parent	A forebear to a particular context node, if that source has a parent
preceding	Any node, related or not, processed properly before a particular context node is processed — not including descendant, attribute, or namespace nodes
preceding-sibling	Any node having the same parent as the context node and processed properly before the named node is processed
self	The current context node

Using location paths

XPointers use location paths, based on generations of elements and other document components, to find a specific target. A location path combines keywords and syntax to find a specific place or component in a target document. You can combine one or more absolute location terms and/or relative location terms to pinpoint a particular location to which to link:

- An *absolute location term* is analogous to an absolute URI. Its address is a complete reference to the final target location.

- A *relative location term* is analogous to a relative URI. Its address starts with the current (absolute) location and uses a partial reference to link to the next location on the way to the target. The *argument* (the value or expression used to find the location in the document) for a relative location term can include an instance number, node name or type, attribute name and/or value, several keywords, and string.

Each location path builds on the previous one, using the hierarchical structure (root element/child element/child of child, and so on) of XML documents to point to a distinct location in a document. Each argument that you add to a location path refines the search for the specific document component even more.

The following example shows an XPointer with an absolute URI:

```
<anchor xlink type="extended"
href="http://example.com/test.xml#ID(sect_01)">
Sample Document
</anchor>
```

The following example contains a relative URI and a longer (therefore more refined) XPointer:

```
<anchor xlink:extended
 href="/test.xml#child(3,#element,art,5)">
 Sample Document
</anchor>
```

An absolute location path specifies a specific location. When you use an absolute location path, you don't need to go through any intermediate locations first. An absolute location path allows you to set a specific starting point for a containing resource. Then you can add other types of location path to further refine the link. You can combine absolute location path and relative location path in a single argument. In fact, when you use relative location paths, you usually start the argument with an absolute location path. A location step has an *axis* (which shows the tree relationship between the selected node and the context node), a *node test* (which names the node type and expanded qualifier name, with a prefix, of the selected node), and optional *predicates* (which filter the selected nodes set to a greater extent). Use the following symbols to join absolute and relative location steps in an XPointer.

- / is a character that indicates the separation between one location step and another.
- // are characters that represent /descendant-or-self:: node()/.
- . is a character that represents self::node().

Following is a fragment from an XPointer:

```
string-range(//chap05).child(section,"intro")[2]
```

Enter the string-range keyword to find a range that contains a particular string. Start with the descendant, chap05. Then, select the second occurrence (2) of the intro string in the section child element.

```
string-range(//chap05).fsibling(section,"intro")[2]
```

The only difference between this and the prior fragments is that section must be a following sibling instead of a child.

This example from the XPointer candidate recommendation illustrates how to find a particular punctuation mark (!) and the character that immediately follows it:

```
string-range(/,"!",1,2)[5]
```

The expression uses the slash (/) to indicate the starting text-node location step, indicates the punctuation mark is a string by enclosing it within quotation marks, instructs that the fifth ([5]) exclamation mark is the first selection (1), and that the following character (2) is also included.

Now that you have gotten an overview of XLinks and XPointers, it's time to move on to a brand-new topic — styling XML documents with Extensible Style sheet Language (XSL) style sheets. To learn more, continue to Chapter 7, "Styling Documents with XSL."

6

in plain english in pl
sh in plain english in
glish in plain english
in plain english in pl
sh in plain english in
glish in plain english
in plain english in pl
glish in plain english
in plain english in pl
sh in plain english in
glish in plain english
in plain english in pl
sh in plain english in
glish in plain english
in plain english in pl
lish in plain english
in plain english in pl
sh in plain english in
glish in plain english
in plain english in pl
sh in plain english in
lish in plain english
in plain english in pl
glish in plain english

Styling Documents with XSL

Extensible Stylesheet Language (XSL) allows writers and editors to write documents with which to transform, format, and enhance XML document output, using nested DSSSL Online (DSSSL-O) rules. This chapter provides an overview of XSL style sheets and examples based on the current XSL working draft.

●—NOTE

At the time of this writing, XSL is a working draft. Because the W3C has not announced a formal XSL recommendation, the language will probably undergo further changes. Because of this and the fact that the cascading-style-sheet recommendation is relatively stable (although not supported by all browsers), consider using cascading style sheets (CSS) rather than XSL. To follow the progress of XSL—especially when it becomes a recommendation—make sure that you check the XSL homepage at `http://www.w3c.org/TR/XSL/`.

XSL incorporates CSS and DSSSL features into a language specifically created for XML documents. XSL documents are constructed in the same way as XML documents; once you have learned how to use XML, you are well on your way to creating properly constructed XSL documents. The XSL namespace is located at `http://www.w3.org/1999/XSL/Format`. By default, refer to the XSL namespace by using the prefix `fo:`.

Learning About DSSSL and DSSSL-0

XSL is based on both cascading style sheets and Document Style Semantics and Specification Language (DSSSL). DSSSL is a comprehensive and lengthy standard used for transforming and styling documents — including SGML and now XML. The DSSSL standard, ISO/IEC 10179:1996, documents both the transformation and styling languages for specifying document transformation and formatting in a manner that ignores particular platforms or programs. You can use DSSSL with any document format for which a property set can be defined according to the Property Set Definition Requirements of ISO/IEC 10744. In particular, you can use DSSSL to specify the presentation of documents marked up according to ISO 8879:1996, Standard Generalized Markup Language (SGML).

●─NOTE────────────────────────

To learn more about cascading style sheets, you can refer to a Web site or book that covers the subject. For example, look at *XHTML In Plain English* by Sandra E. Eddy, published by IDG Books Worldwide. *XHTML In Plain English* includes a comprehensive CSS reference and a tutorial chapter, which provides an introduction to cascading style sheets.

DSSSL Online (or DSSSL-O) comprises a subset of DSSSL characteristics that enable developers to style electronic documents read by SGML, XML, and XHTML browsers. XSL uses DSSSL flow object classes as the basis for identifying particular elements, attributes, and other components of documents or finding certain occurrences of components.

DSSSL is made up of many elements, known as characteristics, with which you can apply many types of styles to flow objects, objects that fill a defined area in document output. Typical flow objects include hyperlinks, characters, paragraphs, pages, groups of adjacent pages, graphics, and tables. Flow object classes, which are groups of related flow objects, include both named formatting attributes and named *ports*, locations to which ordered lists of flow objects are attached. This allows the organization of flow objects as flow-object trees, which demonstrate specific ancestor-and-descendant relationships. When a flow object tree is created, each flow object is associated with its own formatting characteristics. Formats of parent flow objects can control the formats of child flow objects, or the child flow objects can have their own formats.

The output of a formatted flow object "flows" into an *area*, which is a rectangle with a set height and width. In many ways, an area is analogous to a frame in a word processing document — especially if you consider the fact that a frame can include document elements as diverse as text and graphics.

A *sosofo* (an acronym for "specification of a sequence of flow objects") specifies both the placement and formatting of particular elements in a document. A sosofo allows you to nest one or more child elements under a parent and specify particular formats for all or for particular elements. Under DSSSL, elements, attributes, and other objects in a document are known as *nodes*.

Style sheets use rules to select a document element and apply formats and enhancements, and a cascading style sheet rule is composed of a selector (the element) and a declaration (the property and value). DSSSL rules are also composed of two parts: A *query* "finds" one or more nodes, and a *make_expression* forms a flow object from the node.

The DSSSL standard specifies categories of flow object classes, most of which are supported by DSSSL-O. DSSSL-O supports the following flow object classes: aligned-column, box, character, display-group, external-graphic, leader, line-field, link, marginalia, multi-mode, paragraph, paragraph-break, rule, score, scroll, sideline, simple-page-sequence, table, table-border, table-cell, table-column, table-part, and table-row.

Introducing XSL

XSL both transforms and styles XML documents. The XSLT (Transformations) language handles the job of transforming documents (which is known as *tree transformation*), and a style sheet language uses declarations to create output. When you use XSL, you create an external XSL document — similar to an XML document — that sets formats and enhancements for one or more elements in XML documents. For example, you can define all level-one headings as bold, red, set in the Helvetica typeface, and set to a 16-point size. You can also specify properties for families of elements: You can apply certain formats or enhancements for a parent element to descendant and ancestor elements. With XSL, you can also style elements by their position and value, generate text and graphics, and define formatting macros. You can write XSL documents for all types of printed and electronic output.

When you declare a style, you define a *tree construction rule* (known in previous XSL drafts as a template rule) for each format or enhancement. A tree construction rule is composed of a pattern and a template, which identify the input element types to be styled and the output flow objects. The *pattern* is a string that names one or more input element types in the *source tree*, which contains all the elements defined in the XML document's DTD. The *action* specifies a *subtree* (that is, the elements that match the pattern) of flow objects, styled objects that fill a defined area. Examples of flow objects include hyperlinks, pages, groups of adjacent pages, graphics, and links. Look at the following example:

```
<?xml version="1.0"?>
<xsl:stylesheet
    xmlns:xsl="http://www.w3.org/1999/XSL/Transform"
    xmlns:fo="http://www.w3.org/1999/XSL/Format"
    version="1.0">

<xsl:template match="redtext">
  <fo:block text-align="center">
    <xsl:apply-templates/>
  </fo:block>
</xsl:template>
```

The first line states that the document is based on XML 1.0. The following three lines call the XML namespace and declare the version, 1.0. Using the `target-element` keyword and attributes of the matched element, the pattern statement `match="redtext"` targets (that is, identifies) the `redtext` element type for the styling action, center alignment. Using the action, the XML processor acts on the target element and its children: It places the contents of all instances of the `redtext` element in a paragraph and changes the element as the template instructs.

A pattern can also include references to ancestors and descendants of a single target element with the *area tree*, which is the result of processing and formatting. Referring to specific relatives of elements allows you to select certain elements in a document while ignoring others of the same type, or to style the same element type in different ways depending on the context in which it appears in a document.

You can use the following criteria to select a particular target element:

- All its ancestors
- All its descendants
- Certain descendants or ancestors (use wildcard characters to pinpoint the selection)
- One or more particular element attributes, their values, or both
- The location of the element among its sibling elements
- A specific factor that differentiates the element from its sibling elements

The target element is the focus of a pattern; from the target element flow generations of ancestors and descendants and their attributes.

●—NOTE

In each case of a series of nested elements, an XSL processor relies on *recursion*, in which processing of all elements is not complete until the last (and most insignificant) child element is processed. The processing for the target element relies on the processing for the child element nested immediately below it, which in turn relies on its child, and so on, until the "least" child is processed. In other words, each processing result affects the element above it. Recursion allows the processor to work on individual elements rather than process the entire set of elements as a whole — as long as the set is under one rule. In addition, recursion does not take place unless there is at least one child element of the target element.

You can match two instances of a target element and cause two different actions with the mode attribute. To differentiate between the occurrences, simply declare a mode for one of them.

```
<?xml version="1.0"?>
<xsl:stylesheet
    xmlns:xsl="http://www.w3.org/1999/XSL/Transform"
    xmlns:fo="http://www.w3.org/1999/XSL/Format"
    version="1.0">

<xsl:template match="manual">
  <xsl:apply-templates
      select="part/sect_head" mode="toc"/>
  <xsl:apply-templates/>
</xsl:template>
    other lines
<xsl:template match="part/sect_head" mode="toc">
```

This example, which is based on an example in the XSL working draft, creates a table of contents for a manual made up of parts and sections.

Evaluating Examples

Perhaps the best way to understand XSL is to review a few examples.

The first example applies various styles (boldface, 14-point size, and blue) to the text in a paragraph element, para:

```
<?xml version="1.0"?>
<xsl:stylesheet
    xmlns:xsl="http://www.w3.org/1999/XSL/Transform"
    xmlns:fo="http://www.w3.org/1999/XSL/Format"
                version="1.0">

<xsl:template match="para">
  <fo:block>
    <fo:initial-property-set
      font-weight="bold"
      font-size="14pt"
      color="blue"/>
    <xsl:apply-templates/>
  </fo:block>
</xsl:template>


</xsl:stylesheet>
```

The following example segment, based on an example in a previous XSL working draft, styles a photograph and its caption:

```
<xsl:template match="photo">
  <fo:block text-align="center">
    <fo:external-graphic src="{@image}"/>
  </fo:block>
</xsl:template>

<xsl:template match="caption">
  <fo:block space-before="3pt" text-align="center"
    start-indent="10mm" end-indent="10mm">
    <xsl:apply-templates/>
  </fo:block>
</xsl:template>
```

The statements center-align the block-element, photo, and call the graphic using the src attribute. The caption is centered and indented. In addition, an extra three points are inserted above the caption.

The following example, from the XSL working draft, styles an ordered list:

```
<?xml version='1.0'?>
<xsl:stylesheet
   xmlns:xsl="http://www.w3.org/1999/XSL/Transform"
   xmlns:fo="http://www.w3.org/1999/XSL/Format"
             version='1.0'>

<xsl:template match="ol">
   <fo:list-block provisional-distance-between-starts="15mm"
   provisional-label-separation="5mm">
     <xsl:apply-templates/>
   </fo:list-block>
</xsl:template>

<xsl:template match="ol/item">
   <fo:list-item>
     <fo:list-item-label start-indent="5mm"
       end-indent="label-end()">
       <fo:block>
         <xsl:number format="a."/>
       </fo:block>
     </fo:list-item-label>
     <fo:list-item-body start-indent="body-start()">
       <fo:block>
         <xsl:apply-templates/>
       </fo:block>
     </fo:list-item-body>
   </fo:list-item>
</xsl:template>

</xsl:stylesheet>
```

The first xsl:template statement, which matches the ol element, styles the entire ordered list. The provisional-distance-between-starts property sets the length between the end of a start indent of a list-item label and the beginning of the list item itself, and provisional-label-separation sets the length between the end of a list-item label and the beginning of the list item. Because both properties apply to the entire list, every list item is styled the same way. The second xsl:template statement refers to list items within the ordered list (ol/item). The start-indent property acts on the item label (fo:list-item-label), setting the number format to a with a period. The next statement applies the body-start() function to the text in each list item (fo:list-item-body). Finally, a series of end tags closes the style sheet.

The following segment lays out a page named layout:

```
<fo:simple-page-master master-name="layout"
  page-height="8in" page-width="5in"
  margin-top="1in" margin-bottom="1in"
  margin-left="1.25in" margin-right="1.25in">
</fo:simple-page-master>
```

The properties in the segment set the page height, page width, and all four margins.

The following example from the XSL working draft lays out a table:

```
<?xml version='1.0'?>
<xsl:stylesheet
    xmlns:xsl="http://www.w3.org/1999/XSL/Transform"
    xmlns:fo="http://www.w3.org/1999/XSL/Format"
                version='1.0'>

<xsl:template match="p">
  <fo:block>
    <xsl:apply-templates/>
  </fo:block>
</xsl:template>

<xsl:template match="table">
  <fo:table width="12cm" table-layout="fixed">
    <xsl:apply-templates/>
  </fo:table>
</xsl:template>

<xsl:template match="colspec">
  <fo:table-column>
    <xsl:attribute name="column-number">
      <xsl:number count="colspec"/>
    </xsl:attribute>
    <xsl:attribute name="column-width">
      <xsl:call-template name="calc.column.width">
        <xsl:with-param name="colwidth">
          <xsl:value-of select="@colwidth"/>
        </xsl:with-param>
      </xsl:call-template>
    </xsl:attribute>
  </fo:table-column>
</xsl:template>

<xsl:template match="tbody">
  <fo:table-body>
    <xsl:apply-templates/>
```

```
    </fo:table-body>
  </xsl:template>

  <xsl:template match="row">
    <fo:table-row>
      <xsl:apply-templates/>
    </fo:table-row>
  </xsl:template>

  <xsl:template match="entry">
    <fo:table-cell column-number="{@colnum}">
      <xsl:if test="@valign">
        <xsl:choose>
          <xsl:when test="@valign='middle'">
            <xsl:attribute
              name="display-align">center
            </xsl:attribute>
          </xsl:when>
          <xsl:otherwise>
            <xsl:attribute name="display-align">
              <xsl:value-of select="@valign"/>
            </xsl:attribute>
          </xsl:otherwise>
        </xsl:choose>
      </xsl:if>
      <xsl:if test="@align">
        <xsl:attribute name="text-align">
          <xsl:value-of select="@align"/>
        </xsl:attribute>
      </xsl:if>
      <xsl:apply-templates/>
    </fo:table-cell>
  </xsl:template>
```

The first statements match the paragraph (p) element and declare that it has a block format. The second statements set the table width and table layout. The third statements act on table columns — numbering them and setting the width. The next statements set the table body (tbody) and row (row) elements. The last statements specify conditions for data entry, including the column number and alignment.

The following example from the XSL working draft sets colors of various document components, including links, visited links, active links, hover buttons, and objects in current focus:

```
<?xml version='1.0'?>
<xsl:style sheet
  xmlns:xsl="http://www.w3.org/1999/XSL/Transform"
```

```
        xmlns:fo="http://www.w3.org/1999/XSL/Format"
                    version='1.0'>

<xsl:template match="p">
 <fo:block>
 <xsl:apply-templates/>
 </fo:block>
</xsl:template>

<xsl:template match="xlink:mylink"
xmlns:xlink="http://www.w3.org/1999/xlink">
 <xsl:variable name="show">
 <xsl:value-of select="@xlink:show"/>
  </xsl:variable>
   <fo:multi-properties text-decoration="underline">
    <fo:multi-property-set active-state="link"
           color="blue"/>
    <fo:multi-property-set active-state="visited"
           color="red"/>
    <fo:multi-property-set active-state="active"
           color="green"/>
    <fo:multi-property-set active-state="hover"
           text-decoration="blink"/>
    <fo:multi-property-set active-state="focus"
           color="yellow"/>
    <fo:wrapper color="merge-property-values()"
        text-decoration="merge-property-values()">
     <fo:simple-link
          external-destination="http://w3.org/TR"
          show-destination="{$show}">
      <xsl:attribute name="role">
      <xsl:value-of select="@xlink:title"/>
      </xsl:attribute>
      <xsl:apply-templates/>
     </fo:simple-link>
    </fo:wrapper>
   </fo:multi-properties>
</xsl:template>

</xsl:stylesheet>
```

This chapter concludes the tutorial. Please keep in mind that the chapters in the tutorial just touch the surface of XML and are based on a "snapshot" of the technology at a particular time. Be sure to check the W3C Web site (http://www.w3.org/) often to make sure that you stay up to date with the XML language and the technologies related to XML.

in plain english in p
sh in plain english ir
glish in plain english
in plain english in p
sh in plain english ir
glish in plain english
in plain english in p
glish in plain english
in plain english in p
sh in plain english ir
glish in plain english
in plain english in p
sh in plain english ir
glish in plain english
in plain english in p
lish in plain english
in plain english in p
sh in plain english ir
glish in plain english
in plain english in p
sh in plain english ir
lish in plain english
in plain english in p
lish in plain english

Unicode Characters
and Character Sets

In the past, software and electronic-document developers used the ASCII and Latin-1 characters. Now, XML supports the entire Unicode character set — almost 60,000 codes in Unicode 3.0.1, which is the current version at the time of this writing. In addition to ASCII and Latin-1 characters, which are a small part of the Unicode character set, Unicode includes many other special characters and — to completely support the internationalization of XML documents — alphabets from many languages.

This appendix is made up of sections for each character-class production, based on a subset of the almost 50,000 codes in Unicode 2.1. Starting each section is one or more tables that illustrate and describe characters from character sets that are commonly used by English speakers. The "Other Supported Character Sets" sections contain information about supported characters within non-English character sets. For more information about Unicode and its many character sets, characters, and symbols, go to the Unicode home page (http://www.unicode. org/) and browse through the pages at the site.

Legal or special characters allow you to embed alphabetic characters, symbols, and nonkeyboard characters in a document. XML's character-class productions (`BaseChar`, `CombiningChar`, `Digit`, `Extender`, `Ideographic`, and `Letter`) support the special characters listed in the following tables.

For more information about character-class productions, including the syntax and specific characters supported by each, see "XML Syntax" (p. ___) in Part I. Please keep in mind that XML supports the entire Unicode character set — whether or not they are listed in the XML recommendation.

●─NOTE ────────────────────────────────

The `Char` production supports any Unicode character, including those documented in this part, but excluding #xFFFE and #xFFFF.

Tables A-1 through A-21 each include some or all of the following column headings:

Char (Character)	A typed character.
Glyph	An image of the character or symbol, the counterpart to Char.
UTC Code	The code assigned by the Unicode Organization's Unicode Technical Committee.
Entity Name	The approved syntax for the characters. In most cases, you should use this syntax instead of the numeric entry reference.
Numeric Entry Reference	A numeric code counterpart to the entity name.
Description	A brief description of the character.

●─NOTE ────────────────────────────────

In addition to the characters specified in this part, XML also supports four standard control characters and the Euro character for the European Monetary Union:

#x9 (Unicode code #x0009), which inserts a tab (HT)
#xA (Unicode code #x000A), which inserts a line feed (LF)
#xD (Unicode code #x000D), which inserts a carriage return (CR)
#x20 (Unicode code #x0020), which inserts a space
#20AC, which inserts a Euro character

BaseChar Characters and Character Sets

This section covers characters and character sets specified for the BaseChar production in the XML 1.0 recommendation.

Latin 1 Uppercase and Lowercase

Table A-1 contains the alphabetic characters in the Special Characters — Latin 1 Uppercase and Lowercase set, specified in the BaseChar production.

Table A-1 *BaseChar Special Characters — Latin 1 Uppercase and Lowercase*

Char.	UTC Code	Char.	UTC Code	Char.	UTC Code	Char.	UTC Code
A	#x0041	N	#x004E	a	#x0061	n	#x006E
B	#x0042	O	#x004F	b	#x0062	o	#x006F
C	#x0043	P	#x0050	c	#x0063	p	#x0070
D	#x0044	Q	#x0051	d	#x0064	q	#x0071
E	#x0045	R	#x0052	e	#x0065	r	#x0072
F	#x0046	S	#x0053	f	#x0066	s	#x0073
G	#x0047	T	#x0054	g	#x0067	t	#x0074
H	#x0048	U	#x0055	h	#x0068	u	#x0075
I	#x0049	V	#x0056	i	#x0069	v	#x0076
J	#x004A	W	#x0057	j	#x006A	w	#x0077
K	#x004B	X	#x0058	k	#x006B	x	#x0078
L	#x004C	Y	#x0059	l	#x006C	y	#x0079
M	#x004D	Z	#x005A	m	#x006D	z	#x007A

Latin 1 Supplementary

Table A-2 contains characters in the Latin 1 Supplementary set, specified in the BaseChar production.

Table A-2 *BaseChar Special Characters — Latin 1 Supplementary*

Glyph	UTC Code	Entity Name	Numeric Entry Reference	Description
À	#x00C0	À	À	Grave Accent A
Á	#x00C1	&Aacute	Á	Acute Accent A
Â	#x00C2	Â	Â	Circumflex Above A
Ã	#x00C3	Ã	Ã	Tilde Above A
Ä	#x00C4	Ä	Ä	Umlaut Above A
Å	#x00C5	Å	Å	Ring Above A
Æ	#x00C6	Æ	Æ	Ligature AE
Ç	#x00C7	Ç	Ç	Cedilla C
È	#x00C8	È	È	Grave Accent E
É	#x00C9	É	É	Acute Accent E
Ê	#x00CA	Ê	Ê	Circumflex Above E
Ë	#x00CB	Ë	Ë	Umlaut Above E
Ì	#x00CC	Ì	&#204:	Grave Accent I
Í	#x00CD	Í	Í	Acute Accent I
Î	#x00CE	Î	Î	Circumflex Above I
Ï	#x00CF	Ï	Ï	Umlaut Above I
Ð	#x00D0	Ð	Ð	Icelandic ETH
Ñ	#x00D1	Ñ	Ñ	Tilde Above N
Ò	#x00D2	Ò	Ò	Grave Accent O
Ó	#x00D3	Ó	Ó	Acute Accent O
Ô	#x00D4	Ô	Ô	Circumflex Above O
Õ	#x00D5	Õ	Õ	Tilde Above O
Ö	#x00D6	Ö	Ö	Umlaut Above O
Ø	#x00D8	Ø	Ø	Stroke or Slash O
Ù	#x00D9	Ù	Ù	Grave Accent U
Ú	#x00DA	Ú	Ú	Acute Accent U
Û	#x00DB	Û	Û	Circumflex Above U
Ü	#x00DC	Ü	Ü	Umlaut Above U
Ý	#x00DD	Ý	Ý	Acute Accent Y

A

Glyph	UTC Code	Entity Name	Numeric Entry Reference	Description
Þ	#x00DE	Þ	Þ	Icelandic THORN
ß	#x00DF	ß	ß	Sharp s
à	#x00E0	à	à	Grave Accent a
á	#x00E1	á	á	Acute Accent a
â	#x00E2	â	â	Circumflex Above a
ã	#x00E3	ã	ã	Tilde Above a
ä	#x00E4	ä	ä	Umlaut Above a
å	#x00E5	å	å	Ring Above a
æ	#x00E6	æ	æ	Ligature ae
ç	#x00E7	ç	ç	Cedilla c
è	#x00E8	è	è	Grave Accent e
é	#x00E9	é	é	Acute Accent e
ê	#x00EA	ê	ê	Circumflex Above e
ë	#x00EB	ë	ë	Umlaut Above e
ì	#x00EC	ì	ì	Grave Accent i
í	#x00ED	í	í	Acute Accent i
î	#x00EE	î	î	Circumflex Above i
ï	#x00EF	ï	ï	Umlaut Above i
ð	#x00F0	ð	ð	Icelandic eth
ñ	#x00F1	ñ	ñ	Tilde Above n
ò	#x00F2	ò	ò	Grave Accent o
ó	#x00F3	ó	ó	Acute Accent o
ô	#x00F4	ô	ô	Circumflex Above o
õ	#x00F5	õ	õ	Tilde Above o
ö	#x00F6	ö	ö	Umlaut Above o
ø	#x00F8	ø	ø	Stroke or Slash o
ù	#x00F9	ù	ù	Grave Accent u
ú	#x00FA	ú	ú	Acute Accent u
û	#x00FB	û	û	Circumflex Above u
ü	#x00FC	ü	ü	Umlaut Above u
ý	#x00FD	ý	ý	Acute Accent y

Continued

Table A-2 *Continued*

Glyph	UTC Code	Entity Name	Numeric Entry Reference	Description
þ	#x00FE	þ	þ	Icelandic thorn
ÿ	#x00FF	ÿ	ÿ	Umlaut Above y

Extended Latin-A

Table A-3 contains characters in the Extended Latin-A set, specified in the BaseChar production.

Table A-3 *BaseChar Special Characters — Extended Latin-A*

Glyph	UTC Code	Entity Name	Description
Ā	#x0100	Ā	Macron A
ā	#x0101	ā	Macron a
Ă	#x0102	Ă	Breve Above A
ă	#x0103	ă	Breve Above a
Ą	#x0104	Ą	Ogonek A
ą	#x0105	ą	Ogonek a
Ć	#x0106	Ć	Acute Accent C
ć	#x0107	ć	Acute Accent c
Ĉ	#x0108	Ĉ	Circumflex Above C
ĉ	#x0109	ĉ	Circumflex Above c
Ċ	#x010A	Ċ	Dot Above C
ċ	#x010B	ċ	Dot Above c
Č	#x010C	Č	Caron C
č	#x010D	č	Caron c
Ď	#x010E	Ď	Caron D
ď	#x010F	ď	Caron d
Đ	#x0110	Đ	Stroke D
đ	#x0111	đ	Stroke d
Ē	#x0112	Ē	Macron E
ē	#x0113	ē	Macron e
Ĕ	#x0114	n/a	Breve Above E

Glyph	UTC Code	Entity Name	Description
ĕ	#x0115	n/a	Breve Above e
Ė	#x0116	Ė	Dot Above E
ė	#x0117	ė	Dot Above e
Ę	#x0118	Ę	Ogonek E
ę	#x0119	ę	Ogonek e
Ě	#x011A	Ě	Caron E
ě	#x011B	ě	Caron e
Ĝ	#x011C	Ĝ	Circumflex Above G
ĝ	#x011D	ĝ	Circumflex Above g
Ğ	#x011E	Ğ	Breve Above G
ğ	#x011F	ğ	Breve Above g
Ġ	#x0120	Ġ	Dot Above G
ġ	#x0121	ġ	Dot Above g
Ģ	#x0122	Ģ	Cedilla G
ģ	#x0123	n/a	Cedilla g
Ĥ	#x0124	Ĥ	Circumflex Above H
ĥ	#x0125	ĥ	Circumflex Above h
Ħ	#x0126	Ħ	Stroke H
ħ	#x0127	ħ	Stroke h
Ĩ	#x0128	Ĩ	Tilde Above I
ĩ	#x0129	ĩ	Tilde Above i
Ī	#x012A	Ī	Macron I
ī	#x012B	ī	Macron i
Ĭ	#x012C	n/a	Breve Above I
ĭ	#x012D	n/a	Breve Above i
Į	#x012E	Į	Ogonek I
į	#x012F	į	Ogonek i
İ	#x0130	İ	Dot Above I
ı	#x0131	ı	Dotless i
Ĵ	#x0134	Ĵ	Circumflex Above J
ĵ	#x0135	ĵ	Circumflex Above j
Ķ	#x0136	Ķ	Cedilla K
ķ	#x0137	ķ	Cedilla k

Continued

A

Table A-3 *Continued*

Glyph	UTC Code	Entity Name	Description
κ	#x0138	n/a	kra
Ĺ	#x0139	Ĺ	Acute Accent L
ĺ	#x013A	ĺ	Acute Accent l
Ļ	#x013B	Ļ	Cedilla L
ļ	#x013C	ļ	Cedilla l
Ľ	#x013D	Ľ	Caron L
ľ	#x013E	ľ	Caron l
Ł	#x0141	Ł	Stroke L
ł	#x0142	ł	Stroke l
Ń	#x0143	Ń	Acute Accent N
ń	#x0144	ń	Acute Accent n
Ņ	#x0145	Ņ	Cedilla N
ņ	#x0146	ņ	Cedilla n
Ň	#x0147	Ň	Caron N
ň	#x0148	ň	Caron n
Ŋ	#x014A	Ŋ	ENG
ŋ	#x014B	ŋ	eng
Ō	#x014C	Ō	Macron O
ō	#x014D	ō	Macron o
Ŏ	#x014E	n/a	Breve Above O
ŏ	#x014F	n/a	Breve Above o
Ő	#x0150	Ő	Double Acute Accent O
ő	#x0151	ő	Double Acute Accent o
Œ	#x0152	Œ	Ligature OE
œ	#x0153	œ	Ligature oe
Ŕ	#x0154	Ŕ	Acute Accent R
ŕ	#x0155	ŕ	Acute Accent r
Ŗ	#x0156	Ŗ	Cedilla R
ŗ	#x0157	ŗ	Cedilla r
Ř	#x0158	Ř	Caron R
ř	#x0159	ř	Caron r
Ś	#x015A	Ś	Acute Accent S

Glyph	UTC Code	Entity Name	Description
ś	#x015B	ś	Acute Accent s
Ŝ	#x015C	Ŝ	Circumflex Above S
ŝ	#x015D	ŝ	Circumflex Above s
Ş	#x015E	Ş	Cedilla S
ş	#x015F	ş	Cedilla s
Š	#x0160	Š	Caron S
š	#x0161	š	Caron s
Ţ	#x0162	Ţ	Cedilla T
ţ	#x0163	ţ	Cedilla t
Ť	#x0164	Ť	Caron T
ť	#x0165	ť	Caron t
Ŧ	#x0166	Ŧ	Stroke T
ŧ	#x0167	ŧ	Stroke t
Ũ	#x0168	Ũ	Tilde Above U
ũ	#x0169	ũ	Tilde Above u
Ū	#x016A	Ū	Macron U
ū	#x016B	ū	Macron u
Ŭ	#x016C	Ŭ	Breve Above U
ŭ	#x016D	ŭ	Breve Above u
Ů	#x016E	Ů	Ring Above U
ů	#x016F	ů	Ring Above u
Ű	#x0170	Ű	Double Acute Accent U
ű	#x0171	ű	Double Acute Accent u
Ų	#x0172	Ų	Ogonek U
ų	#x0173	ų	Ogonek u
Ŵ	#x0174	Ŵ	Circumflex Above W
ŵ	#x0175	ŵ	Circumflex Above w
Ŷ	#x0176	Ŷ	Circumflex Above Y
ŷ	#x0177	ŷ	Circumflex Above y
Ÿ	#x0178	Ÿ	Umlaut Above Y
Ź	#x0179	Ź	Acute Accent Z
ź	#x017A	ź	Acute Accent z
Ż	#x017B	Ż	Dot Above Z

Continued

Table A-3 *Continued*

Glyph	UTC Code	Entity Name	Description
ż	#x017C	ż	Dot Above z
Ž	#x017D	Ž	Caron Z
ž	#x017E	ž	Caron z

Extended Latin-B

Table A-4 contains characters in the Extended Latin-B set, specified in the BaseChar production.

Table A-4 *BaseChar Special Characters — Extended Latin-B*

Glyph	UTC Code	Description
b	#x0180	Stroke b
B	#x0181	Hook B
Ƃ	#x0182	Topbar B
ƃ	#x0183	Topbar b
Ƅ	#x0184	Tone SIX
ƅ	#x0185	Tone six
Ɔ	#x0186	Open O
Ƈ	#x0187	Hook C
ƈ	#x0188	Hook c
Ɖ	#x0189	African D
Ɗ	#x018A	Hook D
Ƌ	#x018B	Topbar D
ƌ	#x018C	Topbard d
ƍ	#x018D	Turned delta
Ǝ	#x018E	Reversed E
Ə	#x018F	SCHWA
Ɛ	#x0190	Open E
Ƒ	#x0191	Hook F
ƒ	#x0192	Hook f
Ɠ	#x0193	Hook G
Ɣ	#x0194	GAMMA

Glyph	UTC Code	Description
ɦʋ	#x0195	hv
ι	#x0196	IOTA
ɪ	#x0197	Stroke I
Ƙ	#x0198	Hook K
ƙ	#x0199	Hook k
ł	#x019A	Bar l
ƛ	#x019B	Stroke lambda
ɯ	#x019C	Turned M
Ɲ	#x019D	Left Hook N
ŋ	#x019E	Long Right Leg n
ɵ	#x019F	Middle Tilde O
Ơ	#x01A0	Horn O
ơ	#x01A1	Horn o
Ƣ	#x01A2	OI
ƣ	#x01A3	oi
Ƥ	#x01A4	Hook P
ƥ	#x01A5	Hook p
Ʀ	#x01A6	YR
Ƨ	#x01A7	Tone TWO
ƨ	#x01A8	Tone two
Ʃ	#x01A9	ESH
ƪ	#x01AA	Reversed ESH Loop
ƫ	#x01AB	Palatal Hook t
Ƭ	#x01AC	Hook T
ƭ	#x01AD	Hook t
Ʈ	#x01AE	Retroflex Hook T
Ư	#x01AF	Horn U
ư	#x01B0	Horn u
Ʊ	#x01B1	UPSILON
Ʋ	#x01B2	Hook V
Ƴ	#x01B3	Hook Y
ƴ	#x01B4	Hook y
Ƶ	#x01B5	Stroke Z

Continued

Table A-4   *Continued*

Glyph	UTC Code	Description
ƶ	#x01B6	Stroke z
Ʒ	#x01B7	EZH
Ƹ	#x01B8	EZH Reversed
ƹ	#x01B9	ezh Reversed
ƺ	#x01BA	ezh Tail
ƻ	#x01BB	Stroke 2
Ƽ	#x01BC	Tone FIVE
ƽ	#x01BD	Tone five
ƾ	#x01BE	Stroke Inverted Glottal Stop
Ƿ	#x01BF	Wynn
ǀ	#x01C0	Dental Click
ǁ	#x01C1	Lateral Click
ǂ	#x01C2	Alveolar Click
ǃ	#x01C3	Retroflex Click
Ǎ	#x01CD	Caron A
ǎ	#x01CE	Caron a
Ǐ	#x01CF	Caron I
ǐ	#x01D0	Caron i
Ǒ	#x01D1	Caron O
ǒ	#x01D2	Caron o
Ǔ	#x01D3	Caron U
ǔ	#x01D4	Caron u
Ǖ	#x01D5	Umlaut Above Macron U
ǖ	#x01D6	Umlaut Above Macron u
Ǘ	#x01D7	Umlaut Above Acute Accent U
ǘ	#x01D8	Umlaut Acute Accent u
Ǚ	#x01D9	Umlaut Above Caron U
ǚ	#x01DA	Umlaut Above Caron u
Ǜ	#x01DB	Umlaut Above Grave Accent U
ǜ	#x01DC	Umlaut Above Grave Accent u
ǝ	#x01DD	Turned e
Ǟ	#x01DE	Umlaut Above Macron A

Glyph	UTC Code	Description
ǟ	#x01DF	UmlautAbove Macron a
Ǡ	#x01E0	Dot Above Macron A
ǡ	#x01E1	Dot Above Macron a
Ǣ	#x01E2	Macron AE
ǣ	#x01E3	Macron ae
Ǥ	#x01E4	Stroke G
ǥ	#x01E5	Stroke g
Ǧ	#x01E6	Caron G
ǧ	#x01E7	Caron g
Ǩ	#x01E8	Caron K
ǩ	#x01E9	Caron k
Ǫ	#x01EA	Ogonek O
ǫ	#x01EB	Ogonek o
Ǭ	#x01EC	Ogonek Macron O
ǭ	#x01ED	Ogonek Macron o
Ǯ	#x01EE	Caron EZH
ǯ	#x01EF	Caron ezh
ǰ	#x01F0	Caron j
Ǵ	#x01F4	Acute Accent G
ǵ	#x01F5	Acute Accent g
Ǻ	#x01FA	Ring Above Acute Accent A
ǻ	#x01FB	Ring Above Acute Accent a
Ǽ	#x01FC	Acute Accent AE
ǽ	#x01FD	Acute Accent ae
Ǿ	#x01FE	Stroke Acute Accent O
ǿ	#x01FF	Stroke Acute Accent o
Ȁ	#x0200	Double Grave Accent A
ȁ	#x0201	Double Grave Accent a
Ȃ	#x0202	Inverted Breve A
ȃ	#x0203	Inverted Breve a
Ȅ	#x0204	Double Grave Accent E
ȅ	#x0205	Double Grave Accent e
Ȇ	#x0206	Inverted Breve E

Continued

Table A-4 *Continued*

Glyph	UTC Code	Description
ȇ	#x0207	Inverted Breve e
Ȉ	#x0208	Double Grave Accent I
ȉ	#x0209	Double Grave Accent i
Ȋ	#x020A	Inverted Breve I
ȋ	#x020B	Inverted Breve i
Ȍ	#x020C	Double Grave Accent O
ȍ	#x020D	Double Grave Accent o
Ȏ	#x020E	Inverted Breve O
ȏ	#x020F	Inverted Breve o
Ȑ	#x0210	Double Grave Accent R
ȑ	#x0211	Double Grave Accent r
Ȓ	#x0212	Inverted Breve R
ȓ	#x0213	Inverted Breve r
Ȕ	#x0214	Double Grave Accent U
ȕ	#x0215	Double Grave Accent u
Ȗ	#x0216	Inverted Breve U
ȗ	#x0217	Inverted Breve u

IPA Extensions

Table A-5 contains characters in the IPA Extensions set, specified in the BaseChar production.

Table A-5 *BaseChar Special Characters — IPA Extensions*

Glyph	UTC Code	Description
ɐ	#x0250	Turned a
ɑ	#x0251	alpha
ɒ	#x0252	Turned alpha
ɓ	#x0253	Hook b
ɔ	#x0254	Open o
ɕ	#x0255	Curl c
ɖ	#x0256	Tail d

Glyph	UTC Code	Description
ɗ	#x0257	Hook d
ɘ	#x0258	Reversed e
ə	#x0259	schwa
ɚ	#x025A	Hook schwa
ɛ	#x025B	Open e
ɜ	#x025C	Reversed Open e
ɝ	#x025D	Hook Reversed Open e
ɞ	#x025E	Closed Reversed Open e
ɟ	#x025F	Dotless Stroke j
ɠ	#x0260	Hook g
ɡ	#x0261	Script g
ɢ	#x0262	Small G
ɣ	#x0263	gamma
ɤ	#x0264	Rams horn
ɥ	#x0265	Turned h
ɦ	#x0266	Hook h
ɧ	#x0267	Hook heng
ɨ	#x0268	Stroke i
ɩ	#x0269	iota
ɪ	#x026A	Small I
ɫ	#x026B	Middle Tilde l
ɬ	#x026C	Belt l
ɭ	#x026D	Retroflex Hook l
ɮ	#x026E	lezh
ɯ	#x026F	Turned m
ɰ	#x0270	Turned Long leg m
ɱ	#x0271	Hook m
ɲ	#x0272	Left Hook n
ɳ	#x0273	Retroflex Hook n
ɴ	#x0274	Small N
ɵ	#x0275	Barred o
ɶ	#x0276	Small OE
ɷ	#x0277	Closed omega

Continued

Table A-5 *Continued*

Glyph	UTC Code	Description
ɸ	#x0278	Small PHI
ɹ	#x0279	Turned r
ɺ	#x027A	Turned Long Leg r
ɻ	#x027B	Hook Turned r
ɼ	#x027C	Long Leg r
ɽ	#x027D	Tail r
ɾ	#x027E	Fishhook r
ɿ	#x027F	Reversed Fishhook r
ʀ	#x0280	Small R
ʁ	#x0281	Inverted Small R
ʂ	#x0282	Hook s
ʃ	#x0283	esh
ʄ	#x0284	Stroke Hook Dotless j
ʅ	#x0285	Squat Reversed esh
ʆ	#x0286	Curl esh
ʇ	#x0287	Turned t
ʈ	#x0288	Retroflex Hook t
ʉ	#x0289	Bar u
ʊ	#x028A	upsilon
ʋ	#x028B	Hook v
ʌ	#x028C	Turned v
ʍ	#x028D	Turned w
ʎ	#x028E	Turned y
ʏ	#x028F	Small Y
ʐ	#x0290	Retroflex Hook z
ʑ	#x0291	Curl z
ʒ	#x0292	ezh
ʓ	#x0293	Curl ezh
ʔ	#x0294	Glottal Stop
ʕ	#x0295	Pharyngeal Voiced Fricative
ʖ	#x0296	Inverted Glottal Stop
ʗ	#x0297	Stretched C

A

Glyph	UTC Code	Description
ʘ	#x0298	Bilabial Click
ʙ	#x0299	Small B
ɚ	#x029A	Closed Open e
ɛ	#x029B	Small Hook G
ʜ	#x029C	Small H
ʝ	#x029D	Crossed-Tail j
ʞ	#x029E	Turned k
ʟ	#x029F	Small L
ɋ	#x02A0	Hook q
ʡ	#x02A1	Stroke Glottal Stop
ʢ	#x02A2	Stroke Reversed Glottal Stop
ʣ	#x02A3	dz Digraph
ʤ	#x02A4	dezh Digraph
ʥ	#x02A5	Curl dz Digraph
ʦ	#x02A6	ts Digraph
ʧ	#x02A7	tesh Digraph
ʨ	#x02A8	Curl tc Digraph

Spacing Modifier Letters

Table A-6 contains characters in the Spacing Modifier Letters set, specified in the BaseChar production.

Table A-6 *BaseChar Special Characters — Spacing Modifier Letters*

Glyph	UTC Code	Description
ʻ	#x02BB	Prime
ʼ	#x02BC	Double Prime
ʽ	#x02BD	Reversed Comma
ʾ	#x02BE	Right Half Ring
ʿ	#x02BF	Left Half Ring
ˀ	#x02C0	Glottal Stop
ˁ	#x02C1	Reversed Glottal Stop

Greek and Coptic

Table A-7 contains characters in the Greek and Coptic set, specified in the BaseChar production.

Table A-7 *BaseChar Special Characters — Greek and Coptic*

Glyph	UTC Code	Entity Name	Description
Ά	#x0386	n/a	Tonos ALPHA
Έ	#x0388	n/a	Tonos EPSILON
Ή	#x0389	n/a	Tonos ETA
Ί	#x038A	n/a	Tonos IOTA
Ό	#x038C	n/a	Tonos OMICRON
Ύ	#x038E	n/a	Tonos UPSILON
Ώ	#x038F	n/a	Tonos OMEGA
ΐ	#x0390	n/a	Dialytika Tonos iota
A	#x0391	&Agr;	ALPHA
B	#x0392	&Bgr;	BETA
Γ	#x0393	&Ggr;	GAMMA
Δ	#x0394	&Dgr;	DELTA
E	#x0395	&Egr;	EPSILON
Z	#x0396	&Zgr;	ZETA
H	#x0397	&EEgr;	ETA
Θ	#x0398	&THgr;	THETA
I	#x0399	&Igr;	IOTA
K	#x039A	&Kgr;	KAPPA
Λ	#x039B	&Lgr;	LAMBDA
M	#x039C	&Mgr;	MU
N	#x039D	&Ngr;	NU
Ξ	#x039E	&Xgr;	XI
O	#x039F	&Ogr;	OMICRON
Π	#x03A0	&Pgr;	PI
P	#x03A1	&Rgr;	RHO
Σ	#x03A3	&Sgr;	SIGMA
T	#x03A4	&Tgr;	TAU
Y	#x03A5	&Ugr;	UPSILON

Glyph	UTC Code	Entity Name	Description
Φ	#x03A6	&PHgr;	PHI
Χ	#x03A7	&KHgr;	CHI
Ψ	#x03A8	&PSgr;	PSI
Ω	#x03A9	&OHgr;	OMEGA
Ϊ	#x03AA	n/a	Dialytika IOTA
Ϋ	#x03AB	n/a	Dialytika UPSILON
ά	#x03AC	n/a	Tonos alpha
έ	#x03AD	n/a	Tonos epsilon
ή	#x03AE	n/a	Tonos eta
ί	#x03AF	n/a	Tonos iota
ΰ	#x03B0	n/a	Dialytika Tonos upsilon
α	#x03B1	&agr;	alpha
β	#x03B2	&bgr;	beta
γ	#x03B3	&ggr;	gamma
δ	#x03B4	&dgr;	delta
ε	#x03B5	&egr;	epsilon
ζ	#x03B6	&zgr;	zeta
η	#x03B7	&eegr;	eta
θ	#x03B8	&thgr;	theta
ι	#x03B9	&igr;	iota
κ	#x03BA	&kgr;	kappa
λ	#x03BB	&lgr;	lambda
μ	#x03BC	&mgr;	mu
ν	#x03BD	&ngr;	nu
ξ	#x03BE	&xgr;	xi
ο	#x03BF	&ogr;	omicron
π	#x03C0	&pgr;	pi
ρ	#x03C1	&rgr;	rho
ς	#x03C2	&sfgr;	final sigma
σ	#x03C3	&sgr;	sigma
τ	#x03C4	&tgr;	tau
υ	#x03C5	&ugr;	upsilon
φ	#x03C6	&phgr;	phi

Continued

A

Table A-7 *Continued*

Glyph	UTC Code	Entity Name	Description
χ	#x03C7	&khgr;	chi
ψ	#x03C8	&psgr;	psi
ω	#x03C9	&ohgr;	omega
ï	#x03CA	n/a	Dialytika iota
ü	#x03CB	n/a	Dialytika upsilon
ó	#x03CC	n/a	Tonos omicron
ú	#x03CD	n/a	Tonos upsilon
ώ	#x03CE	n/a	Tonos omega
ϐ	#x03D0	n/a	Beta Symbol
ϑ	#x03D1	n/a	Theta Symbol
ϒ	#x03D2	n/a	Hook Upsilon
ϓ	#x03D3	n/a	Acute Accent Hook Upsilon
ϔ	#x03D4	n/a	Umlaut Above Hook Upsilon
ϕ	#x03D5	n/a	Phi Symbol
ϖ	#x03D6	n/a	Pi Symbol
Ϛ	#x03DA	n/a	Stigma
Ϝ	#x03DC	n/a	Digamma
Ϟ	#x03DE	n/a	Koppa
Ϡ	#x03E0	n/a	Sampi
Ϣ	#x03E2	n/a	SHEI
ϣ	#x03E3	n/a	shei
Ϥ	#x03E4	n/a	FEI
ϥ	#x03E5	n/a	fei
Ϧ	#x03E6	n/a	KHEI
ϧ	#x03E7	n/a	khei
Ϩ	#x03E8	n/a	HORI
ϩ	#x03E9	n/a	hori
Ϫ	#x03EA	n/a	GANGIA
ϫ	#x03EB	n/a	gangia
Ϭ	#x03EC	n/a	SHIMA
ϭ	#x03ED	n/a	shima
Ϯ	#x03EE	n/a	DEI

Glyph	UTC Code	Entity Name	Description
ϯ	#x03EF	n/a	dei
ϰ	#x03F0	n/a	Kappa Symbol
ϱ	#x03F1	n/a	Rho Symbol
ϲ	#x03F2	n/a	Lunate Sigma Symbol
ϳ	#x03F3	n/a	Yot

Additional Extended Latin

Table A-8 contains characters in the Additional Extended Latin set, specified in the BaseChar production.

Table A-8   *BaseChar Special Characters — Additional Extended Latin*

Glyph	UTC Code	Description
Ḁ	#x1E00	Ring Below A
ḁ	#x1E01	Ring Below a
Ḃ	#x1E02	Dot Above B
ḃ	#x1E03	Dot Above b
Ḅ	#x1E04	Dot Below B
ḅ	#x1E05	Dot Below b
Ḇ	#x1E06	Line Below B
ḇ	#x1E07	Line Below b
Ḉ	#x1E08	Cedilla Acute Accent C
ḉ	#x1E09	Cedilla Acute Accent c
Ḋ	#x1E0A	Dot Above D
ḋ	#x1E0B	Dot Above d
Ḍ	#x1E0C	Dot Below D
ḍ	#x1E0D	Dot Below d
Ḏ	#x1E0E	Line Below D
ḏ	#x1E0F	Line Below d
Ḑ	#x1E10	Cedilla D
ḑ	#x1E11	Cedilla d
Ḓ	#x1E12	Circumflex Below D
ḓ	#x1E13	Circumflex Below d

Continued

Table A-8 *Continued*

Glyph	UTC Code	Description
È̄	#x1E14	Macron Grave Accent E
è̄	#x1E15	Macron Grave Accent e
É̄	#x1E16	Macron Acute Accent E
é̄	#x1E17	Macron Acute Accent e
Ḙ	#x1E18	Circumflex Below E
ḙ	#x1E19	Circumflex Below e
Ḛ	#x1E1A	Tilde Below E
ḛ	#x1E1B	Tilde Below e
Ḝ	#x1E1C	Breve Above Cedilla E
ḝ	#x1E1D	Breve Above Cedilla e
Ḟ	#x1E1E	Dot Above F
ḟ	#x1E1F	Dot Above f
Ḡ	#x1E20	Macron G
ḡ	#x1E21	Macron g
Ḣ	#x1E22	Dot Above H
ḣ	#x1E23	Dot Above h
Ḥ	#x1E24	Dot Below H
ḥ	#x1E25	Dot Below h
Ḧ	#x1E26	Umlaut Above H
ḧ	#x1E27	Umlaut Above h
Ḩ	#x1E28	Cedilla H
ḩ	#x1E29	Cedilla h
Ḫ	#x1E2A	Breve Below H
ḫ	#x1E2B	Breve Below h
Ḭ	#x1E2C	Tilde Below I
ḭ	#x1E2D	Tilde Below i
Ḯ	#x1E2E	Umlaut Above Acute Accent I
ḯ	#x1E2F	Umlaut Above Acute Accent i
Ḱ	#x1E30	Acute Accent K
ḱ	#x1E31	Acute Accent k
Ḳ	#x1E32	Dot Below K
ḳ	#x1E33	Dot Below k

Glyph	UTC Code	Description
Ḵ	#x1E34	Line Below K
ḵ	#x1E35	Line Below k
Ḷ	#x1E36	Dot Below L
ḷ	#x1E37	Dot Below l
Ḹ	#x1E38	Macron Dot Below L
ḹ	#x1E39	Macron Dot Below l
Ḻ	#x1E3A	Line Below L
ḻ	#x1E3B	Line Below l
Ḽ	#x1E3C	Circumflex Below L
ḽ	#x1E3D	Circumflex Below l
Ḿ	#x1E3E	Acute Accent M
ḿ	#x1E3F	Acute Accent m
Ṁ	#x1E40	Dot Above M
ṁ	#x1E41	Dot Above m
Ṃ	#x1E42	Dot Below M
ṃ	#x1E43	Dot Below m
Ṅ	#x1E44	Dot Above N
ṅ	#x1E45	Dot Above n
Ṇ	#x1E46	Dot Below N
ṇ	#x1E47	Dot Below n
Ṉ	#x1E48	Line Below N
ṉ	#x1E49	Line Below n
Ṋ	#x1E4A	Circumflex Below N
ṋ	#x1E4B	Circumflex Below n
Ṍ	#x1E4C	Tilde Above Acute Accent O
ṍ	#x1E4D	Tilde Above Acute Accent o
Ṏ	#x1E4E	Umlaut Tilde Above O
ṏ	#x1E4F	Umlaut Tilde Above o
Ṑ	#x1E50	Macron Grave Accent O
ṑ	#x1E51	Macron Grave Accent o
Ṓ	#x1E52	Macron Acute Accent O
ṓ	#x1E53	Macron Acute Accent o
Ṕ	#x1E54	Acute Accent P

Continued

Table A-8 *Continued*

Glyph	UTC Code	Description
ṕ	#x1E55	Acute Accent p
Ṗ	#x1E56	Dot Above P
ṗ	#x1E57	Dot Above p
Ṙ	#x1E58	Dot Above R
ṙ	#x1E59	Dot Above r
Ṛ	#x1E5A	Dot Below R
ṛ	#x1E5B	Dot Below r
Ṝ	#x1E5C	Dot Below Macron R
ṝ	#x1E5D	Dot Below Macron r
Ṟ	#x1E5E	Line Below R
ṟ	#x1E5F	Line Below r
Ṡ	#x1E60	Dot Above S
ṡ	#x1E61	Dot Above s
Ṣ	#x1E62	Dot Below S
ṣ	#x1E63	Dot Below s
Ṥ	#x1E64	Acute Accent Dot Above S
ṥ	#x1E65	Acute Accent Dot Above s
Ṧ	#x1E66	Caron Dot Above S
ṧ	#x1E67	Caron Dot Above s
Ṩ	#x1E68	Dot Above Dot Below S
ṩ	#x1E69	Dot Above Dot Below s
Ṫ	#x1E6A	Dot Above T
ṫ	#x1E6B	Dot Above t
Ṭ	#x1E6C	Dot Below T
ṭ	#x1E6D	Dot Below t
Ṯ	#x1E6E	Line Below T
ṯ	#x1E6F	Line Below t
Ṱ	#x1E70	Circumflex Below T
ṱ	#x1E71	Circumflex Below t
Ṳ	#x1E72	Umlaut Below U
ṳ	#x1E73	Umlaut Below u
Ṵ	#x1E74	Tilde Below U

Glyph	UTC Code	Description
ṵ	#x1E75	Tilde Below u
Ṷ	#x1E76	Circumflex Below U
ṷ	#x1E77	Circumflex Below u
Ṹ	#x1E78	Tilde Above Acute Accent U
ṹ	#x1E79	Tilde Above Acute Accent u
Ṻ	#x1E7A	Macron Umlaut Above U
ṻ	#x1E7B	Macron Umlaut Above u
Ṽ	#x1E7C	Tilde Above V
ṽ	#x1E7D	Tilde Above v
Ṿ	#x1E7E	Dot Below V
ṿ	#x1E7F	Dot Below v
Ẁ	#x1E80	Grave Accent W
ẁ	#x1E81	Grave Accent w
Ẃ	#x1E82	Acute Accent W
Ẅ	#x1E84	Umlaut Above W
ẇ	#x1E87	Dot Above w
Ẉ	#x1E88	Dot Below W
Ẋ	#x1E8A	Dot Above X
ẍ	#x1E8D	Umlaut Above x
Ẕ	#x1E94	Line Below Z
ẕ	#x1E95	Line Below z
ẖ	#x1E96	Line Below h
ẗ	#x1E97	Umlaut Above t
ẙ	#x1E99	Ring Above y
ẚ	#x1E9A	Right Half Ring Above a
ẛ	#x1E9B	Dot Above Long s
Ạ	#x1EA0	Dot Below A
ạ	#x1EA1	Dot Below a
Ả	#x1EA2	Hook Above A
ả	#x1EA3	Hook Above a
Ấ	#x1EA4	Circumflex Above Acute Accent A
ấ	#x1EA5	Circumflex Above Acute Accent a
Ầ	#x1EA6	Circumflex Above Grave Accent A

Continued

Table A-8 *Continued*

Glyph	UTC Code	Description
ầ	#x1EA7	Circumflex Above Grave Accent a
Ẩ	#x1EA8	Circumflex Hook Above A
ẩ	#x1EA9	Circumflex Hook Above a
Ẫ	#x1EAA	Circumflex Tilde Above A
ẫ	#x1EAB	Circumflex Tilde Above a
Ậ	#x1EAC	Circumflex Above Dot Below A
ậ	#x1EAD	Circumflex Above Dot Below a
Ắ	#x1EAE	Breve Above Acute Accent A
ắ	#x1EAF	Breve Above Acute Accent a
Ằ	#x1EB0	Breve Above Grave Accent A
ằ	#x1EB1	Breve Above Grave Accent a
Ẳ	#x1EB2	Breve Hook Above A
ẳ	#x1EB3	Breve Hook Above a
Ẵ	#x1EB4	Breve Tilde Above A
ẵ	#x1EB5	Breve Tilde Above a
Ặ	#x1EB6	Breve Above Dot Below A
ặ	#x1EB7	Breve Above Dot Below a
Ẹ	#x1EB8	Dot Below E
ẹ	#x1EB9	Dot Below e
Ẻ	#x1EBA	Hook Above E
ẻ	#x1EBB	Hook Above e
Ẽ	#x1EBC	Tilde Above E
ẽ	#x1EBD	Tilde Above e
Ế	#x1EBE	Circumflex Above Acute Accent E
ế	#x1EBF	Circumflex Above Acute Accent e
Ề	#x1EC0	Circumflex Above Grave Accent E
ề	#x1EC1	Circumflex Above Grave Accent e
Ể	#x1EC2	Circumflex Hook Above E
ể	#x1EC3	Circumflex Hook Above e
Ễ	#x1EC4	Circumflex Tilde Above E
ễ	#x1EC5	Circumflex Tilde Above e
Ệ	#x1EC6	Circumflex Above Dot Below E

Glyph	UTC Code	Description
ệ	#x1EC7	Circumflex Above Dot Below e
Ỉ	#x1EC8	Hook Above I
ỉ	#x1EC9	Hook Above i
Ị	#x1ECA	Dot Below I
ị	#x1ECB	Dot Below i
Ọ	#x1ECC	Dot Below O
ọ	#x1ECD	Dot Below o
Ỏ	#x1ECE	Hook Above O
ỏ	#x1ECF	Hook Above o
Ố	#x1ED0	Circumflex Above Acute Accent O
ố	#x1ED1	Circumflex Above Acute Accent o
Ồ	#x1ED2	Circumflex Above Grave Accent O
ồ	#x1ED3	Circumflex Above Grave Accent o
Ổ	#x1ED4	Circumflex Hook Above O
ổ	#x1ED5	Circumflex Hook Above o
Ỗ	#x1ED6	Circumflex Tilde Above O
ỗ	#x1ED7	Circumflex Tilde Above o
Ộ	#x1ED8	Circumflex Above Dot Below O
ộ	#x1ED9	Circumflex Above Dot Below o
Ớ	#x1EDA	Horn Above Acute Accent O
ớ	#x1EDB	Horn Above Acute Accent o
Ờ	#x1EDC	Horn Above Grave Accent O
ờ	#x1EDD	Horn Above Grave Accent o
Ở	#x1EDE	Horn Hook Above O
ở	#x1EDF	Horn Hook Above o
Ỡ	#x1EE0	Horn Tilde Above O
ỡ	#x1EE1	Horn Tilde Above o
Ợ	#x1EE2	Horn Above Dot Below O
ợ	#x1EE3	Horn Above Dot Below O
Ụ	#x1EE4	Dot Below U
ụ	#x1EE5	Dot Below u
Ủ	#x1EE6	Hook Above U
ủ	#x1EE7	Hook Above u

Continued

Table A-8 *Continued*

Glyph	UTC Code	Description
Ứ	#x1EE8	Horn Above Acute Accent U
ứ	#x1EE9	Horn Above Acute Accent u
Ừ	#x1EEA	Horn Above Grave Accent U
ừ	#x1EEB	Horn Above Grave Accent u
Ử	#x1EEC	Horn Hook Above U
ử	#x1EED	Horn Hook Above u
Ữ	#x1EEE	Horn Tilde Above U
ữ	#x1EEF	Horn Tilde Above u
Ự	#x1EF0	Horn Above Dot Below U
ự	#x1EF1	Horn Above Dot Below u
Ỳ	#x1EF2	Grave Accent Y
ỳ	#x1EF3	Grave Accent y
Ỵ	#x1EF4	Dot Below Y
ỵ	#x1EF5	Dot Below y
Ỷ	#x1EF6	Hook Above Y
ỷ	#x1EF7	Hook Above y
Ỹ	#x1EF8	Tilde Above Y
ỹ	#x1EF9	Tilde Above y

Letterlike Symbols

Table A-9 contains characters in the Letterlike Symbols set, specified in the BaseChar production.

Table A-9 *BaseChar Special Characters – Letter-like Symbols*

Glyph	UTC Code	Description
Ω	#x2126	Ohm Sign
K	#x212A	Kelvin Sign
Å	#x212B	Angstrom Sign
e	#x212E	Estimated Symbol

Number Forms

Table A-10 contains characters in the Number Forms set, specified in the BaseChar production.

Table A-10 *BaseChar Special Characters — Number Forms*

Glyph	UTC Code	Description
⅀	#x2180	Roman Numeral 1000
⅁	#x2181	Roman Numeral 5000
⅂	#x2182	Roman Numeral 10000

Other Character Sets

Table A-11 lists other BaseChar character sets and characters for each.

●—NOTE

Because it is difficult to use American fonts to display non-English special characters, the following table does not contain illustrations of the glyphs. To view the characters in this table, go to the Unicode Consortium's Web site (http://www.unicode.org/).

Table A-11 *Other BaseChar Character Sets*

Character Set	Supported Characters
Arabic Presentation Forms	#xFB50 - #xFBB1, #xFBD3 - #xFD3D, #xFD50 - #xFD8F, #xFD92 - #xFDC7, #xFDF0 - #xFDFB, #xFE70 - #xFE72, #xFE74, #xFE76 - #xFEFC
Arabic	#x0621 - #x063A, #x0641 - #x064A, #x0671 - #x06B7, #x06BA - #x06BE, #x06C0 - #x06CE, #x06D0 - #x06D3, #x06D5, #x06E5, #x06E6
Armenian	#x0531 - #x0556, #x0559, #x0561 - #x0586
Bengali	#x0985 - #x098C, #x098F, #x0990, #x0993 - #x09A8, #x09AA - #x09B0, #x09B2, #x09B6 - #x09B9, #x09DC, #x09DD, #x09DF - #x09E1, #x09F0, #x09F1
Bopomofo	#x3105 - #x312C
Cyrillic	#x0401 - #x040C, #x040E - #x044F, #x0451 - #x045C, #x045E - #x0481, #x0490 - #x04C4, #x04C7 - #x04C8, #x04CB - #x04CC, #x04D0 - #x04EB, #x04EE - #x04F5, #x04F8, #x04F9

Continued

Table A-11 *Continued*

Character Set	Supported Characters
Devanagari	#x0905 - #x0939, #x093D, #x0958 - #x0961
Georgian	#x10A0 - #x10C5, #x10D0 - #x10F6
Greek Extensions	#x1F00 - #x1F15, #x1F18 - #x1F1D, #x1F20 - #x1F45, #x1F48 - #x1F4D, #x1F50 - #x1F57, #x1F59, #x1F5B, #x1F5D, #x1F5F - #x1F7D, #x1F80 - #x1FB4, #x1FB6 - #x1FBC, #x1FBE, #x1FC2 - #x1FC4, #x1FC6 - #x1FCC, #x1FD0 - #x1FD3, #x1FD6 - #x1FDB, #x1FE0 - #x1FEC, #x1FF2 - #x1FF4, #x1FF6 - #x1FFC
Gujarati	#x0A8F - #x0A91, #x0A93 - #x0AA8, #x0AAA - #x0AB0, #x0AB2, #x0AB3, #x0AB5 - #x0AB9, #x0ABD, #x0AE0
Gurmukhi	#x0A05 - #x0A0A, #x0A0F, #x0A10, #x0A13 - #x0A28, #x0A2A - #x0A30, #x0A32, #x0A33, #x0A35, #x0A36, #x0A38, #x0A39, #x0A59 - #x0A5C, #x0A5E, #x0A72 - #x0A74, #x0A85 - #x0A8B, #x0A8D
Hangul Jamo	#x1100, #x1102 - #x1103, #x1105 - #x1107, #x1109, #x110B, #x110C, #x110E - #x1112, #x113C, #x113E, #x1140, #x114C, #x114E, #x1150, #x1154, #x1155, #x1159, #x115F - #x1161, #x1163, #x1165, #x1167, #x1169, #x116D, #x116E, #x1172, #x1173, #x1175, #x119E, #x11A8, #x11AB, #x11AE, #x11AF, #x11B7, #x11B8, #x11BA, #x11BC - #x11C2, #x11EB, #x11F0, #x11F9
Hangul Compatibility Jamo	#x3131 - #x318E
Hangul Syllables	#xAC00 - #xD7A3
Hebrew	#x05D0 - #x05EA, #x05F0 - #x05F2
Hiragana	#x3041 - #x3094
Kannada	#x0C85 - #x0C8C, #x0C8E - #x0C90, #x0C92 - #x0CA8, #x0CAA - #x0CB3, #x0CB5 - #x0CB9, #x0CDE, #x0CE0, #x0CE1
Katakana	#x30A1 - #x30FA
Lao	#x0E81, #x0E82, #x0E84, #x0E87, #x0E88, #x0E8A, #x0E8D, #x0E94 - #x0E97, #x0E99 - #x0E9F, #x0EA1 - #x0EA3, #x0EA5, #x0EA7, #x0EAA, #x0EAB, #x0EAD, #x0EAE, #x0EB0, #x0EB2, #x0EB3, #x0EBD, #x0EC0 - #x0EC4

Character Set	Supported Characters
Malayalam	#x0D05 - #x0D0C, #x0D0E - #x0D10, #x0D12 - #x0D28, #x0D2A - #x0D39, #x0D60, #x0D61
Oriya	#x0B05 - #x0B0C, #x0B0F, #x0B10, #x0B13 - #x0B28, #x0B2A - #x0B30, #x0B32, #x0B33, #x0B36 - #x0B39, #x0B3D, #x0B5C, #x0B5D, #x0B5F - #x0B61
Tamil	#x0B85 - #x0B8A, #x0B8E - #x0B90, #x0B92 - #x0B95, #x0B99, #x0B9A, #x0B9C, #x0B9E, #x0B9F, #x0BA3, #x0BA4, #x0BA8 - #x0BAA, #x0BAE - #x0BB5, #x0BB7 - #x0BB9
Telugu	#x0C05 - #x0C0C, #x0C0E - #x0C10, #x0C12 - #x0C28, #x0C2A - #x0C33, #x0C35 - #x0C39, #x0C60, #x0C61
Thai	#x0E01 - #x0E2E, #x0E30, #x0E32, #x0E33, #x0E40 - #x0E45
Tibetan	#x0F40 - #x0F47, #x0F49 - #x0F69

CombiningChar Characters and Character Sets

This section covers characters and character sets specified for the CombiningChar production in the XML 1.0 recommendation.

Combining Diacritical Marks

Table A-12 contains characters in the Combining Diacritical Marks set, specified in the CombiningChar production.

Table A-12 *CombiningChar Special Characters — Combining Diacritical Marks*

Glyph	UTC Code	Description
à	#x0300	Grave Accent Above
á	#x0301	Acute Accent Above
â	#x0302	Circumflex Above
ã	#x0303	Tilde Above
ā	#x0304	Macron Above

Continued

Table A-12 *Continued*

Glyph	UTC Code	Description
ā	#x0305	Overline
ă	#x0306	Breve Above
ȧ	#x0307	Dot Above
ä	#x0308	Dieresis Above
ả	#x0309	Hook Above
å	#x030A	Ring Above
a̋	#x030B	Double Acute Accent
ǎ	#x030C	Caron Above
a̍	#x030D	Vertical Line Above
a̎	#x030E	Double Vertical Line Above
ȁ	#x030F	Double Grave Accent
a̐	#x0310	Candrabindu
ȃ	#x0311	Inverted Breve Above
a̒	#x0312	Turned Comma Above
a̓	#x0313	Comma Above
a̔	#x0314	Reversed Comma Above
a̕	#x0315	Comma Above Right
a̖	#x0316	Grave Accent Below
a̗	#x0317	Acute Accent Below
a̘	#x0318	Left Tack Below
a̙	#x0319	Right Tack Below
a̚	#x031A	Left Angle Above
a̛	#x031B	Horn
a̜	#x031C	Left Half Ring Below
a̝	#x031D	Up Tack Below
a̞	#x031E	Down Tack Below
a̟	#x031F	Plus Sign Below
a̠	#x0320	Minus Sign Below
a̡	#x0321	Palatalized Hook Below
a̢	#x0322	Retroflex Hook Below
ạ	#x0323	Dot Below
a̤	#x0324	Dieresis Below

Glyph	UTC Code	Description
ą	#x0325	Ring Below
ą	#x0326	Comma Below
ą	#x0327	Cedilla
ą	#x0328	Ogonek
ą	#x0329	Vertical Line Below
ą	#x032A	Bridge Below
ą	#x032B	Inverted Double Arch Below
ą	#x032C	Caron Below
ą	#x032D	Circumflex Below
ą	#x032E	Breve Below
ą	#x032F	Inverted Breve Below
ą	#x0330	Tilde Below
ą	#x0331	Macron Below
ą	#x0332	Low Line
ą	#x0333	Double Low Line
ą	#x0334	Tilde Overlay
ą	#x0335	Short Stroke Overlay
ą	#x0336	Long Stroke Overlay
ą	#x0337	Short Solidus Overlay
ą	#x0338	Long Solidus Overlay
ą	#x0339	Right Half Ring Below
ą	#x033A	Inverted Bridge Below
ą	#x033B	Square Below
ą	#x033C	Seagull Below
ą	#x033D	X Above
ą	#x033E	Vertical Tilde
ą	#x033F	Double Overline
à	#x0340	Grave Tone Mark
á	#x0341	Acute Tone Mark
ã	#x0342	Greek Perispomeni
ą	#x0343	Greek Koronis
ä	#x0344	Greek Dialytika Tonos

Continued

Table A-12 *Continued*

Glyph	UTC Code	Description
ą	#x0345	Greek Ypogegrammeni
ẫ	#x0360	Double Tilde
ẫ	#x0361	Double Inverted Breve

Combining Diacritical Marks for Symbols

Table A-13 contains characters in the Combining Diacritical Marks for Symbols set, specified in the CombiningChar production.

Table A-13 *CombiningChar Special Characters — Combining Diacritical Marks for Symbols*

Glyph	UTC Code	Description
ȃ	#x20D0	Left Harpoon Above
ȃ	#x20D1	Right Harpoon Above
ȃ	#x20D2	Long Vertical Line Overlay
ȃ	#x20D3	Short Vertical Line Overlay
ȃ	#x20D4	Anticlockwise Arrow Above
ȃ	#x20D5	Clockwise Arrow Above
ȃ	#x20D6	Left Arrow Above
ȃ	#x20D7	Right Arrow Above
ȃ	#x20D8	Ring Overlay
ȃ	#x20D9	Clockwise Ring Overlay
ȃ	#x20DA	Anticlockwise Ring Overlay
ȃ	#x20DB	Three Dots Above
ȃ	#x20DC	Four Dots Above
ȃ	#x20E1	Left Right Arrow Above

CJK Symbols and Punctuation

Table A-14 contains characters in the CJK Symbols and Punctuation set, specified in the CombiningChar production.

●—NOTE

In this table, the lowercase *a* is in the background of each character to show the position of that character from the baseline.

Table A-14 *CombiningChar Special Characters — CJK Symbols and Punctuation*

Glyph	UTC Code	Description
ặ	#x302A	Level Tone Mark
ặ	#x302B	Rising Tone Mark
a̋	#x302C	Departing Tone Mark
ạ̖	#x302D	Entering Tone Mark
·a	#x302E	Hangul Single Dot Tone Mark
：a	#x302F	Hangul Double Dot Tone Mark

Other CombiningChar Character Sets

Table A-15 lists other specified CombiningChar character sets and characters for each.

●—NOTE

Because using American fonts to display non-English special characters is difficult, the following table does not contain illustrations of the glyphs. To view the characters in this table, go to the Unicode Consortium's Web site (http://www.unicode.org/).

Table A-15 *Other Combining Char Character Sets*

Character Set	Supported Characters
Cyrillic	#x0483 - #x0486
Hebrew	#x0591 - #x05A1, #x05A3 - #x05B9, #x05BB - #x05BD, #x05BF, #x05C1 - #x05C2, #x05C4
Arabic	#x064B - #x0652, #x0670, #x06D6 - #x06DC, #x06DD - #x06DF, #x06E0 - #x6E4, #x06E7 - #x06E8, #x06EA - #x06ED
Devanagari	#x0901 - #x0903, #x093C, #x093E - #x094C, #x094D, #x0951 - #x0954, #x0962 - #x963

Continued

Table A-15 *Continued*

Character Set	Supported Characters
Bengali	#x0981 - #x0983, #x09BC, #x09BE, #x09BF, #x09C0 - #x09C4, #x09C7 - #x09C8, #x09CB - #x09CD, #x09D7, #x09E2 - #x09E3
Gurmukhi	#x0A02, #x0A3C, #x0A3E, #x0A3F, #x0A40 - #x0A42, #x0A47 - #x0A48, #x0A4B - #x0A4D, #x0A70 - #x0A71
Gujarati	#x0A81 - #x0A83, #x0ABC, #x0ABE - #x0AC5, #x0AC7 - #x0AC9, #x0ACB - #x0ACD
Oriya	#x0B01 - #x0B03, #x0B3C, #x0B3E - #x0B43, #x0B47 - #x0B48, #x0B4B - #x0B4D, #x0B56 - #x0B57
Tamil	#x0B82 - #x0B83, #x0BBE - #x0BC2, #x0BC6 - #x0BC8, #x0BCA - #x0BCD, #x0BD7
Telugu	#x0C01 - #x0C03, #x0C3E - #x0C44, #x0C46 - #x0C48, #x0C4A - #x0C4D, #x0C55 - #x0C56
Kannada	#x0C82 - #x0C83, #x0CBE - #x0CC4, #x0CC6 - #x0CC8, #x0CCA - #x0CCD, #x0CD5 - #x0CD6
Malayalam	#x0D02 - #x0D03, #x0D3E - #x0D43, #x0D46 - #x0D48, #x0D4A - #x0D4D, #x0D57
Thai	#x0E34 - #x0E3A, #x0E47 - #x0E4E
Lao	#x0EB1, #x0EB4 - #x0EB9, #x0EBB - #x0EBC, #x0EC8 - #x0ECD
Tibetan	#x0F18 - #x0F19, #x0F35, #x0F37, #x0F39, #x0F3E, #x0F3F, #x0F71 - #x0F84, #x0F86 - #x0F8B, #x0F90 - #x0F95, #x0F97, #x0F99 - #x0FAD, #x0FB1 - #x0FB7, #x0FB9
Hiragama	#x3099, #x309A

Digit

This section covers the characters and character sets specified in the Digit production in the XML 1.0 recommendation.

ISO 646 Digits

Table A-16 contains characters in the ISO 646 Digits set, specified in the Digit production.

Table A-16 *Digit Special Characters — ISO 646 Digits*

Glyph	UTC Code	Description
0	#x0030	Digit Zero
1	#x0031	Digit One
2	#x0032	Digit Two
3	#x0033	Digit Three
4	#x0034	Digit Four
5	#x0035	Digit Five
6	#x0036	Digit Six
7	#x0037	Digit Seven
8	#x0038	Digit Eight
9	#x0039	Digit Nine

Other Digit Character Sets

Table A-17 lists other Digit character sets and characters for each.

● **NOTE** ───────────────────────────────

Because it is difficult to use American fonts to display non-English special characters, the following table does not contain illustrations of the glyphs. To view the characters in this table, go to the Unicode Consortium's Web site (http://www.unicode.org/).

Table A-17 *Other Digit Character Sets*

Character Set	Supported Characters
Arabic-Indic Digits	#x0660 - #x0669
Eastern Arabic-Indic Digits	#x06F0 - #x06F9
Devanagari Digits	#x0966 - #x096F
Bengali Digits	#x09E6 - #x09EF
Gurmukhi Digits	#x0A66 - #x0A6F
Gujarati Digits	#x0AE6 - #x0AEF
Oriya Digits	#x0B66 - #x0B6F

Continued

Table A-17 *Continued*

Character Set	Supported Characters
Tamil Digits (no zero)	#x0BE7 - #x0BEF
Telugu Digits	#x0C66 - #x0C6F
Kannada Digits	#x0CE6 - #x0CEF
Malayalam Digits	#x0D66 - #x0D6F
Thai Digits	#x0E50 - #x0E59
Lao Digits	#x0ED0 - #x0ED9
Tibetan Digits	#x0F20 - #x0F29

Extender

This section covers the characters and character sets specified for the Extender production in the XML 1.0 recommendation.

Extender Special Characters

Table A-18 contains characters for the Extender production. The character sets in which the characters are located are within parentheses.

Table A-18 *Extender Special Characters*

Glyph	UTC Code	Description
··	#x00B7	Middle Dot (C1 Controls and Latin-1 Supplement)
ː	#x02D0	Triangular Colon (Spacing Modifier Letters)
ˑ	#x02D1	Half Triangular Colon (Spacing Modifier Letters)
々	#x3005	Ideographic Iteration Mark (CJK Symbols and Punctuation)
〱	#x3031	Vertical Kana Repeat Mark (CJK Symbols and Punctuation)
〲	#x3032	Vertical Kana Repeat with Voiced Sound Mark (CJK Symbols and Punctuation)
〳	#x3033	Vertical Kana Repeat Mark Upper Half (CJK Symbols and Punctuation)

Glyph	UTC Code	Description
/˙	#x3034	Vertical Kana Repeat with Voiced Sound Mark Upper Half (CJK Symbols and Punctuation)
\	#x3035	Vertical Kana Repeat Mark Lower Half (CJK Symbols and Punctuation)

Other Extender Character Sets

Table A-19 lists other Extender character sets and characters for each.

Table A-19 *Other Extender Character Sets*

Character Set	Supported Characters
Greek	#x0387
Arabic	#x0640
Thai	#x0E46
Lao	#x0EC6
Hiragana	#x309D - #x309E
Katakana	#x30FC - #x30FE

Ideographic

This section covers characters and character sets specified for the Ideographic production in the XML 1.0 recommendation.

CJK Symbols and Punctuation

Table A-20 contains characters specified in the Ideographic production.

Table A-20 *Ideographic Special Characters — CJK Symbols and Punctuation*

Glyph	UTC Code	Description
〇	#x3007	Number Zero
〡	#x3021	Hangzhou Numeral One

Continued

Table A-20 *Continued*

Glyph	UTC Code	Description
I I	#x3022	Hangzhou Numeral Two
I I I	#x3023	Hangzhou Numeral Three
X	#x3024	Hangzhou Numeral Four
Ƽ	#x3025	Hangzhou Numeral Five
⊥	#x3026	Hangzhou Numeral Six
⊥	#x3027	Hangzhou Numeral Seven
三	#x3028	Hangzhou Numeral Eight
夂	#x3029	Hangzhou Numeral Nine

Additional Ideographic Character Set

Table A-21 lists the additional Ideographic character set and its characters.

●─NOTE

Because it is difficult to use American fonts to display non-English special characters, the following table does not contain illustrations of the glyphs. To view the characters in this table, go to the Unicode Consortium's Web site (http://www.unicode.org/).

Table A-21 *Additional Ideographic Character Set*

Character Set	Supported Characters
CJK Unified Ideographs	#x4E00 - #x9FA5

Country Codes

This appendix lists country name codes based on those in the ISO 3166 standard. Country names are listed alphabetically. Note that when you use a country code in a document, it is common practice to express it in uppercase. In contrast, the language code is usually expressed in lowercase (see Appendix C [p. 805]).

ISO 3166 Country Codes

Country	Code	Country	Code
Afghanistan	AF	Canada	CA
Albania	AL	Cape Verde	CV
Algeria	DZ	Cayman Islands	KY
American Samoa	AS	Central African Republic	CF
Andorra	AD	Chad	TD
Angola	AO	Chile	CL
Anguilla	AI	China	CN
Antarctica	AQ	Christmas Island	CX
Antigua and Barbuda	AG	Cocos (Keeling) Islands	CC
Argentina	AR	Colombia	CO
Armenia	AM	Comoros	KM
Aruba	AW	Congo, The Democratic	CG
Australia	AU	Republic of the	
Austria	AT	Cook Islands	CK
Azerbaijan	AZ	Costa Rica	CR
Bahamas	BS	Cote D'Ivoire	CI
Bahrain	BH	Croatia	HR
Bangladesh	BD	Cuba	CU
Barbados	BB	Cyprus	CY
Belarus	BY	Czech Republic	CZ
Belgium	BE	Denmark	DK
Belize	BZ	Djibouti	DJ
Benin	BJ	Dominica	DM
Bermuda	BM	Dominican Republic	DO
Bhutan	BT	East Timor	TP
Bolivia	BO	Ecuador	EC
Bosnia and Herzegovina	BA	Egypt	EG
Botswana	BW	El Salvador	SV
Bouvet Island	BV	Equatorial Guinea	GQ
Brazil	BR	Eritrea	ER
British Indian Ocean Territory	IO	Estonia	EE
Brunei Darussalam	BN	Ethiopia	ET
Bulgaria	BG	Falkland Islands (Malvinas)	FK
Burkina Faso	BF	Faroe Islands	FO
Burundi	BI	Fiji	FJ
Cambodia	KH	Finland	FI
Cameroon	CM	France	FR

B

ISO 3166 Country Codes

Country	Code	Country	Code
France, Metropolitan	FX	Kazakhstan	KZ
French Guiana	GF	Kenya	KE
French Polynesia	PF	Kiribati	KI
French Southern Territories	TF	Korea, Democratic People's Republic of (North)	KP
Gabon	GA		
Gambia	GM	Korea, Republic of (South)	KR
Georgia	GE	Kuwait	KW
Germany	DE	Kyrgyzstan	KG
Ghana	GH	Laos, People's Democratic Republic of	LA
Gibraltar	GI		
Greece	GR	Latvia	LV
Greenland	GL	Lebanon	LB
Grenada	GD	Lesotho	LS
Guadeloupe	GP	Liberia	LR
Guam	GU	Libyan Arab Jamahiriya	LY
Guatemala	GT	Liechtenstein	LI
Guinea	GN	Lithuania	LT
Guinea-Bissau	GW	Luxembourg	LU
Guyana	GY	Macau	MO
Haiti	HT	Macedonia	MK
Heard Island and McDonald Islands	HM	Madagascar	MG
		Malawi	MW
Holy See (Vatican City State)	VA	Malaysia	MY
Honduras	HN	Maldives	MV
Hong Kong	HK	Mali	ML
Hungary	HU	Malta	MT
Iceland	IS	Marshall Islands	MH
India	IN	Martinique	MQ
Indonesia	ID	Mauritania	MR
Iran	IR	Mauritius	MU
Iraq	IQ	Mayotte	YT
Ireland	IE	Mexico	MX
Israel	IL	Micronesia, Federated States of	FM
Italy	IT	Moldova, Republic of	MD
Jamaica	JM	Monaco	MC
Japan	JP	Mongolia	MN
Jordan	JO	Montserrat	MS

B

Continued

ISO 3166 Country Codes (continued)

Country	Code	Country	Code
Morocco	MA	Saint Lucia	LC
Mozambique	MZ	Saint Pierre and Miquelon	PM
Myanmar (Burma)	MM	Saint Vincent and	VC
Namibia	NA	The Grenadines	
Nauru	NR	Samoa	WS
Nepal	NP	San Marino	SM
Netherland Antilles	AN	Sao Tome and Principe	ST
Netherlands	NL	Saudi Arabia	SA
New Caledonia	NC	Senegal	SN
New Zealand	NZ	Seychelles	SC
Nicaragua	NI	Sierra Leone	SL
Niger	NE	Singapore	SG
Nigeria	NG	Slovakia	SK
Niue	NU	Slovenia	SI
Norfolk Island	NF	Solomon Islands	SB
Northern Mariana Islands	MP	Somalia	SO
Norway	NO	South Africa	ZA
Oman	OM	South Georgia and The South	GS
Pakistan	PK	Sandwich Islands	
Palau	PW	Spain	ES
Palestinian Territory, Occupied	PS	Sri Lanka	LK
Panama	PA	Sudan	SD
Papua New Guinea	PG	Suriname	SR
Paraguay	PY	Svalbard and Jan Mayen	SJ
Peru	PE	Islands	
Philippines	PH	Swaziland	SZ
Pitcairn	PN	Sweden	SE
Poland	PL	Switzerland	CH
Portugal	PT	Syrian Arab Republic (Syria)	SY
Puerto Rico	PR	Taiwan, Province of China	TW
Qatar	QA	Tajikistan	TJ
Reunion	RE	Tanzania, United Republic of	TZ
Romania	RO	Thailand	TH
Russian Federation	RU	Togo	TG
Rwanda	RW	Tokelau	TK
Saint Helena	SH	Tonga	TO
Saint Kitts and Nevis	KN	Trinidad and Tobago	TT

B

ISO 3166 Country Codes

Country	Code	Country	Code
Tunisia	TN	Uzbekistan	UZ
Turkey	TR	Vanuatu	VU
Turkmenistan	TM	Venezuela	VE
Turks and Caicos Islands	TC	Viet Nam	VN
Tuvalu	TV	Virgin Islands, British	VG
Uganda	UG	Virgin Islands, U.S.	VI
Ukraine	UA	Wallis and Futuna	WF
United Arab Emirates	AE	Western Sahara	EH
United Kingdom	GB	Yemen	YE
United States Minor Outlying Islands	UM	Yugoslavia	YU
		Zaire	ZR
United States	US	Zambia	ZM
Uruguay	UY	Zimbabwe	ZW

B

Language Codes

This appendix lists language name codes based on those in the ISO 639: 1988 standard. Language names are listed alphabetically. Note that when you use a language code in a document, it is common practice to express it in lowercase. In contrast, the country code is usually expressed in uppercase (see Appendix B [p. 799]).

ISO 639 Language Codes

Language	Code	Language	Code	Language	Code
Abkhazian	ab	Chinese	zh	Hausa	ha
Afar	aa	Corsican	co	Hebrew	he
Afrikaans	af	Croatian	hr	Hindi	hi
Albanian	sq	Czech	cs	Hungarian	hu
Amharic	am	Danish	da	Icelandic	is
Arabic	ar	Dutch	nl	Indonesian	id
Armenian	hy	English	en	Interlingua	ia
Assamese	as	Esperanto	eo	Interlingue	ie
Aymara	ay	Estonian	et	Inuktitut	iu
Azerbaijani	az	Faroese	fo	Inupiak	ik
Bashkir	ba	Fiji	fj	Irish Gaelic	ga
Basque	eu	Finnish	fi	Italian	it
Bengali	bn	French	fr	Japanese	ja
Bhutani	dz	Frisian	fy	Javanese	jw
Bihari	bh	Scottish Gaelic	gd	Kannada	kn
Bislama	bi	Galician	gl	Kashmiri	ks
Breton	br	Georgian	ka	Kazakh	kk
Bulgarian	bg	German	de	Kinyarwanda	rw
Burmese	my	Greek	el	Kirghiz	ky
Belarusian	be	Greenlandic	kl	Kirundi	rn
Cambodian	km	Guarani	gn	Korean	ko
Catalan	ca	Gujarati	gu	Kurdish	ku
Laotian	lo	Quechua	qu	Tatar	tt
Latin	la	Rhaeto-Romance	rm	Tegulu	te
Latvian	lv	Romanian	ro	Thai	th
Lingala	ln	Russian	ru	Tibetan	bo
Lithuanian	lt	Samoan	sm	Tigrinya	ti
Macedonian	mk	Sangho	sg	Tonga	to
Malagasy	mg	Sanskrit	sa	Tsonga	ts
Malay	ms	Serbian	sr	Turkish	tr
Malayalam	ml	Serbo-Croatian	sh	Turkmen	tk

Language	Code	Language	Code	Language	Code
Maltese	mt	Sesotho	st	Twi	tw
Maori	mi	Setswana	tn	Uigar	ug
Marathi	mr	Shona	sn	Ukrainian	uk
Moldavian	mo	Sindhi	sd	Urdu	ur
Mongolian	mn	Singhalese	si	Uzbek	uz
Nauru	na	Siswati	ss	Vietnamese	vi
Nepali	ne	Slovak	sk	Volapük	vo
Norwegian	no	Slovenian	sl	Welsh	cy
Occitan	oc	Somali	so	Wolof	wo
Oriya	or	Spanish	es	Xhosa	xh
Oromo	om	Sudanese	su	Yiddish	yi
Pashto	ps	Swahili	sw	Yoruba	yo
Persian	fa	Swedish	sv	Zhuang	za
Polish	pl	Tagalog	tl	Zulu	zu
Portuguese	pt	Tajik	tg		
Punjabi	pa	Tamil	ta		

C

EBNF Reference

Using Extended Backus-Naur Form (EBNF) notation, a developer writes a DTD to specify the elements, attributes, entities, and special characters for one document or a document set. A DTD also sets the rules, limitations, and values for each of the components. XHTML documents are associated with one of three DTDs: strict, transitional, or frameset.

This appendix contains tables of EBNF syntax. To learn how to use EBNF, refer to page 654 in Chapter 1, "Introducing XHTML" and Chapter 4, "Constructing a Basic XML Document" (p. 699).

Table D-1 lists basic EBNF syntax. Under each entry is a short description.

Table D-1 *Extended Backus-Naur Form (EBNF) Notation*

Syntax	Description
#xN	Enter #x and N, a hexadecimal integer matching any UCS-4 code value in ISO/IEC 10646 standard.
[ ]	Brackets indicate that the grouped content within is optional.
[a-zA-Z], [#xN-#xN]	Enter one of the characters within the range a to z, A to Z, or #xN to #xN.
[^a-z], [^#xN-#xN]	Do *not* enter any of the characters within the range adjacent to the NOT character. In other words, enter any character outside the range.
[^abc], [^#xN#xN#xN]	Do *not* enter any of the characters adjacent to the NOT character. In other words, enter any character not listed.
"string"|'string'	Enter the literal string enclosed within the quotation marks or single quote marks. Do *not* mix quotation marks and single quote marks in an expression.
( )	Parentheses contain an expression in the same way that you would use them to contain a mathematical expression.
(expression)	Enter an expression consisting of a combination of the previously listed parts of syntax in this table. To combine expressions, use the syntax in Table D-2.

Table D-2 lists the EBNF syntax for expressions and components, where A indicates an expression (within parentheses) or a component (without parentheses). With each entry is a short description.

Table D-2 *Extended Backus-Naur Form (EBNF) Expression Syntax*

Syntax	Description
A?	An expression or component followed by a question mark indicates that the expression is optional but must match if it's provided.
A B	One expression or component followed by another must be matched exactly.

Syntax	Description
A|B	Expressions or components separated by pipe symbols indicate ORs. Choose one expression OR the other — in other words, just choose one. In this book, pipes appear in a larger point size to differentiate them from pipe characters within elements.
A − B	The first expression or component must be present, and the expression or component following the minus sign must be absent. Note that a range (for example, A-B) contains no spaces, but the minus sign indicating an absent expression or component (A − B) is both preceded and followed by a space.
A+	An expression or component followed by a plus sign indicates that the expression *must* appear one or more times.
A*	An expression or component followed by an asterisk indicates that the expression *may* appear one or more times.

Table D-3 lists the EBNF symbols used as delimiters, connectors, and indicators. Under each entry is a short description. Note that some of these symbols have appeared in Tables D-1 and D-2.

Table D-3 *Extended Backus-Naur Form (EBNF) Symbols*

Symbols	Description
< and >	Delimit the start and end of a declaration or tag, respectively.
/	With < (for example, </), indicates the beginning of an end tag. With > (for example, />), indicates the end of an empty-element tag.
::=	Represents the separator between the symbol and the expression making up a production: symbol|Symbol ::= expression.
!	Indicates that a reserved keyword follows.
−	Indicates either a range, if the expressions (A-B) do not include spaces, *or* subtraction, if the expressions (A - B) do include spaces.
^	Indicates that you must not select any of the characters that follow.
&	Starts a parsed general entity.
&#	Starts a decimal character reference.
&#x	Starts a hexadecimal character reference.
%	Starts a parameter entity or parameter entity reference.

Continued

D

Table D-3 *Continued*

Symbols	Description
;	Ends an entity.
?	Indicates that a content particle can occur up to one time.
+	Indicates that a content particle *must* occur one or more times.
*	Indicates that a content particle can occur an unlimited number of times but doesn't have to occur at all.
|	Connects content particles and states that a Web page developer can select the listed components in any order. Within brackets, indicates a choice.
,	Connects content particles and states that a Web page developer *must* select the listed components in the order in which they appear.
/* and */	Delimits the start and end of a comment.
(and)	Delimits the start and end of an expression to be evaluated as a whole.
" and '	Delimits the start and end of a string. Do not mix quotation marks and single quote marks for the same string.
<? and ?>	Delimits the start and end of a processing instruction.
[and]	Delimits the start and end of a range; [delimits the start of an internal DTD.
]>	Delimits the end of an internal DTD.
<![and]]>	Delimits the start and end of a CDATA section.

Index

', 676
- component, 185, 213, 228, 374, 560, 633
!= component, 193, 213
    !DOCTYPE declaration, 661
!DOCTYPE keyword, 61, 662
!ELEMENT keyword, 66, 662, 685
!ENTITY keyword, 89, 112, 695
!NOTATION keyword, 110
", 676
#, 165, 443, 692
#default keyword, 347
#FIXED, 58, 59, 148, 154, 160, 691
#IMPLIED, 58, 59, 91, 135, 146, 148, 150,
    151, 152, 154, 155, 158, 159, 691
#PCDATA keyword, 101
#PCDATA, defined, 687
#REQUIRED, 58, 59, 91, 135, 151, 160, 690
#x0009 or #x9, 124
#x000A or #xA, 121, 124
#x000D or #xD, 120, 124
#x0020 or #x20, 120, 124
$, 229
%, 78, 112, 115, 460, 693, 694
&, 77, 78, 662, 691, 692
&#, 78, 693, 694
&#x, 78, 693, 694

(, 81, 101, 111, 128, 195, 199, 208, 217, 324,
    460, 511, 585, 676
), 81, 101, 111, 128, 195, 199, 208, 217, 325,
    460, 511, 585, 676
*, 44, 56, 205, 207, 686
,, 128, 195, 199, 325, 511
., 184, 195, 211, 464, 555, 742
.., 195
/, 166, 184, 212, 215, 219, 326, 663, 742
//, 182, 183, 213, 215, 326, 742
/>, 69
/1, 166
:, 207
::, 189, 195, 320
;, 77, 97, 115, 692, 693, 694
?, 44, 56, 686
?>, 117, 133, 138
@ , 183, 195
[, 61, 95, 97, 195, 216, 676, 701
], 61, 195, 216, 676
]]>, 95, 96, 97
]> delimiter, 701
^, 173, 175, 677
|, 46, 81, 101, 111, 326, 676
+, 45, 56, 185, 213, 374, 560, 686
<, 213, 218, 662, 663, 676, 691, 692

<!-, 49, 685
<![, 95, 96, 97
</, 83
<?, 117
<?xml, 133, 137
<?xml-stylesheet, 142
<=, 213, 218
=, 82, 193, 213
>, 83, 213, 218, 662, 663
->, 49, 685
>=, 213, 218
100 - 900 keywords, 491

A

abbreviated axis specifier, providing, 320-321
AbbreviatedAbsoluteLocationPath XPath
    production, 182, 185
AbbreviatedAxisSpecifier XPath
    production, 182-183, 189, 320
AbbreviatedRelativeLocationPath XPath
    production, 183-184, 219
AbbreviatedStep XPath production, 184, 222
abbreviating
        absolute location path, 182
        axis specifier, 182-183
        relative location path, 183-184
        step, 184
above keyword, 456
abs keyword, 370
abs() XSL function, 370-371
absolute and relative steps to target location,
    specifying series of, 203-204
absolute keyword, 372, 657
absolute length, indicating, 371
absolute location path, abbreviating, 182
absolute location term, defined, 741
absolute or relative floating-point number in
    expression, representing, 558-559
absolute position of fo:block-container, speci-
    fying, 372
absolute step and optional relative steps to target
    location, specifying, 184-185
absolute unit of measure, representing, 372-373
absolute URI, defined, 734
absolute value
        returning for argument, 370-371
        representing number with, 371-372
absolute-colorimetric keyword, 594
AbsoluteLength XSL production, 371
AbsoluteLocationPath XPath production,
    184-185, 204
AbsoluteNumeric XSL production, 371-372,
    558
absolute-position XSL property, 372
AbsoluteUnitName XSL production, 371, 372-73
acting on

expressions through multiplication, division,
    or finding modulus, 204-205, 554-555
expressions through addition or subtraction,
    185-186, 374-375
action, defined, 748
active keyword, 373
Active Server Pages, 725
active-state XSL property, 373-374, 754
actuate XLink attribute, 146-147, 161, 735, 738
adding lines to text, 628-629
addition or subtraction, acting on expressions
    through, 185-186, 374-375
additional level of embedding for element,
    opening, 634-635
AdditiveExpr XPath production, 185-186,
    374-375, 460
adjusting aspect value of font, 487-488
after keyword, 437, 454
alias for another namespace URI, declaring style
    sheet's and result tree namespace URI is,
    347-348
aligning
        element vertically, 635-636
        fo:leader formatting objects with same con-
            tent and values, 532-533
        table caption, 437-438
alignment
        setting horizontal alignment of last line of
            text, 625-626
        setting horizontal alignment of text, 625-626
        specifying between areas in block-progression-
            dimension, 591
        specifying block-progression-direction
            alignment of reference-area children,
            454-455
alignment point, determining default, 395-397
alignment-adjust XSL property, 375-376
alignments of elements, allowing precise, 375-376
all keyword, 612
allowing
        browser to choose application to render
            element, 447-448
        for specification of color profile rendering
            intent other than default, 594
        precise alignments of elements, 375-376
alphabet, specifying letter of current, 98
alphabetic characters or decimal or hexadecimal
        numbers, representing, 376
alphabetic keyword, 349, 387, 455
alphabetic letters and other characters, combining,
    47-49
AlphaOrDigits XSL production, 376, 443
alternate document processors
        defined, 598
        specifying role of formatting object for,
            598-599

alternate page-masters, producing pages sequence from recurring occurrences of, 498–499

`alternate` pseudo-attribute, 143

alternate set of properties, setting, 480–481

`always` keyword, 526, 528, 572, 573, 614

`ancestor` axis-name keyword, 187, 740

`ancestor-or-self` axis-name keyword, 188, 740

and logical expression, 186

`AndExpr` XPath production, 186–187, 214

ANY keyword, 53, 54, 65, 66

any keyword, 349, 390, 559, 576

Apple, 655

application

  allowing browser to choose to render element, 447–448

  naming for processing instruction target, 118–119

  specifying process to be performed within a target, 117–118

applying

  block-level formats to table caption, 505

  shadow effects to text, 630–631

  template rules to all children of current node, 330–331

arc content, specifying role of, 148

arc link

  defined, 737

  specifying end point of, 158–60

  specifying starting point of, 149–150

`arc` XLink element type, 147–148, 160

`arcrole` XLink attribute, 148, 736, 738

area tree, defined, 748

area, defined, 370, 747

area's block progression dimension for block-level and replaced-elements areas, specifying, 390–391

areas that belong to destination resource are shown, specifying whether, 523

argument

  defined, 741

  representing, 187, 376–377

  returning absolute value of, 370–371

  returning concatenation of strings in, 190–191

  returning rounded integer closest in value to, 220–221, 599

  returning value of property whose name matches, 551–552

  returning one that has been converted to boolean, 189–190

  returning one that has been converted to number, 210–211

  returning one with excess whitespace stripped out, 209–210

  returning one with translated characters, 226–227

argument node-set's first node, returning namespace URI of expanded-name of, 206–207

argument string

  returning true or false depending on whether it contains other argument string, 191

  returning true or false depending on whether it starts with the other argument string, 221

`Argument` XPath production, 187, 199, 376–377, 511

arguments

  returning minimum of two numeric, 552

  returning maximum of two numeric, 548

"As We May Think", 655

`ascending` keyword, 356

ASP, 725

aspect value of font, adjusting, 487–488

associating

  random number of resources, 148–149

  title with document, 508

Atlantic Monthly, 655

`AttDef` XML production, 28–29, 30

ATTLIST declaration, 29, 679

`AttlistDecl` XML production, 29–31, 99

attribute

  declaring whether it is required, optional, or fixed, 57–60

  naming, 31–32

  providing, 320–321

`attribute` axis-name keyword, 188, 320, 740

attribute list, declaring element type's, 29–31

attribute lists, 687

attribute set, specifying and naming, 332–334

attribute specification, defined, 28

attribute type

  indicating character data string, 130–131

  indicating that it is composed of enumerated notation names or name tokens, 80–81

  indicating that it is tokenized set, 134–135

  specifying, 32–33

attribute types, 688–690

attribute value

  providing, 31–32

  stating, 33–34

attribute values, 687, 691–692

`Attribute` XML production, 69, 129

attribute-list declaration, 679

attributes, 664–665, 704–705

  `actuate`, 735, 738

  `arcrole`, 736, 738

  creating them for elements produced by `xsl:element`, 331–332

  defined, 656

Continued

attributes *(continued)*
defining, 28-29
from, 738
href, 735, 738
label, 738
role, 736, 738
show, 736, 738
title, 736, 738
to, 738
type, 735, 738
AttType XML production, 28, 32-33
AttValue XML production, 31, 33-34, 58
auditory cue
sounding after element, 450-451
sounding before and/or after element, 449-450
sounding before element, 451-452
auto keyword, 372, 375, 390, 434, 435, 436, 440,
447, 448, 454, 513, 515, 524, 525, 526,
528, 535, 542, 543, 544, 545, 546, 561,
572, 573, 575, 576, 582, 592, 594, 598,
602, 605, 621, 623, 632, 633, 642, 648
automatic processing, selecting node-sets for,
342-343
auto-restore XSL property, 377
autosense-script keyword, 455
avoid keyword, 572, 573
axis name and predefined specifier, specifying,
188-189
axis name, giving predefined one to context node,
187-188
axis specifier
abbreviating, 182-183
providing abbreviated, 320-321
axis, defined, 204, 742
axis-name keyword, 740-741
AxisName XPath production, 187-188, 189, 195
AxisSpecifier XPath production, 189-189, 222
azimuth XSL property, 377-379

B
background color, specifying, 381-382
background image
repeating onscreen, 386-387
specifying, 382-383
specifying initial horizontal position of, 385
specifying initial vertical position of, 385-386
specifying starting position for, 383-385
specifying whether it is fixed or scrolls in
page background, 380-381
background or border, formatting inline text with,
473-474
background XSL property, 379-380
background-attachment XSL property, 380-381
background-color XSL property, 381-382
background-image XSL property, 382-383

background-position XSL property, 383-385
background-position-horizontal XSL property, 385
background-position-vertical XSL property,
385-386
background-repeat XSL property, 386-387
backslant keyword, 489
bare names, 168
BaseChar XML production, 34-37, 98
baseline
moving away from default location, 388-389
setting line-spacing height of font above,
485-486
setting line-spacing height of font below,
484-485
baseline keyword, 387, 591, 635
baseline, redetermining dominant, 455-456
baseline-identifier XSL property, 387-388
baseline-shift XSL property, 388-389
baseline-table, reestablishing font-size for, 455-456
before keyword, 437, 454, 591
before-edge keyword, 387
beginning of character data section, marking,
40-41
beginning of list item, setting length between end
of list-item label and, 587-588
behind keyword, 378
below keyword, 456
Berners-Lee, Tim, 730
bidi-override keyword, 634
bidirectionality writing direction for inline script,
overriding, 465-466
bitmapped graphics, specifying scaling tradeoff
when formatting, 602
blank keyword, 390
blank or filled, making page-master eligible for
selection depending on whether it is,
389-390
blank-or-not-blank XSL property, 389
blink keyword, 628
blinking text, 628-629
block
controlling location of left edge of box from
left edge of, 535
controlling location of right edge of box from
right edge of, 597-598
block progression dimension for block-level and
replaced-elements areas, specifying area's,
390-391
block-level and replaced-element boxes, setting
inline-progression-dimension of, 525-526
block-level box, creating, 467
block-level formats to table caption, applying, 505
block-level selections, formatting, 466-467
block-progression-dimension XSL property,
390-391

`block-progression-dimension`, specifying alignment between areas in, 591
`block-progression-direction` alignment of `reference-area` children, specifying, 454–455
BODY element, 660
`body-start` keyword, 391
`body-start` value for list, returning, 391–392
`body-start()` XSL function, 391–392
`bold` keyword, 491
`bolder` keyword, 491
boldness or lightness of font, specifying, 491–492
boolean after evaluating context-node language and context-node xml:lang attribute, returning, 201
`boolean` keyword, 189
`boolean()` XPath function, 189–190
boolean, returning argument that has been converted to, 189–190
border
  collapsing table-cell, 405–406
  setting
    color of bottom, 402–403
    color of ending edge of, 408–409
    color of leading edge of, 397–398
    color of left, 413–414
    color of right, 418–419
    color of starting edge of, 422–424
    color of top, 429–430
    color of trailing edge of, 393–395
    style of bottom, 403–404
    style of ending edge of, 409–410
    style of leading edge of, 398–399
    style of left, 414–415
    style of right, 419
    style of starting edge of, 424–425
    style of top, 430–432
    style of trailing edge of, 395–396
    width of bottom, 404–405
    width of ending edge of, 410–411
    width of leading edge of, 399–400
    width of left, 415–416
    width of right, 420–421
    width of starting edge of, 425–426
    width of top, 432
    width of trailing edge of, 396–397
  specifying
    color, style, and/or width of bottom box, 400
    color, style, and/or width of left box, 411
    color, style, and/or width of right box, 416
    color, style, and/or width of top box, 427
    one or more colors for, 406–408
border or background, formatting inline text with, 473–474
`border` XSL property, 392–393

`border-after-color` XSL property, 393–395
`border-after-style` XSL property, 395–396
`border-after-width` XSL property, 396–397
`border-before-color` XSL property, 397–398
`border-before-style` XSL property, 398–399
`border-before-width` XSL property, 399–400
`border-bottom` XSL property, 400–402
`border-bottom-color` XSL property, 402–403
`border-bottom-style` XSL property, 403–404
`border-bottom-width` XSL property, 404–405
`border-collapse` XSL property, 405–406
`border-color` XSL property, 406–408
`border-end-color` XSL property, 408–409
`border-end-style` XSL property, 409–410
`border-end-width` XSL property, 410–411
`border-left` XSL property, 411–413
`border-left-color` XSL property, 413–414
`border-left-style` XSL property, 414–415
`border-left-width` XSL property, 415–416
`border-right` XSL property, 416–418
`border-right-color` XSL property, 418–419
`border-right-style` XSL property, 419
`border-right-width` XSL property, 420–421
borders
  separating cell border from adjacent, 422
  setting style of one or more, 426–427
  setting width of one or more, 432–434
  specifying color, style, and/or width of all four box, 392–393
borders around empty table cells, showing or hiding, 457
borders of adjacent cells, specifying distance between, 421–422
`border-separation` XSL property, 421–422
`border-spacing` XSL property, 422
`border-start-color` XSL property, 422–424
`border-start-style` XSL property, 424–425
`border-start-width` XSL property, 425–426
`border-style` XSL property, 426–427
`border-top` XSL property, 427–429
`border-top-color` XSL property, 429–430
`border-top-style` XSL property, 430–432
`border-top-width` XSL property, 432
`border-width` XSL property, 432–434
`both` keyword, 440
bottom border
  setting color of, 402–403
  setting style of, 403–404
  setting width of, 404–405
bottom edge of box, controlling location of, 434–435
`bottom` keyword, 384, 385, 437, 635
bottom margin of box
  setting, 543–544
  turning on or off, 543–544

bottom padding of box
  setting size of, 564–566
  turning on or off, 564–566
bottom XSL property, 434–435
boundary contained within fo:marker,
  retrieving, 594–595
box
  changing
    orientation of horizontally displayed text
      glyphs with, 512–513
    orientation of selection with, 588–589
    orientation of vertically displayed text
      glyphs with, 513–514
  controlling
    location of bottom edge of, 434–435
    location of left edge of, 535
    location of right edge of, 597–598
    location of top edge of, 632–633
  creating
    block-level, 467
    inline, 474–475
  defining clipping area of, 440–441
  inserting
    page break after page, 572–573
    page break before page, 573–574
    page break inside page, 574–575
  setting
    bottom margin size, 543–544
    bottom padding size, 564–566
    dimensions and orientation of page, 605–606
    ending-edge-padding size of, 567–568
    leading-edge padding size, 564
    left margin size, 544–545
    left padding size, 640–641
    level of one in stack of elements, 648
    margin size, 542–543
    padding size, 562–564
    right margin size, 545–546
    right padding size, 569–570
    starting-edge-padding size of, 570–571
    top margin size, 546–547
    top padding size, 571–572
    trailing-edge padding size, 564
  specifying
    amount of space between two columns in,
      444–445
    how line breaks occur in, 644–445
    indention at ending edge of, 457–458
    indention at starting edge of, 618–619
    number of columns in, 444
    whether it is visible or invisible, 636–637
  turning on or off
    bottom margin, 543–544
    bottom padding, 564–566
    ending-edge padding of, 567–568
    leading-edge padding, 564

    left margin, 544–545
    left padding, 568–569
    margins, 542–543
    paddings, 562–564
    right margin, 545–546
    right padding, 569–570
    starting-edge padding, 570–571
    top margin, 546–547
    top padding, 571–572
    trailing-edge padding, 564
box border, specifying color, style, and/or width of
  bottom, 400
  left, 411
  right, 416
  top, 427
box borders, specifying color, style, and/or width
  of all four, 392–393
boxes, setting inline-progression-dimension of
  block-level and replaced-element, 525–526
box's
  specifying horizontal part width or vertical
    part height, 461–462
  specifying whether and how contents overflow,
    561–652
break
  specifying whether to omit table footer at
    column or page, 624
  specifying whether to omit table header at
    column or page, 624–625
break-after XSL property, 435–436
break-before XSL property, 436–437
breaking lines within box, 644–645
browser to choose application to render element,
  allowing, 447–448
bt-lr keyword, 645
bt-rl keyword, 645
Bush, Vannevar, 655

C

calling
  function, 198–99, 511–512
  template by name, 334–335
Candidate Recommendations, 658, 734
capitalize keyword, 631
capitalized text,changing to, 631–632
caption
  applying block-level formats to table, 505
  formatting, 466–467
  formatting table and its, 504
  specifying position and alignment of table,
    437–438
caption keyword, 482
caption-side XSL property, 437–438
cascading style sheets, 666, 708, 745
case of text, changing, 631–632
case-name XSL property, 438

case-order keyword, 356
case-sensitivity, 710
case-title XSL property, 438
CDATA attribute type, 131, 688
CData XML production, 37-38, 39
cdata-section-elements keyword, 352
CDEnd XML production, 38-39
CDSect XML production, 39-40, 52
CDStart XML production, 39, 40-41
ceiling keyword, 190, 439
ceiling() XPath function, 190, 439
cell
    containing content for table, 505-506
    defined, 716
cell border, separating from adjacent borders, 422
cell ends table row, indicating whether table, 458-459
cell properties in table column, containing, 506
cell starts table row, indicating whether table, 619-620
cells
    showing or hiding borders around empty table, 457
    specifying distance between borders of adjacent, 421-422
center keyword, 378, 384, 385, 386, 454, 625, 627
center-left keyword, 378
center-right keyword, 378
CERN, 656
CGI, 729
CGI scripts, 725
changing
    case of text, 631-632
    orientation of horizontally displayed text glyphs with box, 512-513
    orientation of selection with its box, 588-589
    orientation of vertically displayed text glyphs with box, 513-514
Char XML production, 37, 41-42, 49, 94, 117, 142
character
    specifying hyphen, 517
    specifying if it should be treated as word-space or normal character, 633
    specifying one in name, 104-105
    specifying one mapped to glyph, 467-468
    specifying public identifier within public identifier literal, 120-121
    specifying Unicode, 439-440
    specifying way in which linefeed character is treated, 537-538
    tokenizing expression by, 460-461
character data
    indicating any nonmarkup, 42-43

instructing XML to process language code in which it is written, 647-648
instructing XML to process it using specific XML language code, 138-140
representing in character data section, 37-38
character data section
    marking beginning of, 40-41
    representing character data in, 37-38
character data string, indicating attribute type is, 130-131
character entities, 705, 706-707
character reference or entity reference, naming, 123-124
character references
    decimal, 693
    hexadecimal, 693
character sets, ISO/IEC 10646, 43
character XSL property, 439-440
character-data section
    marking, 38-39
    marking entire, 39-40
characteristics
    returning for computer-system font, 623
    setting formatting of fo:block's first line, 473
    setting formatting of footnote citation, 472-473
    setting table-cell header speak, 614-615
character-point, defined, 169
characters
    combining alphabetic letters and other characters, 47-49
    indicating whether strikethrough characters are drawn over spaces, 602-603
    returning argument with translated, 226-227
    returning number in argument's string, 223-224
    setting spacing between, 535-537
    specifying minimum number in word after hyphenation character, 519-520
    specifying minimum number in word before hyphenation character, 520-521
    specifying way in which contiguous white-space characters are treated, 640-641
CharData XML production, 42-43, 52
CharRef XML production, 43, 123, 142
charset pseudo-attribute, 143
checking on
    namespace name collection or node name, 207-208
    node for type and expanded name of location-step nodes set, 208
child, providing, 320-321
child axis-name keyword, 740
child component, 320
child elements, 683, 687, 702, 723
    forcing user to use in specific order, 127-129
Continued

child elements *(continued)*
  listing, 44–46
  locating target element by navigating through
    integer values for, 166–167
child flow objects, determining which fo:multi-
    property-sets will format, 373–374
child keyword, 188, 637
child sequences, 168
ChildOrAttributeAxisSpecifier XSLT
    production, 320–321, 328
children XML production, 44–46, 54
children, specifying block-progression-
    direction alignment of reference-
    area, 454–455
ChildSeq XPointer production, 166–167, 176
choice list, defined, 686
choice XML production, 44, 46–47, 56
choosing first true xsl:when condition, 335–336
citation, setting formatting characteristics of
    footnote, 472–473
citing page number containing first box from
    formatting object, 492–493
clear XSL property, 440
clip XSL property, 440–441
clipping area of box, defining, 440–441
code
  identifying RGB hexadecimal color, 443
  specifying RFC-1766 country, 448–449
  specifying RFC-1766 language, 530–531
code keyword, 616
collapse keyword, 405, 636
collapsed range, defined, 170
collapsing table-cell border, 405–406
color, 750, 754
  returning RGB, 596–957
  setting for bottom border, 402–403
  setting for ending edge of border, 408–409
  setting for leading edge of border, 397–398
  setting for left border, 413–414
  setting for right border, 418–419
  setting for starting edge of border, 422–424
  setting for top border, 429–430
  setting for trailing edge of border, 393–395
color code, identifying RGB hexadecimal, 443
color name, returning computer-system, 622–623
color profile name of internal reference, specify-
    ing, 443–444
color profile rendering intent other than default,
    allowing for specification of, 594
color value from ICC Color Profile, returning, 521
Color XSL production, 443, 585
color XSL property, 441–443
color
  specifying background, 381–382
  specifying text foreground, 441–443

color, style, and/or width, specifying for
  all four box borders, 392–393
  bottom border, 400
  left border, 411
  right border, 416
  top border, 427
color-profile-name XSL property, 443–344
colors, specifying one or more border, 406–408
column
  containing cell properties in table, 506
  specifying number of first in table-cell span,
    445–446
column keyword, 435, 436, 518, 527, 528
column number, returning inherited value of
  property from fo:table-column with
  matching, 510–511
column or page break
  specifying whether to omit table footer at, 624
  specifying whether to omit table header at,
    624–625
column-centric, 717, 720
column-centric, defined, 717
column-count XSL property, 444
column-gap XSL property, 444–445
column-number property, setting width of column
  specified in, 446
column-number XSL property, 445–446, 753
columns
  determining whether they are spanned within
    multi-column area, 612–613
  setting number of spanned by table cells,
    556–557
columns in box
  specifying amount of space between two,
    444–445
  specifying number of, 444
column-width XSL property, 446
CombiningChar XML production, 47–49, 104
comma separator, 685
comment keyword, 169, 209
comment node in result tree, creating, 336
Comment XML production, 49–50, 52, 99, 100
comment, indicating nonprinting, nonparsed,
  49–50
comments, 685, 702
comparing operands for equality or nonequality,
  192–194
component, creating from contiguous flow objects, 471–472
Computer Lib/Dream Machines, 655
computer-system color name, returning, 622–623
computer-system font, returning characteristic
  of, 623
concat() XPath function, 190–191

concatenation of strings in argument, returning, 190–191

condensed keyword, 488

condensed or expanded version of font, selecting, 488–489

condition

  falling back to template when condition is false, 341–342

  testing if condition is true, 365–367

conditional section, indicating, 50–52

conditionality, 611

conditionality keyword, 536, 607, 608, 610, 643

conditionally ignored section, naming, 94–95

conditionalSect XML production, 50–52, 89

conditions, naming page-master used if some are true, 469

consider-shifts keyword, 539

containing

  all layout masters for document, 475–476

  all portions of floating note, 472

  cell properties in table column, 506

  content for table cell, 505–506

  content of floating object, 471

  list-item body, 478–479

  properties for table rows, 507–508

  properties for table-footer rows, 506–507

  properties for table-header rows, 507

content XML production, 52–53, 64, 86

content for table cell, containing, 505–506

content of floating object, containing, 471

content of object, specifying width of, 448

content particles, defined, 46

content type, specifying element's, 53–55

content

  declaring element and, 66–68

  specifying type of, 447–448

content-height XSL property, 446–447

content-particle grammar in child-elements list, specifying, 55–57

contents, defining ignored section's, 95–97

contentspec XML production, 53–55, 66

content-type XSL property, 447–448

content-width XSL property, 448

context node

  defined, 204

  giving predefined axis name to, 187–188

context position, returning number that equals, 216

context size, returning number that equals, 201–202

context-node language and context-node xml:lang attribute, returning boolean after evaluating, 201

contiguous flow objects, creating single component from, 471–472

contiguous lines are positioned to each other, determining how, 540–541

contiguous whitespace characters are treated, specifying way in which, 640–641

continuous keyword, 615

controlling

  how numerals are spoken, 615

  how punctuation is spoken, 615–616

  location of bottom edge of box, 434–435

  location of left edge of box from left edge of block containing it, 535

  location of right edge of box from right edge of block containing it, 597–598

  location of top edge of box, 632–633

  speaking rate, 616–617

controls, defined, 726

copying

  current node and its namespace nodes, 336–337

  fragment of result tree into same result tree, 337–338

count keyword, 192, 349, 752

count of number of nodes in argument's node-set, returning, 191–192

count() XPath function, 191–192

country code, specifying RFC-1766, 448–449

country XSL property, 448–449

covering range, defined, 170

cp XML production, 46, 55–57, 128

creating

  attributes for elements produced by xsl:element, 331–332

  block-level box, 467

  comment node in result tree, 336

  element with template for its attributes and child elements, 340–341

  inline box, 474–475

  leader connecting two formatting objects, 476–477

  override for element using Unicode bidirectional algorithm, 634–635

  path by composing location path and filter expression, 215–216

  processing-instruction node, 354–355

  result-tree output, 351–353

  single component from contiguous flow objects, 471–472

  text node in template, 360–361

cross-reference identifier, specifying, 589–590

CSS, 666, 745

CSS2, 666, 715

cue XSL property, 449–450

cue-after XSL property, 450–451

cue-before XSL property, 451–452

current flow, naming, 465

current keyword, 321

current node and its namespace nodes, copying, 336–337

`current()` XSLT function, 321
`cursive` keyword, 484

D

`dashed` keyword, 395, 398, 403, 410, 414, 419,
        424, 426, 431, 600
data, setting inline graphic with descendant, 475
data entities, 696
data entity, 705
databases, XML, 720–725
`data-type` keyword, 356
decimal character references, 693
decimal format, specifying, 338–340
decimal or hexadecimal character code,
        specifying, 43–44
decimal or hexadecimal numbers or alphabetic
        characters, representing, 376
decimal-separator keyword, 339
declaration, defined, 666
declarations
        attribute-list (ATTLIST), 679
        document type (DOCTYPE), 660, 661, 673,
                674, 683
        element, 660, 673, 675, 677, 685, 686
        encoding, 661
        entity, 675
        inserting parameter-entity reference or space
                between, 57–58
        standalone, 661
        standalone, defined, 661
        XML, 660, 661, 673, 674, 682–683, 700–701
declaring
        document type, 61–63
        document's encoding name, 71–73
        element and content, 66–68
        element type's attribute list, 29–31
        external subset markup, conditions, and para-
                meter-entity references, 88–89
        general entity, 89–91
        general or parameter entity, 74–76
        ICC Color Profile for style sheet, 468–469
        list elements, 714–715
        markup within parameter entities, 98–100
        notation name, 110–111
        parameter entity (PE), 112–114
        style sheet's and result tree namespace URI is
                alias for another namespace URI, 347–348
        unparsed external entity, 106–107
        whether attribute is required, optional, or
                fixed, 57–60
        whether document contains internal subset or
                refers to external subset, 126–127
        XML document, 137–138, 682–683
        XML document type, 61–63
`DeclSep` XML production, 57–58
`DefaultDecl` XML production, 28, 57–60

defined region
        setting viewing area after body of fo:region-
                body, 495–496
        setting viewing area before body of fo:region-
                body, 496
        setting viewing area body of, 496–497
defining
        attribute, 28–29
        clipping area of box, 440–441
        element's end tag, 83–84
        general entity, 76–77
        how object is aligned with its parent, 387–388
        ignored section's contents, 95–97
        parameter entity (PE), 114–115
        start tag for an element, 129–130
definition descriptions, defined, 714
definition list, defined, 714
definition terms, defined, 714
delimiters, 662
`descendant` axis-name keyword, 188, 740
descendant data, setting inline graphic with, 475
`descendant-or-self` axis-name keyword, 188,
        740
`descending` keyword, 356
describing XML document, 119–120
designating fully-formed XPointer, 176–177
destination area, indicating distance from top of
        page to location of first, 452
destination of `fo:simple-link` formatting
        object, indicating, 526
destination or target resource of simple link, indi-
        cating, 462–463
destination resource
        specifying location of, 604–605
        specifying whether areas that belong to it are
                shown, 523
destination-placement-offset XSL property, 452
determining
        default alignment point, 387–388
        how contiguous lines are positioned to each
                other, 540–541
        page height, 575
        page width, 576–577
        precedence of formatting-object regions reach-
                ing into simple-page-master's corners,
                584–585
        whether columns are spanned within multi-
                column area, 612–613
        which `fo:multi-property-sets` will
                format child flow objects, 373–374
        which `fo:multi-property-sets` will
                format related objects, 373–374
digit, specifying, 60–61
`digit` keyword, 339
`Digit` XML production, 60–61, 104
digits, specifying one or more, 192, 452–453

digits keyword, 615
Digits XPath production, 192, 211, 452–453, 464
dimensions and orientation of page box, setting, 605–606
direction
    overriding bidirectionality writing for inline script, 465–466
    setting for inlined or displayed text, 645–647
direction XSL property, 453–454
disable-output-escaping keyword, 360, 362
discard value, 607, 608, 610, 611, 643
display or print direction, specifying text, 453–454
display-align XSL property, 454–455
displayed or hidden flow objects depending on fo:multi-switch, nesting, 480
displayed or inlined, setting direction in which text is, 645–647
displaying
    floating element after prior element is clear, 440
    non-control character at end of line, 621
disregard-shifts keyword, 539
distance
    indicating from top of page to location of first destination area, 452
    specifying between borders of adjacent cells, 421–422
div keyword, 205, 213, 554, 560
division, acting on expressions through, 204–205, 554–555
DOCTYPE declaration, 660, 661, 673, 674, 683
doctypedecl XML production, 61–63, 119
doctype-public keyword, 352
doctype-system keyword, 352
document
    containing all layout masters for, 475–476
    declaring whether it contains internal subset or refers to external subset, 126–127
    describing XML, 119–120
    inserting whitespace in XML, 124–126
    returning one that is not main document, 321–322
document entity, defined, 63
document instance, 662–666
document instance, defined, 660
document keyword, 321, 595
document module, defined, 63
document of formatting-object tree, identifying source, 606–607
document processors, specifying role of formatting object for alternate, 598–599
document prolog, 660–662
document prolog, defined, 660
Document Style Semantics and Specification Language, 657, 667, 746

document type declaration, 656, 660, 661, 673, 674, 683
document type, declaring, 61–63
document type definition, 661
document type definition, defined, 656
document XML production, 63–64
document() XSLT function, 321–322
documents
    valid, 672–673
    well-formed, 671–672
dominant-baseline XSL property, 455–456
dots keyword, 534
dotted keyword, 395, 398, 403, 410, 414, 419, 424, 426, 431, 600
double keyword, 395, 398, 403, 410, 414, 419, 424, 426, 431, 600
DSSSL, 657, 667, 746
DSSSL flow object classes, 746
DSSSL Online, 657, 745
DSSSL-O, 745
DTD
    defined, 656
    external, 661
    internal, 661
    reading, 677–679

E

EBNF, 676
EBNF, defined, 654
effects to text, applying shadow, 630–631
element
    allowing browser to choose application to render, 447–448
    creating element with template for its attributes and child elements, 340–341
    creating override using Unicode bidirectional algorithm, 634–635
    displaying after prior element is clear, 440
    empty, 687
    floating in document, 463
    opening level of embedding using Unicode bidirectional algorithm, 634–635
    pausing after element is spoken, 578–579
    pausing after and/or before element is spoken, 577–578
    pausing before element is spoken, 579–580
    positioning onscreen or in printed format, 583–584
    returning true or false depending on whether instruction element is named, 322
    setting vertical alignment of, 635–636
    specifying height of, 514–515
    specifying maximum height of, 548–549
    specifying maximum width of, 550–551
    specifying minimum height of, 552–553

Continued

element *(continued)*
    specifying minimum width of, 553–554
    specifying relative-position of, 591–592
    specifying whether box in which it resides is
        visible or invisible, 636–637
    specifying width of, 642–643
element and content, declaring, 66–68
element content within tags, representing, 52–53
element declaration, 660, 673, 675, 677, 685, 686
element type, defined, 31
element type's attribute list, declaring, 29–31
element XML production, 52, 63, 64–66
element-available() XSLT function, 322
elementdecl XML production, 66–68, 99
elements
    allowing precise alignments of, 375–376
    child, 702, 723
    declaring list, 714–715
    defined, 656
    empty, 663–664, 703–704
    listing child, 44–46
    preserving whitespace in list of, 354
    returning by ID value, 200–201
    root, 702, 723
    setting level of box in stack of, 648
    stripping whitespace from list of, 357
element's content
    playing sound while it is spoken, 582–583
    specifying type, 53–55
elements keyword, 354, 357
elevation XSL property, 456–457
embed keyword, 155, 634
embedding for element, opening additional level
    of, 634–635
EMPTY, 53, 54, 65, 66, 68, 69
empty elements, 663–64, 687, 703–704
empty table cells, showing or hiding borders
    around, 457
empty-cells XSL property, 457
empty-element tag, writing, 68–70
EmptyElemTag XML production, 64, 68–70
enabling user to choose child-element order,
    46–47
EncName XML production, 70–71
encoding
    information, 701
    information and version about external subset
        or external parameter entity, providing,
        132–134
encoding component, 71
encoding declaration, 661
encoding declaration, defined, 661
encoding keyword, 351
encoding name
    declaring document's, 71–73
    specifying, 70–71

EncodingDecl XML production, 71–73, 133, 138
encompassing entire XML document, 63–64
end keyword, 437, 625, 627
end of line is printed or displayed, indicating
    whether non-control character at, 621
end of list-item label and beginning of list item,
    setting length between, 587–588
end point of arc link, specifying, 158–160
end tag, defining element's, 83–84
end tags, 663, 702
end-indent XSL property, 457–58, 746
ending edge of border, setting color of, 408–409
ending edge of border, setting style of, 409–410
ending edge of border, setting width of, 410–411
ending edge of box, specifying indention at,
    457–458
ending indention for last line of paragraph flow
    object, setting amount of, 531–532
ending-edge padding of box, turning on or off,
    567–568
ending-edge-padding size of box, setting, 567–568
end-point type locations, returning, 167
end-point() XPointer function, 167
ends-row XSL property, 458–459
enhancements, specifying text, 489–490
enhancing text with lines or blinking, 628–629
ensuring that string is enclosed within pair of
    parentheses, 178
entities, 665–666
    character, 705, 706–707
    data, 696, 705
    declaring markup within parameter, 98–100
    external, 692, 695
    external, defined, 666
    general, 692, 705–706
    general, defined, 666
    internal, 692
    internal, defined, 666
    parameter, 694, 705, 707–708
    parameter, defined, 666
    parsed, 692
    parsed general, 693
    parsed, defined, 666
    unparsed, 692
    unparsed external, 696
    unparsed, defined, 666
ENTITIES XML attribute, 73, 134, 689, 696
entity
    declaring general, 89–91
    declaring parameter, 112–114
    declaring unparsed external, 106–107
    defining parameter, 114–115
    providing version and encoding information
        about external subset or external parameter,
        132–134

specifying well-formed external general
parsed, 86–87
entity declaration, 675
entity reference
naming, 123–124
specifying, 77–79
entity references, 666, 706
ENTITY XML attribute, 73–74, 134, 689, 696
entity
defined, 692
specifying general, 73–74
EntityDecl XML production, 74–76, 99
EntityDef XML production, 76–77, 90
EntityRef XML production, 77–79, 123
entity-reference delimiter, 692
EntityValue XML production, 76, 79–80, 114
enumerated NOTATION attribute type, 690
enumerated notation names or name tokens, indicating that attribute type is composed of,
80–81
EnumeratedType XML production, 32, 80–81
enumeration token, providing NCName for, 459
Enumeration XML production, 80, 81–82
enumeration, defined, 81
EnumerationToken XSL property, 491, 492, 659
Eq XML production, 31, 71, 82–83, 126, 136
equal sign, indicating, 82–83
equality or nonequality, comparing operands for,
192–194
EqualityExpr XPath production, 186, 192–194
error message, defined, 29
ETag XML production, 64, 83–84
European Laboratory for Particle Physics, 656
evaluating
expression, 511–512
expression and returning template based on
true and false conditions, 343–344
operands to find if each is true or false,
214–215
two operands to find if both are true or false,
186–187
evaluating and processing an expression and calling function, 198–199
even keyword, 494, 559
even or odd position in page sequence, making
page-master eligible for selection depending on its, 559
even-page keyword, 435, 436
exclude-result-prefixes keyword, 358, 361
expanded keyword, 488
expanded or condensed version of font, selecting,
488–489
expanded-name of argument node-set's first node
returning namespace URI of, 206–207
returning QName representing, 206

expanded-name of first node in argument's node-
set, returning local part of, 203
Expr XPath production, 177, 187, 194, 217, 376,
459–460, 585
expression
evaluating and processing, 511–512
generating text using, 362–363
indicating, 194, 459–460
inserting whitespace in, 196–197, 461
negating, 228, 633–634
representing absolute or relative
floating-point number in, 558–559
representing predicate, 217
symbolizing primary, 217–218, 558
tokenizing, 194–196
tokenizing character by character or name by
name, 460–461
uniting path, 228–229
uniting path expression and another union,
228–229
expression and location path, creating path by
composing filter, 215–216
expression and predicate, filtering primary expression or combination of filter, 197–198
expression and returning template based on true
and false conditions, evaluating, 343–344
expression or combination of filter expression and
predicate, filtering primary, 216–217
expressions
acting on through addition or subtraction,
185–186, 374–375
acting on through multiplication, division, or
finding a modulus, 204–205, 554–555
testing relationship of two, 218–219
ExprToken XPath production, 194–196, 460–461
ExprWhitespace XPath production, 196–197, 461
Extended Backus-Naur Form, 676–677
Extended Backus-Naur Form, defined, 654
extended links, defined, 145, 737–739
extended pointers, 739–743
extended XLink type, 148–149, 160
Extender production, 104
extender symbol, inserting, 84
Extender XML production, 84
Extensible HyperText Markup Language, 656
Extensible Stylesheet Language, 657, 666, 745–754
extensible, defined, 659
extension-element-prefixes keyword, 358, 361
extent XSL property, 461–462
external DTD, 661
external DTD subsets, 674–676, 684, 701
external DTD subsets, defined, 672
external entities, 692, 695
external entity
declaring unparsed, 106–107
defined, 75, 666

external general parsed entity, specifying well-formed, 86-87
external graphic
  indicating one placed inline, 470-471
  setting scaling of, 601-602
external identifier
  resolving into system identifier, 122-123
  specifying URI of, 131-132
external linkset, defined, 154
external parameter entity or external subset, providing version and encoding information about, 132-134
external subset
  declaring markup, conditions, and parameter-entity references, 88-89
  declaring whether document contains internal subset or refers to, 126-127
  defined, 62
  providing version and encoding information about, 132-134
  specifying, 87-88
external-destination XSL property, 462-63, 754
ExternalID XML production, 61, 76, 84-86, 110, 114
extParsedEnt XML production, 86-87
extra-condensed keyword, 488
extra-expanded keyword, 489
extSubset XML production, 88-89
extSubsetDecl XML production, 88-89, 97

F

factor units of proportional measure, returning proportional, 585-586
falling back to template when condition is false, 341-342
false and true conditions, evaluating expression and returning template based on, 343-344
false keyword, 197, 516, 584, 603, 640
false or true
  evaluating two operands to find if both are, 186-187
  returning depending on whether argument string contains other argument string, 191
  returning depending on whether function is in function library, 323-324
  returning depending on whether instruction element is named, 322
  returning depending on whether one argument string starts with the other argument string, 221
false() XPath function, 197
false
  falling back to template when condition is, 341-342

returning value of true if argument is, 210
family or name
  specifying fonts by, 483-484
  specifying voices by, 637-638
fantasy keyword, 484
far-left keyword, 377
far-right keyword, 378
fast keyword, 617
faster keyword, 617
female keyword, 637
field, defined, 722
file, specifying median volume of waveform, 638-639
filled or blank, making page-master eligible for selection depending on whether it is, 389-390
filter expression and location path, creating path by composing, 215-216
filter expression and predicate, filtering primary expression or combination of, 197-198
FilterExpr XPath production, 197-198, 215
filtering primary expression or combination of filter expression and predicate, 197-198
filters nodes in location path, inserting predicate expression that, 216-217
finding
  modulus, 554-555
  modulus, acting on expressions through, 204-205
first column in table-cell span, specifying number of, 445-446
first destination area, indicating distance from top of page to location of, 452
first fo:multi-case formatting object is restored when fo:multi-switch formatting object is concealed by ancestor, indicating, 377
first keyword, 576
first line of text, indenting, 629-630
first true xsl:when condition, choosing, 335-336
first-including-carryover keyword, 596
first-page number in pages sequence, setting, 524-525
first-starting-within-page keyword, 596
five regions of page, generating up to, 501-502
fixed keyword, 372, 380, 583, 623
fixing background image in page background, 380-381
float XSL property, 463
floating element in document, 463
floating element, displaying after prior element is clear, 440
floating note, containing all portions of, 472
floating object, containing content of, 471

floating-point number
 defined, 464
 representing absolute or relative in expression,
 558–559
 representing, 210–211, 463–464, 555–556
FloatingPointNumber XSL property, 463–464,
 555
floor() XPath function, 198, 464–465
flow object
 indicating whether output stays together,
 526–527
 indicating whether page break is inserted after, 435–436
 indicating whether page break is inserted before, 436–437
 indicating whether to keepwith following one,
 527–528
 indicating whether to keepwith prior one,
 528–529
 setting amount of ending indention for last
 line of paragraph, 531–532
flow object classes, 747
flow objects
 creating single component from contiguous,
 471–472
 defined, 369
 determining which fo:multi-property-
 sets will format child, 373–374
 nesting displayed or hidden depending on
 fo:multi-switch, 480
flow, naming current, 465
flow-name XSL property, 465
flow-object area
 inserting space after, 607–608
 inserting space at end of inline, 609–610
 inserting space at start of inline, 610–611
 inserting space before, 608–609
flows, defined, 493
fo:bidi-override XSL formatting object,
 465–466
fo:block XSL formatting object, 466–467, 748,
 750, 751, 752
fo:block's first line, setting formatting characteristics of, 473
fo:block-container XSL flow object, 467
fo:block-container, specifying absolute
 position of, 372
fo:character XSL flow object, 467–468
fo:color-profile XSL formatting object,
 468–469
fo:conditional-page-master-reference XSL formatting object, 469
fo:declarations XSL formatting object,
 469–470

fo:external-graphic XSL flow object,
 470–471, 750
fo:external-graphic, specifying URI of,
 617–618
fo:float XSL formatting object, 471
fo:flow XSL formatting object, 471–472
fo:footnote XSL formatting object, 472
fo:footnote-body XSL formatting object,
 472–473
fo:initial-property-set XSL formatting
 object, 473, 750
fo:inline XSL formatting object, 473–474
fo:inline-container XSL formatting object,
 474–475
fo:instream-foreign-object XSL formatting
 object, 475
fo:layout-master-set XSL formatting object,
 475–476
fo:leader XSL formatting object, 476–477
fo:leader formatting objects with same content
 and values are aligned, indicating
 whether, 532–533
fo:list-block XSL formatting object, 477–478,
 751
fo:list-item XSL formatting object, 478, 751
fo:list-item-body XSL formatting object,
 478–479, 751
fo:list-item-label XSL formatting object,
 479, 751
fo:marker
 identifying group name for multiple formatting objects, 547
 producing running headers and running footers with, 499–500
 retrieving boundary contained within, 594–595
 specifying preference for fo:retrieve-
 marker to retrieve children of, 595–596
fo:marker XSL formatting object, 479–480
fo:multi-case
 indicating whether first formatting object is
 restored when fo:multi-switch formatting object is concealed by ancestor, 377
 indicating whether formatting objectis displayed first, 619
 naming, 438
 providing title for, 438
 switching to, 621–622
 toggling from one to another, 481–482
fo:multi-case XSL formatting object, 480
fo:multi-properties XSL formatting object,
 480, 754
fo:multi-property-set XSL formatting object,
 480–481, 754
fo:multi-property-sets, determining which
 will format related objects, 373–374

fo:multi-switch
  indicating whether first fo:multi-case for-
    matting object is restored when it is con-
    cealed by ancestor, 377
  nesting displayed or hidden flow objects de-
    pending on, 480
fo:multi-switch XSL formatting object, 481
fo:multi-toggle XSL formatting object, 481–482
fo:page-number XSL formatting object, 492
fo:page-number-citation XSL formatting
  object, 492–493
fo:page-sequence XSL formatting object,
  493–494
fo:page-sequence-master XSL formatting
  object, 494
fo:region-after XSL formatting object, 495–496
fo:region-before XSL formatting object, 496
fo:region-body XSL formatting object, 496–497
fo:region-body
  setting viewing area after body of defined
    region, 495–496
  setting viewing area before body of defined
    region, 496
fo:region-end XSL formatting object, 497
fo:region-start XSL formatting object, 497–498
fo:repeatable-page-master-alternatives XSL formatting object, 498–499
fo:repeatable-page-master-reference XSL formatting object, 499
fo:retrieve-marker
  producing running headers and running foot-
    ers with, 479–480
  specifying preference to retrieve children of
    fo:marker, 595–596
fo:retrieve-marker XSL formatting object,
  499–500
fo:root XSL formatting object, 500
fo:simple-link
  indicating destination or target resource of,
    526
  indicating, 462–463
fo:simple-link XSL formatting object, 500–501,
  754
fo:simple-page-master XSL formatting object,
  501–502, 752
fo:single-page-master-reference XSL formatting
  object, 502
fo:static-content XSL formatting object,
  502–503
fo:table XSL formatting object, 503–504, 752
fo:table-and-caption XSL formatting object,
  504
fo:table-body XSL formatting object, 504–505,
  752
fo:table-caption XSL formatting object, 505

fo:table-cell XSL formatting object, 505–506,
  753
fo:table-column with matching column number,
  returning inherited value of property
  from, 510–511
fo:table-column XSL formatting object, 506,
  752
fo:table-footer XSL formatting object, 506–507
fo:table-header XSL formatting object, 507
fo:table-row XSL formatting object, 507–508,
  753
fo:title XSL formatting object, 508
fo:wrapper XSL formatting object, 508–509, 754
focus keyword, 373
following axis-name keyword, 188, 740
following-sibling axis-name keyword, 188, 740
font
  adjusting aspect value of, 487–88
  returning characteristic of computer-system,
    623
  selecting condensed or expanded version of,
    488–489
  setting line-spacing height of font above
    baseline, 485–486
  setting line-spacing height of font below
    baseline, 484–485
  specifying boldness or lightness of, 491–492
  specifying enhancements to, 489–490
font properties, specifying, 482–483
font size, specifying, 486–487
font variations, specifying, 490–491
font XSL property, 482–483
font-family XSL property, 483–484
font-height keyword, 540
font-height-override-after XSL property, 484–485
font-height-override-before XSL property, 485–486
fonts by name or family, specifying, 483–484
font-size for baseline-table, reestablishing, 455–456
font-size XSL property, 486–487, 750
font-size-adjust XSL property, 487–488
font-stretch XSL property, 488–489
font-style XSL property, 489–490
font-variant XSL property, 490–491
font-weight XSL property, 491–492, 750
footer, specifying whether to omit table at column
  or page break, 624
footers and headers with fo:marker, producing
  running, 499–500
footers and headers with fo:retrieve-marker,
  producing running, 479–80
footnote citation, setting formatting characteristics
  of, 472–473
force-page-count XSL property, 494–495
foreground color, specifying, 441–443
form, defined, 722

format keyword, 349

format, specifying decimal, 338–340

format-number() XSLT function, 322–323

formats to table caption, applying block-level, 505

formatted string, returning number as, 322–323

formatting
and inserting number in result tree, 348–350
inline text with background or border, 473–474
list or list item, 477–478
paragraphs, captions, headings, and other block-level selections, 466–467
set of pages, 493–494
table, 503–504
table and its caption, 504
table body, 504–505

formatting bitmapped graphics, specifying scaling tradeoff when, 602

formatting characteristics of fo:block's first line, setting, 473

formatting characteristics of footnote citation, setting, 472–473

formatting object
citing page number containing first box from, 492–493
returning value of property from nearest-ancestor, 509–510
returning value of property from parent, 510

formatting object for alternate document processors, specifying role of, 598–599

formatting object is restored when fo:multi-switch formatting object is concealed by ancestor, indicating first fo:multi-case, 377

formatting objects
creating leader connecting two, 476–477
defined, 369

formatting-object regions reaching into simple-page-master's corners, determining precedence of, 584–585

formatting-object subtrees, switching to, 481

formatting-object tree, identifying source document of, 606–607

formatting-objects group, setting properties inherited by, 508–509

fragment identifiers, defined, 165, 735

fragment of result tree into same result tree, placing, 337–338

from XLink attribute, 149–150, 161, 349, 738

from-nearest-specified-value keyword, 509

from-nearest-specified-value() XSL function, 509–510

from-parent() XSL function, 510

from-table-column() XSL function, 510–511

full XPointer
identifying XPointer parts that make up, 167–168

or FullXPtr, locating target element by specifying part of, 177–178

FullXPtr XPointer component, 167–168, 176

fully-formed XPointer, designating, 176–177

function
providing NCName for, 512
providing QName for, 199–200

function library, returning true or false depending on whether function is in, 323–324

function-available() XSLT function, 323–324

FunctionCall XSL production, 198–199, 218, 511–512, 585

FunctionName XSL production, 195, 199–200, 460, 511, 512

functions, calling, 511–512

G

GEDecl XML production, 74, 89–91

general entities, 705–706

general entities, specifying list of valid XML, 73

general entity, 692
declaring, 74–76, 89–91
defined, 75, 666
defining, 76–77
specifying, 73–74

general-entity references, 696

generate-id() XSLT function, 324

generating
text using expression, 362–363
up to five regions of page, 501–502

generic identifier, defined, 60

giving
predefined axis name to context node, 187–188
unique identifier to formatting object within fo:namespace formatting object, 521–523

global declarations for style sheet, grouping, 469–470

glyph, indicating character mapped to, 467–468

glyph-orientation-horizontal XSL property, 512–513

glyph-orientation-vertical XSL property, 513–514

glyphs
changing orientation of horizontally displayed text with box, 512–513
changing orientation of vertically displayed text with box, 513–514

grammar, defined, 676

graphic
setting scaling of external, 601–602
specifying URI of fo:external-graphic, 617–618

graphic file or target link, indicating URI for, 515–516

graphic placed inline, indicating external, 470–471

graphic with descendant data, setting inline, 475

graphics, specifying scaling tradeoff when formatting bitmapped, 602

groove keyword, 395, 398, 403, 410, 415, 419, 424, 426, 431, 600
group name for multiple fo:marker formatting objects, identifying, 547
grouping, global declarations for style sheet, 469–470

H

hanging keyword, 387, 455
HEAD element, 660
header at column or page break, specifying whether to omit table, 624–625
header speak characteristics, setting table-cell, 614–615
headers and footers with fo:marker, producing running, 499–500
headers and footers with fo:retrieve-marker, producing running, 479–480
headings, formatting, 466–467
height
    determining page, 575
    specifying for element, 514–515
height of element
    specifying maximum, 548–549
    specifying minimum, 552–553
height of font
    setting line-spacing above baseline, 485–486
    setting line-spacing below baseline, 484–485
height of object, specifying content, 446–447
height XSL property, 514–515
height, specifying box's vertical part, 461–462
here() XPointer function, 168
hexadecimal character references, 693
hexadecimal color code, identifying RGB, 443
hexadecimal or decimal character code, specifying, 43–44
hexadecimal or decimal numbers or alphabetic characters, representing, 376
hidden keyword, 395, 398, 403, 409, 414, 419, 424, 426, 431, 636
hidden or displayed flow objects depending on fo:multi-switch, nesting, 480
hide keyword, 457, 619
hiding
    borders around empty table cells, 457
    table-cell border, 405–406
high keyword, 580
higher keyword, 456
highest integer, returning, 198, 464–465
horizontal alignment of text, setting, 625–626
horizontal part width of box, specifying, 461–462
horizontal position of background-image, specifying initial, 385
horizontal rule
    setting pattern for, 599–600
    setting thickness of, 600–601

horizontally displayed text glyphs with box, changing orientation of, 512–513
host name, defined, 734
hover keyword, 373
href XSL property, 515–516
HTML, 656, 657
HTML element, 660
html keyword, 351
http, 656
HTTP protocol, 725, 730
Hypercard, 655
hypermedia, 655
hypertext, 655
HyperText Markup Language, 656
Hypertext Transport Protocol, 656
hyphenate XSL property, 516–517
hyphenated word, setting location of both parts of, 517–518
hyphenation, indicating whether it is allowed, 516–517
hyphenation character
    specifying, 517
    specifying maximum number of lines in row that can end with, 518–519
    specifying minimum number of characters in word after, 519–520
    specifying minimum number of characters in word before, 520–521
hyphenation-character XSL property, 517
hyphenation-keep XSL property, 517–518
hyphenation-ladder-count XSL property, 518–519
hyphenation-push-character-count XSL property, 519–520
hyphenation-remain-character-count XSL property, 520–521

I

IANA, 139
ICC Color Profile
    declaring for style sheet, 468–469
    returning color value from, 521
icc-color() XSL function, 521
icon keyword, 482
ID attribute type, 134, 688, 689, 695
id keyword, 200, 324, 358, 361
ID value, returning elements by, 200–201
ID XML attribute, 91
id XSL property, 575–577
id() XPath function, 200–201
identifier
    indicating that XML identifier follows, 91
    indicating that XML identifier cross-reference follows, 92–93
    resolving external identifier into system identifier, 122–123

returning string identifier for node in first node-set, 324

specifying identifier for cross-reference, 589–590

identifiers and keys to locate node, specifying pattern of, 324–325

identifying

group name for multiple fo:marker formatting objects, 547

node type or number, 208–209

notation used to express XPointer, 172–173

parsed external entity, 84–86

region, 590–591

RGB hexadecimal color code, 443

source document of formatting-object tree, 606–607

specific node location type, 168–170

XPointer parts that make up full XPointer, 167–168

ideogram, defined, 91

ideogram, specifying, 91–92

ideographic keyword, 387, 455

Ideographic XML production, 91–92, 98

IdKeyPattern XSLT production, 324–325, 326

IDREF XML attribute, 92–93, 134, 689

IDREFS XML attribute, 93–94, 134, 689

IEC, 694

Ignore XML production, 94, 95, 96

ignored section, indicating included section nested in an, 94

ignored section, naming conditionally, 94–95

ignored section's contents, defining, 95–97

ignoreSect XML production, 50, 94–95

ignoreSectContents XML production, 95–97

ignoring contiguous whitespace characters, 640–641

image

specifying background, 382–383

specifying starting position for background, 383–385

imported style sheet, instructing processor to override template rule in, 329–330

importing XSL style sheet, 344–345

inbound, defined, 737

INCLUDE keyword, 97

included section nested in an ignored section, indicating, 94

included section, indicating, 97–98

includeSect XML production, 50, 97–98

including

another XSLT style sheet, 345

label and list-item body, 478

list-item label, 479

indefinite keyword, 575, 576

indent keyword, 352

indenting first line of text, 629–630

indention

setting amount of ending for last line of paragraph flow object, 588–590

specifying at ending edge of box, , 457–458

specifying at starting edge of box, 618–619

indicate-destination XSL property, 523

indicating

absolute length, 371

any nonmarkup character data, 42–43

attribute type is character data string, 130–131

attribute type is tokenized set, 134–135

character mapped to glyph, 467–468

conditional section, 50–52

destination or target resource of fo:simple-link formatting object, 526

destination or target resource of simple link, 462–463

distance from top of page to location of first destination area, 452

equal sign, 82–83

expression, 194, 459–460

external graphic placed inline, 470–471

first fo:multi-case formatting object is restored when fo:multi-switch formatting object is concealed by ancestor, 377

fo:simple-link, 462–463

how link resource is displayed onscreen, 155–156

included section, 97–98

included section nested in an ignored section, 94

link that associates one local resource and one remote resource, 156–157

list of XML cross-references follows, 93–94

local resource for link, 153

miscellaneous information, 100–101

mixed element content, 101–102

nonprinting, nonparsed comment, 49–50

page number, 492

path of link transversal, 147–148

relative length ending with name of relative unit of measure, 592–593

remote resource for link, 152–153

root node of result tree, 500

start of simple link, 500–501

synonym of XSL style sheet, 361–362

that attribute type is composed of enumerated notation names or name tokens, 80–81

that valid XML identifier cross-reference follows, 92–93

that valid XML identifier follows, 91

URI for target link or graphic file, 515–516

Continued

indicating *(continued)*
  valid XML name token follows, 107–108
  whether fo:leaders formatting objects with
    same content and values are aligned,
    532–533
  whether fo:multi-case formatting object is
    displayed first, 619
  whether hyphenation is allowed, 516–517
  whether line height is modified for subscript
    or superscript characters, 539–540
  whether non-control character at end of line
    is printed or displayed, 621
  whether output produced by flow object stays
    together, 526–527
  whether page break is inserted after flow ob-
    ject, 435–436
  whether page break is inserted before flow
    object, 436–437
  whether strikethrough characters are drawn
    over spaces, 602–603
  whether table cell ends table row, 458–459
  whether table cell starts table row, 619–620
  whether to keep flow object with following
    one, 527–528
  whether to keep flow object with prior one,
    528–529
  XSL style sheet, 357–358
infinity keyword, 339
inflection in voice, specifying highest level of,
  620–621
inherit keyword, 372, 375, 378, 380, 382, 384,
  385, 386, 388, 389, 390, 391, 392, 394,
  395, 396, 397, 399, 400, 402, 404, 405,
  407, 409, 410, 411, 412, 414, 415, 416,
  417, 418, 419, 420, 421, 422, 423, 424,
  425, 427, 428, 430, 431, 432, 433, 434,
  435, 436, 437, 440, 441, 442, 443, 444,
  445, 447, 448, 449, 450, 451, 453, 454,
  456, 457, 458, 462, 463, 483, 484, 485,
  487, 489, 490, 491, 495, 513, 514, 515,
  516, 517, 518, 519, 520, 524, 525, 527,
  528, 529, 530, 531, 533, 534, 535, 536,
  537, 538, 539, 540, 542, 543, 544, 545,
  546, 547, 549, 550, 552, 553, 559, 561,
  564, 565, 566, 567, 568, 569, 570, 571,
  572, 573, 575, 576, 577, 578, 579, 580,
  581, 582, 583, 584, 586, 587, 588, 589,
  590, 591, 592, 594, 597, 598, 600, 601,
  602, 603, 604, 605, 606, 607, 609, 610,
  611, 612, 613, 614, 615, 616, 617, 618,
  620, 621, 623, 626, 627, 628, 629, 631,
  632, 633, 634, 635, 636, 637, 638, 639,
  640, 641, 642, 643, 644, 646, 648
inherited property value, returning, 523–524

inherited value of property from fo:table-
  column with matching column number,
  returning, 510–511
inherited-property-value() XSL function, 523
initial-page-number XSL property, 524–525
inline box, creating, 475–475
inline flow-object area
  inserting space at end of, 609–610
  inserting space at start of, 610–611
inline graphic, setting with descendant data, 475
inline script, overriding bidirectionality writing
  direction for, 465–466
inline text with background or border, formatting,
  473–474
inline, indicating external graphic placed, 470–471
inlined or displayed, setting direction in which
  text is, 645–647
inline-progression-dimension of block-level and
  replaced-element boxes, setting, 525–526
inline-progression-dimension XSL property,
  525–526
input form, defined, 722
inserting
  and formatting number in result tree, 348–350
  element in document, 463
  extender symbol, 84
  multiply operator, 205–206, 555
  page break after page box, 572–573
  page break before page box, 573–574
  page break inside page box, 574–575
  parameter-entity reference or space between
    declarations, 57–58
  predicate expression that filters nodes in
    location path, 216–217
  space after flow-object area, 607–608
  space at end of inline flow-object area, 609–610
  space at start of inline flow-object area, 610–611
  space before flow-object area, 608–609
  whitespace in expression, 461
  whitespace in XML document, 124–126
  whitespace into expression, 196–197
inset keyword, 395, 399, 403, 410, 419, 424, 427,
  431
inside keyword, 625, 627
instance, 662–666
instance, defined, 660
instructing
  processor to override template rule in im-
    ported style sheet, 329–330
  Unicode bidirectional algorithm to open
    additional level of embedding or create
    override for element, 634–635
  XML processor in correct way to interpret
    xpointer scheme, 177
  XML processor on how to interpret named
    non-xpointer scheme, 173

XML processor to use named style sheet, 141–143

XML to process character data using specific XML language code, 138–140

XML to process language code in which character data is written, 647–648

instruction element is named, returning true or false depending on whether, 322

instructions, processing, defined, 661

integer

returning highest, 198, 464–465

returning lowest integer closest to negative infinity that is not less than argument, 190

returning lowest, 439

returning rounded integer closest in value to argument, 599

integer-pixels keyword, 602

internal DTD subset, defined, 672

internal DTD subsets, 661, 673–674, 683–684, 701

internal entity, defined, 74, 666

internal reference, specifying color profile name of, 443–444

internal subset

declaring whether document contains one or refers to external subset, 126–127

defined, 62

internal-destination XSL property, 526

internal-entity value, specifying, 79–80

International Electrotechnical Commission, 676

International Standards Organization (ISO), 656

interpreting xpointer scheme, 177

invisible or visible, specifying whether box in which element resides is, 636–637

ISO 10646, 665

ISO 15924, 604

ISO 3166, 449

ISO 8879:1996, 746

ISO/IEC 10646, 43, 694

ISO/IEC 10744, 746

ISO/IEC 14977: 1996, 676

italic keyword, 489

J

justify keyword, 625, 627

K

keep flow object with following one, indicating whether to, 527–528

keep flow object with prior one, indicating whether to, 528–529

keep-together XSL property, 526–527

keep-with-next XSL property, 527–528

keep-with-previous XSL property, 528–529

key, returning node-set that matches, 325

key keyword, 324, 325

key() XSLT function, 325

keys and identifiers to locate node, specifying pattern of, 324–325

keyword, representing reserved, 529–530

Keyword XSL production, 529–530, 585

L

label and list-item body, including, 478

label attribute, 161, 738

label of locator or resource type XLink, specifying, 151–152

label XLink attribute, 151–152

label-end keyword, 530

label-end value for list, returning, 530

label-end() XSL function, 530

landscape keyword, 605

lang() XPath function, 201, 349, 355

language code

instructing XML to process language code in which character data is written, 647–648

specifying RFC-1766, 530–531

language or script for composing selected lines, naming, 603–604

language XSL property, 530–531

large keyword, 486

larger keyword, 487

last keyword, 576

last line of paragraph flow object, setting amount of ending indention for, 531–532

last line of text, setting horizontal alignment of, 625–626

last() XPath function, 201–202

last-ending-within-page keyword, 596

last-line-end-indent XSL property, 531–532

last-starting-within-page keyword, 596

laying out pages set from page-master, 502

layout masters for document, containing all, 475–476

layout, specifying table, 623–624

leader connecting two formatting objects, creating, 476–477

leader length, specifying maximum and minimum, 533

leader pattern, specifying, 533–534

leader-alignment XSL property, 532–533

leader-length XSL property, 533

leader-pattern width, specifying, 534–535

leader-pattern XSL property, 533–534

leader-pattern-width XSL property, 534–535

leading edge of border

setting color of, 397–398

setting style of, 398–399

setting width of, 399–400

leading-edge padding of box

sizing, 564

turning on or off, 564

left border
  setting color of, 413-414
  setting style of, 414-415
  setting width of, 415-416
left edge of box from left edge of block containing
  it, controlling location of, 535
left keyword, 378, 384, 385, 437, 440, 463, 572,
  573, 626, 627
left margin of box
  sizing, 608-609
  turning on or off, 544-545
left padding of box
  turning on or off, 640-641
  sizing, 544-545
left XSL property, 535
left-side keyword, 377
left-to-right stereo speaker location of sound file,
  specifying, 377-379
leftwards keyword, 378
legal hexadecimal or decimal character code,
  specifying, 43-44
length
  indicating absolute, 371
  indicating relative length, 592-593
  setting between end of list-item label and
    beginning of list item, 587-588
  setting between end of start indent of list-item
    label and beginning of list item, 586-587
length keyword, 385
letter of current alphabet, specifying, 98
Letter XML production, 98, 103, 104, 757
letter-spacing XSL property, 535-537
letter-value keyword, 349
level keyword, 349, 456
level of box in stack of elements, setting, 648
library, returning true or false depending on
  whether function is in function, 323-324
lighter keyword, 491
lightness or boldness of font, specifying, 491-492
limiting number of pages in page sequence in
  another page sequence, 549-550
line breaks occur in box, specifying how, 644-645
line height is modified for subscript or superscript
  characters, indicating whether, 539-540
line is printed or displayed, indicating whether
  non-control character at end of, 621
line of text, indenting first, 629-630
linefeed character is treated, specifying way in
  which, 537-538
linefeed-treatment XSL property, 537-538
line-height XSL property, 538-539, 540
line-height-shift-adjustment XSL property,
  539-540
lines are positioned to each other, determining
  how contiguous, 540-541

lines
  naming language or script for composing
    selected, 603-604
  specifying maximum number of lines in a row
    that can end with hyphen, 518-519
line-spacing
  setting height of font above baseline, 485-486
  setting height of font below baseline, 484-485
line-stacking-strategy XSL production,
  540-541
line-through keyword, 628
link
  indicating local resource for, 153
  indicating one that associates one local resource
    and one remote resource, 156-157
  indicating remote resource for, 152-153
  indicating target resource or destination of
    simple, 462-463
  providing title information with, 157
  specifying end point of arc, 158-160
  specifying starting point of arc, 149-150
link attribute and attribute value or namespace
  URI follows, signaling that, 161-162
link content, specifying role of, 153-155
link keyword, 373
link resource
  indicating how it is displayed onscreen,
    155-156
  specifying title of a, 157-158
link transversal, indicating path of, 147-148
link type, specifying, 160-162
linkbase, defined, 155
linking resource, specifying way in which it is
  retrieved, 146-147
links
  extended, 737-739
  simple, 735-737
list
  declaring element type's attribute, 29-31
  returning body-start value for, 391-392
  returning label-end value for, 530
  specifying content-particle grammar in child-
    elements, 55-57
  specifying valid XML general entities, 73
  specifying valid XML name tokens, 109-110
list elements, declaring, 714-715
list item
  defined, 714
  setting length between end of list-item label
    and beginning of, 587-588
list of elements
  preserving whitespace in, 354
  stripping whitespace from, 357
list of mathematical and logical operators,
  providing, 212-213

list of mathematical operators, providing, 559–560

list of XML cross-references follows, indicating, 93–94

list or list item, formatting, 477–478

listing

    all possible notation-type names, 111–112

    attributes, 687

    child elements, 44–46

    name tokens for an attribute, 81–82

    valid XML names, 105–106

list-item body and label, including, 478

list-item body, containing, 478–479

list-item label

    setting length between end of label and beginning of list item, 587–588

    setting length between end of start indent of label and beginning of list item, 586–587

list-item label, including, 479

lists

    definition, 714

    nesting, 716

    ordered, 714

    unordered, 714

literal

    naming public identifier, 121–122

    representing, 541–542

    specifying public identifier character within public identifier, 120–121

Literal XSL production, 195, 202–203, 208, 218, 324, 541–542, 585

literal

    defined, 202, 541–542

    representing, 202–203

local links, defined, 145

local part of expanded-name of first node in argument's node-set, returning, 203

local resource for link, indicating, 153

local-name() XPath function, 203

locating

    node with pattern of identifiers and keys, 324–325

    target element by navigating through integer values for child elements, 166–167

    target element by specifying part of full XPointer or FullXPtr, 177–178

location of destination resource, specifying, 604–605

location path

    abbreviating absolute, 182

    abbreviating relative, 183–184

    creating path by composing location path and filter expression, 215–216

    defined, 741

    inserting predicate expression that filters nodes in, 216–217

specifying contents, 221–222

specifying set of patterns, 326–327

location paths, 741–743

location paths, specifying pattern to locate node, 325–326

location terms, absolute and relative, 741

location type, identifying specific node, 168–170

LocationPath XPath production, 203–204, 215

LocationPathPattern XSLT production, 325–326

locations, returning of

    end-point type, 167

    start-point type, 173–174

location-set

    returning one with one location for out-of-line link, 170–171

    returning one with one location, 168

    returning ranges for each location in specified, 171

    returning true if it contains one location, 175–176

location-step nodes set, checking on node for type and expanded name of, 208

locator keyword, 160

locator link type, defined, 737

locator or resource type XLink, specifying label of, 151–152

locator XLink type, 152–153

locator, specifying remote resource, 150–151

logical and mathematical operators, providing list of, 212–213

logical or mathematical operator, naming, 213–214, 560–561

logical structure, defined, 662

loud keyword, 638

low keyword, 580

lower keyword, 456

lowercase keyword, 631

lowercase text, changing to, 631–632

lower-first keyword, 356

lowest integer

    returning, 439

    returning one closest to negative infinity that is not less than argument, 190

lr keyword, 645

lr-alternating-rl-bt keyword, 646

lr-alternating-rl-tb keyword, 646

lr-bt keyword, 645

lr-inverting-rl-bt keyword, 646

lr-inverting-rl-tb keyword, 646

lr-tb keyword, 645

ltr keyword, 453

M

Mac Help system, 655
making
    page-master eligible for selection depending
        on its odd or even position in page
        sequence, 559
    page-master eligible for selection depending
        on its page-sequence position, 575–576
    page-master eligible for selection depending
        on whether it is blank or filled, 389–390
male keyword, 637
mapped to glyph, indicating character, 467–468
margin of box, sizing, 542–543
margin XSL property, 542–543
margin-bottom XSL property, 543–544, 752
margin-left XSL property, 544–545, 752
margin-right XSL property, 545–546, 752
margins of box, turning on or off, 542–543
margin-top XSL property, 546–547, 752
marker-class-name XSL property, 547
marking
    beginning of character data section, 40–41
    character-data section, 38–39
    character-data section, 39–40
markup
    declaring within parameter entities, 98–100
    defined, 656, 662
markupdecl XML production, 61, 89, 98–100
master-name XSL property, 611–612, 752
masters for document, containing all layout,
    475–476
match keyword, 345, 359, 749, 750, 751, 752, 753,
    754
mathematical and logical operators, providing list
    of, 212–213
mathematical keyword, 388, 455
Mathematical Markup Language (MathML), 662
mathematical operators, providing list of, 626–628
mathematical or logical operator, naming, 213–214,
    560–561
max() XSL function, 548, 684
max-height XSL property, 540
maximum, 611
maximum and minimum leader length, specifying,
    533
maximum height of element, specifying, 548–549
maximum keyword, 533, 536, 538, 607, 608, 610,
    643
maximum number of lines in row that can end with
    hyphenation character, specifying, 518–519
maximum of two numeric arguments, returning,
    548
maximum width of element, specifying, 550–551
maximum-repeats XSL property, 549–550
max-uniform keyword, 601

max-width XSL property, 550–551
measure
    indicating relative length ending with name of
        relative unit of, 592–593
    representing absolute unit of, 372–373
    representing relative unit of, 593–594
    returning proportional factor units of propor-
        tional, 585–586
media pseudo-attribute, 143
median volume of waveform file, specifying,
    638–639
media-type keyword, 352
medium keyword, 396, 399, 404, 411, 415, 420,
    425, 432, 433, 486, 580, 617, 638
menu keyword, 482
merge-property-values() XSL function,
    551–552, 754
message-box keyword, 482
messages, warning and error, defined, 29
metalanguage, defined, 676
method keyword, 351
middle keyword, 387, 635
min keyword, 552
min() XSL function, 552
min-height XSL property, 552–553
minimum, 610
minimum and maximum leader length,
    specifying, 533
minimum height of element, specifying, 552–553
minimum keyword, 533, 536, 538, 607, 608, 609,
    643
minimum
    specifying number of characters in word after
        hyphenation character, 519–520
    specifying number of characters in word
        before hyphenation character, 520–521
    specifying number of paragraph-lines left
        at bottom of page, 561
    specifying number of paragraph-lines left at
        top of page, 641–642
minimum of two numeric arguments, returning,
    552
minimum width of element, specifying, 553–554
minus-sign keyword, 339
min-width XSL property, 553–554
Misc XML production, 63, 100–101, 119
miscellaneous information, indicating,
    100–101
mix keyword, 582
mixed element content
    defined, 102
    indicating, 101–102
Mixed XML production, 53, 101–102
mod keyword, 205, 213, 554, 560
mode keyword, 331, 359, 749

modulus
finding, 554–555
finding by acting on expressions, 204–205
monospace keyword, 484
moving baseline away from default location,
388–389
multi-column area, determining whether columns
are spanned within, 612–613
multiple keyword, 349
multiple properties, switching between, 480
multiplication, acting on expressions through,
204–205, 554–555
MultiplicativeExpr XSL production, 185,
204–205, 374, 554–555
multiply operator, inserting, 205–206, 555
MultiplyOperator XSL production, 204,
205–206, 212, 554, 555, 560

N

Name production, 28, 29, 31, 56, 61, 66, 68, 77,
83, 90, 101, 105, 106, 110, 111, 113, 115,
118, 129, 142, 166, 180
name keyword, 206, 332, 333, 334, 339, 340, 345,
353, 355, 359, 363, 367
name matches argument, returning value of
property whose, 551–552
name
providing name of vendor that developed
XSLT processor, 364–365
returning for computer-system color, 622–623
specifying color profile of internal reference,
443–444
specifying name of retrieve-class-marker
XSL property, 595
name or family
specifying fonts by, 483–484
specifying voices by, 637–638
name token, indicating valid XML, 107–108
name tokens
defined, 689
listing for an attribute, 81–82
specifying list of, 108–109
name tokens or notation names, indicating that
attribute type is composed of enumerated,
80–81
Name XML production, 102–104, 166, 176
name() XPath function, 206
name
specifying character in, 104–105
specifying valid XML, 102–104
tokenizing expression by, 460–461
NameChar XML production, 103, 104–105, 107
named non-xpointer scheme, instructing XML
processor on how to interpret, 169
names
listing valid XML, 105–106

Names XML production, 105–106
namespace axis-name keyword, 188, 333, 340, 740
namespace name collection or node name, checking on, 207–208
namespace nodes, copying current node and its,
336–337
namespace
declaring style sheet's and result tree URI is
alias for another namespace URI, 347–348
defined, 734
returning URI of expanded-name of argument
node-set's first node, 206–207
signaling that URI or link attribute and
attribute value follows, 161–162
namespaces, 103
namespace-uri() XPath function, 206–207
NameTest XPath production, 195, 207–208
naming
attribute, 31–32
attribute set, 332–334
conditionally ignored section, 94–95
current flow, 465
entity reference or character reference,
123–124
fo:multi-case formatting object, 438
language or script for composing selected
lines, 603–604
logical or mathematical operator, 213–214,
560–561
page-master, 547–548
page-master used if some conditions are true,
469
parameter-entity reference, 115–117
public identifier literal, 121–122
region, 590–591
target application for processing instruction,
118–119
NaN, 220, 339
narrower keyword, 488
NCName
component, 207, 459
providing for enumeration token, 459
providing for function, 512
NDATA keyword, 696
NDataDecl XML production, 76, 106–107
nearest-ancestor formatting object, returning
value of property from, 509–510
negating expression, 228, 633–634
Nelson, Theodor Holm (Ted), 655
nesting
displayed or hidden flow objects depending
on fo:multi-switch, 480
lists, 716
XML elements, 665
new keyword, 155, 604

NMTOKEN XML attribute, 107–108, 134, 150, 152, 159, 689

Nmtoken XML production, 81, 107, 108

NMTOKENS XML attribute, 109–110, 134, 689

Nmtokens XML production, 108–109

no keyword, 346, 351, 352, 360, 362, 377, 458, 523, 619, 624, 625, 633

no true condition, producing template based on, 350–351

no-change keyword, 455

node
applying template rules to all children of current, 330–331
checking on node for type and expanded name of location-step nodes set, 208
copying current node and its namespace nodes, 336–337
creating processing-instruction, 354–355
creating text node in template, 360–361
defined, 169
identifying type or number, 208–209
returning local part of expanded-name of first node in argument's node-set, 203
returning string identifier for node in first node-set, 324
specifying pattern of location paths to locate, 325–326
specifying pattern of relative paths to locate, 327–328
specifying pattern of steps to locate, 328

node keyword, 169, 209

node location type, identifying specific, 168–170

node name or namespace name collection, checking on, 207–208

node test, defined, 204, 742

node-point, defined, 169

nodes
defined, 747
inserting predicate expression that filters nodes in location path, 216–217
returning count of number in argument's node-set, 191–192
returning sum of all in node-set, 226
sorting selected, 355–357

node-set
returning local part of expanded-name of first node in argument's, 203
returning node-set containing current node, 321
returning node-set that matches key, 325

node-set's first node, returning QName representing expanded-name of argument, 206

node-sets for automatic processing, selecting, 342–343

NodeTest XPath production, 208, 222, 328

NodeType XPath/XPointer production, 168–170, 195, 199, 208–209

no-force keyword, 495

no-limit keyword, 549

nonblank keyword, 390

non-control character at end of line is printed or displayed, indicating whether, 621

none keyword, 146, 155, 160, 382, 389, 395, 398, 403, 409, 414, 419, 424, 426, 431, 440, 448, 449, 450, 451, 463, 487, 518, 530, 548, 550, 582, 598, 600, 604, 606, 612, 613, 616, 628, 630, 631

nonequality or equality, comparing operands for, 192–194

nonmarkup character data, indicating any, 42–43

nonprinting, nonparsed comment, indicating, 49–50

nonvalidating XML processor, defined, 62

non-xpointer scheme, instructing XML processor on how to interpret named, 172–173

no-repeat keyword, 386

normal character or word-space, specifying if character should be treated as, 633

normal keyword, 488, 489, 490, 491, 536, 538, 613, 634, 639, 643

normalize-space() XPath function, 209–210

not() XPath function, 210

Not-a-Number, 220, 339, 556

NOTATION attribute type, 111, 690

notation name, declaring, 110–211

notation used to express XPointer, identifying, 172–173

notation, defined, 80, 110, 656, 688

NotationDecl XML production, 99, 110–111

notation-type names, listing all possible, 111–112

NotationType XML production, 80, 111–112

note, containing all portions of floating, 472

nowrap keyword, 639, 644

number
formatting and inserting in result tree, 348–350
indicating page, 492
representing absolute or relative floating-point in expression, 558–559
representing floating-point, 210–211, 463–464, 555–556
representing XML version, 136–137
returning argument that has been converted to, 210–211
returning as formatted string, 322–323
returning characters in argument's string, 223–224
symbolizing followed by percent-sign symbol, 580

Number component, 195, 211, 218, 356, 371, 653, 670

number of columns
   specifying, 444
   setting those spanned by table cells, 556–557
number of first column in table-cell span, specifying, 445–446
number of pages in page sequence in another page sequence, limiting, 549–550
number of paragraph-lines
   specifying minimum left at bottom of page, 561
   specifying minimum left at top of page, 641–642
number of resources, associating, 148–149
number of rows spanned by table cells, setting, 557
number of times table-column property is repeated, setting, 556–557
number that equals context position, returning, 216
number that equals context size, returning, 201–202
number with absolute value, representing, 371–372
number with value relative to other values, representing, 593
Number XPath production, 210–211, 555–556
number() XPath function, 211–212
number-columns-repeated XSL property, 556–557
number-columns-spanned XSL property, 556–557
number-rows-spanned XSL property, 557
numbers or alphabetic characters, representing hexadecimal or decimal, 376
numerals are spoken, controlling how, 700
numeric arguments, returning maximum of two, 548
numeric arguments, returning minimum of two, 552
Numeric XSL production, 558–559

O

object
   containing content of floating, 471
   defining how it is aligned with its parent, 387–388
   returning one that indicates system-properties value, 328–329
   returning string converted from, 222–223
   specifying content-height of, 446–447
   specifying width of content of, 448
objects
   creating leader connecting two formatting, 476–477
   creating single component from contiguous flow, 471–472
   determining which fo:multi-property-sets will format related, 373–374
oblique keyword, 489
odd keyword, 495, 559

odd or even position in page sequence, making page-master eligible for selection depending on its, 559
odd-or-even XSL property, 435, 436, 559
omitting
   table footer at column or page break, 624
   table header at column or page break, 624–625
omit-xml-declaration keyword, 351
once keyword, 614
one or more borders
   setting style of, 426–427
   setting width of, 432–434
onLoad keyword, 146
onRequest keyword, 146
onscreen or in printed format, positioning element, 583–584
opening additional level of embedding for element, 634–635
operands
   comparing for equality or nonequality, 192–194
   evaluating to find if both are true or false, 186–187
   evaluting to find if each is true or false, 214–215
operator
   inserting multiply, 205–206, 555
   naming logical or mathematical, 213–214, 560–561
Operator XPath production, 195, 212–213, 460, 559–560
OperatorName XPath production, 212, 213–214, 560–561
operators
   order of precedence for, 186
   providing list of mathematical and logical, 212–213
   providing list of mathematical, 559–560
optimum keyword, 533, 536, 538, 607, 608, 610, 643
or keyword, 213, 214
order keyword, 356
order
   enabling user to choose child-element, 46–47
   of precedence for operators, 186
ordered lists, defined, 714
OrExpr XPath production, 194, 214–215
orientation and dimensions of page box, setting, 605–606
orientation of horizontally displayed text glyphs with box, changing, 512–513
orientation of selection with its box, changing, 588–589
orientation of vertically displayed text glyphs with box, changing, 513–514

origin() XPointer function, 170–171
orphans XSL property, 561
other keyword, 146, 155
outbound, defined, 735, 737
out-of-line link, returning location-set with one
  location for, 170–171
output produced by flow object stays together,
  indicating whether, 526–527
output, creating result-tree, 351–353
outset keyword, 395, 399, 403, 410, 415, 419,
  424, 427, 431
outside keyword, 625, 627
overflow XSL property, 561–562
overflow, specifying whether and how box's
  contents, 561–562
overline keyword, 628
override for element using Unicode bidirectional
  algorithm, creating, 634–635
overriding
  bidirectionality writing direction for inline
    script, 465–466
  template rule in imported style sheet, 329–330

P

padding of box
  sizing, 632–34
  turning on or off all, 562–64
  turning on or off ending-edge, 567–568
  turning on or off starting-edge, 570–571
padding XSL property, 562–564
padding-after XSL property, 564
padding-before XSL property, 564
padding-bottom XSL property, 564–566
padding-end XSL property, 567–568
padding-left XSL property, 568–569
padding-right XSL property, 569–570
padding-start XSL property, 570–571
padding-top XSL property, 571–572
page
  generating up to five regions of, 501–502
  specifying minimum number of paragraph-
    lines left at bottom of, 561
  specifying minimum number of paragraph-
    lines left at top of, 641–642
page background, specifying whether background
  image is fixed or scrolls in, 380–381
page box
  inserting page break after, 572–573
  inserting page break before, 573–574
  inserting page break inside, 574–575
  setting dimensions and orientation of, 605–606
page break
  indicating whether it is inserted after flow
    object, 435–436
  indicating whether it is inserted before flow
    object, 436–437

inserting after page box, 572–573
inserting before page box, 573–574
inserting inside page box, 574–575
page height, determining, 575
page keyword, 435, 436, 518, 527, 528, 595
page number
  citing one containing first box from formatting
    object, 492–493
  indicating, 492
page or column break
  specifying whether to omit table footer at, 624
  specifying whether to omit table header at,
    624–625
page sequence
  making page-master eligible for selection
    depending on its odd or even position in,
    559
  setting page-masters that produce, 494
page sequence in another page sequence, limiting
  number of pages in, 549–550
page width, determining, 576–577
page-background properties, specifying one or
  more, 379–380
page-break-after XSL property, 572–573
page-break-before XSL property, 573–574
page-break-inside XSL property, 574–575
page-height XSL property, 575, 752
page-master
  making eligible for selection depending on its
    odd or even position in page sequence,
    559
  making eligible for selection depending on its
    page-sequence position, 575–576
  making eligible for selection depending on
    whether it is blank or filled, 389–390
  naming one that is used if some conditions
    are true, 469
  naming, 547–548
  producing pages sequence from recurring
    occurrences of, 545
page-masters that produce page sequence, setting,
  494
page-position XSL property, 575–576
pages
  formatting set of, 493–494
  limiting number in page sequence in another
    page sequence, 549–550
pages sequence
  producing from recurring occurrences of
    alternate page-masters, 498–499
  producing from recurring occurrences of
    page-master, 499
  setting first-page number in, 524–525
pages set from page-master, laying out, 502
page-sequence keyword, 595

page-sequence position, making page-master eligible for selection depending on its, 575–576
page type at end of pages sequence, forcing, 539–540
page-width XSL property, 649–650, 752
paragraph flow object, setting amount of ending indention for last line of, 588–590
paragraph-lines
  specifying minimum number left at bottom of page, 630
  specifying minimum number left at top of page, 735–736
paragraphs, formatting, 466–467
parameter entities, 693, 694, 705, 707
parameter entity
  declaring markup within, 98–100
  declaring, 74–76, 112–114
  defined, 75, 666
  defining, 114–115
parameter-entity reference
  inserting between declarations, 57–58
  naming, 115–117
parameter-entity references, declaring external subset markup, conditions, and, 88–89
parameters for templates, providing, 367–368
parent axis-name keyword, 741
parent keyword, 188
parent, defining how object is aligned with its, 387–388
parentheses, ensuring that string is enclosed within pair of, 175
parsed character data, defined, 687
parsed entity, 692
parsed entity, defined, 74, 666
parsed external entity, identifying, 84–86
parsed general entity, 693
path and filter expression, creating path by composing location, 215–216
path, creating by composing location path and filter expression, 215–216
path expression
  uniting with another union expression, 228–229
  uniting, 228–229
path of link transversal, indicating, 147–148
PathExpr XPath production, 215–216, 228
Pattern component, 326
pattern
  defined, 320, 748
  specifying leader, 591–593
  setting for rule, 599–600
  specifying one of identifiers and keys to locate node, 324–325
  specifying one of location paths to locate node, 325–326

specifying one of relative paths to locate node, 327–328
specifying one of steps to locate node, 328
Pattern XSLT production, 326–327
pattern-separator keyword, 339
pause XSL property, 577–578
pause-after XSL property, 578–579
pause-before XSL property, 579–580
pausing
  after and/or before element is spoken, 577–578
  after element is spoken, 578–579
  before element is spoken, 579–580
PE
  declaring, 112–114
  defined, 666
  defining, 114–115
PEDecl XML production, 74, 112–114
PEDef XML production, 113, 114–115
percent keyword, 339
Percent XSL production, 580, 593
percentage keyword, 447
percent-sign symbol, symbolizing number followed by, 580
perceptual keyword, 594
PEReference XML production, 57, 79, 115–117
per-mille keyword, 339
PEs, 705, 707–708
physical structure, defined, 662
PI XML production, 52, 99, 100, 117–118
pipe symbol (|), 685
PITarget XML production, 117, 118–119
pitch of speaking voice
  setting, 580–581
  varying range of, 581–582
pitch XSL property, 580–581
pitch-range XSL property, 581–582
placing
  fragment of result tree into same result tree, 337–338
  table caption, 437–438
play-during XSL property, 582–583
playing sound while element's content is spoken, 582–583
point keyword, 169
point, determining default alignment, 387–388
pointers, extended, 739–743
portrait keyword, 605
ports, defined, 746
position keyword, 216
position of fo:block-container, specifying absolute, 372
position XSL property, 583–584
position() XPath function, 216
positioning element onscreen or in printed format, 657–658

pre keyword, 639
precedence for operators, order of, 186
precedence keyword, 536, 607, 609, 610, 643
precedence of formatting-object regions reaching
    into simple-page-master's corners, deter-
    mining, 584–585
precedence XSL property, 536, 607, 609, 610,
    643
preceding axis-name keyword, 741
preceding keyword, 188
preceding-sibling axis-name keyword, 188,
    741
precise alignments of elements, allowing, 377–78
PredefEntityRef component, 141, 142
predefined axis name to context node, giving,
    187–188
predicate expression
    inserting one that filters nodes in location
        path, 216–217
    representing, 217
Predicate XPath production, 197, 216–217, 222,
    328
predicate
    defined, 176
    filtering primary expression or combination of
        filter expression and, 197–198
PredicateExpr XPath production, 216, 217
predicates, defined, 204, 742
preference for fo:retrieve-marker to retrieve
    children of fo:marker, specifying, 676–677
preserve keyword, 537, 611
preserving whitespace in list of elements, 354
primary expression
    filteringof one or combination of filter expres-
        sion and predicate, 197–198
    symbolizing, 217–218, 585
PrimaryExpr XPath production, 197, 217–218,
    585, 633
print or display direction, specifying text, 453–454
printed or onscreen, positioning element, 583–584
printing non-control character at end of line, 621
priority keyword, 359
process to be performed within a target application,
    specifying, 117–118
processing expression, 511–512
processing expression and calling function,
    198–199
processing instructions, defined, 49, 661
processing, selecting node-sets for automatic,
    342–343
processing-instruction keyword, 169, 208, 209
processing-instruction node, creating, 354–355
processor
    instructing to override template rule in
        imported style sheet, 329–330
    providing version of XSLT, 365

specifying role of formatting object for alter-
    nate document, 598–599
producing
    pages sequence from recurring occurrences of
        alternate page-masters, 498–499
    pages sequence from recurring occurrences of
        page-master, 499
    running headers and running footers with
        fo:marker, 499–500
    running headers and running footers with
        fo:retrieve-marker, 479–480
    template based on no condition being true,
        350–351
production, defined, 676
Project Xanadu, 655
prolog, 660–662
prolog XML production, 63, 119–120
prolog, defined, 660
properties
    containing cell in table column, 554
    containing those for table rows, 506–507
    containing those for table-footer rows, 554–556
    containing those for table-header rows, 507
    setting alternate set of, 480–481
    setting those inherited by formatting-objects
        group, 508–509
    specifying font, 482–483
    switching between multiple, 480
property
    returning inherited value from fo:table-
        column with matching column number,
        510–511
    returning value from parent formatting object,
        510
    returning value of property from nearest-
        ancestor formatting object, 509–510
    Property Set Definition Requirements, 746
property value, returning inherited, 523–524
property whose name matches argument,
    returning value of, 551–552
proportional factor units of proportional measure,
    returning, 585–586
proportional-column-width() XSL function,
    585–586
providing
    abbreviated axis specifier, child, attribute, or
        separator, 320–321
    attribute value, 31–32
    list of mathematical and logical operators,
        212–213
    list of mathematical operators, 559–560
    name of vendor that developed XSLT
        processor, 364–365
    NCName for enumeration token, 459
    NCName for function, 512
    parameters for templates, 367–368

QName for function, 199–200
title for fo:multi-case formatting object, 438
title information with link, 157
URL for vendor's company, 365
version and encoding information about external subset or external parameter entity, 132–134
version of XSLT processor, 365
XML version, 135–136
provisional-distance-between-starts XSL property, 586–587
provisional-label-separation XSL property, 587–858
PseudoAtt component, 141, 142
pseudo-attributes, 142
PseudoAttValue component, 141, 142
PubidChar XML production, 120–121
PubidLiteral XML production, 85, 121–122
public identifier character within public identifier literal, specifying, 120–121
public identifier literal
    naming, 121–122
    specifying public identifier character within, 120–121
PUBLIC keyword, 85, 122, 684, 695
PublicID XML production, 110, 122–123
punctuation is spoken, controlling how, 615–616

Q

QName
    component, 172, 199, 207, 229
    providing for function, 199–200
    returning representing expanded-name of argument node-set's first node, 206
qualified name of variable reference, specifying, 229
qualified name, defined, 332
query, defined, 747

R

range
    returningor each location in expression, 172
    returning range location for each string match that does not overlap 174–175
    varying range of pitch of speaking voice, 581–582
range() XPointer function, 171
RangeExpr component, 177
range-inside() XPointer function, 171–172
ranges for each location in specified location-set, returning, 171
range-to() XPointer function, 172
rate, controlling speaking, 616–617
reading DTD, 677–679
record, defined, 722
recursion, defined, 749

redetermining dominant-baseline, 455–456
reestablishing font-size for baseline-table, 455–456
Reference XML production, 33, 52, 79, 123–124
reference
    naming entity or character, 123–124
    naming parameter-entity, 115–117
    specifying color profile name of internal, 443–444
    specifying qualified name of variable, 229
reference-area children, specifying block-progression-direction alignment of, 454–455
reference-orientation XSL property, 665–666
referring external subset or declaring whether document contains internal subset, 126–127
ref-id XSL property, 589–590
region body
    setting viewing area at end of, 497
    setting viewing area at start of, 497–498
region
    naming or identifying, 590–591
    setting viewing area after body of defined fo:region-body, 540–541
    setting viewing area before body of defined fo:region-body, 541
region-name XSL property, 590–591
regions of page, generating up to five, 548–549
regions, setting static content for, 501–502
related objects, determining which fo:multi-property-sets will format, 373–374
RelationalExpr XPath production, 193, 218–219
relationship of two expressions, testing, 218–219
relative keyword, 583, 592, 627
relative length ending with name of relative unit of measure, indicating, 592–593
relative location path
    abbreviating, 183–184
    defined, 741
relative paths to locate node, specifying pattern of, 327–328
relative steps to target location
    specifying absolute step and optional, 184–185
    specifying series of absolute and, 203–204
    specifying series of, 219–220
relative unit of measure
    indicating relative length ending with name of, 592–593
    representing, 593–594
relative URI, defined, 734
relative-align XSL property, 591
relative-colorimetric keyword, 594
RelativeLength XSL production, 592–593
RelativeLocationPath XPath production, 182, 183, 184, 203, 215, 219–220

RelativeNumeric XSL production, 558, 593, 625, 672
RelativePathPattern XSLT production, 326, 327-328
relative-position of element, specifying, 591-592
relative-position XSL property, 591-592
RelativeUnitName XSL production, 592, 591-592
remote link, defined, 145
remote resource for link, indicating, 152-153
remote resource locator, specifying, 150-151
rendering-intent XSL property, 594
repeat keyword, 386, 582
repeating background image onscreen, 386-387
repeat-x keyword, 386
repeat-y keyword, 386
replace keyword, 155, 688
replaced-element and block-level boxes, setting inline-progression-dimension of, 525-526
replaced-elements areas, specifying area's block progression dimension for block-level and, 390-391
representing
 absolute or relative floating-point number in expression, 558-559
 absolute unit of measure, 372-373
 alphabetic characters or decimal or hexadecimal numbers, 376
 argument, 187, 376-377
 character data in character data section, 37-38
 element content within tags, 52-53
 floating-point number, 463-464, 555-556
 literal, 202-203, 541-542
 number with absolute value, 371-372
 number with value relative to other values, 593
 predicate expression, 217
 relative unit of measure, 672-674
 reserved keyword, 586-587
 XML version number, 136-137
resample-any-method keyword, 602
reserved keyword, representing, 529-530
resolving external identifier into system identifier, 122-123
resource error, defined, 166
resource link type, defined, 737
resource or locator type XLink, specifying label of, 151-152
resource XLink type, 153, 160
resources, associating number of, 148-149
rest keyword, 576
result tree
 creating comment node in, 336
 creating result-tree output, 351-353
 formatting and inserting number in, 348-350
 indicating root node of, 500
 placing fragment into same result tree, 337-338

result tree namespace
 URI is alias for another namespace URI, declaring style sheet's and, 347-348
result-prefix keyword, 347
retain keyword, 621
retain value, 607, 608, 610, 611, 643
retrieve-boundary XSL property, 594-595
retrieve-class-marker XSL property, specifying name of, 595
retrieve-class-name XSL property, 595
retrieve-position XSL property, 595-596
retrieving boundary contained within fo:marker, 594-595
returning
 absolute value of argument, 370-371
 argument that has been converted to boolean, 189-190
 argument that has been converted to number, 210-211
 argument with excess whitespace stripped out, 209-210
 argument with translated characters, 226-227
 body-start value for list, 391-392
 boolean after evaluating context-node language and context-node xml:lang attribute, 201
 characteristic of computer-system font, 623
 color value from ICC Color Profile, 521
 concatenation of strings in argument, 190-191
 count of number of nodes in argument's node-set, 191-192
 elements by ID value, 200-201
 evaluating expression and template based on true and false conditions, 343-344
 false value, 197
 highest integer, 198, 464-465
 inherited property value, 523-524
 inherited value of property from fo:table-column with matching column number, 510-511
 label-end value for list, 530
 local part of expanded-name of first node in argument's node-set, 203
 locations of end-point type, 167
 locations of start-point type, 173-174
 location-set with one location, 168
 location-set with one location for out-of-line link, 170-171
 lowest integer, 439
 lowest integer closest to negative infinity that is not less than argument, 190
 maximum of two numeric arguments, 552
 minimum of two numeric arguments, 552
 name of computer-system color, 622-623
 namespace URI of expanded-name of argument node-set's first node, 206-207
 node-set containing current node, 321

node-set that matches key, 325
number as formatted string, 322-323
number of characters in argument's string, 223-224
number that equals context position, 216
number that equals context size, 201-202
object indicating system-properties value, 328-329
proportional factor units of proportional measure, 585-586
QName representing expanded-name of argument node-set's first node, 206
range for each location in expression, 172
range location for each string match that does not overlap, 174-175
ranges for each location in specified location-set, 171
RGB color, 596-597
rounded integer closest in value to argument, 599
rounded integer closest to argument value, 220-221
string converted from object, 222-223
string identifier for node in first node-set, 324
substring after occurrence of second argument, 225
substring before occurrence of second argument, 225-226
substring depending on second and third arguments, 224-225
sum of all nodes in node-set, 226
true if location-set contains one location, 175-176
true or false depending on whether argument string contains other argument string, 191
true or false depending on whether function is in function library, 323-324
true or false depending on whether instruction element is named, 322
true or false depending on whether one argument string starts with the other argument string, 221
true value, 227-228
value of property from nearest-ancestor formatting object, 509-510
value of property from parent formatting object, 510
value of property whose name matches argument, 551-552
value of true if argument is false and false if argument is true, 210
XML document that is not main document, 321-322
RFC-1766 country code, specifying, 448-449
RFC-1766 language code, specifying, 530-531
RGB color, returning, 596-597

RGB hexadecimal color code, identifying, 443
rgb keyword, 381, 394, 397, 402, 407, 408, 413, 418, 423, 430, 442, 596, 630
rgb() XSL function, 596-597
richness of voice, specifying, 597
richness XSL property, 597
ridge keyword, 395, 399, 403, 410, 415, 419, 424, 427, 431, 600
right border
    setting color of, 418-419
    setting style of, 419
    setting width of, 420-421
right edge of box from right edge of block containing it, controlling location of, 597-598
right keyword, 378, 384, 385, 437, 440, 463, 572, 573, 626, 627
right margin of box
    sizing, 545-546
    turning on or off, 545-546
right padding of box
    sizing, 569-570
    turning on or off, 569-570
right XSL property, 597-598
right-side keyword, 378
rightwards keyword, 378
rl keyword, 645
rl-bt keyword, 645
rl-tb keyword, 645
role attribute, 161, 736, 738
role of arc content, specifying, 148
role of formatting object for alternate document processors, specifying, 598-599
role of link content, specifying, 153-155
role XLink attribute, 153-155
role XSL property, 598-599
root element, 701, 702, 709, 723
root node of result tree, indicating, 500
round keyword, 220, 599
round() XPath function, 220-221, 599
rounded integer, returning one closest in value to argument, 220-221, 599
row
    indicating whether table cell ends table, 458-559
    indicating whether table cell starts table, 619-620
    specifying maximum number of lines in one that can end with hyphenation character, 518-519
row-centric, 717, 720
row-centric, defined, 717
rows
    containing properties for table, 507-508
    containing properties for table-footer, 506-507

Continued

rows *(continued)*
  containing properties for table-header, 556
  setting number of rows spanned by table
    cells, 507
rtl keyword, 453
rule
  defined, 676
  setting pattern for, 599–600
  setting thickness of, 600–601
  specifying template, 358–360
rule keyword, 534
rule-style XSL property, 599–600
rule-thickness XSL property, 600–601
running headers and running footers with
    fo:marker, producing, 499–500
running headers and running footers with
    fo:retrieve-marker, producing, 479–480

S

S XML production, 28, 29, 46, 57, 58, 61, 66, 69,
    71, 81, 82, 83, 85, 90, 95, 97, 100, 101,
    105, 106, 108, 110, 111, 112, 117, 122,
    124–126, 128, 129, 133, 136, 138, 142,
    146, 150, 151, 152, 155, 158, 159, 160,
    168, 196, 461
sans-serif keyword, 484
saturation keyword, 594
scaling of external graphic, setting, 601–602
scaling tradeoff when formatting bitmapped
    graphics, specifying, 602
scaling XSL property, 601–602
scaling-method XSL property, 602
Scheme XPointer production, 172–173, 182
scheme, instructing XML processor on how to
    interpret named non-xpointer, 173
SchemeSpecificExpr XPointer production, 173, 177
score-spaces XSL property, 602–603
script or language for composing selected lines,
    naming, 603–604
script XSL property, 603–604
script, overriding bidirectionality writing
    direction for inline, 465–466
scroll keyword, 380, 561
scrolling background image in page background,
    380–381
SDDecl XML production, 126–127, 138
section
  indicating conditional, 50–52
  marking character-data, 38–39
select keyword, 330, 338, 342, 353, 355, 362,
    363, 367, 752, 753, 754
selecting
  condensed or expanded version of font,
    488–489
  node-sets for automatic processing, 342–343

selector, defined, 666
self axis-name keyword, 741
self keyword, 188
self::node(), 184
semi-condensed keyword, 488
semi-expanded keyword, 488
separate keyword, 405
separating
  cell border from adjacent borders, 422
  table-cell border, 405–406
separator, providing, 320–321
seq XML production, 44, 56, 127–129
sequence list, defined, 686
series of relative steps to target location, specify-
    ing, 219–220
serif keyword, 484
set of location path patterns, specifying, 326–327
set of pages, formatting, 493–494
set of properties, setting alternate, 480–481
setting
  alternate set of properties, 480–481
  amount of ending indention for last line of
    paragraph flow object, 531–532
  bottom-margin size of box, 543–544, 564
  bottom-padding size of box, 564–566
  color of bottom border, 402–403
  color of ending edge of border, 408–409
  color of leading edge of border, 397–398
  color of left border, 413–414
  color of right border, 418–419
  color of starting edge of border, 422–424
  color of top border, 429–430
  color of trailing edge of border, 393–395
  dimensions and orientation of page box,
    689–691
  direction in which text is displayed or inlined,
    645–647
  ending-edge-padding size of box, 567–568
  first-page number in pages sequence, 524–525
  formatting characteristics of fo:block's first
    line, 473
  formatting characteristics of footnote citation,
    472–473
  horizontal alignment of last line of text,
    625–626
  horizontal alignment of text, 625–626
  inline graphic with descendant data, 475
  inline-progression-dimension of block-level
    and replaced-element boxes, 525–526
  left-margin size of box, 544–545
  left-padding size of box, 568–569
  length between end of list-item label and
    beginning of list item, 587–588
  length between end of start indent of list-item
    label and beginning of list item, 586–587

level of box in stack of elements, 648
line-spacing height of font above baseline,
    485–486
line-spacing height of font below baseline,
    484–485
location of both parts of hyphenated word,
    569–570
margin size of box, 542–543
number of columns spanned by table cells,
    556–557
number of rows spanned by table cells, 557
number of times table-column property is re-
    peated, 556–557
padding size of box, 562–564
page-masters that produce page sequence, 494
pattern for rule, 599–600
pitch of speaking voice, 580–581
properties inherited by formatting-objects
    group, 508–509
right-margin size of box, 545–546
right-padding size of box, 569–570
scaling of external graphic, 601–602
spacing between characters, 535–537
spacing between words, 643–644
starting-edge-padding size of box, 643–644
static content for regions, 502–503
style of bottom border, 403–404
style of ending edge of border, 409–410
style of leading edge of border, 398–399
style of left border, 414–415
style of one or more borders, 426–427
style of right border, 419
style of starting edge of border, 424–425
style of top border, 430–432
style of trailing edge of border, 395–396
table-cell header speak characteristics, 614–615
thickness of rule, 600–601
top-margin size of box, 546–547
top-padding size of box, 571–572
value for variable, 363–364
variable's default value, 353–354
vertical alignment of element, 635–636
viewing area after body of defined region,
    fo:region-body, 495–496
viewing area at end of region body, 497
viewing area at start of region body, 497–498
viewing area before body of defined region,
    fo:region-body, 496
viewing area body of defined region, 496–497
width of bottom border, 404–405
width of column specified in column-number
    property, 446
width of ending edge of border, 410–411
width of leading edge of border, 399–400
width of left border, 415–416

width of one or more borders, 432–434
width of right border, 420–421
width of starting edge of border, 425–426
width of top border, 432
width of trailing edge of border, 396–397
SGML, 656, 667, 746
shadowing text, 630–631
shifting baseline away from default location,
    388–389
show XLink attribute, 155–156, 161, 457, 619,
    736, 738
show-destination XSL property, 604–605, 754
showing borders around empty table cells, 457
signaling that namespace URI or link attribute
    and attribute value follows, 161–162
silent keyword, 638
simple keyword, 160
simple link
    defined, 145, 735–737
    indicating destination or target resource of,
        526
    indicating start of, 500–501
    indicating target resource or destination of,
        462–463
simple XLink type, 156–157
simple-page-master's corners, determining prece-
    dence of formatting-object regions reach-
    ing into, 584–585
single keyword, 349
size, specifying font, 486–487
size of box
    setting bottom margin, 543–544
    setting bottom padding, 564–566
    setting leading-edge padding, 564
    setting left margin, 544–545
    setting left padding, 568–569
    setting margin, 542–543
    setting padding, 562–564
    setting right margin, 545–546
    setting right padding, 569–570
    setting top margin, 546–547
    setting top padding, 571–572
    setting trailing-edge padding, 564
size XSL property, 605–606
slow keyword, 616
slower keyword, 617
small keyword, 486
small-caps keyword, 490
small-caption keyword, 482
smaller keyword, 487
soft keyword, 638
solid keyword, 395, 398, 403, 410, 414, 419, 424,
    426, 431, 600
sorting selected nodes, 355–357
sosofo, defined, 747

sound file
  specifying left-to-right stereo speaker location of, 377–379
  specifying top-to-bottom stereo speaker location of, 456–457
sound while element's content is spoken, playing, 582–583
sounding
  auditory cue after element, 450–451
  auditory cue before and/or after element, 449–450
  auditory cue before element, 451–452
source document of formatting-object tree, identifying, 606–607
source tree, defined, 320, 748
source-document XSL property, 606–607
space
  inserting after flow-object area, 607–608
  inserting at end of inline flow-object area, 609–610
  inserting at start of inline flow-object area, 695–696
  inserting before flow-object area, 693–694
  inserting between declarations, 57–58
  specifying amount between two columns in box, 444–445
space keyword, 534, 538, 607
space-after XSL property, 607–608
space-before XSL property, 608–609, 750
space-end XSL property, 609–610
spaces
  specifying way in which spaces and white-space characters are treated, 611–612
  indicating whether strikethrough characters are drawn over, 602–603
space-start XSL property, 610–611
space-treatment XSL property, 611–612
spacing
  setting between characters, 535–537
  setting between words, 643–644
span XSL property, 612–613
span, specifying number of first column in table-cell, 445–446
spanning
  columns within multi-column area, 612–613
  table-cell columns, 556–557
  table-cell rows, 557
speak characteristics, setting table-cell header, 614–615
speak XSL property, 613–614
speaker location of sound file, specifying top-to-bottom stereo, 456–457
speak-header XSL property, 614–615
speaking
  controlling rate of, 616–617

numerals, 615
punctuation, 615–616
text, 613–614
speaking voice
  setting pitch of, 580–581
  varying range of pitch of, 581–582
speak-numeral XSL property, 615
speak-punctuation XSL property, 615–616
specific order, forcing user to use child elements in, 127–129
specification of color profile rendering intent other than default, allowing for, 594
specifier
  abbreviating axis, 182–183
  providing abbreviated axis, 320–321
  specifying axis name and predefined, 188–189
specifying
  absolute position of fo:block-container, 372
  absolute step and optional relative steps to target location, 184–185
  alignment between areas in block-progression-dimension, 591
  amount of space between two columns in box, 444–445
  and naming attribute set, 332–334
  area's block progression dimension for block-level and replaced-elements areas, 390–391
  attribute type, 32–33
  axis name and predefined specifier, 188–189
  background color, 381–382
  background image, 382–383
  block-progression-direction alignment of reference-area children, 454–455
  boldness or lightness of font, 491–492
  character that combines alphabetic letters and other characters, 47–49
  color for element's document text, 441–443
  color profile name of internal reference, 443–444
  color, style, and/or width of all four box borders, 392–393
  color, style, and/or width of bottom border, 400
  color, style, and/or width of left border, 411
  color, style, and/or width of right border, 416
  color, style, and/or width of top border, 427
  content-height of object, 446–447
  content-particle grammar in child-elements list, 55–57
  decimal format, 338–340
  digit, 60–61
  distance between borders of adjacent cells, 421–422
  element height, 514–515
  element width, 642–643

element's content type, 53–55
encoding name, 70–71
end point of arc link, 158–160
entity reference, 77–79
extent of width of box's horizontal part or
    height of vertical part, 461–462
external subset, 87–88
font properties, 482–483
font size, 486–487
font variations, 490–491
fonts by name or family, 483–484
height of text line from baseline to baseline,
    538–539
highest level of inflection in voice, 620–621
how line breaks occur in box, 644–645
hyphen character, 517
identifier for cross-reference, 589–590
ideogram, 91–92
if character should be treated as word-space
    or normal character, 633
indention at ending edge of box, 457–458
indention at starting edge of box, 618–619
initial horizontal position of background-image,
    385
initial vertical position of background-image,
    385–386
internal-entity value, 79–80
label of locator or resource type XLink,
    151–152
leader pattern, 533–534
leader-pattern width, 534–535
left-to-right stereo speaker location of sound
    file, 377–379
legal hexadecimal or decimal character code,
    43–44
letter of current alphabet, 98
link type, 160–161
list of valid XML general entities, 73
list of valid XML name tokens, 109–110
location of destination resource, 604–605
location path contents, 221–222
maximum and minimum leader length, 533
maximum height of element, 548–549
maximum number of lines in row that can
    end with hyphenation character, 518–519
maximum width of element, 550–551
median volume of waveform file, 638–639
minimum height of element, 552–553
minimum number of characters in word after
    hyphenation character, 519–520
minimum number of characters in word be-
    fore hyphenation character, 520–521
minimum number of paragraph-lines left at
    bottom of page, 561

minimum number of paragraph-lines left at
    top of page, 641–642
minimum width of element, 553–554
name of retrieve-class-marker XSL property,
    595
number of columns in box, 444
number of first column in table-cell span,
    445–446
one character in name, 104–105
one legal character, 41–42
one or more border colors, 406–408
one or more digits, 452–453
one or more page-background properties,
    379–380
pattern of identifiers and keys to locate node,
    324–325
pattern of location paths to locate node,
    325–326
pattern of relative paths to locate node,
    327–328
pattern of steps to locate node, 328
position and alignment of table caption,
    460–462
preference for fo:retrieve-marker to retrieve
    children of fo:marker, 676–677
process to be performed within a target appli-
    cation, 117–118
public identifier character within public iden-
    tifier literal, 120–121
qualified name of variable reference, 229
relative-position of element, 668–670
remote resource locator, 150–151
RFC-1766 country code, 448–449
RFC-1766 language code, 530–531
richness of voice, 597
role of arc content, 148
role of formatting object for alternate docu-
    ment processors, 598–599
role of link content, 153–155
scaling tradeoff when formatting bitmapped
    graphics, 602
series of absolute and relative steps to target
    location, 203–204
series of relative steps to target location,
    219–220
set of location path patterns, 326–327
starting point of arc link, 149–150
starting position for background image,
    383–385
table layout, 623–624
template rule, 358–360
text display or print direction, 453–454
text enhancements, 489–490
text foreground color, 466–468
title of a link resource, 157–158

Continued

specifying *(continued)*
  top-to-bottom stereo speaker location of sound file, 456–457
  type of content, 447–448
  Unicode character, 439–440
  URI of external identifier, 131–132
  URI of fo:external-graphic, 617–618
  valid XML general entity, 73–74
  valid XML name, 102–104
  valid XML name token, 107
  valid XML name tokens, 108–109
  voices by name or family, 637–638
  way in which contiguous whitespace characters are treated, 640–641
  way in which linefeed character is treated, 537–538
  way in which linking resource is retrieved, 146–147
  way in which spaces and whitespace characters are treated, 611–612
  well-formed external general parsed entity, 86–87
  whether and how box's contents overflow, 561–562
  whether areas that belong to destination resource are shown, 523
  whether background image is fixed or scrolls in page background, 380–381
  whether box in which element resides is visible or invisible, 636–637
  whether text is spoken, 613–614
  whether to omit table footer at column or page break, 624
  whether to omit table header at column or page break, 624–625
  width of content of object, 448
  XML element, 64–66
speech-rate XSL property, 616–617
spell-out keyword, 613
spoken, playing sound while element's content is, 582–583
spread keyword, 518
src XSL property, 617–618, 750
stack of elements, setting level of box in, 648
STag XML production, 64, 129–130
standalone, 682, 701
standalone declaration, 661
standalone keyword, 126, 352
Standard Generalized Markup Language, 656, 746
start indent of list-item label and beginning of list item, setting length between end of, 586–587
start keyword, 437, 625, 627
start of simple link, indicating, 500–501
start tag for an element, defining, 129–130

start tags, 663, 702
start-indent XSL property, 618–619, 750, 751
starting edge of border
  setting color of, 422–424
  setting style of, 424–425
  setting width of, 425–426
starting edge of box, specifying indention at, 618–619
starting point of arc link, specifying, 149–150
starting position for background image, specifying, 389–392
starting-edge padding of box
  turning on or off, 570–571
  sizing, 570–571
starting-state XSL property, 619
start-point keyword, 174
start-point type, returning locations of, 173–174
start-point() XPointer function, 173–174
starts-row XSL property, 619–620
starts-with keyword, 221
starts-with() XPath function, 221
static content, defined, 502
static content, setting for regions, 502–503
static keyword, 583, 592
stating attribute value, 33–34
status-bar keyword, 483
Step XPath production, 183, 219, 221–222
step, abbreviating, 184
StepPattern XSLT production, 327, 328
steps to locate node, specifying pattern of, 328
stereo speaker location of sound file, specifying left-to-right, 380–384
stress XSL property, 620–621
strikethrough characters are drawn over spaces, indicating whether, 602–603
string
  returning number as formatted, 322–323
  returning number of characters in argument's, 223–224
  returning one converted from object, 222–223
string identifier for node in first node-set, returning, 324
string is enclosed within pair of parentheses, ensuring that, 175
string keyword, 222
string match that does not overlap, returning range location for each, 174–175
string() XPath function, 222–223
string-length keyword, 224
string-length() XPath function, 223–224
string-range keyword, 174
string-range() XPointer function, 174–175
StringType XML production, 32, 130–131
StringWithBalancedParens XPointer production, 173, 175

stripping whitespace from list of elements, 357
style, setting for
  bottom border, 403–404
  ending edge of border, 409–410
  leading edge of border, 398–399
  left border, 414–415
  one or more borders, 426–427
  right border, 419
  starting edge of border, 424–425
  top border, 430–432
  trailing edge of border, 395–396
style sheet
  declaring ICC Color Profile for, 468–469
  grouping global declarations for, 469–470
  importing XSL, 344–345
  including another XSLT, 345
  indicating synonym of XSL, 361–362
  indicating XSL, 357–358
  instructing processor to override template rule in imported, 329–330
  instructing XML processor to use named, 141–143
style sheets, cascading, 708, 745
style sheet's and result tree namespace URI is alias for another namespace URI, declaring, 347–348
style, color, and/or width, specifying
  all four box borders, specifying, 392–393
  for bottom border, 400
  for left border, 416
  for right border, 434
  for top border, 427
StyleSheetPI component, 141
stylesheet-prefix keyword, 347
sub keyword, 398, 635
sub-resource error, defined, 166
subscript or superscript characters, indicating whether line height is modified for, 539–540
subset, specifying external, 87–88
substring
  returning after occurrence of second argument, 225
  returning before occurrence of second argument, 225–226
  returning depending on second and third arguments, 224–225
substring( ) XPath function, 223–224
substring-after( ) XPath function, 225
substring-before( ) XPath function, 225–226
subtraction or addition
  acting on expressions through, 376–377
  acting on one or more expressions through, 185–186
subtree, defined, 748

subtrees, switching formatting-object, 481
sum keyword, 226
sum of all nodes in node-set, returning, 226
sum( ) XPath function, 226
super keyword, 389
superscript or subscript characters, indicating whether line height is modified for, 601–603
suppress keyword, 621
suppress-at-line-break XSL property, 621
switching
  between multiple properties, 480
  to fo:multi-case formatting object, 621–622
  to formatting-object subtrees, 481
switch-to XSL property, 621–622
syllabic base character, defined, 104
symbolizing
  number followed by percent-sign symbol, 580
  primary expression, 217–218, 585
synonym of XSL style sheet, indicating, 361–362
syntactic, defined, 676
syntax error, defined, 166
system color name, returning, 622
system font, returning characteristic of, 623
system identifier
  defined, 132
  resolving external identifier into, 122–123
SYSTEM keyword, 85, 684, 695
system-color( ) XSL function, 622
system-font( ) XSL function, 623
SystemLiteral XML production, 85, 131–132
system-properties value, returning object indicating, 328–329
system-property keyword, 328
system-property( ) XSLT function, 328–329

T

table and its caption, formatting, 504
table body, formatting, 504–505
table caption
  applying block-level formats to, 505
  specifying position and alignment of, 437–438
table cell
  containing content for, 505–506
  defined, 716
  indicating whether it ends table row, 458–459
  indicating whether it starts table row, 619–620
table cells
  setting number of columns spanned by, 622–623
  setting number of rows spanned by, 557
  showing or hiding borders around empty, 457
table column, containing cell properties in, 506
table layout, specifying, 623–624, 752
table rows, containing properties for, 507–508

table, formatting, 503–504
table-cell border, collapsing, 405–406
table-cell header speak characteristics, setting, 614–615
table-cell span, specifying number of first column in, 445–446
table-column property is repeated, setting number of times, 556–557
table-footer rows, containing properties for, 506–507
table-header rows, containing properties for, 507
table-layout XSL property, 623–624
table-omit-footer-at-break XSL property, 624
table-omit-header-at-break XSL property, 624–625
tag, writing empty-element, 68–70
tags, representing element content within, 52–53
target application
    naming for processing instruction, 118–119
    specifying process to be performed within a, 117–118
target element
    locating by navigating through integer values for child elements, 166–167
    locating by specifying part of full XPointer or FullXPtr, 177–178
target link or graphic file, indicating URI for, 515–516
target location
    specifying absolute step and optional relative steps to, 184–185
    specifying series of absolute and relative steps to, 203–204
    specifying series of relative steps to, 219–220
target resource
    specifying location of, 604–605
    indicating location of fo:simple-link formatting object, 526
tb keyword, 645
tb-lr keyword, 645
tb-rl keyword, 645
tb-rl-in-rl-pairs keyword, 646
template
    calling by name, 334–335
    creating text node in, 360–361
    evaluating expression and returning it based on true and false conditions, 343–344
    producing template based on no condition being true, 350–351
template rule, 748
template rule, specifying, 358–360
template rules to all children of current node, applying, 330–331
template when condition is false, falling back to, 341–342

templates, providing parameters for, 367–368
terminate keyword, 346
test keyword, 343, 367, 753
testing
    if condition is true, 365–367
    relationship of two expressions, 218–219
text
    applying shadow effects to, 630–631
    changing case of, 631–632
    enhancing with lines or blinking, 628–629
    indenting first line of, 629–630
    setting horizontal alignment of, 625–626
    setting horizontal alignment of last line of, 625–626
    specifying display or print direction, 453–454
    specifying enhancements to, 489–490
    specifying foreground color, 441–443
text declaration, 132–134
text glyphs with box
    changing orientation of horizontally displayed, 512–513
    changing orientation of vertically displayed, 513–514
text
    generating using expression, 362–363
    setting direction in which it is displayed or in-lined, 740–743
    specifying whether it is spoken, 698–699
text keyword, 169, 209, 351, 356
text node in template, creating, 360–361
text-after-edge keyword, 387
text-align XSL property, 625–626, 750
text-align-last XSL property, 626–628
text-before-edge keyword, 387
text-bottom keyword, 635
TextDecl XML production, 86, 87, 135–137
text-decoration XSL property, 628–629, 754
text-indent XSL property, 629–630
text-line height, specifying from baseline to baseline, 538–539
text-shadow XSL property, 630–631
text-top keyword, 635
text-transform XSL property, 631–632
thick keyword, 396, 399, 404, 411, 415, 420, 425, 432, 433
thickness of rule, setting, 600–601
thin keyword, 396, 399, 404, 411, 415, 420, 425, 432, 433
third-party, defined, 737
title attribute, 161, 737, 741
title
    associating with document, 508
    providing for fo:multi-case formatting object, 438
    specifying for a link resource, 157–158

title information with link, providing, 157
title keyword, 158, 160
title link type, defined, 737
title pseudo-attribute, 143
title XLink attribute, 157–158
to attribute, 161, 738
to keyword, 159
to XLink attribute, 158–160
toggling from one fo:multi-case to another,
    481–482
token, defined, 460
token, providing NCName for enumeration, 459
tokenized set, indicating attribute type is, 134–135
TokenizedType XML production, 32, 134–135
tokenizing
    expression, 194–196
    expression character by character or name by
      name, 460–461
tokens, defined, 688
top border
    setting color of, 429–430
    setting style of, 430–432
    setting width of, 432
top edge of box, controlling location of, 632–633
top keyword, 384, 385, 437, 635
top margin of box, turning
    on or off, 610–611
top margin size of box, setting, 610–611
top padding of box, turning on or off, 546–547
top padding size of box, setting, 571–572
top XSL property, 632–633
top-to-bottom stereo speaker location of sound
    file, specifying, 456–457
traditional keyword, 349
trailing edge of border
    setting color of, 393–395
    setting style of, 395–396
    setting width of, 396–397
trailing-edge padding of box
    setting, 564
    turning on or off, 634
translate keyword, 227
translate() XPath function, 226–227
translated characters, returning argument with,
    226–227
transparent keyword, 388, 415, 422
treat-as-space keyword, 537
treat-as-word-space XSL property, 633
treating linefeed character, 537–538
tree, identifying source document of formatting-
    object, 691–692
tree construction rule, defined, 748
tree transformation, defined, 747
true
    evaluating expression and returning template
      based on truth, 343–344

naming page-master used if some conditions
    are, 469
producing template based on no condition be-
    ing, 350–351
returning if location-set contains one location,
    175–176
returning value if argument is false, 210
returning value of false if argument is, 210
testing if condition is, 365–367
true or false
    evaluating two operands to find if both are,
      186–187
    returning depending on whether argument
      string contains other argument string, 191
    returning depending on whether function is
      in function library, 323–324
    returning depending on whether instruction
      element is named, 322
    returning depending on whether one
      argument string starts with the other
      argument string, 221
true keyword, 227, 516, 584, 603, 640
true value, returning, 227–228
true xsl:when condition, choosing first, 335–336
true() XPath function, 227–228
turning on or off
    bottom margin of box, 543–544
    bottom padding of box, 564–566
    ending-edge padding of box, 567–568
    leading-edge padding of box, 564
    left margin of box, 544–545
    left padding of box, 568–569
    margins of box, 542–543
    paddings of box, 569–570
    right margin of box, 545–546
    right padding of box, 641–642
    starting-edge padding of box, 570–571
    top margin of box, 546–547
    top padding of box, 571–572
    trailing-edge padding of box, 564
    whitespace, 639–640
two numeric arguments
    returning maximum of, 548
    returning minimum of, 552
type attribute, 161, 735, 738
type keyword, 160
type of content, specifying, 475–477
type pseudo-attribute, 143
type XLink attribute, 160–161
type, specifying link, 160–161

U

UCS, 657
ultra-condensed keyword, 488
ultra-expanded keyword, 552

UnaryExpr XPath production, 204, 228, 554, 633–634
underline keyword, 715
Unicode bidirectional algorithm to open additional level of embedding or create override for element, instructing, 634–635
Unicode character, specifying, 439–440
unicode-bidi XSL property, 634–635
union expression, uniting path expression and another, 228–229
UnionExpr XPath production, 228–229
unique keyword, 176
unique() XPointer function, 175–176
Universal Character Set, 657
unordered lists, defined, 714
unparsed entity, 692
unparsed entity, defined, 74, 666
unparsed external entities, 696
unparsed external entity, declaring, 106–107
unparsed-entity-uri() XSLT function, 329
uppercase keyword, 631
uppercase text,changing to, 631–632
upper-first keyword, 356
URIs
    absolute, 734
    indicating for target link or graphic file, 515–516
    relative, 734
    specifying for external identifier, 131–132
uri keyword, 388, 478, 479, 480, 656
URL for vendor's company, providing, 365
URLs, defined, 655
use keyword, 345
use-attribute-sets keyword, 333, 337, 340
use-content keyword, 534
use-font-metrics keyword, 484, 485, 534
user to use child elements in specific order, forcing, 127–129

V

valid documents, 672–673
valid XML name token
    indicating that it follows, 107–108
    specifying, 107
valid XML name, specifying, 102–104
valid XML names, listing, 105–106
value
    returning object indicating system-properties, 328–329
    setting for variable, 363–364
    setting variable's default, 353–354
value keyword, 349
value of property
    returning inherited value from fo:table-column with matching column number, 559–561

returning from nearest-ancestor formatting object, 558–559
returning from parent formatting object, 510
returning value whose name matches argument, 551–552
variable, setting value for, 363–364
variable reference, specifying qualified name of, 229
VariableReference XPath production, 195, 217, 229
variable's default value, setting, 353–354
variations, specifying font, 533–534
varying, range of pitch of speaking voice, 655–656
vendor that developed XSLT processor, providing name of, 364–365
vendor's company, providing URL for, 365
version and encoding information about external subset or external parameter entity, providing, 132–134
version keyword, 351, 358, 361
version number, representing XML, 136–137
version of XSLT processor, providing, 365
version, providing XML, 135–136
VersionInfo XML production, 133, 135–36, 137, 673
VersionNum XML production, 136–137
vertical alignment of element, setting, 635–636
vertical part height of box, specifying, 461–462
vertical position of background-image, specifying initial, 385–386
vertical-align XSL property, 635–636
vertically displayed text glyphs with box, changing orientation of, 513–514
viewing area, setting
    after body of defined region, fo:region-body, 495–496
    at end of region body, 497
    before body of defined region, fo:region-body, 496
    body of defined region, 496–497
    start of region body, 497–498
visibility XSL property, 636–637
visible keyword, 561, 636
visible or invisible, specifying whether box in which element resides is, 636–637
visited keyword, 373
voice
    setting pitch of speaking, 580–581
    specifying highest level of inflection in, 620–621
    specifying richness of, 597
    varying range of pitch of speaking, 581–582
voice-family XSL property, 638–639
voices by name or family, specifying, 637–638
volume, specifying median of waveform file, 638–639
volume XSL property, 638–639

W

warning message, defined, 29
waveform file, specifying median volume of,
    638–639
Web browsing, defined, 656
well-formed documents, 671–672, 709
well-formed external general parsed entity,
    specifying, 86–87
whitespace
    controlling in XML document, 140–141
    inserting in expression, 196–197
    inserting in XML document, 124–126
    preserving in list of elements, 354
    returning argument with excess stripped out,
        209–210
    specifying way in which characters and
        spaces are treated, 611–612
    specifying way in which contiguous charac-
        ters are treated, 640–641
    stripping from list of elements, 357
    turning on or off, 639–640
white-space XSL property, 639–640
white-space-collapse XSL property, 640–641
wider keyword, 488
widows XSL property, 641–642
width
    determining page, 576–577
    setting for bottom border, 404–405
    setting for ending edge of border, 410–411
    setting for leading edge of border, 399–400
    setting for left border, 415–416
    setting for one or more borders, 432–434
    setting for right border, 420–421
    setting for starting edge of border, 425–426
    setting for top border, 432
    setting for trailing edge of border, 396–397
    setting of column specified in column-number
        property, 446
    specifying box's horizontal part, 494–495
    specifying for content of object, 477
    specifying for element, 736–737
width XSL property, 736–737
Windows Help system, 655
words, setting spacing between, 737–739
word-space or normal character, specifying if
    character should be treated as, 722
word-spacing XSL property, 643–644
wrap keyword, 644
wrap-option XSL property, 644–645
writing empty-element tag, 68–70
writing direction for inline script, overriding
    bidirectionality, 465–466
writing-mode XSL property, 645–647

X

x-fast keyword, 617
XForms, 725
x-high keyword, 580
XHTML, 656, 657
XHTML In Plain English, 658, 667
x-large keyword, 487
XLink, 658
XLink attributes
    actuate, 146–147
    arc, 147–148
    arcrole, 148
    from, 149–150
    href, 150–151
    label, 151–152
    role, 153–155
    show, 155–156
    title, 157–158
    to, 158–160
    type, 160–161
XLink types
    extended, 148–149
    locator, 152–153
    resource, 153
    simple, 156–157
    title, 157
xlink: keyword, 161, 737
XLinks, 145–162
x-loud keyword, 638
x-low keyword, 580
XML, 657
XML cross-references follows, indicating list of,
    93–94
XML databases, 720–725
XML document
    controlling whitespace in, 140–141
    declaring, 137–138, 682–683
    describing, 119–120
    encompassing entire, 63–64
    inserting whitespace in, 124–126
    returning document that is not main
        document, 321–322
XML document type, declaring, 61–63
XML element, specifying, 64–66
XML elements, nesting, 665
XML general entity, specifying, 73–74
XML identifier cross-reference follows, indicating
    that, 92–93
XML identifier follows, indicating that, 91
xml keyword, 351
XML language code, instructing XML to process
    character data using specific, 138–140
XML name token follows, indicating, 107–108
XML name token, specifying, 107
XML name tokens, specifying, 108–109
    list of, 109–110

XML name, specifying valid, 102–104
XML names, listing, 105–106
XML processing instructions
    xml-stylesheet, 141–143
XML processor
    instructing in correct way to interpret
        xpointer scheme, 177
    instructing on how to interpret named non-
        xpointer scheme, 173
    instructing to use named style sheet, 141–143
XML productions
    AttDef, 28–29
    AttlistDecl, 29–31
    Attribute, 31–32
    AttType, 32–33
    AttValue, 33–34
    BaseChar, 34–37
    CData, 37–38
    CDEnd, 38–39
    CDSect, 39–40
    CDStart, 40–41
    Char, 41–42
    CharData, 42–43
    CharRef, 43
    children, 44–46
    choice, 46–47
    CombiningChar, 47–49
    Comment, 49–50
    conditionalSect, 50–52
    content, 52–53
    contentspec, 53–55
    cp, 55–57
    DeclSep, 57–58
    DefaultDecl, 57–60
    Digit, 60–61
    doctypedecl, 61–63
    document, 63–64
    element, 64–66
    elementdecl, 66–68
    EmptyElemTag, 68–70
    EncName, 70–71
    EncodingDecl, 71–73
    EntityDecl, 74–76
    EntityDef, 76–77
    EntityRef, 77–79
    EntityValue, 79–80
    EnumeratedType, 80–81
    Enumeration, 81–82
    Eq, 82–83
    ETag, 83–84
    Extender, 84
    ExternalID, 84–86
    extParsedEnt, 86–87
    extSubset, 87–88
    extSubsetDecl, 88–89
    GEDecl, 89–91

Ideographic, 91–92
Ignore, 94
ignoreSect, 94–95
ignoreSectContents, 95–97
includeSect, 97–98
Letter, 98
markupdecl, 98–100
Misc, 100–101
Mixed, 101–102
Name, 102–104
NameChar, 104–105
Names, 105–106
NDataDecl, 106–107
Nmtoken, 107
Nmtokens, 108–109
NotationDecl, 110–111
NotationType, 111–112
PEDecl, 112–114
PEDef, 114–115
PEReference, 115–117
PI, 117–118
PITarget, 118–119
prolog, 119–120
PubidChar, 120–121
PubidLiteral, 121–122
PublicID, 122–123
Reference, 123–124
S, 124–126
SDDecl, 126–127
seq, 127–129
STag, 129–130
StringType, 130–131
SystemLiteral, 131–132
TextDecl, 132–134
TokenizedType, 134–135
VersionInfo, 135–136
VersionNum, 136–137
XMLDecl, 137–138
XML to process character data using specific
    XML language code, instructing, 138–140
XML to process language code in which character
    data is written, instructing, 647–648
XML version number, representing, 136–137
XML version, providing, 135–136
xml:lang processing instruction, 139
xml:space
    processing instruction, 140
    XML attribute, 140–141
XMLDecl XML production, 119, 137–138
xmlns keyword, 161, 734, 748, 749, 750
xml-stylesheet XML processing instruction,
    141–143
XPath functions
    boolean(), 189–190
    ceiling(), 190
    concat(), 190–191

contains(), 191
count(), 191-192
false(), 197
floor(), 198
id(), 200-201
lang(), 201
last(), 201-202
local-name(), 203
name(), 206
namespace-uri(), 206-207
normalize-space(), 209-210
not(), 210
number(), 211-212
position(), 216
round(), 220-221
starts-with(), 221
string(), 222-223
string-length(), 223-224
substring(), 224-225
substring-after(), 225
substring-before(), 225-226
sum(), 226
translate(), 226-227
true(), 227-228
XPath productions
  AbbreviatedAbsoluteLocationPath, 182
  AbbreviatedAxisSpecifier, 182-183
  AbbreviatedRelativeLocationPath,
    183-184
  AbbreviatedStep, 184
  AbsoluteLocationPath, 184-185
  AdditiveExpr, 185-186
  AndExpr, 186-187
  Argument, 187
  AxisName, 187-188
  AxisSpecifier, 188-189
  Digits, 192
  EqualityExpr, 192-194
  Expr, 194
  ExprToken, 194-196
  ExprWhitespace, 196-197
  FilterExpr, 197-198
  FunctionCall, 198-199
  FunctionName, 199-200
  Literal, 202-203
  LocationPath, 203-204
  MultiplicativeExpr, 204-205
  MultiplyOperator, 205-206
  NameTest, 207-208
  NodeTest, 208
  NodeType, 208-209
  Number, 210-211
  Operator, 212-213
  OperatorName, 213-214
  OrExpr, 214-215
  PathExpr, 215-216

Predicate, 216-217
PredicateExpr, 217
PrimaryExpr, 217-218
RelationalExpr, 218-219
RelativeLocationPath, 219-220
Step, 221-222
UnaryExpr, 228
UnionExpr, 228-229
VariableReference, 229
XPointer functions
  end-point(), 167
  here(), 168
  origin(), 170-171
  range(), 171
  range-inside(), 171-172
  range-to(), 172
  start-point(), 173-174
  string-range(), 174-175
  unique(), 175-176
xpointer keyword, 172, 177
XPointer location, defined, 169
XPointer parts that make up full XPointer, identifying, 167-168
xpointer scheme, instructing XML processor in correct way to interpret, 177
XPointer, designating fully-formed, 176-177
XPointer, identifying notation used to express, 172-173
XPtrExpr XPointer production, 177
XPtrPart keyword, 167, 177-178
XSL examples, 746, 750-754
XSL functions
  abs(), 370-371
  body-start(), 391-392
  ceiling(), 439
  floor(), 464-465
  from-nearest-specified-value(), 509-510
  from-parent(), 510
  from-table-column(), 510-511
  icc-color(), 521
  inherited-property-value(), 523-524
  label-end(), 530
  max(), 548
  merge-property-values(), 551-552
  min(), 552
  proportional-column-width(), 585-586
  rgb(), 596-597
  round(), 599
  system-color(), 622-623
  system-font(), 623
XSL productions
  AbsoluteLength, 371
  AbsoluteUnitName, 372-373
  AdditiveExpr, 374-375

Continued

XSL productions *(continued)*
   AlphaOrDigits, 376
   Argument, 376-377
   Color, 443
   Digits, 452-453
   Expr, 459-460
   ExprToken, 460-461
   ExprWhitespace, 461
   FunctionCall, 511-512
   FunctionName, 512
   Keyword, 529-530
   Literal, 541-542
   MultiplicativeExpr, 554-555
   MultiplyOperator, 555
   Number, 555-556
   Numeric, 558-559
   Operator, 559-560
   OperatorName, 560-561
   Percent, 580
   PrimaryExpr, 585
   RelativeLength, 592-593
   RelativeNumeric, 593
   RelativeUnitName, 593-594
   UnaryExpr, 633-634
XSL style sheet, importing, 344-345
XSL style sheet, indicating, 357-358
XSL style sheet, indicating synonym of, 361-362
XSL Transformations, 658
xsl:apply-imports XSLT element, 329-330
xsl:apply-templates XSLT element, 330-331,
   748, 749, 750, 751, 752, 753
xsl:attribute XSLT element, 331-332, 333,
   752, 753, 754
xsl:attribute-set XSLT element, 332-334
xsl:call-template XSLT element, 334-335, 752
xsl:choose XSLT element, 335-336, 753
xsl:comment XSLT element, 336
xsl:copy XSLT element, 336-337
xsl:copy-of XSLT element, 337-338
xsl:decimal-format XSLT element, 338-340
xsl:element, creating attributes for elements
   produced by, 331-332
xsl:element XSLT element, 340-341
xsl:fallback XSLT element, 341-342
xsl:for-each XSLT element, 342-343
xsl:if XSLT element, 343-344, 753
xsl:import XSLT element, 344-345, 359, 361
xsl:include XSLT element, 345
xsl:key XSLT element, 345-346
xsl:message XSLT element, 346-347
xsl:namespace-alias XSLT element, 347-348
xsl:number XSLT element, 348-350, 751, 752
xsl:otherwise XSLT element, 335, 350-351, 753
xsl:output XSLT element, 351-353

xsl:param XSLT element, 353-354, 359
xsl:preserve-space XSLT element, 354
xsl:processing-instruction XSLT element,
   354-355
xsl:sort XSLT element, 331, 342, 355-357
xsl:strip-space XSLT element, 357
xsl:stylesheet XSLT element, 357-358, 748,
   749, 750, 751, 752, 753
xsl:template XSLT element, 358-360, 748, 749,
   750, 751, 752, 753, 754
xsl:text XSLT element, 360-361
xsl:transform XSLT element, 361-362
xsl:value-of XSLT element, 362-363, 752,
   753, 754
xsl:variable XSLT element, 363-364, 754
xsl:vendor XSLT element, 364-365
xsl:vendor-url XSLT element, 365
xsl:version XSLT element, 365
xsl:when, choosing first true condition, 335-336
xsl:when XSLT element, 335, 365-367, 753
xsl:with-param XSLT element, 331, 334,
   367-368, 752
XSLT functions
   current(), 321
   document(), 321-322
   element-available(), 322
   format-number(), 322-323
   function-available(), 323-324
   generate-id(), 324
   key(), 325
   system-property(), 328-329
   unparsed-entity-uri(), 329
XSLT processor, providing version of, 365
XSLT productions
   ChildOrAttributeAxisSpecifier, 320-321
   IdKeyPattern, 324-325
   LocationPathPattern, 325-326
   Pattern, 326-327
   RelativePathPattern, 327-328
   StepPattern, 328
XSLT style sheet, including another, 345
x-small keyword, 528
x-soft keyword, 638
xx-large keyword, 529
xx-small keyword, 528
yes keyword, 346, 351, 352, 360, 362
zero-digit keyword, 339
z-index XSL property, 648

Two Books in One!

my2cents. books.com